395-428
375-394

THE MODERN MIDDLE EAST

The Modern Middle East: A Reader

Edited by

ALBERT HOURANI, PHILIP KHOURY
and MARY C. WILSON

I.B.TAURIS
LONDON · NEW YORK

Reprinted in 2005 by I.B. Tauris & Co. Ltd
New edition published in 2004
First published in 1993
6 Salem Road, London W2 4BU
175 Fifth Avenue, New York NY 10010
www.ibtauris.com

In the United States of America and in Canada distributed by Palgrave Macmillan,
a division of St Martins Press, 175 Fifth Avenue, New York NY 10010

ISBN 1 86064 963 7
EAN 978 1 86064 963 9

A full CIP record for this book is available from the British Library
A full CIP record for this book is available from the Library of Congress

Library of Congress catalog card: available

Typeset by Rowlands Phototypesetting, Suffolk, UK
Printed and bound in India by Replika Press Pvt. Ltd.

Contents

Preface to the Second Edition

It is now ten years since the original edition of The *Modern Middle East: A Reader.* Changes in the present volume have been limited to Part IV, "The Middle East Since the Second World War." The passage of ten years has allowed some important themes of the period since 1945 to emerge with greater clarity. In that time as well scholars have plumbed new sources and developed new approaches to historical narrative and analysis. We have tried to capture some of this in our new Part IV.

The first edition of *The Modern Middle East: A Reader*, which was published in 1993, emerged from a series of conversations over the years with our teacher, friend and, ultimately, collaborator, the late Albert Hourani, who died in Oxford on 17 January 1993. In the 1970s, we had the privilege of attending Albert Hourani's lectures at Harvard and in Oxford that were to form the foundation of his magisterial *A History of the Arab Peoples.* During that time he introduced us to the best periodical and other essay-length literature on the modern history of the Middle East. Since then this literature has grown in size and improved in quality, in part owing to his encouragement of three generations of Middle East scholars. As teachers ourselves, we wished to make this literature more accessible.

The Reader is designed to complement Parts III-V of *A History of the Arab Peoples*: The Ottoman Age, the Age of European Empires, and the Age of Nation-States. It expands in one direction and narrows in another the geographical scope of the Hourani book in that non-Arab parts of the Middle East such as Iran and Turkey are given attention here, but Arab North Africa is not. We have attempted to highlight a range of themes and topics concerned with the changing politics, economy, society and intellectual climate of the Middle East during the previous two hundred years. Nevertheless, we acknowledge that the *Reader* does not address all relevant themes and topics. Inevitably, there are many more articles or book chapters that we might have incorporated had space permitted; some could easily have been substituted for those we did finally select.

Albert Hourani made his main contribution to this enterprise far in advance of ours. He counseled us on what to include in the *Reader*, reminding us that the articles should illustrate important themes in the modern history of the Middle East or the uses of new kinds of sources. He encouraged us to include a few articles because the authors have original ideas about their subjects that deserve to be considered. He also contributed the introductory essay.

In the preparation of the first edition we were and remain indebted to Lynn Withey of the University of California Press and to the dozen anonymous historians—our peers—whom she consulted. Their written comments were especially useful. We are also grateful to Margaret Owen, who translated André Raymond's article on Cairo and to those who assisted us in the voluminous correspondence with authors and publishers necessary for the first edition: Ram Manikkalingam. Elisabeth Stark, and Josephine Bennett, all of M.I.T. Finally, the first edition would not have seen the light of day without the publication and editorial staff at I.B. Tauris in the early 1990s: Helen Simpson, Roger Wells, Deirdre Clark, Sally Crawford, Emma Sinclair-Webb, Russell Townsend, John Crabb, and, above all, Anna Enayat, our principal editor. She was herself a close friend and colleague of Albert Hourani, and gave unstintingly of her time and energy.

In the preparation of the second edition our thanks go to all the authors who have generously allowed us to reprint their work, to Turi Munthe, our editor at I.B. Tauris whose encouragement and patience made the present volume possible, and to Margo Collett of M.I.T. and Alice Izer of the University of Massachusetts at Amherst who helped with correspondence and other technical matters. We are very grateful to all involved in the production of this edition.

Mary C. Wilson
Philip S. Khoury

Leverett, Massachusetts
January 2003

Acknowledgements

We wish to thank the following publishers and journals for giving us permission to reprint the journal articles and chapters from books contained in this volume.

Ervand Abrahamian, 'The Crowd in the Persian Revolution,' *Iranian Studies* II, 4 (1969), 128-150. Reprinted by permission of *Iranian Studies.*

Feroz Ahmad, 'War and Society under the Young Turks, 1908-1918', *Review* XI, 2 (1988), 265-286. Reprinted by permission of *Review.*

Hanna Batatu, 'Of the Diversity of the Iraqis, the Incohesiveness of their Society and their Progress in the Monarchic Period toward a Consolidated Political Structure,' in *The Old Social Classes and the Revolutionary Movements of Iraq* (Princeton, 1978), 13-36. Reprinted by permission of Princeton University Press.

Joel Beinin and Zachary Lockman, '1919: Labor Upsurge and National Revolution,' in *Workers on the Nile* (Princeton, 1988), 83-120. Reprinted by permission of Princeton University Press.

Kenneth M. Cuno, 'The Origins of Private Ownership of Land in Egypt: a Reappraisal,' *International Journal of Middle East Studies* 12 (1980), 245-275. Reprinted by permission of Cambridge University Press.

Roderic H. Davison, 'Turkish Attitudes Concerning Christian-Muslim Equality in the Nineteenth Century,' in *Essays in Ottoman and Turkish History, 1774-1923* (Austin, 1990), 110-132. Reprinted by permission of the University of Texas Press.

C. Ernest Dawn, 'From Ottomanism to Arabism: The Origin of an Ideology,' in *From Ottomanism to Arabism: Essays on the Origins of Arab Nationalism* (Urbana, 1973), 122-147. Reprinted by permission of the University of Illinois Press.

Paul Dumont, 'Said Bey—The Everyday Life of an Istanbul Townsman at the Beginning of the Twentieth Century,' in Hans Georg Majer (ed.), *Osmanistische*

Studien zur Wirtschafts und Sozialgeschichte. In Memoriam Vanlo Bofkov (Wiesbaden, 1986), 1-16. Reprinted by permission of Otto Harrassowitz.

Mamoun Fandy, 'Religion, Social Structure, and Political Dissent in Saudi Arabia,' Adapted from Mamoun Fandy, *Saudi Arabia and the Politics of Dissent* (London, 1999), 221-60. Copyright © Mamoun Fandy. Adapted and reprinted by permission of Palgrave Macmillan and the author.

Joel Gordon, 'Nasser 56/Cairo 96,' in Walter Armbrust (ed.), *Mass Mediations: New Approaches to Popular Culture in the Middle East and Beyond* (Berkeley and Los Angeles, 2000), 161-181. Copyright © The Regents of the University of California. Reprinted by permission of the University of California Press and the author.

Uriel Heyd, 'The Ottoman 'Ulema and Westernization in the Time of Selim III and Mabmud II,' in Heyd (ed.), *Studies in Islamic History* (Jerusalem, 1961), 63-96. Reprinted by permission of Magnes Press.

Albert Hourani, 'Ottoman Reform and the Politics of Notables,' in *The Emergence of the Modern Middle East* (London, 1981), 36-66. Reprinted by permission of Macmillan Press Ltd.

R. Stephen Humphreys, 'The Strange Career of Pan Arabism,' in R. Stephen Humphreys, *Between Memory and Desire. The Middle East in a Troubled Age* (Berkeley and Los Angeles, 1999), 60-82. Copyright © The Regents of the University of California. Reprinted with permission of the University of California Press and the author.

Charles Issawi, 'Middle East Economic Development, 1815-1914: the General and the Specific,' in M. A. Cook (ed.), *Studies in the Economic History of the Middle East from the Rise of Islam to the Present Day* (London, 1970), 395-411. Reprinted by permission of Oxford University Press.

Nikki R. Keddie, 'Iranian Revolutions in Comparative Perspective,' *American Historical Review* 88 (1983), 579-598. Reprinted by permission of the *American Historical Review* and the author.

Philip S. Khoury, 'Syrian Urban Politics in Transition: The Quarters of Damascus during the French Mandate,' *International Journal of Middle East Studies* 16 (1984), 507-540. Reprinted by permission of Cambridge University Press.

Ann K. S. Lambton, 'Social Change in Persia in the Nineteenth Century,' in

Qajar Persia: Eleven Studies (Austin: University of Texas Press, 1987), 194-222. Copyright © 1987 by Ann K. S. Lambton.

Şerif Mardin, 'Religion and Secularism in Turkey,' in Ali Kazancigil and Ergun Özbudun (eds.), *Ataturk: Founder of a Modern State* (London, 1981), 191-219. Reprinted by permission of C. Hurst and Co.

David McDowall, 'Dilemmas of the Jewish State,' in his *Palestine and Israel: The Uprising and Beyond* (London: I. B. Tauris, 1989), 163-181, 291-296. Author has revised the original chapter for the purposes of this publication.

Roger Owen, 'Egypt and Europe: from French Expedition to British Occupation' in Owen and Bob Sutcliffe (eds.), *Studies in the Theory of Imperialism* (London, 1972). Reprinted by permission of the author.

Donald Quataert, 'Ottoman Women, Households, and Textile Manufacturing, 1800-1914,' in Nikki R. Keddie and Beth Baron (eds.), *Women in Middle Eastern History* (New Haven, 1991), 161-176. Reprinted by permission of Yale University Press.

André Raymond, 'Le Caire,' in *L'Egypte d'aujourd'hui: Permanence et Changements 1805-1976* (Paris, 1977), 214-241. By permission of the Centre National de la Recherche Scientifique and the author.

Olivier Roy, "The Crisis of Religious Legitimacy in Iran," *Middle East Journal* 53/2 (Spring 1999), 201-216. Reprinted by permission of *Middle East Journal* and the author.

Avi Shlaim, 'Israel and the Arab Coalition in 1948,' in Eugene Rogan and Avi Shlaim (eds.), *The War for Palestine: Rewriting the History of 1948* (Cambridge, 2001), 79-103. Copyright © Cambridge University Press. Reprinted by permission of Cambridge University Press and the author.

Ted Swedenburg, 'The Role of the Palestinian Peasantry in the Great Revolt (1936-1939),' in Edmund Burke III and Ira M. Lapidus (eds.), *Islam, Politics, and Social Movements* (Berkeley, 1988), 169-203. Copyright © 1988 The Regents of the University of California. Reprinted by permission of the University of California Press.

Judith Tucker, 'Decline of the Family Economy in Mid-Nineteenth-Century Egypt,' *Arab Studies Quarterly* vol. 1, no 3 (1979), 245-271. Reprinted by permission of *Arab Studies Quarterly*.

Note on Presentation

In the preparation of this volume, the integrity of the different authors' own systems of transliteration has been respected; and no attempt has been made to impose uniform spelling of personal or place names. The presentation of material like tables has been standardized but the material itself has not. Similarly footnotes have been extracted from the text and presented in all cases as chapter notes, but the content of the notes has not been altered. Where there is a reference in text or notes to another chapter of the book in which a particular article originally appeared, the reference has been expanded to give the full publication details of the original source. And where there is a reference to a 'forthcoming' work that has since appeared, full publication details are provided.

Introduction

Albert Hourani

I

The study of the modern Middle East, by scholars trained in the concepts and methods of modern historiography and using them in order to throw light upon their subject, has existed for some thirty or forty years, but it is only in the last few years that there has emerged—in North America and Europe, as well as in the region itself—a critical mass of scholars and students large enough to ensure that the study is carried on at a high level. It is in these last years too that some of the basic sources for it have become easily available.

It takes time for the ideas and conclusions of scholars, working on materials hitherto unused in order to throw light on a more or less unexplored and unexplained subject, to find their way into books, and particularly into textbooks. The normal method of stating and explaining one's conclusions, particularly if they are still tentative, is by means of articles in specialized periodicals, and the proceedings of conferences. It has therefore seemed to us worthwhile to make a selection of some of the more significant and stimulating articles on the subject, in order to supplement the few general surveys which exist.

The articles in this book have been chosen by the editors on the basis of their own personal judgements, but also after wide-ranging inquiries among teachers of Middle Eastern history in several countries. They have tried to find articles which convey the flavour of a particular author's work or the ideas of a school of thought, which address themselves to important aspects of the subject, or which make use of the kinds of material which seem likely to be important for future research.

For the purposes of this book, the 'Middle East' is regarded as including the area covered by what are now the states of Turkey, Iran, and Israel, and the Arab states from Egypt eastwards. This definition, like all such definitions, is to some extent arbitrary. It would have been possible to look westwards from Egypt to the Arab countries of North Africa, or eastwards from Iran to Afghanistan and south Asia, or westwards again from Turkey to those parts of south-eastern Europe which for so long formed part of the Ottoman or 'Turkish' Empire. That the area has been defined in this way can be explained partly by the limits and design of most university courses on the 'modern history of the Middle East', partly by the limits of space in this book, but also, and mainly, by the fact that this area has a sufficient unity of historical experience to enable it to be an intelligible unit of study.

Broad similarities of physical environment and climate have created comparable economic and social systems: certain relationships between city and countryside, a certain fragile balance between different uses of land, for settled agriculture and for nomadic pasturage. The situation of the region in the world, lying as it does between the Indian Ocean and the Mediterranean Sea, with Russia and central Asia to the north and Africa to the south, has given it, to a great extent, a common political destiny: much of it has formed part of great empires, some of them created within the region itself (those of Egypt and Mesopotamia in ancient times, then of Byzantium and the 'Abbasid caliphate, then of the Ottomans and Safavids in early modern times) or having their centres outside (that of Rome and, in modern times, those of Britain and France). The region was the heartland where the religion of Islam first appeared and its first great empire grew up; within the empire there developed a distinctive society, created by the formation of new links between the countries of the Indian Ocean and those of the Mediterranean, and a civilization in which the thought and art of the Greek and Persian worlds were given new forms and directions by the acceptance of the religion of Islam, and of Arabic as a language of high culture.

The unity should not be exaggerated, however. Each region, and even each city, had its own historical experience and its distinctive and continuing interests. Within each district, there were always differences and tensions between the high literate culture and the folk-culture of the urban poor and of peasants and nomads. In many cities and villages, although Islam became the religion of the majority and of power, Christian, Jewish and other communities continued to exist.

A broad division gradually appeared between the western part of the Islamic world, where Arabic was the main language of culture and for centuries the ruling elites were drawn from Turkish or other immigrant groups from central Asia, and the eastern part, where Persian was a language of high culture alongside Arabic and where other ruling elites held power, although they too tended to be of Turkish origin. This division found expression, in early modern times, in the formation of two great empires, those of the Ottomans in the west and of the Safavids in the east. Political conflicts between them expressed themselves in religious terms: the Ottomans maintained the Sunni form of Islam, while the Safavids proclaimed Shiʿism as the official religion of their state.

II

This book confines itself to the 'modern' period, that is to say, the nineteenth and twentieth centuries. All divisions of the continuum of historical time are bound to some extent to be arbitrary, but the changes which have taken place in the Middle East, as in the rest of the world, during the last two centuries have been so great and have gone so deep that they can be regarded as forming a new and distinctive period in the history of the world.

Of course, it would not be correct to talk in terms of a complete break with the past, as if what had existed earlier had been totally replaced by something new. It is more accurate to think of the process as having been created by a complex interaction between two rhythms of change. On the one hand, there were ancient societies, created by certain uses of limited natural resources, given shape and direction by the laws, practices and doctrines of a dominant religion, Islam, and ruled by Muslim imperial governments; this society was not static, but was changing by processes generated from within itself and limited by the resources made available by the technology of the time. On the other hand, there were changes of other kinds and at different paces, made possible by the use of new technology and the consequent accumulation of greater resources in north-western Europe in the eighteenth and nineteenth centuries. These changes were communicated to the Middle East, as to other parts of the world, by way of international trade, new kinds of communication and education, and new forms of administration and law, imposed either by indigenous governments wishing to acquire the strength of the European states, or else by those states themselves as they expanded their empires by means of the military strength given them by the changes in their societies.

An earlier generation of historians of the Middle East tended to look only at this second kind of change, and to assume that the ancient societies into which it was introduced were stagnant or in decay, and powerless to resist. Seen in this light, the modern history of the Middle East would be that of the imposition of various kinds of European domination over passive and unresisting societies.

This is the way in which European diplomatic historians tended to look at the history of the region: as a history of the 'Eastern Question', that is to say of the Middle East as a problem in the relations between the great European states. In another sense, it is the way in which those who view history in integral Islamic terms might see it: as the history of Muslim societies which have their own inherited norms of communal behaviour and for which the modern period has been marked by attempts made by foreign powers, or by local ruling groups unfaithful to their traditions, to impose an artificial order upon society.

It would be better, however, to see the history of this period as that of a complex interaction: of the will of ancient and stable societies to reconstitute themselves, preserving what they have of their own while making the necessary changes in order to survive in a modern world increasingly organized on other principles, and where the centres of world power have lain for long, and still lie, outside the Middle East.

III

When this process which we can call 'modern' began, the greater part of the Middle East was ruled by the two great empires, those of the Ottomans and Safavids. In spite of differences between them, the societies which they ruled had great similarities: they were the product of the whole process of Islamic civilization to which they were the heirs. Except for some outlying parts—most of the Arabian peninsula, and the regions of the southern Nile valley—they were societies dominated by cities, and by the relations between city populations and those who ruled them.

The great cities were centres of manufacture by traditional methods, but still more of international trade between countries lying to the east and west of them. The dominant elements of urban societies were a combination of three groups: merchants, in particular those engaged in the international trade in valuable goods; masters of crafts; and the *'ulama*, those engaged in studying, transmitting, interpreting and administering the *shari'a*, the body of laws derived from the teachings of Islam, which formed the only formal legal system, the guarantee of order and justice without which the complex life of a city, and the commercial relations between cities far apart from each other, could not have been carried on.

The cities were the centres of political power. Although successive dynasties had come to power by means of military forces provided by men of the countryside, the mountains or the steppe, and although some of those dynasties were themselves of similar origin, to survive and flourish they had to link their interests with those of the cities, and more specifically with those of the urban elites. The rulers could give the city order and maintenance of the fabric of law, and could defend and extend trade routes. The city for its part could give the ruler the money, by way of taxes and special levies, in order to maintain his government and army, the fine products of its crafts to show his magnificence, and the educated officials to run his chancery and treasury. The *'ulama* in particular held the keys of legitimacy: by recognizing him as a just Muslim ruler they could turn his power into legitimate authority.

They had a common interest too in controlling the countryside, and bringing in the surplus of rural production on favourable terms: this provided revenue, in cash or in kind, for the government and army, food for the urban population, and raw materials for industry. It was by the exercise of control over the countryside that landownership was created: the landowner was a military officer, an official or an urban notable who was able to establish an effective claim to part of the rural surplus. This rule by government and landowners did not extend over the whole countryside, however. Beyond the areas of direct rule there lay others where the urban government could maintain its ultimate control by supporting local intermediaries, lords of a valley or chiefs of a nomadic group, a 'tribe'. Beyond that again there lay regions of steppe, desert or mountain where even this degree of control was impossible, and where small market towns lived in some degree of subjection to the chiefs of pastoral tribes.

IV

By the late eighteenth century, the system of control by the great imperial governments had changed. The Ottoman Sultan in Istanbul still ruled almost all the lands his ancestors had conquered, not only in what we have defined as the Middle East but in North Africa and south-eastern Europe. The final authority of the central government still existed: the Ottoman army and navy could keep the main routes open, and local governors still maintained the major interests of the empire. The Sultan could still claim to have legitimate authority: he dispensed justice in the name of the *shari'a*; the judges were appointed and paid by him and played an important part in local administration; the annual pilgrimage to Mecca, by pilgrims gathering in Cairo and Damascus, two great cities of the empire, was organized and protected by his government, and was an annual assertion of his authority and unique position in the heart of the world of Islam.

The balance between central and local authorities had changed, however. Apart from regions near Istanbul and those on some principal trade routes, many of the provinces were ruled by governors or ruling groups which had their own sources of local power and in some places were able to make their rule hereditary. In some provinces—Saida in Syria, Baghdad in Iraq, and Cairo—power was in the hands of local military groups (*mamluks*), perpetuating their power by recruits from the Caucasus or elsewhere.

Another balance also had changed. In some parts of the Empire, the rural area under direct control of the cities had shrunk, and that under control of lords of the valleys or tribal chiefs had expanded; this might lead to an extension of the area used for pastoralism as opposed to sedentary agriculture. It was therefore more difficult for Ottoman governors to collect the revenue needed to maintain their armies and administration.

It was only on the outskirts of the Empire, however, that there was a challenge to the final authority of the Ottoman Sultan. In the upper Nile valley, a local sultanate, that of the Funj, was created in the seventeenth century. In central Arabia, the rulers of a market town, the Al Sa'ud, founded a state which expanded to include much of the Arabian peninsula. This was a challenge of a new kind, for the Al Sa'ud were allied with a religious reformer, Muhammad ibn 'Abd al-Wahhab, who called for a return to the purity of the first century of Islam and rejected the kind of Islam which the Ottomans supported. At the beginning of the nineteenth century the Sa'udi ruler occupied the holy cities of Mecca and Madina, and thus cast doubt on one of the claims of the Ottomans to have a special authority in the world of Islam.

In Iran, the weakening of central authority had gone further. The rule of the Safavids came to an end in the early eighteenth century, and for a time Iran was divided between a number of local rulers, based in one or other of the great cities. A brief attempt at uniting the former empire of the Safavids was made by a soldier of fortune, Nadir Shah, coming from the north-eastern region of Khurasan and expanding his rule westwards into Iraq and eastwards into northern India, but this fell to pieces when he died. It was not until the last years of the century that the ancient pattern repeated itself. A powerful leader of a tribal coalition was able to establish a new dynasty, that of the Qajars, and extend its rule over the whole of Iran. In some ways, however, it was a precarious rule. It was not based on the great cities, but in a comparatively new regional centre, Tehran in the north; it did not have the same kind of large, disciplined army as the Ottomans could rely on. It could not claim the same religious legitimacy as the Safavids had had and the Ottomans still possessed; some of the Shi'i *'ulama* were willing to serve it, but others, in the Shi'i holy cities of Iraq, lying beyond the power of the rulers, kept their distance from it.

By the last quarter of the eighteenth century, relations between the Middle East, or at least some parts of it, and Europe were changing. There was a different pattern of international trade: European merchants in the main ports and trading cities were buying silk, cotton and other raw materials, and selling spices and coffee grown in the European colonies in the East and West Indies, and textiles woven in their factories. The shadow of European military power came closer. From the north, Russia had expanded to the coast of the Black Sea, and a war with the Ottoman Empire ended in 1774 with a treaty which showed the unequal power of the two empires and led to the loss of a Muslim territory, the Crimea. To the east, the British East India Company took over the government and revenues of Bengal, an important province of a third great Muslim Empire, that of the Mughals, and was extending its influence in the Persian Gulf and southern Iraq.

V

A new phase can be said to start around the beginning of the nineteenth century, with a two-fold advance in European influence and power. The wars of the French Revolution generated a greater military power, based on new kinds of organization and military technique. A sign of this was the brief occupation of Egypt by the French in 1798. It did not last long, but the intrusion of a European power into the heart of the Muslim world had repercussions far beyond; it led to the involvement of the Ottoman government in alliances with the enemies of France. Of more lasting importance was the advance of Russia from the north, for a time in the European provinces of the Ottoman Empire and more permanently in the Caucasus. The ancient Christian kingdom of Georgia and part of the Iranian region of Azerbaijan were absorbed, and a treaty with Iran in 1828 showed Russia's superior power. The influence of British India increased in the Persian Gulf, where the first agreements were made with some of the rulers of small ports, and as the British expanded westwards in India their pressure upon the Qajars increased.

There was also a change in the nature of trade. Once the wars of the French Revolution ended in 1815, European merchant ships returned to the ports of the eastern Mediterranean, bringing with them goods of a new kind, those produced in the factories of northern Europe: above all, cotton textiles and iron products. From the 1830s onwards these goods began to be carried in a new way, by steamships; in the 1850s and 1860s the extension of telegraphs brought the Middle Eastern cities closer in many ways to those of Europe and America. The result of these innovations was a change in the terms of trade. The Middle Eastern countries were able to pay for the goods they imported only by producing raw materials for the factories of Europe, in particular the high-grade cotton which began to be produced in Egypt on a large scale from the 1830s onwards.

Indigenous governments tried to respond to the new threats and pressures from Europe by changing their own methods of work. The Ottoman government began to create a new army on the European model; its methods of administration also changed, and new legal codes were brought in, modelled upon those of western Europe. They carried with them the idea of citizenship, of rights and duties, of equality between citizens of different religions, and of the existence of an 'Ottoman nation'; in the Treaty of Paris of 1856 which ended a war in which the Ottoman Empire was allied with Britain and France against Russia, the Sultan was recognized as a member of the European states-system.

Such changes strengthened the power of the central government, but only within limits. The westernmost province of the Empire, Algiers, was occupied by France in 1830–47. Some of the European provinces were the scene of local revolts in the name of the new idea of nationalism: Serbia became autonomous in the early years of the century, and Greece became an independent kingdom in 1833, after a revolt in 1821, a long attempt by the Ottomans to crush it, and intervention by the European powers.

Even in the regions still lying within the Empire, the freedom of action of the central government was limited. On the one hand, the European ambassadors and consuls exercised a growing influence; on the other, some provincial rulers were able to secure almost autonomous power. In Tunis, a local dynasty which had ruled beneath Ottoman sovereignty since the early eighteenth century was able to create a more modern system of administration, in collaboration with the European merchants. In Egypt, a Turkish soldier of fortune, Muhammad 'Ali, made himself governor with a new military elite from the Balkans and Anatolia; he created a new army and a more effective administration, established conditions in which European merchants could work more freely, and changed the nature of trade by encouraging the cultivation of cotton. For a time he extended his rule into Syria and Arabia, but he met with opposition from most of the European powers, which did not wish the Ottoman government to be weakened too far; he was compelled to withdraw from his conquests but was given recognition as hereditary ruler of Egypt. (It was to check his expansion in Arabia that the British government in India established the first British colony in the Middle East, Aden.)

Rather similar attempts at reform were made in Iran, but in more difficult circumstances. The Qajars continued to rule. At the beginning of the long reign of Nasir al-Din Shah, a reforming minister tried to initiate changes, but with little result: the bureaucracy and army were not strong enough to impose and administer them; the pressure of European merchants and governments was weaker than in the countries round the Mediterranean; caught between contending pressures from Russia and British India, the Shah had less freedom of action.

How far did societies change in the first half of the nineteenth century? There was a certain change in the structure of social power in the cities, at least in those cities which were centres of reforming governments and foreign trade. Since the government was taking an increasing part in the regulation of social life, bureaucrats—in particular the higher bureaucrats—were acquiring greater power. In the countries under Ottoman control, former local ruling dynasties were eliminated, but the urban notables who had grown up around them continued to be influential as intermediaries between administrators sent from Istanbul and the urban population. Merchants engaged in trade with Europe grew richer and more powerful; in the Ottoman cities and in Egypt they were mainly Europeans or local Christians and Jews, in Iran largely Muslims. On the other hand, merchants engaged in the older kinds of trade by land routes lost some of their position, and so did masters of crafts whose products were displaced by the new kinds of import from Europe. In Istanbul, Cairo and Tunis, a class of men was emerging educated in the new European fashion—army officers, officials, teachers and doctors—but they were still too marginal to have much impact on society; the moral conscience of communities was still controlled by those learned in the religious sciences.

In the countryside, the domination of large landowners grew greater as the control of the government extended. In Egypt, Muhammad ʿAli expropriated many of the former holders of land and himself became the chief landowner, but by the mid-century much of the land had been given to officials of the dynasty and officers in the army. In the Ottoman provinces, a land law of 1858 led to the formation of large estates by merchants, urban notables, and tribal chieftains. The rhythm of production in the countryside proceeded much as before, except in those parts which were producing raw materials for Europe: silk in Lebanon, above all cotton in Egypt, where the extension of perennial irrigation was beginning to affect ancient patterns of seasonal production.

VI

The half-century which stretched roughly from 1860 to the outbreak of World War I in 1914 saw, in some ways, a continuation of processes begun earlier in the century. The extension of control by the government was carried further. Thanks to the coming of new methods of communication—railways, telegraphs and steamships—it was possible to establish direct administration at the expense of local chieftains. The opening of the Suez Canal in 1869, and the building of the Hijaz railway in the early twentieth century, made it possible for Ottoman administration to extend to Hijaz and Yemen; in central Arabia, a dynasty supported by the Ottomans expanded southwards into territory controlled by the Al Saʿud, who had been crushed by Muhammad ʿAli but had revived later. The power of Cairo stretched southwards into upper Egypt and the Sudan, but a religious reformer, the Mahdi, was able to remove Egyptian rule in the 1880s and create a system of Islamic government. Such changes were slower and less complete in Iran until the last quarter of the nineteenth century; communications were still limited, except for the opening to international trade of the valley of the Karun river in the south-west.

These changes took place within an environment marked by closer European control. In order to finance the changes, indigenous governments fell into debt to European bankers, supported by their governments, which came to exercise a closer control over the finances. In Egypt, this control was the first step towards something else: the imposition of rule by a single European power, Great Britain, for which Egypt had increasing importance after the opening of the Suez Canal, the main artery of communication with India, East Asia and Australia. In 1882, after a crisis in which control of the country seemed to be passing into the hands of military officers with ideas of Egyptian independence, Britain occupied the country; henceforth, although formally Egypt continued to be ruled by the family of Muhammad 'Ali under Ottoman suzerainty, Britain had effective control. A similar process had already taken place in Tunisia, occupied by France in 1881, and it was to continue as the division of the world between the great European powers went further. Britain extended its rule southwards from Egypt into the Sudan in the last years of the century, and it increased its control over the rulers of the Persian Gulf by a series of treaties in which they placed their relations with the outside world in British hands. Similarly, France established a protectorate over the kingdom of Morocco in 1912, and Italy began to occupy the Ottoman province of Tripoli (Libya) in 1911.

The Ottoman government was able, however, to maintain some freedom of action in its central provinces, because European rivalries were too strong to allow any one Power to occupy them, but Britain, France, Russia and later Germany all made it clear that they had special interests in various parts of it. In Iran, contrary pressures from the British in India and from Russia, extending its empire in central Asia, enabled the Shah's government to maintain a precarious independence, but in 1907 an Anglo-Russian agreement virtually divided the country into spheres of influence. The discovery and exploitation of oil in Iran gave Britain a new interest in the country: by 1914 the British government had a controlling interest in the Anglo-Persian Oil Company.

The extension of government control and of European influence brought about further changes in society. In the capital cities, Istanbul and Cairo, and in the centres of foreign trade there grew up a dual society: popular quarters, where the poor lived in much the same way as before, not yet changed by mass immigration from the countryside; and new quarters, where high officials, European merchants, a new class of indigenous merchants and a growing professional class lived in houses of European design and had the amenities of European urban life. In the countryside, the area of settled agriculture grew larger at the expense of that of nomadic pastoralism, particularly where cash crops could be grown for the European market. New land laws in Egypt and the Ottoman Empire gave greater assurance to private property, and once more it was largely those who could make use of urban laws and the power of the government who profited from it. There does not seem to have been any great increase in the rural population beyond the means of subsistence; in some regions there may have been a rise in living standards.

In this period a new element in the population began to grow in importance: those with a modern education, a knowledge of what was happening in the outside world, and a mastery of one or other of the techniques essential for thriving in modern society. By now education had spread beyond the small number of those sent abroad by reforming governments or trained in special schools. Governments were creating networks of schools at every level, and European and American religious missions also established schools, including some higher colleges and some schools for girls. The traditional religious schools still existed for the training of *'ulama*, but the opportunities for their graduates were more limited, as codes of law based on European models replaced those derived from the *shari'a*, except in the sphere of family and personal law, and as the activities of a modern government, army and society required men trained in a new way.

This growing literate class could now make use of different media of communication. Printing was becoming widespread, and the presses of Istanbul, Beirut, Cairo and Tehran were producing a growing number of books in Turkish, Arabic and Persian, many of them translations or adaptations from European literature, but also works of poetry and a new kind of simplified expository prose. More influential than books were newspapers and periodicals; they imparted news of the outside world brought by the telegraph, explained the techniques and social forms of Europe and America, and discussed the problems and prospects of their own societies.

Thus there grew up an intelligentsia, not wholly absorbed into government service and having its own ideas about the way in which society should be organized. The official ideologies of the states were those of national solidarity and unity around the ruling families: there was an Ottoman or Egyptian or Persian nation gathered around the throne. As the nineteenth century approached its end, however, there spread other ideas which carried within them a criticism of existing forms of government. In the Ottoman Empire, the idea of an Ottoman nation was developed in two directions: on the one hand, towards the idea of a constitution and control by the people; on the other, towards an idea of Islamic unity around the Ottoman sultan. In 1876 a constitution was granted, but it was soon suspended. It was restored after a revolution in 1908; this was largely carried out by army officers, who from this time onwards were to play an important political role. The weakening of the Sultan's control and the growth of European influence gave various ethnic elements in the Empire the opportunity to put forward their claims to independence. By 1914 most of the European provinces had been absorbed into nation-states; the Armenians had made a bid for independence but had been suppressed; Turkish and Arab nationalism had both begun to become important.

Similarly, in Iran a movement which involved various strata of the population led in 1906 to the granting of a constitution; this did not last long, however, because it was thought by the two dominant powers to run counter to their interests. In Egypt, the national movement which had been suppressed by the British occupation revived in the first years of the twentieth century.

These new national movements were beginning to acquire a content of ideas about the way in which national communities should be organized. One of the constituent elements in this content was the idea of the emancipation of women, put forward by women writers in periodicals, and also by some men who supported them.

VII

Shortly after the outbreak of war in 1914, the Ottoman government entered on the side of Germany and Austria-Hungary; the end of the war was to see the disappearance of the Ottoman Empire, as of other empires of Europe. In 1914 the British extinguished Ottoman sovereignty in Egypt and made the country a protectorate; by 1918, military campaigns in Ottoman territory had led to British and French occupation of the Arab provinces of the Empire, and allied control of Istanbul and the central government. In the next few years, the Arab regions were placed under British and French administrations subject to some supervision by the League of Nations (the 'Mandate system'): the French in Syria and Lebanon; the British in Iraq, Palestine and Transjordan, with a special obligation in Palestine to facilitate the creation of a 'Jewish national home'. Of other Ottoman territories, Anatolia and the district round Istanbul became the state of Turkey, after a strong Turkish resistance to plans of partition drawn up by the British and their allies. In the Arabian peninsula, Hijaz and Yemen became independent states, but in the 1920s the former was absorbed into a larger unit, the state of Saudi Arabia, created by a member of the Al Sa'ud, 'Abd al-'Aziz ('Ibn Saud'). Iran had not been officially involved in the war, but in fact much of its territory had come under Russian or British control, and by its end the government of the Qajars was very much under British domination. Soon afterwards the dynasty was deposed by a military officer, Reza Pahlevi, who made himself Shah in 1926.

Of the states which were formally independent, the only one which was fully so was Turkey. Ruled by an Ottoman general who had led the national resistance to the plans to divide it, Mùstafa Kemal (Atatürk), and with the advantage of being able to build a state around the structure of the Ottoman central administration and army, the new Turkey began a policy of radical change. It was to be a national state: the main ethnic minorities, the Greeks and Armenians, for the most part had been eliminated, by massacre or expulsion, during and after the war. It was to be a secular state, taking its inspiration from what its leaders believed to be the principles of the modern civilization of Europe: it would be secular, deriving its laws from the popular will and national interest; it would try to acquire the strength necessary to survive in the modern world by industrialization, national education and the emancipation of women.

The example of Turkey was followed by Reza Shah in Iran, within the limits imposed by a slower process of change and the strength of British influence. It also had a deep impact on the nationalist movements in the countries placed under British and French control. During the next twenty years Britain and, more hesitantly, France moved towards accommodation with movements demanding national independence. In Egypt, Britain was able to reach agreement with the organized nationalist party, the Wafd, by a treaty in 1936 which recognized Egypt's independence within limits but which preserved a British military presence for a number of years. A similar treaty had been made a few years earlier with Iraq, where a member of the Hashimite family, the rulers of Mecca who had been allied with Britain during the Syrian campaign during the war, had been made king; another member of the family was made Amir of Transjordan. In Syria and Lebanon, France tried in 1936 to make similar treaties but failed because of the weakness of French governments. In Palestine it was impossible to move in this direction because of the British commitment to the creation of a Jewish national home; by 1939 the Jewish population had increased considerably through immigration from Europe, and Arab opposition to the policy had also increased.

During the later 1930s the British and French hold over the Middle East was challenged by the rise of German and Italian power. When World War II broke out in 1939, parts of the Middle East became theatres of military operations. First Italian then German threats to the British position in Egypt were not decisively defeated until 1943; the danger of German control in Syria led to its occupation by British and Free French forces, and a similar fear in Iraq also led to British military occupation of the country. Turkey remained neutral. Iran, although also neutral, was an important channel of communication between the Western allies and Russia, and it was occupied by British and Russian armies; in 1941 Reza Shah abdicated and was replaced by his son.

This was a period when the two rhythms of change in society became more closely connected with each other. The social domination of landowners and merchants continued to exist, and was strengthened by the increasing control of governments over society, the extension of cultivation, and the virtual end of nomadic pastoralism as an economically viable way of using land. The spread of education was creating an expanding middle class of small business men and professional men and—increasingly—women. It was these two classes which dominated the nationalist movements against foreign rule, and the indigenous governments to the extent to which they became self-governing. In Turkey and Egypt, more than in other countries, modern industry was expanding, and there were the beginnings of labour organization and activity. In this period the growth of population began to be marked, and the surplus population of the countryside was moving into the large cities.

These changes were scarcely beginning in the two main states of the Arabian peninsula, Saudi Arabia and Yemen, where absolute monarchs claiming a religious sanction for their rule governed societies that were organized on the basis of tribal loyalties and barely touched by modern economic and social changes. In some parts of the peninsula, however, a new kind of change was imminent, as the oil resources of the area round the Gulf became more important in the economic life of the world. In addition to those in Iran, those in northern Iraq were exploited from the 1930s by an international company, with British, French, Dutch and American participation. After 1945, the exploitation of wells in Kuwait and the east of Saudi Arabia began on a considerable scale. The implications of this were far-reaching: on the one hand, domination of the economies of the producing countries by the foreign companies, and an increasing strategic interest in them by Europe and the United States; on the other, royalties to the producing countries made economic development possible, and the training of technicians added a new element to the educated class.

An expanding literate population in the cities was more exposed than before to new ideas, and the spread of them was made easier by improved communications: the coming of the automobile, even across the desert, the beginnings of air routes, the spread of newspapers and radio, and its use by the competing Powers during World War II. The dominant idea was that of nationalism: the creation of independent states. The example of Turkey was strong everywhere, particularly in Iran. In some Arab countries, but not in Egypt, the idea of an Arab state, reuniting the former Ottoman provinces which had been divided by Britain and France, was stronger than that of limited nation-states. At the end of World War II it seemed to have found its first embodiment in the creation of a League of Arab States.

In intricate relationship with the ideas of nationalism was another complex of ideas: that of a re-structuring of society on the basis of Islamic law and social morality, adapted to the needs of the modern world. This was given an impetus by the creation of Saudi Arabia, a state based on a strict version of

Islam, and also by the emergence of the Muslim Brothers in Egypt, a movement in the lower ranks of the urban literate population. In Turkey the power of the *ʿulama* and what they stood for seemed to have disappeared; in Iran, the Shiʿi *ʿulama* were far from the centre of political power but still had a great influence over the masses of the population.

VIII

The half-century after the end of World War II saw the disappearance of the European empires in the Middle East. After a series of crises, France withdrew from Syria and Lebanon in 1946. Faced with an organized Jewish community in Palestine demanding immigration for the remnants of European Jewry and supported by the United States, Britain withdrew from Palestine in 1948, in circumstances which led to the creation of the state of Israel in the greater part of Palestine, the amalgamation of most of the remainder with Transjordan in the state of Jordan, and the dispossession of the majority of the Palestinian Arab population. In Egypt and Iraq, the withdrawal of British forces took place under treaty agreements; the agreement with Egypt led to the independence of the Sudan.

The withdrawal was less complete than it might have seemed: both Britain and the United States had a major interest in controlling the production of oil, and Britain for a time wished to maintain its position as the dominant power in the Middle East. This gave rise to a series of crises. In Iran, an attempt by a government led by Musaddiq to ensure real national independence by nationalizing the oil company was thwarted by Anglo-American intervention in 1953. In Egypt, the nationalization of the Suez Canal Company in 1956 was the occasion for an Anglo-French attempt to reassert control over the country, but this failed because it was opposed to the interests of the new super-powers. In 1958, a revolution in Iraq ended the monarchy and British ultimate domination. In the next few years, the vestiges of British power, in the small states of the Gulf, and in Aden and the protectorate of small states around it, disappeared.

As British and French power waned, the life of the newly independent states was lived in the context of the 'Cold War' between the two super-powers, the USA and the USSR, which gave them a certain freedom of policy. Turkey and some other states were firmly in the Western camp, but the dominant tendency in most of the other states was towards 'non-alignment' between the two blocs. Internally, most states began their independent life with some kind of constitutional government, but this proved to be fragile. In Turkey and the Sudan, there were alternations between periods of constitutional government and military rule. In Iran, the end of Musaddiq's bid for power was followed by 25 years of rule by the Shah. In Egypt, the monarchy and constitution were overturned by a military coup in 1952 and the ascendancy of a powerful dictator, Jamal 'Abd al-Nasir; similar coups took place in Syria and Iraq. In Yemen too the rule of the monarch, the Imam, was ended by a revolution; elsewhere in the Arabian peninsula, however, absolute rule of a traditional kind continued. In Jordan the monarchy continued, and King Husayn was able to retain power in the midst of conflicting forces. Lebanon remained a constitutional republic, but a combination of internal and external pressures led to a long period of civil war, the collapse of central authority, and the domination of Syria over most of the country; nevertheless, the idea and forms of constitutional government continued. Israel too maintained a constitutional regime, the nature of which changed as new immigrant groups altered the structure of the population.

Two factors dominated the changes in society during this period. One was the rapid growth of population everywhere, largely because of improvements in public health and medical services, but also because of changes in patterns of marriage and child-bearing. This had important consequences. First, there was an exodus of population from the countryside, where most governments tended to give less importance to the development of agriculture than to industry; the capital cities in particular grew and became homes to a mass of displaced peasantry not accustomed to the restraints of urban life. Secondly, there was a change in the age-structure of the population; in almost all countries, those under the age of twenty formed the majority of the population; this had implications both for views of the past and for expectations for the future.

The second dominant factor was the rapid and vast expansion of the oil industry. Saudi Arabia, Kuwait, the United Arab Emirates and other Gulf states became very important centres of production; together with the older-established oil-producing states, Iran and Iraq, they held a large proportion of the known oil reserves of the world. In different ways, all the countries took control of production from the foreign companies during the 1970s, and the formation of a strong cartel, OPEC, gave them considerable influence over prices. The great increase in oil prices in the 1970s produced wealth for lavish expenditure and, in some countries, capital development. The result was a shift in power between countries which had oil and those which had none; the difference was alleviated but not eliminated by loans and grants from the richer to the poorer. Another result was large-scale migration from the poorer countries with surplus population to the richer ones which needed labour at various levels: Yemenis, Egyptians and Palestinians went in large numbers to Saudi Arabia and the smaller states of the Gulf.

The growth of a young, literate urban population with too few outlets for work had its impact upon ideas about the organization of society. At least until the end of the 1970s, nationalism continued to be the dominant ideology, but socialism became important in the constellation of ideas which surrounded it: that is, the idea that social justice, national strength and therefore genuine independence involved control of the productive resources of the state by the government, and division of wealth in the direction of greater equality. In some countries, large landed estates were broken up, and landowners ceased to play the dominant role in most societies. In Arab countries, the dominant form of nationalism was 'Nasirism', the mixture of ideas put forward in the name of ʿAbd al-Nasir and spread by the new mass media: Arab unity, socialism and neutralism. The desire for restoration of the rights of the Palestinian Arabs was an essential ingredient of it. Nasirism met with defeat in 1967, when a war between Israel and a coalition of Arab states—Egypt, Syria and Jordan—led to the Israeli occupation of the remainder of Palestine. From that time, support for Palestinian claims passed mainly to the Palestinians themselves, and to the Palestinian Liberation Organization which spoke in their name; in the 1980s the Palestinians under Israeli occupation were to take a more active role in a long-drawn-out movement of virtual rejection of an Israeli role. From that time too the nature of Israeli politics changed, as Israel faced new problems: whether to withdraw from the occupied territories in return for peace, or to hold on to them and use their land and water for Jewish settlements.

In the 1970s two other significant changes took place. One was a certain rejection, in Egypt and other Arab countries, of the tendency towards state control of economic life, and a new opening towards the capitalist economies of the West. This movement was led by Nasir's successor in Egypt, Anwar Sadat, who also opened a new phase in the relations between Israel and its Arab neighbours by making peace in return for Egyptian land controlled by Israel since the 1967 war.

The other change was the downfall in 1979 of the autocratic government of the Shah in Iran, in a way which had repercussions throughout the Islamic world. It was overthrown by a mass uprising which several political forces helped to organize. In the event, the force which emerged as pre-eminent was that of a movement to restore the domination of Islamic law and social morality in society. Its leader and spokesman was a Shiʿi divine, Ruhullah Khomeini, whose ideas, circulated by the new medium of the cassette, met with a response among the new urban masses. Khomeini became the effective head of the government; this was a new departure, but the content of his ideas and programme was not new. Often described as 'fundamentalism', it could better be called 'Islamic conservatism', the desire to preserve the moral heritage of the past and to relate change to unchanging principles. It linked the social morality which had been developed over the centuries by Shiʿi divines with ideas drawn from the popular nationalism of the age: social justice for the poor, and hostility to the super-powers. In at least one respect it broke with the immediate past: in its attempt to confine women to traditional roles in society.

The challenge of this kind of Islamic revival was felt throughout the world of Islam. It gave a stimulus to analogous movements in other countries. It had a specially close impact upon Iran's western neighbour, Iraq, the home of a more secular, populist, Arab nationalist regime under Saddam Husayn. A long war between the two (1980–88) ended in military stalemate, but in the process Iraq had generated such military strength, with the aid of Western states, as to make possible an attempt in 1990 to overthrow the existing order in the Gulf states. The occupation of Kuwait by Iraq seemed to pose a threat not only to the existing order in the Gulf but also to two essential interests of the United States: the security of Saudi Arabia and that of Israel. Various common interests brought together a broad coalition of forces which compelled Iraq to withdraw from Kuwait after a brief war. The success of US armed forces in this war, and the simultaneous decline in the position of the USSR in the world, left America the dominant power in the region; but in 1991 it was still too early to say how that power would be used.

IX

The study by historians of this long period of complex change has passed through several stages. The first serious documented studies concerned the relations between the great European states, their agreements and disagreements in regard to the Near East (the so-called 'Eastern Question'). The states and peoples of the region came into the picture as passive bodies, over which the Powers pursued their interests. In a later phase, more attention was given to indigenous governments and elites which were trying to change armies, methods of administration, systems of law and ways of thought and life, in order to make them conform to the model provided by Western Europe. Together with this, there was an emphasis upon the work of writers, connected with the reforming elites and rulers, who tried to give a direction to change, and to justify it, in terms of those ideas—of civilization, of citizenship and nationalism, of secularism and the re-formulation of religious beliefs—which they thought to contain the secret of European strength. Later still, more attention has been paid to changes in social and economic structures: to the growth and changing shape of cities, changes in patterns of production and exchange, and changes too in the distribution of wealth and the formation of social strata or classes.

The writing of each period was marked by a distinctive use of sources, and to some extent this is shown in the articles included in this book. Thus studies of the 'Eastern Question' were based, by necessity, on the archives of the great European governments, and in particular those of Britain and

France. To a great extent those of the second period also made use of these European archives. Some historians were aware, however, of the danger inherent in the use of them to throw light on the process of internal change; they might reflect the views of indigenous governments and reformers, who were eager to talk to European diplomats in order to win their sympathy, but they did so at one remove and with a danger of distortion. Such archives of Middle Eastern governments as had become available were beginning to be used by those with access to them. In particular, this was the period when some historians (mostly Turkish) were exploring the vast archives of the Ottoman government: for the earlier period of Ottoman rule, tax-records and the records of business brought to the imperial council and decisions made there; for the period of reform in the nineteenth century, the administrative papers of the various ministries. In a similar way, a number of historians, both European and Arab, were able to explore the papers of the government of Egypt, from the time of Muhammad 'Ali onwards. When various regions came under British or French rule, the archives of those governments and their local administrations took on a new importance. The ideas which underlay, or could be used to justify, reform were explored by way of memoirs, newspapers and cultural periodicals from the mid-nineteenth century onwards.

During the third phase, in which more attention was given to social and economic history, European sources continued to be important, in particular reports of consuls and the papers of trading companies, when they were available. Historians were aware, however, of the danger of relying too much on such sources: the picture they gave of the societies they described was seen in the perspective of the commercial and financial interests of European governments and traders, and of the indigenous merchants associated with them; they tended to ignore other sectors of the economy and other strata of society. In the last twenty years or so, some scholars of a younger generation have begun to make systematic use of other kinds of sources: the instructions (*awamir*) sent by the central government to its local representatives, and the records of the *mahkama*, the court of the *qadi* or judge of Islamic law (the *shari'a*). Until changes in the law and its administration in the nineteenth century, the *qadi* had a central role in Ottoman government and society: he not only decided legal disputes, he was responsible for the distribution of the property of deceased persons in accordance with the prescriptions of the *shari'a*; he kept a record of transactions between individuals and families (marriage contracts and transfers of property); he also kept registers of orders issued by the government in Istanbul to its local representatives. Archives of the *mahkama* can be found wherever Ottoman direct rule existed, and they are being used by a growing number of scholars to throw light upon such matters as changes in the distribution of property, relations between and within families, and 'political economy' – that is to say, the relationship between wealth and social power. (In Iran, such documents also exist, but the use of them has scarcely begun.) When the place of the *shari'a* and its judges became less important in the second half of the nineteenth century, the papers of the new administrative units, the ministries, can be used for similar purposes, and so can those of European colonial administrations when and where they were created. For the period since 1945, there is now a mass of more or less reliable, quantitative evidence to be found in documents produced by agencies of the United Nations and other international bodies.

It seems likely that most historians now working will continue to be attracted to subjects of this sort and will learn to use the kinds of sources which are now available. To a great extent, however, Middle Eastern historiography is a reflection of what is current in studies of other parts of the world, and it may be that more attention will be given to two other kinds of historical enquiry which have become important in European and American historiography of the present day. First, there may be greater interest in the study of movements of the collective consciousness, changes in the *mentalités* (to use a French term which has now become current) of whole strata of society. These are particularly important in a period of growth of urban populations and mass participation in political activity: the Iranian revolution of 1979, for example, showed how important and almost unforeseen such movements might be. The study of *mentalités* is rather different from the older kind of intellectual history, which laid its emphasis upon individual thinkers believed to be important or influential, and the relations between them. European and American historians have found ways of writing this kind of history, on the basis of such sources as newspaper articles, speeches and sermons, advertisements, inscriptions on tombstones, popular songs, and the records of the lives of 'ordinary people', and similar sources exist in the Middle East.

Secondly, there is likely to be a greater concern with 'women's history', and by this is meant not only the history of the changing roles of women in society, but something broader: the attempt to discern, by the use of whatever sources are available, the specific ways in which Middle Eastern women have experienced historical events and processes and, by so doing, to arrive at a new kind of understanding of them.

I

Reforming Elites and Changing Relations with Europe, 1789–1918

Introduction

MARY C. WILSON

There were many sources of the social and political changes that transformed the Middle East in the nineteenth century. Historians differ in their analyses of these changes, in their judgements of the relative importance of internal and external factors, and in their estimations of the impact of economic, social, political and intellectual forces. Which came first and when? Some historians look back to the worldwide economic changes of the sixteenth century, some only look as far as the new ideas of the French Revolution, and some see the sultans of the seventeenth and eighteenth centuries taking on problems of social disturbance and administration in ways not unlike those of their nineteenth-century descendants. What historians do agree about is that in the nineteenth century the impulse to control alterations in social and political life, and to reshape government and change its relationship to society, came primarily from the ruler and those closest to him. Reform in the Middle East in the nineteenth century was reform from above.

Five articles in this section are about reform in the Ottoman Empire and Egypt which, though nominally part of the Ottoman Empire until 1914, followed an increasingly independent path of state formation after the brief French occupation of 1798–1801. The sixth article presents an overview of Iran in the nineteenth century; implicitly it invites comparison with the Ottoman and Egyptian cases. The time frame is a conventional one. Selim III, whose reign began in 1789, has long been viewed as the first sultan to initiate reforms aimed at reorganizing the Ottoman government along lines conventionally referred to as modern. That is, with his reign began those cumulative, self-conscious changes aimed at centralizing, rationalizing and secularizing the Ottoman state within the changed historical context of the long nineteenth century. The year 1918 marks the defeat of the Ottoman Empire in the First World War and of those elites who had either overseen and benefited from the changes of the preceding century or been created by them.

The central story of the Ottoman and Egyptian reforms of the long nineteenth century—the achievements and setbacks of Selim III, Mahmud II and Muhammad ʿAli, the imperial edicts and laws of the Tanzimat, the accelerated centralization of power in the hands of Abdulhamid II and the Young Turks, the loss of control in Egypt to Britain—is well known and will not be retold here. Rather, the articles included in this section discuss the participation of certain elites in reform and the impact of reform on them. They also address the part that Europe played. Each poses questions that, at the time of writing, had not yet been adequately addressed; some of these questions still await investigation. Some establish analytical categories that have proven of great use to later historians.

Over 30 years ago Uriel Heyd took a careful look at *ʿulama* attitudes towards the legislative and institutional reforms proposed by Selim III and Mahmud II and made two important discoveries. First, he found 'the elements of class struggle within the *ʿulemā* corps' and outlined a social gulf between the highest *ʿulama* families, whose power, influence and wealth were passed on from generation to generation, and the humble theological student (*softa*), often of provincial origin, waiting half a lifetime for a degree and a post and the wherewithal to support a wife and family. It is still true, as he noted at the time, that class struggle among the Ottoman *ʿulama* has not been adequately studied. Second, he found that a significant proportion of the highest *ʿulama* supported reform, and did so not simply from a position of dependence on the sultan's favour, but from the conviction that any means to ensure the survival of the empire was ultimately justifiable.

The highest *ʿulama* supported reform from positions of great trust and responsibility within the ruling bureaucracy. Heyd's conclusion, that the integration of *ʿulama* into the ruling class did no great service to religion and did not result in a more Islamic state, deserves attention. It helps to qualify the meaning of 'Islamic' as commonly used to describe the Ottoman state and may be useful to us in thinking about the impact of Islamic political groups and movements in our own time.

An incident of apostasy in 1843 related by Heyd presented the highest *ʿulama* of the empire, who also tended to be the most reform-minded, with an impossible dilemma. European representatives were quick to protest at the death sentence mandated by the *sharīʿa* and the *ʿulama* closest to the sultan had to give their advice in a case where religious law and realpolitik were in clear contradiction. Roderic Davison tells us the end of the story. In 1844 the sultan 'engaged not to enforce the death penalty for apostasy from Islam'.

Two conclusions can perhaps be drawn from this story: that the influence of the European powers on Istanbul was growing, and that the customary laws and attitudes regulating religious identity and behaviour in the Ottoman Empire were changing. The two are related, though it is with the latter that Davison is mainly concerned.

The position of non-Muslims in the Ottoman Empire was a subject of disproportionate concern both to European states in the nineteenth century and to Western historians of the empire in the twentieth. In an article published in 1954, Davison begins to redress the balance of historical attention by focusing on Muslim attitudes towards Christians and the attempt to legislate equality between the two. Davison breaks with prior historians in his judgement that Tanzimat statesmen were sincere in their attempts to legislate equality between Muslim and non-Muslim. In the context of the changing Ottoman state of the nineteenth century, he sees this effort as part of the process by which Ottoman subjects, grouped into corporate identities in varied relationships to the state, were to be redefined as individuals sharing equally in the rights and duties of citizenship. Osmanlılık, the new ideology of identity propagated to subsume the corporate identities of the past, was most warmly received, however, not by the Christians of the empire, but by a new Muslim intelligentsia which emerged towards the end of the Tanzimat, the Young (or New) Ottomans. It failed to bind errant Christians to the empire—they came to prefer independence to equality—but helped instead to lay the intellectual foundations for the later development of Turkish and Arab nationalism.

If Davison attempted in 1954 to shift the light of historical attention from Christians to Muslim attitudes towards Christians, Albert Hourani in 1966 turned the spotlight full on the neglected Muslim town-dwellers of the empire. In the process he established a category, 'urban notables', and named a type of politics 'the politics of notables', which have proved of lasting value to historians of the Ottoman provinces and the successor states in the period from the eighteenth century to the mid-twentieth century.

The urban notable was a man of local prominence who occupied an intermediary position between the distant power of Istanbul and local society. As a man of property and substance, he was interested in maintaining the status quo. Hence he remained loyal to a government that guaranteed the customs of the country and served, when necessary, as a conduit for its power. As a man of local standing and leadership, he hoped to keep governmental interference at bay and voiced, when unavoidable or when useful to himself, his clients' interests to the central government. The legislative and administrative reforms emanating from Istanbul throughout the nineteenth century which aimed at the centralization of power and the breakdown of corporate identities tended to encroach on the urban notable's range of independent action. With his own interests threatened, the urban notable was moved to expression, and we can hear through him the voices of Muslim urban society raised at moments of crisis precipitated by the vast changes of the period.

The emergence of new types of historical sources not only makes new types of history possible, but may indicate historical shifts themselves. Hourani points out that, beginning about 1760, European diplomatic and consular correspondence assumes importance in the writing of Ottoman social and political history; the proliferation and increased accuracy of such sources signals 'the growing weight of European interests in the Middle East', which Roger Owen demonstrates in his 1972 essay on imperialism in Egypt.

European interests in Egypt expanded rapidly throughout the nineteenth century. As a classic case of European expansion, the British occupation of Egypt became, in Owen's words, 'a battleground for rival theories' of imperialism. He eschews that battle to look behind the immediate crisis which brought British troops to Egypt in 1882, and beyond questions of motive. In the century before the British occupation, Egypt was subject to two forces, themselves related: the expanding capitalist economy of Europe and the centralizing state of Muhammad 'Ali and his descendants. The interaction of these two—the government's newly imposed control of the countryside and its need for revenue, and the extension of European laws and financial practices—transformed Egyptian society. In the process Europe was drawn increasingly into Egypt's affairs, ending finally in the British occupation. In this, Owen sees a pattern. 'The loss of economic independence not only preceded the loss of political independence, it also prepared the way for it.'

The Ottoman Empire followed a similar pattern, with differences of rhythm and timing. Outright loss of political control was put off until the occupation of Istanbul after the First World War, though some historians argue that the substance of political independence had been lost before that. Feroz Ahmad describes how the Young Turks, convinced that the empire could not survive without a European protector, managed finally to sign an alliance with Germany on the eve of the First World War. Economic dependence on Europe was such that the Ottoman economy was paralyzed when the war interrupted the supply of European goods and capital.

Despite great economic hardship, the war gave the empire new opportunities for freedom of action; the capitulations were abolished and, in Ahmad's words, 'the Turks were finally masters of their house'. The Young Turk policies of the war years—the forays into mass political mobilization, economic planning, new social services and the encouragement of women in the labour force—laid the foundations, both social and psychological, for the creation of a citizenry that had been the goal of the nineteenth-century reforms all along. That the citizen-state which finally emerged did not conform geographically with the boundaries of the empire was perhaps inevitable. The Ottoman Empire had travelled a long way from 1801 when, as Heyd tells us, 'softas armed with slippers and stones attacked and expelled the Russian ambassador and his party, including other diplomats and a few ladies, who by special permission of the Ottoman Government were visiting the Suleymaniye Mosque'.

Qajar Iran, beyond the eastern border of the Ottoman Empire, experienced the changes of the nineteenth century differently. There, the governing elite did not attempt to take change in hand through a programme of reform as happened in the Ottoman Empire and Egypt. In Ann Lambton's 1981 analysis, social change in Iran in the nineteenth century was bounded by two things: the Shiʿi attitude towards temporal power and the intrusion of European powers. The former caused a gap between the *ʿulama* and government and a certain abdication of responsibility on the part of the *ʿulama.* The latter provided the impetus for change. As a result, official engagement with change was superficial. For example, when Britain requested redress of certain Christian grievances, the specific matter was settled to the satisfaction of Christians and the European powers, but no general statement of policy or new legislation ensued, as had occurred in the Ottoman Empire.

As the century passed there was a melding of elites—upper *ʿulama,* large-scale merchants, court bureaucrats, tribal leaders and large landowners—through intermarriage and shared interests. There remained, however, deep vertical cleavages among the peoples of Iran and a vast social and political gulf between the elites and their subjects. By the end of the century, in Lambton's words, 'the fundamental issue in social change, which concerns the relationship of man to man and the purposes of society, [had] received little consideration and it was, perhaps, because of this that social change still remained very limited'.

The Ottoman ʿUlemā and Westernization in the Time of Selīm III and Maḥmūd II

URIEL HEYD

'My Sublime State is a Muhammedan State.' (Sultan Maḥmūd II to Grand Vizier Ṣāliḥ Pasha, April 1821)
'The Turkish Empire is evidently hastening to its dissolution, and an approach to the civilization of Christendom affords the only chance of keeping it together for any length of time.' (Stratford Canning, British Ambassador at Constantinople, to Lord Palmerston, 7 March 1832)

I

THE ATTITUDE OF THE ʿULEMĀ

The real 'Eastern Question' of the nineteenth century was the success or failure of the attempts at modernizing the Ottoman State and society on Western lines; the problem usually so termed actually was, to a large extent, a reflection of this process in the field of international politics. The outcome of the attempts at modernization depended greatly on the attitude of the ʿulemā, the powerful corps of Muslim learned men who dominated the religious institutions, the judiciary and education of the Empire, and, in addition, held most important positions in public administration, diplomacy and politics. An investigation of their attitude and the reasons why they adopted it is important not only for the study of this particular period in Ottoman history. It may also be of some relevance for the understanding of the position taken by Muslim religious leaders in general with regard to modernization and Westernization.[1]

Support of Westernization

The early modernizing reforms of the Ottoman Sultans were carried out with the active cooperation of many of the highest ʿulemā. Printing, for instance, was introduced in 1727 after the şeyḫü'l-islām of the time had issued a fetvā permitting the use of this European invention within certain limits and several leading ʿulemā had also expressed a favourable opinion of the new art.[2] Almost fifty years later a şeyḫü'l-islām blessed the Western bayonets with which Baron de Tott had armed the soldiers of his new artillery corps, the *sürʿatçi*.[3] Sultan Selīm III, who initiated systematic reforms in the Empire was strongly supported by several şeyḫü'l-islāms as well as by the ḳāḍī-ʿaskers, Velī-żāde Meḥmed Emīn and Tatarcık ʿAbdu'llāh. The şeyḫü'l-islāms, Meḥmed Ṭāhir (1825–28), ʿAbdü'l-Vehhāb (1821–22, 1828–33) and Muṣṭafā ʿĀṣım (1818–19, 1823–25, 1833–46), the mollās, Meḥmed Esʿad, Muṣṭafā Behcet and many others, loyally cooperated with his successor, Sultan Maḥmūd II, in destroying the Janissaries, abolishing the Bektashi order and modernizing the army and State.

Leading ʿulemā not only sanctioned and supported the innovations initiated by the Sultans and their military and civil advisers, both Ottoman and European. Some of them also played a major role in conceiving, suggesting and planning reforms on European lines. Tatarcık ʿAbdu'llāh, in a project (*lāyiḥa*) of reforms he submitted to Sultan Selīm, ardently demanded the adoption of Western military science and drill, the systematic translation of European technical works into Turkish and the employment of foreign instructors and experts.[4]

Even more novel and statesmanlike ideas were put forward a generation later by Mollā Keçeci-zāde Meḥmed ʿİzzet[5] in a less known memorandum written after the destruction of the Janissaries in 1826. He proposed payment of fixed salaries to all officials, including the ʿulemā; establishment of a consultative assembly of ʿulemā and high officials; and reorganization of many other aspects of public administration. Among the most noteworthy of his recommendations are perhaps those relating to economics. He stressed the need for arousing a greater interest in trade and industry among the (Muslim) population of the Empire and appealed in particular to the upper classes of Ottoman society to give up their traditional disdain of profit-making. The Government should consistently support new enterprises by providing them with capital and exempting them from taxation during the first three years, as was customary in Europe. Imports should be drastically curtailed and many commodities hitherto imported should be produced in factories to be established chiefly outside Istanbul where wages were lower. Moreover, the standard of living of the upper classes (which included his own, the ʿulemā) should be lowered and the unproductive building of luxurious houses be restricted.[6] The exposition of such ideas by a high-ranking mollā more than ten years before the beginning of the Tanẓīmāt period deserves attention. It is a very instructive example of the important contributions made by ʿulemā at that time to progressive political and economic thought.

In the early nineteenth century the large majority of the educated Muslims in the Ottoman Empire still belonged to the ʿulemā class. For the propagation of new ideas the reformers therefore largely depended on support given by the ʿulemā in their writings, and such support several of them gave to a considerable extent. Sultan Maḥmūd's early reforms were fervently defended by Meḥmed Esʿad, one of the mollās mentioned above, in his chronicles of the Empire for the year 1241 (1825–26) and in his work entitled *Üss-i Żafer*, the famous account of the extirpation of the Janissaries. He was not the only ʿālim who wrote official history with this tendency. The major imperial historiographers (*vaḳʿa-nüvīs*) of the reign of Maḥmūd II—Ṣānī-zāde ʿAṭā'ullāh before Meḥmed Esʿad, as well as Aḥmed Cevdet and Aḥmed Luṭfī in the following generation—were also ʿulemā and in their works wholeheartedly emphasized the advantages and legality of the Western innovations.

On a popular level a similar function was often fulfilled by the imāms of the various quarters of Istanbul who were instructed by the cadi of the capital to act against any criticism of the new military institutions expressed in coffee-houses and other places.[7] When the fez was introduced in the new Ottoman army in 1243 (1827–28), several prominent public preachers (*ders-i ʿāmm*) not only approved the innovation in the Council of State but also took it upon themselves to explain its legality to the people.[8] The imāms and *ḫōcās* were the main instruments of Government propaganda until the first Turkish newspaper, the official *Taḳvīm-i Veḳāyiʿ*, appeared in 1831. Approximately a hundred years earlier ʿulemā (and a dervish şeyḫ) had been appointed proof-readers, assistants, and, later, directors of the newly established printing press of İbrāhīm Müteferriḳa, which had aroused so many misgivings among the reactionaries. It was probably for the same reason that Sultan Maḥmūd now made Mollā Meḥmed Esʿad editor of the newspaper and another ʿālim its proof-reader.[9] Similarly, when in 1830–31 the first modern general census of the Ottoman Empire was to be carried out, ʿulemā were appointed to head many of the regional teams (Meḥmed Esʿad, for instance, in Sofia) in order to dispel the suspicions of the people.[10]

Another valuable service rendered by this same mollā was connected with Sultan Maḥmūd's revolutionary measures against the plague. The popular religious belief in predestination prevented the taking of any precautions against this disease, which from time to time caused havoc among the population of the Ottoman Empire. In 1812, for example, over seventy thousand people were estimated to have died from it in Istanbul and the vicinity.[11] The most effective way to fight the plague was of course to keep it from being imported from abroad. Meḥmed ʿAlī had introduced quarantine in Egypt earlier in the century, but in Istanbul the ʿulemā were reported to have opposed Sultan Maḥmūd's wish to follow his example.[12] The young Prussian officer, Helmuth von Moltke, who in the 1830s spent several years in Turkey, wrote in a letter of February 1837, 'Die Pest wird bestehen, so lange es Ulemas giebt'.[13] He was, however, soon to be proved wrong. In 1838 the Sultan overrode all opposition and decided to establish a quarantine station near Istanbul with the help of Austrian experts. A fetvā sanctioning this innovation was obtained and an article in the official newspaper *Taḳvīm-i Veḳāyiʿ* put forward a series of religious and logical arguments against the popular prejudice.[14] Among the three officials charged with launching the project were two ʿulemā, Meḥmed Esʿad and the Chief Physician of the Sultan (*ḥekīm-başı*), ʿAbdü'l-Ḥaḳḳ.[15] Their cooperation with the Government helped without doubt to overcome the opposition among the people and the lower ʿulemā. The fact that for many years to come these laudable decisions remained largely on paper[16] should not detract from the importance of the liberal attitude of the ʿulemā leaders with regard to this delicate question.

Though less devastating than the plague, cholera, too, took a large toll among the Ottomans in that period. By order of Sultan Maḥmūd, his Chief Physician and confidant, ḳāḍī-ʿasker Muṣṭafā Behcet, wrote a treatise in Turkish on the cholera morbus in which he made use of an Austrian manual. After giving an account of the history of the disease, the author described its symptoms and recommended precautionary measures and modes of treatment.[17] Several thousand copies of this treatise were printed at the Imperial Press and in August 1831 were distributed free of charge among the civil population and soldiers in Istanbul and the provinces.[18]

The same ʿālim, Muṣṭafā Behcet, also took an active part in the early development of medical studies. During his third term as Chief Physician, and largely on his initiative, the new army medical school, the *ṭıbb-ḫāne* or *ṭıbbīye*, was founded in 1827.[19] The new institution had to overcome a strong traditional prejudice against the dissection of human bodies. A few years before the opening of the medical school Sultan Maḥmūd had, by a *ḫaṭṭ-ı hümāyūn*, ordered the printing of a work on anatomy entitled *Mir'āt al-Abdān fī Tashrīḥ Aʿẓā' al-Insān*, written by Şānī-zāde Meḥmed ʿAṭā'ullāh, the mollā mentioned above. This book, which was published in 1820 and aroused much interest in Europe, as well, contained a large number of engravings illustrating the text.[20] The publication of pictures of the human form was also contrary to Ottoman-Muslim tradition. It is certainly worthy of notice that the man who ignored two such powerful religious prejudices and composed this pioneer work on modern medicine was a high-ranking member of the ʿulemā corps.

The ʿulemā did not limit their cooperation in educational reform to the medical school. In 1838–39 the first steps were taken to establish *rüşdīye*, i.e. middle schools, and İmām-zāde Meḥmed Esʿad, titular ḳāḍī-ʿasker of Anatolia, was appointed their superintendent with the title of (*mekteb-i*) *maʿārif-i ʿadlīye nāẓırı*.[21] A few years after Sultan Maḥmūd's death the abovementioned ʿālim and historian, Ṣaḥḥāflar-Şeyḫi-zāde Meḥmed Esʿad, concluded his career as first Ottoman Minister of Education.[22]

In their support for, or their acquiescence in, the Westernizing reforms of Selīm III and Maḥmūd II the ʿulemā leadership joined forces with certain dervish orders. Traditionally, many high ʿulemā had strong ṣūfī inclinations. Several şeyḫü'l-islāms of the eighteenth and early nineteenth centuries are known to have belonged to the Naḳshbendī order or to the Mevlevī order,[23] while others built or supported dervish convents.[24] The Mevlevīs enjoyed the special favour of Sultan Selīm III and therefore of high society in his time. They became the most powerful order politically, thus superseding the popular Bektashis who were closely associated with the reactionary Janissary corps.[25] Under Maḥmūd II the Mevlevīs continued to support reforms. During his reign some adherents of the order occupied very influential positions in the Government and at Court. The most important among them, Meḥmed Saʿīd Ḥālet, was for many years the Sultan's chief confidant and the virtual arbiter of the Empire's destiny.[26] In Maḥmūd's later years one of his favourite courtiers and companions was ʿAbdī Bey, a devout Mevlevī.[27] Another one, Aḥmed Ṣādiḳ Zīver Efendi, was appointed one of the six members of the new *meclis-i vālā-yı aḥkām-ı ʿadlīye* set up in 1838.[28] Strong rumours circulating in Istanbul in the late 1830s had it that the Sultan continually obtained secret information on home affairs through Mevlevī channels.[29] According to the assertion of the Moldavian prince, Ghika, the şeyḫ of the famous Mevlevī convent at Galata (Pera), also a personal friend of Maḥmūd II, did more than anyone else to help the Sultan overcome the opposition of the ʿulemā to his reforms.[30]

Opposition to Reforms

The attitude of the mollās who supported the Westernizing reforms of Selīm III and Maḥmūd II was certainly not typical of the entire ʿulemā corps. As a result of the revolution of 1807 reactionary elements in the ʿulemā leadership succeeded temporarily in stopping these reforms by force. The rebellious Janissaries were actively helped and guided by Şeyḫü'l-İslām Meḥmed ʿAṭā'ullāh, 'l'âme de la révolution', his teacher Meḥmed Münīb, the cadi of Istanbul Murād-zāde Meḥmed Murād and several other mollās who signed a *ḥüccet-i şerʿīye* condemning the reforms of the New Order (*niżām-ı cedīd*) as unprecedented illegal innovations (*bidʿat*) and reprehensible imitations of the infidels.[31] After the accession of Sultan Maḥmūd in the following year,[32] the conservative ʿulemā were, however, increasingly forced into a purely defensive position, offering only passive resistance to, or acquiescing in, the reform policy of the Government.

Yet, on one issue, which at first sight may seem to be of rather minor importance, the ʿulemā leadership successfully opposed Maḥmūd's wishes. In 1828 the Sultan is said to have demanded that the ʿulemā should also wear the red fez, the new headgear which was made compulsory for all Government officials and soldiers and was worn by the sovereign himself. Şeyḫü'l-İslām Meḥmed Ṭāhir, who had cooperated with the Sultan in the destruction of the Janissaries and had sanctioned all subsequent reforms, staunchly refused to agree to this innovation.[33] Maḥmūd dismissed him, but the war with Russia which broke out at about that time made any serious quarrel with the 'ulemā most inopportune. The project was therefore laid aside[34] and the 'ulemā saved their white turbans, which distinguished them from the rest of the people, until Atatürk's reform a hundred years later.

After the end of the war in 1829 Maḥmūd felt free to resume his reforms with greater vigour and on a much larger scale. His introduction of another European custom led to a new clash with the 'ulemā, but this time the Sultan completely ignored their opinion. Maḥmūd, like Selīm before him, had his portrait painted several times, though the şeyḫü'l-islām is thought to have objected to this offence against religious tradition.[35] In 1832 the Sultan went so far as to send the şeyḫü'l-islām his portrait set with brilliants as a sign of his favour,[36] and such presents to high officials and foreign rulers became customary.[37] When, however, in 1836 the monarch's portrait was solemnly displayed in various barracks and Government offices, many people, especially among the 'ulemā, reportedly expressed their discontent.[38] The exhibition of the portrait was preceded by a great military procession and was accompanied by music, gun salvoes and fireworks. But it is interesting to note that the religious ceremonies in its honour were performed by dervish şeyḫs and not by 'ulemā.[39] The opposition of the 'ulemā seems to have stemmed from their fear that the public display of the portrait might give rise to the impression that it was to be worshipped by the people.[40]

Though the leadership of the 'ulemā corps generally supported Sultan Maḥmūd or at least submitted to his will, many 'ulemā in the lower ranks remained extremely hostile to European innovations. Unfortunately, the opinions of the opponents of Westernization cannot be adequately studied, since very few of them dared to express their views in writing. Even if they had, the copying or printing of their works would hardly have been allowed. Some information on opposition to the reforms is found in European sources, but many of these, in particular the innumerable travel books of the period under review, are not reliable and are to be used with great caution.

However, even the Turkish chronicles for the years of intensive reforms following the Peace of Adrianople record a number of disturbances in which reactionary 'ulemā were involved. In 1829, for instance, several ḫōcās were exiled for criticizing the new institutions in their Ramaḍān sermons in the mosques.[41] One of them, a Bosnian müderris, had publicly objected to the new European dress and pronounced those adopting it misbelievers. There is evidence that he later joined a dangerous rebel in the Aydın region who claimed to have been sent by Allah to defend the poor and drew into his force remnants of the Janissaries and other outlaws.[42] A little later the muftī and another 'ālim at Tosya, south-east of Kastamonu, supported local rebels, many of whom were said to have been Janissaries expelled from Istanbul in 1826.[43]

One of the main centres of opposition to many reforms of Ottoman Government and society on Western lines was the students of the religious colleges (*medrese*), the so-called *ṭalebe-yi 'ulūm* or softas. Their number was very large. According to detailed lists for 1784,[44] there were about 1500 softas in Istanbul, not counting their *çömez* or 'fags', who served the students in return for board, lodging and private tuition. In addition there were many external students, who lived outside the medreses. More than three thousand softas, it is claimed,[45] took part in the annihilation of the Janissaries in 1826. In the 1830s and 1840s the total of medrese students in the capital was estimated at about five thousand.[46] The softas pursued their studies over a long period of years, often living in very difficult conditions. Many of them were undernourished, receiving—according to European observers[47] — only one free meal a day. Though a considerable number were no longer young, they were generally unmarried. Many of them had to wait a long time before they were able to obtain any remunerative post.

Throughout the history of the Ottoman Empire the softas had been a breeding ground of discontent and trouble-making.[48] In the eighteenth and early nineteenth centuries their dissatisfaction grew as a result of the scandalous corruption in the 'ulemā leadership. It may safely be assumed that the poor softas (and low-ranking 'ulemā) regarded with deep envy the enormously rich heads of their corps, most of whom belonged, as will be pointed out later, to a small number of aristocratic families. The abuse they resented in particular was the ever increasing tendency to grant the higher positions in the corps to members of these clans, in many cases ignorant and otherwise unworthy.[49] While the softa of lower, especially provincial, origin had to study ten or twenty years and to pass several difficult examinations before becoming a müderris, the son of a high mollā of a distinguished family was sometimes granted that rank at the age of six![50] Similar discrimination was evident in subsequent promotions. Instead of rising to higher positions in accordance with the traditional consideration of seniority, members of this privileged group often 'jumped the queue' (*ṭafra*).[51] As the chiefs of the 'ulemā corps occupied high positions in Government, the animosity of the softas and lower 'ulemā naturally turned against all authority. These elements of class struggle within the 'ulemā corps—a struggle not yet adequately studied—were bound to lead to serious trouble in periods of military disasters, great political and social changes, and drastic attempts at reforms, as in the days of Selīm III and Maḥmūd II.

During the first part of Maḥmūd's reign the softas several times openly challenged the authority of the Government, including that of the high ʿulemā. A famous example is the Incident of the Candle (*vaḳʿa-yı mūm*) in winter 1817–18. A quarrel resulting from the refusal of a grocer to sell more than one candle to each customer led to a serious clash between Janissary guards and students of the famous medrese of Meḥmed the Conqueror who from olden days had enjoyed the privilege of possessing arms. The softas rose in protest and caused the resignation of the şeyḫü'l-islām.[52] A few years later, in 1821, many hundreds of softas demonstrated before the palace of the şeyḫü'l-islām, demanding the liberation of one of their professors who had been condemned to exile because of his anti-government speeches. The Grand Vizier was compelled personally to assuage the angry and dangerous crowd.[53]

Moreover, since the studies at the medrese were strictly limited to the traditional subjects of Muslim learning, the softas objected violently to European reforms; in all probability they considered them a danger not only to their religious beliefs but also to their economic prospects. It is therefore not surprising that their fanaticism and narrow-mindedness often far surpassed those of the ʿulemā leaders. In April 1801, for example, softas armed with slippers and stones attacked and expelled the Russian ambassador and his party, including other diplomats and a few ladies, who by special permission of the Ottoman Government were visiting the Süleymānīye Mosque. Deeply embarrassed, the Porte ordered several softas to be executed and many others to be bastinadoed and banished.[54] When in spring 1833 French-supported Meḥmed ʿAlī Pasha threatened the very existence of the Ottoman State and the Government had to appeal to the Russians for help, measures were considered to expel fanatical anti-foreign softas from Istanbul.[55]

Just as the progressive attitude of the ʿulemā leadership did not affect the opposition of the softas and lower ʿulemā to Maḥmūd's reforms, so the cooperation of the Mevlevīs and other orders with the Sultan was not shared by all dervishes. In particular, many members of the popular orders and unattached itinerant dervishes objected violently to the policy of reforms. During the Friday prayers in the Süleymānīye Mosque in 1829 an ecstatic dervish loudly cursed and reviled the şeyḫü'l-islām, who attended the service together with other State dignitaries, for influencing the Sultan to adopt 'false rites'.[56] Even more outrageous was the outburst of another fanatical dervish, known as Şeyḫ Saçlı, who in 1837 stopped Sultan Maḥmūd on the new Galata bridge, called him 'infidel Sultan' and accused him of destroying the religion of Islam. The dervish, whom the people considered a saint, was arrested and executed, and a martyr legend quickly sprang up among the masses.[57]

The Ideology of Reform

The high 'ulemā who in their writings or their speeches in the Councils of State expressed approval of the reforms defended their attitude by arguments either taken from religious law and early Islamic history or based on reason and common sense.[58]

Djihād, the holy war against the infidels, they argued, was one of the foremost duties of believers. To strengthen the army of Islam by every means was therefore an important religious obligation. It had become a most urgent necessity in the days when the Ottoman State, the last bulwark of Islam, suffered defeat after defeat at the hands of superior Christian forces. The existence of the Empire and therewith of Islam could no longer be safeguarded without the adoption of European military technique.

To learn from the infidel enemy would not constitute a religiously illicit innovation (*bid'at*) but would be an application of the legitimate maxim of *muḳābele bi-'l-mis̱l* or reciprocation, that is, fighting the enemy with his own weapons. Such conduct was sanctioned by several passages in the Qur'ān, such as chapter VIII, verse 60, '... and prepare against them (the enemies) what force ye are able'. The passage (ch. IX, v. 36), '... and fight against the idolators altogether (*kāffatan*) as they fight against you altogether' is traditionally understood as allowing the Muslims to make war 'in all' months, including the four sacred ones.[59] Apologists for Maḥmūd's reforms, however, interpreted it as permitting them to make use of all the arms and tactics used by their opponents, or even explained *kāffatan* in the sense of fighting 'in a united and compact formation'.[60] The last interpretation was specifically meant to legalize the new European drill officially styled *ta'līm-i şer'ī*, i.e. drill according to the religious law,[61] and the Western battle order introduced by Selīm III and Maḥmūd II. An even more explicit basis for them was discovered in ch. LXI, v. 4, 'Verily God loveth those who fight for his religion in battle array, as though they were a well compacted building (*bunyān marṣūṣ*)'.[62]

Further arguments were based on precedents in ancient Muslim history. Ibn Khaldūn had already shown, they said, that the early Muslims gave up the pagan Arab custom of individual combat in the 'hit and run' fashion (*al-karr wa-'l-farr*) and adopted the higher military technique of their Persian and Byzantine foes who fought in lines of battle (*ṣufūf*).[63] Similarly, Aḥmed Cevdet added,[64] the Prophet did not hesitate to learn from the Zoroastrian Persians the technique, until then unknown in Arabia, of digging a trench (*khandaḳ*) round his capital, Medina. Others asserted[65] that the early Muslims borrowed the use of *bārūt* invented by the infidels, referring, it seems, to the Greek fire or similar incendiary material hurled at the enemy,[66] but possibly also to gunpower which the Ottomans adopted many centuries later. The

Prophet of Islam, it was further argued, did not limit his borrowings from the unbelievers to military matters. After the battle of Badr he employed several prisoners taken from the infidel Meccans to teach reading and writing to Muslim children in Medina.[67]

Learning from the infidels should not give rise to any feeling of inferiority among the Muslims. They should keep in mind that the progress of Christian Europe in military science was but the reaction of the frightened West to the superiority of Ottoman arms and Muslim heroism over many centuries.[68] Also Western economic principles which the Ottomans should adopt, such as payment of fixed salaries to Government officials, were ideas which the Europeans 'had taken from our (Islamic) religious law'.[69] The Muslims would only take back what originally had been borrowed from them. The ideologists of Western reforms among the 'ulemā[70] hotly rejected the argument of their adversaries that *man tashabbaha bi-qawm fa-huwa minhum*, 'Who imitates a(nother) people becomes one of them', meaning that the imitation of Europe by Muslims would lead to the complete loss of their identity.

A more practical and apparently widespread objection which the reformers had to meet was the contention that since Western methods were contrary to those customary in the Muslim world their adoption was bound to end in disastrous failure. To invalidate this argument, Keçeci-zāde[71] quoted the example of Egypt, likewise a Muslim country, which in his opinion had been ruined even more than Turkey. But 'an illiterate vizier of our Padishah (referring to Meḥmed 'Alī, the ruler of Egypt), a man of mediocre intelligence, has turned that old Egypt into a new country'.[72] It is after all well known, Keçeci-zāde added, 'that our (Turkish) 'ulemā are in every respect superior to the 'ulemā of al-Azhar and that our high Government officials and clerks are more intelligent than his (Meḥmed 'Alī's) Dīvān Efendisi'.

Keçeci-zāde strongly rebuked those fatalist Muslims who claimed that nothing could be done until the arrival of the Mahdī. Quoting the Arabic proverb, 'Men's exertions uproot mountains', he rejected the pessimism of those who did not believe that the old Ottoman Empire could be reorganized. He drew their attention to the infidel Austrians, Prussians and French who, 'though deprived of divine support', had succeeded by rational measures (*tedābīr-i 'aḳlīye*) in reconstructing and rejuvenating their states after most serious defeats.[73] In his last memorandum written shortly before his banishment and death,[74] the mollā called on the Ottomans not merely to rely on divine help, which was not always forthcoming, but to devise ways and means to reform their State.

The final argument of all the 'ulemā who favoured modernization was the religious obligation of every Muslim to follow the orders of the Sultan, as long as they were not contrary to the holy law. Verse 59 of the fourth chapter of the Qur'ān, 'O true believers, obey God, and obey the apostle and those who are in authority among you', was a stock phrase in the polemic arsenal of all reformers.

Many of the arguments presented by the ʿulemā in favour of reforms were certainly no more than an ideological 'superstructure' which concealed the real reasons for their attitude. Retrospectively, the support given by the high ʿulemā to the policy of opening the Ottoman Empire to European secular ideas and institutions seems a suicidal policy from the point of view of the interest of their corps. Why then did the ʿulemā leadership cooperate with Selīm III and Maḥmūd II and, in the teeth of very strong popular opposition, help them to carry out their reforms? The reasons for their attitude, which form the subject of the second part of this paper, cannot be understood without an inquiry into the position of the ʿulemā in the Ottoman Empire, the character of the State and the policy of the Sultans in this period.

II

REASONS FOR ʿULEMĀ SUPPORT OF REFORM

Decline of Power

One reason for the attitude of the high ʿulemā was their fear of the Sultan, particularly of Maḥmūd II. This strong ruler ruthlessly eliminated the powerful feudal lords (*dere-beyi*) and local notables (*aʿyān*). He crowned his establishment of an absolute and autocratic monarchy by the annihilation of the Janissaries, who had so often been the collaborators or instruments of the ʿulemā in checking the power of the Sultans. On various occasions Maḥmūd showed that he demanded submission to his will from all his servants, including the ʿulemā, and dismissed and banished şeyḫü'l-islāms and other mollās who refused to comply with his wishes. In this way he succeeded not merely in silencing their opposition to his reforms but even in having them help him to carry out his policy. A number of examples quoted above show how the Sultan made use of the ʿulemā's spiritual influence on the people in order to obtain religious sanction and secure popular respect for his innovations.

Maḥmūd II's success in mastering the ʿulemā is spectacular in view of the enormous power this corps had wielded for many generations, especially after the decline of the military classes. In the middle of the eighteenth century a British ambassador at Constantinople[75] was deeply impressed by the political influence of the ʿulemā. In his opinion their discontent alone would be enough to shake the Sultan's throne. His French colleague reported in 1786 that 'ce n'est pas ici comme en France, où le roi est le seul maître; il faut persuader les ulémas, les gens de loi, les ministres qui sont en place, et ceux qui n'y sont plus'.[76] A few years earlier the Prussian envoy claimed in one of his despatches that the ʿulemā dreamed of the establishment of a kind of aristocratic government of which they would be the main pillars and the Sultan a mere decoration.[77]

However, towards the end of the eighteenth century the ʿulemā's power gradually declined. Lack of unity among them was one of the fundamental causes for this. Not only, as mentioned above, were the leading ʿulemā families and high mollās separated by a deep gulf from the rank and file, but within the leadership itself the struggle for promotion to the highest positions led to constant intrigues. These became particularly violent when in the eighteenth century an excessively large number of müderrises and mollās were appointed because of favouritism and nepotism, thus increasing the number of candidates for the few top positions in the corps.[78] Hence it should not be surprising that a mollā was often willing to yield to the Sultan's wishes and even agree to innovations of Western origin, as the price for gaining ascendancy over a rival.

Moreover, the prestige of the ʿulemā had declined greatly during preceding generations because of the growing corruption in their ranks.[79] Posts were given or even sold to unsuitable men, such as followers and servants of high ʿulemā. In some cases people who were not even able to read their names were appointed cadis.[80] The venality of the judges had become proverbial. While in olden times, a leading ʿālim[81] lamented, people came to the cadi to complain of oppression by the governor and his subordinates, it was now the other way round. Instead of the ʿulemā restraining the Government from infringing upon the holy law, the Sultan had to issue innumerable firmans warning the judges not to violate the sharīʿa.[82]

The moral fibre of the ʿulemā corps had weakened to an alarming extent. When during the military and financial crisis of the first years of his rule Sultan Selīm III ordered all subjects to deliver their gold and silver objects to the mint, many rich ʿulemā refused to do so, though the use of such utensils was also forbidden by religious law. Some of them even dared to express criticism of the Sultan's order.[83] According to ʿĀṣım,[84] at the beginning of Selīm III's reign an ʿālim and his students enthusiastically volunteered to join the war against the Russian infidels. But such cases appear to have become rare in the early nineteenth century. In the Great Council held in 1821 the şeyḫü'l-islām dramatically declared that he himself would pick up a rifle, bind a shawl around his head and go to war against the Greek rebels.[85] Needless to say, he never left his comfortable palace. The moral decline of the ʿulemā corps lost it some of the traditional respect and trust of the common people and thereby further weakened its power of resistance to the Sultan's pressure.

Hostility to Janissaries and Bektashis

A further reason for the support of the reform policy by the high 'ulemā was their hatred of the Janissaries and their associates. True, in the revolutions of 1703, 1730, and 1807–8 many leading 'ulemā had made common cause with the Janissary insurgents. But such short-lived cooperation should not conceal the basic conflict and hostility that existed between the Janissaries, who belonged to the illiterate working class, and the higher 'ulemā, who formed the only aristocracy in Ottoman society.

Until Maḥmūd II's time the mollās were the most privileged class in the State. They could be dismissed and exiled but, unlike other Government officials, were almost never executed. Their great fortunes, not subject to taxation, could be freely left to their descendants, whereas those of other dignitaries were—until 1826[86]—confiscated by the Sultan after their owner's death, if not earlier. No wonder that the mollās, especially the leading families among them, were staunch supporters of public law and order and feared all revolutionary actions of the rabble led by the Janissaries, 'this collection of grocers, boatmen, fishermen, porters, coffee-house keepers, and such like persons'.[87]

The 'ulemā seem never to have forgotten[88] the tragic end of the famous Şeyḫü'l-İslām Feyżu'llāh who was murdered in 1703 by the rebellious Janissaries and whose corpse was ignominiously dragged through the streets of Adrianople and finally thrown into the river. They knew by bitter experience that rebels against the Government were often tempted to vent their rage on the rich and powerful 'ulemā. The case of an ex-mollā of Aleppo in the reign of 'Abdü'l-Ḥamīd I may be considered typical: while returning to the capital, he was attacked by a horde of insurgents, robbed of his very considerable belongings, stripped of his clothes, and given the bastinado to the accompaniment of malicious sneering and laughter by the rebels.[89] The 'ulemā writers who supported Maḥmūd II's reforms made every effort to prove that the Janissaries were bad Muslims who violated the religious law and even cut copies of the Qur'ān into pieces during their rebellions.[90]

Even stronger accusations of this sort were directed against the Bektashi order which was closely associated with the Janissaries. The higher 'ulemā took a most hostile attitude to this proletarian and unintellectual, or even anti-intellectual, order in which uneducated men could rise to the highest ranks. They strongly criticized the unorthodox behaviour of the Bektashis, accusing them of drinking wine even during the month of Ramaḍān, neglecting public prayers, rejecting the first three caliphs in Shiite fashion, etc. The Bektashis reciprocated by heaping scorn and ridicule upon the pompous 'ulemā, imputing hypocrisy and many other vices to them. In their contest with these dangerous rivals the 'ulemā won a resounding victory. In July 1826 they, or at least many of their leaders, supported the Sultan in abolishing the order, destroying many of its convents, and confiscating a large part of its endowments for the Public Treasury.[91]

Connections with the Court

The negative reasons discussed so far were not the only, and not even the principal, motives for the cooperation of the high-ranking 'ulemā with Selīm III and Maḥmūd II. Several of these 'ulemā were bound to their sovereign from early youth by ties of personal friendship. Three examples may serve as an illustration.

Velī-zāde Meḥmed Emīn, who during Selīm's reign had three times held the position of ḳāḍī-'asker of Rūmeli and strongly advocated the *Niẓām-ı Cedīd*, stood in a peculiar sentimental relationship to the Sultan. His father, the former şeyḫü'l-islām, Velīyü'd-Dīn, is said to have presented to Sultan Muṣṭafā III a beautiful Georgian slave-girl named Mihr-i Şāh who became the mother of Selīm. After her son's accession to the throne she, as Vālide Sulṭān, had a most powerful influence on him and, through her steward, Yūsuf Agha, on the affairs of State. She reportedly retained an affectionate feeling for her former master and she as well as her son, the Sultan, showed kindness to Velī-zāde.[92] His death in 1805[93] was a severe blow to Selīm and the reform party.

Another striking example is Ḫalīl Efendi, commonly known as Çerkes Ḫalīl. Born in Circassia of an unknown father, he was brought as a slave-boy into the Imperial harem where his mother served as a wet-nurse to Hibetu'l-lāh Sulṭān, baby daughter of Sultan Muṣṭafā III. In the Sarāy, Ḫalīl became a personal attendant to young Prince Selīm. When the latter came to the throne in 1789, he appointed his friend to the lucrative post of superintendent of his Private Treasury (*ḫazīne ketḫüdāsı*). About thirteen years later Ḫalīl resigned from service in the Palace and obtained the office of Mollā of Ġalata, thus joining the highest class of the 'ulemā. Though he is said to have studied religious sciences from early youth, such appointment of a complete outsider to a mollāship was regarded by many of his fellow 'ulemā as a shocking novelty. They did not dare, however, to object to a friend and favourite of the Sultan. After the accession of Maḥmūd II in 1808 Ḫalīl gained great personal influence on the young Sultan, who may have known him from the time of his service in the Sarāy. He became a member of the State Council and representative at meetings with foreign envoys, was twice appointed ḳāḍī-'asker of Rūmeli, and in 1819 reached the highest position in the 'ulemā corps.[94]

This irregular elevation of a Circassian slave to the office of şeyḫü'l-islām was received by the great ʿulemā families as an outrageous affront to the traditions of their corps.[95] But Maḥmūd did not hesitate to force his personal favourite upon them, just as he had elevated the low-born clerk, Ḥālet Efendi, to a dominant position in the political affairs of the State and his Chief Barber to a similar position at the Palace.

The third ʿālim of this type, Yasinci-zāde ʿAbdü'l-Vehhāb, was of even greater importance for the success of the reforms. As a child he, too, was taken into the Sarāy and became a companion of young Selīm. After studying under a well-known ʿālim at the Palace he obtained the rank of müderris, rose in the hierarchy, and finally twice became şeyḫü'l-islām. The second time he served during the most decisive period of Western reforms, the years 1828–33. He consistently supported Maḥmūd II, who showed him much favour. When ʿAbdü'l-Vehhāb died in 1834 the Sultan himself attended the funeral prayers at the Fātiḥ Mosque. It is significant that this loyal mollā wrote a treatise entitled *Khulāṣat al-Burhān fī Iṭāʿat al-Sulṭān*, 'The Essence of the Proof concerning Obedience to the Sultan'.[96]

The three high ʿulemā mentioned were not the only members of their corps who maintained strong ties with the Sarāy. Close connections between the high ʿulemā and the Court existed at all times and were another reason for their cooperation with the Sultans. According to long-established custom, four important charges at Court were always held by ʿulemā of the highest class—the posts of the Sultan's Chief Physician (*ḥekīm-başı*),[97] Chief Astrologer (*müneccim-başı*) and, of course, the two Private Imams (*ḫünkār imāmı* or *imām-ı sulṭānī*). These dignitaries, who before and after their service at the Palace filled the highest positions in the ʿulemā hierarchy, maintained close contacts with the chief courtiers and in many cases with the Sultan himself.[98] An excellent example is Muṣṭafā Mesʿūd, the Chief Physician whose exceptional studies at Vienna will be discussed later on. He won Maḥmūd II's confidence to such an extent that in 1812 the Sultan instructed the new hospodar of one of the Rumanian principalities to send his secret reports on the international scene by Austrian diplomatic pouch and address them to Mesʿūd Efendi. The Ottoman cabinet ministers were not to know of this arrangement by which the Sultan hoped to obtain sufficient information to be able to supervise his Government's activities.[99]

In Selīm's and Maḥmūd's times several high ʿulemā and Mevlevī şeyḫs joined a number of Court officials and formed a circle of intellectuals interested in music and literature. They often met at the Sarāy and were even allowed into the Sultan's presence.[100]

During the eighteenth and early nineteenth centuries the traditional division between the ʿulemā and the Men of the Sword, who occupied the military and higher administrative positions, became less pronounced. Many pashas were said to have one or more of their sons join the ʿulemā corps with a view to being able to transfer their property to their heirs, thus safeguarding it against confiscation after their death.[101] İbrāhīm, who was şeyḫü'l-islām in 1774–75 and 1785, carried the title Bey Efendi, because he was the son of a pasha, Grand Vizier ʿİvaẓ Meḥmed. One of his brothers, Ḫalīl Pasha, also became Grand Vizier.[102] Similarly, both the father and grandfather of İbrāhīm ʿİṣmet Bey Efendi, one of the chief ʿulemā in Selīm III's time, were pashas of vizier rank.[103] An Austrian diplomat who met him as Ottoman plenipotentiary at the Sistova peace conference in 1791 describes him as haughty and very proud of his illustrious origin.[104] Under Maḥmūd II's reign a son of Grand Vizier Ḫalīl Ḥamīd Pasha, Meḥmed ʿĀrif Bey Efendi, was repeatedly ḳāḍī-ʿasker of Rūmeli.[105] Many more such cases could be added.

The fact that many of the leading ʿulemā had close relatives who had served or were serving in the highest secular offices of the State was bound to influence their outlook. It brought them into personal contact with the political and military leaders of their time and helped them to gain clearer insight into the major problems of the Empire.

ʿUlemā in Government

Inasmuch as their corps was strongly represented in the Government and the supreme consultative bodies of the Ottoman State, the high ʿulemā needed understanding of current political affairs. As of old, the two ḳāḍī-ʿaskers were prominent members of the Imperial Dīvān. Another member, the nişāncı, at times also belonged to the ʿulemā class.

The State Council (*encümen-i meşveret* or *meclis-i şūrā*), which was convened to discuss important political questions, often met at the palace of the şeyḫü'l-islām. Among those usually invited were, apart from the şeyḫü'l-islām,[106] the present and former ḳāḍī-ʿaskers, the cadi of Istanbul, and many other ʿulemā, such as the şeyḫs of the Aya Sofya and other Imperial mosques, the naḳībü'l-eşrāf (the head of the descendants of Muḥammad), the Chief Physician, ḫōcās of the Palace, public lecturers, and others.[107] These ʿulemā often regarded themselves as a separate group within the Council, deliberating among themselves before their spokesman expressed his opinion.[108]

The inclusion of the chiefs of the ʿulemā corps was also considered necessary in order to make them share the responsibility for grave and unpopular decisions and to prevent them from subsequently criticizing the Government's policy either openly or secretly.[109] On the other hand, in Council meetings the ʿulemā often tried not to commit themselves or their corps on delicate questions.[110]

ʿUlemā also took an active part in the new councils set up by Selīm III and Maḥmūd II to enact their reform programme. The earliest of these was the special council of high officials which was established by Selīm for the execution of the *Nizām-ı Cedīd* and for some time superseded the Dīvān in importance. Among its three chief members was a well-known 'ālim, Tatarcık 'Abdu'llāh. He and his two colleagues—Yūsuf Agha, the superintendent of the mint, and Meḥmed Rāşid, çavuş-başı and later re'īsü'l-küttāb—secretly discussed and decided upon all major problems and, in the words of the Austrian envoy at Constantinople, 'really governed the Ottoman Empire'.[111]

In the permanent councils set up towards the end of Maḥmūd II's rule the 'ulemā were represented on a rather limited scale, a sign of their declining political power. The new Military Council (*dār-ı şūrā-yı 'askerī*), which was opened in 1837, consisted of military men and civil officials. It had only one member from among the 'ulemā, the muftī of the Council, who according to its statutes was to fulfil two functions—to examine and solve problems of religious law which might arise in the Council, and to lead the prayers of its members at the fixed hours.[112] In the *meclis-i vālā-yı aḥkām-ı 'adlīye* set up in 1838 there was one 'ālim among six and in the *dār-ı şūrā-yı bāb-ı 'ālī* one among (at first) seven members.[113] A müderris was appointed member of the new *nāfi'a meclisi*.[114]

During the whole period under review the 'ulemā exerted a considerable influence on the foreign policy of the Empire. This was due not only to their participation in the various councils but to the fact that many leading 'ulemā held important diplomatic posts. When in 1810–11 Maḥmūd II wanted to establish a common Muslim front against Russia which was threatening both the Ottoman Empire and Persia, he sent a high-ranking 'ālim, the future şeyḫü'l-islām Yasinci-zāde 'Abdü'l-Vehhāb, as ambassador to Iran.[115] The same position was entrusted twenty-five years later to the famous historian, Meḥmed Es'ad, at that time Cadi of Istanbul.[116]

'Ulemā were apparently not willing to serve as visiting or—after the late eighteenth century—resident diplomatic representatives in Christian countries. They were, however, conspicuous among the Ottoman plenipotentiaries at armistice and peace negotiations with European Powers. Yasinci-zāde 'Os̱mān, father of the above-mentioned ambassador to Persia and at that time preacher of the Aya Sofya Mosque, was in 1772 appointed second Ottoman representative at the abortive peace talks with the Russians at Focşani.[117] Mollā İbrāhīm 'İşmet Bey Efendi, also mentioned above, was one of the Sultan's plenipotentiaries at the peace conference with Austria at Sistova and with Russia at Jassy in 1791–92. Under Maḥmūd II one of the Turkish representatives who negotiated with the Russians at Bucharest (1812), Akkerman (1826) and Adrianople (1829) was in each case a mollā.[118]

In the capital, 'ulemā took a leading part in official talks and negotiations with foreign diplomats. Their participation at such meetings was institutionalized by the appointment of a high-ranking member of the corps as 'commissary at conferences' (*mükālemeye me'mūr, meclis-i mükāleme me'mūru*).[119] In despatches sent by Austrian envoys from Constantinople these officials are termed 'président des (aux) conférences'.

Among those charged with this function in the late eighteenth century were the future şeyḫü'l-islāms, Muftī-zāde Aḥmed, Meḥmed Kāmil, and Ḥamīdī-zāde Muṣṭafā.[120] At the turn of the century the above-mentioned Mollā İbrāhīm 'İṣmet held this position and showed considerable diplomatic skill in the negotiations with Russia and England after the French invasion of Egypt.[121] The Sultans often appointed 'ulemā of their confidence to this post in order to control talks with foreign diplomats. So, for example, Tatarcık 'Abdu'llāh, a fervent supporter of Sultan Selīm's reforms, took part in such meetings over a long period of time. In the beginning of Maḥmūd II's reign his confidant, ḳāḍī-'asker Ḫalīl Efendi, for many years fulfilled this duty.

According to despatches in the Austrian archives, some of these 'ulemā representatives remained silent spectators but others played an active role in the talks and sometimes took a more intransigent position than their colleague, the re'īsü'l-küttāb.[122] Such difference of opinion among the Ottoman representatives may not always have been real. It certainly allowed the Re'īs Efendi to demonstrate to the foreign diplomat the pressure of Ottoman public opinion or the willingness of his Government to make concessions even to the point of disregarding the religious scruples and objections of the 'ulemā.[123]

The great influence of the 'ulemā on foreign affairs continued through the period of Maḥmūd's reforms. The *président des conférences*, Meḥmed 'Arif, a distinguished 'ālim mentioned above, was said to be a most important member of the Government in 1829. The Austrian Internuntius of that time reported[124] that in order to influence the Sultan he approached Meḥmed 'Arif (and the Chief Astrologer, another high-ranking 'ālim). In the early 1830s the same position was held by Muṣṭafā Behcet, repeatedly Chief Physician and ḳāḍī-'asker of Rūmeli, who also wielded great influence in the Dīvān.

To be able to discharge diplomatic functions of such responsibility the top members of the 'ulemā hierarchy had to be carefully selected. In his memorandum to Sultan Selīm, Tartarcık 'Abdu'llāh stated in reference to the high 'ulemā:[125] 'Some persons who have come from the provinces (*taşra*), however much learning they have acquired and studies completed, are uncouth and uncultured people (*nā-puḫte ve bī-terbiye*) who are unaware of the customs of Government and careless of the established usages of social intercourse and intimacy. When such persons are all at once promoted to high 'ulemā positions they sometimes conduct themselves in an improper manner.' These responsible posts could be adequately filled only by men who, in the words of the historian, Süleymān 'İzzī,[126] 'possessed knowledge of worldly concerns and were familiar with external affairs'. Such ʿulemā were not many, especially after the decline of the corps in the late eighteenth century,[127] but ʿulemā like Tatarcık ʿAbdu'llāh, İbrāhīm ʿİṣmet and several others certainly left their mark on the conduct of Ottoman foreign policy. Only towards the end of the reign of Maḥmūd II were the ʿulemā superseded as diplomats by the *ḫōcegān-ı dīvān*, the higher 'civil servants', who in the eighteenth and early nineteenth centuries had grown in numbers, education and political influence.[128] They had a better training and longer experience in international affairs and in particular knew foreign languages which in the 1830s 'ceased to be, as in former times, a reproach and became a distinction in Turkey'.[129]

In addition to their positions in the highest Government councils and diplomatic service, the ʿulemā fulfilled most important governmental functions in their capacity as cadis. As is well known, the authority of an Ottoman cadi was not limited to the administration of justice. He was at the same time head of the civil administration of his district (*ḳażā*) and had to deal with taxation, the census of population and land, the supply and prices of various commodities and many other subjects.

Raison d'état

In view of these facts, it is hardly surprising that the Ottoman ʿulemā, especially of the higher class, were deeply convinced that not only the fate of Islam but their own depended on the existence and stability of the Empire. They knew that the Sultans were right when, in appealing to them and the other high dignitaries, they declared, 'We are all in the same boat' (*cümlemiz bir sefīne içinde*).[130] The *raison d'état* was therefore a primary consideration in their minds. A high ʿālim of the eighteenth century is reported[131] to have stated that the religious law could be accommodated to the circumstances of the State whenever this would yield any advantage, because in his opinion the sharīʿa had been laid down with a view to helping in the propagation of the Muslim faith and not to placing obstacles in its way.

The more the Ottoman Empire lost its former might and had to submit to the will of the Great Powers, the oftener the high ʿulemā, who took part in deciding its political affairs, faced a difficult choice between the requirements of the holy law and the needs of the State. Several articles of the Ottoman-Austrian peace treaty of Sistova of 1791, for instance, could hardly be carried out without violating the sharīʿa. According to the treaty, Austrian citizens who had been captured and made slaves by the Turks were to be returned; but the ḳāḍī-ʿasker negotiating with the Austrian envoy strongly objected, on religious grounds, to the liberation of those who in the meantime had embraced Islam, though in many cases under duress or as children.[132]

Other problems of this kind were the status of the non-Muslim subjects who had entered the consular service of a European country; the status of children of Frankish residents in Turkey and Ottoman Christian wives; and the status of Christian subjects who had spent some time in Austrian territory and had become naturalized citizens there before returning to the Ottoman Empire. The claims of the Sultan's Government that all these people were to be considered his subjects clashed with treaty obligations and the objections of the European Powers.[133]

A similar problem arose as to the right of foreign residents in the Ottoman Empire to possess real estate without thereby becoming *z̲immīs*, i.e. non-Muslim Ottoman subjects. The ʿulemā members of the Government pointed out that this was contrary to the religious law, but had to acquiesce in the *status quo* granting the foreigners certain rights in this respect.[134] But there were even more serious questions. Alliances with Christian Powers, though according to some ʿulemā contrary to a Qur'ānic injunction, became imperative and were sanctioned by the şeyḫü'l-islām and the highest mollās.[135] Since the shariʿa forbids ceding any part of the Muslim dominions to the infidels, the recognition of Russian rule in the Crimea, a Muslim-populated province, brought the ʿulemā into great difficulties.[136] Similarly, when in 1830 the Ottoman Government could no longer resist the pressure of the Great Powers, the şeyḫü'l-islām had to issue a fetvā[137] in which he agreed to the recognition of an independent Greek State.

Thus the high ʿulemā were willing to bow to political necessity even where it conflicted with the holy law. They quoted the old maxim, *al-ḍarūrāt tubīḥ al-maḥẓūrāt*, 'Necessity permits what is prohibited', and claimed that according to the sharīʿa one had in certain circumstances to choose the 'lesser of two evils' (*şerreynin̄ ehveni*).[138] This problem reached its breaking-point a few years after Maḥmūd II's death. In 1843 the execution of an apostate from Islam, as required by the religious law, aroused the strong protests of ambassadors of friendly states, especially Stratford Canning, the powerful British envoy. The Grand Vizier at first refused to budge and told the Interpreter of the British Embassy that it had been 'necessary to obey the (holy) law, otherwise the Ulemas would have risen against us'.[139] However, the şeyḫü'l-islām, Muṣṭafā ʿĀṣım, who had served many years under Sultan Maḥmūd, took a more liberal attitude than some members of the Dīvān did. He was reported to have advised the ministers not to bring such cases to his notice, as he had no choice but to state the religious law. Yet, he added, where State necessity existed, the Sublime Porte would herself be found the most competent judge.[140] This attitude of the ʿulemā leadership found classical expression in the later part of ʿAbdü'l-Mecīd's reign. When Meḥmed ʿĀrif, the liberal şeyḫü'l-islām, was asked in the Privy Council for a fetvā legalizing a proposed innovation, he is said to have replied to the minister, 'Sir, don't ask our opinion on everything. If we are not asked, we do not interfere with what you are doing.'[141]

Unlike the fanatical masses of the Muslim population, including the softas and many lower 'ulemā, most members of the higher classes of the corps understood, in the period under review, the need for good relations with the European Powers. They also seem to have generally taken a friendlier attitude than the average Muslim towards the Christian foreigner, resident or visitor. As far back as the middle of the seventeenth century the French diplomat and traveller, d'Arvieux, established a personal friendship with the learned cadi of Sidon who often supped with him and after the local people had retired freely discussed with him various matters, not excluding religion.[142] Travellers in the eighteenth century made friends with their teachers of Turkish, in one instance a mollā of Istanbul who invited the foreigner into his home.[143] Baron de Tott, who lived many years in Istanbul during the third quarter of the eighteenth century, became very friendly with rich Mollā Murād of the famous Dāmād-zāde family of şeyḫü'l-islāms. The mollā often spent long hours in de Tott's company and, animated by several bottles of good maraschino, talked with him about various subjects in the frankest way.[144]

Foreign tourists had similar experiences in the provinces. A Frenchman who travelled through Anatolia in the time of Maḥmūd II reported[145] that both at Amasya and Osmancık the local cadi invited him to come secretly to his house, so as not to arouse the people's suspicion. Both these 'ulemā, one of whom originated from Istanbul and the other from Smyrna, told him how happy they were to spend some hours with an educated guest, complaining bitterly about the ignorant and uncultured people in whose midst they had to live.

The increasing interest in, and closer contacts with, Europe and European culture in Selīm III's time affected even the 'ulemā class. In 1801 es-seyyid Muṣṭafā Mes'ūd, son of the ḥekīm-başı Nu'mān Efendi, suddenly left Istanbul for Vienna to study medicine there. The event caused a sensation in the Ottoman capital. This was the first time, it was pointed out, that a member of a distinguished Muslim family, an 'ālim and emīr (descendant of the Prophet), had gone to study in the lands of the infidels. The young Efendi, whom the Austrian envoy at Constantinople describes[146] as a very studious young man of high morals and an ascetic behaviour, is said by Turkish sources[147] to have spent his time in Vienna at theatres and balls instead of studying. In any case, the course of studies of this 'ālim, who, as mentioned above, obtained his father's post as Chief Physician under Maḥmūd II, remained an exception.

Islamic Character of the State

Despite Westernizing reforms and growing contacts with Europe and Europeans, the 'ulemā under Selīm III and Maḥmūd II apparently were not apprehensive of any serious threat of secularization. Indeed, until the last third of Maḥmūd's reign, and in many aspects even longer, the Ottoman Empire remained a Muslim State based on Islamic law, permeated by Muhammedan ideals and actually based upon its Muslim population only. The disastrous wars against European states in the second and third decades of the nineteenth century even increased the Ottomans' feeling that they faced a concerted attack of the Christian world on the last bulwark of Islam.

The French invading Egypt in 1798, the Russians defeating the Turkish armies in 1810 and later, the Greeks revolting in 1821—all of them were considered and styled *a'dā-yı dīn*, 'enemies of the faith', whose aim was the destruction of Islam.[148] Very illuminating is the wording of an official Ottoman note sent in August 1821 to the Russian ambassador. It refers to 'this Muhammedan State and Aḥmedī (i.e. Muslim) nation [which] ... was born 1200 years ago ... and from absolute nothingness has become such a powerful body'.[149] Even in a document like this, which was not intended for home consumption, Sultan Maḥmūd's Empire was not regarded as a successor to the State founded by 'Os̱mān and made great by Meḥmed II, Selīm I and Süleymān I; the Ottomans prided themselves rather on being the heirs of that tiny Arab body politic of Medina established in 622 by the founder of Islam.

The frequent reference of European statesmen of that time to the need for Christian solidarity against the barbarian Muslim Turks and the important role Orthodox priests played in leading the Greek revolt were bound to strengthen the conviction of Ottomans of all classes that they were fighting religious wars. In particular the joint attack of the British, French and Russian fleets at Navarino in 1827 seemed to them once more to vindicate the old Muslim saying that all infidels were *milla wāḥida*, 'one [hostile] nation'.[150] It is significant that even after the decisive step towards the modernization of the Empire, the destruction of the Janissaries in 1826, Maḥmūd II named his new European-styled army 'The Victorious Muhammedan Troops' (*'asākir-i manṣūre-yi Muḥammedīye*).

In a State so strongly pledged to continuous holy war against the infidels, the 'ulemā rightly felt that they were a most important and leading class. In 1825–26 a Turkish translation by a contemporary mollā, Meḥmed Münīb, of al-Shaybānī's *al-Siyar al-Kabīr* (with al-Sarakhsī's commentary) was printed and distributed by order of Sultan Maḥmūd 'to arouse the believers to fight against the polytheists and to urge them to obey the Leader of the Muslims (the Sultan)'.[151] On the eve of a new war against Russia 'ulemā were sent in 1827–28 to Albania, Lāzistān and other provinces to call the people to join the holy war.[152]

However, the shattering victories of the Russians in this war, their occupation of Adrianople and threat to Istanbul brought about a deep change. With the Peace of Adrianople of 1829 a completely new era opened in Ottoman relations with Europe. Now the Turkish leaders understood that without maintaining very close relations with at least one major Christian Power the Empire was lost.[153] In November 1828 the Re'īs Efendi, Pertev, in a conversation expressed the surprising idea of convening a general European congress to settle the Ottoman-Russian confict. The Austrian Internuntius in Constantinople understood him to wish that the Ottoman Empire be admitted into, and guaranteed as part of, the political system of Europe.[154]

Under these circumstances the traditional hostility to the Christian world as a whole could no longer be maintained. The time-honoured slogan of holy war against the unbelievers could no longer be the main, or at least the only, appeal to the people in times of foreign wars. Nor could the faithful from now on be called upon to heed the precept of the Qur'ān (ch. IV, v. 144), 'O true believers, take not the unbelievers for [your] protectors', or similar sayings in the Ḥadīth.[155] The change was brutally driven home to the consciousness of the Ottomans when a few years later, in 1832–33 and again in 1839–40, the very existence of their State was threatened by a Muslim foe, Meḥmed 'Alī of Egypt, and they were rescued only by the intervention of the infidels—first the Russians, then the British and their allies.

Parallel to this development and closely interrelated with it, the attitude of the Ottoman Government towards its non-Muslim citizens began to change in the late 1820s. Maḥmūd II seems to have become convinced that the traditional gulf between the Muslim community and the re'āyā had to be bridged, both for political and economic reasons. The last instance of large-scale anti-Christian measures was the expulsion of the Armenian Catholic community of Istanbul early in 1828. After the end of the Russian war in the following year the Sultan made many efforts to prove his liberal and benevolent attitude to his non-Muslim subjects. However, in Maḥmūd's life-time this policy did not go so far as to frighten the 'ulemā by undermining the predominance of Islam and the Muslim citizens in the Empire.

Moreover, some of the modernizing reforms even strengthened the Islamic institutions of the State. An example is the firman issued shortly after the destruction of the Janissaries which prohibited the governors from inflicting the death penalty without a formal sentence of a competent cadi.[156] Similarly, with a view to separating the executive and judicial powers, the tribunal of the Grand Vizier was abolished in 1838 and its functions transferred to the highest 'ulemā.[157]

Nevertheless, many 'ulemā, especially of the lower ranks, were, as has been shown, strongly opposed to the reforms. In order to appease these 'ulemā, Selīm III and Maḥmūd II did their best to convince them, and the people, of their—at least outward—attachment to religion. Both rulers repaired and restored a very large number of mosques, holy tombs, dervish convents, and other religious buildings in the capital and the provinces.[158]

Two new mosques were built by Maḥmūd in Istanbul, the Hidāyet in 1813–14 and the Nuṣret in 1826.[159] The Sultans scrupulously observed their obligation to attend public prayer and frequently also visited convents of dervish orders, especially of the Mevlevīs and Naḳshbendīs.[160] Strict orders were repeatedly issued by the Sultans enjoining all Muslims to perform the daily prayers in groups, either in the mosques or in their offices, houses and mansions.[161] Particular attention was given to providing religious services and instruction to the soldiers of the new army. Special imāms were attached to every unit of Selīm's *Niżām-ı Cedīd* troops.[162] According to the first paragraph of the Regulations of Maḥmūd's modernized army,[163] the imāms of every regiment are to teach the soldiers in their free time the elements of Islam (*şurūṭ-ı ṣalāt, ʿilm-i ḥāl,* etc.) and see to it that they observe their religious duties. The Sultan also gave orders to appoint special imāms and religious teachers for various Government departments.[164]

Maḥmūd demonstrated his respect and support not only for religion but also for its representatives, the ʿulemā. To the ceremony of the beginning of the religious studies of his son and heir, ʿAbdül-Mecīd, in 1831 he invited a much larger number of ʿulemā than had been customary in the past.[165] In Ramaḍān 1251 (January 1836) the *ṣudūr dersi*, a discussion of Qurʾān verses among the foremost ʿulemā in the presence of the Sultan, was reintroduced after it had been abandoned for a long time.[166] On frequent occasions the Sultan bestowed gifts on the ʿulemā, softas and loyal dervishes.[167] Maḥmūd probably knew that one of the reasons for the dissatisfaction and agitation of the lower ʿulemā in the past was their poverty.[168] He ordered increases in the salaries of the imāms and other employees of the waqf institutions. Shortly before his death he also raised the salaries of the politically important public preachers (*vāʿiẓ*) who, unlike the *ḫuṭabā*, addressed the people in simple Turkish and often discussed topical issues in their sermons.[169] In recognition of the support of the ʿulemā leadership in suppressing the Janissaries in 1826 the Sultan assigned the palace of the Janissary commander-in-chief as residence of the şeyḫüʾl-islāms and abrogated the old rule according to which a şeyḫüʾl-islām after his dismissal was cut off from all contact with officials in active service.[170]

Maḥmūd II is said to have contemplated following the example of Meḥmed ʿAlī in Egypt and taking over the enormous waqf properties which to a large extent were administered by, and conferred benefits on, the ʿulemā. He did not dare, however, to harm their economic interests so openly and limited himself to establishing some form of State control over the waqf income of certain major religious and charitable institutions.[171] Nevertheless these changes, together with some other economic factors,[172] eventually led to impoverishment of the ʿulemā. In the late 1830s and the 1840s European travellers already claimed that many medreses were declining, their professors living in great straits and their students starving.[173] In 1847 an observer stated, possibly with some exaggeration, that 'the higher class of Oulema, who derived large incomes from the endowments of the mosques, are nearly all sunk into poverty'.[174] However, this serious deterioration became obvious only under ʿAbdü'l-Mecīd. Until the end of Maḥmūd's reign the ʿulemā generally succeeded in maintaining most of their economic and social privileges. When Mekkī-zāde Muṣṭafā ʿĀṣım, the last şeyḫü'l-islām to serve under Maḥmūd II, died in 1846 he was reported to have left property worth twenty million piasters.[175]

III

CONCLUSION

The support of the ʿulemā leaders for the Westernizing reforms of Selīm III and Maḥmūd II is understandable in view of their integration in the ruling class and their active participation in the Government of the Ottoman Empire which still retained its strongly Islamic character. In their hostility to the reactionary Janissaries and Bektashis they found themselves to be natural allies of the reforming Sultans. They feared Maḥmūd II and realized that the internal weakening of their corps had made open resistance to his policy no longer possible. The consistent efforts of both Sultans to prove their religious orthodoxy and appease the ʿulemā also made it difficult for the latter to oppose innovations and helped them set their conscience at rest. Finally, the great changes under Selīm III and Maḥmūd II were not made in the name of a new ideology; they were not based on, or accompanied by, a novel set of values. On the contrary, all the important reforms were, as has been shown, presented as being required and sanctioned by Islam. Everything was done 'for the sake of religion and State'.

It has often been observed that the ʿulemā in various periods and different countries were more concerned with upholding the ideas and theoretical values of Islam than with fighting for the preservation of Muslim institutions in practice. From far back they were accustomed to bowing to the will of the secular rulers and tolerating the violation of the holy law by Muslim society. What mattered in their opinion were the divine doctrines of Islam, while reality was in any case temporary, fleeting and morally evil. They believed, as Snouck Hurgronje put it,[176] that 'on devient mécréant, non pas en négligeant presque toute la loi, ni en la violant, mais bien en doutant de la valeur éternelle d'un de ses principes, en voulant les améliorer ou les réformer'. Selīm III and Maḥmūd II went out of their way to stress that nothing could be further from their mind than doing the latter. Legal reforms started only under ʿAbdü'l-Mecīd, open discussion of religious reforms even much later.

Yet, it remains somewhat astonishing that the leading ʿulemā in Selīm's and

Maḥmūd's time were not farsighted enough to realize that the Westernizing reforms supported by them would eventually destroy the Islamic character of the Ottoman State and society. This lack of perspicacity was, no doubt, due to their unbounded confidence in the superiority and eternal strength of their religion and, at the same time, to their limited knowledge and understanding of historical developments in the West. Even those among them who were aware of the decline of religion and the power of the clergy in contemporary Europe failed to draw the logical conclusion that modernization might lead to a similar result in the lands of Islam.

By making the ʿulemā an essential part of the Government, the Ottomans had largely succeeded in bridging the traditional gulf between the *umarā'* and the *fuḳahā'*, between political-administrative reality and religious-legal theory. However, while thus preventing a clash of the European type between Church and State, they caused a deep split both within the ʿulemā corps and in the minds of the leading ʿulemā. The integration of the ʿulemā in the ruling class of the Empire may have been beneficial for the unity of the Ottoman State but had most serious consequences for religion, at least in its official form. It caused the higher ʿulemā to devote their main attention to politics and administration and, along with other factors, hampered the free spiritual development of Islam during the decisive period of its confrontation with Western civilization.

This article is reprinted from Uriel Heyd (ed.), *Studies in Islamic History* (Jerusalem, 1961), pp. 63–96. Reprinted with permission of Magnes Press.

NOTES

1. I wish to take this opportunity to express my gratitude to the Rockefeller Foundation, New York, for the grant which enabled me, *inter alia*, to collect material for this study. My sincere thanks are also due to the Director of the Österreichisches Staatsarchiv. Abt. Haus-, Hof- und Staatsarchiv, at Vienna for allowing me to study the despatches of the Austrian envoys (Internuntii) in Constantinople during the reign of Selīm III and Maḥmūd II.

The documents will be quoted as follows: 'Despatch of Austr. Internunt., or Envoy, [dated] 11 Oct. 1830 (VI/51, no. 321 A)', which stands for '*Türkei*, Reihe VI, Karton 51, Dokument No. 321 A'.

2. The texts of the fetvā and the *taḳrīẓ* of the ʿulemā are found in the Preface to Vānḳūlī's dictionary, the first work printed. See also Fr. Babinger, *Stambuler Buchwesen im 18. Jahrhundert*, Leipzig, 1919, pp. 9–10.

3. Baron de Tott, *Mémoires sur les Turcs et les Tartares*, Amsterdam, 1785, III, 123–24.

4. *Ta'rīḫ-i ʿOs̱mānī Encümeni Mecmūʿası* (*TOEM*), VII, no. 41 (1332), pp. 257 ff.

5. On the life and views of this interesting personality see *TOEM*, VII, no. 41, pp. 285–97; *Tarih Vesikaları*, I, no. 3 (1941), pp. 162–66; and *İslâm Ansiklop.*, s.v. 'İzzet Molla'.

6. A manuscript of this memorandum is to be found in the library of the Türk Tarih Kurumu, Ankara (Y 556). On this memorandum see also İbnül Emin Mahmut Kemal, *Son Asır Türk Şairleri*, IV, Istanbul, 1937, pp. 739–40.

7. Meḥmed Esʿad, *Üss-i Żafer*, Istanbul, 1293, p. 65.

8. See the *taḳrīr* submitted by the Grand Vizier to Sultan Maḥmūd II, published by İ. H. Uzunçarşılı in Türk Tarih Kurumu, *Belleten, XVIII* (1954), p. 229.

9. Meḥmed Süreyyā, *Sicill-i 'Os̱mānī* (*SO*), II, 83; Ahmet Refik, *Hicrî On İkinci Asırda Istanbul Hayatı*, Istanbul, 1930, p. 168; Aḥmed Luṭfī, *Ta'rīḫ*, III, 157; Aḥmed Rāsim, *'Os̱mānlı Ta'rīḫi*, IV, Istanbul, 1328–30, p. 1855, note.

10. Luṭfī, III, 142; Despatch of Austr. Internunt., 11 Oct. 1830 (VI/51, no. 321 A).

11. Despatches of same, 10 Sept. and 10 Oct. 1812 (VI/4 A, no. 22 & 24).

12. Despatch of same, 7 Dec. 1836 (VI/65, no. 207); Aḥmed Cevdet, *Ta'rīḫ*, X (1309), p. 95.

13. Helmuth von Moltke, *Briefe über Zustände und Begebenheiten in der Türkei*, 6. Aufl., Berlin, 1893, p. 122.

14. Luṭfī, V, 125; Despatch of Austr. Internunt., 21 Mar. 1838 (VI/67, no. 275).

15. Luṭfī, III, 142; V, 152.

16. L.-P.-B. D'Aubignosc, *La Turquie nouvelle*, Paris, 1839, I, 232–35.

17. For a detailed summary of the treatise in English see *Sketches of Turkey in 1831 and 1832* by An American [Dr J. E. De Kay], New York, 1833, pp. 518–20.

18. Luṭfī, III, 167; V. 126; R. Walsh, *A Residence at Constantinople*, London, 1836, II, 305; Despatch of Austr. Internunt., 10 Oct. 1831 (VIII/3, no. 337).

19. Despatch of same, 10 May 1827 (VI/27, no. 171); *Tanzimat*, I, Istanbul, 1940, p. 937; Osman Ergin, *Türkiye Maarif Tarihi*, I, Istanbul, 1939, pp. 282 ff.

20. T.-X. Bianchi, *Notice sur le premier ouvrage d'anatomie et de médecine, imprimé en turc*, Paris, 1821; Şānī-zāde Meḥmed 'Atā'ullāh, *Ta'rīḫ*, II, 336–37; Cevdet, X, 213; Fr. Babinger, *Geschichtsschreiber der Osmanen*, Leipzig, 1927, pp. 346–47; *Tanzimat*, I, 935–36.

21. Luṭfī, V, 137; *Tarih Vesikaları*, I, no. 3 (1941), pp. 212 ff.; *SO*, I, 341; Rāsim, IV, 1769, note.

22. *SO*, I, 339.

23. For instance, Paşmakçı-zāde 'Alī, Dāmād-zāde Aḥmed, Çelebi-zāde İsmā'īl 'Āṣım, and Ḥamīdī-zāde Muṣṭafā (see their biographies in İ. H. Uzunçarşılı, *Osmanlı Tarihi*, IV, Part 2, Ankara, 1959).

24. For example, Feyẓu'llāh-zāde Muṣṭafā, Ṣamānī-zāde 'Ömer Ḫulūsī, a. o. (ibid.).

25. Cevdet, V (1278), p. 273; VI (1286), p. 166.

26. See *İslâm Ansiklop.*, s.v. 'Hâlet Efendi'.

27. Luṭfī, V, 25.

28. Luṭfī, V, 107; *SO*, II, 437–38.

29. D'Aubignosc, I, 201–6.

30. Charles Rolland, *La Turquie contemporaine*, Paris, 1854, p. 223.

31. Despatches of Austr. Internunt., 31 May and 18 July 1807 (VI/1, no. 17 & 21); *'Aṭā* (Ṭayyār-zāde Aḥmed 'Aṭā'ullāh), *Ta'rīḫ*, III, 82–83; Aḥmed 'Āṣım, *Ta'rīḫ*, II, 46–49 (text of the *ḥüccet*); but see also 'Āṣım's defence of the Şeyḫü'l-İslām (I, 337).

32. In the uprising against Bayraḳdār in 1808 the high 'ulemā, though strongly opposed to his régime, did not come into the open but are said to have left the task of inciting the people to the imāms and dervishes (Ch. MacFarlane, *Constantinople in 1828*, London, 1829, II, 94; Juchereau de St.-Denys, *Histoire de l'empire ottoman*, Paris, 1844, II, 211 ff.).

33. MacFarlane, II, 44–46.

34. A. Slade, *Records of Travels in Turkey ... in the years 1829, 1830, and 1831*, II, London, 1833, pp. 207–8. The statement in MacFarlane (II, 346–47) that in 1829 even the 'ulemā wore the fez is mistaken (see Luṭfī, II, 148, 195, 269–73); MacFarlane had left Turkey in October 1828.

35. Walsh, II, 299.

36. Luṭfī, IV, 65.

37. Luṭfī, V, 98.

38. Despatch of Austr. Internunt., 10 Aug. 1836 (VI/65, no. 190 C); H. Southgate, *Narrative of a Tour through Armenia ... and Mesopotamia*, New York, 1840, I, 79–81; J. M. Jouannin et J. van Gaver, *Turquie*, Paris, 1840, p. 428.

39. Luṭfī, V, 50–52.

40. See Luṭfī's apology (ibid., 51).

41. Luṭfī, II, 144.

42. Luṭfī, II, 169.

43. Luṭfī, III, 146; IV, 56.

44. Tonderini, *De la littérature des Turcs*, Paris, 1789, II, 6–25; J. Dallaway, *Constantinople*, London, 1797, pp. 63–64.
45. *Üss-i Żafer*, 187–88; Luṭfī, I, 147.
46. *Sketches of Turkey*, 257; Ch. White, *Three Years in Constantinople*, London, 1845, II, 217.
47. Toderini, II, 25; White, II, 217.
48. For their misdeeds in Anatolia in the seventeenth century, for example, see, Ç. Uluçay, *XVII. Asırda Saruhanda Eşkiyalık*, Istanbul, 1944, pp. 23–30.
49. 'Āṣım, I, 297, 334–36; Cevdet, I (1271), p. 118.
50. As in the case of Dürrī-zāde Meḥmed 'Aṭā'ullāh (see Rif'at Efendi, *Devḥatü'l-Meşāyiḫ*, [Istanbul, lithogr.], p. 108.
51. Cevdet, IV (1275), p. 163; Slade, I, 229.
52. Şānī-zāde, II, 358–61; Despatch of Austr. Internunt., 26 Jan. 1818 (VI/8, no. 2).
53. Despatch of same, 24 Dec. 1821 (VI/12, no. 116 A & I).
54. Despatch of same, 25 Apr. 1801 (II/125, no. 18); F. C. H. L. Pouqueville, *Voyage en Morée, à Constantinople, etc.*, Paris, 1805, II, 185–86; J.-E. Beauvoisins, *Notice sur la cour du Grand-Seigneur*, Paris, 1809, pp. 84–86.
55. Despatch of Austr. Internunt., 7 Apr. 1833 (VI/57, no. 6 G)
56. Luṭfī, II, 94.
57. Jouannin-Gaver, 429.
58. For the following see *Üss-i Żafer*, especially the *ḥüccet-i şer'iye* of 21 Şevvāl 1241 (29 May 1826) (pp. 36–40), the *lāyiḥa* of Tatarcık 'Abdu'llāh, and that of Keçeci-zāde 'İzzet (see above, notes 4 and 6).
59. See, for instance, *Tafsīr al-Djalālayn* on this verse.
60. *Üss-i Żafer*, 42.
61. Ibid., 114.
62. Ibid., 37, 44.
63. Ibid., 49; cf. Ibn Khaldūn, *Muḳaddima*, Beirut, 1900, pp. 271–73.
64. Cevdet, II (1271), p. 256.
65. *Üss-i Żafer*, 37–38.
66. See *Encyclop. of Islam*, N.E., s.v. 'Bārūd', I, VI; cf. also Toderini, II, 2, chapter 3, §XII.
67. Meḥmed Es'ad, *Ta'rīḫ*. Österr. Nationalbibl., Vienna, H. O. 210 (Flügel, no. 1141), f. 202 a-b.
68. Tatarcık's *lāyiḥa* (*TOEM*, VII, 260 ff.); *Üss-i Żafer*, 55.
69. Es'ad, *Ta'rīḫ*, 200 a.
70. E.g., Şānī-zāde, I, 101.
71. In his memorandum (Türk Tarih Kurumu Library, Ankara, Y 556, f. 4 b).
72. Keçeci-zāde uses the term *yeñi dünyā*, 'new world', the usual epithet for America, as an antonym of *eski 'ālem* (ibid., 4 a).
73. Ibid., 4 a, 5 a.
74. 'Aṭā, III, 261.
75. Sir James Porter, *Observations sur la religion . . . des Turcs*, Londres, 1769, I, 113.
76. Choiseul-Gouffier to Vergennes, quoted in L. Pingaud, *Choiseul-Gouffier, la France en Orient sous Louis XVI*, Paris, 1887, p. 82.
77. J. W. Zinkeisen, *Geschichte des osmanischen Reiches*, VI, Gotha, 1859, p. 19, n. 2.
78. See Tatarcık's *lāyiḥa* (*TOEM*, VII, 273); G. A. Olivier, *Voyage dans l'Empire othoman*, I, Paris, an 9, pp. 155–56.
79. Cevdet, V, 175 ff.; VIII (1288), pp. 412 ff.
80. *TOEM*, VII, 274.
81. Keçeci-zāde 'İzzet (see Türk Tarih Kurumu Library, Y 556, f. 22 a).
82. Luṭfī, V, 94.
83. Cevdet, IV, 371–72; E. Z. Karal, *Selim III.ün Hatt-ı Humayunlari*, Ankara, 1942, pp. 34–36.
84. 'Āṣım, I, 16.
85. Şānī-zāde, IV, 201.
86. Comte Andréossy, *Constantinople et le Bosphore*, Paris, 1828, p. 69; Luṭfī, I, 144–45.
87. Memorandum by Çelebi Efendi [Köse Ketḫüdā Muṣṭafā Reşīd] written in 1804 to explain and defend the Niẓām-ı Cedīd and published, in translation, in William Wilkinson, *An Account of the Principalities of Wallachia and Moldavia*, London, 1820, pp. 220–21.

88. *Üss-i Żafer*, 158.

89. See copy of a petition in a *mecmū'a* in the Bibl. Nationale, Paris, Suppl. turc, no. 1027, f. 219 a-b.

90. *Üss-i Żafer*, 113, 159.

91. Ibid., 199–211; Es'ad, *Ta'rīḫ*, 183 a-184 a; Lutfī, I, 149–51.

92. Beauvoisins, 11–13.

93. Cevdet, VIII, 58.

94. 'Aṭā, II, 184–85; *Devḥa*, 125–26; Despatches of Austr. Internunt., 10 Mar. 1812 and 10 Sept. 1819 (VI/4 A, no. 5; VI/8, no. 33 A & C) (detailed biography).

95. Ibid., 33 C.

96. 'Aṭā, II, 186–89.

97. Aḥmed Necīb, Chief Physician in 1836/7, who did not belong to the 'ulemā corps, was an exception (Luṭfī, V, 70; *SO*, I, 296).

98. See Cevdet, X, 214.

99. Secret despatch (in code) of Austr. Internunt., 25 Nov. 1812 (VI/5, no. 29). For Mes'ūd's biography see Şānī-zāde, III, 135–38.

100. 'Aṭā, III, 193–94.

101. Cevdet, V, 179; Olivier, I, 155–56.

102. *Devḥa*, 105–6; *SO*, I, 143–44.

103. *SO*, III, 472. 'İṣmet's ṣon, 'Ārif Ḥikmet, was a famous şeyḫü'l-islām in 'Abdü'l-Mecīd's time.

104. Despatch of Austr. Envoy. 26 Aug. 1791 (II/97, no. 1).

105. *SO*, III, 272.

106. Former holders of this office used to be barred from political life (see Rāsim, IV, 1820) until the abrogation of this rule in 1826 (see below, note 170, and Luṭfī, I, 91, 291; II, 86).

107. See, for instance, *Üss-i Żafer*, 15–16.

108. Cevdet, II, 203, 206.

109. Cevdet, IV, 163.

110. See, for example, the deliberations in December 1783 whether war should be made on Russia (Cevdet, II, 196 ff.).

111. Despatch of Austr. Internunt., 25 Sept. 1792 (II/100, no. 32).

112. 'Aṭā, III, 121–22, 295–96.

113. Luṭfī, V, 107.

114. Ibid., 140.

115. Şānī-zāde, I, 399–402. A picture of the ambassador is reproduced in *Tarih Vesikaları*, I, no. 5 (1942), after p. 370.

116. Luṭfī, V, 12.

117. J. von Hammer, *Geschichte des Osmanischen Reiches*, 2. Ausg., IV, 630 ff.; *SO*, III, 432.

118. Şānī-zāde, II, 96; Cevdet, X, 10–11; Luṭfī, I, 119; II, 103; *SO*, I, 156; III, 349.

119. Şānī-zāde, IV, 23; Cevdet, IV, 164.

120. *Devḥa*, 114; *SO*, I, 271; IV, 67–68.

121. 'Āṣım, I, 62, 295–96; Karal, 58–59.

122. Despatches of Austr. Internunt., 10 Sept. 1819, 10 Jan. 1792, and 25 Nov. 1827 (VI/8, no. 33 C; II/98, no. 2, P.S. 2; VI/28, no. 199 B).

123. For a typical example see the talks with the Russian representative early in 1776 (Zinkeisen, VI, 19).

124. Despatch of Austr. Internunt., 25 May 1829 (VI/37, no. 265 A).

125. *TOEM*, VII, 271.

126. Süleymān 'İzzī, *Ta'rīḫ*, Istanbul, 1199, f. 143 b.

127. Cevdet, XI, 197.

128. Cevdet, IV, 163.

129. *Sketches of Turkey*, 141.

130. 'Abdü'l-Hamīd I in a *ḫaṭṭ-ı hümāyūn* near the end of his reign (Cevdet, IV, 164) and Selīm III in an early *ḫaṭṭ* (E. Z. Karal, *Selim III'ün Hat-tı Hümayunları, Nizam-i Cedit*, Ankara, 1946, p. 150).

131. [J. A.] Guer, *Moeurs et usages des Turcs*, Paris, 1746–47, II, 131.

132. Despatches of Austr. Envoy, 26 Nov. 1791 and 10 Jan. 1792 (II/97, no. 9, P.S. 2; 10, P.S. 1; and II/98, no. 2, P.S. 1). There were many thousands of Austrian subjects, mainly Wallachians, in Turkish slavery.

133. Despatches of same, 24 Dec. 1791 and 25 Febr. 1792 (II/97, no. 12, P.S. 4; II/98, no. 6, P.S. 2).

134. Ibid. Some violations of the holy law with respect to foreign residents were not new. They had existed for centuries as a result of the capitulations granted to European rulers.

135. E. Z. Karal, *Osmanlı Tarihi, V*, Ankara, 1947, p. 20; id., *Hatt-ı Humay.*, 1942, pp. 59–60.

136. See, for instance, Cevdet, II, 196–207.

137. For its text see Luṭfī, II, 14.

138. E.g., Cevdet, II, 203.

139. Report by Mr. Pisani of 24 August 1843.

140. St. Lane-Poole, *The Life of the R.H. Stratford Canning*, London, 1888, II, 91.

141. ʿAbdu' r-Raḥmān Şeref, *Ta'riḫ Muṣaḥabeleri*, Istanbul, 1339, p. 303.

142. Chevalier d'Arvieux, *Mémoires*, Paris, 1735, I, 444.

143. J. Otter, *Voyage en Turquie et en Perse*, Paris, 1748, I, 23.

144. Baron de Tott, I, 12, 34 ff.; cf. *SO*, IV, 358–59.

145. V. Fontanier, *Voyages en Orient*, Paris, 1829, pp. 219, 263–68.

146. Despatch of Austr. Internunt., 10 July 1801 (II/125, no. 24, P.S. 7).

147. Cevdet, X, 214. Şānī-zāde (II, 344–45) relates even more damaging gossip.

148. See, for instance, Karal, *Osm. Tarihi, V*, 39–40; Şānī-zāde. I, 365; Luṭfī, II, 123.

149. The Turkish text is attached to Despatch of Austr. Internunt., 5 Aug. 1821 (VI/12, no. 100 A).

150. G. Rosen, *Geschichte der Türkei*, I, Leipzig, 1866, p. 58. The adage is already used in an *ʿahd-nāme* of 934 (1527/8) (Bibl. Nationale, Paris, Ancien fonds turc, no. 81, f. 99 b).

151. *Üss-i Ẓafer*, 157–58; Esʿad, *Ta'riḫ*, 46a–47a

152. Luṭfī, I, 102, 260.

153. The Ottomans had a foretaste of such a predicament when they had to enter anti-French alliances with Russia and England at the time of Napoleon's invasion of Egypt.

154. Despatch of Austr. Internunt., 10 Nov. 1828 (VI/34, no. 241 B).

155. ʿĀṣım, I, 238–39.

156. ʿAṭā, III, 138; MacFarlane, II, 138.

157. Jouannin-Gaver, 434; Despatch of Austr. Internunt., 4 Apr. 1838 (VI/67, no. 277 B).

158. Cevdet, V, 108, 273; ʿAṭā, III, 139–43; Luṭfī, IV, 72, 160, 166; V, 10–11; VI, 36.

159. Şānī-zāde, II, 212; ʿAṭā, III, 141; Esʿad, *Ta'rīḫ*, 84 a–b.

160. Despatch of Austr. Internunt., 2 Dec. 1834 (VI/61, no. 98); Luṭfī, V, 21.

161. Luṭfī, V, 65–66; Southgate, I, 168–69.

162. ʿĀṣım, I, 39.

163. *Ḳānūn-nāme-yi ʿAsākir-i Manṣūre-yi Muḥammedīye*, Istanbul, 1244.

164. Esʿad, *Ta'rīḫ*, 49 b-50a, 56 a.

165. Luṭfī, III, 163.

166. Luṭfī, V, 38–39.

167. E.g., Luṭfī, II, 144–45; III, 170; *Moniteur Ottoman*, Istanbul, no. 90, 9 Şevvāl 1250 (7 Febr. 1835).

168. See ʿĀṣım, I, 332–33 on the situation in 1807.

169. Luṭfī, IV, 166; V, 4, 65; VI, 29.

170. *Üss-i Ẓafer*, 116, 125–26; Luṭfī, I, 144, 148. When the Janissary revolt broke out in 1826, several former şeyḫü'l-islāms were urgently invited to join the headquarters of the loyal forces (Esʿad, *Ta'rīḫ*, 147 a-b).

171. Despatch of Austr. Internunt., 25 June 1827 (VI/27, no. 178 D); A. Ubicini, *Lettres sur la Turquie*, I, Paris, 1851, p. 190; ʿAṭā, III, 138.

172. Ubicini, I, 211–12.

173. Southgate, II, 166–67 (for Baghdad in 1838); Ch. MacFarlane, *Turkey and Its Destiny*, London, 1850, I, 396–97; II, 52–56, 535.

174. MacFarlane, I, 106.

175. ʿAbdu'r-Raḥmān Şeref, 301.

176. *Selected Works of C. Snouck Hurgronje*, ed. by G.-H. Bousquet and J. Schacht, Leiden, 1957, p. 248.

Turkish Attitudes Concerning Christian–Muslim Equality in the Nineteenth Century

RODERIC H. DAVISON

Every modern society has been faced with problems arising from inequalities among the various groups of which it is composed, particularly since the eighteenth-century proclamation in America that 'all men are created equal,' and the elaboration in France of the Declaration of the Rights of Man and the Citizen. The differences which produced inequality have been various—economic, social, racial, linguistic, religious, political—and variously intertwined. In the Near East until very recent times the major boundary lines between groups, and therefore the principal barriers to a homogeneous society of equals, have been religious. Although today social and economic disparities in Near Eastern society have vastly increased as modern technology and finance have provided greater opportunities for getting and spending, and although nationalist rivalries now challenge the primacy of religious rivalries, it is still often true that religion is the dividing line, and that a man's creed is his distinguishing mark.

In the Ottoman empire of the early nineteenth century his religion provided a man's label, both in his own conceptual scheme and in the eyes of his neighbors and his governors. He was a Muslim, Greek Orthodox, Gregorian Armenian, Jew, Catholic, or Protestant before he was a Turk or Arab, a Greek or Bulgar, in the national sense, and also before he felt himself an Ottoman citizen. The Ottoman government, by granting official recognition to these *millet*s, as the religious communities were called, had preserved and even emphasized the religious distinctions. The empire itself was governed by Muslims; its law was based on the religious law of Islam. But within this

Reprinted by permission from *American Historical Review* 59:4 (July 1954): 844–864.

empire the several Christian communities and the Jewish community enjoyed a partial autonomy, whereby the ecclesiastical hierarchy which administered the *millet* supervised not only the religious, educational, and charitable affairs of its flock; it controlled also such matters of personal status as marriage, divorce, and inheritance, and it collected some taxes. This mosaic pattern, in which a Christian and a Muslim living side by side in the same state under the same sovereign were subject to different law and different officials, had served the Ottoman empire well for four centuries. In the Near East law was still, as it had formerly been in the West also, personal rather than territorial.

The semiautonomy of the Christian *millet*s did not, however, mean complete equality among the subjects of the empire. The Muslim *millet* was dominant. This did not lead to any systematic persecution of Christians by Muslims, nor to any systematic oppression of Christians by the Ottoman government. Indeed, inefficient or corrupt and extortionate government in the empire often bore more heavily on Muslim Turks and Arabs than it did on Christians. Pasha and tax-farmer alike found the piastres they could squeeze from Muslims just as sound as Christian money and did not vary their harshness or their methods with the religion of the victim. Despite all this, it was still incontestable that Christians were looked down upon as second-class citizens both by the Muslim public and by the government. They suffered unequal treatment in various ways. Their dress was distinctive, and if Christian or Jew wore the fez he was required to sew on it a strip of black ribbon or cloth, not to be concealed by the tassel. Sometimes the unequal treatment was in purely ecclesiastical matters, as for example on those occasions when the Sublime Porte denied permits to one of the Christian sects for the repair of churches. One aspect of religious inequality was particularly galling, though it arose infrequently as a concrete issue—Christians could not so easily make converts from among the Muslims as could Muslims from among the Christians, since Islamic law demanded that apostasy be punished by death. In addition, the Christians suffered certain specific disabilities in public life. They were, for example, denied opportunity for appointment to the highest administrative posts, they could not serve in the armed forces but had to pay an exemption tax; Christian evidence was discounted in a Muslim court of law. Neither the concept nor the practice of citizenship, involving equal rights and duties, existed in the Ottoman Empire before the nineteenth century.[1]

After 1800, the attention of the Ottoman government was forcibly directed toward the question of equality in several ways. First, as Christian groups in the empire absorbed Western ideas of liberty and nationality, and as education and literacy increased among them, they complained more frequently and loudly about the lack of equality. Second, they found ready hearers among the several great powers who traditionally acted as protectors of Christians in the Near East and who, for mixed motives of humanitarianism and power politics, magnified the volume of these complaints in the Sublime Porte's ear and pressed for changes. Third, Ottoman statesmen who were concerned to check the territorial disintegration of the empire, and its internal decline, embarked on a program of reorganization and incipient westernization which inevitably brought them up against the same problem of equality as they moved to adopt or adapt elements of the Western state's political pattern. The question of the equality of Christian, Muslim, and Jew was by no means the major question faced by these statesmen, but it ran like a thread through many phases of the larger problem of Ottoman reform and westernization. Should Christians be given equal opportunity as students in the schools to be established in a reformed educational system? Should they be allowed to serve in a rejuvenated army? Should they be admitted to the highest administrative posts as the bureaucracy was improved? Should the contemplated revisions and codifications of law apply equally to Christian and Muslim? And, if any sort of representative government were established, whether on a provincial scale or in the form of a constitutional monarchy, should Christians be represented, and how?

It is, therefore, one of the most significant aspects of Ottoman history in the nineteenth century that the doctrine of equality did, in fact, become official policy. Sultan Mahmud II (1808–1839), who took some crucial steps toward reform in his own vigorous way, frequently made it plain that in his view all his subjects, of whatever creed, were equal.[2] But it was during the Tanzimat period of 1839 to 1876, a new era in Ottoman efforts at reform and westernization, that the doctrine of the equality of Christian and Muslim was proclaimed in the most solemn manner and came to play a prominent role in the central question of Ottoman revival.[3]

I

An imperial edict of reforms, the Hatt-i Sherif of Gülhane, opened the new era on November 3, 1839.[4] After public proclamation before an impressive assembly of diplomats and Ottoman notables, the edict was sworn to by the young sultan Abdul Medjid [Abdülmecid] and his high officials in the room where the mantle of the prophet Muhammad was preserved. Much of the Hatt-i Sherif had a profoundly Muslim ring. It laid the decline of the empire directly to the nonobservance of 'the precepts of the glorious Kuran.' In the next breath it then attempted to reconcile Muslim tradition and progress, promising new institutions which should not contravene Muslim law but should conform to its demands. Security of life, honor, and property was guaranteed, along with reforms in taxing and conscription methods. But the Hatt-i Sherif was most remarkable neither for its Muslim overtones, for its promises of 'life, liberty, and property,' nor for its pledge to correct specific evils, though all this was important. The most novel aspect of the *hatt* arose from its official declaration of equality. 'These imperial concessions,' affirmed Abdul Medjid in his edict, 'are extended to all our subjects, of whatever religion or sect they may be.'

The new policy was confirmed in a more extensive Hatt-i Humayun of 1856, which promised equal treatment for adherents of all creeds in such specific matters as educational opportunity, appointment to government posts, and the administration of justice, as well as in taxation and military service.[5] An interesting antidefamation clause was included also, forbidding 'every distinction or designation tending to make any class whatever of the subjects of my Empire inferior to another class, on account of their religion, language, or race.' Legal action would ensue against anyone, whether public official or private individual, who used 'any injurious or offensive term.' Even name-calling was forbidden in the name of equality.

At frequent intervals the theme was restated, with variations. The next sultan, Abdul Aziz [Abdülaziz], opened his new Council of State [Şûray-ı Devlet] in 1868 with a speech which referred to adherents of all creeds as 'children of the same fatherland.'[6] His successor, Murad V, echoed these sentiments in his first *hatt*.[7] The trend culminated in December, 1876, with the promulgation of the first written constitution in Ottoman history, establishing a limited monarchy all of whose subjects were considered 'Osmanli, whatever religion or creed they hold.' The constitution further affirmed that 'all Osmanli are equal before the law . . . without distinction as to religion.'[8]

From 1839 to 1876 many efforts—some valiant, some half-hearted, some merely for the record; some spontaneous, some under diplomatic pressure—were made by the Ottoman government to translate the promises of equality into fact. The sultan in 1844 engaged not to enforce the death penalty for apostasy from Islam. Some Christians were appointed, and some later were elected, to local advisory councils [*meclisler*] established in each province, and also to the Grand Council of State [*Meclis-i Vâlâ-yı Ahkâm-ı Adliye*] in 1856. Christians and Muslims were accepted together as students in the newly established imperial *lycée* of Galata Saray in 1867. These and many other measures did something to raise the status of the non-Muslims of the empire, but the advance was slow and piecemeal. No genuine equality was ever attained.

Many European writers of the time, and many Western historians since, have dealt with the Tanzimat period, and the equality question that ran through it, in one of two ways. Some look on it from the outside as a phase of the Eastern Question, during which European diplomats in the service of their own national interests had constantly to prod the Ottoman government to live up to its professions of reform and equality, and to carry them out in a

French, Russian, or English fashion. Others consider it primarily as a phase of the long-continued internal decay of the empire, when all efforts to restore the 'sick man' to health were unavailing. In either case, most writers have assumed the inability or the unwillingness of the Turks to carry out any significant change. Measuring achievement against promise, they have frequently concluded that the Ottoman statesmen either publicly professed what they did not believe or publicly promised what they knew they could not effect. Such viewpoints, together with the abundant evidence of partial successes, failures, and sins of omission in the Ottoman reform efforts, have often led to the judgment that the promises, particularly the promise of equality, were largely hypocrisy—dust to throw in the eyes of the West, to ward off foreign intervention in favor of the subject peoples of the empire, and to blind observers to the continuance of an oppressive Turkish rule over downtrodden Christians.[9]

Careful reassessment of the Tanzimat period is likely to show that such views are based on an inadequate understanding of the aims of the Ottoman statesmen, of the results actually obtained, and of the formidable obstacles to progress and equality. There is need for more penetrating investigation and analysis of the Tanzimat period than has yet been undertaken either by Turkish or Western historians.[10] Among the subjects demanding attention is that of Turkish attitudes on the various phases of reform. An inquiry into the attitudes of Turkish statesmen and people on the subject of Muslim-Christian equality can help to explain what changes the then climate of opinion might or might not accept and why the official program of equality was only partly realized. A complete explanation would of course involve all aspects of the reform question. It would involve also a reconsideration of the degree and nature of Ottoman lag behind European civilization, of the impediments which great-power diplomacy offered to Ottoman reform, and of the situation of multinational empires in an age of clamoring nationalisms. But Turkish attitudes were obviously among the most important forces at work in this period. Some useful indications can be given in answer to three crucial questions: what in reality were the attitudes of leading Ottoman statesmen toward these promises of equality? what traditions and what experience shaped the basic attitudes of Turks toward Christians, a century ago? and what attitudes were then current among them on the proclamation of Christian equality with Muslims?

II

Four Ottoman statesmen initiated and carried through most of the reform measures in this period—Reshid, Ali, Fuad, and Midhat.[11] Each was grand vizier [*sadrazam*] at least twice, and each occupied high public office throughout most of his adult life. As individuals they were completely different, and often rivals for power. But they were alike in their lack of bigotry and fanaticism.[12] Each had a fair acquaintance with Western political ideas and practices, and with some phases of European life and culture, though Ali was less 'Europeanized' than the others in his manner of life and of speech. Each of the four, in his struggles with the administration of the unwieldy empire, came to believe that a degree of westernization was necessary to strengthen the empire. They agreed, further, that this process of reform demanded that all subjects of the empire be treated alike, regardless of creed. They differed as to how fast and by what measures the goal of equality might be reached. Often they waited to be pushed by events. Midhat, who had the greatest energy but the least finesse of the four Tanzimat statesmen, was the most inclined to brush aside legitimate doubts and the cautions born of experience, and to shoulder his way ahead against general prejudices.

It is quite true, as their Western critics charged, that the Tanzimat statesmen used some of the great declarations involving the principle of equality as weapons of diplomacy in times of international crisis, and not solely as programs for domestic reform. The Hatt-i Sherif of 1839 was proclaimed at a time when Muhammad Ali of Egypt threatened the empire's integrity and when the Ottoman government sorely needed the European support which such a promise of reform might help to secure. The Hatt-i Humayun of 1856 was issued under diplomatic pressure as a means of avoiding foreign supervision of Ottoman reform after the Crimean War. Again, the constitution of 1876 was announced dramatically just as a conference of European diplomats got under way in Constantinople to draw up a reform program for parts of the empire. Midhat, who was both the principal author of the constitution and grand vizier at the moment, used his constitution to thwart foreign intervention by proclaiming that the empire was already reforming itself in fundamental fashion. But specific crises alone did not dictate the content of reform promises or the views of the Ottoman statesmen, although they often dictated the time and manner of proclamation. Sometimes, as in 1876, crisis facilitated reform, since at other less turbulent periods there might be more objection from the sultan, from other ministers, or from the public, on the score that no such radical measures were warranted. Crisis, therefore, helped to crystallize and precipitate reform projects already considered by responsible viziers, and also to induce a readier reception. The impact of crises on the Tanzimat statesmen was also, naturally, a strong influence on their attitudes toward equality, but their attitudes did not then fluctuate constantly.

Ali was the most conservative Muslim of the four and cautious in moving ahead with reform measures. His views, therefore, are probably the most significant gauge of the advance of attitudes among leading statesmen on

Muslim-Christian equality. Ali believed firmly that the Ottoman Turk was best fitted to govern the conglomeration of peoples in the empire.[13] He believed further that the prestige of this government rested on the prestige of Islam, against which he would allow no propaganda, though he was quite willing that Christians should enjoy freedom of belief and worship.[14] But under the pressure of events, including both the rebellions of native Christians and the interventions of the great powers, Ali's views on the status of Christians changed slowly. In 1867, when he was dealing with the rebellion in Crete, Ali wrote for the Sublime Porte a remarkable memorandum recommending a speedier application of the policy of equality. The Christians would cease to be revolutionaries, said Ali, as their hopes were fulfilled. Therefore they must be given every opportunity for education and tenure of public office, for which they were well fitted, even better prepared than Muslims generally at the moment. The Christians would then no longer regard themselves as held in subjection by a Muslim state but as subjects of a monarch who protected all equally. 'In short,' concluded Ali, 'the fusion of all subjects ... with the exception of purely religious affairs ... is the only means.'[15] There is no reason to question Ali's sincerity here, though it is obvious that he was pushed to his conclusions by the rush of events and not by thinking in a vacuum about the virtues of equality.

The other three statesmen came more easily to such opinions. Reshid was certainly influenced by a desire for praise for his liberal views from European courts but was apparently convinced that reforms which should guarantee equality to all peoples of the empire would ensure their devotion to the Ottoman government.[16] Fuad expressed in a private memorandum his belief that the grant of liberties to the non-Muslim peoples of the empire would dull their nationalist and separatist enthusiasms.[17] Midhat had as a provincial governor in Bulgaria (the Tuna or Danube *vilayet*) shown that he believed in treating Christians and Muslims on an equal basis, while at the same time he suppressed ruthlessly any separatist or revolutionary moves among the Bulgars. He continued to maintain, even after his political star sank in Abdul Hamid II's reign, that the chaotic condition of the empire could be remedied only by a rule of law under which Christians were brought to complete equality with Muslims.[18]

What the four Tanzimat statemen believed boiled down to this—that to save the empire, a new egalitarian citizenship and concept of patriotism, *Osmanlılık* or 'Ottomanism,' had to be created. Sometimes they expressed this as the 'fusion,' sometimes as the 'brotherhood' of all Ottoman subjects. Official documents began to speak more of 'imperial subjects,' 'subjects of the Sultanate,' and 'subjects of the Exalted [Ottoman] state,' in a composite or collective sense, as if to convey a concept of Ottoman citizenship unbroken by *millet* boundaries.[19] The idea of patriotism, or 'compatriotism,' was also expressed in the Hatt-i Humayun of 1856.[20] Though the statesmen knew that the concept of *Osmanlılık* was a break with the past, it is hard to say whether they fully realized what a tremendous revolution in traditional views was involved here, and what the logical outcome would be. They were not consciously trying to undermine the dominant position of the Muslim Turk. Yet by fostering an egalitarian citizenship, and by attempting to blur the demarcation lines between *millet*'s, they were taking a significant step on the road to a purely secular concept of state and citizenship. A nationality law of 1869, intended to combat the evils of the foreign protection of native Ottoman subjects, had also the effect of putting the acquisition and retention of citizenship on a purely territorial basis, unconnected with religion.[21] When the 1876 constitution specified that all peoples of the empire were to be called Osmanli, the unspoken corollary ran that henceforth their primary allegiance was to the state, and only secondarily were they Muslim, Jew, or Greek.

With this program of *Osmanlılık*, which would swallow up the narrower concept of Christian equality with Muslims, the Tanzimat statesmen sought to promote reform, fend off the powers, and forestall rebellion. They knew that reform measures would be hard to put across. '*L'on ne saurait improviser la réforme des mœurs*,' said Fuad in 1867, explaining to the European powers why more had not been accomplished in the way of reform since the Hatt-i-Humayun of 1856.[22] But in the view of the statesmen, Ottomanism was necessary for the salvation of the empire. They wanted to regain a viable and competitive status in a world increasingly ordered by European power and civilization and to prevent the Balkan provinces and Egypt, in particular, from breaking away. Like Winston Churchill, none of them took office in order to preside over the liquidation of empire. Because this was a self-interested version of the doctrine of equality, it was no less honestly meant by its proponents. They are open to criticism not so much on the grounds of hypocrisy as because they failed to understand the driving force of the nationalistic spirit which at this very period was growing stronger among the Greeks, Serbs, and Rumanians of the empire and beginning also to infect Bulgars and Armenians. Because the virulent forms of modern nationalism were not fully comprehensible to them, the Tanzimat statesmen tended to regard such movements as discontent with local conditions, or the product of foreign agitators, or plain insolent rebellion.

One might proceed from this point to argue that the program of equality between Christian and Muslim in the empire remained largely unrealized not because of bad faith on the part of leading Ottoman statesmen but because many of the Christians wanted it to fail. The demand in Crete was basically for autonomy or union with Greece, not for equality. Other Greeks in the empire wanted the same thing. In 1862, for instance, five thousand of them held a banquet on the Bosporus, agitating for the extension of Greek rule to

Macedonia and Thessaly.[23] Serbs wanted not equality but union with the autonomous principality of Serbia. Serbia and Rumania, still within the empire, wanted no sort of equality but national independence. When Midhat Pasha in 1872 began work on a scheme of converting the Ottoman Empire into a federal state like Bismarck's new Germany, with Rumania and Serbia playing Bavaria and Württemberg to the Porte's Prussia, he got a blunt rebuff from them.[24] They were not interested even in a sort of corporate equality within the empire.

The ecclesiastical hierarchies that ruled the Christian *millet*'s also opposed equality. *Osmalılık* would both decrease their authority and lighten their purses. This was especially true of the Greek Orthodox hierarchy, which had the most extensive prerogatives and by far the largest flock. When the Hatt-i Sherif was solemnly read in 1839 and then put back into its red satin pouch it is reported that the Greek Orthodox patriarch, who was present among the notables, said, '*Inşallah*—God grant that it not be taken out of this bag again.'[25] In short, the doctrine of equality faced formidable opposition from Christians of the empire who were leaders in the churches and the nationalist movements. Ottoman brotherhood was only a remote possibility, if the Christians continued in these directions.

But equality and brotherhood had also to contend with the fundamental Turkish view of Christians. Not only the specific reactions of the Muslim Turks to the proclamations of equality but their basic attitudes toward Christians showed from the beginning that *Osmanlılık* would have hard sledding.

III

If there were a possibility that Muslim Turks could accept an Ottoman fusion in which Christians were their equals, it would be owing to two strong currents in their religious tradition and development. As Muslims, the Turks inherited an attitude of toleration for 'peoples of the book' [*ehl-i kitap*]—those who, like Christians and Jews, possessed a book of divine revelation and paid tribute to the Muslim government. At various times the Ottoman government had offered sanctuary to non-Muslims, notably in the sixteenth century to the Jews driven from Spain. A Turk was likely to say to a Christian that 'your faith is a faith, and my faith is a faith.'

The tolerant attitude was often reinforced among the people by the remarkable degree of religious syncretism which had existed in Anatolia, and also in the Balkans, since the earliest days of Turkish penetration. The racial mixtures of the Ottoman Empire had been accompanied by religious mixtures of all sorts. Folk-Islam among the Turks was unorthodox in many ways, bearing marks not only of Shiite mysticism but of belief in various Christian miracle stories, saints, and shrines. The widespread Bektashi order, which claimed some seven million adherents, embodied in its beliefs many heterodox notions and helped to provide a climate which might be sympathetic to Christianity and Christians. During the Tanzimat period, American missionaries at work in the Ottoman empire were occasionally excited to discover what they at first thought might be a fertile field for their evangelism—groups of Muslims who read the Christian scriptures or heard Christ preached by their leaders. Some of these were Bektashi. One such group, not specifically Bektashi, was reported to have 10,000 adherents and twice that number of sympathizers.[26]

Despite the toleration and the syncretism, however, there remained among the Turks an intense Muslim feeling which could sometimes burst into open fanaticism. Such outbursts characteristically came at times of political crisis, particularly in the 1870s, when the internal chaos in the empire, and the external pressures on it, produced a distinct Muslim reaction, the counterpart of what later would have been a nationalist reaction. More important than the possibility of fanatic outbursts, however, was the innate attitude of superiority which the Muslim Turk possessed. Islam was for him the true religion. Christianity was only a partial revelation of the truth, which Muhammad finally revealed in full; therefore Christians were not equal to Muslims in possession of truth. Islam was not only a way of worship, it was a way of life as well. It prescribed man's relations to man, as well as to God, and was the basis for society, for law, and for government. Christians therefore were inevitably considered second-class citizens in the light of religious revelation—as well as by reason of the plain fact that they had been conquered by the Ottomans. This whole Muslim outlook was often summed up in the common term *gâvur* (or *kâfir*), which meant 'unbeliever' or 'infidel,' with emotional and quite uncomplimentary overtones. To associate closely or on terms of equality with the *gâvur* was dubious at best. 'Familiar association with heathens and infidels is forbidden to the people of Islam,' said Asim, an early nineteenth-century historian, 'and friendly and intimate intercourse between two parties that are to one another as darkness and light is far from desirable.'[27]

Islam embodied also a strong prejudice against innovation [*bid'at*]. A declaration of equality might encounter this prejudice not only among Muslim theologians but among the ruling group of the empire who traditionally served faith and state, not state alone. And to the popular mind the promotion of second-class citizens to equal status would undoubtedly be innovation, even if considered only against the background of popular conservatism, rather than as the sort of innovation proscribed by Islam. The whole reform program of the Tanzimat period inevitably ran up against these two intermingled conservatisms of inertia and Islam. Not only that, but the trend of the Tanzimat toward new institutions carried a profound psychological shock in its implication that the traditional Ottoman way of life was not in all respects the best, and that in Christian Europe some things were done better. Imponderables like these confronted the doctrine of Muslim-Christian equality.

Attitudes from their Muslim and Ottoman past were strengthened by the Turks' reactions to the recent impact of Christians on Ottoman life and affairs. The impact seemed generally bad. The Christians of the empire made constant trouble with their sectarian squabbles, whether argument over privileges in the Holy Places, the question of whether Bulgars should be subject to the Greek hierarchy, or the Hassounist controversy over papal authority among the Catholic Armenians. Some Christians made trouble by shifting from one *millet* to another in search of political advantage and foreign protection. The Christian sectarian quarrels were not only unedifying to the Muslims; they were positive nuisances to the Porte and offered in addition excuses for great power intervention.

The other general experience which Muslim Turks had of native Christians was that increasingly the latter tended to become rebels against legitimate authority. It is true that many Turkish and Arab lords had defied central authority, but the matter was not quite the same in Muslim eyes. Turkish *derebey*'s, or 'lords of the valley,' had governed various districts without regard to the Porte's decrees, but many were benevolent despots who held the esteem of their subjects and whose downfall at the hands of Mahmud II was often regretted. Muhammad Ali of Egypt was a rebel, but he was a Muslim, and many Turks had thought of him as a possible saviour from the infidel ideas of the reform edict of 1839.[28] Christian rebellion, on the other hand, antagonized Muslim sentiment and eventually provoked among some Turks a reaction which was Ottoman and patriotic but would later become Turkish and nationalist. The events of 1867, for example, when Crete was in revolt and when the last Turkish garrison was forced to withdraw from Belgrade, aroused some Turks to a pitch of frenzy.[29] Their anger mounted both against the rebel Christians and against the weakness of the Ottoman government in dealing with rebellion. A similar reaction was natural in the critical years 1875–76, when uprisings in Bosnia, Herzegovina, and Bulgaria were followed by open war against the sultan by two of his vassal states, Serbia and Montenegro.

The continuous interference of the great powers of Europe in Ottoman affairs also angered the Turks. These powers were all, of course, Christian by profession, if not in conduct. Russia, an enemy of long standing, was in a category by itself. But England and France also, despite the fact that they had assisted the empire with their armies in the Crimean War, and at other times with diplomatic pressure, were often detested because these services were overshadowed in the Turkish view by frequent and often high-handed interference. One such instance, which rankled particularly in connection with Muslim-Christian equality, was the fact that the Hatt-i Humayun of 1856 was not purely an autochthonous edict, but that large parts of it had in effect been dictated by the British, French, and Austrian ambassadors. The British ambassador, Lord Stratford de Redcliffe, had in many ways done great service for the Ottoman Empire, but in this period Ali three times asked London to recall him. Stratford would not allow the sultan to reign along with him, said Ali, and demanded that his own influence should be 'so paramount and notorious' that the Porte lost prestige in the eyes of its own public.[30] Years after Stratford had left Constantinople, Ali still spoke of him with real hatred.[31] Fuad, who with his social graces, fluent French, and Europeanized witticisms got along well with foreign diplomats, nevertheless voiced almost the identical criticism of a sympathetic French Ambassador, M. Bourée, because 'whatever good thing was done must be advertised as a benefit conferred by France . . .'[32]

Foreign interference rankled particularly when it was based on the capitulatory privileges which the great powers stretched and abused. Many ordinary Turks became aware of this when they saw the support given by Christian diplomats and consuls to thousands of protégés, largely Ottoman Christians who had never seen their protecting country but who were shielded against the taxes and courts of their own state and were often granted foreign passports. Many of the protégés were decidedly shady characters, and their number was considerably augmented in the Crimean War period by riffraff and adventurers of European origin who raised the crime rate in Constantinople.[33] At the end of the Crimean War the Austrian internuncio felt that 'the only respectable people, at least so it appears, are the Turks whom we are going to civilize and initiate into the mysteries of our progress.'[34]

The conduct of the more respectable representatives of Christendom in the empire might elicit Turkish approval but might also arouse resentment. It is not apparent that the little colonies of foreign workers, such as the English dockyard workers at Hasköy or the German Swiss at Amasya, had any noticeable impact. Some of the Polish and Hungarian refugees who came after the revolutions of 1830 and 1848 fitted in well with the Ottoman scene, and some became Muslims. There were always respected individual westerners like the English merchant of Beirut, James Black. It was reported that when a Muslim of the area wanted to use an oath stronger than 'by the beard of Muhammad' he swore 'by the word of Black, the Englishman.'[35] But westerners of the utmost personal respectability could often rub Turks the wrong way. Some of the British consuls in the empire were found even by their own superiors to be shallow and vain, and to supply their personal deficiencies 'by borrowing largely from the national dignity,' which they then dragged into every private affair.[36] Missionaries of impeccable character often annoyed Muslims by their evangelical persistence. An extreme example concerns two English missionaries who one day affixed a poster to the mosque of St. Sophia advertising that on the morrow from its steps they would denounce the prophet Muhammad as an impostor.[37]

IV

Given such a background of the innate Muslim conviction of superiority, and the unfortunate experiences of Turks with Christians, a preponderance of opinion against the official doctrine of Muslim-Christian equality was natural. Turkish resistance to the doctrine varied with the individual, the locality, and the moment. Some Turks, quite a few of them in the Ottoman bureaucracy, accepted it at least superficially, but wholehearted acceptance was rare. No great uprisings against the reform edicts occurred, though in some localities there was rioting. In part, the opposition came from the mere fact of the proclamation of unpopular principles, whereas the slow introduction of specific measures, with no fanfare, might have gone unnoticed. Many Turks muttered their resentment against the authors of the doctrine of equality and other infidel concepts. Each of the four Tanzimat statesmen was called the '*gâvur paşa*,' the 'unbeliever of a pasha,' though Ali probably less frequently than the others. The mere idea of equality, especially the antidefamation clause of 1856, offended the Turks' inherent sense of the rightness of things. 'Now we can't call a *gâvur* a *gâvur*,' it was said, sometimes bitterly, sometimes in matter-of-fact explanation that under the new dispensation the plain truth could no longer be spoken openly.[38] Could reforms be acceptable which forbade calling a spade a spade?

Events which followed the two great reform proclamations serve to illustrate the general antipathy to their promises of equality. One example is related to the touchy question of military service. Both in 1839 and 1856 the sultan proclaimed that his Christian subjects should be equally privileged to serve in the armed forces along with the Muslims, instead of paying an exemption tax as they had previously done. It soon became obvious that the Christians would rather continue to pay than serve, despite the step toward equality which military service might mean. It also became obvious that the Turks wanted Christians to be equally liable to service so far as sharing the burdens and dangers went but balked at giving the Christians equal opportunity for promotion to the officer corps. Muslim Turks did not want to serve under native Christian officers. In theory the equal right to serve in the armed forces remained, but in fact the whole matter was quietly buried, and the old exemption tax reappeared under a different name. Both Turks and Christians were satisfied to see the inequality continue.[39]

Another illustration of Turkish reactions is found in the experience of the considerable group of American Congregational missionaries in the empire. They reported in general a decrease in Muslim fanaticism and in interference with their work. One missionary who knew the country well observed that only the *ulema*, the Muslim theologians, kept up any semblance of old-style bigotry by the 1860s, and that merely in order to keep what influence they could among the people and 'spunge' off the wealthy.[40] Another calculated that 'before the Hatti-Humayoun [of 1856] there were more cases of persecution reported to us every week than there are now in a whole year.'[41] This situation continued until the new rise in Muslim sentiment with the recurrent crises of the 1870s.

But most of the proselytizing efforts of the Congregationalists, and most of their converts, were among the Armenians. Muslim opinion, therefore, was not directly touched. When, however, any case of apostasy from Islam was involved, public fury could easily be aroused. Governmental protection might be secured in such cases, especially in the capital, but the Turkish public was not willing to recognize equal opportunity of conversion in either direction despite the Porte's assurance that 'the Musselman is now as free to become a Christian as the Christian is free to become a Musselman. The government will know no difference in the two cases.'[42] The outstanding case of a fanatical Muslim outburst over transfer of religious affiliation came in the Saloniki incident of 1876. A Bulgarian girl of dubious morals came to Saloniki from her native village to register with the authorities her conversion from Orthodoxy to Islam. When some Greeks of the city kidnapped her, apparently to prevent the transfer of allegiance, an angry Muslim mob sought her out. In the process the mob murdered the French and German consuls who had taken refuge, along with the Turkish governor, in a mosque. The incident occurred at a time when the empire was under great strain from the rebellions in Bosnia and Herzegovina.[43]

When the question of religious equality and conversion involved only competing Christian denominations, Ottoman officials were more likely to act to preserve fair play, and undoubtedly proclaimed equality with greater conviction and delight than when Muslims were involved. A classic example occurred in a town near Ankara following a local persecution of Protestants by Armenians. The governor investigated, and then sent forth a herald to cry: 'It is commanded by the ruling authorities that all subjects cease to deride one another as Moslems and Rayahs, as Armenians and Protestants, since all are equally the dependent subjects of the royal government, and it is further commanded that mutually respecting and honoring one another, all shall dwell together in brotherly love.'[44] In its way this pithy proclamation was a masterly summary of the official policy of equality among adherents of all creeds, of the concept of Ottoman citizenship, and of the antidefamation clause, revealing that the provincial governor understood perfectly what the central government had announced. That the civil authority should also command all men to live together in brotherly love was undoubtedly commendable—and unenforceable.

Another measure of Turkish attitudes on the question of Christian equality is provided by the views of participants in the conspiracy of 1859. The plot, directed against Abdul Medjid and his ministers, was betrayed to the authorities. Some forty-odd participants, many of them army officers and Muslim theological professors and students, were arrested. Interrogation revealed that through their rather fuzzy ideas there ran a general dissatisfaction with the Ottoman government, caused more by the proclamations of Christian equality than by any other single factor. The conspiracy's leading spirit and theoretician, one Sheikh [Şeyh] Ahmet, indicated that he regarded the reform edicts of 1839 and 1856 as contraventions of Muslim law, the *Şeriat*, because they allowed Christians equal rights with Muslims. According to the deposition of another conspirator, Sheikh Ahmet had been teaching in the *medrese* that the Christians got these privileges with the help of foreign powers.[45] The Kuleli incident, as this abortive conspiracy has since been known, provides a good index to widespread Turkish attitudes. It revealed an ill-defined resentment against the mere concept of equality, a conscious support of 'religious law,' and condemnation of the government both for its reform edicts and for its apparent submission to foreign influence.[46] The doctrine of equality seemed bad if for no other reason than that it proclaimed to be equal adherents of religions that were not equal. And *Osmanlılık*, as a purely political concept of the allegiance of peoples of all creeds to a ruler who treated them equally, was unreal, because the traditional concept of 'Osmanli' had always carried strong implications of Muslim orthodoxy as well as of loyalty to the Ottoman state.

Any sample of Turkish opinion in the Tanzimat period must include the one group which was forward-looking, politically conscious, constantly vocal, and therefore influential out of proportion to its small size. This was the New Ottoman Committee, composed principally of writers and would-be reformers who for a short time in the late 1860s coalesced into the nearest approximation to a political party that existed in the empire. Its members were an extraordinary collection of individualists. They quarreled among themselves but were united in their ardent desire to preserve the Ottoman Empire. This group has often been called the 'Young Turks.' Its members were, in fact, the spiritual fathers of the true Young Turks of 1908, and the spiritual grandfathers of the Turks who created the nationalist republic of today. From their writings the later development of a genuinely 'Turkish' consciousness derived great impetus. But by preference the leaders of this group of the 1860s called themselves the New Ottomans [*Yeni Osmanlılar*]. The name is a good indication of their outlook.

The New Ottomans represented a more deeply felt patriotism, a devotion to *Osmanlılık* as they conceived it, than such statesmen as Ali and Fuad were hoping to inculcate. New Ottoman patriotism meant an equal co-operation of peoples of all creeds in a devoted effort to preserve the empire, but opposition to any special concessions to Christians. The New Ottomans believed that the empire could be reformed and revived within the framework of Muslim tradition and religious law, which they thought was sound enough, and progressive and elastic enough, to allow also the adaptation of new institutions from Europe. Most of them seem also to have believed in Muslim Turkish superiority among the united peoples of a united empire. Sometimes, therefore, their writings seem self-contradictory. Ali Suavi, probably the most extravagant and fanatic Muslim among them, could write that 'all the populations composing the Ottoman Empire today form only one nationality: the Osmanli.'[47] Mustafa Fazil Pasha, an Egyptian prince of broad views who was for a time leader of the New Ottomans because his financial resources supported the group, said in a public statement for them that 'it does not matter whether one is Muslim, Catholic, or Greek Orthodox to be able to place the public welfare ahead of private interests. For that it suffices to be a man of progress or a good patriot.'[48] In a bold letter to Abdul Aziz, he contended that the Christian revolts in the empire were but a symptom of a malady—backwardness and bad government—that afflicted the uncomplaining Muslims even more than the Christians. The line of division ran, said Mustafa Fazil, only between oppressors and oppressed, not between Christian and Muslim.[49]

The emphasis on Ottoman patriotism, on preservation of the fatherland from internal decay and external attack, led the New Ottomans to voice retroactive approval of the Hatt-i Sherif of 1839, since in their view Reshid Pasha had with the Gülhane edict started the empire on the road to progress and self-preservation. But they tended to regard the Hatt-i Humayūn of 1856 and most of the subsequent acts of the Porte as harmful, seeing in them concessions to Christians in response to pressures exerted by great powers and by domestic rebellion. This, in the New Ottoman view, led to inequality, not equality. Namik Kemal, the most admirable of the group, castigated the Porte and the powers for enumerating the privileges of Christians in the edict of 1856 when, he said, there should rather have been progress toward constitutional government and the elimination of foreign intervention.[50] Namik Kemal here reflected a view common to many Turks which led them to argue against reform programs proposed by European powers for particular peoples or provinces of the empire, such as the proposals for Bosnia and

Herzegovina in 1875–76, by saying that these measures represented special privilege, injustice to Muslims, and therefore inequality.[51]

In 1867, the year when New Ottoman criticism of the government forced many of the group into European exile, Ali and Fuad were unmercifully excoriated for making concessions to the Cretan rebels and for agreeing, under pressure, that the last Turks would evacuate Belgrade. Again the New Ottomans raised the point that this was inequality, that Muslims in Belgrade and Crete were being unfairly treated.[52] Obviously the weakness of the Sublime Porte in the face of European pressures only increased the exasperation of the New Ottomans over the inequities of the situation. Ziya, next to Namik Kemal the most influential of the New Ottoman writers, expressed the common complaint that equality could never be attained so long as Christians within the empire could have recourse not only to the Ottoman government, and to their *millet* representatives, but also to foreign protectors. For example, said Ziya, if a guilty Christian is jailed, he is suddenly released without cause because someone influential has intervened. But if an innocent Muslim fall into the toils of justice and be imprisoned without cause, who is there to help him? 'Is this equality?' he asks bitterly.[53]

V

In the face of such attitudes, the realization of Ottoman equality, involving the equality of Muslims and Christians, faced extraordinary difficulties.[54] Though Reshid, Ali, Fuad, and Midhat hoped to find salvation for the empire by creating among its peoples the bond of equal citizenship based on Ottoman nationality, the obstacles they faced were too great and the time too late. The Turkish mind, conditioned by centuries of Muslim and Ottoman dominance, was not yet ready to accept any absolute equality, much less to endorse the grant of particular privileges to Christians. And the Christian minorities of the empire continued to push toward separatism. Despite the various steps taken toward it, Ottoman equality was not attained in the Tanzimat period, nor yet after the Young Turk revolution of 1908 when, for a few wild and enthusiastic days, Ottoman brotherhood seemed to have arrived with the end of Abdul Hamid's personal rule and the resurrection of Midhat's constitution of 1876. Then, after this short emotional spree, competing nationalisms again crowded out the concept of *Osmanlılık*. This was true not only among the Christians of the empire but now among the Muslims as well. While Arab nationalism developed, like the Christian nationalisms, as a reaction to Ottoman Turkish control, the Turks themselves found the source for a nationalism of their own in the *Osmanlılık* of the Tanzimat, especially in the more patriotic version of Namik Kemal and other New Ottomans.

In the end, the sort of Ottoman equality at which the Tanzimat statesmen aimed, though it had never been given a full and fair trial, was discredited as an idea both among Muslims and among Christians. Instead of the equality of Christian and Muslim within a heterogeneous empire, based on 'fusion' and 'brotherhood,' there emerged finally a different sort—the corporate equality of competing national sovereign states.

This article is reprinted from Roderic H. Davison, *Essays in Turkish History, 1774–1923* (Austin, 1990). Reprinted by permission of the University of Texas Press.

NOTES

1. There is no adequate study on the status of Christians in the Ottoman Empire. Voluminous sources exist, many of them dealing only with a particular district or period, and many have a distinctive bias. Among the best accounts for the mid-nineteenth century are Abdolonyme Ubicini, *Letters on Turkey*, tr. by Lady Easthope (London, 1856), II; and *Accounts and Papers*, 1861, LXVII, 'Reports ... relating to the Condition of Christians,' a collection of statements by British consuls in different parts of the empire.

2. See the convenient collection of such statements in Harold Temperley, *England and the Near East: The Crimea* (London, 1936), pp. 40–41.

3. The doctrine of equality of course included Jews as well. But Christians were far more numerous in the empire and provided most of the problems. Among the 14,000,000 non-Muslims in an empire of some 35,000,000, Christians were an overwhelming majority. There were perhaps 150,000 Jews. All figures for the nineteenth century are inaccurate approximations. These follow Ubicini, I, 18–26. His estimates, probably low, have found the widest acceptance. For practical reasons, I shall limit the discussion to the status of Christians.

4. Western writers have ordinarily referred to the edict of 1839 as the Hatt-i Sherif [Illustrious Rescript], which was its title in the official French translation distributed by the Sublime Porte to foreign diplomats. See facsimile of French as well as Turkish texts in Yavuz Abadan, 'Tanzimat Fermanın Tahlili' [Analysis of the Tanzimat Edict], *Tanzimat* (Istanbul, 1940), I, following p. 48. Turkish historians usually say *Hatt-ı Humayun* [Imperial Rescript], or else *Gülhane Fermanı* or *Tanzimat Fermanı*. A *ferman* is a decree or edict. I shall continue here to follow the customary Western terminology in order to avoid confusion and to provide a convenient distinction from the Hatt-i Humayun of 1856 (see note 5). Similarly, where Turkish names first occur, their Western forms are used, followed by the modern Turkish spelling in brackets. The official French text of the Hatt-i Sherif is available in many places, for instance in Ubicini and Pavet de Courteille, *Etat présent de L'Empire ottoman* (Paris, 1876), pp. 231–34.

5. Westerners usually call this edict the Hatt-i Humayun, but Turks call it the *Islahat Fermanı* [Reform Edict]. See explanation in note 4. The most useful text, both Turkish and French, is Thomas X. Bianchi, *Khaththy Humaïoun* ... (Paris, 1856).

6. Text in Ignaz von Testa, *Recueil des traités de la Porte ottomane* ... (Paris, 1864–1911), VII, 521–23.

7. Text in *Das Staatsarchiv*, XXX (1877), no. 5702.

8. Articles 8 and 17. Text in *Das Staatsarchiv*, XXXI (1877), no. 5948.

9. Many examples might be cited. Edward A. Freeman, *The Ottoman Power in Europe* (London, 1877), is a gem—three hundred pages of magnificently righteous anti-Turkish tirade. On reform promises see especially pp. 189, 197, 225.

10. There is as yet no scholarly history of the Tanzimat period. The best account of the reforms is still Edouard Engelhardt, *La Turquie et le Tanzimat* ... (Paris, 1882–84), 2 vols. The most satisfactory general history on the first half of the period is Georg Rosen, *Geschichte der Türkei von dem Siege der Reform im Jahre 1826 bis ... 1856* (Leipzig, 1866–67), 2 vols. Many Turkish scholars have studied aspects of the period, but none has yet produced a full-scale consecutive history. The most important single volume is a 1000-page product by some thirty Turkish

scholars, ***Tanzimat, Yüzüncü Yıldönömü Münasebetile*** [The Tanzimat, on the Occasion of its Hundredth Anniversary], I (Istanbul, 1940). Volume II never appeared.

11. Mustafa Reşid Paşa (1800–58); Mehmed Emin Ali Paşa (1815–71); Keçecizade Mehmed Fuad Paşa (1815–69); Ahmed Şefik Midhat Paşa (1822–84).

12. It is interesting to note that Reshid, Ali, and Fuad were all Freemasons: Ebüzziya Tevfik, ***Mecmuai Ebüzziya*** [Ebüzziya's Journal] (Haziran, 1911), cited in Mustafa Nihat, ***Metinlerle Muasır Türk Edebiyatı Tarihi*** [History of Contemporary Turkish Literature with Texts] (Istanbul, 1934), p. 27 n. I am not sure whether or not Midhat was a Freemason, but he came from a family with Bektashi affiliations and heterodox proclivities. See above, p. 69, on the Bektashi.

13. See Ali to Thouvenel, Nov. 28, 1858, in L. Thouvenel, ***Trois années de la question d'Orient*** (Paris, 1897), p. 316.

14. Ali to Musurus, Nov. 30, 1864, enclosed in Morris to Seward, no. 108, Mar. 29, 1865, Turkey no. 18, State, U.S. Archives.

15. Text in Andreas D. Mordtmann, ***Stambul und das moderne Türkenthum*** (Leipzig, 1877–78), I, 75–90. Ali recommended also new educational measures, a reformed civil law code, etc.

16. See for instance his memorandum of Aug. 12, 1839, printed in Frank E. Bailey, ***British Policy and the Turkish Reform Movement . . . 1826–1853*** (Cambridge, Mass., 1942), pp. 271–76.

17. Holographic draft of a memorandum on reforms for the state, in private collection of Salih Keçeci, cited in Orhan F. Köprülü, 'Fuad Paşa,' ***Islam Ansiklopedisi***, IV, 679.

18. Yıldız Palace Archives, Midhat's reply to interrogation of May 8, 1297 [1880], partly reproduced in Ibnülemin Mahmud Kemal Inal, ***Osmanlı Devrinde Son Sadrıazamlar*** [The Last Grand Viziers in the Ottoman Period] (Istanbul, 1940–50), III, 339.

19. The Hatt-i Humayun of 1856 used all these expressions: ***tebaai şahane, tebaai saltanati, tebaai Devlet-i Aliyye.*** See the note on this trend in Reuben Levy, ***Introduction to the Sociology of Islam*** (London, c. 1930–33), II, 259.

20. The term used was ***vatandaş***, which Bianchi (***Khaththy Humaïoun***, p. 4 and n. 1) says was a new form. The basic word, ***vatan***, had meant 'native place' or 'home' but was coming to be equated to ***patrie***, fatherland, since the permeation of French ideas after 1789. See the comments on the meaning of ***vatan*** in Bernard Lewis, 'The Impact of the French Revolution on Turkey,' ***Journal of World History***, I (July, 1953), 107–108.

21. Text in George Young, ***Corps de droit ottoman*** (Oxford, 1905–1906), II, 226–29. See above, p. 72, on the abuses of the capitulations at which the law was aimed.

22. 'Considérations sur l'exécution du Firman Impérial du 18 février 1856,' in Grégoire Aristarchi Bey, ***Législation ottomane*** (Constantinople, 1873–88), II, 26.

23. Morris-Seward, no. 33, Nov. 6, 1862, Turkey no. 17, State, U.S. Archives.

24. 'Zapiski Grapha N. P. Ignatyeva (1864–1874),' ***Izvestiia Ministerstvo Inostrannykh Dyel***, 1915, I, 170–72.

25. Enver Ziya Karal, ***Osmanlı Tarihi V: Nizam-i Cedit ve Tanzimat Devirleri*** [Ottoman History V: Periods of Nizam-i Cedit and Tanzimat] (Ankara, 1947), p. 191. Englehardt, ***La Turquie***, I, 142, attributes a similar remark to the archbishop of Nicomedia at the proclamation of the Hatt-i Humayun of 1856. It should also be pointed out that the Greek hierarchy opposed a democratization of its own ***millet*** structure whereby lay participation in ***millet*** administration would increase.

26. The missionary reports are in the archives of the American Board of Commissioners for Foreign Missions (ABCFM), Armenian Mission, VIII, nos. 79, 88, 92, 93, all Schauffler to Anderson, of Mar. 11, Nov. 16, Dec. 12 and 27, 1859. On the Bektashi order see John Kingsley Birge, ***The Bektashi Order of Dervishes*** (London, 1937). It would serve no purpose to cite here a bibliography on Islam. There is a considerable and scattered literature on syncretism. Frederick W. Hasluck, ***Christianity and Islam under the Sultans*** (Oxford, 1929), 2 vols., is full of information.

27. ***Asim Tarihi*** (Istanbul, n.d.), I, 376, quoted in Bernard Lewis, 'The Impact of the French Revolution on Turkey,' ***Jour. World Hist.***, I, 118, n. 35.

28. Edouard Driault, ***L'Egypte et l'Europe, la crise de 1839–1841*** (Cairo, 1930–), I, letter 79, Sept. 20, 1839, and II, letter 7, Nov. 19, 1839. These Turks did not realize how much of a reformer Muhammad Ali was in Egypt.

29. Prominent among them the New Ottomans, on whom see above, pp. 75–77.

30. Clarendon to Stratford, Jan. 4, 1856, Private Stratford MSS, FO 352/44, Public Record

Office (PRO), quoted in Harold Temperley, 'The Last Phase of Stratford de Redcliffe, 1855–58,' *English Historical Review*, XLVII (1932), 218.

31. L. Raschdau, ed. 'Diplomatenleben am Bosporus, Aus dem literarischen Nachlass ... Dr. Busch,' *Deutsche Rundschau*, CXXXVIII (1909), 384.

32. Elliot to Stanley, no. 68 conf., Dec. 17, 1867, FO 78/1965, PRO.

33. See, for example, the comments of Sir Edmund Hornby, judge of a British consular court in this period, in his *Autobiography* (London, 1928), p. 93. (Marco Antonio) Canini, *Vingt ans d'exil* (Paris, 1868), pp. 111-42, gives a good picture of the riffraff in the capital.

34. Prokesch to Buol, Jan. 10, 1856, Politisches Archiv XII/56, Haus-, Hof- und Staatsarchiv.

35. Henry Harris Jessup, *Fifty-Three Years in Syria* (New York, 1910), I, 49; II, 465.

36. Bulwer to Russell, no. 177, Sept. 27, 1859, enclosing Bulwer to C. Alison of same date, FO 78/1435, PRO.

37. Hornby, pp. 124–25.

38. See the story from Abdurrahman Şeref in Karal, *Osmanlı Tarihi V*, p. 190; also Gad Franco, *Développements constitutionnels en Turquie* (Paris, 1925), p. 12.

39. Dr. K., *Erinnerungen aus dem Leben des Serdar Ekrem Omer Pascha* ... (Sarajevo, 1885), pp. 47, 252. Ömer served on this commission. For a sample of Turkish complaints on Christian exemption see Felix Kanitz, *Donau-Bulgarien und der Balkan* (Leipzig, 1875–79), III, 151.

40. Henry J. Van Lennep, *Travels in Little-Known Parts of Asia Minor* (London, 1870), I, 118–19. Some of the *ulema* were bigoted and narrowly educated, but not all. Jevdet [Cevdet] is an outstanding example of one of the *ulema* of this period who was a staunch Muslim but no bigot.

41. Goodell to Anderson, Nov. 6, 1860, ABCFM, Vol. 284, no. 382. Much of the reported persecution was by other Christians, not Muslims.

42. The statement of a government commission investigating one of the rare cases of conversion from Islam to Christianity: Hamlin to Anderson, Sept. 5, 1857, ABCFM, Armenian Mission, V, no. 276.

43. Documentary account of this in *Das Staatsarchiv*, XXX (1877), nos. 5733–58.

44. Farnsworth to Board Secretaries, Sept. 21, 1865, ABCFM, Vol. 284, no. 331. *Râya* or *reaya* was the customary term for the tributary non-Muslim peoples of the empire, and originally meant 'cattle' or 'flocks.' Presumably the Hatt-i Humayun banned this term also.

45. The conspiracy is analyzed on the basis of documentary evidence, chiefly the interrogation reports, in Uluğ Iğdemir, *Kuleli Vakası Hakkında bir Araştırma* [An Investigation of the Kuleli Affair] (Ankara, 1937). The *medrese* is a school for instruction in Muslim law and theology.

46. The whole reform program was of course often condemned as contrary to religious law by men whose interest was not at all in the *Şeriat* but only in their vested interests in sources of power and income. Such were numerous officials, tax-farmers, moneylenders, etc.

47. Ali Suavi, *A propos de l'Herzégovine* (Paris, 1875), p. 16.

48. Letter of Feb. 5, 1867, in *Le Nord* (Brussels), Feb. 7, 1867.

49. S.A. le Prince Mustapha-Fazyl Pacha, *Lettre adressée à S.M. le Sultan* (n.p., n.d.) [presumably March, 1867], pp. 1–11.

50. In *Hürriyet*, no. 4 (July 20, 1868), reproduced in Ihsan Sungu, 'Tanzimat ve Yeni Osmanlılar' [The Tanzimat and the New Ottomans], in *Tanzimat*, I, 795–96. Sungu's chapter, pp. 777–857 in this volume, is almost entirely a collection of newspaper articles by Namik Kemal and Ziya on questions of the day.

51. See, for example, the 'Manifesto of the Muslim Patriots,' of Mar. 9, 1876, probably written by Midhat or one of his entourage: *Le Stamboul*, June 2, 1876.

52. In their newspaper *Muhbir*, date of issue not given; translation in FO 195/893, no. 120, Mar. 25, 1868, PRO. In his poem, the 'Zafer-name,' Ziya uses heavy irony to attack Ali on the same issues of Crete and Belgrade. He further proclaims acidly that Ali has brought the equality of rights to perfection not only by such concessions but by appointing Greeks and Armenians to high office. English translation and Turkish text of about half the poem are in Elias J. W. Gibb, *A History of Ottoman Poetry* (London, 1900–1909), V, 96–111, and VI, 370–78.

53. In *Hürriyet*, no. 15 (Oct. 5, 1868), reproduced in Sungu, p. 797.

54. There were of course many obstacles to the realization of a doctrine of equality other than those discussed here as 'attitudes.' One of the most important, especially as it affected the relations of Christian and Muslim in the Balkans, was the system of land tenure, with resulting

social and economic inequalities and groups which had a vested interest in maintaining them. A good analysis of this situation in a part of the Balkans in the period up to 1850 is Halil Inalcik, *Tanzimat ve Bulgar Meselesi* [The Tanzimat and the Bulgar Question] (Ankara, 1943).

Added Note: Note 10 says that there is no scholarly history of the Tanzimat period. Since that was written, a book of mine attempted to fill the gap: *Reform in the Ottoman Empire, 1856–1876* (Princeton, 1963), though it is not full on the early Tanzimat years beginning in 1839. Several of the contributions to Benjamin Braude and Bernard Lewis, eds., *Christians and Jews in the Ottoman Empire: The Functioning of a Plural Society*, 2 vols. (New York, 1982), bear on the subject of this essay in one way or another. Two books help to illuminate the more general intellectual climate of the period: Şerif Mardin, *The Genesis of Young Ottoman Thought: A Study in the Modernization of Turkish Political Ideas* (Princeton, 1962), and Niyazi Berkes, *The Development of Secularism in Turkey* (Montreal, 1964). Two others look more specifically at Ottomanism: I. L. Fadeeva, *Offitsialnie Doktrini v Ideologii i Politike Osmanskoi Imperii: Osmanism—Panislamism, XIX-Nachalo XX v.* (Moscow, 1985), and R. A. Safrastian, *Doktrina Osmanisma v Politicheskoi Zhizni Osmanskoi Imperii* (Erevan, 1985).

Ottoman Reform and the Politics of Notables

ALBERT HOURANI

This paper was presented to a conference on the beginnings of modernization in the Middle East, held at the University of Chicago in 1966. It was intended as a brief first statement of certain ideas which I hoped to formulate more fully and to justify in a longer work. I did not therefore think it necessary at the time to provide full references for what I wrote, and now it is too late. I have given references only to a few works which are explicitly or implicitly mentioned, and to one or two more recent ones in the light of which some of my statements might need to be revised. I acknowledge with thanks a number of useful criticisms and suggestions made by Professors J. Berque, P. M. Holt and Stanford J. Shaw and Dr. E. R. J. Owen.

I

It is a commonplace that we cut up history into periods at our peril: the artificial frontiers made for convenience may seem to be real, and a new generation of historians will have to spend time removing them. Nevertheless, to think we must distinguish, and the best we can do is to try to make divisions which reveal something important about the process we are studying. The old division of history in terms of states and dynasties was not without its value; the imposition for example of Ottoman rule on the western part of the Muslim world was an event of great importance, however we look at it. But it is too simple and therefore misleading to go beyond that and make a further distinction simply in terms of the strength or weakness of Ottoman rule; the traditional division of a period of Ottoman greatness followed by one of Ottoman decline does not help us much to find out what really happened. Perhaps it would be more satisfactory to begin by making a distinction in terms of the kind of sources which we as historians must use; this might have a significance beyond itself, both because the sources we use help to determine the emphasis we place within the complex whole of the historical process, and because the appearance of a new and important type of source, or the disappearance of an old one, may reveal a change in the social order or intellectual life.

From this point of view we may make a very rough division of Ottoman history into four phases. In the first, we must rely mainly on Islamic literary sources (using the term 'literary' in its widest sense) and archaeological evidence. In the second, we must add to these the Ottoman archives; they form a unique source for the study of how a great Islamic government worked, but one which must be used in combination with the literary sources if we wish to study also how Ottoman society changed. In the third—stretching roughly, we may say, from 1760 to 1860—the relative value of types of source changes once more. The control of the central government over Ottoman society weakens or is exercised in a more indirect way; the archives in Istanbul keep their value as showing what the Ottoman government thought or intended, but that may have been very different from what actually happened. In some provincial centres important archives exist—Cairo and Tunis are obvious examples; but in others those kinds of document which Professor Shaw has used to good effect[1] may not have survived. In most great cities we can probably find documents kept in the *qadi's* court, but once the reforms began the *qadi* lost his central position in the provincial administration, and the documents we most want to see may not have been registered in his court. Once new courts were established to administer new legal codes, however, their records were systematically kept and can be used to throw light on the effects of the reforms upon Ottoman society.

In this third period the European sources come to have the importance which an earlier generation of historians thought they had for the second. We refer not so much to the travellers; their books are usually to be treated with suspicion unless like Russell they spent a long period in the place they are describing, and in the nineteenth century they are perhaps even less reliable than for earlier times, because the coming of the steamship made it possible to travel rapidly and superficially, the power and wealth of Europe cut the traveller off from the people among whom he moved semi-regally, and romanticism cast the shadow of the observer's own temperament across what he was supposed to be observing. We refer rather to the reports of European diplomats and consuls, and also of Europeans in the Ottoman or Egyptian service. In this period they contain evidence of more direct importance than before for both political and economic history (although rarely for the history of thought). Even a serious and well-informed ambassador, in the seventeenth century, found it difficult to know what was really going on in the *saray*. But by the early nineteenth the ambassadors and consuls of the major powers were not just repeating information picked up haphazardly and from a distance. The growing weight of European interests in the Middle East made it necessary for the governments of Europe to be fully and precisely informed, while the desire of the Ottoman government (and the dependent governments in Egypt and Tunisia) to maintain their independence and reform their methods obliged them and their local governors to take the representatives of the European states at least partly into their confidence.

The process of change which took place in this period was one which, by and large, the population of the empire and its dependent states—even the educated part of it—did not understand. It was change imposed from above, not yet accepted by most elements in the population, affecting the system of law and administration but not as yet the organization of society. For this reason the indigenous 'literary' sources change in nature and value. The Muslim tradition of chronicles, biographies and descriptions continues for a time: apart from al-Jabarti, we may point in a later generation to Ibn Abi Diya'f in Tunis, al-Bitar in Damascus, Sulayman Fa'iq in Baghdad, 'Ali Mubarak in Cairo, and the official historiographers in Istanbul. But those who write within the religious tradition now have a different relationship with authority. The faith in the continued existence of a strong, autonomous and God-preserved Islamic *umma* has been shaken, and the impulse to record the names and virtues of those who have preserved and transmitted the heritage of Islam through history grows weaker; the men of the old culture, looking on their rulers as alien in ways of thought, no longer find it possible or desirable to record their acts. On the other hand, a new school of Christian writers arises in Syria and Lebanon, the product of a new education which has taught them both better Arabic and the languages and ways of thought of Europe. But they too are far from the sources of power, and (except in regard to the princely government in Lebanon itself) possess neither the knowledge nor the self-identification with power which is necessary for the political historian.

In the fourth period, which begins roughly in 1860, the importance of this last factor changes and the historian can use a new combination of sources. The importance of the diplomatic and consular records continues; that of the Ottoman and Egyptian documents increases, as the governments impose a more direct and pervasive control over society, and thus require and are able to obtain fuller and more accurate information. But what distinguishes this fourth from the third period is that the changes which had been imposed from above are now increasingly understood and accepted. There is a new self-awareness and, linked to it, a new and more active interest in the political process, a new concern to take part in the movement of change and determine its direction. We are entering the modern age of the continuously and consciously self-changing society, and once more the indigenous literary sources become important: not so much works of history (although modern history-writing begins with Muhammad Bayram and Cevdet Pasha) as the play, the novel and most of all the press-article aiming to inform, advise, criticize or arouse feeling, written not by the *'alim* responsible to an existing order regarded as of eternal value, but by the politician concerned with power or the intellectual acknowledging no sovereign except his own vision of what should or what must be.

II

We are here concerned with 'the beginnings of modernization'; that is to say, with the third of our four periods. What kinds of source are important for this period we have already said, and in regard to each of them we can ask a further question: what can we expect it to tell us? Each of them can of course be used for one purpose at least, to throw light on the opinions or assumptions of those who wrote it; but can it be used beyond that, and for what?

There is no need to answer this question in detail here. Some of the main lines of an answer are clear. The archives of governments, in a region and age where outside the large cities custom was still king, tell us what rulers or officials wanted to happen but not always what really happened. To take an obvious example, that of land-tenure: as Professor Lambton has shown,[2] the relationship which existed between landlord and peasant was never in exact conformity with the theory of ownership laid down by law, whether *shari'a* or modern statute. Again, diplomatic and consular reports must be treated with caution because those who wrote them were themselves actors in the political process, and wrote their reports not simply as a historical record of events but, often, to justify themselves to their government or persuade it to adopt a certain line of action; moreover, ambassadors and consuls tended to be drawn into the struggles of parties in central or local government, and so reflect (sometimes more than they knew) the views of the party which looked to them for help and to which therefore they had access.

One limitation is common to most of our sources, and it is this which concerns us here. The voice of an important part of the population is scarcely heard in them, or heard only in a muted, indirect and even distorted form: that of the Muslim town-dwellers and their traditional and 'natural' leaders, the urban notables. For example, from all our vast documentation about the events of 1860 in Syria and Lebanon, we can discover with some precision and from within the attitudes and reaction of Maronites, Druzes, Turks, and European governments, but we have scarcely an authentic record of the attitude of the Muslim population and its leaders, except for a short work by al-Hasibi and some passages in al-Bitar's collection of biographies. Again, from our still vaster material about Muhammad 'Ali, we can trace in detail the development of each aspect of his policy, and the growth of a new ruling caste, but we cannot easily discover how the Muslim urban population and its leaders reacted to it. Some reaction there must have been, and we come on traces of it in the later pages of al-Jabarti or when 'Umar Makram is sent into exile. But it is not easy to build anything from these hints, and our usual picture of Egypt in the nineteenth century is an odd one: at one end, a gradual increase in the political activity of the urban population, going on throughout the eighteenth century and reaching its height in the period between the first revolt against French rule and the movement which carried Muhammad 'Ali to power; much later, in the 1870s, a sudden upsurge; and in between virtually nothing, a political vacuum.

This is an important gap in our knowledge, for the urban politics of the Ottoman provinces (at least of the Muslim provinces) cannot be understood unless we see them in terms of a 'politics of notables' or, to use Max Weber's phrase, a 'patriciate'. There are many examples in history of 'patrician' politics. They differ from one place and time to another, but perhaps have certain things in common. This type of politics seems to arise when certain conditions exist: first, when society is ordered according to relations of personal dependence—the artisan in the city producing mainly for patrician patrons, and the peasant in the countryside, whether nominally free or not, also producing mainly for a landowner, either because he cannot otherwise finance himself or because the landowner holds the key to the urban market; secondly, when society is dominated by ***urban*** notables, by great families which (like those of medieval Italy but unlike medieval England and France) reside mainly in the city, draw their main strength from there, and *because* of their position in the city are able to dominate also a rural hinterland; and, thirdly, when these notables have some freedom of political action. This freedom may be of either of two kinds. The city may be self-governing, and the notables its rulers, a 'patriciate' in Max Weber's full sense; or else the city may be subject to a monarchical power, but one on which the urban population wishes and is able to impose limits or exercise influence.

It is this second kind of situation which we find in Muslim history. Very rare exceptions apart, what exists is not the republic ruled by patricians, but monarchy, rooted in one or more cities and ruling their hinterland in cooperation with, and in the interests of, their dominant classes. In such circumstances we find certain typical modes of political action. The political influence of the notables rests on two factors: on the one hand, they must possess 'access' to authority, and so be able to advise, to warn, and in general to speak for society or some part of it at the ruler's court; on the other, they must have some social power of their own, whatever its form and origin, which is not dependent on the ruler and gives them a position of accepted and 'natural' leadership. Around the central core of this independent power they can, if they are skilful, create a coalition of forces both urban and rural. But this process does not necessarily end in one notable or one party of notables drawing all the forces of society into its coalition. In such political systems there is a tendency towards the formation of two or more coalitions roughly balancing one another, and for this several reasons may be given: leadership of this kind is not an institution, and there will always be those who challenge it; since the leader has to combine so many interests, and to balance them against the interests of the ruler, he is bound to disappoint some groups, who therefore tend to leave his coalition for another; and it is in the interest of the ruler to create and maintain rivalries among his powerful subjects, as otherwise he may find the whole of society drawn up against him.

The two aspects of the notable's power are of course closely connected with each other. It is because he has access to authority that he can act as leader, and it is because he has a separate power of his own in society that authority needs him and must give him access. But for this reason, his modes of action must in normal circumstances be cautious and even ambiguous. At moments of crisis direct action may be possible and even be needed. The notables lead a revolution against the ruler, or themselves become rulers during an interregnum; when one dynasty is displaced by another, it is the notables who act as caretakers and surrender the city to its new master. But at other times they must act with care so as not to lose touch with either pole of their power. They must not appear to the city to be simply the instruments of authority; but also they must not appear to be the enemies of authority, and so risk being deprived of their access, or, through the full exercise of the ruler's power, of the very basis of their position in society. Thus in general their actions must be circumspect: the use of influence in private; the cautious expression of discontent, by absenting themselves from the ruler's presence; the discreet encouragement of opposition—but not up to the point where it may call down the fatal blow of the ruler's anger.

III

Ottoman Istanbul was above all a centre of government, comparable, as a Muslim city, not so much to those great organic growths which held the deposit of many ages of Islamic history, but rather to the imperial foundations by which new dynasties marked their greatness. The greatest strength of the government was naturally concentrated in its capital, and there was almost no local countervailing power independent of it. Istanbul had not existed as a Muslim city before the conquest, and the conquerors found there no ancient Islamic society with its inner structure already full grown and having its 'natural' leaders in ancient families with an inherited social prestige. Trade was largely in the hands of foreigners or members of religious minorities, who as such were not able to exercise leadership or obtain power (except for such derived influence as the Phanariot Greeks had for a time); and the obvious need to keep the capital supplied with food made it necessary for the government to prevent that growth of urban domination over the rural hinterland which in other places made it possible for city notables to control the economic exchanges between countryside and town.

Moreover, the class which, in other cities, provided the spokesmen for popular grievances and demands—the *'ulama*—was here very much of an official class, owing its influence to the holding of high religious office in the government, and therefore nearer to the ruler than to the subject; in course of time too it tended to be dominated by privileged families passing on wealth and the tradition of state service from one generation to another. It is true that, at least in the later Ottoman period, the Janissary organization gave the members of the regiments a means of expressing their discontent. But while they could disturb the government they could not themselves control it, and they were themselves indeed the instruments of political forces inside the government. The politics of Istanbul were not the 'politics of notables' as we have defined them but something different, court or bureaucratic politics. The political 'leaders', those who formed and led combinations and struggled for power, were themselves servants of the ruler and derived the core of their power from that, not from their independent position in society. But, as Professor Itzkowitz has shown,[3] the path to power and leadership within the government changed from one Ottoman age to another: in the sixteenth century, it had led through the schools and service of the palace, but by the eighteenth it was more common for civil servants to rise to the top.

In the provincial centres, however, Ottoman power took a different form. Here the distinction of *'askar* and *ra'aya* could have many undertones, ethnic, religious and other. Ottoman governors and officials came from far off, spoke often a different language, did not usually stay long enough to strike roots; the standing forces they could rely on were normally not sufficient to allow them to impose their authority unaided. To rule at all they had to rely on local intermediaries, and these they found already existing. At least in Asia and Africa, the lands the Ottomans conquered were lands of ancient Islamic culture, with a long tradition of urban life and separate political existence; both by necessity and because of a certain view of government, the Ottomans when they came tried not to crush and absorb but to preserve or even revive good local customs. In such conditions, when authority can only maintain itself with local help, a 'politics of notables' can grow up.

But who were the 'notables'? The concept of a 'notable', as we shall use it, is a political and not a sociological one. We mean by it those who can play a certain political role as intermediaries between government and people, and—within certain limits—as leaders of the urban population. But in different circumstances it is different groups which can play this role, groups with different kinds of social power. In the Arab provinces there were three such groups. First there were the traditional spokesmen of the Islamic city, the *'ulama*, whose power was derived from their religious position. They were necessary to the Ottoman government because they alone could confer legitimacy on its acts. But while in Istanbul they were an official group, in the provinces they were local groups: apart from the *qadi*, the others—*muftis, naqibs, na'ibs*—were drawn from local families. Their positions alone would have given them influence, but they derived it also from other sources: from the inherited reputation of certain religious families, going back many centuries perhaps to some saint whose tomb lay at the heart of the city; from the fact that, in spite of this, the corps of *'ulama* lay open to all Muslims; from the connection of the local *'ulama* with the whole religious order and thus with the palace and the imperial *divan*; and from their wealth, built up through the custody of *waqfs* or the traditional connection with the commercial bourgeoisie, and relatively safe from the danger of confiscation because of their religious position.

Secondly, there were the leaders of the local garrisons. They too were necessary to the government because they had immediate control of armed force, but they also had a certain independence of action. They could rely to some extent on the *esprit de corps* which an armed and disciplined body of men develops; and the leaders of the Janissaries in particular controlled the local citadels under direct orders from Istanbul and were not responsible to the local governor. In some places also the Janissaries in course of time took roots in the city: they enlisted local auxiliary troops; membership of a regiment became heredity; particular regiments indeed became closely identified with particular quarters of the city. Thus they served not only as military bodies but as organizations for defence or political action.

Thirdly, there were those whom we might call 'secular notables' (*a'yan, ağas, amirs*): that is to say, individuals or families whose power might be rooted in some political or military tradition, the memory of some ancestor or predecessor; or in the *'asabiyya* of a family or of some other group which could serve as its equivalent; or in the control of agricultural production through possession of *malikanes* or supervision of *waqfs*. (This last factor was of particular importance, not so much because it gave them wealth as because it enabled them to control the grain-supply of the city, and thus indirectly to affect public order and put pressure on the government.)

From whichever of these three groups the local leadership arises, we find it acting politically in much the same way. On the one hand, its leaders or their representatives are members of the governor's *divan*, and thus have formal access to him. On the other, around the core of their own independent power they build up a coalition, combining other notable families, *'ulama*, leaders of armed forces, and also the organizations which embody the active force of the population at large: some of the groups of craftsmen (in particular that of the butchers), the Janissaries in places where they have become a popular group, *shaykhs* of the more turbulent quarters, and those unofficial mobilizers of opinion and organizers of popular action who, under one name or another, go back into the distant past of the Islamic city. The combination may even spread beyond the city and its immediate hinterland and include Beduin chieftains or lords of the mountains. But it is a precarious combination: forces attracted into the orbit of one notable can be drawn away into that of another, or can themselves become independent agents, or can be won back to direct dependence on the government.

This much was true of all the provincial centres, but there were great differences between the provinces in regard to which group of the three took the lead, and how far it could go vis à vis the Ottoman government along a spectrum stretching as far as complete and permanent seizure of power. At one extreme, in the North African provinces, distance from Istanbul and the loss by the Ottoman navy of control of the central Mediterranean made it possible for certain local forces to take over the government, to rule in the name of the sultan and with his investiture, and to hand on their rule to their chosen successors.

In Cairo, however, the balance was more even. True, the local Ottoman power was comparatively weak once the first phase was over, and was unable to maintain a large enough standing army to impose its authority. Nevertheless, Egypt was too important from many points of view for the Ottomans to let it go. Ottoman sea power still counted for something in the eastern Mediterranean, and so did the prestige of the sultan as defender of Sunni Islam and protector of the Holy Places; it was still possible for the Ottoman government to assert its authority, either by a direct act of force or by balancing local groups against each other. But the Ottoman administration in Egypt never rested, as it did in Anatolia and the Balkans, on a social basis of Turkish military landholders. It was thus possible for local leaders to rise, and hope to strengthen and consolidate their position by seizing hold of the land and the land tax. The nature and development of this local leadership has been made clearer by the recent writings of Professors Ayalon, Holt and Shaw.[4] It did not come either from the religious class or from the leaders of the military corps. It is true, the religious leaders (not so much the teachers of the Azhar as the heads of families which possessed a hereditary leadership of important *turuq*) had certain weapons in their hands: a connection with the Muslim merchants who engaged in the Nile and Red Sea trade, control of *waqfs*, a close link with the population of the small towns and the countryside, and of course the prestige of religious ancestry and learning. But the long experience of military rule, and the whole tradition of the Sunni *'ulama*, had taught them to play a discreet and secondary role, and taught the people to look elsewhere for political leadership. The leaders of the 'seven regiments' also had certain obvious advantages; but it may be that, once the military corps began to be drawn into Egyptian society and military discipline to relax, the solidarity of the regiments was not enough to provide that *'asabiyya* which was necessary for one who wished to seize and hold power. In the absence of local families with a tradition of leadership, the only groups which could provide the needed *'asabiyya* were the 'Mamluk' households: these were not military corps but élites created by men possessing political or military power, composed of freedmen trained in the service of the current heads of the household, and held together by a solidarity which would last a lifetime. The training and tradition of the household produced individuals who knew how to gather around them religious leaders, the commanders of the regiments, popular guilds, and behind them one or other of the loose rural alliances *Nisf Haram* and *Nisf Sa'd*, and then, with this combination, to secure real power—to obtain for themselves and their followers from the governor the rank of *bey* and therefore access to the great offices to which *beys* were appointed, and to seize control of the tax farms. But the combination was fragile: one household might be destroyed by others, as the Qasimiyya were destroyed by an alliance of the Faqariyya and Qazdughliyya; but in its turn the new dominant party might split, as did the Faqariyya and Qazdughliyya, or might have to face new rivals; and the Ottoman governors, as well perhaps as other local forces, could use their rivalries to weaken them all.

In the Arab provinces to the east of Egypt also there existed 'notables', but in different forms. In two provincial centres, Sayda (later Acre) and Baghdad, we find the same phenomenon of the Mamluk household as in Egypt. In both of them, however, we find a single Mamluk household, which has a tendency to split but still keeps its solidarity. In each of them, the household has been formed by a strong governor, and after his death secures the governorship for itself and keeps it until the 1830s. Why was it that the Ottoman government accepted this formal monopoly of power by a household? Various reasons may be suggested. First, both Baghdad and Acre were 'frontier' posts. Baghdad lay on the disturbed frontier with Persia, and with a potentially disloyal Shi'i population all around, and Acre lay near the frontier of almost independent Egypt and open to the Mediterranean, and also at the foot of the hill country of northern Palestine and southern Lebanon, whose inhabitants had in the past shown more than velleities of independence and a willingness to ally themselves with outside forces; in the 1770s a combination of semi-autonomous mountain rulers, Egyptian forces coming up the coastal road through Palestine, and Greco-Russian sea forces in the eastern Mediterranean had gravely threatened the Ottoman hold over southern Syria. In both places (as in some other provinces of the empire) it was therefore in the interest of the Porte to acquiesce in the rule of a group which could maintain efficient armed forces, collect taxes, and keep its province loyal to the sultan in the last resort.

In both of them, again, the rural hinterland had been gradually eaten away: in Acre-Sayda by the lords of the Palestinian and Lebanese hills, in Baghdad by such tribal leaders as the *shaykhs* of the Muntafik, who controlled the greater part of the land and therefore the collection of the land tax, as well as many customs posts. There did not therefore exist the same spur to the ambitions and rivalries of urban forces as was provided by the *iltizams* of Egypt. Moreover, those urban forces were weaker than in Cairo, and therefore there was less scope for the creation of powerful combinations. Sayda and Acre were small towns, without great religious families; their hinterland was largely in the possession of Christian, Druzes and Shiʿis, and did not contain large *waqfs*. In Baghdad there were great families of Sunni *ʿulama*, but their social power must have been limited by the hold of Shiʿi divines and tribal chiefs over the countryside. In both of them, commerce was controlled largely by foreigners or members of minorities, Jews and Armenians in Baghdad, Orthodox or Uniate Christians in Sayda and Acre.

Mosul again showed a different picture. It was like Acre and Baghdad in that a local group was able to impose itself on the Ottoman government and insist on a governor drawn from the city itself, but unlike them in that the governor came not from a Mamluk household but from a family, that of Jalili, and one which as so often in Islamic history came from outside (it was probably of Christian origin) and so was able to serve as the focal point for many different groups. Perhaps here too we can find an explanation for these facts in certain characteristics of the city. Mosul had a small hinterland. The range of influence of the urban economy scarcely stretched beyond the plains and river valley immediately around it; beyond that lay Beduin territory and the principalities of the Kurdish mountains. Within this small enclave, almost a city-state, urban politics could work themselves out without much interference. The city itself was a centre of orthodox Muslim education, and around its mosques and schools had grown up some families with a religious tradition and prestige, like the ʿUmaris, the guardians of the religious orthodoxy of northern Iraq. It was also an important centre of trade, lying on the main route from Istanbul and Asia Minor to Baghdad and the Gulf, and being a collecting and distributing centre for parts of Anatolia and Persia; and its trade was largely in Muslim hands. Here once more we find the combination of a religious group with a commercial bourgeoisie. Moreover, it was not a military centre of the same importance as Baghdad. The main armed forces were local ones raised by the Jalili governors, and the Janissaries had become mainly a political organization of the city quarters and under the control of local leaders. There was therefore no military body which could counterbalance the ascendancy of the local notables.

There remain to be considered the cities of Syria and the Hijaz: Damascus, Aleppo, the Holy Cities and their dependencies. Here we find the 'politics of notables' in their purest form. On the one hand, Ottoman authority remained real; it *had* to be a reality, because its legitimacy, in the eyes of the Muslim world, was bound up with its control of the Holy Cities and the pilgrim routes, and also because it was control of the Fertile Crescent which determined that Istanbul, not Cairo or Isfahan, should dominate the heart of the Muslim world. Although this authority might appear to be ceded to a local group, as with the 'Azms in Damascus throughout most of the eighteenth century, it could be taken back either by the time-honoured method of setting one governor against another, or by direct military methods: the imperial road to Syria and the Hijaz lay open.

On the other hand, the power of the notables was particularly great in these cities; and here the 'notables' were not a Mamluk group but an ancient bourgeoisie with its leaders, the *sharifs* in the Hijaz, the great families in Damascus, Aleppo and the smaller Syrian towns, some of them with a religious and learned tradition (and in Aleppo and its province claiming the title and privileges of *sharifs*). This class was strong enough to absorb into itself families of military origin around whom rival loyalties and Mamluk households might have grown up, to restrain the power of the local governor or at least ensure that it was exercised in its own interest, and at times even to revolt successfully against the governor and itself rule the city for short periods (in Aleppo several times, in Damascus in 1830).

In both Aleppo and Damascus, this class was represented in the governor's *divan* and so had access to the governor. In Aleppo the members of the *divan* included the *muhassil*, a local notable who had the farm of the most important taxes; the *serdar* of the Janissaries who, as we shall see, was open to influence by the notables; the *mufti*, the *naqib*, and the principal *'ulama*; and the *a'yan* in the restricted technical sense of those notables who were hereditary members of the *divan*. In Damascus the composition of the *divan* was similar. But the notables not only had access to the governor, they also were in a position to make it impossible for him to rule without them. They controlled the sources of power in the city, not only the wealthy and established classes but the populace. This control was exercised through the religious institutions, the popular quarters, and above all the Janissaries. In both cities there was a formal distinction between *kapikul*, imperial Janissaries, and *yerliye*, local auxiliaries or their descendants. In Aleppo however this distinction had lost its meaning and both alike were local groups open therefore to local influences, while in Damascus the *kapikul* were imperial troops sent from Istanbul, but the fact that they were not under the control of the local governor, only under the distant control of their *ağa* in Istanbul, meant that they too were exposed to local pressures. In both cities they had close connections with certain trades (once more here we come upon the ubiquitous butcher) and with certain popular quarters where immigrants from the countryside and men engaged in the caravan trade gathered: in Aleppo the Banqusa and Bab Nayrab quarters, in Damascus the Maydan, which a French consul called 'le faubourg révolutionnaire' of the city. They and through them the notables could make and unmake public order; they could also control the urban tax system, since taxes were collected through the *shaykhs* of quarters and crafts.

The notables derived their wealth from two sources, trade and the land. Historians have relied so much on consular reports that they have tended to exaggerate the importance of the trade with Europe, with which of course the consuls were mainly concerned. But the wealth of Damascus and Aleppo came very largely by other routes, the pilgrimage route and those across the desert to Baghdad, Persia and the Gulf, and at this time the first of these was wholly and the second partly in Muslim hands. The wealthy Muslim trader appears less in the consular records than the Armenian or Uniate or Jew, but was perhaps more important in this period. As for the land, the orchards of Damascus and the rich plains around the cities were to a large extent virtually owned by the notables, either as *malikanes* or as *waqfs*; when they were not so owned, the notables could hope to obtain the tax farms. Whatever form their control of the villages took, it gave them control of the urban wheat supply, and in both cities we can see them using this in order to create artificial scarcities, and so not only to raise prices and gain wealth but to dominate the governor by causing disorders which only they could quell.

In Syria as in Egypt indeed it may be that the struggles of factions were mainly about control of the food supply and the land tax, both for their own sake and as political instruments. It was for this that political combinations were formed, and because of this that they could be formed. But simply because the prize was so great the combinations were fragile. By the beginning of the nineteenth century, at least in Aleppo, the notables as such seem to have been losing their hold over the combinations they had formed, and power to be passing to their former instruments the Janissary chiefs. It was these who were now obtaining control of the villages and making alliances not only with the forces of the city but with the Beduin and Kurdish chieftains of the countryside. But their power too was more fragile perhaps than that of the Mamluks in Egypt, because urban and settled life in Syria was so much more precarious: the independent power of Kurd and Beduin chiefs was eating up the countryside.

IV

It is clear that the reforms of the *tanzimat* period in the Ottoman Empire and the similar reforms in Egypt (as also in Tunisia) would, if carried to their logical conclusion, have destroyed the independent power of the notables and the mode of political action it made possible. The aim of the reforms was to establish a uniform and centralized administration, linked directly with each citizen, and working in accordance with its own rational principles of justice, applied equally to all. But these aims, although they could be fulfilled to some extent, could not be carried out completely, and in Istanbul and Cairo alike the effect of the reforms was deflected and made more complicated by such factors as the existence of an absolute ruler who was only willing to apply the new ideas so far as they did not threaten but instead strengthened his own position; the gradual development of a public consciousness among certain groups, who were no longer willing to be ruled for their own good from above but wished to take part in the process; and the very size and variety of the Ottoman system of government, which worked differently in different places.

In Cairo (and also, it would seem, in Tunis)[5] the reforms worked primarily in favour of the ruler. In fact, the first and main aim of Muhammad ʿAli was to destroy all rivals to his power. The destruction of the Mamluk notables has been much written about, although perhaps too much attention has been paid to the famous lunch party, and too little to an event of more permanent importance, the abolition of the *iltizams*. The control of the Mamluks over the *iltizams* had been weakened by the French occupation, and this made it easier for Muhammad ʿAli to end the system. This act destroyed both the means by which the military households had secured power and the goal of their ambitions. By collecting the taxes directly, Muhammad ʿAli ensured that no new class of *multazims* should arise; when, towards the end of his reign, a new class of landowners began to come into existence, they did not at first possess the same means as the Mamluks of putting pressure on the government. It is true that they were soon able to achieve a position of much power in the rural economy, but landownership by itself did not create political power once more until Ismaʿil began to need their help and support in the 1870s.

The ascendancy of the Mamluk households in the eighteenth century had prevented in Cairo the process which had taken place in Istanbul, the growth of the political power of the civil servants. They were therefore not an independent force for Muhammad ʿAli to reckon with, and they lost their importance as a new kind of administration grew up for which new types of skill were needed. The new administrators were often Copts or other Christians, who as such had no power of their own, or else men of humble origin trained in the educational missions or the special schools and owing their advancement to the ruler's favour. The old religious families too, although clearly their social prestige remained in great part, lost their political power and freedom of action, which had been at their greatest in the years after the French occupation. The abolition of the *iltizams* (from which they had profited in the confusion caused by the French defeat of the Mamluks), the weakening of the *waqf* system, the development of new legal codes and Muhammad 'Ali's neglect of the old system of religious education, all these helped to weaken them. At the same time the old merchant class lost much of its power and prosperity, with the opening of the Red Sea to steam navigation in the middle of the nineteenth century (even before the Suez Canal was made), and the growth of the large-scale trade in cotton with Europe, which was almost entirely in the hands of Europeans or local Christians or Jews.

The former possessors of power were replaced by Muhammad 'Ali. Like them he built up his own army and his own group of high officers and officials to control it. But he succeeded in doing what his predecessors had failed to do and created around himself a single unchallenged 'Mamluk' household: soldiers of fortune or young boys, Turks, Kurds, Circassians and Albanians (with a few Europeans and Armenians for special purposes); strangers to Egypt, trained in his service, owing their advancement to him, with something of the *'asabiyya* of a Mamluk household but with something else as well, a European education, a knowledge of modern military or administrative sciences, and of the French language through which it came. (Here too we may refer in passing to a similar development in Tunisia: Khayr al-Din can be taken as typical of these last groups of Europeanized Mamluks.)

No doubt there was discontent with the predominance of the ruler and his household, and this was to find expression much later (first of all in the events of 1879–82), and later still to become a recurrent theme of Egyptian nationalism. But in the time of Muhammad 'Ali it could not express itself because the instruments of political action had also been destroyed. The tax farms had gone; the associations of craftsmen remained, as Professor Baer has shown,[6] later than had been thought, and so did the *turuq*, but the stricter policing of the streets and bazaars made popular action more difficult. In the countryside, the sedentarization of the Beduin, and the growth in the power of the *'umda*, the government's agent in the villages, destroyed other possible means of action.[7] It seems too that Muhammad 'Ali set himself deliberately to dispose of those popular leaders who, in the period of confusion before he came to power, had served as mobilizers of popular support in favour of the contenders for power, and, in particular, 'Umar Makram; for, although modern Egyptian historians tend to look on 'Umar Makram as a national leader, it would be better to think of him as an intermediary, someone who as *naqib* had access to the military chiefs but also had a popular following. He had indeed used his talents on behalf of Muhammad 'Ali himself: but in regard to him as to the Albanian soldiers, Muhammad 'Ali knew that the first act of a prudent despot is to destroy those with whose help he has seized power.

It is these two factors, the preponderant power of the government and the absence of instruments of political action, which explain why politics (except for 'court politics') virtually disappeared in Egypt, during the period from the

1820s to the 1870s. In the late 1870s, however, the situation changed. The power of the ruler weakened as foreign pressure on Isma'il grew, and new channels of opinion and action sprang up, as an unofficial press was established, the urban population increased, rural security broke down, the Azhar revived under the khedive's patronage, and Egyptians of peasant origin became officers in the army. Once more then we find political activity, and once more it is the 'politics of notables'. The leaders who arise come, as might be expected, from the 'Mamluk' household formed by Muhammad 'Ali. It was beginning to split up, and its leading members had greater independence of action because by now they had become landowners, through land grants by the ruler and in other ways. Riaz, Nubar, Sharif, Barudi are the new politicians, and behind them one can see in the shadows different groups inside the ruling family. As politicians they still work in the traditional way, by building up their own 'households' and systems of clients. 'Urabi and the army officers were not in the first instance leaders so much as instruments used by the politicians: we have perhaps paid too much attention to 'Urabi, too little to Mahmud Sami al-Barudi and others like him. It was the shock of the Anglo-French intervention which destroyed the politicians' delicate game of manoeuvre and the balancing of forces; the sword, struck from the hand which wielded it, for a moment seemed to have a power of its own as it flew through the air, before falling to the ground.[8]

After the first shock of the British occupation, however, the 'politics of notables' began once more. British rule was indirect; its official purpose was to make possible the end of the occupation, and for many years it was unsure of itself; it needed intermediaries, even after Cromer had found a policy and secured the essential positions of power in the government. Moreover, there was a certain polarization of authority, between the agency and the palace. In such circumstances the notables could play a part, and as usual an ambiguous one, supporting the British occupation but also discreetly serving as the focal points of discontent. It was not until the middle 1890s that their role became less important, as Cromer began to rule more directly through British advisers and puppet ministers, while on the other hand the new khedive began to experiment with a new type of politics, that of the nationalist students and the urban mass.

In Cairo then the effect of the reforms of Muhammad 'Ali was to destroy the old political leadership and replace it by an absolute ruler supported by a new military household; but in Istanbul the process was not so simple, for many reasons but mainly perhaps because of the existence of old and deeply rooted institutions. The reforms brought about the destruction of one such institution, the Janissary regiments. Another was weakened, but only up to a point. The palace was no longer the only source of fear and favour: its wealth was more limited, its men fewer and it could only rule through a skilled and specialized bureaucracy, although, on the other hand, the house of Osman was still the focal point of loyalty, and a whole complex of political habits still gave the sultan a final ascendancy over his officials and subjects. But a third institution increased in power: the higher bureaucracy. Their military rivals had been eliminated. Apart from that, they were needed more than ever because they were the only people who could work the new administrative system; and, as Sharif Mardin's classic book has made clear,[9] that system largely embodied their ideas, or at least the ideas of those who had been trained as diplomats or translators, about how society should be ruled. They were a solid enough group to remain in control; they were held together by certain common values—belief in the empire, belief in modern European civilization, a certain interpretation of the strength of Europe in terms of justice, rationality, efficiency; to a great extent they were a hereditary group, belonging to families with a long tradition of public service, and when the ancient system by which the property of dead or disgraced officials was seized by the state came to an end, their wealth and therefore their stake in the existing order grew.

The division of power between palace and civil service, the differing interests and intervention of the European powers, and the very size and complexity of the civil service, all led to a certain political activity. But it was still court or bureaucratic politics rather than that of notables: the politics of men whose power was based ultimately on their position in the public service, struggling to ensure their dominance and that of their ideas. Here, even more than in Egypt, the conditions of a more open type of political activity had been destroyed. The Janissaries had gone, and, apart from a few isolated incidents, the mob of Istanbul played no great political part until towards the end of the century. The new army officers were not drawn into politics by contending groups, perhaps because the memory of the Janissaries was still there to teach the danger of it. The *ʿulama* lost much of their importance, as in Egypt, as their official functions in the systems of law and education dwindled. The upper *ʿulama*, as Professor Heyd has explained,[10] were to a great extent supporters of reform, for many different reasons: they too in their way wished the empire to be strong again, some of them understood the conditions of its becoming strong, out of conviction and interest they were on the side of established order, and the bureaucratic ideal of rule from above in the light of a principle of justice was not without its appeal to men brought up in the Sunni tradition of politics.

To make up for the loss of internal instruments of action there were, it is true, certain outside forces which could be brought in. Different groups of officials were linked with different European embassies. There were also links with powerful forces in the provinces or dependencies of the empire. The relations between Muhammad ʿAli and the reforming groups in Istanbul need to be studied further, but it is clear from the diplomatic sources that between 1838 and 1840 one aim of Muhammad 'Ali's forward policy in Syria and Asia Minor was to bring to power in Istanbul his own friends among the Turkish court politicians. Again, the possibility that there were links between groups in Istanbul which were opposed to the reforms and such movements as that of Damascus in 1860 needs to be explored.

But such external forces could not make up for the lack of instruments of political action inside Istanbul. Here as in Cairo the period of the *tanzimat* was one of political quiescence, but here too a change begins in the 1860s and 1870s, and for similar reasons: on the one hand the weakening of the power of the government and the growth of European pressure; on the other, the appearance of new instruments of action—the press, the intelligentsia (officials and officers of humble origin and rank, students and graduates of the higher schools), and the new ideas of the Young Ottomans, forming as they did a powerful critique of the principles underlying the reforms.

Thus once more there was scope for the politicians, but who were the politicians? Here as in Cairo they came from inside the system of government. For all his panoply of a traditional Muslim despot, Sultan Abdülhamid II was in a sense the foremost politician of the empire: the first sultan who descended into the political fray, using various means to generate popular feeling and mobilize support vis à vis his own government as well as the European powers. But once the monarchy became political, it could no longer serve as a rallying point for all the forces of society. Other members of the Ottoman family, and of the related Egyptian khedivial family, began to come forward as points around which loyalty or discontent could crystallize. What was more important still, Abdülhamid broke the connection between palace and higher bureaucracy which had continued in spite of strains throughout the period of the *tanzimat*: some of the high officials, with an inherited position and wealth, supported by the official class and one or other European embassy, became rallying points for discreet opposition. The situation was radically changed by the process which began with the Young Turk Revolution and brought Turkey into the modern age of mass-politics. But it is significant that the leaders of the Young Turk Revolution, and of the Kemalist Revolution which followed it, were also drawn from the ranks of the Ottoman officials and officers. Modern Turkey like the later Ottoman Empire was built around the framework of strong and well-rooted institutions of government.

Both in Cairo and Istanbul therefore the reforms worked in favour of the power of the government as against that of the subject, although in each city a different element in the government drew the main profit from the change. In the provinces of Arab Asia however this development was not to come until towards the end of the century, and even then not completely. Before this, the reforms, in so far as they were applied, did not weaken the power of the urban notables and in some ways strengthened it.

There were many reasons for this. It would not be enough to explain it by the distance of Damascus, Aleppo, Baghdad and Jidda from Istanbul. Distance may it is true have counted for something in regard to Baghdad, but Syria and western Arabia felt the impact of modern means of communication even before the Suez Canal was opened and the first railways were built. Steamship lines were opened from the 1830s onwards (at the time of the events of 1860 in Syria, it was possible to reinforce the Ottoman army there rapidly by sea), and telegraph lines were laid in the 1860s. For the main reasons why the Arab provincial cities reacted in a different way to the *tanzimat* we must look elsewhere, and first of all to the very fact that they *were* provincial cities. The hand of the government was less heavy there than in the capital, and there is plenty of evidence that, as the century went on, it came to be regarded as in some sense alien, as it had not been earlier when political thought and sentiment naturally took a religious form. Both the Egyptian government which ruled Syria and the Hijaz in the 1830s, and the Ottoman government which replaced it, were regarded by the Muslim city-dwellers as westernizing governments going against religious tradition and against the ancient principle of Muslim supremacy; and it seems that this view of the new Turkish officials as innovators, almost infidels, sharpened the perception that they were Turks.

Moreover, the long tradition of leadership by the local *a'yan* and *'ulama* was too strong to be broken. It is true, in each of the provinces Ottoman control was sharply imposed or reimposed: in Baghdad and Mosul by military expeditions in the 1830s, in Syria and the Hijaz after the Egyptian withdrawal in 1840. This experience certainly left its mark. It meant that old ruling groups or families lost the power they had had in the eighteenth century, but it did not necessarily mean that they were destroyed, and during the nineteenth century there was perhaps a tendency for families of 'Turkish' or Mamluk military origins to blend with those of 'Arab' and religious origin to form a single class with social prestige. This class still had at its disposal the instruments of political action which had been weakened in Cairo and Istanbul. The *'ulama* remained more important than in the capital, both because they were largely drawn from a locally rooted aristocracy and not an élite of service, and because the religious schools, although in decline, still had a monopoly of religious education. There were no modern professional high schools in the provincial centres, and it was not until towards the end of the century that Muslim families of standing began to send their children to the French and American mission schools or the professional schools of Istanbul.

The 'popular' organizations still remained. Ottoman policing of the cities was less effective than Egyptian, and the quarter remained very much of a s local leadership. The associations of craftsmen still existed, and e evidence that they had more autonomy in Syria at least than in nbul: for what it is worth, Iliya Qudsi speaks of the *shaykhs* of the crafts as being elected by the members,[11] and it seems that in Jerusalem the *shaykhs* were drawn from the poorer *sharifs* and under the control of the *naqib*. The Janissaries also, although formally dissolved in the 1820s, continued to be an important political force for at least another generation. They were largely responsible for the rising of 1854 in Mosul, and they were reported to be still meeting secretly in Aleppo in 1860. There was perhaps greater popular discontent to build on than before. The coming in of European textiles led to a rapid decline of local crafts: raw materials which had previously been manufactured for a wide market in Aleppo or Damascus were now exported to the factories of western Europe. The number of looms fell sharply: in Aleppo, from 10,000 to 4,000 at most during the 1850s. This meant a decline in the prosperity of the artisans and of the merchants whose work was bound up with theirs: a decline the more sharply felt because at the same time a new merchant class was rising to deal with the trade with Europe, and this class tended not be drawn from the local Muslim population. In Damascus, it is true, some Muslim merchants held their own even in the European trade. But in Baghdad it was Jewish and Armenian merchants who prospered; in Aleppo, local Jews and Christians and Europeans; in Beirut, local Christians; in Jidda, Europeans as against the Hadrami merchants.

Again, in spite of efforts the Ottoman control of the Syrian and Iraqi countryside was to remain limited and precarious until much later. It gradually spread over the more accessible plains, but in the hills some degree of autonomy continued, and the power of the Beduin chiefs remained as it was. As late as the 1850s indeed, when in Egypt the process of sedentarization was well under way, the opposite process was still taking place in some parts of Syria, and peasants were abandoning their lands to the pastoral nomads. The traditional connection of the urban *a'yan* with the mountain or Beduin chiefs could still therefore play a role in the politics of the cities.

In some ways indeed the influence of the notables was even strengthened in the first phase of the *tanzimat*. The Ottoman governors needed them more than before. A governor was sent, usually for a short period, to a city he did not know, with a small number of officials to help him, no organized police force or gendarmerie, and inadequate armed forces. He was sent not simply to carry on as before, but to apply a new reforming policy which was bound to arouse opposition. In these circumstances, he could only rule with the help of the local notables: without their local knowledge and their credit with the population he could scarcely hope, for example, to raise conscripts or new taxes. Some at least of the new governors moreover were men out of sympathy with the reforms and for that reason exiled by the central government to posts in different provinces. It was no doubt for these reasons that, with the acquiescence of the government, the local *majlis* in most provincial centres came to be controlled by the notables. The *majlis* included several Muslim notables either appointed by the governor or in some sense elected, as well as the *qadi* and the *mufti* and perhaps the *naqib* ex officio. All the consular reports agree that, at least until the 1860s, this local Muslim element dominated the *majlis*. The Jewish and Christian members, who had played an active part during the Egyptian occupation, were reduced to silence, and in one way or another the *a'yan* were able to do as they wanted with the Turkish officials.

Not only were the notables needed more by the government, their intervention was also more sought after by the population in its dealings with the government. Conscription, new legal codes, new methods of assessing and collecting taxes, the establishment of garrisons or government offices in smaller towns, the attempt to weaken or destroy the local autonomies, all meant that more than ever before the population was brought into connection with the government and the notables could play their traditional role of intermediaries. This strengthened their control over the city, and extended it over the countryside. Notables became 'patrons' of villages, and this was one of the ways in which they came to establish their claims to ownership over them. They also created useful alliances with country notables. In Lebanon, for example, the abolition of the princedom meant that the government in Beirut and Damascus could intervene more than before. Different families or factions in the mountain began to find powerful friends and supporters in the provincial capitals: it was in this period for example that the connection between Druze chiefs of the Shuf and Muslim notables of Beirut grew up. The destruction of the Kurdish principalities had similar effects. Disaffected Kurdish chiefs like Badr Khan formed alliances with discontented urban notables in Mosul; some of the Kurdish ruling families, like that of Baban, themselves settled in Baghdad, became urban notables, but from the city still had a certain influence over their former territories. In those territories, their place as local leaders was taken by the hereditary *shaykhs* of religious orders, like the Barzanji *shaykhs* of the Qadiri order and the Naqshbandi *shaykhs* of Barzan; these too had connections through their orders with the religious aristocracy of the cities.

The notables used their possibilities of action fully in this period. On the whole they threw their influence against the reforms, not only from prejudice or conviction, but because the general direction of the reforms ran contrary to their interests: the political conception underlying the *tanzimat* was that of a direct and identical relationship between the government and each of its citizens, and this was not compatible either with the privileges of Muslim notables or with their role as intermediaries. As was to be expected, they also used their power to increase their wealth. They no less than other classes were deeply affected by the change which was taking place in the trading system. The trade from which their wealth had come was in decline. Long before the Suez Canal was opened, steam communications between Istanbul and Egypt, as well as the disturbed state of Persia and of the desert routes, had cut down the number of pilgrims going to the Holy Cities by the difficult overland route from Damascus: as early as 1843 it was reported that no pilgrims had come to Damascus from Persia, and only 200 from Asia Minor, compared to several thousand in previous years. The merchants of Damascus suffered most from this; those of other cities in Syria, Iraq and the Hijaz suffered also from the decline of the old textile crafts, the insecurity of the transdesert routes, and the opening of steamship communications between Iraq and India. On the other hand there were new possibilities of becoming wealthy from the land, and notables and merchants made the most of them. After the restoration of control by the central Ottoman government, many of the *malikanes* seem to have been abolished, but the land tax as well as other taxes was farmed annually. When the farms were auctioned, the large merchants and notables, in collusion with Ottoman officials, were in a good position to obtain them. The land tax was now paid in kind, while previously it had been paid in money. The tax-farmer would delay levying the tax, under some pretext or other; but the cultivator could not send the rest of his produce to the city market until the tax had been paid. This caused an artificial scarcity in the city, prices went up, and the merchants could then release the stocks of grain they had stored up for this purpose and sell them at a high price. Such manoeuvres, which we find described again and again in the consular sources, were the more profitable because the control of the government was being extended from the city over the more accessible countryside; regions like the Biqaʿ, which had for a long time been under the control of the mountain lords, now came under that of Damascus, and their tax-farms went to Damascene families or Ottoman officials. Later, when the new Land Law was issued, it was used from the beginning by members of the *majlis* and their partners in the Ottoman administration to obtain the title to villages.

In the Syrian and Iraqi provinces, the balance of power between notables and government did not swing decisively in favour of the latter until towards the end of the nineteenth century, when the control of Istanbul grew much more effective for various reasons. But even then this did not mean the end of the local predominance of the notables. Under Abdülhamid they began to send their sons to Ottoman professional schools and from there into the civil or military service; they could preserve their position by becoming part of the Ottoman aristocracy of service. Later, under the Young Turks and then the

Mandatory governments, the idea of Arab nationalism provided them with a new instrument of resistance. Here indeed we find one of the ways in which the history of Syria and Iraq in modern times has differed from that of Turkey and Egypt. The nationalist movement was led by the urban aristocracy and moulded in their image; the change did not begin to come until after 1945.

V

Thus far we have talked in terms of two factors: the government, and the urban notables acting as a focus for local forces and able either to oppose the government or else oblige it to act through them. But there was a third factor involved: the European embassies and consulates, particularly those of England, France and Russia. Their influence was changing in scope and nature. Since the early seventeenth century the European states had had interests of their own to preserve, and had done so by allying themselves with one or other party in the palace, the imperial *divan* or the provincial *divans*. But in the nineteenth century a new situation came into existence. Their power and interests were now so great that they were no longer willing simply to act through whatever government existed, or in other words to allow the Ottoman central or local governments to provide the framework within which the activities of Europe should be conducted. They were now in a position to put pressure on the government to become the kind of government they needed. In particular, they were not willing to deal with the various populations of the empire through the government. European trade with the empire (in particular the textile trade) was growing quickly, and this meant, not only that European merchants should be protected, but that those involved in the trade with Europe, whether foreigners or Ottomans, should be able to deal directly with the population: to travel freely, not to bear vexatious burdens and impositions, to widen the market for imports, to collect materials for export, to tell producers what to produce and lend them the money to do it. At the same time, for various reasons different groups in the population wanted the protection of the European powers, who were willing to give it them. Rich and prominent individuals could be protected by attaching them in some way to the consulates and embassies, and during the 1830s something new happened: for the first time Ottoman subjects were themselves made consular agents. But beyond that, whole communities were taken under protection. A policy of protection, which had been pursued by the French since the seventeenth and the Russians since the late eighteenth century, was pursued by them and others more consciously and deliberately in the 1840s and 1850s; it was then that the British government, which had no obvious protégés of its own, established a connection with the Jews in

Palestine, some of the Druzes in Lebanon, and the new Protestant churches. Behind the protection of trade and religious minorities there lay something else, the major political and strategic interests of the powers, and these also might make necessary a direct connection with the peoples of the empire: British communications with India must be kept open, and for this purpose British consuls must have direct and friendly relations with the chiefs of Beduin tribes which lay across the routes.

In their own interests therefore the European powers needed a certain kind of Ottoman government and a certain position for themselves inside the empire; to obtain this they were prepared to put pressure on the government, and they were able to do so both because of their military strength and because of their connection with different groups in the empire. The Ottoman government for its part needed *them*: only the armies of one European power could protect it from the threats of another. In addition, political groups inside the government looked more than before to the support of European embassies and consulates in their struggles with other groups; this in its turn strengthened the position of the ambassadors and consuls even further.

In general, their influence was used in favour of the reforms of the *tanzimat*. They wanted a better position for their Christian and Jewish protégés, and they wanted an efficient and rational government with which to deal. (This is probably true of the Russian not less than other governments, although we shall not know definitely until the Russian sources are fully used. We should beware of what is written about Russian policy on the basis of British and French sources; there seems no reason to doubt that in this period of change Russia like other states wanted reform, so long as that did not mean the domination of some other power.)

But European help to the reformers was given on one condition: that the reforms did not harm the interests of the European states, and in particular their free and direct access to the peoples of the empire. The decisive struggle in this connection was that between the British government and Muhammad ʻAli in the 1830s. The aim of Muhammad ʻAli's policy, so far as his relations with Europe were concerned, was to create a new framework within which European activities could be pursued, but to make sure that Europe would deal with his territories through *him*, not only as ruler but as merchant-in-chief, principal broker between the rural cultivator and the European market. This claim was not acceptable to the British government, and battle was joined over a number of matters: the rights and privileges of consular agents, the British expedition to open up the Euphrates to navigation, and above all the question of monopolies. After the defeat of Muhammad ʻAli, the claims of Europe were generally accepted. Ottoman and Egyptian reformers needed European help too much to risk a major quarrel, even had they had the strength to pursue it.

The consequence of this was not only that foreigners and protégés secured a better position, and that merchants, consuls and missionaries could travel and work more freely than before, but also that ambassadors and consuls came to have a larger role in the politics of the empire. Once more the role was different in Istanbul, Cairo and the cities of the Fertile Crescent. In Istanbul, no power could allow any of the others to establish a permanent ascendancy; the embassies remained in a permanent tension, each on its guard against the others but all (until the last years before World War I) conscious of the overriding need to prevent the outbreak of war and to preserve the common interests of Europe in the Middle East. Since Istanbul was the capital and its politics, as we have seen, were primarily those of a court and a bureaucracy, the embassies served as centres not so much for the independent forces of society as for groups at court or in the government. In Cairo, at the other extreme, the British military occupation of 1882 meant that one of the foreign representatives became in effect ruler of Egypt, in uneasy collaboration with the palace; this conferred on the other representatives, in particular that of France, and on the Ottoman high commissioner, a new importance as the only possible foci of opposition but also limited their efficacy, since the presence of a British army gave the British consul-general a power which they could not challenge.

In the cities of the Fertile Crescent the influence of the consuls was exercised within a different framework again. Because they were known to have power with the government, and because they had free access to the population, their intervention was sought, and they began to play the part of intermediaries which had belonged for so long to the notables. Innumerable examples of this could be given. To take a few at random: in 1822, after the great earthquake in Aleppo, the *a'yan* asked the French consul to intervene with the government so that the city could be exempted from taxation for five years; in 1830, the *shaykhs* of the Mawali and Anaza tribes asked him to make peace for them with the governor of Aleppo, who himself was willing to accept this intervention; in the 1850s the revolt of Jabal Druze against conscription was ended by the intervention of both the British and the French consuls. Such intervention tended to place the consuls in direct opposition to the interests of the notables. It gave the consuls, whether or not they wanted it, a role in local politics. Both in the town and countryside they could mobilize political forces for local political ends: in fact, they could scarcely avoid doing so. The famous intervention of 'Abd al-Qadir in the Damascus massacres of 1860 is a good example of this. His action to save and protect Christians has usually been regarded as an act of Muslim *noblesse*, and no doubt in a sense it was. But it is clear from the French records that it was the French acting consul who, in anticipation of what happened, distributed arms to the Algerians and agreed that they should act as they did. Seen in this light, it is the French consulate which now plays the traditional part of the notable, and 'Abd al-Qadir and his Algerians that of his clients. The *noblesse* of 'Abd al-Qadir's action remains, but mixed with it is something else: the desire to win the favour of the government of Napoleon III, through whom his own political plans might be accomplished.

The rise of the consulates also threatened the economic power of the notables. While the old trading system declined, the growth of the European trade gave wealth and economic power to Christian or Jewish merchants who were for the most part either formal protégés of one or other consulate or morally attached to it. Even the hold of the notables over the land was challenged. As Chevallier has shown,[12] in parts of Syria the merchant from the seaport was replacing the local landowner as provider of capital for the peasant and organizer of his production. Even more widely, Christian and Jewish merchants were becoming moneylenders and thus acquiring some of the claims of landowners, and were looking to the foreign consulates to support their claims against the peasant: in the early 1860s a large proportion of the village debts in the province of Damascus were owed to Jewish protégés of the British consulate.

The opposition of the notables to the centralizing tendency of reform was in this way coloured with anti-European and anti-Christian feeling, and the growing influence of the European governments and their local protégés provided a common grievance through which the notables could hope to mobilize popular support. The great disturbances of the 1850s (Aleppo in 1850, Mosul in 1854, Nablus in 1856, Jidda in 1858, Damascus in 1860) follow a common pattern. In Mosul for example the events were organized by the relics of the Janissaries, in agreement with the *'ulama*, aiming to restore their own former position, linked with the Kurdish *ağas* who were fighting for their own position in the mountains, strengthened by control of the tax-farms of the villages, which the governor had given back to them, and using anti-Christian feeling to win popular support. Again, in Jidda in 1858, those who set on foot the revolt were some of the large merchants and *'ulama*, with the help or acquiescence of some Ottoman officials, and they used the grievances of the Hadrami traders against the foreign merchants who were replacing them.

After 1860 the fire dies down for a generation, but the rivalry of notable families and consulates as intermediaries, political organizers and potential claimants to rule continued. As one Arab province after another fell under European rule it came to the surface in a new form, the opposition of alien ruler and nationalist movement.

This article is reprinted from Albert Hourani, *The Emergence of the Modern Middle East* (London, 1981), pp. 36–66. Reprinted by permission of Macmillan Press Ltd.

NOTES

1. S. J. Shaw, *Financial and Administrative Organization and Development of Ottoman Egypt 1517–1798* (Princeton, 1962).

2. A. K. S. Lambton, *Landlord and Peasant in Persia* (London, 1953).

3. N. Itzkowitz, 'Eighteenth century Ottoman realities' in *Studia Islamica*, 16 (1962) pp. 73–94.

4. D. Ayalon, 'Studies in al-Jabarti I. Notes on the transformation of Mamluk society in Egypt under the Ottomans' in *Journal of the Economic and Social History of the Orient*, 3 (1960) pp. 275–325; P. M. Holt, *Egypt and the Fertile Crescent 1516–1922* (London, 1966), chapters 5, 6; Shaw, *Financial and Administrative Organization*. See now A. Raymond, *Artisans et commerçants au Caire au XVIIIe siècle* 2 vols (Damascus, 1973–4), in the light of which this account of the relationship between *beys*, leaders of military corps and merchants needs to be revised.

5. See now L. C. Brown, *The Tunisia of Ahmad Bey 1837–1855* (Princeton, 1974).

6. G. Baer, *Egyptian Guilds in Modern Times* (Jerusalem, 1964).

7. G. Baer, 'The Settlement of the Beduins', 'The Dissolution of the Village Community', 'The Village Shaykh 1800–1950', all in *Studies in the Social History of Modern Egypt* (Chicago, 1969) pp. 3–61.

8. A. Schölch, *Ägypten den Ägyptern: die politische und gesellschaftliche Krise der Jahre 1878–1882 in Ägypten* (Zurich, 1973) now throws new light on this.

9. Ş. Mardin, *The Genesis of Young Ottoman Thought* (Princeton, 1962).

10. U. Heyd, 'The Ottoman 'ulemā and westernization in the time of Selīm III and Maḥmūd II' in Heyd (ed), *Studies in Islamic History and Civilization* (Jerusalem, 1961) pp. 63–96, which is reprinted in this volume, pp. 29–59..

11. Iliya Qudsi, 'Notice sur les corporations de Damas', in *Actes du VIème Congrès des Orientalistes* (Leiden, 1885).

12. D. Chevallier, 'Aspects sociaux de la question d'Orient: aux origines des troubles agraires libanais en 1858' in *Annales*, 14 (1959) pp. 35–64.

Egypt and Europe: from French Expedition to British Occupation

ROGER OWEN

The absorption of a country as a dependent state within the imperialist system was more protracted than dramatic occupations, like that of Egypt in 1882, might suggest. In Egypt it involved a long-term transformation of the economy. Efforts to use the state to promote independent industrialization failed as the economy was dragged into the international division of labour; and, as in India, the state lost its autonomy in relation to outside powers (see Patnaik, IX).

Owen argues that much of what happened in Egypt in the nineteenth century is well accounted for in the theories of Marx, Hobson, Luxemburg, Hilferding and Baran. But there remain three areas where the theories do not provide an adequate framework: the role of the metropolitan states in relation to their capitalists, the nature of the Egyptian state and the changes in the Egyptian social structure which imperial penetration produced.

The bombardment of Alexandria and the invasion of Egypt by British troops in 1882 roused something of the same passions that were later to be let loose by the Anglo-French attack on Suez in 1956. Government policy was bitterly attacked in Parliament by Radical and Irish M.P.s. It was also the subject of hostile comment in a series of books and pamphlets such as J. S. Keay's *Spoiling the Egyptians*. A minister, John Bright, resigned from the cabinet in protest.

Among the opponents of the attack on Egypt a single theme predominated: the assertion that it was undertaken to insure that the Egyptian government continued to pay the interest on the country's large external debt. 'It is a stock-jobbers' war', wrote one of John Bright's friends, 'we shall very likely have more of this sort of thing.'[1] For the first time in Britain's history it was the financial community rather than the soldiers or colonial officials who were held to be chiefly responsible for an act of imperial expansion. This point of view was soon to become the stimulus to a new and more radical critique of empire which paid increasing attention to the notion that colonies were obtained because they were a source of profit to certain groups of businessmen and financiers, one which found its most vigorous exponent in J. A. Hobson, whose *Imperialism: a study* appeared in 1902. The invasion of Egypt thus occupies a central role in the genesis of theories of capitalist imperialism.

It was for reasons of this same type that the invasion continued to be seen not merely as just another example of European expansion but as one of its classic cases. As such it has an important place in the books of early writers on capitalist imperialism like Hobson[2] as well as those who have continued to write in the same tradition, such as John Strachey.[3] It follows that the invasion also occupies a central position in the works of writers like Robinson and Gallagher[4] and D. C. M. Platt[5] who are concerned to demonstrate that Egypt was taken for strategic rather than economic motives. Once the British occupation was presented as one of the prime exhibits of nineteenth-century imperialism it was inevitable that it should become a battleground for rival theories.

Whether this is a particularly fruitful way of looking either at the phenomenon of imperialism or at Egyptian history is another matter: my belief is that it is not. It is a major argument of the present case study that the British occupation cannot be studied in isolation, that it can only be understood in terms of an important series of developments which had been taking place since 1798, most of which were related to the transformation of the economy as a result of the policies of the Egyptian state and of its incorporation, as a producer of raw materials, within the European economic system. Seen in these terms an analysis of the relations between Egypt and Europe in the nineteenth century becomes a very different type of case study from those which concentrate simply on the events leading up to the British occupation. It is concerned with changes in the character of European economic expansion over many decades and with the impact of these changes on all sections of Egyptian society. Again, it involves a study of the crisis of the years between bankruptcy in 1875 and occupation in 1882, not so much in its own terms but rather as one of those periods in which, under the pressure of events, basic processes of economic and social change are laid bare for our examination.

An approach of this type has a number of advantages. It allows us to focus attention on one of the special characteristics of nineteenth-century imperialism: the way in which, in many cases, the colonization of an African or Asian territory was preceded by a breakdown of local political and social institutions resulting from a period of enforced contact with the European economy. Again, it enables us to take a new look at major works on the theory of imperialism to discover which of them provide useful guidance not simply about the occupation of Egypt but also about the whole character of European expansion and its effect on non-European societies. In addition, such a study is made more interesting by two other considerations. First, Egypt contained what was certainly one of the most varied societies which Europe encountered in Africa. This was partly a function of the fact that there had been settled life in the Nile valley for so many thousands of years. Furthermore, Egypt had always stood across important routes of international trade. It had been occupied many times and incorporated in a series of world empires. In the early Middle Ages it was Egyptian merchants who had introduced such vital commercial techniques as the bill of exchange to Europe. Even in 1798, when little of its former political or economic importance remained, when Napoleon is credited with having reintroduced the wheeled carriage to Egypt, its long history continued to be reflected in the fact that it contained one of the oldest universities in the world, a complicated system of municipal organization, a high degree of commercial consciousness and an agricultural population, many of whom were well used to growing cash crops for export or for sale in numerous market towns. Second, more information exists about nineteenth-century Egypt than about almost any other African or Asian country. From the *Description de l'Egypte* produced by the scholars of Napoleon's expedition and the works of the great Egyptian historian al-Jabarti to Ali Mubarak's voluminous encyclopaedia, *al-Khitat al-Taufiqiya al-Jadida* and the works of contemporary Egyptian writers like Anouar Abdel-Malek, there are a vast number of books by authors anxious to trace the impact of Europe on Egyptian society. In addition, there is a wealth of material in the Egyptian, Turkish and other government archives.

What follows is a brief analysis of the major economic and social developments in Egypt between 1798 and 1882. It will begin with a description of the transformation of the economy. There will then be an account of changes in the position of certain important social groups inside Egypt. Finally, it will conclude with a schematic account of the prolonged crisis of the years 1875 to 1882.

1. THE TRANSFORMATION OF THE ECONOMY[6]

Egypt in 1798 was a country of some 2,500,000 to 3,000,000 people, of whom perhaps a tenth lived in Cairo, far and away the largest city. The great bulk of the population worked in agriculture. In Upper Egypt peasants concentrated on the cultivation of winter cereals watered by the annual Nile flood. But in Lower Egypt (the Delta) one-eighth or so of the cultivated area was devoted to the production of high value crops like flax and short-staple cotton which required larger amounts of capital and a more complex system of irrigation to provide them with water through the summer months when the river was at its lowest. Another difference between Upper and Lower Egypt lay in the fact that in the Delta taxes often seem to have been collected in cash rather than kind with the result that cultivators were forced to sell a portion of their harvest in the nearest market. For this and other reasons most peasants in the Delta had some experience of operating on the fringes of a money economy, while in a number of areas cash seems to have been as important as custom or tradition as a basis for rural relations.

Meanwhile, the towns served as markets for rural products as well as centres for the production of those manufactured articles, notably linen and silk, which required greater skill, capital and organization than could be provided at village level. Some of the larger ones were also important centres of consumption of the luxury goods which made up the greater part of the merchandise which then entered international trade.

By the end of the eighteenth century the power of the government was weak. Not only was the central administration unable to maintain security in country areas or to supervise the upkeep of the major canals but it had also virtually lost control over the system of rural administration and tax collection. As a result the bulk of the agricultural surplus did not reach the government treasury but remained in the hands of a caste of hereditary tax-farmers who used it largely to provide themselves with the private armies they required in their endless struggles with one another for wealth and power.[7]

In the early years of the nineteenth century this predominantly agricultural economy was acted on by two new sets of forces. One was the efforts of a series of rulers—Muhammad Ali (1805–49), Said (1845–62), and Ismail (1863–79)—to modernize the army and the bureaucracy or, as they saw it, to lay the foundations of a modern state. The other was the impact of the expanding European economy, first through increasing trade, then through the export of European capital. Let us take them in order.

Muhammad Ali. Once he had seized power in 1805 Muhammad Ali's basic aim was to preserve his own rule by building up a large army and navy. During the first years of his regime he relied almost exclusively on foreign mercenaries. But during the 1820s he began to recruit native Egyptians and by the early 1830s he may have had as many as 100,000 men under arms. Such an army obviously required large sums of money and he was quick to see that the key to this was to increase the amount obtained from the land tax by replacing the tax-farmers with a system of direct collection by government agents. This had the further advantage of destroying alternative centres of political power and allowing the government to put an end to the anarchic conditions in the countryside. In addition, further sums were raised by an extension of the state monopolies to cover almost every type of agricultural produce. Crops were taken from the peasants in lieu of taxes and sold abroad on government account, leaving the cultivator little more than enough for bare existence. Finally, a labour tax, the corvée, was imposed on every adult male. In this way Muhammad Ali sought to perfect a system by which the government was able to appropriate the greater part of the rural surplus, using it either for military purposes or for an ambitious attempt to develop the country's resources. Unlike his predecessors Egypt's new ruler seems to have been fully aware of the fact that a continuous increase in government revenues was impossible without a continuous expansion of economic activity. It was for this reason that he was so anxious to encourage the introduction of new crops like long-staple cotton which had a growing market in Europe, to build new canals, and to improve communications. Later, in an effort to reduce imports, Egyptian textile workers were taken from their workshops and placed in government factories producing cotton cloth (much of it for army uniforms) with European machinery. Meanwhile an increasing number of young Egyptians were sent abroad to learn the most modern industrial techniques.

However, Muhammad Ali's attempt to set the state at the centre of the development of the Egyptian economy soon proved too much for the country's rudimentary system of administration and from the late 1830s onwards factories began to be closed or handed over to private individuals and much of the land assigned to senior officials and members of the royal family who themselves were made responsible for supervising agricultural production and collecting taxes. This process was hastened by the Anglo-Turkish Commercial Convention of 1838 which outlawed state monopolies and established a low external tariff of 8 per cent. Three years later the size of the Egyptian army was reduced, by order of the Ottoman government, to 18,000 thus depriving Muhammad Ali of a protected market for the products of his factories. As a result further industrialization was made very much more difficult while, once Egypt's ruler was finally forced to abandon his monopolies in the mid-1840s, the government lost the considerable sums it had derived from its control over agricultural exports.

European commercial expansion. Muhammad Ali's attempts to develop the economy required European assistance and European markets, but he was anxious to reduce the impact of Europe to a minimum. European merchants were confined to Alexandria and forbidden to make contact with the peasants in the interior. Professional schools were established and young Egyptians sent abroad in order to reduce the need for European technical expertise. Strenuous efforts were made to replace European imports with locally manufactured goods. This policy came to an end in the 1840s, however. As a result of European political pressure, first at Istanbul, then on Egypt itself, the country was rapidly opened up to foreign trade, a process which was undoubtedly assisted by Egypt's own large landed proprietors who were anxious to end the monopoly system so that they could sell their produce direct to European merchants rather than to the government. The export of cotton increased by 300 per cent between 1840 and 1860 as moneylenders established themselves throughout the Delta to provide the credit previously supplied by the government, as steam gins were introduced, and as the first railway was built linking Cairo with Alexandria. This paved the way for the rapid expansion of production during the American Civil War (1861–65) when the area placed under cotton increased five times and the size of the harvest by four. Meanwhile, the growing importance of the close ties which were being developed with the British economy can be seen from the fact that between 1848 and 1860 Egypt rose from twenty-sixth to twelfth place as a market for British exports while between 1854 and 1860 it moved from being the tenth most important supplier of British imports to the sixth.

European financial expansion. Increasing trade with Europe was followed by a rapid growth in the import of capital. During the 1850s the first European banks were established in Alexandria. At the same time the construction of more public works, further modernization of the army and of the bureaucracy, and, above all, the need to finance the great part of de Lesseps's Suez Canal project meant that government expenditure rapidly began to outstrip current receipts. Said began to borrow heavily from local bankers and merchants, then (perhaps at de Lesseps's suggestion) to issue treasury bonds. Finally, in 1862, he obtained his first foreign loan. This was followed by many others until by 1875 Egypt had borrowed a nominal sum of nearly £100 million from Europe, of which the Treasury had actually obtained no more than £68 million.

David Landes has described this process from the European side: how the end of the railway boom in the 1840s was followed by the development of new financial institutions, notably the finance company, which were able to obtain large sums of money from new groups of investors; how the particular character of these institutions drove them to seek speculative outlets for their capital abroad; how European money was drawn to the Middle East by the lure of the fabulous rates of interest which, it was supposed, could be obtained from lending money to merchants and agriculturalists.[8] Other writers, notably J. Bouvier, have described the way in which in the early 1870s, a number of French finance companies became heavily dependent on lending money to the Egyptian government.[9]

But how was the money borrowed from Europe used? In brief, Ismail had the same general aims as his grandfather, Muhammad Ali. These were: to build up a modern state, to assert Egypt's independence against both Turkey and Europe, and to diversify the economy. Unfortunately they proved to be mutually contradictory. All his efforts to use European capital to build up a state and an economy strong enough to withstand European pressures only led to increasing dependence on Europe. This can be seen clearly in his efforts to develop the economy. Here three factors were important. First, in so far as the money borrowed from Europe was put to good use and not just wasted it was employed in infrastructural investment of a type which could only benefit government revenue in the medium to long term. Meanwhile government efforts to raise more money from the land tax were thwarted by an inefficient system of collection and the fact that the bulk of the land was passing into the hands of powerful officials. In these circumstances, failure to meet interest payments on the foreign loans was inevitable. Second, efforts to diversify the economy were inhibited by the growing strength and importance of the cotton sector. As an ever-increasing proportion of Egypt's resources were being devoted to the production and export of this one crop it became more and more difficult to develop alternative forms of economic activity. The rich landed proprietors who grew the cotton, the merchants who sold it, were all united in their efforts to defend their particular interests and to make sure that they were the first to benefit from expenditure of government money, changes in the legal system or any other aspect of state activity. Third, unlike the rulers of Japan after 1868 Ismail was unable to place any barriers between the Egyptian economy and that of Europe. His attempts to create a sugar industry, for example, were hindered by the fact that he was unable to prevent the import of cheap government-subsidized sugar from Russia and Germany. The result of all these three factors was Egypt's incorporation, as a producer of cotton and a market for manufactured goods, within the European economic system. However hard he may have striven for independence Ismail was destined to end up by serving the purposes of Europe.

2. CHANGES IN THE POSITION OF IMPORTANT SOCIAL GROUPS[10]

The transformation of the Egyptian economy during the nineteenth century led to significant changes in the position of a number of social groups. Four are of particular importance.

The foreign community. The number of Europeans in Egypt rose from approximately 8,000 to 10,000 in 1838 to over 90,000 in 1881. The majority were concerned with the production and export of cotton or with banking and finance. But there were a growing number who were employed by the government itself, either as officials or experts. By the end of the 1860s, for example, there were over a hundred Europeans in the police.[11] Later, as a result of the report of the Commission of Inquiry in 1878 over 1,300 foreign officials were brought into the administration.[12] The European community occupied a privileged position as a result of the Capitulations, the treaties governing the status of foreigners within the Ottoman Empire. Europeans were virtually beyond the scope of the Egyptian law until the introduction of the Mixed Courts in 1876. They imported goods at their own valuation. They could only be taxed with the greatest difficulty. In addition, with the support of their consuls, they became an increasingly powerful pressure group, committed to defending their own interests as bankers and exporters as well as, by virtue of their extensive holdings of Egyptian bonds, to ensuring that the government maintain payment of interest on the various loans.

Egyptian landed proprietors. The growth of a class of Egyptian landed proprietors came about in three ways. First, in the late 1830s and early 1840s much of the best land in Egypt was parcelled out in estates and placed under the control of members of the royal family and senior officials. Although some of these estates were taken back from their owners during the rule of Abbas (1849–54) a large number remained in private hands. At the same time many local notables, particularly the village shaikhs, were able to take advantage of their position as agents of the central government to obtain land for themselves. There was every incentive to do this, of course, once the production of cotton and other crops became increasingly profitable. Finally, during Ismail's reign palace favourites, army officers, bureaucrats and others were given land either as a gift or in lieu of a pension. Meanwhile, the ruler himself added extensively to the lands owned by the royal family until, at the end of his reign, he controlled something like a fifth of the whole cultivated area.

As yet no historian has been able to make a satisfactory distinction between landed proprietiors of various types, but there is no doubt that, as a group, they occupied a particularly favourable position, often working their estates with corvées of local labour, diverting water from the canals to their own fields whenever they needed it, and paying lower taxes than their peasant neighbours. In addition, it was the landed proprietors who were the major beneficiaries of all the public money spent on digging new canals and building the railway system. It was they, as much as the European consuls, who were responsible for the abolition of Muhammad Ali's agricultural monopolies; they too who may well have put pressure on successive Egyptian governments to pass the laws necessary to create a system of private property in land.

For the most part the large and medium-sized estates created between 1840 and 1880 came from land formerly worked by peasants on their own account. The majority of these peasants remained as agricultural labourers in their villages, or were grouped together on the new estates in hamlets known as *ezbas*. Cotton production is particularly labour-intensive and the landed proprietors seem to have been concerned to maintain the old labour force more or less intact. These labourers were either paid in kind or, more usually, by being allowed to cultivate a tiny plot of land.

The bureaucrats. Efforts to create a modern state required an increasing number of civil servants. These were found at most levels, from among the graduates of Muhammad Ali's and Ismail's schools and from the many young Egyptians sent to Europe to study. As time went on the bureaucracy was subject to a process of rationalization. Separate ministries were formed; jobs were made more specific; pensions were introduced. As a result there developed something which Abdel-Malek is certainly right to characterize as a special bureaucratic interest.[13] Civil servants tended to share common ideas about the role of the state. Further, in the 1870s, they were more or less united in their desire to prevent any increase in the numbers and the privileges of Europeans within the government service. On the other hand, it is often difficult to make a clear distinction between the bureaucrats as a group and the landowners, once the former began to be given estates of their own.

The Turco-Circassian ruling class. During the eighteenth century almost all the senior posts in government and in the army were held by a Turkish-speaking minority, the descendants of Mamluk slaves or of officials sent from Istanbul. Later, during the early nineteenth century many of them were replaced by Ottoman soldiers of fortune who had served in Muhammad Ali's army. In the course of time their importance as a separate group began to diminish, particularly once the administration became more 'Egyptianized' as a result of the increasing employment of native Egyptians and the regulations providing for the use of Arabic in the government service. Meanwhile, for their part, more and more of the Turco-Circassians married Egyptian wives, took up posts in the district administration or in other ways became more closely incorporated within Egyptian society. Nevertheless, their power and prestige was still resented particularly in the army where, in the 1870s, they held every position above that of colonel.

3. BANKRUPTCY AND OCCUPATION 1875–1882 [14]

Egypt's bankruptcy in 1875 marked the beginning of a seven-year period of rapidly accelerating change in many areas of Egyptian government and society. A series of financial arrangements designed to ensure that the country paid its debts paved the way for increasing European control over the administration. This, in turn, provoked a strong Egyptian response, led first by Ismail, for which he was deposed in 1879, and then by a growing number of soldiers and officials. Finally, the emergence of a popular, national movement in 1881 and 1882 seemed sufficiently threatening to European interests to call for the occupation of Egypt by British troops.

Efforts to explain these developments generally concentrate, on the one hand, on tracing the genesis of the national movement; on the other, on seeking to discover what were the motives for increasing European intervention. This method has two major drawbacks. First, it encourages writers to ignore the socio-economic context in which these developments were taking place. Second, most accounts of the crisis, by concentrating either on the Egyptian or on the European side of the story, tend to underestimate the importance of the constant interaction between these two elements. What follows is an attempt to make a few brief points about the crisis in the light of these two considerations.

(*a*) The Egyptian national movement is best seen as a coalition of different groups all of which were, in some way, affected by the financial regime imposed on Egypt by its European creditors after the declaration of bankruptcy. These included the landowners (who were anxious to block the attempts being made by Egypt's European financial controllers to raise more revenue by increasing their taxes), the bureaucrats (disturbed by the numbers of Europeans being employed in the civil service), the Egyptian army officers (many of whom were threatened with premature retirement as a result of plans to economize on military expenditure), and the *ulama* or religious notables.

(*b*) In the late 1870s the fears of members of these four groups were encouraged by the Khedive Ismail for his own purposes but, just before his deposition in 1879, they began to cooperate more closely on the basis of a programme aimed at limiting the powers of the ruler by the introduction of a liberal constitution. This movement continued under Ismail's successor, Taufiq, even though it remained largely ineffectual until the summer of 1881. It was only when the civilian constitutionalists began to ally themselves more closely with the nationalist army officers led by Colonel Arabi that they obtained sufficient power to force a change of regime.

(*c*) The coalition of different interests which went to make up the Egyptian national movement was at its most cohesive in the last months of 1881 and the early part of 1882 when its strength was constantly being revived by the efforts of the British and French government to maintain Taufiq's failing authority. It also gained strength from a constant appeal to social groups which had previously had no part to play in the country's politics, notably the small landowners who were worried about the amount of land which was being seized for non-payment of debt following the introduction of a European type of mortgage law in 1876. Later, however, as the threat of European intervention became more real and as the leaders of the national movement became more successful in obtaining widespread popular support, many of those with important economic interests to defend left the movement and went over to the side of the Khedive and the Europeans.

(*d*) From a European point of view a distinction must be made between the interests and activities of the British and French bondholders and the British and French governments. In the first few months after the announcement of Egypt's bankruptcy it was the bondholders, not their governments, who managed to patch up their differences sufficiently to obtain a financial settlement which would protect all their interests. This was the so-called Goschen-Joubart arrangement of 1877. It was only when this arrangement threatened to break down that the British and French governments intervened more directly, first by instituting a Commission of Enquiry into Egypt's financial situation, then by forcing Ismail to accept a cabinet containing two European ministers to implement the recommendation of the report. The next year they intervened again when it seemed that he was about to alter the existing arrangements.

(*e*) Anglo-French cooperation hid important differences of aim. On the whole the French were more anxious to protect the interests of their bondholders, the British to prevent the situation deteriorating to such an extent that another power might intervene in Egypt and thus stand across the route to India. Nevertheless, both governments were able to act in concert, first in support of a programme of upholding whatever financial arrangement had been made on the bondholder's behalf, then in 1882, in seeking to strengthen the authority of Egypt's ruler against the national movement. It was this last policy which led directly to the British occupation.

(*f*) Finally, the events of the years 1875 to 1882, cutting as they do across a period of rapid economic and social change, help to expose the essential nature of the transformation then taking place. The nature of the links which bound the Egyptian economy to that of Europe are clear; so too is the way in which they were reinforced by the presence of powerful groups within Egypt. Again, the composition of the national movement shows the extent of hostility to European encroachment present in almost all sections of Egyptian society, just as it also reveals something of the division between those who were prepared to resist further foreign intervention by force if necessary and those who were not.

4. CONCLUSION

What I have been trying to describe in this case study is a process analysed in part by a number of theorists. Marx and Hobson have provided an account of the way in which Europe entered the non-European world by means of trade and the export of capital,[15] while Rosa Luxemburg has written of the economic and social dislocation which this caused.[16] Baran and others have described the process by which a country's enforced incorporation within the European economic system imposes a straitjacket on further development by forcing it to concentrate all its effort and resources on the export of primary produce.[17] Hobson and Hilferding pointed to the way in which the expansion of Europe led, inevitably, to the creation of movements of national liberation.[18]

But I have also been trying to suggest, if only by implication, that a study of relations between Egypt and Europe in the nineteenth century reveals a number of areas in which existing theories give little guidance. Three of these are of more than usual importance. The first concerns the role of the European state and, in particular, its relations with its own business community. To take only one example, in the period after 1815 Britain, and, to a lesser extent, France, consciously used state power to open up the Eastern Mediterranean to their own trade. This process was marked, among other things, by the Anglo-Turkish Commercial Convention of 1838, which established what was virtually free trade for British and French goods in the area. Again, each state was willing to use its local representation to intervene on behalf of its own nationals in their pursuit of profit. One way of characterizing these efforts might be to say that a primary aim of the capitalist state in the nineteenth century was to extend its own economic system—its own laws, its own commercial practices, its own pattern of relations between government and merchants and industrialists—out beyond its own borders. But too little work has been done on the relationship between economic and political power to be dogmatic. (See, however, Platt's 'Economic imperialism and the businessman: Britain and Latin America before 1914' [ch. XIII of *Studies in the Theory of Imperialism*].)

A second area in which there is little theoretical guidance concerns the nature of the Egyptian state. Rosa Luxemburg's characterization of it as an 'oriental despotism'[19] is certainly misleading. For one thing there is the fact that, throughout the nineteenth century, Egypt's rulers made continuous efforts to organize the machinery of government along more rational lines and to provide it with the expertise to carry out an increasing number of ever more complicated tasks. Again, in the sphere of ideology, there was the introduction into Egypt of the new and increasingly powerful European notions that growth was natural to an economy and that this growth could be encouraged by judicious state action. But did this also mean that Egypt was necessarily committed to a 'European' pattern of development along capitalist lines? The question remains an open one.

Finally, there are the problems posed by the attempt to analyse the changes produced in Egyptian society by the country's incorporation within a world economic system. How far, for instance, is it possible to talk about the creation of classes in Egypt before 1882? To some extent this is part of the general difficulty surrounding the use of such terms when talking about a pre-industrial society. It also stems from a situation peculiar to Egypt in which there was no definite category of 'landowner' and in which many of those who held agricultural estates were also merchants or bureaucrats or army officers or religious notables. In these circumstances it may be better to look at nineteenth-century Egyptian social development less in terms of classes, strictly defined, more in terms of the creation of a number of overlapping interest groups the members of which 'form a class only in so far as they have to carry on a common battle against another class'.[20]

Nevertheless, these problems aside, the broad lines of the developing relationship between Egypt and Europe in the nineteenth century are clear. Once Muhammad Ali's attempts at economic autarchy had been brought to an end, the international division of labour rapidly asserted itself and Egypt was drawn into the world capitalist system as a producer of industrial raw materials, as a market for manufactured goods, and as a field for the investment of European capital. This, in turn, had a profound effect on the structure of Egyptian society and led, among other things, to the emergence of a movement of national protest and then to foreign occupation. The pattern is simple: the loss of economic independence not only preceded the loss of political independence, it also prepared the way for it.

This article is reprinted from Roger Owen and Bob Sutcliffe (eds), *Studies in the Theory of Imperialism* (London, 1972). Reprinted with permission of the author.

NOTES

1. G. M. Trevelyan, *The Life of John Bright*, 2nd edn (London, Constable, 1925), p. 434.
2. Hobson, *Imperialism: a study* (London, Nisbet, 1902), p. 54–5, 108, 199.
3. *The End of Empire* (London, Gollancz, 1959), pp. 97, 118.
4. *Africa and the Victorians* (London, Macmillan, 1961), ch iv.
5. *Finance, Trade, and Politics* (London, Oxford Univ. Press, 1968), pt iii, ch vii.
6. cf. G. Baer, *A History of Landownership in Modern Egypt 1800–1950* (London, Oxford Univ. Press, 1962); A. E. Crouchley, *The Economic Development of Modern Egypt* (London, Longman, 1938); A-M. Hamza, *The Public Debt of Egypt 1854–1876* (Cairo, 1944); E. R. J. Owen, *Cotton and the Egyptian Economy 1820–1914* (London, Oxford Univ. Press, 1969); and S. J. Shaw, *Ottoman Egypt in the Age of the French Revolution* (Cambridge, Mass., Harvard Univ. Press, 1964).

7. cf. S. J. Shaw, *The Financial and Administrative Organisation and Development of Ottoman Egypt 1715–1798* (Princeton Univ. Press, 1958). pp. 62–3, 95 and A. Raymond, 'Essai de géographie des quartiers de résidence aristocratique au Caire au XVIIIème siècle'. *Journal of the Economic and Social History of the Orient*, 6 (1963), p. 84–5, 95.

8. D. Landes, *Bankers and Pashas* (London, Heinemann Education, 1958). pp. 47–68.

9. 'Les intérêts financiers et la question d'Egypt (1875–76)', *Revue Historique*, 224, July-Sept., 1960.

10. cf. A. Abdel-Malek, *Idéologie et Renaissance Nationale: L'Egypt Moderne* (Paris, 1969); I. Abu-Lughod, 'The transformation of the Egyptian elite: prelude to the Urabi revolt', *Middle East Journal*, 21, (Summer, 1967); G. Baer, *Studies in the Social History of Modern Egypt* (Univ. of Chicago Press, 1969); S. Nour Ed-Dine, 'Conditions des fellahs en Egypte', *Revue d'Islam* (1898).

11. Stanton, 7 Oct. 1869: FO 78/2093 (Public Record Office, London).

12. Malet, 18 May 1882: FO 78/3436.

13. Abdel-Malek, pp. 420–3.

14. cf. Abdel-Malek, ch 12, Bouvier, *op. cit*: P. J. Vatikiotis, *The Modern History of Egypt*, (London, Weidenfield & Nicolson, 1969), ch 6 and 7.

15. Marx, *Capital*, vol. i. pt viii, chs xxi and xxiii; Hobson, pp. 76–79.

16. Luxemburg, *The Accumulation of Capital* (London, Routledge, 1963), ch 29.

17. P. A. Baran, *The Political Economy of Growth* (New York, Monthly Review Press; 1962 edn) pp. 163 ff.

18. Hobson, p. 11; R. Hilferding, *Das Finanzcapital* (Vienna, 1923), pp. 384–9.

19. Luxemburg, p. 358.

20. Marx. *Pre-capitalist Economic Formations*, with an introduction by E. Hobsbawn (London, Lawrence and Wishart, 1964), p. 132.

War and Society under the Young Turks, 1908–18

FEROZ AHMAD

Anyone seeking an appropriate period in order to study the impact of war on society is unlikely to find one more suitable for this purpose than the decade 1908–18 in the history of the late Ottoman Empire. This decade witnessed political strife, violence, and war on an unprecedented scale; throughout these ten years, and beyond to at least 1922, there was hardly a year when the empire was at peace. The Turks were no strangers to warfare, having built their state and empire on the foundations of conquest extending to three continents. Later, they were forced to engage in a long rear-guard action as European armies pushed them back towards the borders of their original state in Asia Minor. In a sense, Ottoman society was already organized as a military society and therefore one should not expect any substantial impact during the decade under discussion. In fact, there was a dramatic difference in the way society was mobilized for war by the Young Turks, reflecting the radical character of the new regime spawned by the constitutional revolution of 1908. The impact of the new regime is almost comparable to that of the revolutionary governments in France after 1789, especially the Jacobins. In any case, the most radical wing of the Young Turks, the Unionists—members of the Committee of Union and Progress (CUP) which led the constitutional movement—were deeply inspired by the Jacobin example and tried to emulate their policies, though not with similar success.

Following the establishment of a constitutional regime by the Young Turks in July 1908, they were confronted with a number of crises which threatened the new regime. Bulgaria threw off the authority of the Sultan and declared itself independent on September 5, 1908; next day, Austria announced the annexation of Bosnia-Herzegovina, provinces she had occupied in 1878. On the same day, Crete announced its decision to unite with Greece. There was little that the Sublime Porte could do but protest to the Great Powers who had signed the Treaty of Berlin in 1878, since the first two acts were a violation of that treaty, while the status of Crete was also guaranteed by the Powers. The Powers, however, informed Istanbul that they would not interfere on behalf of Turkey. As a result, the Turks were forced to fend for themselves. In the next three years there were rebellions in the Yemen, Macedonia, and Albania requiring military intervention. By 1911, the Turks were at war with Italy in Libya, abandoning that province to Rome when they were attacked by a coalition of Balkan states in October, 1912. The Balkan Wars of 1912–13 were a disaster on a scale that neither the Ottoman general staff nor the people had imagined possible. Not only did the Ottoman Empire lose virtually all its European possessions to the enemy, but invading armies penetrated to the outskirts of the capital and threatened the very existence of the Empire.

Istanbul did not fall, and the Turks even regained some territory in Thrace in the second Balkan War. But it is impossible to exaggerate the impact of these military and diplomatic disasters on the Young Turks. Some amongst them had become so demoralized and so full of despair that they were convinced that the Empire could survive only under Western tutelage. Others, notably the Unionists, believed that the Empire could be saved through a program of radical reform. They were also convinced that, in order to buy time to implement such a program, the Porte had to become a member of one of the two alliances that divided Europe, preferably the Triple Entente. Neutrality meant isolation, and isolation, as the Porte's experience during the Balkan Wars had demonstrated, would spell total disaster in another major conflict. Therefore, the Young Turks tried to end their diplomatic isolation by seeking alliances in Europe during the brief interlude without war between the summer of 1913 and August, 1914. With great difficulty, they finally managed to sign an alliance with Germany on August 2, just as the First World War broke out. Initially, Istanbul observed a precarious armed neutrality which lasted three months; by November, she was forced by circumstances, not completely in her control, to enter the War. For the next four years, Turkey was engaged in a struggle that required the mobilization of all its resources, human and material.[1]

II

Confronted with such a series of crises, any regime would have been hard put to provide suitable responses. The old regime of the Sultan would have succumbed to partition under international pressure after making token protests, and would have accepted the *fait accompli*, so long as the regime was permitted to survive in some form or other. Its interests were restricted to those of the Ottoman family and a very small elite that monopolized power in the Palace and in the upper reaches of the civil and military bureaucracy. The Unionists, who constituted the most radical wing of the Young Turk movement, represented what may be described as Gramsci's 'subordinate class.' In the late Ottoman Empire, this class had become politically organized and articulate, demanding a place for Ottoman Muslims in the social and economic structure, a constitutional state, and a new intellectual and moral order to go with it. Thus, immediately after the constitution was restored, the Unionists began to discuss the need to carry out a social revolution. They talked about transforming their society to bring it to the level of advanced societies of the West or Japan which had become a source of inspiration for them. They were proud to consider themselves as the 'Japan' of the Near East (Ahmad, 1969: 23, n. 1). The setbacks they suffered as a result of the crises and the defeats in war forced the Unionists to push for reform. Only after they had seized power during the Balkan Wars through the *coup d'état* of January, 1913, could they implement a program of reform and reorganization. Even then, they could not go very far without running into the barrier of the capitulations, unequal treaties which restricted Ottoman sovereignty and which the Great Powers refused to abrogate. The outbreak of war in 1914 provided the Porte with the opportunity to abrogate the capitulations unilaterally without the fear of intervention from Europe. These hated treaties were abolished in September, 1914, and the Turks were finally masters of their house, free to guide their own destiny.

Even before they had acquired the power and the autonomy to transform their society, the Unionists introduced new methods into politics. The restoration of the constitution had been marked by an explosion of popular sentiment for the new regime. Some of this may have been spontaneous, but much of it was organized by the CUP wherever it had its clubs. Thereafter, organized crowds and mass meetings, addressed by popular figures in the Committee, such as Hüseyin Cahid, the journalist, Riza Tevfik, the 'philosopher,' or Halide Edip, the feminist novelist, soon came to play an important role in the political activity of the CUP. This was especially true during crises and in wartime.

The Unionists used urban masses for the first time when they organized boycotts against Austria's annexationist policies and Greece's union with Crete (Quataert, 1983; Yavuz, 1978). Later, during the Balkan Wars, organized demonstrations were used to keep off balance a government hostile to the CUP. Finally, a popular demonstration was organized against the anti-unionist government of Kâmil Pasha (thought to be arriving at a consensus to sign an ignoble peace with the victorious Balkan coalition) in preparation for the coup of January 23, 1913.

It is worth emphasizing that the initiative to mobilize urban crowds and use them for political ends came from the Committee of Union and Progress and not from the government. In fact, the governments of the period were opposed to popular participation in politics, fearing that such activity might provide the foreign powers with the pretext to intervene. Nevertheless, the CUP organized boycotts against Austrian and Greek enterprises, and the boycott of Austrian goods played a significant role in forcing Vienna to pay compensation for the territories it annexed.

Defeat in war, or even a major diplomatic setback, forces the defeated society to assess its strengths and weaknesses. There is a tendency to try to make better use of existing resources, to remove defects in the internal fabric—in the social structure, in the instrument of power, and, above all, in the armed forces. Talk of reform becomes the order of the day. Defeat can also trigger an imperialist response as a way to seek compensation in another area. This was the case with Russia after the Crimean War, and with France under the Third Republic. In Turkey, too, the rise of an aggressive nationalism which took the form of pan-Turkism or pan-Turanism, may be seen in similar terms. But it was a weak impulse and did not dominate politics, except briefly in 1917–18 during the revolution in Russia, simply because the Ottoman state lacked the power and the means necessary to implement an aggressive policy. Instead, defeats, first in the Balkan Wars and then during the World War, led to the rise of a populist movement inspired in part by the Russian Narodniks. This movement, known as 'To the People' (*Halka doğru*), began to emphasize a Turkish nationalism rooted in Anatolia rather than the Balkans, so recently lost, or Central Asia, under Russian occupation.

III

After this brief introduction, it is time to look more closely at how the Young Turks responded to the problems of mobilizing society for actual war. The Turco-Italian conflict broke out on September 29, 1911. The government of Ibrahim Hakki Pasha was taken by surprise and resigned. The new government responded in the usual bureaucratic manner: it tried to parry the Italian blow 'by raining telegrams upon its ambassadors and diplomatic notes upon the Powers' (Pacha, 1924: 136). But, as usual, the European powers refused to lift a finger in defense of Ottoman sovereignty.[2]

Meanwhile, the CUP had been making preparations to hold its annual congress in Salonika, the site of its headquarters until the city was lost to Greece in 1912. On the day the Italian ultimatum was delivered (September 28), delegates from all over the empire had begun to arrive. The issue of war naturally became the principal concern of the Congress. On October 5, after days of heated discussion, the Committee issued a manifesto inaugurating the Committee of National Defense (CND—*Mudafaa-i Milliye Cemiyeti*). This body was composed of eight members from the Salonika CUP, the organization that had provided the leadership of the constitutional movement both before and after 1908. Generally speaking, the CND's main function was to aid the war effort in any possible way. But it was an unofficial body, acting independently of the government in Istanbul, which soon became openly hostile to the CUP. The inspiration for this populist method of mobilizing for war came directly from the example of the Jacobin Republic of 1792–94. However much the Unionists may have wanted to emulate the Jacobins, their actions could only be superficial. They lacked the support of any independent mass organization like that of the *sans-culottes*, though they did use the guilds, like those of the porters and the boatmen, to build the semblance of a popular power base. More importantly, they did not attempt to win over the peasantry by distributing land as the Jacobins had done, thus rejecting the classical path of the bourgeois revolution, of which the French Revolution was the archetype (Soboul, 1965: 163–64).[3]

Nevertheless, the analogy of the French Revolution and the Jacobins continued to be applied to Unionist methods of mobilization, especially after they seized power in January, 1913. The British ambassador observed in his dispatch of February 5:

> I have the honour to note that the Committee of Union and Progress, which styles the Mahmoud Shevket Pasha Cabinet as the 'Cabinet of National Defence,' has also formed a committee of national defence on the lines of the French revolutionaries of 1793 and the Communists in 1870. They have issued rousing appeals to the 'nation' and all parties to rally to the cry of the 'country in danger,' and have declared the whole Ottoman nation in a state of mobilisation ... The committee of national defence ... is raising subscriptions and organising the country for a 'last ditch' effort ... The new Sheik-ul-Islam [Esat Efendi] has sent a religious appeal, for the defence of the Moslem fatherland, to his subordinates in the provinces, while committee agents have been preaching a holy war in Saint Sophia and other mosques (Pacha, 1924: 136).[4]

The Committee of National Defense remained an unofficial body, without any power, until the Unionist coup. In late 1912, the position of the CUP, which won the fraudulent election in the spring, had become so precarious that it was threatened with destruction by an opposition movement with support in the army. The disaster of the Balkan War gave the CUP a new lease of life, enabling it to appear as the only body with a program and the will to fight.

On Friday, January 31, 1913, a week after the Unionists formed the cabinet with General Mahmud Şevket Pasha as grand *vezir*, they held a meeting at the *darülfünün*, the university in Istanbul, to formally establish the CND. Prior to the meeting, the CUP had issued a proclamation inviting the opposition as well as the Armenian political organizations—the Dashnaks and the Hunchak—to cooperate in the defense effort, declaring that the entire nation had to be in a state of total mobilization in order to meet the threat from the enemy. The formation of the CND under these circumstances suggests that the Unionists intended to undertake tasks that would touch upon almost every aspect of Ottoman society. The primary goal was to raise volunteers for the army and money for the war effort, but sub-committees were formed to take charge of sanitation and health or to carry out propaganda. Thereafter, sub-committees were created on an ad hoc basis to meet new needs and solve problems as they arose. During the First World War, some of these committees became deeply involved in economic activity in order to create what was described as a 'national economy.'[5]

It should come as no surprise to us to find that the inevitable outcome of the CUP's involvement in the economy was widespread corruption. Patronage was one way to reward and enrich loyal party members and to create the bourgeois class missing from the Ottoman-Muslim social structure. It would be more accurate to say that rather than creating a new class out of nothing, the Unionists were providing economic opportunities for established groups and attempting to instil in them the spirit of capitalism. Being a Unionist naturally improved one's chances of benefiting from patronage. A reading of the diary of an American diplomat in wartime Istanbul gives us an idea of what was going on in this sphere. On August 6, 1915, Lewis Einstein noted that, 'The Committee of National Defense is now making money rapidly by its monopolies of sugar and petrol *et cetera.* Their declared intention is to accumulate a capital which they can afterwards use to get the trade of the country in Moslem hands.' On the 17th, he observed that, 'The Committee ... has monopolized all commodities and doles them out at enormous profit' (1918: 218, 243).[6]

The corruption and profiteering led to tension between Şeyhülislam Hayri Efendi and Ismet Bey, Prefect of Istanbul. The cause seems to have been the scarcity of bread in the capital while the sub-committee responsible for this commodity was said to be making 'four thousand [Turkish] pounds daily.' Şükrü Bey, the Minister of Education, was asked to investigate the matter, but it seems that he too was involved in the profiteering! (Einstein, 1918: 247). Not missing a trick, the CND ordered M. Weyl, director of the French Tobacco Regie, to sell tobacco to the Ottoman army through the agency of the committee. Weyl complied. But instead of the tobacco being sold to the army at regulated prices, it was sold in the towns at great profit. The army blamed M. Weyl whom the CND denounced as a French spy, forcing him to leave the country (Einstein, 1918: 260–61).

Wartime necessity forced the Unionists to be creative and rational in regulating the affairs of state at every level. Money was raised at home and abroad, and missions were sent off to distant India and Egypt for this purpose. At home, the most common method was public collection, which not only raised substantial sums of money for various purposes, but also raised public consciousness about politics and foreign affairs. For example, the Fleet Committee (*Dkonan a Cemiyeti*) was reinstituted in February, 1914; it had been originally set up in June, 1909, in response to the crisis with Greece over the island of Crete. But it became defunct and was revived in order to collect funds for the purchase of ships to meet the Greek naval challenge in the Aegean Sea. Branches were set up in almost every town, and government officials were expected to give up a month's salary for the cause. Even European companies were being asked to contribute, and those with business interests in the Empire did so. Much of the money used to order the two battleships from British shipyards came from public subscription. That is why Great Britain's decision to confiscate these vessels on July 31, 1914, before the outbreak of war and before the signing of the alliance with Germany, aroused great indignation among the Turkish people who saw it as 'an act of piracy' (Gilbert, 1971: 193).[7] After this event, it was easier to manipulate public opinion against Great Britain and in favor of Germany, and the 'purchase' of the two German ships, the *Goeben* and the *Breslau*, was greeted with jubilation, as though an insult had been avenged.

Propaganda and intelligence came to be taken more seriously as a result of war. The *Teşkilat-ı Mahsusa* (the 'Special Organization') had been set up by the CUP in 1911 and had played an important role in organizing resistance to the Italians in Libya. This body continued to grow during the war in the Balkans and came into its own after the Unionist seizure of power. On the advice of Riza Bey, the former *mutassarif* of Gumülcine, a town recently lost to the Serbs, the functions of this organization were broadened. Guerilla bands were formed from the local Muslim population of Macedonia, very much in keeping with the tradition of the region, as a way of keeping up resistance while Istanbul negotiated. The *Teşkilat* became more active in collecting intelligence, reconnoitering, and carrying out acts of sabotage, even assassinations. The CUP had used assassins in order to achieve its political aims both before and after 1908; that too was in keeping with the political traditions of the Balkans where the Committee was born. When Noel Buxton, President of the Balkan Committee, arrived in Sofia in mid-September, 1914, the Istanbul press became paranoid, convinced that he had come to intrigue against the Porte. There was speculation that London, using the good offices of the Balkan Committee, was attempting to resurrect a new Balkan alliance against Istanbul, hoping to purchase Bulgaria with the offer of Edirne and Thrace. The Unionists responded by dispatching a Special Organization assassination team to kill Buxton, 'whose name is enough to spell hostility to Turkey,'

Tasvir-i Efkâr had noted on September 17, 1914. The attempt on Buxton's life failed and he was only wounded; but *Tasvir-i Efkâr*, believing that Buxton was dead, opined that 'he had received his punishment,' marking 'the end of an enemy of Islam' (Oct. 16, 1914).

During the period of armed neutrality, the CND was placed under the supervision of the War Ministry under Enver Pasha, no doubt to strengthen the hand of the war minister against his civilian rivals within the CUP. This body was no longer to concern itself with anything political; instead, it was to devote all its efforts to advancing agriculture, industry, commerce, and education. And as though to add prestige to this body, the Sultan was made president, and the heir apparent a member of the board of directors in Istanbul (*Tanin*, Aug. 1, 2, 1914). Throughout the war, the CUP, using a variety of affiliates of the CND, continued its efforts to organize the Ottoman Muslim masses and introduced all sorts of innovations to Turkish society.

The CND, working with the Red Crescent, the Muslim counterpart of the Red Cross, organized orphanages in Anatolia to teach trades and modern farming methods to the ever-increasing number of war orphans. In June, 1915, the government passed a law to establish educational institutions, scientific and technical, to meet the needs of orphans. The budget in these institutions was to be met by taxes on alcoholic beverages and tobacco, as well as by taxes on letters and telegrams. War also caused much destitution among the families of soldiers killed in battle. An association of women was set up to help such families, and its president was the wife of a prominent Unionist, İsmail Canbulat. Members of the committee included the daughter of the German general, Liman von Sanders, as well as the wives of other Unionists and high officials. Whatever the committees may have lacked, they did not lack prestige, provided in abundance by members of the Unionist elite!

IV

It is not at all clear how much solace such organizations brought to the population suffering from the hardships of war. But one may conclude from all these initiatives that the Young Turks recognized the need for social peace if the Empire was to survive a long and terrible war. The situation of the Ottoman Empire was in many ways far worse than that of any of the other belligerents, and it was least equipped to wage war on such a scale. The Turks may have had an empire, but it was an empire dominated and exploited by all the Great Powers of Europe and totally dependent on them. The dependent character of the Empire was soon exposed in a dramatic manner as Europe prepared to go to war in August, 1914; the Ottoman economy was completely paralyzed.

The first consequence of the outbreak of the crisis in Europe in late July, 1914, was the closure of the foreign-controlled bourse in Istanbul and Izmir, with disastrous effect on the commerce of both cities. There was panic on the market, and the Porte was forced to intervene on July 31, suspending all transactions in transferable commodities. Foreign-owned shipping companies, operating in the coastal waters of the empire, suspended their services, disrupting all imports and exports. Insurance companies, again all foreign-owned, refused to insure goods that they believed might be confiscated as contraband of war by belligerent powers. The premium for goods that they were willing to insure rose sharply, naturally affecting prices for the consumer. All these factors led to shortages and an explosion in prices; to make matters worse, the situation was exploited by merchants and traders who were still predominantly non-Muslim. This aggravated the chauvinism among Muslims and Turks.

The outbreak of war between the Great Powers during the first week of August increased the panic in Istanbul. There was a run on the banks—again all European-owned—which were rapidly running short of cash because no more was available from their headquarters in Europe. The people with money stopped making deposits, aggravating the crisis. On August 4, the government intervened, and a moratorium on payments went into effect.

People in the cities, especially in the capital, speculated that there would be shortages of all commodities and began to hoard, as did the shopkeepers. Naturally prices rose out of control, particularly food prices; by August 5, the price of bread in Istanbul had risen from 5 to 55 para.[8] Faced with shortages in the capital, the Porte began to requisition grain in the provinces and made arrangements to import wheat from Romania. The social-democrat revolutionary, Alexander Israel Helphand, better known as Parvus, who was residing in Istanbul at the time, is said to have made a fortune by organizing the import of Romanian grain for the Porte.

The government tried to regulate prices and stamp out hoarding, but with little success. Despite raids by the police in the capital, the press continued to complain that shopkeepers were charging whatever they wished. There are reports of fines being imposed, but that did not deter the profiteers. Apart from the price of bread, which kept rising, the price of potatoes rose 40 per cent during the first week of August; sugar imported from Austria rose 200 per cent, and kerosene 100 per cent. If the price of imported commodities rose sharply, that of local products that could neither be exported nor brought to the capital fell equally sharply. The fruit harvest was bountiful in the Marmara-Aegean region that summer, but it remained unsold. Bursa peaches and İzmir grapes rotted for the want of buyers. The silk industry of Bursa suffered a similar fate.

The situation in the capital may have been bad. But it seems that the situation in the provincial towns, about which there is a dearth of information because the local press has yet to be studied, was much worse. But the consular reports of the foreign powers provide a sketch of the provincial scene. There too, the European crisis and the outbreak of war led to economic paralysis. In Baghdad, where Anglo-Indian trade was dominant, all business came to a standstill. The same was true for towns in Syria as well as Anatolian commercial centers such as Adana. Money was in such short supply in the provinces that even the staff in a number of American consulates could not be paid their salaries. The situation of the treasury in Istanbul was equally critical; the French loan of TL 35,200,000, negotiated earlier in the summer, had been virtually exhausted, and the Finance Ministry was left with a mere TL 92,000 as petty cash on August 3, 1914. The bankruptcy of the treasury became an important factor in bringing about Turkey's entry into the war on the German side three months later.

The Turks had long been aware of their total dependence on, and subordination to, the Great Powers. The outbreak of war served only to confirm the depth and extent of their subjugation. Western domination over the empire was maintained through the institution of unequal treaties known as the capitulations. The Sublime Porte, especially after 1908, had made great efforts to negotiate the abrogation of these treaties, but with no success. Whatever their differences, the Powers were unanimous about maintaining their control over the Turks. The outbreak of hostilities prevented them from intervening in Turkey's affairs and provided the Unionist government with the opportunity to denounce unilaterally the hated capitulations. Thus, on September 9, 1914, the ambassadors of all the Powers received a note informing them that privileges acquired through the capitulations would no longer be recognized on October 1. The Ottoman Empire had become a sovereign state at last.[9]

V

One has only to read the Turkish press of the period to sense the great psychological impact of this unilateral act on the population at large. It seemed as though Turkey, far from being an empire, was a country that had just been liberated from generations of colonial rule; that is how oppressive the capitulations had been. There was a feeling of euphoria which the Unionists exploited by organizing marches and rallies, and making patriotic speeches in the main squares of the capital. September 9 came to be regarded as a national holiday and was given the same status as July 23, the day the constitution was restored. Here was another event—the recapture of Edirne and the 'purchase' of the two German ships being earlier occasions—that enhanced the collective charisma of the CUP and increased its popularity among the Muslims of the empire.

Freed from the restraints of the capitulations, the Unionists set about the task of nationalizing or Turkifying their state and society by eliminating cosmopolitan elements. Ironically, this process gathered momentum precisely at a moment when the empire was threatened with destruction by Allied forces at Gallipoli and the Russian army in eastern Anatolia. Just to give a few examples of this process: the official news agency was described as 'national' rather than 'Ottoman'; Turkish was prescribed as the language to be used by the post office, as well as the language to be used in all communications with the Ministry of Finance. This was followed by a decree requiring all shop signs to be in Turkish. These messages helped to instil a sense of national awareness in the population. But some ideologues among the Unionists understood that Turkish nationalism without strong socio-economic foundations would be a futile experiment. In August, 1917, Yusuf Akçura, one of the most important nationalist thinkers of the period, again issued the warning to the Turks that if they failed 'to produce among themselves a bourgeois class by profiting from [the example of] European capitalism, the chances of survival of a Turkish society composed only of peasants and officials [would] be very slim' (quoted in Berkes, 1964: 426).[10]

This warning had been heeded, and towards the end of the war, thanks to a variety of wartime measures to encourage commercial and industrial activity, it was possible to observe the emergence of a 'national economy.' Not only was there a nascent Turkish bourgeoisie to complement this development, but also a small working class. The author of an article entitled 'The Phase of Capitalism is Beginning' noted this fact and remarked that 'this state of affairs could not fail to provoke conflict between capital and labor in our country' (*İktisadiyat Mecmuası*, Nov. 8, 1917: 1–2). There may be some exaggeration in this observation, but it aptly describes the great transformation that had taken place in Turkish society during this brief period of ten years. Since 1914, the government's principal concern may have been the war, but its preoccupation with economic matters was never far behind.

Anyone perusing the press of wartime Istanbul is bound to be struck by the amount of column space that was devoted to social and economic issues. Despite the war, or perhaps because of it, the problems of agriculture, commerce, or industry were always in the forefront; in fact some journals were founded specifically for this purpose, *İktisadiyat Mecmuası* (*Journal of Economics*), published in February, 1915, being the most notable. Alongside articles on the military situation, there were invariably articles on all sorts of issues that affected the economic life of the country and the war effort. The size and quality of the harvest in various provinces was always worthy of attention; so were the measures taken by the peasants, the authorities, or even experts brought from Germany or Austria-Hungary to combat vermin, which seemed a constant threat to crops and cattle. There are reports of meteorological stations being set up in the capital and in the provinces for more accurate forecasting, and discussions of new laws for the preservation of forests. Chambers of commerce were being founded by the 'new bourgeoisie' in towns around Anatolia and organizations set up to promote this or that industry. One also reads reports of local fairs where peasants were shown new implements and encouraged to adopt modern techniques. In the past, students had been sent to Europe to acquire a western education; during the war, workers were also being sent to Germany to learn to use modern machines. From all this evidence, it is no exaggeration to conclude that wartime Turkey was in the process of a social and economic renaissance.

VI

Ottoman-Turkish society paid a heavy price for this renaissance, though the burden was shared unequally by the various segments. A small minority, the 'nascent bourgeoisie,' derived almost all the benefits of this transformation, retaining the lion's share of the wealth accumulated from wartime profiteering. It is no coincidence that the Koç family, still the owner of the foremost commercial-industry holding company in Turkey today, traces its rise from modest circumstances during the First World War.[11]

The people who bore the heaviest burden were the urban consumers and the peasants. The consumers paid exorbitant prices for shoddy goods and enriched the new class of war profiteers; the '*332 tuccarı* or 'the merchants of 1916,' as they were called, became notorious for their exactions. Such was the popular outcry against their activities, the government was forced to set up commissions of investigation and pass laws to control prices. The peasantry, on the other hand, having no collective voice that could be heard in the capital, suffered silently though not without bitterness and hatred towards the state.

The wars had the most detrimental effect on agriculture. Not only were the peasants conscripted and sent off to fight, but their animals—buffaloes, donkeys, and horses—were also requisitioned. Thus the task of tilling the soil became even more formidable. Ottoman agriculture had suffered, not from the lack of land, but from the scarcity of labor, and constant warfare made the problem more acute. There was great disruption in the countryside during the Balkan Wars, and again in August, 1914, when the Porte declared general mobilization. Once Turkey became a belligerent and had to prepare to fight a long war, the Unionist government responded by virtually legalizing forced labor in order to maintain agricultural production, enforcing these measures ruthlessly throughout the war. With the men being killed and wounded in the different theaters of war, women and chil were forced to assume some of the heaviest tasks on the home front. O cannot talk about the 'liberation' of peasant women because they alway worked, though perhaps not as hard as they were forced to work during the war. But there was a certain amount of 'liberation'—if 'liberation' is the appropriate term—for urban Turkish women, especially in the capital, as a result of war.

Ever since the revolution of 1908, the Young Turks had attempted to involve Turkish middle-class women in activity outside the home. There was a conviction, often expressed in polemical articles, that Turkish society could not be transformed until women were permitted to play an appropriate role. The new regime had tried to improve the situation, but with limited success in the major cities like Istanbul and İzmir. The government opened schools, trained women teachers, and prepared better text books. The liberal Islamic establishment close to the CUP interpreted Islam progressively for this purpose. Supported by Sultan Mehmet Reşad and the Şeyhülislâm, the *ulema*—the doctors of Islamic law and theology—argued that Muslim women were not being treated as the Prophet Muhammad had intended them to be, and that He had also opposed polygamy, as quotations from the *Quran* demonstrated. But Turkish-Muslim society as a whole remained conservative, and in some towns of Anatolia a man speaking to a woman in public was still liable to be fined and the woman flogged.

Wartime necessity forced Turkish society to utilize female labor on a substantial scale. Women began to work in factories, and middle-class women in offices or establishments like the new telephone exchange, until then the domain of non-Muslim women. Women had become such an active part of the labor force in the greater Istanbul region that an organization, whose name may be translated roughly as 'The Society for Muslim Working Women,' was set up in the capital in August, 1916. It had three branches: in Istanbul, Pera, and Üsküdar, which gives us some idea where their working places were concentrated. Its president, no doubt serving in an honorary capacity, was Enver Pasha's wife, Naciye Sultan, while the Pasha himself was listed as a patron.[12]

The Istanbul daily, *Tanin*, commenting on the founding of this body, noted that thousands of women were doing jobs they had never conceived of doing before the war. This was especially true in Istanbul. The object of this society was to publicize this activity, to give it official support in order to make it more acceptable—thus the patronage from the highest circles of Turkish society—and to organize and promote work for women by opening more work places (Aug. 12, 1916). The initial aim was to provide work for another ten thousand women.

Peasant women played an even more vital role, particularly during the harvest of 1916. Tekinalp eulogized their contribution, observing that:

> While the men found themselves at the front struggling heroically for the very life and existence of the country, the women have remained at home struggling equally hard with all their might to provide food for the country and guaranteeing its economic future. In several places, women have succeeded through their labour in not allowing the shortage of men to be felt.
>
> This activity of peasant women [he observed] is to be noted above all in the province of Konya. Semih Bey, the *vali* of Konya, had decided to build a monument to perpetuate the memory of this noble activity by Turkish women during the historic epoch through which we are passing (1916: 1–2).[13]

Despite the imposition of forced labor and the massive contribution of peasant women to agriculture, the area under cultivation continued to decline throughout the war. When the Chamber discussed a new law for compulsory agricultural service in February, 1917, the minister reported that the area under cultivation had declined dramatically from 60 million *donums* in 1913–14 to 30 million in 1914–15, and to 24 million *donums* in 1916. The government hoped to restore cultivation to 30 million *donums* in 1917.[14] The Unionists intended to meet the acute shortage of labor by mechanizing agriculture, and farm machinery as well as Austrian and German experts were imported for this purpose. This was bound to have a great impact on peasant society in Anatolia.

The Unionists were in fact trying to carry out a structural change in agriculture, which undermined the position of the small peasant. In 1916, the government passed a decree introducing the regimentation of farming. The German economic review, *Wirtschaftszeitung der Zentralmachte* wrote that:

> The farmers will not be able to sow and work as they please, but everything will be done in common under State supervision. The State will supply all appliances, manure, and other necessaries in sufficient quantities, and even labour where required. By this means one of the greatest drawbacks of Turkish agriculture, 'small farming' as it is called, will be abolished. In Anatolia the land is very much broken up among small owners, hence intensive cultivation is difficult, but it will now be made possible by the nationalisation of agriculture and the joint cultivation of the soil (Oct. 16, 1916; quoted in *Daily Review of the Foreign Press*, Oct. 28, 1916).

Thus, despite the exploitation of the vast majority of the peasantry, a small class of prosperous 'middle peasants' began to emerge, at least in western Anatolia where capitalist agriculture was most developed. An interview with Dr. Nâzim, a high-ranking Unionist, provides an illustration of this phenomenon.

Dr. Nâzim, who had just been instrumental in setting up an association in İzmir for 'the moral and physical improvement of the peasantry,' claimed that the war had enriched the population of Turkey, and this was especially true of the region around İzmir.

> In nearly all parts of the town one can see traces of our economic revival. The coffee-houses which used to line the quayside before the war have made way for shops. Wherever you look you see signs of newly formed limited companies. The value of money has fallen to such an extent that our peasants, who have made fortunes through the unwarranted rise in the price of food . . . , can pay three liras for a pair of stockings for their daughters (1918: 2–3).

Wartime policies resulted in strengthening the position of the landlords who had emerged as a political force following the Land Code of 1858. Their position was further bolstered by the newly created 'middle peasant.' Both groups benefited by acquiring lands left vacant by peasants killed in war, and by the expulsion and massacre of Greek and Armenian peasants. However, most of the vacated land was resettled by Turkish peasants fleeing from the Balkans and the Caucasus.

In contrast, the position of the Turkish peasantry as a whole deteriorated sharply. How did they respond to their increasing exploitation and oppression? In most cases they seemed to bear their loss with a large dose of fatalism. But sources also reveal a massive increase in banditry and brigandage, not new phenomena in Anatolia. News about this activity is abundant in the press of wartime Istanbul, especially after political and military censorship was lifted in June, 1918. Thereafter, the press carried reports of bandits who were hampering the vital activity of the summer harvest as the peasants were constantly threatened by marauding bands.[15] Many of the brigands were deserters from the army, and there are reports of Turkish deserters seeking refuge with Greek bands in the Black Sea region. By 1918, brigandage (*eşkiyalik*) had become so widespread that small provincial towns were insecure, and public life was threatened.

The situation became sufficiently serious for the Talat Pasha government, which came to power in February, 1917, to appoint İsmail Canbulat, a retired officer and dedicated Unionist, Minister of the Interior. He was expected to deal with this problem energetically, but he too failed to crush the bands. He resigned in September, 1918, after bandits had attacked the train at Bandirma for the second time. He complained that the government was simply not strong enough to cope with the situation (Cavit, 1945). After the war, the nationalist movement inherited the problem of a disgruntled and alienated peasantry and therefore had to rely on the traditional notables to mobilize the countryside. This proved to be an unfortunate legacy for the Republican regime after 1923, as it prevented virtually any reform that threatened the interests of the landlords from being passed in the Assembly.

Another important contribution made by wartime Unionist practices to the Republican regime was the role that the state began to play in social and economic engineering. The Young Turks, including the Unionist wing, intended to follow, as closely as circumstances permitted, the path of individual initiative and free enterprise in creating a modern capitalist economy. But the situation created by a long war forced the state to intervene in order to guarantee the very survival of its people. The ruling party—the Committee of Union and Progress—and the state became involved in every sphere of social and economic activity, from organizing companies to protecting consumers. The proponents of capitalism, inspired and reassured by Germany's wartime example, recognized the necessity of state intervention in a backward society. They began to talk of a 'new' economic model, which was described as '*devlet iktisadiyati*,' or state economy, in which the state would assume those responsibilities that private enterprise could not or would not. These ideas were adopted by the republic in the 1930s, becoming '*devletcilik*' or *étatisme*, one of the 'six arrows' of Kemalist ideology.

One must also consider how and to what extent the mentality of Turkish Muslims was altered by the events of this decade, especially under the impact of war. This matter needs to be studied and, like so many topics in modern Turkish history, awaits its historian. For the moment, one can only note the observations of a contemporary. Dr. Riza Nur, who played a very active oppositional role in the Young Turk period and was also an acute observer of events and trends, remembered how conservative his society had been as the constitutional period commenced. When Riza Tevfik proposed in parliament the introduction of European time, the conservatives came out in opposition claiming that 'the abolition of our time [based on the movements of the sun] will mean the end of prayer.' When the voters of Samsun saw a picture of their deputy in a hat, they said reproachfully: 'The deputy for Samsun went to Europe and wore a hat. He became an infidel. The dirty pig.' Ten years later, in 1919, Riza Nur returned to his old constituency, Sinop on the Black Sea, after his long exile in Europe. He was apprehensive about his reception, especially as he now had a European wife. But he was pleasantly surprised when people asked: 'Did you wear a hat, did your wife move around without a veil?' Riza Nur noted that ideas had changed greatly in the ten years and remarked how attendance to the Alaettin Mosque in Sinop had dropped sharply (Nur, 1967: 281–82). One can see how the ground had been prepared for the reforms of Mustafa Kemal Atatürk.

VII

Such, in broad outlines, is the sketch of war and society during the Young Turk decade. Despite the great transformation that took place during this brief period, the historian must resist the temptation to exaggerate the accomplishments of the Young Turks. Much of Anatolia and Turkish society remained unchanged, indeed untouched, by the reforms, because of the failure to ameliorate the lot of the peasantry, the vast majority of the population. Nevertheless, the reform of society was sufficient to create classes, both in the towns and in the countryside, with a strong commitment to the survival of a Turkish nation state in Anatolia, 'discovered' during the war. These classes sided with the nationalists in the struggle against imperialism and in the civil war against the old regime. They were the dynamic element in Turkish society, the creation of wartime policies. The *Tanin* recognized this and acknowledged the benefits war had brought, liberating the Turks from the strait-jacket the Powers had forced them to wear (Sept. 19, 1917). A German journalist, who spent the years 1915–16 in Istanbul, provides a fitting conclusion to a discussion of the impact of war on Turkish society:

> The war with its enormous intellectual activity has certainly brought all the political and economic resources of the Turks ... to the highest possible stage of development, and we ought not to be surprised if we often find that measures, whether of a beneficial or injurious character, are characterised by modern exactness, clever technicality, and thoroughness of conception ... No one can doubt that it will enormously intensify zeal in the fight for the existence of the Turkey of the future, freed from jingoistic outgrowths, once more come to its senses and confined to its own proper sphere of activity, Anatolia, the core of the Empire (Stuermer, 1917: 1–2).

This article is reprinted from *Review* XI, 2, Spring 1988, pp. 265–288. Reprinted by permission of *Review*.

NOTES

1. For the diplomacy of this period see Kent (1984), Heller (1983), Trumpener (1968), Weber (1970), and Ahmad (1966).

2. Only the International Socialist Bureau tried to mobilize European public opinion against Italian aggression, but with no success (see Haupt, 1972: 56–68).

3. On the reason for Unionist failure to carry out a radical policy towards the peasants see Feroz Ahmad (1983).

4. Lowther to Grey, no. 92 con., Constantinople, 5 February 1913, F.O. 371/1788/6200. The American Embassy also described the Committee of National Defense in similar terms as '*Comité de Salut Public*.' See the dispatch from Constantinople, February 13, 1913, 867.00/485 no. 412. Some documents on the CND may be found in Tarık Zafer Tunaya's invaluable study *Türkiye'de Siyasal Partiler* (1984: 448–57). See also *Tanin*, Jan. 30, 31, Feb. 1, 1913.

5. On the question of 'national economy' see Toprak (1982). This must be the last word on the subject. See also Ahmad (1980).

6. Such a work has a tendency to belittle the Turks since it was obviously published as a part of the U.S. propaganda campaign against Turkey. But Einstein is quite accurate about the corruption prevailing in the capital at the time. Plenty of other sources could be cited.

7. The *Donanma Cemiyeti*, modelled on the German 'Flotten Verein' and the British 'Navy League,' was founded on June 9, 1909, according to its proclamation, given to me by Dr. Aydoğan

Demir of İzmir University, to whom sincere thanks. However, Fahir Çoker, a retired admiral and naval historian, gives July 19, 1909, as the date (1965).

8. 10 *paras* were worth roughly one cent.

9. It is worth quoting the note of the Turkish ambassador in Washington, Ahmed Rüstem Bey, to the Secretary of State to have a sense of what the capitulations and their abolition meant to the Turks.

> Sir: I have the honor to inform you that by Imperial irade the Ottoman Government has abrogated as from the first of October next the conventions known as the capitulations restricting the sovereignty of Turkey in her relations with certain powers. All privileges and immunities accessory to these conventions or issuing therefrom are equally repealed. Having thus freed itself from what was an intolerable obstacle to all progress in the empire, the Imperial Government has adopted as basis of its relations with the other powers the general principle of international law (U.S. Government, 1914: 1090).

10. A French translation of this article, which originally appeared in *Türk Yurdu* (No. 140, 12 Aug. 1333 [1917]), is available in François Georgeon's excellent monograph on Yusuf Akçura.

11. See Vehbi Koç's autobiography *Hayat Hikâyem* (1973) and the more entertaining but historically-accurate fictionalized account by Erol Toy (1973).

12. *'Kadınları Çalıştırma Cemiyet-i İslâmiyesi'* translated in French as 'Société du travail des femmes mussulmanes,' *İktisadiyat Mecmuası*, Vol. I, no. 23, 10 Aug. 1916: 2–3 and Vol. I, no. 25, 31 Aug. 1916: 7. For women's organizations in this period see Tunaya (1984: 476–82).

13. On Tekinalp see Landau (1984). A telegram from Istanbul published in the *Rheinisch Westfalische Zeitung* (n.d.) and quoted in *The Near East* (London), reported that: 'Women are being admitted to the Turkish army. The Ottoman Association for Women's Work publishes a call to all women between 18 and 30 to join the recently created Women Workers' Battalion. The battalion was to be attached to the First Army Corps and would work eight hours daily behind the front. The overseers and officers would first be men, but would gradually be replaced by women' (Feb. 22, 1918: 153).

14. *Echo de Bulgarie*, Mar. 1, 1917, excerpted in War Ministry (London), *Daily Review of the Foreign Press DREP*, Mar. 17, 1917; Novichev (1935: 19–20). Novichev provides a most interesting account of wartime Turkey.

15. Ahmed Emin [Yalman] writes that in many regions: 'peasants had to pay regular tributes to brigands in addition to their official contribution to the Government' (1930: 80).

REFERENCES

Ahmad, Feroz (1966). 'Great Britain's Relations with the Young Turks, 1908–1914,' *Middle Eastern Studies*, II, 4, July, 302–29.

Ahmad, Feroz (1969). *The Young Turks*. Oxford: Clarendon.

Ahmad, Feroz (1980). 'Vanguard of a Nascent Bourgeoisie: The Social and Economic Policies of the Young Turks, 1908–1918,' in Osman Okyar & Halil İnalcık, eds., *Türkiye'nin Sosyal ve Ekonomik Tarihi (1071–1920)*. Ankara: Meteksan, 329–50.

Ahmad, Feroz (1983). 'The Agrarian Policy of the Young Turks, 1908–1918,' in Jean-Louis Bacqué-Grammont & Paul Dumont, eds., *Economie et sociétés dans L'Empire Ottoman (fin du XVII—début du XXe siècle)*. Paris: Ed. du C.N.R.S., 275–88.

Berkes, Niyazi (1964). *The Development of Secularism in Turkey*. Montreal: McGill University Press.

Cavit, Mehmet (1945). 'Meşrutiyet devrine ait Cavit Beyin Hatiralari,' *Tanin*, Aug. 2.

Cooker, Fahri (1965). 'Donanma Cemiyeti İhyasi mı?' *Cumhuriyet*, May 3.

Einstein, Lewis (1918). *Inside Constantinople*. New York.

Emin, Ahmed [Yalman] (1930). *Turkey in the World War*. New Haven.

Georgeon, François (1980). *Aux origines du nationalisme turc—Yusuf Akçura (1876–1935)*. Paris: A.D.P.F.

Gilbert, Martin (1971). *Winston S. Churchill*, III. Boston: Houghton Mifflin.
Haupt, Georges (1972). *Socialism and the Great War*. Oxford: Clarendon.
Heller, Joseph (1983). *British Policy towards the Ottoman Empire, 1908–1914*. London: Frank Cass.
Kent, Marian, ed. (1984). *The Great Powers and the End of the Ottoman Empire*. London: Allen & Unwin.
Koç, Vehbi (1973). *Hayat Hikâyem*. Istanbul: s.n.
Landau, J. M. (1984). *Tekinalp, Turkish Patriot, 1883–1961*. Leiden: Brill.
Novichev, A. D. (1935). *Ekonomika Turtsi v period mirovoi voiny*. Leningrad.
Nur, Riza (1967). *Hayat ve Hatiratim*. Istanbul: Altindag Yayinevi.
Pacha, Mahmoud Moukthat (1924). *La Turquie, l'Allemagne et l'Europe depuis le Traité de Berlin*. Paris.
Quataert, Donald (1983). *Social Disintegration and Popular Resistance in the Ottoman Empire, 1881–1901*. New York: New York Univ. Press.
Soboul, Albert (1965). *A Short History of the French Revolution, 1789–1799*. Berkeley: Univ. of California Press.
Stuermer, Harry (1917). *Two War Years in Constantinople* (*Sketches of German and Young Turkish Ethics and Politics*). London.
Tekinalp (1916). 'Bu seneki mahsulümüz,' *Iktisadiyat Mecmuası*. Vol. I, July 21/27, 1–2.
Toprak, Zafer (1982). *Türkiye' de milli İktisat* (*1908–1918*). Ankara: Yurt.
Toy, Erol (1973). *Imperator*. Istanbul: May Yayınları.
Trumperner, Ulrich (1968). *Germany and the Ottoman Empire, 1914–1918*. Princeton: Princeton Univ. Press.
Tunaya, Tarik Zafer (1984). *Türkiye' de Siyasal Partiler*. Vol. I, *İkinci Meşrutiyet Dönemi*. Istanbul: Hürriyet Vakfi.
United States Government (1914). *Foreign Relations of the United States, 1914*. Washington.
Weber, Frank (1970). *Eagles on the Crescent*. Ithaca: Cornell Univ. Press.
Yavuz, Erdal (1978). '1908 Boykotu,' in Orta Doğu Teknik Universitesi, *Gelisme Dergisi*. Ankara: Ozel Sayısı-Türkiye iktisat tarihi üzerine araştırmalar, 163–81.

Social Change in Persia in the Nineteenth Century

ANN K. S. LAMBTON

It is, I think, impossible to understand the attitude of the Persian people to social change in the nineteenth century or towards the government and political change without some consideration first of the Shi'i doctrine towards the holders of political power and secondly of the intrusion of the Great Powers into Persia. In this paper I shall, therefore, first examine these two matters in order to indicate how they limited social and political change, and how the latter also encouraged such changes. Inevitably, there is much that I shall have to omit. I shall not discuss the intellectual movements which led up to the Constitutional Revolution—I have touched upon them elsewhere and others have discussed them more fully. Nor shall I discuss literary movements, partly because these are concerned, for the most part, with political rather than social change. Another omission, and perhaps a more important one in the context of social change, is a discussion of the position of women and of slaves.

Persia is a country of great variety. Generalizations, inevitably inaccurate, are likely to be especially so with regard to Persia. Change there has been, sometimes in one field and sometimes in another, but on the whole the basic patterns of society and administration have shown a striking continuity. The fragmentation of the Abbasid empire, and the rise and fall of the Saljūq, Ilkhanid, Timurid and Safavid empires all brought about political, economic, social and cultural changes, but the dominant feature has nevertheless been continuity in political and social life.

The rise of the Safavid empire, the last of the great empires before the Qājārs, was, at least in one respect, an exception to this. The establishment of Ithnā 'Asharī (Imāmī) Shi'ism as the official religion of the country by Ismā'īl

Safavid empire— establishment of shi'ism

prior— had been Sunni

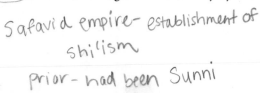

led to a profound change in the ethos of society and the attitude of the people to political power. Prior to this the majority had been Sunnī, Shiʿism being confined to certain districts only. Under the Safavids Persia became a national state with recognizable frontiers, separated by its acceptance of Shiʿism from its neighbours.

Whereas the Sunnī *ʿulamāʾ* so far as they accepted office under an unjust government, i.e. a government to which power had not been lawfully delegated, deliberately sought to give validity to its exercise of power in order that *sharʿī* government might continue, the Imāmī *fuqahāʾ*, although they co-operated for specific purposes with the holders of power, refused to accept any responsibility for the existence of an unjust government—for them all governments during the occultation of the hidden Imām were unjust, even if they were Shīʿī. They were not concerned, as were the Sunnīs, with the valid delegation of power; and their acceptance of office at the hands of unjust rulers in no way legitimized the power of the latter. Practising *taqiyya*, they saw themselves as deputies of the *imām*, not of the ruler, who thus became in their theory, in a sense, irrelevant. In order to understand the ambivalent attitude of the *ʿulamāʾ* (and to some extent of the population in general) towards the government, it is appropriate to consider the views of the early leaders of the Imāmī Shīʿa, views which continued down to, and throughout, the nineteenth century to influence the attitude of the faithful towards authority.

In his discussion of the duty to enjoin the good and to forbid evil, which is a duty incumbent upon all Muslims who are *mukallaf*, i.e. fully responsible and therefore bound to fulfil religious duties, Muḥammad b. al-Ḥasan al-Ṭūsī (d. 460/1067), whose work lies at the base of the writings of almost all later Imāmī *fuqahāʾ*, illustrates both the limitations placed upon the believer's actions by *taqiyya* and the political irresponsibility which results from its practice. He states:

> It is incumbent to enjoin the good and to forbid evil in the heart, by the spoken word and by act whenever the *mukallaf* is able to do this and knows, or considers, that it will not lead to harm to him or to a believer at that time or in the future. If he knows that it will lead to harm to him or to a third party at that time or in the future, or thinks this probable, it is not incumbent upon him in any way—it is only incumbent if he is safe from harm in all cases.[1]

The circumstances in which a believer might accept office from a usurper are laid down by al-Murtaḍā ʿAlam al-Hudā (d. 436/1044) and were broadly accepted by later authorities. According to him, if the one accepting office knew or considered it likely on the basis of clear indications that he would be able, through his tenure of office, to support a right or to reject a false claim or to enjoin the good and forbid evil, and that nothing of this would be accomplished but for his holding office, it was obligatory upon him to accept office. If he feared for some property of his or was afraid of some harm befalling him, the like of which could be borne, it was permissible for him to accept, but if he was forced by the sword, or if he considered it likely that his blood would be shed if he did not accept, he was obliged to accept. Al-Murtażā claims that

> Pious men and scholars have always at various times accepted offices on behalf of the unjust rulers for some of the reasons we have mentioned. The tenure of office on behalf of an unjust ruler is, when there is something of the aforementioned in it that makes it good, only in appearance on behalf of the unjust ruler. Intrinsically, it is on behalf of the true *imāms*—peace be upon them—because they have given permission for the tenure of office under the conditions we have mentioned ... Sound tradition has been transmitted that it is permissible for anyone in this situation to administer the legal punishments, cut the hands of thieves and do whatever the law requires in these matters.

Al-Murtażā's argument in justification of acceptance of office continues as follows:

> If it is said: Is it not the case that through his tenure of office he is strengthening the unjust ruler and giving the appearance that obedience to him is a religious duty? ... We say: If the unjust ruler has gained control of the religion, it is inevitable for everyone who is in his country and belongs in appearance to his subjects that he extol him, display reverence to him, and submit to his orders as if obedience to him were a religious duty ... His holding office thus does not lead him into anything which would not have been necessary for him if he had not accepted the office, while through the office he is enabled to order what is proper and to prohibit what is reprehensible. Thus it is obligatory that he seek to attain to that through the office.[2]

On the question of giving judgement al-Ṭūsī states that

> The true *imāms*, upon them be peace, have cast [the mantle of] judgement (*ḥukūma*) on the *fuqahā'* of the Shī'a during such time as they themselves are not in a position to exercise it in person ... If a *faqīh* exercises authority (*wilāya*) on behalf of a tyrant, let him think that in applying the penalties of the law in giving judgement he is acting on behalf of the true *imām* and let him undertake [these duties] according to the requirements of the *sharī'a* of the faith ... It is not permissible for anyone to choose to exercise oversight on behalf of tyrants unless he has [first] determined that he will not transgress what is obligatory and will only execute what is right and that he will allocate things such as *ṣadaqāt, akhmās*, and so on to their proper use. If he knows that he will not be able to control these things, it is not permissible for him to undertake that work voluntarily, but if he is compelled to do so, it is permissible.

Following the example of the early Imāmī *fuqahā'*, the doctrine of 'the prevention of harm' (*daf'-i mażarrat*) was developed. Under this doctrine it was held that co-operation with, and the acceptance of office from, an unjust ruler was permissible in order to prevent harm. This gave rise to an ambivalent attitude towards government, not only on the part of the religious classes but also on the part of the population generally, while the practice of *taqiyya*, both by the religious classes and the population at large, encouraged and fostered a general reluctance to accept moral and political responsibility.[3] Whereas the Safavids had claimed descent from the Imam Mūsā al-Kāẓim and the early Safavid rulers, or their partisans, had claimed that they ruled in succession to, or on behalf of, the *imāms*, the Qājārs could make no such claim. As a result the demarcation between the religious and the political institution became clearer. There was once more a religious institution standing over against the state and not wholly incorporated into it. The balance, however, was a delicate one. The *fuqahā'*, who asserted their claim to be *nā'ib 'āmm* of the *imām* more openly in the nineteenth century, could, if they so wished, declare the ruler to be the *nā'ib khāṣṣ* of the *imām* for some special purpose, as indeed Shaykh Ja'far Kāshif al-Ghiṭā' did when he declared Fatḥ 'Alī Shāh the *nā'ib khāṣṣ* for the purpose of defensive war against the Russians.[4] Broadly speaking, obedience to the government, although it was illegitimate, was normal, because it gave protection against insecurity and disorder. It would nevertheless appear that the question of war against rebels, which had been forbidden during the occultation by earlier Imāmī *fuqahā'*, was re-opened. Shaykh Ja'far widened the issue, which had earlier been seen essentially in terms of rebellion against the *imām*. For him tyranny (*ẓulm*) was rebellion and every tyrant (*ẓālim*) was a rebel. 'Anyone', he states, 'who rebels against the *imām* or his *nā'ib 'āmm* or his *nā'ib khāṣṣ* in what he commands or prohibits and whoever acts contrary [to his command and prohibition] in withholding *zakāt* or *khums* or in performing his due obligations [*ḥuqūq*] must be fought.' The only question was at what moment action should be taken against the rebel. Since no process was devised to decide when the ruler became a rebel or how a tyrant could be called to account, the question remained largely theoretical. But by the end of the nineteenth century the position of the *'ulamā'* had undergone considerable change; the gulf between them and the government had widened, and it was unlikely, if not inconceivable, that one of the great *mujtahids* of the day would have declared the ruler the *nā'ib khāṣṣ* of the *imām*. Āqā Muḥammad Khān and Fatḥ 'Alī Shāh treated the *'ulamā'* with great respect and sought to secure their support. Muḥammad Shāh and his minister Ḥājjī Mīrzā Āqāsī were Ṣūfīs and less attentive to the orthodox *'ulamā'*. Nāṣir al-Dīn Shāh and his minister the Amīr Niẓām (Mīrzā Taqī Khān), in their attempt to increase the power of the central government, sought to reduce that of the *'ulamā'*. Shaykh Ja'far had written at the beginning of the century that every tyrant (*ẓālim*) was a rebel and at the end of the century it was still tyranny (*ẓulm*) which eventually provoked action against the holders of power. As the movement for constitutional reform spread, the feeling that the weight of tyranny was intolerable and that it was threatening the Islamic way of life rallied religious and popular support to the movement.

From the end of the eighteenth century Persia, situated on India's western borders, assumed in the eyes of those concerned with the affairs of the East India Company in London and Calcutta an importance which grew in relation to their concern about the threat from external enemies to their possessions in India. This involved Britain to an ever increasing extent in Persia. Afghanistan, France and Russia, in turn, appeared to threaten India and the primary British interest in Persia was seen to be the maintenance of the independence and integrity of Persia as an element in the defence of their Indian empire. Britain had no territorial aims in Persia and in the nineteenth century her interest in Persia did not arise primarily out of her relations with Persia but rather out of her relations with those powers which had gained or might gain influence in Persia and might threaten India. This accounts, in part at least, for the vacillations in British policy towards Persia. It was not a situation which Persia could be expected either to understand or to appreciate and it created resentment. Russia, on the other hand, had expansionist designs in Persia and deprived her of all her provinces north of the Aras River in the early years of the century and of territory in the north-east in the middle of the century. This gave rise not only to resentment but also to fear. By the middle of the century, if not considerably before, both the realization by Persians that Persian independence and territorial integrity depended upon the balance of power between Britain and Russia and the fear of foreign intervention limited political experiment and economic and social change. The Persians did not wish for the tutelage of either power and much energy was devoted to playing off the one power against the other. At the same time, the humiliation of military defeat in the Russian wars at the beginning of the century and in the Anglo-Persian war of 1856–57 produced a desire to emulate the progress and technical advances of Western Europe in order to resist the encroachment of foreign powers. It also heightened the sense of distinctiveness and separation felt between Persia as an Islamic society and non-Islamic societies. It produced hostility towards the alien civilization of Europe among all classes, but especially among the religious classes, by whom it was most openly expressed. Ultimately, it also produced nationalism, but a nationalism articulated in terms of Islam.

The memory of the old Persian empire had lived on in the works of Firdawsī, though the details were blurred and legend triumphed over history. A sense of 'being a Persian' (*īrāniyyat*), which was kept alive largely by literary traditions expressed in the Persian language, ran through Persian society, but the emphasis was on culture rather than nationality and this memory and sense of 'being a Persian' did not provide an adequate basis for nationalism in the modern sense. There was no clear and definite memory of common government or of 'good' government and because of lack of communications no close contact between individuals of different regions or of different classes. Many towns and districts were also rent by faction.[5] Such contact and common interests as there were came mainly from a sharing of interests belonging to the locality, the craft or the tribe and, among the educated classes, a sharing of literary interests. Transcending all were religious interests and such common feeling as there was among the people as a whole was religious, not national, and came primarily from the sense of sharing a common religious background. At the same time it was also in the sharing of their literary tradition that Persians, especially the educated classes, felt a common bond and a superiority to other peoples.

As Western techniques were gradually applied to Persia in the nineteenth century, political organizations were able to make their authority effective to an increasing degree, and with this there was to some extent a transition from the old religious loyalties to national loyalties, though patriotism still remained largely a religious sentiment. So far as loyalties transcended the quarter, the city, the craft or the tribe, they were still primarily to Islam. The shah was still *padishāh-i islām* and Persia the *mamālik-i islām*. When eventually in the late nineteenth century the desire among the intellectuals for modernization became stronger, it was largely as a result first of military and diplomatic pressures and then of economic pressure. The religious classes and others continued their resistance to foreign intrusion in a new form, equating modernization with a return to Islam. In other words, they attempted, as Malkam Khān had already done in some of his essays, to clothe modernization in an Islamic garb, just as the Islamic philosophers had sought in the early centuries to equate the learning of the ancient world with Islam and to incorporate it into Islam. In both the early centuries and the nineteenth century the religious classes in general were opposed to change, but as the pressures grew they adopted new tactics in order to control and nullify the demands for change. A somewhat extreme example of the attempt to equate Islam with modernization is the *Ḥuqūq bayn al-islām* by Sayf al-Salṭana, written about 1904 or 1905. His thesis is that all knowledge (including modern sciences) is summed up in the Qur'ān and that Western nations in their modernization were putting into practice the precepts of the Qur'ān and that the reason for the backwardness of Islamic nations was their failure to put such precepts into practice. He claims that all European progressive ideas were borrowed from Islam: the concepts of justice, equality and a consultative assembly were all, he alleges, foreshadowed in the Qur'ān.

Other writers, such as Furṣat, were more moderate and contented themselves with equating the government of the law with the *sharī'a.*

Already in the late eighteenth century there is some evidence of new trends in political thought, notably in the *Rustam al-tawārīkh*, in which the author, Rustam al-Ḥukamā', shows, for example, an incipient awareness of the interaction of political and economic affairs. There is also evidence in his work of fear of British intrusion coupled with a recognition of the decay and tyranny prevalent in Persia. Rustam al-Ḥukamā' lived in Iṣfahān. Those in the south and south-east tended, on the whole, to look to India and therefore to be especially conscious of British influence. At the time the British had no diplomatic representative in Persia: any business that might arise was dealt with by the representatives of the East India Company, whose headquarters had been transferred from Basra to Bushire in 1778. It is unlikely that Rustam al-Ḥukamā''s book had widespread influence but its composition suggests that there was a 'reading public' not merely among men of letters but also, perhaps, among those who were beginning to question traditional attitudes.[6] By the middle of the nineteenth century the desire for change had become more broadly based. Lady Sheil, a percipient observer of the Persian scene, writing of 1850 and the civil and religious disturbances which took place in Persia in that year, states: 'There is a spirit of change abroad among the Persians.' Elsewhere, remarking on the growing demand for luxuries, she noted that the satisfaction of this would increase Persia's dependence upon Europe. She writes:

> With all their alacrity to endure a life of roughness, or even hardship, they [the Persians] have a vast aptitude for luxury and enjoyment. Their wants are increasing daily, and these wants must be supplied from Europe.[7]

The patterns of change in the nineteenth century were complex. The first impulse for change almost certainly came from contact with the alien civilization of Europe in the military and diplomatic fields. A series of diplomatic missions, foreign military instructors, advisers and adventurers were to be found in Persia in the early years of the century. A curious feature of the Persian army in the reign of Fatḥ 'Alī was a corps of Russian (Muslim) deserters, until it was disbanded in 1840. The influence of the military missions in the military field was small. Some progress was made in elementary tactics and organization but none, or almost none, in the matter of discipline, regularity of pay, supplies and the formation of a professional officer corps. Indirectly, however, the military missions encouraged political and social change. As a result of their presence and the need felt for military reform, 'Abbās Mīrzā sent two young Persians to study in England in 1811 and five more in 1815. One of these, Mīrzā Ṣāliḥ, who later played an important part in spreading knowledge of Western Europe in Persia, was to learn English and French, a second was to study medicine, a third engineering and fortifications, a fourth the duties of an artillery and a cavalry officer, and the fifth the art of the gunsmith.[8]

Indirectly, the military and diplomatic missions also played a part in overcoming suspicion of Western medicine, though there were no modern medical services run by the Persian government until towards the end of the century, and even then they were of an elementary and very limited nature. The British missions, military and diplomatic, had attached to them doctors, many of whom by their medical skill attracted the confidence of the ruling and other leading families. At first they met with opposition both from Persian doctors and from the government. In the winter of 1811–12 the surgeons of the British mission endeavoured to introduce vaccination. Cowpox was obtained from Constantinople and some 300 children were vaccinated in Tehran. Women, mainly from the poor, thronged their premises bringing their offspring to be vaccinated. This apparently aroused the opposition of the Persian doctors and, perhaps, also the suspicion of the government. Whatever the reason, the government placed *farrāshes* at the gates of the premises of the mission, ostensibly as a mark of attention to the head of the mission but in fact to prevent the entry of the women.[9]

Among the first English surgeons and doctors who worked in Persia was Dr. Charles Cormick, who had been a member of the military mission provided under the Preliminary Treaty between Persia and Britain and had stayed in Persia after the mission left. He married an Armenian lady and settled in Tabrīz and became ʿAbbās Mīrzā's physician. His son William, who was trained in England and practised in London and Paris, was summoned back to Persia by Muḥammad Shāh in 1844. He, too, settled in Tabrīz and in addition to treating the late ʿAbbās Mīrzā's family had a flourishing apothecary's business. One of the most successful of the doctors was John McNeill, who first came to Persia as assistant surgeon to the legation in 1821 and later became British minister. He successfully treated Tāj al-Dawla, Fatḥ ʿAlī Shāh's favourite wife, in 1826. Thereafter he regularly attended members of the shah's *ḥaram*. After the rupture of Anglo-Persian relations in 1838 a succession of French doctors were employed by the royal family, among them a French surgeon, M. Labat, who treated Muḥammad Shāh successfully in 1844, and Dr. Cloquet. In 1845 a young Persian, Mīrzā Ṣādiq, was sent by the shah to England to study medicine. Shortly afterwards three or four other young men were sent to France to study general science. Dr. Joseph Dickson, who became doctor to the British legation in 1848 and held his appointment until 1887, was called in from time to time to treat Nāṣir al-Dīn Shāh, and at the latter's request accompanied him on his first European tour in 1873. In 1890 Dr. Hugh Adcock was appointed personal physician to Muẓaffar al-Dīn, the *valī ʿahd*, who was then residing in Tabrīz. When he succeeded in 1896,

Adcock accompanied him to Tehran and for ten years held the position of consulting physician in chief to the shah. Medical treatment was also given by the doctors of the British military and diplomatic missions to the poor in Tabrīz and Tehran. In 1837 a visitor to Tabrīz remarked that:

> from morning to night the steps of the British Palace were thronged with sick, who sought relief from the European skill. Both here and in Tehran the good which is done by the medical gentlemen belonging to the Embassy is incalculable.[10]

The medical treatment offered to the poor first in Tabrīz, Tehran and Bushire was later extended to other parts of the country where British consulates were opened. The Indo-European Telegraph department, which became operational in 1865, also had doctors attached to it; they, too, ran dispensaries for the poor.[11]

Although a medical class was opened in the Dār al-Funūn, which was founded in 1851, the Persian government did not concern itself with public health until 1868. In that year a Sanitary Council was established on which doctors from the British, French and Russian legations also served. The first modern Persian hospital was opened with German help in Tehran in the following year.[12] The development of hospital services was slow. Among the first modern hospitals and dispensaries were those set up by Christian missionary societies. The first to be opened was a dispensary in Urūmiyyeh, where the American Justin Perkins of the American Board of Commissioners for Foreign Missions founded a mission, which worked mainly among the Armenians and Nestorians, in 1835. Mary Bird of the Church Missionary Society opened a dispensary for Muslim women in the Iṣfahān bazaar in 1891. Despite much opposition from the *mullās*, who preached against her and sought to prevent her access to the bazaar, she won the devotion of her many patients and appears to have had access to families of all classes. In 1896 a hospital and dispensary were opened by the Church Missionary Society in Julfā (Iṣfahān) and between 1897 and 1900 they established hospitals in Kirmān, Yazd and Shīrāz.

In the first half of the nineteenth century there were virtually no modern schools in Persia. Education was given in *maktabs* and *madrasas*. In the former, Persian and a little Arabic sufficient for reading the Qur'ān, and sometimes a little arithmetic, were taught. The pupils were mainly, though not entirely, boys. The *maktabs*, run by *mullās*, were not under any kind of government control. The pay for tuition varied but was usually small. *Madrasas* existed in many towns; some were attached to mosques and the teachers, who were *'ulamā'*, were paid from the *awqāf* of the *madrasa* or mosque. In them young men were taught, fed and frequently lodged. They were instructed in all or some of the following: the religious sciences, Arabic, logic, philosophy and Persian literature. Modern sciences were neglected. Families with means employed private tutors or arranged small private classes for their sons; female tutors were sometimes employed to teach their daughters.

It was again under the influence of military considerations that some of the early steps to modernize education were taken. In 1851 the Dār al-Funūn college was founded by Nāṣir al-Dīn's minister, the Amīr Niẓām (Mīrzā Taqī Khān). Its purpose was to train officers for the army and officials for the bureaucracy. Dā'ūd Khān, an Armenian, who had once been a Russian officer and was subsequently appointed chief military instructor by Muḥammad Shāh towards the end of his reign, was sent to Vienna to engage military and civilian teachers. Seven men, four of whom were military men, the fifth a mineralogist, the sixth a chemist and the seventh a doctor, came out. A few days before their arrival Amīr Niẓām was dismissed. His successor, Mīrzā Āqā Khān Nūrī, was not in favour of the college. The Austrians began work under difficulties in 1852. The results of their work in the military field were negligible. A number of books on military sciences and scientific matters were, however, translated into Persian and published between 1853 and 1858. By 1859 the Austrians had all left, except the doctor, J. E. Polak, who became the shah's physician. He resigned in 1860, having been supplanted by Dr. Tholozan, a surgeon-major of the French army, whom the French government had sent out to Persia and who had become the chief medical adviser to the shah in 1859 and remained so until Nāṣir al-Dīn's death.

Pupils entered the Dār al-Funūn at fourteen after passing an elementary examination. In addition to military classes, civilian classes were also formed for geology, medicine, mathematics, Persian, Arabic, English, Russian, music, physics and geography. Although few of the pupils were in fact enrolled in the army, a modern education was given to numbers of young men, many of whom entered the bureaucracy. In the later years of Nāṣir al-Dīn Shāh's reign, the Dār al-Funūn decayed for lack of finance and interest, but revived later and became one of the foremost schools of the country. A rival college, the Nāṣirī College, was founded by the Nā'ib al-Salṭana, Nāṣir al-Dīn's third son, but it had little more than a nominal existence and virtually ceased to exist with the retirement of its founder on the death of Nāṣir al-Dīn. Another military college, the Madrasa-i Niẓāmiyya, established at the prompting of Mīrzā Ḥusayn Khān Mushīr al-Dawla, one of Nāṣir al-Dīn's ministers, also had a very short life.

As in the case of hospitals, the Christian missionary societies played an important part in the foundation of modern schools. Justin Perkins founded schools in Urūmiyyeh and the neighbourhood. By 1841, 17 schools had been set up in 16 villages and by 1851 the number had increased to 45. Their pupils were mostly Assyrians (Nestorians) but a school for Muslims was also run. In 1840 Perkins received a farman from Muḥammad Shāh, on the instigation of Malik Qāsim Mīrzā, requesting him to increase his efforts and instruction among the young, and with an even greater zeal than hitherto to teach them the science of history, geography, geometry and mathematics.[13] The American Board of Foreign Missions of the Presbyterian Church in the United States also founded schools in Tehran (1872), Tabrīz (1873) and Hamadān (1880). Their educational work was at first confined mainly to the Assyrian and Armenian minorities. A start was also made in female education, a school for girls being opened in Tehran in 1874. The London Society for promoting Christianity among the Jews also set up small schools in Tehran (1876), Iṣfahān (1889) and Hamadān (1889). None of these, however, initially had influence among the Muslim population. The Archbishop of Canterbury's mission to the Assyrians, founded in 1886, also carried on educational work among Assyrians. In 1896 Dr. Jordan of the American Presbyterian Mission to Persia arrived from America and founded a new school, which by 1901 had all the classes necessary for a complete high school and had among its pupils Muslims as well as members of the minorities. This college, together with the Stuart Memorial College, later founded by the Church Missionary Society in Iṣfahān, played an important part in education in Persia in the first half of the twentieth century.

Few steps were taken by the Persian authorities to make modern education available. Muẓaffar al-Dīn, shortly after his accession, expressed a desire that something should be done for public instruction and in the following year a committee was set up. In 1898 a number of schools were opened in Tehran and other places and were placed under the ministry for public instruction in 1899. Modern education, however, was still only provided for a small minority. There were also a number of Europeans who were employed as tutors to the sons of Qājār princes and well-to-do families. They may have had some influence in the introduction of new ways of thought. Probably the first of these was Charles Burgess, who came to Persia in a commercial capacity in 1828 and was later for a period tutor to some of the royal princes in Tabrīz.[14]

Apart from the European diplomatic and military missions and the missionary and merchant communities, occasional travellers also visited Persia—some like Martyn and Wolff were freelance missionaries, some like Layard and Browne were scholars, others, like Curzon, were persons travelling to gather information, and a few, like Isabella Bird, were women. Their impact was confined to the fairly small circle of persons they met on their travels.

In the middle of the nineteenth century there were some 150 Europeans in Persia; by the 1890s there were some 800 and by 1900 about 1,000. The increase in their numbers was due mainly to the growth in the activity of European trading firms and other companies.[15] They were mainly concentrated in Tehran and only thinly scattered through the provinces. Their contacts were mostly with the official and trading classes. Some had wider contacts, notably the employees of the carpet companies, which in Sulṭānābād were in close contact with the weavers in the town and the surrounding villages.

It was not only the advent of foreigners to Persia which aroused interest in the outside world and stimulated a desire for change and led to the provision of some modern education and medicine—even if it produced at the same time hostility. Increasing travel abroad by Persians for diplomatic, commercial and educational purposes was also of great importance in stimulating change, but this was primarily, perhaps, in the intellectual rather than the social field, though clearly it led to some, perhaps rather superficial, changes in dress and household furniture. It was largely through the channel of foreign travel that the main currents for reform came in the second half of the nineteenth century.[16]

The growth in foreign trade and new patterns of internal trade were other factors which influenced social change. Here again, the attitude of the government towards the extension of commerce was equivocal. Although not opposed to it on economic grounds, they had a lively fear, induced partly by the example of the British in India and by Russian action in the north, that the extension of foreign commerce would be a prelude to political domination. For this reason they resisted the consular articles of the treaties of Gulistān and Turkomānchāy and were reluctant to conclude a commercial treaty with Britain. Foreign trade in fact increased. However, there was also in the second half of the nineteenth century a settlement of Persian merchants in Istanbul, Cairo, Damascus, Karachi, Bombay and the neighbouring Russian territories; and members of these Persian commercial communities in foreign cities played an important role in the transmission of ideas and in stimulating modernization in Persia.

No roads

Although communication with the outside world increased during the nineteenth century, inside Persia the lack of roads and transport was a major constraint on development and movement and, perhaps, also on social change. Famine in one region could not easily be relieved by the transport of surpluses from another region.[17] Troops could not be quickly moved to deal with disorders or rebellion in outlying districts. There were no metalled roads until the 1870s and by the end of the century their aggregate length was less than 800 miles. Three metalled roads, the first from Tehran to Qazvīn, Rasht and Enzelī, the second from Mashhad via Qūchān to Ashqābād, and the third from Julfā to Tabrīz, linked Russian territories with northern Persia. There was also a metalled road from Tehran to Sulṭānābād. The first three roads were constructed with financial help from Russia and the fourth with help from the Imperial Bank of Persia.[18]

The Indo-European Telegraph, mentioned above, the construction of which began in 1862, became operational in 1865. Apart from providing revenue for the Persian treasury, it enabled the central government to make its influence more effectively felt in the provinces and brought Persia into contact with the outside world in a way which had not been the case before. The belief that the telegraph wires ended at the foot of the Persian throne, incidentally, made the telegraph stations into a place of asylum (*bast*). In 1893, for example, 2,000 people, following bread riots, marched on the telegraph office in Shīrāz, insisting that a message be sent to the shah demanding the dismissal of the mayor of Shīrāz and a cut in the price of bread. The crowd swelled to about 10,000 and held the telegraph staff prisoner until an answer was received from Tehran.[19]

The reluctance on the part of the Persian government to improve communications, like their reluctance to improve foreign trade, was also a reaction to the intrusion of foreign powers. Because of the weakness of Persia *vis-à-vis* foreign powers, it was the concern of Nāṣir al-Dīn and his ministers to maintain, not to remove, the obstacles to movement. In 1882 W. J. Dickson, who first went to Persia in 1852, referring to the fact that the want of carriageable roads still obstructed trade, wrote:

> The fact is that a feeling still prevails amongst some of the influential classes that Persia's safest policy is 'to let well alone'; that the requirements of the State are sufficienly [sic] satisfied by the present limited resources of the country, and that so long as it remains in its actual conditions, they will be allowed to manage their own affairs: whereas every step towards improvement might tend to increase the influence of the foreign, to the detriment of the native, element.[20]

The *'ulamā'* also objected to the construction of new roads and railways because they feared that the development of communications would open the country to Europeans, who by their activities would threaten the way of life of believers.[21]

The introduction of the printing press in the first half of the nineteenth century[22] and the foundation of the official gazette in 1851 were also factors making for modernization. In the second half of the nineteenth century a considerable number of books were lithographed in Tehran and Tabrīz. But there was no growth in an independent Persian press until the twentieth century. The Persian press published abroad—in Calcutta, Istanbul, Cairo and, briefly, in London—had a great effect in stimulating political change towards the end of the nineteenth and the beginning of the twentieth century but had perhaps less effect in encouraging social change.

Demographic changes, especially in the latter years of the century, may have increased the contact of different classes and different regions with each other, and may thus, at least marginally, have contributed to social change. Dr. Gilbar has shown that the urban population had increased from about 8 to 9 per cent in the middle of the century to 18 per cent in the early 1900s, though only three towns had 100,000 inhabitants or more: Tehran (about

280,000), Tabrīz (about 200,000) and Iṣfahān (about 100,000). The bulk of the increase in population came from the rural areas and the small towns. Many of the tribal groups—Shahsivans, Afshārs, Kangarlūs and Qarāchurlūs, who had been living in the vicinity of the capital in the middle of the century—also moved into the city in the 1870s and 1880s as a result of the increasing demand for unskilled labour.[23] The growth in the numbers of the latter in the capital increased the danger of bread riots in time of scarcity; it also made it easier for the discontented to mount demonstrations against the government.

Apart from immigration into the towns there was also some migration of labourers and peasants, sometimes of a permanent, but often of a seasonal, nature. In the middle of the century numbers of Armenians and Nestorians migrated from Khwuy, Salmās and Urūmiyyeh to Russia as labourers, though many returned after a few months. It appears that some of the Armenians taken to Russia after the wars in the first quarter of the century also came back to Persia.[24] In the famine years of 1871–2 many thousands of peasants and townsmen emigrated from the central and southern provinces to the Caspian littoral in search of food. In the 1890s there was also a movement of peasants from Āẕarbāyjān, and to a lesser extent from Kirmān and Yazd, to villages in the north-east because of the greater prosperity at that time in Khurāsān.[25]

At the beginning of the nineteenth century Persia was still a traditional Islamic society. Despite the tribal ethos of the Qājārs and their entourage and the apparent laxity in some circles in the observation of some, at least, of the precepts of Islam, the supremacy of the *sharīʿa* was never openly challenged, however much it might be contravened in practice. In the course of the century the scope of *ʿurf* jurisdiction widened,[26] but there was a great reluctance to commit to writing anything which might be regarded as conflicting with, or encroaching upon, the *sharīʿa*. This was illustrated at a meeting in 1881 between Mīrzā Saʿīd Khān, the minister for foreign affairs, and Ronald Thomson, the British minister, at which the question of Nestorian grievances with regard to inheritance and testimony in the courts arising out of regulations issued by the Persian government in 1864 and confirmed in 1881 was discussed. Speaking on the former point, Mīrzā Saʿīd Khān

> positively stated that neither the Shah nor any of his Ministers could view with satisfaction or could have any special object in preserving a Regulation which inflicted manifold injustice on the Christians, and by which a family could be reduced to beggary by one of its members turning Mussulman, and then claiming and obtaining the whole inheritance, to the exclusion of the other relations. Mirza Saïd Khan said that positive orders would be sent to Azerbaijan to have the existing practice discontinued, but he objected to communicating the orders officially to the Legation, as they were in opposition to the religious law, and all he consented to do was to address a

> note to Her Majesty's Minister stating that orders had been sent to the proper authorities with regard to the question of the Nestorian grievances, which had formed the subject of discussion between him and Her Majesty's minister; but that, as these orders referred to delicate matters connected with the Mussulman religious law, it was not advisable to refer to them more specifically.[27]

That which held society together was Islam, and that which moved the populace was an appeal to defend Islam against the encroachment of infidels made by one of the great *mujtahids*. So far as reform was advocated it was seen by the population, except for a small minority, as a return to the norms of Islamic life. Few felt any need for fundamental change in the bases on which society rested. Change was for the infidel, not for the Muslim. There was much latent hostility towards non-Muslims and suspicion of foreigners on the grounds that they would subvert Islam. Invariably, in view of the political situation, religious hostility became bound up with the resentment aroused by the political intrusion of foreign powers. There was much resistance to the adoption of European customs in matters of dress, manners and everyday intercourse. For example, in spite of the repeated outbreaks of cholera and the heavy loss of life in these outbreaks, precautionary measures advocated by Europeans for the prevention of disease were opposed as being aimed at the overthrow of Islam. The strict quarantine required by international regulations, for the administration of which in the ports along the Persian Gulf British doctors became responsible in 1896, was little understood. It provoked intense hostility among local merchants and others whose livelihood was affected, and among pious Muslims, who had to obtain a sanitary certificate before shipping the bodies of their dear ones to Basra for burial at Karbalā. Resentment at foreign interference in these matters is equally clearly seen in the cholera outbreak of 1904. At this time the customs administration was in the hands of the Belgians, and the quarantine organization set up on the Turco-Persian border during the epidemic was run by them and aroused much ill-feeling. Their activities in other fields had already given rise to much annoyance and opposition to foreign intervention had become largely focused on them.[28] Large numbers of pilgrims normally passed over the Turco-Persian border on their way to and from Karbalā and Najaf. The holding of pilgrims in quarantine posts was regarded as an interference with religious duties. At least one of the leading *mujtahids* and his followers refused to submit to the regulations.[29] Precautionary action to control the spread of the epidemic by assuring clean water supplies and the prevention of the indiscriminate washing of the dead, were also regarded as attempts to subvert and suppress Islam.

Another matter which caused irritation because of its supposed infringement of Islamic law was the question of the abolition of the slave trade. The British government made strenuous efforts in the 1840s to put down the slave trade in the Persian Gulf and sought to obtain from the Persian and Turkish governments farmans prohibiting the trade in their respective parts of the Persian Gulf. When the application was made to the Persian government in 1846, Muḥammad Shāh refused to give such a farman on the grounds that it would be contrary to Islam, which, he maintained, sanctioned slavery. His refusal to prohibit the trade was probably due not so much to religious scruple as to the bitterness he felt towards the British government because of the affair of Āqā Khān Maḥallātī[30] and various other matters. Many of the *'ulamā'* however, appear to have supported him in his refusal. Eventually a compromise was reached, but the question of the slave trade and the searching of Persian vessels suspected of slave-trading continued to give rise to disputes into the reign of Nāṣir al-Dīn and later.

Apart from hostility to the infidel—though paradoxically great hospitality and friendship were often shown to individual foreigners—there was no room in society for dissident groups, Islamic or otherwise, as shown by the severity and cruelty with which the Bābī rebellion was suppressed in the middle of the century. Political opposition and heresy were still, as they had been in the Middle Ages, inextricably mixed. Christians, Jews and Zoroastrians were second-class citizens, they lived in conditions of insecurity and fear and were subject intermittently to persecution. The most numerous of the minority groups were the Christians, consisting mainly of Armenians (orthodox and catholic) concentrated in Āẕarbāyjān and Iṣfahān, and Nestorians in Urūmiyyeh and Kurdistān. Because of the fundamental insecurity of their position, they sought foreign protection. So far as they were successful, their circumstances were temporarily alleviated, but because of the protection they enjoyed they were almost inevitably suspected of being spies and traitors. Their integration into society was thus made even more difficult than would, perhaps, otherwise have been the case.

In the course of the nineteenth century the protection of *ẕimmīs* became confused with the issues of protection generally and asylum, which latter was an old-established custom. The most common place in which asylum was sought was a mosque or shrine. From Safavid times onwards the tombs of the great religious leaders had been regarded as sanctuaries. The gateway of the royal palace at Iṣfahān, the royal kitchen and the royal stables were similarly regarded. In Qājār times, apart from shrines and mosques and the houses of religious leaders, the royal stables and the telegraph office were recognized as places of asylum, as also was the neighbourhood of a cannon, though this was not of very general validity. Sanctuary was taken both by those who sought refuge from injustice and also by those who sought to escape the law. In the latter case it was not infrequent for them to be removed from their place of sanctuary. As the century progressed, asylum was increasingly used to protest against injustice or supposed injustice. Its use to make a collective protest and a demand for reform reached its culmination in the early years of the twentieth century at the time of the Constitutional Revolution. Muḥammad Shāh and Nāṣir al-Dīn Shāh both sought, without success, to limit or abolish sanctuary.

With the establishment of foreign missions in Persia in the nineteenth century a new aspect was given to asylum, which was now also sought in the premises of the foreign missions. This was not normally granted to common malefactors but rather to political figures, princes of the royal house, governors and ministers, who had fallen into disfavour and whose lives were in danger, and it was normally accompanied by protection at least as long as the individual concerned remained on the mission premises.

It was recognized by society at large that because of the arbitrary nature of the power of the Persian government and the absence of any generally accepted processes of law, asylum provided some protection to the subject. Foreign missions also claimed the right to grant asylum, partly because of the arbitrary nature of the government and partly because the practice was commonly accepted in Persia. Initially their claim to do so does not appear to have given rise to any objections. Towards the end of Muḥammad Shāh's reign, however, it became the subject of acrimonious discussion between the government and foreign missions, partly, perhaps, because it had become bound up also with the question of succession to the throne. It remained a bone of contention into the twentieth century.

In the nineteenth century although writers on the state no longer put forward the medieval theory of the organization of society, its basis was in fact still hierarchical. Each class had its own functions and norms of behaviour. In this respect society was extremely formal: each person was expected to dress and conduct himself according to what was expected of his class. A failure to do so threatened the *status quo* and this caused alarm. There were, however, no impassable barriers between the different classes and men of humble origin could and did rise to the highest positions of state. The traditional dichotomy between 'the men of the sword' and 'the men of the pen' still, broadly speaking, existed. The former were not, however, in any sense professional soldiers; they were also administrators. To them belonged, first and foremost, the Qājār princes (the *shāhzādehs*), other tribal leaders (*khāns* and *begs*) and the great landlords. Their power derived from the number of their followers. They tended to keep large trains of servants and to extort from the peasants in the villages which they owned or farmed the means to provide for their retinues. The Qājār princes were, although proud of their origins, accessible to Europeans and fond of their society.[31] Paradoxically it was mainly from 'the men of the sword' that the early moves for modernization came. The reasons for this, as suggested above, were political and not social, deriving from the reaction to the intrusion of the Great Powers into Persia and their military preponderance.

Under Āqā Muḥammad Khān the structure of the empire was that of a loose tribal empire. In the reign of Fatḥ ʿAlī Shāh the most important posts in the army and many of the provincial governments were held by Qājārs. His court was composed of the khans of the Qājār, Afshār, Shaqāqī and other tribes. To these were added, according to Jaubert, the French traveller, who was in Persia in 1805–6, hostages from those districts in which Fatḥ ʿAlī Shāh had been challenged on his accession and which he had subdued. These hostages, Jaubert alleges, were obliged to present themselves to the shah daily and were held responsible for the slightest disorder in their home districts.[32] The practice of taking hostages was one of the traditional ways of maintaining security and continued to be followed by the Qājārs. In the middle of the century the Gūklān were compelled to furnish 40 or 50 families, who lived in one of the districts of Tehran.[33] By the end of the century the custom of taking hostages had been somewhat modified but had not entirely disappeared.

The 'men of the pen', comprising men of letters and those in the higher echelons of the bureaucracy educated in the traditional branches of learning, were men of education and polish, the heirs of a long tradition of bureaucratic skills. Already under Fatḥ ʿAlī Shāh the bureaucracy began to reassert its position—it had been unimportant under Āqā Muḥammad Shāh—and to establish a centralized organization based largely on the practice of the past, which was further expanded in the reign of Nāṣir al-Dīn Shāh. The existence of a highly centralized bureaucracy did not, however, mean that the Qājārs were able to bring the powerful provincial governors and tribal leaders fully under their control. The great empires of the past, the Saljūq, Ilkhanid and Safavid empires, had all had a centralized bureaucracy, but only the strongest rulers had been able to exert control over the outlying regions. Time and again after the foundation of new empires and kingdoms the 'men of the pen', many of whom came from families who had served successive governments, succeeded in reasserting the traditional bureaucratic forms, but highly centralized and elaborately organized though the bureaucratic administration was, no effective system of financial control was devised. In practice this resulted in a high degree of provincial independence.

As the century progressed, the relative importance of the 'men of the sword' and the 'men of the pen' changed. The latter came to play an increasingly important part in affairs of state and in the entourage of the shah. But whereas the 'men of the sword' had a power base, the 'men of the pen' were the servants of whatever ruler was in power. Their position was fundamentally insecure and their rise and fall subject to the caprice of the ruler. High position inevitably made them the object of the jealousy of their fellows and often of the suspicion of the shah also. Many of those in the highest positions suffered disgrace and humiliation and some lost their lives. In this situation they tended to bend with the wind, to prefer compromise to confrontation. They themselves would, perhaps, have argued that it was their very suppleness and readiness to compromise which enabled Persia to survive political convulsions and which made it possible for them to preserve a balance between Russia and Britain in the nineteenth and twentieth centuries. Theirs was predominantly the world of theory; their weakness was a contempt for practical experience and action, though this was not always the case. Hājjī Mīrzā Ibrāhīm and Amīn al-Dawla both rose, in the early Qājār period, to the position of *ṣadr-i aʿẓam* after experience in local administration in Shīrāz and Iṣfahān respectively. In the later years of the century the tendency was for the high officials of the bureaucracy to be to a greater extent than formerly lacking in experience of local government. It was, incidentally, from them that the early attempts to initiate political reform in the second half of the nineteenth century came, and it is, perhaps, because of their background that they paid little attention to the pragmatic aspects of reform.[34] In addition to the dichotomy between the 'men of the pen' and the 'men of the sword' there was also a tendency on the part of the 'men of the pen' to regard the artisans and craftsmen, 'those who made things' in everyday life, and the peasants and nomads, who had experience in the cultivation of the land and in stock-rearing respectively, with contempt.

Beside the 'men of the sword' and the 'men of the pen' there was a third group, the *ʿulamā'*, ranging from the great *mujtahids* down to itinerant *mullās*. The *ʿulamā'* held a position of great influence in society and among the families of the great *ʿulamā'* there was often a certain continuity. Some of the *ʿulamā'*, the *shaykh al-islām* and the *imām jumʿa* of the major cities, the *khaṭīb* and sometimes the *pīsh-namāz*, were paid by the state and were, to that extent, government servants like the members of the bureaucracy. But apart from those who held such major offices, the government depended upon the general body of *ʿulamā'* for the performance of many public services: they held the *sharʿī* courts, performed marriages and burials, witnessed documents and acted as guardians for orphans and widows. Their position in society was different from that of any other group: their prestige derived not from secular but from religious learning, and the more learned among them were regarded as the representatives of the Hidden Imam, who was, for most of the population, the 'true king'. For these various reasons, and because the mass of the population looked to the *ʿulamā'* (though not to those who had compromised their position by association with the ruler) for support and who were, therefore, the potential leaders of popular discontent, the rulers treated them with respect, even if, when they felt strong enough, they sought to reduce their influence. Thus, Nāṣir al-Dīn Shāh made various attempts to clip their wings.[35] All classes deferred to the great *mujtahids*, but even the lesser *mullās* had influence among the labourers and peasants, and in the incitement of mobs. That large numbers of religious students (*ṭalaba*) lived together in the *madrasas* in the great Shīʿī centres and in other large cities enabled the *ʿulamāʾ* to muster supporters for some cause to which they gave their blessing more easily than other groups. The attitude of the religious classes towards the government was, however, ambivalent. Holding that all governments were usurpers during the absence of the *imām*, some, especially the great *mujtahids*, held themselves aloof from the authorities for fear of jeopardizing their salvation in the next world; others, either because they were venal and corrupt or because they believed that stability best served the interests of the Muslims, co-operated with the authorities on the basis of the principle of *dafʿ-i mażarrat.*

The fourth important group in society was that constituted by the big merchants (*tujjār*), those who traded on a large scale and were engaged in the import-export trade and the bazaar and shopkeepers. Many of them were also money-lenders. Rates of interest were high and considerable riches were accumulated by moneylending. In the absence of banks, the government needed the services of the big merchants both for the provision and the transmission of funds. Armenian merchants from northern Persia and Russian Armenia played an important part in trade, in particular the silk trade, as they had in the eighteenth century. By the second half of the nineteenth century the wool trade between Persia and Transcaucasia was also in their hands. Some of the Armenians were Persian subjects, others Russian, and as such they received Russian protection which often placed them in a favourable position *vis-à-vis* Persian merchants. In southern Persia there were a small number of Indian merchants, who by the middle of the century enjoyed British protection.

In the large cities there was a *malik al-tujjār* appointed by the government but not in receipt of a salary. His duty was to settle disputes, investigate claims and give certificates of solvency. In a farman dated 27 Shawwāl 1259/20 November 1843 issued by Muḥammad Shāh to Bahman Mīrzā, the governor of Āẕarbāyjān, and in one to Ḥusayn Khān, governor of Yazd, issued in Jumādā I 1260/May–June 1844, it was stated, *inter alia*, that a *malik al-tujjār* would be established wherever there was a flourishing commerce.[36] Where a *malik al-tujjār* existed both Persian and foreign protected merchants were under his nominal charge. In Tehran and Tabrīz the *malik al-tujjār* came into conflict with the Russian authorities during the reign of Muḥammad Shāh over the protection of merchants, a matter which continued to give rise to disputes later also.

In some places the merchants were subject in the early years of the nineteenth century to certain disabilities, but this was unusual. Scott Waring, who visited Shīrāz in 1802, states that the merchants were prohibited from wearing scarlet or crimson robes or having silver or gold buttons on them. He contrasts the character of the merchants with that of the military and bureaucratic officers of the state. Whereas the latter were, he alleges, often rapacious, and were accustomed to spend what they acquired, the merchants were 'always intent upon gain'. They were, he states, 'a shrewd, sensible, and thrifty class of people, willing to undergo any hardship if they had a prospect of making money'.[37] Similarly Justin Perkins states that their style of living was frugal, never extravagant and not often beyond their means. Many of them went on the pilgrimage to Mecca and acquired the dignity and sanctity of *ḥājjīs*.[38] It was not uncommon for government officials and others to go into partnership with merchants, Muḥammad Ḥusayn Khān Amīn al-Dawla, governor of Iṣfahān under Āqā Muḥammad Khān, was said to be in partnership with almost every shopkeeper, farmer and merchant in the town, setting up those who were in want of capital and increasing the means of others who were already in trade.[39] Members of the royal family, including the shah, and occasionally members of his *ḥaram*, from time to time engaged in mercantile transactions, putting money out with merchants to be worked by them. Such transactions were presumably carried on under a *mużāraba* contract, for which *sharʿī* law lays down detailed conditions.

Persian merchants, especially those dealing in the import–export trade, became increasingly influential in the latter part of the nineteenth century. Dr. Gilbar has indicated that the big merchants played a central role in bringing about growth in certain sections of the agricultural sector, in traditional and modern industry, transportation and other services.[40] Elsewhere he has shown the importance of their role in the events leading up to the Constitutional Revolution.[41] The interests of the big merchants did not, however, always coincide with those of the bazaar merchants, the shopkeepers and the craft guilds, who played a rather different role in society.

The various groups and classes were not in any way 'closed' groups. Two things in particular served to unite them: marriage alliances and landownership. The 'men of the sword', through inheritance, family connection and especially provincial office, acquired large estates. Often a governor would settle permanently in the province of which he had become the governor and himself and his family after him would become one of the major local landowners. The Nūrī family in Kirmān, who originally came from Māzandarān, is a case in point. The members of the bureaucracy similarly acquired through purchase large estates and in this way the two classes, the 'men of the sword' and the 'men of the pen', became assimilated to each other. The big merchants also tended to invest surplus funds in land, not only or perhaps primarily for economic gain, but because land gave social prestige. Thus the three groups were drawn together by a common interest. But this was not all: the *'ulamā'*, because of the administration of *awqāf*, and because some of the more venal among them used their position as *mutavallīs* to acquire private estates, also shared a common interest with others who owned or held land.

The second factor which united the leaders of the various groups was intermarriage. At all levels marriage alliances played an extremely important part in political life. The shah, the provincial governors, tribal leaders and government officials took into their *ḥarams* the daughters of local notables and gave their women to those whose support they wished to secure. Leading *'ulamā'* and merchants similarly sought to assure their positions and to increase their influence by marriage alliances. The ramifications of the great families were thus often very considerable. As a result of this mobility the differences between the classes were less sharp than might otherwise have been the case. By the end of the century members of the Qājār family were to be found in almost all walks of life; they were not only provincial governors and military commanders, but also ministers and members of the bureaucracy, writers, poets and Ṣūfīs (but very rarely *'ulamā'*). Basically, however, the structure of society had not greatly altered by the end of the nineteenth century. All still lived in the same world. The gulf which was later to appear between the western-educated and the rest was not yet widely felt.

In the early years of the twentieth century change was much more rapid, politically, economically and socially. The Constitutional Revolution, the roots of which go back to the nineteenth century, can, perhaps, be regarded as a watershed. It was not so much that the constraints of the nineteenth century had weakened or disappeared, but that contact with the outside world had increased, not only in the political and commercial fields, but also in the educational and cultural fields, and that economic conditions inside the country were changing—oil was beginning to be exploited and industry to grow. These various developments made for a loosening, and even a disintegration of the bonds of society as they had existed for centuries; but the fundamental issue in social change, which concerns the relationship of man to man and the purposes of society, received little consideration and it was, perhaps, because of this that social change still remained very limited.

NOTES

1. *Al-Nihāya fī mujarrad al-fiqh wa-'l-fatāwā*, Beirut 1390/1970, p. 299; Persian text (ed. Muḥammad Bāqir Sabzavārī), 2 vols., Tehran AHS 1333–4/1954–6, 1, 199.

2. W. Madelung, 'A Treatise of the Sharīf al-Murtaḍā on the legality of working for the government (*mas'ala fi 'l-'amal ma'a 'l-sulṭān*),' *Bulletin of the School of Oriental and African Studies*, XLIII (1980), i, 26–7.

3. *Al-Nihāya*, pp. 301–3; Persian text, 1, 201–2.

4. See further my article 'A nineteenth century view of *jihād*,' *Studia Islamica*, XXXII (1970), i, 181–92. See also *Qājār Persia*, p. xiv n. 7.

5. Rivalry between factions has been a characteristic feature of Persian social and political life since early times. It frequently took the form of rioting between different religious rites, between different wards or groups in a city or between neighbouring towns and villages (see further 'Islamic Society in Persia', in A. K. S. Lambton, *Theory and practice in medieval Persian government*, London 1980, ch. 7, pp. 15 ff.).

6. See further my article 'Some new trends in Islamic political thought in late 18th and early 19th century Persia', *Studia Islamica*, xxxix (1977), i, 95–128. Cf. also Rustam al-Hukamā''s essay entitled '*Aḥkām va ash'ār*' written in 1828–29, quoted by F. Ādamiyyat and Humā Nāṭiq in *Afkār-ijtimāī va siyāsī va iqtiṣādī*, Tehran AHS 1356/1977–8, pp. 27 ff.

7. Lady Sheil, *Glimpses of life and manners in Persia*, London 1856, pp. 181 and 213–14.

8. See further W. Floor, 'Crafts and industry in Qājār Iran', G.G. Gilbar (ed.), *The modern Middle East, 1800–1914: studies in macro-economic history*, forthcoming. See also F. Ādamiyyat, *Fikr-i āzādī*, Tehran AHS 1340/1961, pp. 27–8. After his return to Tabrīz Mīrzā Ṣāliḥ founded a printing press there and started the first Persian newspaper, *Kāghaẕ-i akhbār.* The first number appeared in 1836; its existence, however, was ephmeral (Mīrzā Ṣāliḥ, *Safar-nāmeh-i Mīrzā Ṣāliḥ-i Shīrāzī*, ed. Muḥammad Shahristānī with an introduction by Ismā'īl Rā'in, Tehran AHS 1347/ 1968–9, pp 26 ff.).

9. J. Morier, *A second journey through Persia, Armenia and Asia Minor, to Constantinople, between the years 1810 and 1816*, London 1818, p. 191.

10. R. W. Wilbraham, *Travels in the Transcaucasian provinces of Russia*, quoted by Sir Denis Wright, *The English amongst the Persians*, London 1977, p. 126.

11. Ibid.

12. Ibid.

13. J. Perkins, *A Residence of eight years in Persia*, Andover-New York 1843, p. 420.

14. See *letters from Persia written by Charles and Edward Burgess 1828–1855*, ed. B. Schwarz, New York 1942. See also W. Sparroy, *Persian children of the royal family*, London 1902, for an account of the author's residence in Iṣfahān as tutor to the sons of Ẓill al-Sulṭān.

15. G. G. Gilbar, 'Demographic developments in late Qājār Persia, 1870–1906', *Asian and African Studies*, XI (1976), ii, 152 ff.

16. See Ādamiyyat, op. cit., and idem., *Īdi'ūlūzhī-i nihżat-i mashrūṭiyyat-i Īrān*, Tehran AHS 1355/1976–7; Ādamiyyat and Nāṭiq, op. cit., and B. Fragner, *Persische Memoire Literatur als Quelle zur neueren Geschichte Irans*, Wiesbaden 1979.

17. G. G. Gilbar, 'The Persian economy in the mid-19th century', *Die Welt des Islams*, XIX (1979), iv, 207–8.

18. See further idem., 'A note on the development of transportation in late Qājār Iran', forthcoming.

19. Wright, op. cit., p. 133.

20. Quoted by Gilbar, 'Transportation'.

21. Ibid.

22. A printing press was established in Tabrīz in 1816. By 1839 there were two lithograph presses in Tabrīz, both the property of Persians, vigorously at work printing Persian books (Perkins, op. cit., p. 374). In 1825 'Abbās Mīrzā sent a Persian to Russia to learn the lithographic process and a plant was established in Tabrīz in that year. Shortly afterwards it was transferred to Tehran. See further Floor, 'Crafts and Industry'. See also idem., 'The first printing press in Iran', *Zeitschrift der Deutschen Morgenländischen Gesellschaft*, cxxx (1980), ii, 369–71 for a brief account of the abortive attempts to establish printing presses in Safavid Persia, one by an Armenian in Julfā (Iṣfahān) and the other by the Carmelite fathers in 1629.

23. Gilbar, 'Demographic Developments', 149 ff.

24. United Kingdom. Public Record Office. F.O. 60:107. Bonham to Sheil, no. 21, Tabriz, 12 March 1844.

25. See further Gilbar, 'Demographic Developments', 152.

26. *'Urf* jurisdiction had existed alongside *shar' ī* jurisdiction from earliest times. The latter was administered by the *qāḍīs* and the *shar'ī* officials and was a written law, which in theory could have no rival. *'Urf* was unwritten and administered by the ruler and his deputies and its judgments enforced by the strong hand of power (see further art. 'Maḥkama', *Encyclopaedia of Islam*, 2nd edition, vi, Leiden 1986, 1–44, esp. 11–22).

27. 'Persian regulations respecting the Nestorian community in the district of Oroomiah—1864', in *British and Foreign State Papers*, LXXIII (1881–82), London 1889, 344.

28. On the Belgian customs administration see A. Destrée, *Les fonctionnaires belges au service de la Perse 1898–1915*, Tehran & Liège 1976.

29. R. M. Burrell, 'Aspects of the reign of Muẓaffar al-Dīn Shāh of Persia, 1896–1907', Ph.D. thesis, University of London 1979, pp. 138 ff.

30. Āqā Khān Maḥallātī, the leader of the Ismā'īlīs, was appointed governor of Kirmān in 1835 or 1836. On his withholding revenue from the central government a force was sent to collect arrears. Unable to resist, Āqā Khān Maḥallātī fled in 1837 to Bam, where he was besieged. He surrendered and was sent to Tehran. He was allowed to return to Kirmān and in 1840 he renewed his rebellion. After a number of skirmishes he was defeated and took refuge in Afghanistan and later India, whence, it was alleged, he carried on a secret correspondence with his followers in eastern Persia. The unfounded attribution of his revolt to British instigation is another example of the sensitiveness of Persia to intervention by the Great Powers. The question of Āqā Khān Maḥallātī continued to trouble Anglo-Persian relations throughout the latter years of Muḥammad Shāh's reign.

31. Cf. Perkins, op. cit., p. 51.

32. P. A. Jaubert, *Voyage en Arménie et en Perse*, Paris 1821, p. 239.

33. Lady Sheil, op. cit., pp. 119–20 and 207.

34. See further Shaul Bakhash, *Iran: monarchy, bureaucracy and reform under the Qajars, 1858–1896*, London 1978.

35. See further my article 'The Persian *'ulamā* and Constitutional Reform', reprinted in *Qājār Persia*, pp. 277–300.

36. C. U. Aitchison, *A Collection of treaties, engagements and sanads relating to India and neighbouring countries*, Calcutta 1933, XIII, 72.

37. E. Scott Waring, *A Tour to Sheeraz*, London 1807, pp. 57, 77 and 102–3.

38. Op. cit., p. 151.

39. Morier, op. cit., p. 131.

40. G. G. Gilbar, 'Economic growth in late Qājār Iran' in Gilbar (ed.), *The modern Middle East 1800–1914*.

41. G. G. Gilbar, 'The big merchants (*tujjār*) and the Persian constitutional revolution of 1906', *Asian and African Studies*, XI (1977), I, 292 ff. See also K. Ekbal, 'Der politische Einfluß des persischen Kaufmannsstandes in der frühen Kadscharenzeit, dargestellt am Beispiel von Ḥāǧǧī Ḫalīl Khan Qazwīnī Maliku't-Tuǧǧār', *Der Islam*, LVII (1980), i, 9–35.

II

Transformations in Society and Economy, 1789–1918

Introduction

MARY C. WILSON

The outcome of the reforms initiated by Middle Eastern elites and encouraged by European powers was varied. It included results both desired and inadvertent and had effects which were experienced differently across the social spectrum. The transformations in society and economy that took place in the nineteenth century were not, however, solely the result of self-conscious programmes of reform. Rather, the reforms took place in a world historical context and were themselves in part an attempt to control the powerful impact of that changing context. This section looks at the nineteenth-century Middle East as shaped both by internal reform and by the changing relationship of the Middle East to the rest of the world. It outlines structural change in social and economic relations and describes the way such change altered individual lives.

The lead article by Charles Issawi draws a picture of the nineteenth-century Middle East as profoundly affected by its integration into the expanding world economy dominated by European capital. He gives an overview of change in areas where it can best be quantified: population, investment, transportation and trade. His signal contribution is in comparing the Middle East with India and Japan. He finds that the Middle East had a 'specific pattern of economic development', and suggests several reasons why this might have been so, 'proximity to Europe . . ., social and political backwardness, and the nature of foreign economic and political control'. All of these crippled the growth of a bourgeoisie, and in its absence he sees foreigners as the active agents of change in the Middle East. The picture which he draws of Middle Eastern economic change in the nineteenth century is one of discontinuity with previous Middle Eastern economic patterns, both in its causes and in its effects.

Kenneth Cuno takes the opposite view. Looking at land use in Egypt, he finds that the origins of private ownership lay not in the nineteenth-century expansion of European capitalism, but in seventeenth-century local conditions of a weak state and a raise in agricultural prices. The two together encouraged individuals to act as if land were privately held. Against this backdrop, the early reforms of Muhammad 'Ali resurrected 'the Ottoman land system originally established in Egypt', in order to reassert state control over land. The requirements of state formation, however, caused Muhammad 'Ali and his successors to make a compromise between maximizing revenue through state ownership of land and its produce and co-opting the support of important groups in Egyptian society. One result of this compromise was the legislation of 1854–8 which strengthened ownership rights and represented 'the ascendancy, once again, of landed classes in Egypt'. For Cuno, nineteenth-century legislation did not create private land ownership; rather the practice of private ownership evident from the seventeenth century on was recognized, finally, by nineteenth-century legislation. Thus, in his view, reform—or at least the land reforms of the nineteenth century—exhibited continuity with past land use patterns.

How these pictures of economic and legal change translated to changes in individual economic activity, material life and social organization is the topic of Judith Tucker's inquiry. In her conceptual framework, the motor force of change in nineteenth-century Egypt is the penetration of capitalism. She finds that the reforms legislated in response to this force were not beneficial to all or even to the majority.

For peasants, by far the largest group in Egyptian society, nineteenth-century reform brought increased demands: conscription and forced labour (corvée). Reform also brought loss of control over land and crops, and a drop in peasants' material standard of life. Peasant resistance to these changes included attempts to consolidate family property in order to protect it from state interference. Looking at court cases, Tucker finds that this consolidation was carried out at the 'expense of those family members whose legal and customary rights were weakest', at the expense, in other words, of women. According to her analysis, the assumption that women benefited from 'the impact of the West and the rise of "modern" society should be re-examined'.

The inclusion of women's historical experience and activities can lead to shifts in historical judgement. Reform becomes less positive and, in Donald Quataert's article, the decline of Middle Eastern textile manufacturing in the nineteenth century becomes less absolute. He looks at women's textile production in both city and countryside and concludes that although manufacturing activities changed, owing to the impact of European manufactured goods, they did not cease. He faults prior historians for looking solely at the urban manufacturing sector and, within that, only at the (male) guild structure. The production of silk thread in Bursa, for example, increased ten times by mid-century thanks to mechanization and a female labour force. Over-expansion thereafter meant that silk-spinning factories did not work at full capacity. Owing to the social view of women workers as supplemental wage-earners, however, the factories stayed open, using women as a flexible workforce. Cotton spinning did drop off dramatically under the impact of European imports, but this did not entirely halt local spinning and weaving. Women who could afford to buy imported yarn wove that into cloth. Women who could not afford it continued to spin and weave for home use. At the end of the century handlooms were still a common feature in most Ottoman homes, testifying to the 'flexible responses to changing market opportunities' of the Ottoman household and to continuing textile production.

Women and peasants are often absent from the historical record and are often wrongly judged in their absence as outside history, passive or traditional. Yet their historical experience and sometimes even their voices can be recovered by a careful assessment of known sources and by access to new ones, as has been demonstrated by Tucker and Quataert. The urban scene, and in it the sites of (male) power, of bureaucracy, of schools, is better documented. Yet it, too, has its silences.

Paul Dumont shatters one such silence by uncovering the daily life of an Ottoman functionary. His subject, Said Bey, lived in Istanbul at the beginning of the twentieth century. Said Bey has reaped the benefit of a century of reform: he has had an excellent modern education, he knows French, and he holds several posts. His activities are noted in his ledgers—not what he thought and felt, but how he spent his time and his money. These records are eloquent testimony to the material and cultural life of a certain rank in society and of social relations within that rank. They also testify to the continuities and to the transformations of that century of reform.

Said Bey was comfortable, even well-off. He and his wife had active social lives, each in its proper gendered sphere following the classic lines of Ottoman society. In his material and cultural life European forms jostled but did not overpower the Ottoman. From time to time he went to the theatre to see plays of Western type and to balls and the opera, but he regularly went to Karagoz and Arabic and Turkish musical events and theatre. He bought a blue stoneware stove and a mangal (brazier) in the same year. He and his family observed all religious holidays, although he does not appear to have been personally pious. He also observed public holidays, smoothly accommodating himself to the flow of political events; he celebrated the sultan's accession annually before 1908 and the Young Turk revolution thereafter. The momentous political changes of the new century do not appear to have registered in his daily life. The accumulated change of the past century, however, can be clearly seen in the particular eclecticisms of his material surroundings and of his social and cultural life. It is even more obvious in his political and religious life, which has a decidedly civic cast.

Ervand Abrahamian's article turns from an individual to 'the crowd', from the Ottoman Empire to Qajar Iran, and from the apparently apolitical Said Bey to the pointedly political crowd of the 1905–9 Persian revolution. Of this crowd he asks the question: who took part and why? His theoretical framework is bounded at one end by Gustave Le Bon's 'monstrous mob', activated by irrational and murderous group instinct; at the other end is George Rudé's 'single-minded', 'not fickle [or] peculiarly irrational' crowd. He finds that there was not one crowd in the Persian revolution but two. The first, the 'constitutional crowd', controlled the streets between 1905 and 1907; the second 'conservative crowd' controlled the streets after 1907. He finds both crowds to be of identifiable social make-up with rational goals according to their interests. Thus he comes down firmly on the side of George Rudé. What his article demonstrates is less the changes that had taken place in Iran by the turn of the century, although the slogan of a constitution surely suggests some change, than changes that had begun to take place in the study of Middle East history in the 1960s when it began to branch out from the established fields of political and diplomatic history towards social history.

The city was the site of the Persian revolution of 1905–9; the urban crowd was, for a moment, the arbiter of power. Although Middle Eastern cities had long been the sites of power, they had not always been the sources of power. Cairo, the subject of André Raymond's essay, had seen a succession of rulers whose power came from outside—the mamluks, the Ottoman governors, the French (briefly), Muhammad ʿAli and his descendants, and the British. Although from outside, each had to come to terms with important groups within the city, in particular with *ʿulama* and merchants, in order to stay in power. These two groups were the local groups to reckon with from the time of the medieval historian Maqrizi (1364–1441) until the mid-nineteenth century, and this stability of social organization perhaps accounts for a Cairo relatively unchanged in size or shape from the medieval period until 1863. In 1863 the Khedive Ismaʿil began to build a new, Europeanized Cairo. His efforts ended with the creation of a classic colonial city, the dual city, and with the chain of events that led to the British occupation of Egypt in 1882. The changes wrought by Ismaʿil in Cairo reflected not only his own mentality but also the changed relationship between Egypt and Europe. The new Europeanized quarters with their banks and embassies marked the end of that stable world of *ʿulama* and merchants and a shift of power in favour of Europe and its clients.

Britain's occupation solidified and made rigid the division of Cairo into two cities begun by Ismaʿil. The European city expanded westward to the

Nile and across it owing to the 1902 Aswan barrage, which made possible closer control of Nile flooding and the building of new quarters on the banks and islands of the river and of bridges connecting the western bank to the new city centre. The initial years of growth and prosperity under the British, however, hid the ill effects of a colonial economy.

After World War I the population of Cairo began to grow at a rate which outstripped the population growth of Egypt. Overpopulation of the countryside and a consequent decline in rural standards of living brought rural migrants to the city in large numbers. In 1927 only 64 per cent of Cairo's population had been born there. But work in Cairo was not easy to find because industrialization had been little encouraged by the British. Thus the seeds of Cairo's twentieth-century crisis lay in the nineteenth century's need for rural workers, brought on by an expanding state and the need for increased revenues on the one hand, and by the industrialization of Britain and the need for increased raw materials on the other.

Cairo's burgeoning population, without sufficient work or sufficient urban services for its numbers, has filled and spilled out of the colonial dual city. New suburbs and satellites built since the 1960s never quite meet the needs of the growing middle-class population; the poor live in slums. This third Cairo, the metropolis, has become the symbol of the legacy of imperialism and of the shortcomings of independent governments in the twentieth-century Middle East to which we turn in the second half of this book.

Middle East Economic Development, 1815–1914: the General and the Specific

CHARLES ISSAWI

In the century between the Napoleonic and First World Wars a world economy, based on western Europe, was built. Two aspects of this process may be distinguished. On the one hand, the various regions were successively integrated in a world-wide economic and financial system, through mechanical transport, mass migration, vast capital flows and a huge expansion in international trade. And on the other, the economy of the non-European countries was profoundly transformed. Thanks to the spread of security, the introduction of modern hygiene and the reduction of famine, death rates fell and population increased severalfold. In response to rising European demand for raw materials and helped by a sharp reduction in transport costs, agricultural output greatly expanded and export of cash crops multiplied; this in turn had deep repercussions on systems of land tenure, generally resulting in a shift from communal or tribal ownership to individual property rights. Handicrafts, exposed to the competition of European machine-made goods, were for the most part eliminated; and since, for a variety of economic, social and political reasons, modern factories did not rise to take their place, a process of de-industrialization occurred in many parts of the world. Social systems were also transformed and the already great inequality prevailing in these countries increased. For although the level of living of the masses probably rose in most places over the greater part of the period, the income and wealth of the upper strata grew much more rapidly. Lastly, the active agents of change were mostly foreign—either Europeans or Americans or immigrants from neighbouring countries, e.g. the Chinese and Indians in south-east Asia.

The above description fits the Middle East very closely for the period under review. The purpose of this paper is to examine whether and in what respects the region diverged from the prevailing patterns and trends. For this purpose four topics that lend themselves to quantitative analysis will be examined in some detail: population growth, foreign capital investment, mechanical transport and foreign trade. Five other topics will also be briefly discussed: agriculture, industry, levels of income, educational progress and agents of economic change. Wherever possible, comparison will be made with world totals and with figures for two other regions with sharply contrasting experiences, India and Japan; Japan was chosen as the most successful example of development in recent history while India, on the contrary, represents a country that failed to develop rapidly in spite of a promising start in several fields. Lastly, an attempt will be made to determine whether the Middle East had its own distinctive pattern of development.

It goes without saying that this paper represents only a tentative first approach to a field that has received very little study. Essentially, it raises questions rather than providing answers. Its main purpose is to stimulate discussion and suggest topics for further research.

Population

In the nineteenth century population growth occurred in almost all parts of the world, but its extent varied considerably. The following table gives some crude estimates made by Carr-Saunders and Willcox, respectively.[1]

	Compound Annual Rate of Increase per 1,000					
	1800–1850		1850–1900		1900–1920	
Africa	1·1	0·0	4·7	6·9	7·7	− 0·4
N. America	29·8	29·8	23·0	23·0	18·6	18·6
Latin America	11·1	7·2	13·0	13·0	18·6	18·6
Asia	4·3	2·0	5·4	2·8	2·8	6·1
Europe & USSR	7·1	7·0	8·7	7·0	7·0	7·0
Total	5·1	3·4	7·3	5·9	5·9	7·1

For India, the population has been guessed at about 120 million in 1800. The 1872 census gave a total of 206 million, the 1911 census of 315, and the 1921 census of 319 million; about half the increase in 1872–1911 is attributable to improved methods of enumeration and additional areas covered[2] and the negligible growth in 1911–21 is due to the influenza epidemic. The 'real increase in population (allowing for the inclusion of new territory) in 50 years has been 88.6 million, i.e., 34.9 per cent',[3] giving a compound rate of growth of 6 per thousand. Accepting the 1800 guess of 120 million would imply a rate of growth of 7 for 1800–72, which may err on the side of exaggeration. Japan's population in 1800 was probably around 30 million. The 1872 census showed a figure of 33 million (which should probably be raised to 35 or 36 million) and that of 1920 of 56 million,[4] indicating rates of growth of 1 and 11 per thousand, respectively; however, the first figure should be slightly raised and the second reduced.

For the Middle East estimates are of the very roughest. Egypt's population in 1800 is usually put at 2.5–3 million, but good reasons have been given for raising the figure to at least 3.5 million.[5] The first reliable census, that of 1897, put the total at 9.72 million and the 1917 census at 12.75 million, indicating rates of growth of 11 and 14 per thousand, respectively. For Iraq, where the first census was taken in 1947, Hasan's estimates show annual rates of growth of 13 between 1867 and 1890, 18 in 1890–1905 and 17 in 1905–19.[6] No reliable figures are available for Syria—which term is used throughout this paper to cover 'geographical' or 'greater' Syria. British consular estimates in the 1830s ranged from 1,000,000 to 1,864,000, but most of them fall between 1,250,000 and 1,450,000. Estimates for 1910–15 cluster around 3.5 million.[7] Assuming a figure of 1,350,000 for 1835 and 3.5 million for 1914 would suggest a rate of growth of 12 per thousand; putting the 1835 figure at 1,864,000 would reduce the growth rate to 8. If these figures are at all correct, they would indicate that the rate of growth of the population of the Arab countries was distinctly higher than those of Asia and Africa in general and India and Japan in particular. If this is so, it would mean that a large share of the increment in income achieved during the period under review was swallowed up by population growth. Available data on Algeria point in the same direction.[8] However, it should be remembered that not even an indication of the trend of population in Arabia is available, while that of the Sudan is usually believed to have fallen during the Mahdist period, following an earlier growth under Egyptian rule.[9]

Data for Turkey and Iran are even more fragmentary. The 1831 Ottoman 'census' put the number of males (*erkek*) in Anatolia at 2,384,000. If one assumes this to refer to adult males, a population of some 10 million is indicated—a figure of the same order of magnitude as other very rough estimates given by various European sources.[10] On the eve of the First World War, the population of the territory of what became the Republic of Turkey was put at 14,549,000.[11] Accepting these two figures at their face value would indicate the low growth rate of 5 per thousand in 1831–1914 (but see note 15, below). For Iran it is not even possible to say whether the population in the latter half of the nineteenth century was larger or smaller than it had been at the beginning of that century. Thus Rawlinson put the total in 1850 at 10 million but in 1873 'after two desolating visitations of cholera and famine' at 6 million.[12] Other estimates for the 1880s range between 5 and 10 million, the two least unsatisfactory showing 7,654,000 for 1884 (by Houtum Schindler) and 6 million for 1888 (by a Russian scholar, Zolotarev). A later estimate by Houtum Schindler put the population in 1897 at 9 million, while Lorini gives a figure of 9,332,000 for 1899.[13]

As a very rough check on these figures, one can attempt some backward extrapolation. In 1956, when the first nation-wide Iranian census put the population at 18,955,000, that of Egypt was 23,532,000 and that of Turkey 24,771,000.[14] Assuming the same ratio to have prevailed in 1890 would indicate a figure of around 7 million for Iran, compared to about 9 million for Egypt. However, it seems highly unlikely that in 1890–1956 the Iranian rate of growth was as high as the Egyptian. This might indicate that the higher estimates given by Sir A. Houtum Schindler—a British-German general in the Iranian army, who knew the country well—are nearer the mark, a conclusion that tallies with Curzon's and Lorini's.[15]

As for Iran's rate of growth, for what it is worth, one can quote Curzon's guess, presumably based on the India Office records on which he drew so heavily, that at the time of his journey, a period 'free both from war and famine', the population was growing at 0.75 per cent per annum.[16] And for what they are worth, most of the estimates of town populations quoted by him show some increase in the period 1800–90, often following sharp declines in the eighteenth century; however, there were some important exceptions, e.g. Isfahan and Meshed, whose populations seem to have declined.

Capital investment

A United Nations study, *Capital Movements during the Interwar Period*, has put total long-term foreign investment outstanding in 1914 at $44,000 million. Of this over $2,000 million, or as much as one-twentieth, was in the Middle East.

Total investment in Egypt on the eve of the First World War was over E £200 million, of which 94 million represented the outstanding public debt and the rest investment in the private sector.[17] For Turkey, the outstanding government debt at the time of the Lausanne conference was 161 million Turkish gold pounds, a figure not too significantly different from the one for 1914. Private foreign investment in 1914 was £66.4 million.[18] In Iran the only important private investment was that of the Anglo-Persian Oil Company, whose capital was raised to £4.2 million in 1914; the addition of the few Russian, British and other enterprises (banks, mines, transport, telegraphs, fisheries, etc.) would bring the total to well over £10 million.[19] As for the public debt, at the outbreak of war some £2 million was owed to Britain and the equivalent of about £4.8 million to Russia.[20]

The magnitude of foreign investment in Turkey and Egypt may be gauged by comparing it with the following figures, which represent total foreign investment in both the private and public sectors in 1913: India about £360 million, Japan about £200 million, China about £150 million, Brazil a little over £150 million, Mexico a little over £100 million. Relative to their population, the Ottoman Empire (and, still more strikingly, Egypt) had received an enormous amount of foreign capital. In Iran the scale of foreign investment was much smaller. It may be added that hardly any of the investment in the Ottoman Empire percolated to the Persian Gulf–Red Sea area; the exceptions were the Hijaz railway and some railway and irrigation construction in Iraq. Similarly the Sudan was only just beginning to attract foreign capital at the outbreak of war.

When, however, attention is turned to the *use* made of this foreign investment, the picture looks much less favourable. For whereas the bulk of the Indian and Japanese public debts helped to finance economic development, most of the Ottoman, Egyptian and Iranian public debts was either taken up in commissions and charges, or was used to repay earlier debts or to finance wars, or for indemnity payments, or was spent by the monarchs in various unproductive ways.[21] As a result these countries found themselves saddled with debt charges that absorbed one-eighth of the Iranian budget, nearly a third of the Ottoman and almost half the Egyptian, and yet had very little to show in return.

Transport

Three factors shaped much of the development of transport in the Middle East: the region's location, the pattern of growth of steam navigation and the rivalries of the Great Powers. The high fuel consumption of steamships confined them to rivers and narrow waters for many decades; it was not until the 1870s that the greater part of international trade was carried by steamers rather than sailing ships. But within such waters steam navigation spread rapidly and by the 1830s the Mediterranean was criss-crossed by several lines. In the late 1830s British, French and Austrian lines provided regular services to Egypt, Syria and Turkey. After that progress was swift. Describing the situation around 1860, Farley reported: 'The mails leave London for Syria every Friday via Marseilles and every Monday via Trieste; while English steamers run regularly between Beirut and Liverpool'[22]—to which he could have added the Russian Black Sea line, which started operations in 1845 and served the Levant and Alexandria. And by 1870, there were three Egyptian, three British, five French, four Austrian, two Italian, one Russian and one Turkish steamship lines maintaining regular services to Egypt, and many others with ships calling at irregular intervals.[23] In the meantime, regular steamer services between India and Suez had been established in 1834, and between India and the Persian Gulf in 1861. It may be added that the opening of the Suez Canal not only attracted a vast volume of traffic to the eastern Mediterranean but also strongly stimulated the development of steam navigation in general, by greatly facilitating fuelling on the Europe–Far Eastern route.[24]

Thus one may say that the Middle East was very adequately served by steamship lines connecting it with the outside world. It also had commercial steamboats on its navigable rivers at fairly early dates: the Nile in Egypt by 1841 and in the Sudan by the early 1860s,[25] the Tigris–Euphrates in 1862 and the Kārūn in 1888.

As regards railways, the other principal means of transport in the nineteenth century, the Middle East (with the definite exception of Egypt) was far less well equipped. In 1913 total railway track in the world was over 1,100,000 kilometres; of these 4,300 were in Egypt, 3,500 in the Ottoman Empire and 2,500 in the Sudan, i.e. less than 1 per cent of the world total, a figure commensurate with neither the region's area nor its population. By that date India had 56,000 kilometres of railway and Japan 11,000. Two further facts stand out: the high development of railway transport in Egypt (which accounted for nearly half the regional total) and its absence in Iran.

By 1913 Egypt had a higher railway mileage per unit of *inhabited* area than almost any country in the world, and per unit of population than most countries.[26] It owed this position to an early start: Egypt had its first railway before Sweden or Japan, and it was not until the 1870s that the *total* railway mileage of Argentina and Brazil surpassed that of Egypt, while Japan did not catch up until the 1890s and China until after 1900. This in turn was largely due to the British desire for swift connections between Alexandria and Suez, the two steamship terminals on the route to India. A combination of factors made it possible for the British to push their railway scheme, against French opposition—just as the French were later to carry out the Suez Canal project, much more slowly and laboriously, against British obstruction. And after that the rulers of Egypt—first the viceroys and then the British—had enough freedom of action and sufficient resources to build a large network.

The completion of the trans-Egyptian railway greatly reduced the attraction of the rival route, through Mesopotamia, which also had its supporters in Britain. Other factors holding up railway development in Turkey, Syria and Iran were the weaker financial positions of these countries and the intensity of Great Power rivalries. One has only to read the diplomatic history of the Baghdad railway, or to follow the various projects and counter-projects for railways in Iran drawn by the British and Russians, to realize what an important impediment this constituted. Here, too, except for Egypt and the Sudan, the contrast with India and Japan is striking.

Foreign trade

International trade grew rapidly in the period under review. Rough estimates put the total (exports plus imports) in current prices at £320 million in 1800, £560 million in 1840, £1,450 million in 1860, £2,890 million in 1872–3 and £8,360 in 1913. Since prices were much higher in the period 1800–40 than in 1880–1913, the increase in real terms was greater than the twenty-five-fold rise registered in the above figures.[27]

Taking the Middle East as a whole, the expansion of foreign trade did not match the general advance. The Egyptian figure may indeed have been higher than the world average. The first reliable statistics put total trade in 1823 at E£2.1 million; by 1860 the total stood at E£5.1 million, by 1880 at E£21.8 million and by 1913 at E£60 million, a thirty-fold increase; moreover the 1823 level was probably higher than that of any of the previous fifty years or so.[28] But Ottoman trade almost certainly did not rise as fast, though comparison is vitiated by the fact that the area covered shrank steadily. In 1829 Ottoman trade with Britain and France amounted to £2.6 million, and total trade may be guessed to have been around £4 million. In 1876 the total was estimated at £54 million and in 1911 it stood at £63.5 million—perhaps a fifteen-fold increase[29]—and for the other parts of the region the growth in trade was surely much smaller.

The only available series for Iran, compiled by Entner, refers to that country's trade with Russia and shows a drop from an average of 10 million gold roubles in 1830–1 (a figure higher than that of previous years and reflecting the effects of the Treaty of Turkmanchai of 1828) to 6.9 million in 1860 and a recovery to 10.4 million in 1880; after that there was a rapid rise to a peak of 101.3 million in 1913.[30] In fact, however, Iran's total trade must have risen much less than ten-fold over the whole period. First, because the figures are in gold (1896) roubles, and therefore deflate the value of the 1830–1 totals, when prices were higher. (The figure for 1830–1 in account roubles was 25.2 million.) Secondly, because Russia's share of total trade probably rose appreciably over this period—it grew from 45 per cent of the total in 1901/2 to 63 per cent in 1912/13,[31] and in the late 1880s Curzon had estimated it at about £2 million (a figure that agrees fairly well with the Entner series) out of a total Iranian trade of some £7–8 million,[32] or say 30 per cent.

The few available data on Arabia and the Sudan also indicate that the rate of growth must have been rather low.[33]

Both India and Japan showed faster growth in their foreign trade than did the Middle East. Following the abrogation, in 1813, of the monopoly hitherto enjoyed by the East India Company 'the increase of trade with India [in 1814–32] has been enormous'.[34] By 1835–9 total trade averaged £18.7 million per annum (or about twice the 1814 level)[35] and in 1909–14 slightly over £250 million, a more than twenty-five-fold increase in one hundred years. In Japan total trade rose from an average of 36.0 million yen in 1868–70 to 1,511.4 million in 1913, a more than forty-fold increase.[36]

But although Middle Eastern foreign trade grew more slowly than did that of India and Japan, it played a relatively larger part in the economy of the region. Thus *per capita* trade in Egypt in 1913 amounted to $24.3, in the Ottoman Empire to $15.2, and in Iran to $10.3; the corresponding figures for India were $4.3 and for Japan $12.6. As a proportion of gross national product trade must have been far higher in the Middle East than in Japan and India.[37]

No less important is the difference in the composition of trade. By 1913 the Middle East's exports consisted almost entirely of agricultural produce, with some minerals from Turkey and a very small amount of oil from Iran. The same was true for India, except for some textiles. But Japanese exports already contained an appreciable proportion of cotton and silk textiles and other manufactured goods.

Agriculture

This large population growth and increase in exports presupposes an expansion of agricultural output, and all available evidence points to such a trend in most parts of the region. Generally speaking this was accomplished within the framework of peasant farming rather than plantation farming, and by extension of cultivated area rather than by intensification.[38] Hardly any attempts were made to improve methods of cultivation other than the foundation of the Ottoman Agricultural Bank in 1888 and one or two irrigation projects such as the Konya and Hindiyya dams, and there is no evidence of a rise in yields per acre.

The major exception to this statement was of course Egypt. Here extension of cultivation was impossible without irrigation works, which became steadily more elaborate and expensive in the course of the century. Conversion from basin to perennial irrigation naturally increased total annual yield per acre, since more than one crop could be grown on the same patch of land in a year and there was a shift to more valuable cash crops, especially cotton. But there is also evidence of a sharp rise in yields *per crop* per acre.[39] And at the turn of the century systematic efforts at intensification by means of selective breeding and application of chemical fertilizers were begun.[40]

India's experience recalls both that of Egypt and that of the rest of the Middle East. In most regions there was simply an extension of the cultivated area, with a switch to cash crops unaccompanied by a rise in yields. But there was also an enormous expansion of irrigation, and by 1913 government irrigation works watered an area of 25 million acres while private works accounted for a further 22 million. And starting around 1900 systematic research and experimentation was undertaken.[41]

Japan's development was completely different. Since most of the cultivable land was already under cultivation, growth could come only by raising yields, through intensification. This began as early as the 1870s and has been sustained to a remarkable degree ever since.[42]

Industry

'In India there was a much more definite hiatus than in the West between the decay of the handicrafts and the establishment of factories, during which certain types of demand were largely met by imports.'[43] In the Middle East the hiatus was even greater. For on the one hand the decline of some handicrafts, under the impact of European competition, began as early as the eighteenth century and was sharply accelerated from the 1830s on. And on the other the advent of modern industry was greatly delayed—indeed it was only just beginning to appear at the outbreak of the First World War, and did not really gain a foothold until the 1930s.[44]

India, on the other hand, continued to export handicraft textiles to Europe and elsewhere until early in the nineteenth century—it is worth recalling that Alexander Hamilton's report of 1791 demanded protection as much from Indian as from British goods; the decline of its handicrafts started around 1820 and modern industrialization began earlier than in the Middle East, in the 1860s, gathered strength in the last quarter of the nineteenth century and reached large proportions by 1914, in spite of a slackening after the 1890s.[45] As for Japan, there was practically no hiatus. For the handicrafts were immune to foreign competition until the opening of the country in the 1850s, and after that were greatly helped by the government to modernize and play an important part in the economy. And on the other hand, as early as the 1850s, and much more so after the Meiji restoration of 1868, modern industries were set up by the government or private enterprise, making of Japan a significant industrial power by 1914.[46]

Levels of living

Only the most tentative statements are possible regarding trends in levels of living. In Egypt it is possible that there may have been a fall in levels of living (but surely not in *per capita* income) under Muḥammad 'Alī, followed by a rise under his immediate successors. In the 1860s the cotton boom seems to have appreciably raised levels of living and during the British occupation there is also evidence of a distinct improvement.[47] For Syria, two scholars believe that there was a general impoverishment in the 1840s–50s,[48] but the decline in levels of living, if any, may well have been confined to the towns. It seems probable that from the 1860s until the First World War a steady, if slow, rise in *per capita* incomes and levels of living occurred. As for Iran, 'in periods of peace before the mid-nineteenth century the peasants were apparently better off than they are today'.[49] Clearly, one cannot draw conclusions for the region as a whole.

The course of events in India is at least as obscure. The most recent and authoritative survey of the state of knowledge in this field observes: 'It is dismaying to realize that even within very broad ranges of error we do not know whether during the past century-and-a-half the economy's performance improved, stagnated or actually declined,' and adds, 'This is true whether we attempt to measure performance in terms of *per capita* income or by any reasonable combination of qualitative-quantitative elements.'[50] As for Japan, 'some advance in living standards is evidenced in the decline of mortality rates, in increased *per capita* consumption of food and clothing supplies, and in the growth of public services of various kinds—especially in the cities', but most of the increase in national product was absorbed by population growth, capital investment and armaments.[51]

Educational progress

Here one can be much more definite. Both in mass and in higher education the Middle East—which had started at a very low level in 1800—lagged behind other regions with distinctly lower *per capita* incomes. Thus Egypt's illiteracy rate in 1907 was 93 per cent, a figure equal to that of India but well above Burma's 71 per cent, Ceylon's 69 per cent and the Philippines' 51 per cent—not to mention Japan, where already in the 1850s a male literacy rate of 40–50 per cent had been achieved and by 1914 'virtually the entire population had attained functional literacy, and compulsory school attendance was as close to 100 per cent as it could be'.[52] Illiteracy among the Turks (though not among the minority groups) must have been still higher, since the 1927 figure was 92 per cent (by which time Egypt's had fallen to 85 per cent) and in Iran higher still. As for higher education, by 1914 Egypt had only an embryonic university in Cairo, and Turkey a young and anaemic one in Istanbul,[53] in contrast to the small but far superior Indian universities (three of which were by then over sixty years old) and technical institutes, not to mention the excellent Japanese universities.

The one exception to the above statement is Lebanon, where illiteracy rates were almost certainly not above 50 per cent and which had two good foreign universities.

Agents of economic and social change

Here too the main facts are clear, and very significant. In Japan the impetus for economic development came from the ruling circles, who kept a firm hold over the whole process. Foreign capital investment in the private sector was negligible and although foreign skills played an important part they did so under Japanese supervision and control.[54] In India, by contrast, the main impetus was British—not only through the government, which built the railways, ports and irrigation works, but also in the private sector: in foreign trade, plantations, finance and several industries. But much of the development was carried out by Indians, e.g. the cotton textile industry, which was almost entirely Indian, the steel industry and other branches. In this process Parsees played a leading part, but Hindus, notably the Marwaris, also had their share. The role of Muslims was negligible.[55]

In the Middle East the development that took place before 1914 was achieved almost entirely by foreigners or members of minority groups—Armenians, Greeks, Jews, Christian Lebanese and Syrians. The lack of interest of the Muslim majority—whether Egyptian, Turkish, Arabian or Iraqi—is striking, and has often been commented upon. Only in Syria, Iran and Hadramaut is there any evidence of commercial entrepreneurship among Muslims.[56] It may be added that the only country to receive any appreciable immigration was Egypt, which by 1914 had nearly a quarter of a million Europeans and somewhat fewer Armenians, Lebanese, Syrians and Jews, all of whom played a dominant part in the economy; mention should also be made of Jewish immigration to Palestine.

Conclusion

In drawing conclusions from the foregoing analysis, to see whether there was a specific pattern of economic development in the Middle East, an initial distinction should be made between the Mediterranean portion and the Persian Gulf–Red Sea portion of the region. The latter, which includes Iran, Iraq, Arabia and the Sudan, was relatively little affected by the changes taking place in the world until the exploitation of oil made of it, suddenly, the centre of the Middle East economy. Until the First World War, the impact of the world upon it had been mainly negative since European competition had severely hurt its shipping trade[57] and handicrafts without developing commensurately its other resources.

As for the Mediterranean region, here too there was much diversity, the trends observed being far more advanced in Egypt than in Syria or Turkey; the result of the foregoing discussion may be summarized as follows:

Population growth probably started earlier than in other underdeveloped regions (including India and Japan) and therefore, even assuming that rates of increase were no higher than elsewhere, may have reached greater overall dimensions; this was certainly true of Egypt and possibly of Syria and Iraq.

Foreign capital borrowing this was extremely high, and the proceeds were largely used unproductively, in contrast to India and Japan.

Transport regular steamship connections with Europe were established very early; railways were highly developed in Egypt, much less so in Syria and Turkey.

Foreign trade growth was rapid, though slower than in Japan and, except for Egypt, slower than in India; however, both in *per capita* terms and as a percentage of gross national product, foreign trade was far greater than in India or Japan.

Agriculture expansion of output was obtained by the extension of the cultivated area, not by intensification as in Japan. In Egypt even more than in India, irrigation played a leading part.

Industry Middle Eastern crafts seem to have suffered more from foreign competition than did those of India and Japan; in addition, modern industry came much later.

Education remarkably little progress was made in this field, probably less than in India, not to mention Japan.

Agents of growth these were drawn almost solely from foreign or minority groups, in sharp contrast with Japan and, to a far lesser extent, India.

Underlying the pattern formed by these trends are three basic, and partly interrelated, factors: the region's proximity to Europe and strategic location, its social and political backwardness, and the nature of foreign economic and political control. To them should be added a fourth: the scarcity of those resources on which industry was based until the end of the nineteenth century, notably water-power, wood, coal and iron. Almost the only raw material available for industrialization was cotton.

Proximity accounts for the early date at which Europe began to impinge on the economy of the Middle East. It helps to explain the forging of transport links with Europe, the exposure of Middle Eastern handicrafts to devastating foreign competition, the expansion of Middle Eastern agricultural output in response to foreign demand, and the consequent rapid growth of foreign trade. Proximity may have impelled Europeans to help in establishing quarantines and other hygienic controls in the Middle East, to prevent the spread of epidemics, and in this way may have stimulated population growth.[58] It facilitated the migration to the Middle East of European entrepreneurs and technicians, who made an important contribution to the region's development and imposed on it a certain direction and pattern. And proximity certainly facilitated European economic and political control over the Middle East.[59]

The social and political backwardness of the region helps to account for the nature of its response to the impact of European economic expansion. Three aspects of this may be distinguished. First, the educational and cultural level of the Middle East was very low, even compared to other underdeveloped regions such as Japan and India, not to mention south-eastern Europe and Latin America.[60] Secondly its social structure was unfavourable for development. For various historical reasons, it had failed to produce a vigorous bourgeoisie and lacked autonomous bodies, such as city states, guilds and other corporations which could express, and defend, the interests of classes or groups interested in economic development; instead, control remained firmly in the hands of the military and civilian bureaucracy. Thirdly, and no doubt at least partly as a consequence, the economic ideas and policies of the government were singularly unenlightened. In Europe, the basic tenet of the Mercantilists was the need to promote exports in order to increase the output of local industry, and various measures were used to achieve this end. In the Ottoman Empire, however, exports were taxed at a higher rate than imports. Here prevailed a 'policy of provision', to use Hecksher's expressive term describing the medieval European attitude. The main objectives were not to promote local production but to meet the fiscal needs of the government and to ensure that the principal towns, and in particular Istanbul, would be adequately supplied. Some signs of a more enlightened policy appeared under Selim III but little came of it. And after that Middle Eastern statesmen, such as Reshid Pasha, swallowed the liberal prescription for economic growth and did little to help the economy until the latter part of the nineteenth century.[61]

The very low educational and cultural level of the Middle East, its social structure, and the form of its political institutions, meant that it had neither a half-way efficient government nor a native bourgeoisie that could take the country's economic development in hand and help to guide its course along the desired path. Hence when it was struck by the Industrial Revolution, with its demand for the exploitation of its raw materials, market and transport possibilities, development had to be carried out by Europeans assisted by minority groups—if it was to be achieved at all. But development through such an implanted bourgeoisie had four fatal defects. First, a very large share of the fruits of progress went to foreigners or members of minorities; to take an extreme case, just before the First World War these two groups may have owned 15–20 per cent of Egypt's wealth and absorbed well over 10 per cent of its income. Secondly, the presence of educated foreigners or minority groups weakened the main pressure on the governments for the spread of education and the development of human resources in these countries. Thirdly, the existence and power of this bourgeoisie inhibited the growth of a native Muslim one. Lastly, because of this factor, the whole process of capitalist development in the region remained alien and was regarded as such by its inhabitants, a fact that helps to explain the measures taken against foreigners and minority groups in Turkey in the 1920s and in Egypt in the 1940–50s. It should be added that in Syria and Lebanon foreigners played a different and far smaller part and development was much more indigenous.

Lastly, as regards foreign economic and political control, in a way the Middle East had the worst of both worlds. Japan, never having lost its full independence, was able to carry out the 1868 revolution and thereafter to guide the economy in the direction demanded by the national interest, as interpreted by the ruling group. India, by contrast, was subjected to outright British control. This had many drawbacks, which have been rightly stressed since the time of Adam Smith. But it had some advantages, which were strikingly foretold by Marx (see his brilliant 'The Future Results of British Rule in India', published in the *New York Daily Tribune*, July 1853) though carefully ignored by his followers. After the initial plunder and dislocation, British rule provided honest and efficient administration. It also ensured that the foreign debt was used productively, to build the largest irrigation system in the world and the third largest railway network, and to provide some education, and it transformed the land tenure system. And while not encouraging, and indeed often positively impeding, industrialization it 'laid down the material premises' for it.

In the Middle East, however, there was no complete foreign *political* control, except in Aden and in the Sudan after 1896. In the rest of the region there was much influence by rival powers, which jealously watched and checked each other. This led to the abortion of Muḥammad 'Alī's attempt at development and of two promising revolutions, the Egyptian in 1882 and the Iranian in 1905–9 and to the stultification of much progress that might otherwise have taken place in Turkey, Iran and Syria. Even in Egypt the Capitulations and Caisse de la Dette thwarted many of Cromer's reforms.[62] Yet foreign *economic* control was overwhelming and led not only to the buttressing of the existing social order and to the creation of a deep feeling of discouragement but also to the sucking out of vast sums from the region in the form of payments of interest and dividends. This drain, together with the rapid population growth, wars, royal extravagance and possibly the rise in consumption levels, left little for investment in physical and human capital. The disastrous results of such a situation showed themselves most clearly in Egypt after the First World War, when the limits of cultivation had been reached and terms of trade deteriorated. Fortunately for the Middle East, it got a second chance, in the form of the discovery of its oil resources and a huge amount of foreign aid, and this is enabling it today to carry out a new programme of industrialization and modernization of its economy and society.

This article is reprinted from M. A. Cook (ed.), *Studies in the Economic History of the Middle East from the Rise of Islam to the Present Day* (London, 1970), pp. 395–411. Reprinted by permission of Oxford Unversity Press.

NOTES

1. *Cambridge Economic History of Europe*, vol. vi, Cambridge, 1965, p. 58.
2. *Ibid.*, p. 64.
3. Vera Anstey, *The Economic Development of India*, London, 1957, p. 605.
4. *Cambridge Economic History*, p. 65.
5. Gabriel Baer, 'Urbanization in Egypt, 1820–1907', in W. R. Polk and R. L. Chambers (eds), *The Beginnings of Modernization in the Middle East*, Chicago, 1968.
6. M.S. Hasan, 'Growth and Structure of Iraq's Population, 1867–1947', *Bulletin of the Oxford University Institute of Statistics*, XX, 1958.
7. For sources see Charles Issawi, *The Economic History of the Middle East*, Chicago, 1966, p. 209.
8. For a fuller discussion see Charles Issawi, 'Economic Growth in the Arab World since 1800', *Middle East Economic Papers* (Beirut), 1964.
9. See Issawi, *Economic History*, pp. 332, and 469–70, respectively.
10. See *ibid.*, p. 17.
11. Eliot G. Mears, *Modern Turkey*, New York 1924, p. 580, quoting *Statesman's Yearbook.* This figure is not necessarily incompatible with that of the census of 1927, viz., 13,648,000, in view of Turkey's huge war losses and the exodus of Greeks, Armenians and others.
12. George Curzon, *Persia and the Persian Question*, London, 1892, vol. ii, p. 492.
13. *Ibid.* p. 493, *Encyclopaedia Britannica* (Eleventh Edition), s.v. Persia, and Eteocle Lorini, *La Persia economica*, Rome, 1900, p. 378. L. A. Sobotsinskii, *Persia* (St Petersburg, 1913), p. 12, quotes a 'contemporary' (1909) estimate by Medvedev of 10 million.
14. United Nations, *Monthly Bulletin of Statistics.*
15. The corresponding figure for Turkey would be about 10 million in 1890, which would imply a rate of growth of over 15 per thousand between 1890 and 1914; this figure seems too high, and it is therefore probable that the 1890 figure was well above 10 million. By the same token, the 1831 figure may have been somewhat below 10 million.
16. *Op. cit.*, p. 493.
17. See A. E. Crouchley, *The Investment of Foreign Capital in Egyptian Companies and Public Debt*, Cairo, 1936, and L. A. Fridman, *Kapitalističeskoye razvitiye Yegipta*, Moscow, 1963, p. 13.
18. For details see Issawi, *Economic History*, pp. 94–106.
19. For details see Muḥammad 'Alī Jamālzāde, *Ganj-i Shāygān*, Berlin, 1335 A. H., pp. 98–117. The Russian Discount Bank's capital was 64 million gold roubles and the total value of the Russian property to which the Soviets renounced all claims in 1921 has been put as high as 600 million gold roubles. However, the latter figure includes various military installations and the basis of the valuation is not clear. See S. G. Gorelikov, *Iran*, Moscow, 1961, p. 153, citing M. V. Popov, *Amerikanskiy imperializm v Irane*, Moscow, 1956, p. 5.

20. See Jamālzāde, *op. cit.*, p. 155, and Sir Percy Sykes, *A History of Persia*, London, 1921, vol. ii, p. 523.

21. Issawi, *Economic History*, pp. 94–106, 430–8.

22. J. Farley, *The Resources of Turkey*, London, 1862, p. 209.

23. A. E. Crouchley, *The Economic Development of Modern Egypt*, London, 1938, p. 142. See also Aḥmad al-Ḥitta, *Tārīkh Miṣr al-iqtiṣādī*, Cairo, 1957, and N. Verney and G. Dambmann, *Les Puissances étrangères dans le Levant*, Paris, 1900.

24. See Max E. Fletcher, 'The Suez Canal and World Shipping', *Journal of Economic History*, 1958.

25. See Richard Hill, *Sudan Transport*, London, 1965.

26. See Charles Issawi, 'Asymmetrical Development and Transport in Egypt, 1800–1914', in Polk and Chambers (eds), *op. cit.*

27. Albert H. Imlah, *Economic Elements in the Pax Britannica*, Cambridge, Mass., 1958, pp. 189, 94–8.

28. For details see Issawi, *Economic History*, pp. 363–4.

29. *Ibid.*, p. 30. For Syria the rise may have been of the same order, from say, £500,000 a year, in the 1820s to about £10 million in 1911—both figures referring to sea-borne trade, which rose far more rapidly than land-borne—see *ibid.*, pp. 208–9. For Iraq, Hassan puts average total trade at £438,000 in 1864–71, £1,760,000 in 1880–7, and £6,428,000 in 1912–13—see Muḥammad Salmān Ḥasan, *Al-taṭawwur al-iqtiṣādī*, Beirut, n.d., pp. 95 and 223.

30. Marvin L. Entner, *Russo-Persian Commercial Relations, 1828–1914*, Gainesville, Fla., 1965, p. 8.

31. *Ibid.*, p. 63.

32. Curzon, *op. cit.*, vol. ii, pp. 562, 582. An earlier estimate had put the Russian share much lower. Even after doubling the figure for Persian imports from Russia, to take account of smuggling, total trade between the two countries in 1852–7 was put at 4.4 million thalers, out of a total Persian trade estimated at 42 million, or £6.3 million; however, the latter figure, which includes estimates for trade with Central Asia, may be somewhat too high. See Ernst Otto Blau, *Commerzielle Zustände Persiens*, Berlin, 1858, pp. 164–5.

The League of Nations, *International Statistical Yearbook, 1928*, Geneva, 1929, put Iran's imports in 1913 at $55 million and its exports at $38 million, or a total of $93 million (about £17 million). This would imply a three-fold increase in current prices in the sixty years preceding the First World War. Since price levels in the 1850s were close to those prevailing in 1913, the increase in real terms must also have been about three-fold.

Some increase must also have taken place in the first half of the nineteenth century. This is suggested by the fact that in 1831–56 trade through Trabzon, almost all of which was in transit to or from Iran, multiplied twelve-fold (Blau, *op. cit.*, pp. 235–6). In the early 1850s Trabzon accounted for almost half of Iran's imports and a sixth of its exports.

Earlier figures are contradictory. In 1834 J. B. Fraser estimated Iran's total trade with Europe, including Russia, at £1 million (*ibid.*, p. 165). In 1836, W. Stuart put Britain's exports to Iran at just over £1 million and stated that Russia's were two-thirds higher (Curzon, *op. cit.*, vol. ii, p. 564).

33. See Issawi, *Economic History*, Part V, Introduction, and Part VII, Introduction.

34. Liverpool East India Committee, quoted in I. Durga Parshad, *Some Aspects of Indian Foreign Trade, 1757–1893*, London, 1932, p. 132.

35. *Ibid.*, p. 215.

36. Bank of Japan, *Historical Statistics of the Japanese Economy* (1966).

37. See Issawi, 'Asymmetrical Development'; the foreign trade and population figures were taken from the League of Nations *Statistical Yearbook*, 1928.

38. For details see Issawi, 'Economic Growth', also Hla Myint, *The Economics of the Developing Countries*, London, 1964, chapter 3.

39. See A. E. Crouchley, 'A Century of Economic Development', *L'Egypte Contemporaine*, (Cairo) 1939, and E. R. J. Owen, 'Cotton Production and the Development of the Egyptian Economy', D. Phil. Thesis, Oxford University, 1965.

40. See Robert L. Tignor, *Modernization and British Colonial Rule in Egypt*, Princeton, N. J., 1966, chapter 7.

41. See Anstey, *op. cit.*, chapter 7.

42. See chart in US Department of Agriculture, *Agriculture in 26 Developing Nations, 1948 to 1963,* Washington, D. C., p. 45. The most recent discussion of this question is in James I. Nakamura, *Agricultural Production and the Economic Development of Japan, 1873–1922,* Princeton, N. J., 1966.

43. Anstey, *op. cit.*, p. 207. However, the following judgement by a highly qualified scholar should be noted. 'The vast expansion of British cloth exports to India skimmed off the expanding demand. The handloom weavers were at least no fewer in number and no worse off economically at the end of the period than at the beginning ... The traditional sector, generally speaking, did not decline absolutely in economic significance,' Morris D. Morris, 'Towards a Reinterpretation of Nineteenth-Century Indian Economic History', *Journal of Economic History,* 1963.

44. See Issawi, *Economic History,* pp. 38–59, 452–60. For Muḥammad 'Alī's attempt at industrialization see *ibid.*, pp. 389–402.

45. See Anstey, *op. cit.*, chapter 9, *Cambridge Economic History,* pp. 908–19, and Krishan Saini, 'Some measures of the economic growth of India, 1860–1913', unpublished paper, Columbia University.

46. See *Cambridge Economic History,* pp. 875–99, and William W. Lockwood, *The Economic Development of Japan,* Princeton, N.J., 1954.

47. See Owen, *op. cit.*, and Issawi, *Economic History,* p. 365.

48. I. M. Smilianskaya, 'Razloženiye feodalnikh otnoshenii ...', translated in *ibid.*, pp. 226–47, and Dominique Chevallier, 'Western Development and Eastern Crisis in the Mid-Nineteenth Century', in Polk and Chambers (eds), *op. cit.*

49. Nikki R. Keddie, *Historical Obstacles to Agrarian Change in Iran,* Claremont Asian Studies, Claremont, California, 1960, p. 4. See also A. K. S. Lambton, *Landlord and Peasant in Persia,* London 1953, pp. 143–5.

50. Morris, *op. cit.*; see also Anstey, *op. cit.*, chapter xvi. However, there is evidence of distinct progress in the forty or fifty years preceding the First World War—see Saini, *op. cit.*

51. Lockwood, *op. cit.*, pp. 34, 138–50.

52. Herbert Passin, *Society and Education in Japan,* New York, 1965, p. 11—for details see Issawi, 'Asymmetrical Development'.

53. At that time Robert College drew its students almost solely from minority groups—see Mears, *op. cit.*, chapter 5.

54. Only one field was at first dominated by foreigners, the export trade. But even here 'by 1913 the bulk of overseas commerce was handled by Japanese firms, and half of it already moved in Japanese ships', Lockwood, *op. cit.*, p. 329.

55. See Morris, *op. cit.*, Anstey, *op. cit.*, pp. 109–17, and D.H. Buchanan, *The Development of Capitalistic Enterprise in India,* New York, 1934, chapters vii–xiii.

56. See Issawi, *Economic History,* pp. 114–25, 505–13, Jamālzāde, *op. cit.*, pp. 93–117.

57. Thus the total tonnage of vessels from the Persian Gulf entering Indian ports rose from nearly 100,000 tons per annum in the late 1850s to over 200,000 in the early 1900s and then fell well below its original level by the First World War—see *Statistical Abstract Relating to British India.* Since these figures cover not only Arab and Persian craft but British and other steamers plying between India and the Gulf, the fall in the former must have been very great. The same process occurred in the Red Sea region.

58. For a detailed study see Robert Tignor, 'Public Health Administration under British Rule, 1882–1914', unpublished doctoral dissertation, Yale University, 1960. Rudimentary quarantines were established in several Ottoman ports in the first half of the nineteenth century.

59. The following judgement deserves consideration: 'Had Japan been situated in closer proximity to the great industrialized nations of the West, her pattern of growth and structural change after 1868 would probably have been somewhat different. Both the pressure to industrialize, and the opportunity to do so, might have been somewhat diminished. She would have enjoyed more favorable access to large external markets for her coal, marine products, and high-value farm crops. Western consumer manufactures might also have competed more strongly in Japan than was the case, delaying the progress of industry.' Lockwood, *op. cit.*, p. 353.

60. See Issawi, 'Asymmetrical Development'.

61. *Idem, Economic History,* pp. 52–3.

62. Another important factor was the restrictions imposed on the Middle Eastern governments by international commercial conventions, which prevented them from giving tariff protection to their industries. But these restrictions had their counterpart in India and, until 1899, in Japan.

The Origins of Private Ownership of Land in Egypt: a Reappraisal

KENNETH M. CUNO

In the historiography of Egypt it has long been accepted that private ownership of land was introduced in the nineteenth century.[1] This development in statute law has often been linked analytically to a process of 'modernization.'[2] Modernization theory posits a fundamental dichotomy between two ideal-type societies, the traditional and modern, which implies an equally sharp discontinuity between historical eras: before and after the beginning of modernization. In this view, traditional societies lack the potential for generating significant social change from within. Change results rather from the expansion of communications and diversification of technology worldwide from modern Europe and North America. In the process of modernization, traditional norms and structures break down in the host societies, and new, rational values and institutions emerge in their place. The development of Egypt's new land regime is usually considered one such change.

In most historical studies to date, the impact of Europe and/or the rise of powerful reformers influenced by European ideas have been seen as crucial to the beginnings of modernization in the Middle East. For Egypt, the two events most symbolic of this are the French occupation of 1798–1801 and the reign of Muhammad Ali Pasha, 1805–1848, the 'founder of modern Egypt.'[3] On closer examination of the sources, however, the evidence shows not historical discontinuity but its opposite; not the shattering and replacement of institutions but their dynamic evolution, due as much to indigenous forces as to outside influences.[4] This calls for a reappraisal of socioeconomic change in Egypt, of its relationship to European influences, and of the significance to it of reform legislation.

THE TRANSFORMATION OF PROPERTY RELATIONS

Contrary to the received tradition in most history texts, the transformation of property relations in Egypt and other Ottoman lands was already underway, and had led to the appearance of forms of private ownership of land, long before the famous reforms of the nineteenth century. This becomes evident upon examination of the behavior of landholding elements in the eighteenth and nineteenth centuries, of their struggles to acquire or maintain control of the land at three levels: as a source of revenue, as a disposable source of income, and as a means of production and subsistence.

As these different levels of utility of the land indicate, a hierarchy of shared rights or claims to it and/or its produce existed in the period before Muhammad Ali's rise to power, similar to other precapitalist orders in Europe and Asia.[5] Political, economic, and social relations were intimately connected with property relations. Or, to put it another way, property relations were social relations in the broadest sense of the term, sanctified in law.

The establishment of private ownership of land in place of this system was not the creation of 'rights' where none existed before, nor simply a matter of their transfer from the state to individuals. Rather it involved the consolidation of these shared claims into one sphere and their appropriation by individuals. It represents the establishment of exclusive control of the land by individuals as the prevailing system of property relations in place of shared control.

Ottoman administration of land tenure in Egypt embodied the principle of shared rights.[6] The sultan (i.e. the state) was by law 'owner' of most agricultural land. State authority over the land was in fact limited to taxation and enforced maintenance of the irrigation works through use of the corvée. Second, to carry out taxation and administration in the countryside, the state had turned to a variety of intermediaries who were made responsible for one or more villages, and who received a portion of the revenues from them and from privately held sections of land in them in return for their services. Finally, peasants held traditional rights to till the land and remain on it.

In Lower Egypt and parts of Middle Egypt peasants held their land sections for life, and passed them on to their heirs, as long as taxes were paid (hence the term *athar* or *athariyya*, loosely: 'that which remains'). The annual Nile flood caused more extreme variations in the area of cultivable land in Upper Egypt and the remainder of Middle Egypt, and so land here was annually surveyed and redivided within the village community (*arḍ misāḥa*, 'survey land'). Thus individual security of tenure was guaranteed the holder of athar land, and village clans must have maintained a similar continuous claim to their due portion of misāḥa land. Neither the state nor intermediaries interfered in the production process except indirectly, through tax demands and irrigation works.

J. C. Scott has noted that peasants value greatest and defend most tenaciously these two conditions: security of tenure and control of decision making in the production process. The peasant community's direct control of land and production is its means of maintaining security in face of unpredictable forces—such as weather, or a market economy—and of guaranteeing to itself a culturally defined, minimum, acceptable subsistence. Interference with these traditional rights, or rigid tax/rent demands which threaten to push peasants below the acceptable subsistence level, are more resented and more likely resisted than systems of exploitation which are more flexible but which siphon off a greater amount of their surplus.[7] Ottoman law, significantly, provided for lowered taxes in years of drought or disastrous floods, and also guaranteed the terms of traditional peasant tenure.[8]

Ottoman regulations likewise provided for checks on the intermediaries, to prevent them from tyrannizing the peasantry, from usurping state prerogatives in control of the land, and from pocketing more than their legal share of revenues. Salaried officials were originally employed to oversee cultivation and the collection of taxes. During the seventeenth century tax farms, *iltizāms*, appeared.[9] They were acquired for a year or more through an auction held by the Treasury. With the iltizām, its holder, the *multazim*, received a tax-free section of land, *ūsya*, which he had cultivated for his own profit by wage or corvée labor, or which he rented out. His personal profit, *fā'iḍ*, from ūsya land and excess taxes collected could come to four or five times the taxes remitted, indicating the profitability of iltizāms.[10]

Law must be backed by force to be effective, however, and in a situation such as this where the state is weak, its formal regulations provide little indication of actual practices. Each party to the shared rights to the land of Ottoman Egypt, as elsewhere, could assert or defend them only according to its command of means of coercion—its political power. As Ottoman authority in the provinces weakened, its land laws became increasingly irrelevant, while intermediaries gained increasing control of the land at the state's expense. By the early eighteenth century they had acquired landholding rights in Egypt that established them as landlords in every sense of the term. These included: (1) lifetime possession of the iltizām, as long as taxes were paid; (2) inheritance of it by descendants, wives, or white slaves; (3) the ability to convert land into waqf, thereby guaranteeing the family's continued possession of it; (4) the ability to mortgage the land, (5) to pawn it, or (6) to sell it outright.[11]

These criteria are precisely those used in previous studies of nineteenth-century Egypt to show a movement toward private ownership.[12] Paradigms that see private ownership as appearing in Egypt during the nineteenth century at the earliest should thus be discarded.

The intermediaries' usurpation of state authority over the land was marked by a proliferation of legal fictions used to get around the formal, legally inalienable status of the land. Mortgage and pawning were conducted under the euphemism of 'transfer,' *isqāt*; sales were called 'indefinite transfer,' *isqāt ilā al-abad.*[13] Similar fictions were employed in transactions involving waqf land.[14] The resort to legal fictions should not be surprising since they were used in various times and places, for example to circumvent Qur'ānic prohibitions of risk-taking and interest,[15] and were also used to circumvent restrictions on landownership in parts of contemporary Europe.[16] Developments that caused land to be treated as an alienable commodity led to the use of these fictions, but the continuation of old legal terminology for land tenure on the surface has obscured this transformation.

The re-establishment of a strong state in nineteenth-century Egypt arrested the development toward private ownership in part. Yet, paradoxically, it facilitated this movement over the long term. The state concentrated control of the land as never before in a single sphere, in its own hands. Second, it violated the traditional terms of peasant tenure by interfering in production and transferring tenures as it saw fit. Finally, the weakening of the state after 1840 allowed a new generation of intermediaries and privileged landholders it had created to influence land tenure policies to their own benefit.

If land tenure issues can be appreciated in terms of competition or struggle among various actors over the land and its product, then developments in the nineteenth century appear as but a continuation of trends in the eighteenth century. The legislation of private ownership of land came toward the end of this long-term struggle for control of the land. It legitimized the new order this struggle had wrought, firmly establishing the positions of those who had gained in the process: the large landowners in particular, but also a stratum of wealthy peasants. Finally, it represents a late stage in the transition from shared to exclusive rights to the land.

The circumstances that led to this transformation will require extensive investigation in the future. Here is presented evidence that this process was, in fact, in train, as well as the factors that appear to have influenced it and its outcome. Local and regional economic trends are considered, as well as changes in the nature of the state and its ability to regulate land tenure. The changing relationships among peasants, intermediaries/landlords, and the state, and between them and the land are also followed.

THE EASTERN MEDITERRANEAN BEFORE 1800

The lands of the eastern Mediterranean under Ottoman rule, while separated politically and culturally from Europe, appear to have been linked to it as part of a larger region subject to similar broad economic and demographic trends. The Ottoman Empire felt the effects of the sixteenth-century 'price revolution' and experienced a rise in population then at approximately the same time as did Europe. Population in Europe, at least, began to increase again in the eighteenth century.[17] This and the beginnings of industrial revolution led to a nearly century-long rise in the absolute price of agricultural commodities which is visible in both Europe and the Middle East. The price of land increased in turn, and speculative trading in it—even where legally prohibited—appeared in both regions.[18] New elements shouldered their way in among the landholding classes, and local landholding and/or commercial aristocracies often were able to increase their political strength *vis-à-vis* their monarch and peasantry.

The changing composition of landowning classes is marked in Europe by commoners acquiring noble estates—sometimes openly—even where it was prohibited by law, and in the Ottoman Empire by the entry of merchants into landholding.[19] Landed aristocracies (or their equivalents) were enticed by rising prices and enabled by weakened state authority to increase their control over their holdings. The established sociopolitical orders, connected closely with property relations, were being undermined, and at the same time state authority over land tenure was being whittled away. Both developments laid the bases for institutional change at a later date.

In the sixteenth century, rising prices in the Mediterranean region had led to increased exports of foodstuffs and raw materials from the Ottoman Empire. Venetian ships loaded grain in Egypt's ports at mid-century. Thereafter the Empire's population seems to have caught up with production, and the export of grain to the West was prohibited. The Greek archipelago then became a center for contraband grain trade which flourished in the eighteenth century.[20] Egyptian wheat, rice, and beans found their way to the West according to shifting market demand and the relative ability of the Porte to enforce its trade regulations.

Industrial crops—wool, silk, cotton, flax, leather, oils, and dyestuffs—acquired a new importance in the eighteenth century owing to Europe's industrial expansion.[21] In addition, both regional and European demand for the Levant's fine cottons and silks, and for its spun cotton and wool, led to increased textile production in certain areas. All of this resulted in expanded cash crop production, especially in cotton, producing yet another effect: a trend toward greater regional specialization. The planting of mulberry trees in the Lebanon and Macedonia and expansion of cotton cultivation in Macedonia, Anatolia, and Palestine were accompanied by the development of food and vegetable-dye production in other areas. The Biqāʿ and Hawrān became important grain-producing regions fought over by the amīrs of the Lebanon and the wālīs of Sidon and Damascus. Egyptian foodstuffs supplied Syria, Macedonia, and Istanbul, as well as being marketed in Egypt and the West. Egypt also produced indigo and safflower dyes for internal and export markets. Crop specialization in Egypt is somewhat problematic, as more than one crop per year could be raised in many areas. Different districts did tend to specialize, however, in cotton, flax, dyestuffs, oilseeds, sugar cane, or food crops.[22]

While only a small part of Egypt's external trade was conducted directly with the West, price movements in Cairo during this century clearly show that the country was feeling the effects of the overall increase in trade and the rise in agricultural commodity prices, suggesting that the factors behind the price rise may have been generalized, and not simply a matter of Europe's influence. The price of beans, wheat, rice, cattle, and camels rose two and a half times during the century. Mutton increased three times. Butter, oils, cheese, sugar, and honey rose twofold. Industrial commodities also show price increases: the price of raw cotton increased nearly fivefold, while the price of flax and spun cotton doubled.[23] The export price of safflower dye increased nearly threefold.[24] In Egypt as elsewhere, rising prices enhanced the value placed on land, a major factor in its transformation into private property.

In the sixteenth century the Ottomans had begun to convert Balkan and Anatolian *timār* lands into iltizāms which court circles and urban 'commercial-usury capital' acquired. At the same time these elements began to illegally purchase timārs. Weakening state control and economic opportunities also led those *timārlıs* who could to convert their holdings, illegally, into iltizāms. The seventeenth and eighteenth centuries saw the appearance of life-term tax farms, *malikânes*, following the development of a speculative market in landholdings. These centuries also saw the appearance of the Balkan *çiftliks*, privately owned commercial estates devoid of any obligations to the state. The çiftlik holder owned the land outright, and often the tools, animals, and seeds his tenants used.[25] Here, the process of usurpation of state control was complete, and the terms of peasant tenure had also been altered. Çiftliks spread rapidly throughout the Balkans in the late eighteenth century, associated closely with 'the diffusion of the cultivation of new colonial products: cotton and maize.'[26] The production and trade of such cash crops were the economic basis of the rise of powerful provincial notables, the *a'yān*.[27]

In the Lebanon, the expansion of sericulture was organized by Maronite and Druze shaykhs and the Maronite monastic orders. As in the Balkans, the concentration of land in fewer hands and the increased exploitation of tenants are associated with the spread of market-oriented agriculture. In both regions the conversion of holdings into waqf—property set aside for the ostensible support of pious works—played an important role in the alienation and concentration of land.[28]

The rise of Shaykh Ẓāhir al-'Umar in Palestine is associated with the spread of cotton cultivation. As multazims, Ẓāhir and other shaykhs were able to monopolize cotton by serving as middlemen between peasants and French merchants. His successor as local strongman, the Wālī of Sidon, Ahmad Pasha al-Jazzār, sought to acquire as much land as possible in the form of malikâne. His monopolization of all production and trade anticipates the methods of Muhammad Ali.[29]

Ottoman officials were aware of the fiscal and political dangers of developments in landholding, though not always able to stop them. Attempts to reform the land regime which appear 'modern' in inspiration were actually efforts to re-establish a greater degree of state control over the land. In the seventeenth century, reform-minded Ottomans criticized the malikâne system, and it was decreed abolished under Ahmad III in 1714/1715.[30] Military reverses weakened his position and led to the decree's reversal three years later. He later attempted yet another reform, turning malikâne lands back into short-term iltizāms and placing some under the administration of salaried state officials. Also, 'for the first time in over a century extensive cadastral surveys were made . . .'[31]

Efforts to curb the power of local notables and re-establish state control over the land were revived under Sultans Mustafa III and Abdulhamid I.[32] Administrative and military reforms were always accompanied by fiscal reforms affecting landholding: the well-known reforms of Selim III and Mahmud II followed this pattern. To study Ottoman landholding in this period is to study a multifaceted struggle for the land itself, both between the political center and the provinces, and among the actors in each locale.

THE SITUATION IN EGYPT

While the agrarian history of Egypt in this period has yet to receive detailed examination, it is possible to reconstruct a partial picture of it from the evidence already available. The two more or less constant political-economic factors favoring change in late Ottoman Egypt were the secular rise in agricultural prices and the weakness of state authority. But if conditions favor change, it is still human action and interaction which determine its course and outcome.

Under the conditions of the eighteenth century, intermediaries and peasants responded in a variety of ways affecting landholding and land use. Parallel to changes elsewhere in the Ottoman Empire, multazims in Egypt succeeded in transforming their iltizāms into a form of private property in land. Early in the eighteenth century, their new rights of disposition were expressed in the term 'malikâne,' indicating that lifetime tenure had become common. Conversion of the land into waqf, and bequest, mortgage, pawning, or sale of it—through the device of isqāt—were within the multazim's power. The earliest register devoted to isqāt in Egypt dates from 1728, indicating that by this time this legal fiction was commonly used in transactions involving landholdings.[33]

Cairo's merchants appear among the holders and purchasers of iltizāms in these registers, and speculative transactions appear to have often occurred within an absentee landholding class there. A merchant appears in court records as a holder of three villages in Daqahliyya province as early as 1673,[34] and the Sharā'ibī merchant dynasty in particular increased their landholdings throughout the eighteenth century.[35] T. Walz's study of the *gallāba* merchants, those engaged in the Sudan trade, shows that some lesser merchants also acquired iltizāms. Others rented sections of iltizām or waqf lands, or held mortgages of fallah land.[36] Egypt's wealthier ulama were also active in acquiring iltizāms, primarily in their home districts, in addition to their administration of waqf lands.[37]

The wealthy merchants' involvement in land was part of a general trend of investment in urban and rural properties and tax farms.[38] The wealthiest ulama are hardly distinguishable from the large merchants in these financial dealings.[39] Such investments made sense. The relative stagnation of coffee and textile prices undermined the most profitable commerce in the hands of indigenous merchants,[40] while agricultural commodity prices rose. It is presently impossible to ascertain the extent of merchant involvement in landholding. A. A. Abd al-Rahim's figures show merchants comprising only slightly more than 1 per cent of the total number of multazims on the eve of the French invasion, as opposed to none a century and a half earlier.[41] But the size of their holdings is unfortunately not indicated, nor is the number and extent of the mortgages that they undoubtedly held.

The evidence is also inconclusive concerning the accumulation of iltizāms. Many holdings appear to have been small and scattered: between 1658–1660 and 1797, the total number of multazims increased by more than 250 per cent, although the extent of fractionalization of their holdings varied from one area to the next.[42] On the other hand, some multazims were converting fallah land into ūsya land,[43] a process reminiscent of the engrossment of *demesne* holdings in contemporary eastern Europe, under similar conditions.

The conversion of holdings into waqf is another example of the growth of *de facto* private property in land through the use of legal fictions. Waqf lands paid only a 'protection tax' in this period to safeguard their status. Legally, they could not be divided or sold, nor were they commonly subject to confiscation. 'Family,' or *ahlī*, waqfs, furthermore, remained in the possession of the makers' descendants. They received the bequest's income until the extinction of the line, and only then did the revenues from an ahlī waqf revert to the designated charitable work. Thus conversion of land into ahlī waqf guaranteed the family's continued possession of it, along with important tax exemptions, and many multazims were able to convert their ūsya holdings into waqf. Here, too, the growth of a market in land resulted in the exchange of waqf lands—despite the law—by what amounted to sale. Waqf lands were exploited in a way similar to ūsya lands: the *nāẓir*, administrator, either leased them to a village shaykh or had them cultivated by means of wage labor.[44]

Jabarti reports that waqf lands surveyed in 1813 came to 600,000 faddans in Upper Egypt and the Cairo vicinity. Thus the amount of land converted to waqf in these areas alone came to some 20 per cent of all of Egypt's cultivated land,[45] a measure of the extent to which land was taken out of the state's control in this period. If Jabarti's remarks are any guide, the concentration of waqf lands in the hands of wealthy nāẓirs and notables was indeed common. He mentions one Shams al-Dīn b. Ḥamūda, a shaykh of the village of Birmā, Minufiyya, who told him that his family held 1,000 faddans of waqf land for which no tax was paid, in addition to other lands for which he paid a nominal amount.[46]

Despite the consolidation of property rights and a tendency toward concentration of the land, multazims and nāẓirs do not appear to have been directly engaged in agricultural production nor did they attempt to alter the relations of production. Under the right conditions, investment to raise the productivity of land would have been a plausible response to the era's price trends. But the adequately large income that many iltizāms appear to have offered, and the possibility of losing an iltizām with a change of rulers in Cairo, probably discouraged investment. As occurred in the Balkans, the evidence so far indicates that increased exploitation rather than an increase in surplus production was the most common result of these *rentiers'* activities.[47]

At the village level a variety of responses to the conditions of this century can also be observed. These encompass not only competition for control of the land, but also activities in the sphere of production which indicate a potential for agricultural development. At the present state of our knowledge it will have to suffice to present three situations illustrating these responses.

In Giza and much of the central Delta the Mamluk beys were able to maintain the greatest authority, indicated by the presence of 'Mamluk houses'—residences for their local representatives—in the villages.[48] These regions produced a variety of crops for the market—cotton, flax, oilseeds, dyestuffs, and various food crops.[49] Here, social stratification was visible at the time of the French occupation, the result of control of local political and economic resources. Local police and administrative offices were monopolized by the wealthier village families and tended to be hereditary, starting with the position of village shaykh. He usually represented the most powerful clan in the village and was the supreme police and judicial authority in the village.[50]

In villages where the multazim rented out his ūsya land, it was leased by one of the village shaykhs at a price reflecting the market in land. This varied according to its quality and proximity to a market town: the ūsya lands near Bulaq went at the highest rate. If the multazim had the ūsya cultivated for his own account through wage labor or corvée, the shaykhs and *khūlī*s were responsible for assigning the land and were paid for their services. The khūlī, an official drawn from the village, was also charged with checking the survey and assessment of village lands performed by the multazim's officials—a position of considerable power and potential wealth.[51]

The economic position of the wealthy families was also strengthened through important tax exemptions. The shaykhs, khūlīs, and *shāhid*s (local, professional witnesses for tax purposes) were exempt from *barrānī* taxes on portions of their land. These were extraordinary taxes in kind which the multazims levied in different villages according to their ability to impose them and the villagers' ability to pay. Butter, sheep, cheese, grain, honey, chickens, and other farm products were taken, all of whose prices were increasing in absolute terms and drastically so in terms of the continually debased coinage. Barrānī accounts appear in the tax registers from the seventeenth century on, but along with other taxes they increased greatly during the eighteenth.[52]

The financial and political power of these families also enabled them to acquire additional lands which were kept off the tax registers with the connivance of other local officials.[53] This was facilitated by the land system in the villages of Lower Egypt, since transactions also took place at this level, though legally only concerning usufructuary rights. In these districts, then, a wealthy peasant stratum in alliance with the ruling elite used its political and economic resources to acquire additional lands and tax exemptions, and were also in a position to rent land from absentee holders, either to produce more for the market or to profit from the rising price of land by subleasing.

A quite different phenomenon was the appearance of what could be termed militant peasantries in certain areas. As a political-economic phenomenon, these peasants were protecting and sometimes extending their control over areas of market-oriented agriculture and commerce, as well as using their strength to resist the increasing burden of taxes and fees levied by the multazims and the provincial administration. As a sociological phenomenon, this development is associated with the sedentarization of certain bedouin tribes. Once they have become cultivators, bedouin are nearly indistinguishable from peasants—some even adopted the fallahin's brown woolen dress. Still, they retained a tribal identity and solidarity *vis-à-vis* outsiders. 'Bedouin influence' seems to have been the common factor in those areas which maintained a quasi-independence from the beys.[54]

In parts of lower Sharqiyya and Daqahliyya a sort of bedouin–fallah symbiosis occurred. North of Bilbays, bedouin were described as the 'caste prépondérante . . . sans être la plus nombreuse. . . .'[55] They camped adjacent to fallah villages, engaging in stockbreeding and cultivation as well as in escorting caravans along the route to Syria and the Hijaz. French observers described this region as rich in various field crops, orchards, and especially date groves. The peninsula of Manzala rivaled Damietta as a rice-growing region.[56]

The mutual interests of the bedouin and fallahin here led to military alliances. 'Village wars' were jointly conducted against neighboring districts, and the frequent mention of peasants carrying arms to the fields and of fortified towns and villages attest to this strife.[57] Despite such conflict these reports are silent about any resultant 'devastation.' Village wars were fought for control of water and land, no doubt provoked by the increasing value of land and herds and by occasional variations in the flood level.

An equally important dimension of this symbiosis was the ability to resist the bey's exactions. Tax payments and other relations were a matter of negotiation between the bedouin shaykhs and the Mamluks.[58] Unlike the central Delta region, there is no mention of 'Mamluk houses' for lower Sharqiyya and Daqahliyya, indicating that the beys and their subordinates could establish no permanent presence there.

The presence of a militant peasantry in Middle Egypt also appears to be related to the increasing importance of cash crops, but here the settled bedouin, 'arabes cultivateurs,' subjugated the fallahin and usurped their land. From about the middle of the century one tribe had established itself and taken up cultivation on the right bank of the Nile in the regions of Atfīḥ, Ashmunīn, and Manfalūṭ. At the time of Jomard's observations (1799–1801) they were expanding their control of land across the river. Already they held most of the islands of Middle Egypt and a strip of land a quarter league wide on the left bank. The land seized was planted in tobacco, indigo, sugar cane, date palms, and forage crops, as well as melons, grains, and legumes. The first group of crops was the most important, grown for local and regional markets. Sugar, indigo, and wool were the principal industries of the villages, and these as well as dates were sold to Cairo merchants. Large tracts of forage crops were also planted, as summer cultivation required a supply of cattle to turn the waterwheels, and the military power and communications of these villages depended upon large herds of horses and camels.[59]

In these and other bedouin villages of Middle and Upper Egypt the shaykhs acquired a preponderant political and economic role. It is primarily in these regions that small amounts of village shaykhs' *masmūḥ* land appeared, land held by them free of any tax, said to be 'vols faits par des Arabes qui sont établis par force dans divers villages,' and passed on to their heirs.[60] This observation lays bare the way in which privileged landholding rights could be created at the village level through the exercise of local political power. The displacement of fallahin by bedouin in these districts is one of the most obvious forms that the struggle or competition for land between cultivators took. It was no less real, however, where wealthy peasants, here or in the Delta, acquired land through receiving pawns or mortgages, or through purchase of usufructuary rights—again, aided by their command of local political and economic resources.

In the militant peasant districts of Middle Egypt, 'Mamluk houses' were also unknown, and at the time of the French occupation taxes were collected from them with difficulty or not at all.[61] Here and in lower Sharqiyya the extent of the bey's authority versus the villagers' independence must have been fluid, depending on the military strength either side could marshal at any time. Title to the land in these areas remained in the hands of multazims and taxes were paid,[62] although these peasants may well have escaped the full weight of the period's increasing taxation, which would have enabled them to benefit more from the secular price rise.

In Damietta's rice-growing region, Girard's reports indicate that peasant farmers were responding positively to the market opportunities of the time. Peasants leased land from the multazims for either a cash rent per faddan or a portion of the harvest, the farmer being responsible for all costs. As rice farming required considerable working capital for waterwheels, animals and drivers to turn them, canal maintenance, and planting, thinning, and harvesting, the farmer next turned to Damietta's rice merchants for a loan at interest. After the harvest these merchants purchased the crop, had it milled, and placed it on the market. The farmer employed a permanent workforce as well as seasonal migrant labor, all of whom were paid wages. Girard noted that by such arrangements, 'the exploitation of the rice farms resembles more or less that of our farms of Europe.'[63] This is the clearest example of peasant entrepreneurship and development toward a capitalist organization of the relations of production in agriculture.

To summarize, peasants behaved under the conditions of the times in a variety of ways which reflected their material interests. Peasants acquired and/or protected their holdings through the exercise of local power, including at times armed force. Security of tenure may not have seemed threatened to Damietta's rice farmers, since predictable flood waters and the steady demand for rice must have ensured satisfaction of rental and credit arrangements, and must have made their automatic renewal relatively easy. This, at any rate, is indicated by their willingness to go heavily into debt at the beginning of each season. In each case, peasants retained or enforced security of tenure, and sufficient freedom of action in production to take advantage of the opportunities offered by the rising prices of commodities and land.

POLITICS AND LAND TENURE: FROM ALI BEY TO MUHAMMAD ALI

Both the Ottomans and their local rivals for power in Egypt confronted landholding and commercial interests, and attempted to enlist their support through a mixture of coercion and cooption. But to the extent that these interests were thereby strengthened, the rulers were correspondingly weakened through loss of revenues and at times the loss of control of the countryside. To the extent that the rulers suppressed them, however, they undermined their own political and financial bases of support. It was a dilemma that Egypt's rulers would also face in the nineteenth century.

The seventeenth and eighteenth centuries witnessed a struggle for Egypt's revenues on two levels. Intermediaries were largely successful in acquiring rights to the land, reducing the fiscal and administrative control of the state. Second, the contest between the wālī of Cairo and local political forces would determine who controlled and exploited the urban and rural tax structures.

In the seventeenth and early eighteenth centuries, a number of strong wālīs were able to adjust state taxes to inflation, to extend them to land that had been concealed from the registers, and to reduce diversions of imperial revenues by middlemen, all of which raised state revenues for a time.[64] In the period of Mamluk ascendancy, when strong rulers were able to establish themselves in Cairo, the tendency was also to attempt to tighten control over and take a larger share of the lands' revenues.

With Ali Bey al-Kabir (ruled 1760–72, with interruptions) came the first of a number of attempts at political and economic centralization. Control of customs and land-tax collection was the economic basis of his power. He intervened in the customs houses, ousting the Jewish agents and turning them over to Syrian merchant allies.[65] As for land taxes, the treasury now received them

> as a result of direct negotiations between the Vâlî and the Şeyh ul-Beled [of Cairo, *de facto* ruler of Egypt] of the time rather than by the [former] system of imposition and collection. [Assessment] and collection of the taxes from the cultivators was controlled and executed entirely by the Şeyh ul-Beled and his Mamlûks, who delivered to the Imperial Treasury the amounts agreed on in the negotiations.[66]

Ali Bey and his successors also increased the number and weight of extraordinary taxes levied in the towns and rural areas.[67]

As efforts to establish greater central control affected land tenure, they took the form of replacing multazims of the opposition party with one's own followers. Ali Bey had his rivals banished or killed and distributed their landholdings among his followers, an unprecedented interference in the land regime.[68] The tightening of control over the intermediaries—while still working through them—was a strategy also followed in the short-lived attempts of Hasan Pasha (1786) and Yusuf Pasha (1801) to reassert Imperial control over the province, as it was in Napoleon's reorganization.[69] Muhammad Ali followed a similar route in his first years as wālī until the fruition of these short-term policies and new economic circumstances allowed and induced him to take more drastic measures.

The pace of his reform of the land regime, part of an overall drive for centralization, varied according to the balance of political forces in the country, as it had under his predecessors. But short-term economic and political conditions also pushed policy in the direction of centralization. More than two decades of war in Europe proved a windfall for the rulers of this food-exporting country. Thus Murad Bey had profited from the war of the First Coalition,[70] and Muhammad Ali was in a similar position when war broke out anew. Egyptian grain began to flow to Malta in 1808, the volume increasing two years later when the export price of wheat rose from 26 to 80 piasters per ardeb in less than twelve months under the Pasha's new monopoly. Wheat prices in Cairo at the time ranged from 12 to 18 piasters. In 1811 the export price reached 100 piasters and remained high until 1813. In 1816–17, due to European crop failures, the export price of wheat rose again, during a short export boom, from 60 to 120 piasters per ardeb.[71] Second, the war in Arabia required a transport fleet and maintenance of a large force of mercenaries, adding urgency to the search for new revenues.

The boom in grain sales no doubt enabled Muhammad Ali to pursue his preparations for the Hijaz expedition more quickly, and helped finance the concluding phases of his struggle with the Mamluk amīrs. In addition to the Mamluks' dealings with the English, their control of the grain of Upper Egypt must have drawn him into putting an early end to them. The Citadel massacre followed the Mamluks' repeated violation of agreements to pay tribute—in wheat.[72] Thus the trade boom strengthened the Pasha's hand, and along with the costs of military preparations accelerated his program of centralization. But major changes in the land regime were likely to be attempted in any event. That they were on the way is indicated by the gradual tightening of control over the land which began in 1806, and by the importance that control of the land had taken in the struggles of the previous century.

As the area of Egypt under his control expanded, Muhammad Ali followed a policy toward land tenure which—on the surface—may appear contradictory, owing to the double-edged strategy of coercion and cooption. On the one hand, he allowed the iltizām system to remain during his first ten years in power, granting iltizāms anew to his family and followers. On the other hand, he pursued a policy aimed at undermining the authority of the multazims over the fallahin, collecting some taxes directly from the latter, and encouraging them to voice their grievances against the multazims.[73] The appearance of randomness in the land policy belies the political strategy employed. The aim was control of all the country's resources, but, in order to accomplish this, it was necessary to piece together a ruling elite of family, officers, bureaucrats, and merchants, many of whom were placed in charge of tax farms and tracts of land under varying arrangements, including in some cases an obligation to restore uncultivated land to productivity. Consolidation of power also involved coming to terms with other political forces too powerful or indispensable to suppress entirely—certain ulama, the village shaykhs, and certain bedouin shaykhs. Piecemeal moves to extend his authority reflect Muhammad Ali's understanding that any wholesale changes would have encountered too much resistance. Instead, he proceeded against the weaker targets first, temporizing when strong opposition was met, in order to keep a united opposition from forming.

In 1806, half the multazims' fā'iḍ was claimed. By 1807, masmūḥ lands were being taxed. Toward the end of the same year, Jabarti reports that lands held by the ulama and those under their protection were put under the regular tax. In 1808, receiving reports that many multazims were unable to pay the sums demanded, Muhammad Ali had their villages reassigned to his family and followers. Many of these were in underpopulated Buhayra province. To correct the labor shortage, town dwellers bearing *nisbas* from that province's villages were forcibly relocated there.[74]

In 1809, the Pasha ordered the compiling of a register for the taxation of waqf and ūsya lands and attempted to apply it first in Buhayra. Along with new market taxes, this measure brought a protest from some of the ulama. On more than one occasion deputations were assured that the new taxes would not be imposed, but the persistence of the delegations indicates that some in fact may have been collected. Land taxes were thus selectively and unequally applied in this period, a legacy from the previous century and a reflection of political realities. Jabarti records a meeting of ulama, officers, and notables convened the following year to consider means of improving the country's revenues. The shaykhs were enraged at the suggestion that their lands be taxed at a rate equal with that of the others. Yet shortly thereafter, registers were drawn up to include all land for taxation, including ūsya, waqf, and land held by the village shaykhs untaxed until then.[75]

After 1810 the reorganization of the land regime and agriculture entered a more intensive phase. Even before this time, multazims had faced extreme pressure to meet their tax obligations on time, even if it meant paying out of their pockets or borrowing at interest. If a multazim was unable to meet his obligations he had to surrender the land without being freed of his debt. In 1812, with the conquest of Upper Egypt, nearly all lands there were seized by the state and taxed directly. Waqf lands attached to mosques were taxed at half rate. These taxes were taken in kind, and wheat was already being accepted in place of cash payments in other parts of the country. Wheat not taken in taxation was subject to a state monopoly. Rice was monopolized from 1812. The rice-producing lands were put under the supervision of salaried officials who took the place of merchants in advancing capital to the peasants and purchasing their harvests.[76]

The cadastral survey of Lower Egypt, 1813–14, was the culmination of this phase of centralization. All cultivated and uncultivated land was surveyed. Land was recorded in the names of its holders, or cultivators, or those indicated as tenants at the time—that is, the names of all with a claim to the land were registered.[77] The surveyors used a standard faddan reportedly smaller than most customary ones which ranged in size from 200 to 400 square *qasabas* (a linear measure originally taken from a sugar cane); the new faddan equaled 333⅓ qasabas. Land was classified according to its fertility and a corresponding scale of taxation set.[78] At the cadaster's completion, most intermediary landholders were to be dispossessed for a promised pension.

The organization of a pyramidal administration was completed along with the cadaster and the land confiscations. All officials above the village level were salaried. They were charged with public security, maintenance of the irrigation system, and supervision of cultivation—including the allocation of seeds, implements, and animals as needed—as well as collection of taxes, and the purchase of crops subject to state monopolies.[79] Taxes were unified but not necessarily reduced, and the old intermediate structure, already partly bypassed, was eliminated.

During 1814 the multazims were allowed to collect the harvest on their ūsya lands, although they found that the peasants had heard of the confiscations and now resisted the corvée. The bureau charged with reviewing ahlī waqfs required their holders to present their deeds with supporting statements. Those with titles verified after the Ottoman reconquest of 1801 were to be taxed at half rate. Waqfs assigned to charitable works were incorporated into village lands and taxed accordingly.[80] The rigorous procedure of verification no doubt was designed to bring the maximum amount of land under government control.

It appears that many of Muhammad Ali's mercenaries and their wives had acquired iltizāms by 1815. Their confiscation that year, and an attempt to introduce European-style drill, caused several units in Cairo to mutiny and to riot. As one result, many of these multazims were allowed to retain their ūsya lands, but without any of the old rights to corvée labor to farm them.[81] These and other multazims were promised a pension in compensation for their lost lands, but it was smaller than expected and slow in coming. Ūsya lands were to be tax free, yet Amin Sami's account of the 1817/1818 budget shows these being taxed at the full rate. Finally, in the case of all lands retained by the old intermediaries, they found that their holdings had shrunk due to the new, smaller feddan employed in the survey.[82]

Helen Rivlin has noted the similarity of Muhammad Ali's reorganization to previous plans for reform. 'The revolution in Egyptian land tenure, envisioned in part by Selim III, Napoleon, and Menou,' she writes, 'had been executed by Muhammad Ali . . .'[83] In fact, this was more a resurrection of the Ottoman land system originally established in Egypt. That system had also been designed to maximize the flow of revenue to the capital. It had also consisted of an administrative structure of salaried officials who collected taxes and oversaw irrigation and cultivation.[84] Ottoman attempts to reverse the process of loosening central control in various provinces during the seventeenth and eighteenth centuries had aimed at curtailing if not abolishing tax farming, to return to something like the original system. But the Ottomans lacked the strength to carry this reform through. Instead they were forced to seek the support of the same elements who had usurped state authority over the land, in their efforts to suppress the Mamluk beys. Only vestiges of the original Ottoman land system survived in Egypt by the late eighteenth century, but the scribes who collaborated with the French undoubtedly drew inspiration from that system in helping the French devise their 'new' system.

Muhammad Ali's administrative centralization *was* revolutionary in that it completely altered the structure of political power in Egypt. The notion that in its methods it was something fundamentally new or European-inspired, however, should be discarded. It was but a phase in the recurring pattern of a central authority's struggle with local rivals for control of the land revenues of the country.

1816–1837: CENTRALIZATION AND EXPANSION

Agrarian policy under Muhammad Ali was part of a program of economic expansion in all spheres. At the same time, financial straits resulting from campaigns, diplomatic crises, and fluctuations in international markets added to the pressure on the agricultural sector, always the chief source of revenues.

The relationship of state commerce and industry to agriculture cannot be overemphasized. Muhammad Ali's tightening of control over the land followed and complemented his control of commerce. He acquired control of Cairo's customs in 1805, and the Mediterranean ports' customs in 1807, with the addition of these cities to his domain. The development of the state as a commercial enterprise is symbolized by the career of Boghos Yusufian of Izmir, a member of one of the era's far-flung Armenian merchant families. In Muhammad Ali's service he rose from merchant and farmer of Alexandria's customs to 'minister' of commerce and foreign affairs by the mid-1820s, in step with the development of Egyptian state administration.[85]

The Pasha himself brought to Egypt a considerable knowledge of the eastern Mediterranean's commerce and politics. As one who combined the roles of soldier and merchant in Cavalla, Macedonia, he was typical of his times.[86] Once in control of Egypt, he set about organizing state and parastatal commerce as opportunity permitted. Egypt's Mediterranean fleet was from the beginning a merchant fleet, the acquisition of large warships dating from the Greek revolt of 1821.[87] By patronizing a group of Armenian, Greek, Syrian, Maghribi, and local merchants, Muhammad Ali received important financial services, and tied into a network of commercial and diplomatic intelligence.[88] Before 'modern' state banking and diplomatic structures appeared, then, their functions were being performed by such associates. The flow of information permitted the Pasha to manipulate exports and export prices to his advantage, and to devise policies—including agrarian policies—in light of international conditions.

Nonmilitary industrial projects were undertaken with just such knowledge of past and contemporary economic trends. State efforts to develop Egypt's textile industries led to the introduction of sericulture and the expansion of cotton and indigo production. This entailed the deepening of old canals and the digging of new ones for summer irrigation, even before the discovery of 'Jumel' long-fiber cotton. According to Mustafa Fahmy's figures, of the total cotton-processing capacity installed (not accounting for replacement), 49 per cent of the cards, 22 per cent of the mule jennies, and 57 per cent of Egypt's looms were set up in 1817–21. Five of nine bleaching works and the only two printing works were also established before 1821, the first year of Jumel production.[89] All this indicates an early intent to modernize and expand cotton textile production.

Food crops and other traditional crops such as flax and oil seeds remained important for internal consumption, industry, and export. In addition, large new tracts of olives and vines were planted, opium culture was revived, and merino sheep were imported to supply a new woolen industry. Skilled foreigners were employed to establish or improve the production of silk, indigo, and opium.[90] Land was granted tax free, as *rizqa bi-lā māl*, to those who would plant either acacia trees or horticultural gardens along the new Mahmudiyya Canal. Acacias produced a hardwood used in construction. Tax exemptions on date palms were similarly intended to encourage their cultivation. Experiments were also made in acclimatizing coffee, cochineal, and teak, but were disappointing.[91]

A variety of sources contain estimates and official accounts of the area of land under cultivation, or taxed, in this period. Most reliable accounts for the period 1800–50 indicate that the total cultivated area was between 3 and 4 million faddans (see table 1). All evidence points to increasing areas of land cultivated during this period. Three projects which extended the area of cultivation were completed by 1820: the Mahmudiyya Canal, running from the Rosetta branch of the Nile to Alexandria, the repair of the sea dike near

TABLE 1 *Accounts of Egypt's cultivated and taxed land, 1800–1852*[a]

	Taxed				
	Lower Egypt	Upper Egypt	Total	'Cultivated'	'Cultivable'
1800			3,970	4,038	
1813 (1)	2,373				
1813 (2)					2,905
1813 (3)				3,055	
1815/1816	1,904				
1817/1818	1,970	1,033	3,003		
1820/1821		1,315	3,219		
1822	1,900	1,748	3,647		
1835					3,500
1830s				3,856	
1840				4,491	
1843				3,672	
1844			3,590		
1852			3,525	4,160	

[a] In 1,000s of faddans. Cf. Patrick O'Brien. 'The Long-Term Growth of Agricultural Production in Egypt,' in P. M. Holt, ed., *Political and Social Change in Modern Egypt* (Oxford, 1968), p. 172, table.

Sources:

1800: Pierre Jacotin, 'Tableau de la superficie de l'Egypt.' *Description de L'Egypte, Etat moderne,* XVIII, 2, pp. 102–105. Note that by Jacotin's method, his figures are subject to a large degree of error, after any inaccuracies in the preparation of the French maps of Egypt. The figures used here have been modified by Helen Rivlin to equal 'new' faddans (*The Agricultural Policy of Muhammad Ali in Egypt* [Cambridge, Mass., 1961], p. 265).

1813 (1): Omar Toussoun, *La Géographie de l'Egypte à l'époque Arabe.* Mémoires de la Société Royale de Géographie d'Egypte, VIII. 3 (Cairo, 1928), p. 508.

1813 (2): Yacoub Artin, *La Propriété foncière en Egypte* (Cairo, 1883), p. 325.

1813 (3): Idem, 'Essai sur les causes de renchérissement de la vie matérielle au Caire dans le courant du XIXe siècle,' *Mémoires présentées à l'Institut Egyptien,* V, 2 (Cairo, 1907), 67.

1815/1816: Ali Barakat, *Taṭawwur al-Milkiyya al-Zirāʿiyya fī Miṣr wa Atharuh ʿalā al-Haraka al-Siyāsiyya 1813–1914* (Cairo, 1977), pp. 26–28. See also note 103.

1817/1818: Sami, *Taqwīm al-Nīl,* II. 266–270.

1820/1821: Barakat, *Taṭawwur al-Milkiyya,* pp. 26–28.

1822: Sami, *Taqwīm al-Nīl,* II. 298–302. The increase for Upper Egypt is due at least in part to the extension of the land tax to areas where previously only trees and water-lifting devices were taxed.

1835: John Bowring, 'Report on Egypt and Candia,' *Parliamentary Papers* 1840, XXI, as cited in O'Brien, 'Long-Term Growth of Agricultural Production,' p. 172.

1830s: A. B. Clot, *Aperçu général sur l'Egypte* (2 vols.: Paris, 1840), II, 264–265.

1840: Artin, 'Essai,' p. 68.

1843: de Regny, *Statistique de l'Egypte* (Alexandria, 1870), as cited in O'Brien, 'Long-Term Growth of Agricultural Production,' p. 172.

1852: Butros Ghali, 'Rapport présenté a la commission d'enquête de l'impôt foncier en 1880,' cited in Artin, 'Essai,' p. 68, for the area taxed. The area cultivated is Artin's own figure.

Alexandria, and the reclamation of the Wadi Tumaylat for sericulture, which alone involved the construction of 1,000 *sāqiyas* (waterwheels).[92]

How did the agrarian and land tenure systems evolve in this period? Once the cadaster of 1813–14 had been completed, and with a pattern of extensive state involvement in commerce and industry taking shape, pivotal changes in the agrarian regime were a short and complementary step. In 1816, state monopolies were extended: the fallahin were forbidden to sell their harvests of hemp, sesame, indigo, cotton, wheat, beans, and barley to anyone but government agents. These were taken to government warehouses in each village, bought at a fixed price, and credited to each peasant's account after deductions of taxes. The rice monopoly continued along the lines previously set.[93]

That year the state also entered directly into production—planting and cultivation—as evidenced by an order to the mudirs to see to the doubling of the area devoted to hemp, chick-peas, sesame, and cotton, although the order was unevenly enforced. Scribes were charged with keeping track of crops on the stalk, and were to follow them through each stage of cultivation—not because the fallahin needed instruction but to thwart the thievery which was their response to the new controls. This system was continued through the late 1830s, although the internal trade in grain was freed in 1830.[94]

Land tenure in this period took several forms, with different motives and consequences. State policy was influenced by a desire to increase production, to take from it the maximum surplus possible, but also to insure the loyalty of bureaucratic and military cadres. It was not Muhammad Ali's policy to reward his followers' services with land: '. . . j'en ai trouvé le moyen en leur prodiguant l'argent et les présents, mais en les empêchant de devenir propriétaires et de se créer eux-mêmes une influence personelle sur la population.'[95]

Yet a certain amount of land was alienated. The contradictory aspect of land grants to individuals in a period of increased central control of the land again highlights the compromises necessary to offset opposition to the new order and to attach indispensable elements to it. And the state could confidently grant limited amounts of land as long as it was capable of dictating the terms of land tenure. This, of course, in no way contradicts the thesis that many grants in this period were also aimed at encouraging agricultural investment, experimentation, and land reclamation.

Grants of rizqa bi-lā māl were offered from 1827. Much of the area along the Mahmudiyya Canal had lost population, and cultivation there had declined during the previous century. The capital required to set up waterwheels and plant trees means that these grants must have gone to wealthier individuals.

Uncultivated land, surveyed in the cadasters but not included in the tax registers (hence the term *ib'ādiyya*, 'set apart'), was granted under two different sets of circumstances. One type was granted to individuals who would bring them into production. They were given a deed entitling them to lifetime tenure, although the land was to revert to the state upon their death. The first such grant occurred in 1826: they appear to have been granted both as tax exempt for life and tax exempt for the first few years. They were undertaken by officials, officers, and foreigners, the latter forfeiting any capitulatory privileges. By 1837, these lands came to 103,175 faddans, and by 1848, to 164,960 faddans, nearly exclusively in Middle Egypt. In the registers inspected by Ali Barakat, nearly all recipients of these grants occupied high administrative or military positions.[96] A small amount of cultivated, *ma'mūr*, land was also granted: 8,703 faddans between 1827 and 1848.[97]

Bedouin pastoralists were also granted lands classified as ib'ādiyya, as an inducement to settling, on condition that they cultivate them. But these tribes often found it more convenient to sublet to tenants. Decrees in 1837, 1846, and later prohibited this practice. Bedouin ib'ādiyya grants involved no title deed, but only the Pasha's promise not to tax the bedouin directly, nor to subject them to corvée or conscription.[98] By such arrangements these grants appear to have been a kind of treaty: in return for their special status, bedouin served as auxiliaries in the army. Their revolt and migration were provoked by Abbas's and Said's efforts to tax their lands in the 1850s.[99]

Personal estates held by members of the ruling family came to be called *jifliks* (çiftliks). Their extent in this period is unknown, but it was probably limited due to the alienation of revenues involved. Contemporary sources mention estates held by Muhammad Ali, for example, at Shubra, Ibrahim's estate on Rūda Island, and others.[100] These early estates do not appear in the registers of jifliks, all dating from 1838, which Barakat examined (discussed in the following section). In the case of the early personal estates and the new jifliks granted from 1838, the principle of land given a member of the ruling family is the same. But the later grants were part of a strategy of continuing state control of agriculture in the wake of the Treaty of Balta Liman the same year. The different circumstances and intent of the new jifliks account for the separate registers.

While Muhammad Ali's reorganization had established a salaried bureaucracy in the countryside, state administration at the village level continued to be carried out by prominent villagers much as it had under the old regime. Village shaykhs were appointed from among the wealthier families as before. Not a few such families must have held the office under the beys.[101] Under Muhammad Ali, the village shaykhs received grants of tax-free land, masmūḥ, in lieu of salaries. Grants of masmūh were made in Upper Egypt as early as 1813.[102] The cadaster of Lower Egypt was not completed until 1814, and whether masmūḥ lands were granted there at the time is uncertain. Jabarti first mentions masmūḥ in reference to the cadaster of 1820–21.[103]

Two types of masmūḥ were granted, *masmūh al-mashāyikh* and *masmūḥ al-masṭaba*. The former was intended as compensation for official duties explained below. The latter, sometimes assigned to the same individual, was to support the costs of visitors' and officials' lodging and board. Most shaykhs received four to five faddans of land as masmūḥ out of every 105 faddans of maʿmūr land belonging to the village. The most prominent shaykhs, or *muqaddims*, received 10 faddans out of every 100 faddans of maʿmūr in the village.[104] Differing local conditions and the different periodicity and modes of fiscal and administrative reorganization, however, preclude an assumption of complete uniformity in this system's application. The quality of the masmūḥ lands the shaykhs received, and/or their activities in improving them, caused these lands to be assessed at the highest rates in the villages when Said taxed them in 1857.[105]

In addition to their acquisition of these lands, the shaykhs, their families and protégés continued to be in a position to amass wealth and accumulate additional land, despite the more stringent supervision of land registration and exploitation than before. With the increased involvement of the state in production, the shaykhs' power increased. They were made responsible for assessing and collecting taxes (as in the past), for reassigning athar land on a fallah's death or conscription, for apportioning corvée duty, and for assigning the cultivation of cash crops among the fallahin once the quota to be grown had been fixed.[106] The shaykhs' abuse of their role in reassigning lands is said to have led Said to transfer this function to the provincial governments in 1854.[107] It was these families, the wealthy peasantry, whose members were recruited when the lower provincial offices were opened to native Egyptians in the 1830s.[108] Hamont reports that one such official who rose in the provincial administration of Ṭanṭa held some 500 to 600 faddans of ibʿādiyya land in 1839. It was found that 300 faddans of this land had been 'stolen' from one of Abbas Pasha's jifliks several years earlier.[109] Whether a victim of political intrigue, a real villain, or both, this fallah's career indicates the scale of wealth that a few of the rural elite could reach.

In 1837, noting that there were many landless fallahin in the villages who worked as day laborers, Duhamel observed that '... il n'est pas rare de trouver des Sceiks, qui possèdent ... mille et plus de feddans ...' of athar land.[110] This was an exaggeration in terms of the typical amount of land held, but further testifies to the existence of a distinct stratum of wealthy peasants which, despite the changes in the land regime, was able to maintain and even improve its position.

How did the condition of the peasantry change in this period? To say that under the Mamluk beys the peasants were sheltered from direct contact with the state, implying that this made life easier for them,[111] is to misunderstand the nature of the old and new regimes. Both exploited the peasantry. Under both a peasant family's ability to withstand the burdens imposed and/or to shift them onto others' shoulders was a matter of relative strength. The weak, poor, and unprotected fared the worst in face of the state and the rural elite in both periods. One rough indicator of overall conditions in this period is an upturn in population. 'Civil order,' in the opinion of a recent writer, accounts for lowered mortality.[112] On the other hand, the gains made by wealthy peasants could only have come at their poorer neighbors' expense. In addition, peasants were expropriated in the creation of large estates in the 1840s, and reduced there to wage laborers and tenants.

The new regime did affect the fallah's life more directly in many ways, with the introduction of conscription, the organization of corvée labor for distant projects, the relocation of population on reclaimed land, and the control of agriculture and village industries. Taxation increased and was more effectively enforced. But these new demands did not go without resistance. The later years of Jabarti's chronicle contain references to black-marketing and strenuous efforts to suppress it.[113] Resistance to increasing demands on the populace took the form of indifferent work or sabotage in factories and on the farms, and self-mutilation, endemic stealing, or outright revolt.[114]

Revolt occurs less from absolutely intolerable conditions than from conditions perceived to be intolerable—that is, one's condition and response to it are matters of subjective appraisal. Adequately fed peasants who have recently improved their lot or have something to gain are more likely to revolt than those who are completely ground down.[115] The great peasant revolts of Upper Egypt and the one in Sharqiyya occurred in areas which had enjoyed a quasi-autonomy a generation earlier. These revolts followed the more thorough cadaster of 1820–21 and an increase in rural taxation, and were set off by the beginning of conscription.

THE GROWTH AND ENTRENCHMENT OF PRIVILEGED LANDHOLDINGS FROM 1838

The landholding system as it developed between the first cadaster and the late 1830s was not uniform in regard to the principle of ownership, but rather it reflected the priorities of the state: to increase production, both to fuel the economy and provide revenues, and to provide for and conciliate certain elements indispensable to maintaining the state. The bulk of village lands were taxed and administered directly through the bureaucracy in cooperation with prominent village families. Exempt from taxation were the masmūḥ lands in the hands of the shaykhs, bedouin ibʿādiyya grants, rizqa bi-lā māl and ibʿādiyya grants belonging to officers, officials, and other wealthy individuals, and the personal estates of royal family members and a few high officers and officials.

As long as the state created by Muhammad Ali remained strong it could resist any pressure to remove these lands from its ultimate control. Once created, however, the new bureaucratic machinery was potentially at the disposal of landed interests, should they gain control over it.

The changes in Egypt's land regime during Muhammad Ali's final decade reflect the weakening of the state due to the defeat in Syria (1840) and the imposition of free trade according to the provisions of the Treaty of Balta Liman (1838). The state had also been weakened by a fiscal crisis.

The increasing demands of capital investment, a growing military establishment and constant wars, along with a far from perfect bureaucracy, epidemics, and a capricious Nile, had caused many villages to fall into tax arrears by this time.[116] Agriculture and the land tax accounted for the lion's share of revenue and had to be maintained. At first, a short-lived attempt was made to merge the responsibilities of villages in arrears with those still able to meet their obligations.[117] Finally in 1840, a decree was issued which in essence resurrected the iltizām system of old, in the form of *ʿuhda* grants: high officers, officials, and family members were required to take over responsibility for the bankrupt villages, paying the arrears, and collecting and forwarding each year's taxes thereafter. They were charged with providing working capital as needed by the fallahin, with supervising cultivation and harvesting, and were to act as local arbiters, replacing the middle level of state bureaucracy in these capacities. The creation of the ʿuhdas accomplished a forced contribution from the wealthy with the payment of the arrears, and was designed to insure future revenues, while at the same time cutting administrative costs. Peasants on the ʿuhdas were also thereby relieved of the accumulation of tax arrears. The recipients of these grants, the *mutaʿahhids*, received a section of land in each ʿuhda to cultivate for their own profit.[118]

Following the Treaty of Balta Liman and the defeat in Syria, an acceleration of jiflik grants also took place, and these are said to have included the best cotton lands in the country.[119] Muhammad Ali himself acquired most of these, 239,426 of a total of 334,216 faddans granted between 1838 and 1846. Nearly all the new jifliks created were in Lower Egypt.[120] Administration of the new jifliks was patterned after the bureaucratic regime previously established over the entire country, and all peasants on these estates were reduced to tenancy or wage labor.[121]

Both the ʿuhdas and new jifliks enabled Muhammad Ali to circumvent the intent of Balta Liman tariffs, which would henceforth prevent use of the customs to control the import–export trade, or the use of trade monopolies to manipulate commodity prices. Now that these options were closed, the Pasha retreated into the sphere of production in order to maintain the monopoly of commodities in a new form. As evidence of this he acquired by far the largest amount of his new jifliks in 1841–45, only one jiflik grant in this period going to someone else.[122]

Peasants on ʿuhdas also were expropriated. The mutaʿahhids were required to take over athar lands which destitute peasants lacked the means to cultivate, with the stipulation that as their condition improved these peasants would regain direct responsibility for their lands step by step.[123] It appears in fact that little effort was made to improve the fallahin's lot. The pressure on mutaʿahhids to meet tax payments worked against this in any event, and many fallahin on these estates found themselves reduced to tenancy. Barakat found that of the ʿuhdas held by the royal family in 1846–47, only 99,301 of a total of 228,461 feddans were recorded as remaining in peasant hands.[124]

The apparent lack of resistance to these changes in their status may reflect the truly desperate straits of peasants on ʿuhda and jiflik lands, in which relief from tax arrears and a continued guaranteed livelihood as tenants and laborers would seem to them an improvement. But this rather tranquil picture may also reflect the inadequacy of our sources in showing the peasants' response.

In addition to the obvious fiscal motivations, the pattern of land grants in the 1840s may also reflect court factionalism, which became more pronounced, and a desire to attach the political elite more firmly to the Pasha, in light of this division. New jiflik grants are recorded for the Pasha's two daughters, a nephew, sons Said and Halim, and grandson Abbas, but none for Ibrahim.[125] While the aim of encouraging investment was never absent from policy,[126] the extension of ibʿādiyya holders' rights may also have been a political concession to them. These lands had been made inheritable in 1836; in 1842, full rights of disposition over them were granted.[127]

Aside from ibʿādiyya lands and the new jifliks, further forfeiture of control of the land was avoided. No rights of disposal were given the mutaʿahhids. The law of 1846 codified some of the fallahin's traditional rights over their land—including its transfer—and may have been intended in part as a counterpoise to the mutaʿahhid's power. By reaffirming the fallah's right to return to athar land he had abandoned it appears designed to lure back fugitives, and it dovetails with the intent that destitute peasants were to take back land taken over by the mutaʿahhids as soon as they were able.[128]

This blend of old and new arrangements indicates that while the administration of land tenure was adjusted to meet new exigencies, the aims of policy remained essentially as before: maximization of production and revenue with tight state control over the land. Although the genesis of the land regime of the next generation—with its large estates—is apparent here, such was not the intent. If the state had been able to maintain its policies and to regain sufficient authority over the landholders it had created, then landholding in Egypt after mid-century would have evolved differently from the way in which it actually did.

UNRESOLVED CONTRADICTIONS

The further legislation of formal landownership rights in nineteenth-century Egypt resulted not only from the tendency of larger landholders to take and ask for more, but also from rulers' efforts to resolve a basic contradiction in the very process of state formation. It was the same dilemma faced earlier by Ottoman reformers and their local rivals in Cairo. Maximization of revenue was the *sine qua non* of building and maintaining a strong state, whether one considers Ottoman policy or the efforts of local strongmen attempting to build successor states. This requirement lies behind the variety of fiscal reform schemes the period witnessed, and it tended to push policy in the direction of administrative centralization, the elimination of tax-farming middlemen, and tighter, more direct control of the land. The same principle applied to commerce, as expressed in state policy in regard to appaltos and tax farms of the customs. Thus administrative and fiscal reform went hand in hand with 'military reform,' the creation of forces capable of dominating the countryside and of eliminating independent focuses of power.

On the other hand, the process of reviving a state or of building one anew also required the collaboration of indispensable elements in the society: village shaykhs, merchants, bureaucrats, officers, and so on, many if not all of whom held lands and/or tax-farming offices. To the extent that the state had to rely on their support it could not afford to confiscate or tighten control over their landholdings, mercantile activities, or offices—at least not without significant concessions and exemptions. But to the extent that revenues were needed, the ruler was drawn in this direction, into direct confrontation with landed interests in particular.

Egypt's rulers sought to resolve this dilemma in two ways. One was to establish military dominance in the countryside, and then to allow supporters and collaborators to establish themselves, or remain, as landlords. But this strategy simply reproduced the contradiction in a new form, postponing its resolution. Thus under Ali Bey and his successors, and in Muhammad Ali's early years, such a policy was accompanied by increased tax pressure on the landholders. Similarly, we read of the seemingly erratic behavior of rulers who alternately 'favored' a merchant group and subjected them to degrees of extortion.[129]

The second way out was military expansion. It is not proposed here that this is the only factor behind expansion. But successful conquest might help fill the state's coffers in the short run through booty, and in the long run through control of trade routes and the exploitation of imperial possessions, the latter relieving—at least temporarily—the pressure to raise greater revenues at home. The role of different rulers' merchant allies in Egypt's expansion thus deserves attention. They knew the regions worth conquering and exploiting, they possessed the expertise with which to milk them, and they had an interest in relieving pressure on themselves at home and in trading in conquered territories under state patronage.[130] Expansion also involved—and could pay for—an expanded military, which would enhance the ruler's ability to apply coercion at home.

Conquest, however, was a risky affair. The returns were potentially great, but only if conquered territory could be held and administered without major cost.

Thus the Powers' intervention in 1840 to confine Muhammad Ali's forces to Egypt takes on an added dimension of importance. This event has been seen as confirming the region's movement along the road to economic dependence and underdevelopment. The substantial truth of this proposition, should not, however, be allowed to obscure the importance of sociopolitical processes within Egypt which reinforced this trend. Efforts to retain control of the land and obstruct free trade after 1840 indicate that Egypt's rulers had not given up the game. Administrative reform, education, exploration for minerals, and the irrigation works—that is, the creation of a modern state—continued under Abbas and Said. As before, such activities were intended to meet the requirements of contemporary conditions and were subject to the shifting strength of the rulers and different political factions. Both Abbas and Said sought to consolidate their positions, to increase the state's control of the land, and to raise revenues. Reminiscent of Muhammad Ali, Abbas confiscated from two-thirds to three-quarters of the ʿuhdas for nonpayment of taxes, and attempted to tax bedouin ibʿādiyya lands. He was also accused of attempting to recreate Muhammad Ali's monopolies.[131]

Yet by the late 1840s the state had lost its ability to milk commerce through the customs, its army had been reduced, and future military expansion was ruled out except in the direction of Africa. Such constraints limited the independent maneuverability of Egypt's rulers and enhanced the relative power of indigenous political interests, as reflected in the obvious use of land grants for political patronage.[132] These groups in turn sought to consolidate their positions as landholders, from members of the ruling family and high officials at the top to the rural elite which increasingly rose in the middle levels of the bureaucracy. The value attached to land increased, especially in the 1850s, the result of the irrigation works and rising export prices for cotton and grain.[133] As one indication of the wealthy landholders' increased leverage on the state, the right of fallahin to return to athar land they had abandoned was reduced step by step in this decade. Furthermore, the fallahin's abandonment of land to the state for sale to investors was facilitated.[134] Both measures were a significant reversal of traditional state policy which hastened the concentration of land in fewer hands.

Among all groups able to influence state policy, there was a direct interest in free trade and a more liberal definition of landholders' rights. Indeed, as Baer writes, there was 'a need ... felt to facilitate land transactions,' but not, as he states, simply 'to encourage the development of agriculture.'[135] A century earlier, *de facto* rights of ownership had appeared in usage, the result of the increased value attached to land in a situation where the state was unable to maintain effective control over its disposition. Agricultural development intensified in the nineteenth century, but in a situation where the state's authority had considerably increased and where many of the larger landholders themselves were high state officials. Thus the arena where the struggle for land was played out shifted to the state, and its results were expressed in legislation.

New fiscal needs, large tracts of land alienated by earlier grants, and the continued concealment of athar land from the tax registers led Said to take the well-known measures of the 1850s, which had the effect of further defining and strengthening landholders' rights. He imposed a mild tax, the *'ushur*, on jiflik, ib'ādiyya, and on the remaining 'uhda lands, but at the price of granting full ownership rights to their holders.[136] He succeeded in subjecting bedouin ib'ādiyya lands to the much higher *kharāj* tax, which required a series of expeditions to coerce the tribes. Masmūḥ lands were subjected to the kharāj in 1857 and assimilated to village lands in 1858. But the shaykhs retained most of their local prerogatives, including the duty to assess lands for taxation[137]—that is, they remained able to protect what they held and acquire more—while traditional rights of disposition over peasant lands were confirmed but not extended to absolute private ownership.

The legislation of 1854–58 reflects the ascendancy, once again, of landed classes in Egypt, able to influence land-tenure policy in their own interests. These classes were to prove more powerful and enduring than their counterparts of the eighteenth century. They were able to prosper, the more powerful gaining formal ownership rights over large estates in exchange for extremely low rates of taxation. This, and Egypt's lack of control over customs rates, meant that the full weight of the state's increasing fiscal needs was borne by the small peasantry. Despite the increased exploitation of the peasantry, state expenditures outstripped revenues. Said and Ismail were obliged to look outside of Egypt for financing, to the point of heavy borrowing and eventual bankruptcy.

This article is reprinted from the *International Journal of Middle East Studies*, vol. 12, November 1980, pp. 245–275. Reprinted with the permission of Cambridge University Press.

NOTES

Author's Note: I wish to thank Dr. Afaf Lutfi al-Sayyid-Marsot and Yahya Sadowski for their many helpful suggestions and criticisms during the successive drafts of this paper.

1. See Gabriel Baer, 'The Development of Private Ownership of the Land,' in his *Studies in the Social History of Modern Egypt* (Chicago, 1969); and idem, *A History of Landownership in Modern Egypt 1800–1950* (Oxford, 1962).

2. For a more extensive discussion of modernization theory and its inadequacies, see Samuel P. Huntington, 'The Change to Change: Modernization, Development, and Politics,' *Comparative Politics*, 3, 3 (April 1971), 283–322. A statement of the theory and its application in an Egyptian context is found in Robert Tignor, *Modernization and British Colonial Rule in Egypt 1880–1914* (Princeton, 1966). Writers of this school have differed over whether a change in values is primary, or whether technological change first produces the necessary change from traditional to modern values. See, e.g., Manfred Halpern, *The Politics of Social Change in the Middle East and North Africa* (Princeton, 1963); Daniel J. Lerner, *The Passing of Traditional Society: Modernizing the Middle East* (Glencoe, Ill., 1958); James A. Bill and Carl Leiden, *The Middle East: Politics and Power* (Boston, 1974): and, on the subject of 'technicalization,' Marshall G. S. Hodgson, *The Venture of Islam* (3 vols.: Chicago, 1974), I, 52–53.

3. A recent challenge to the periodicity of the modernization thesis is Peter Gran's *The Islamic Roots of Capitalism* (Texas, 1979).

4. This is not to pose the question of whether 'internal forces' had more effect than 'external' influences in this period. The internal–external dichotomy is as false as the traditional–modern, since in reality processes in both realms were intertwined and cannot be separated.

5. See, for example, Jerome Blum, *The End of the Old Order in Rural Europe* (Princeton, 1978); and James C. Scott, *The Moral Economy of the Peasant: Rebellion and Subsistence in Southeast Asia* (Yale, 1976).

6. This discussion follows the land system's detailed description in Stanford Shaw, 'Landholding and Land-Tax Revenues in Ottoman Egypt,' in P. M. Holt, ed., *Political and Social Change in Modern Egypt* (Oxford, 1968), pp. 91–103; idem, *The Financial and Administrative Organization and Development of Ottoman Egypt, 1517–1798* (Princeton, 1962), pp. 1–50; and Abd al-Rahim Abd al-Rahman Abd al-Rahim, *Al-Rīf al-Miṣrī fī al-Qarn al-Thāmin ʿAshar* (Cairo, 1974), pp. 65–124.

7. Scott, *Moral Economy*, Introduction.

8. Abd al-Rahim, *Al-Rīf al-Miṣrī*, pp. 65–124.

9. The evolution of the role of Egypt's intermediaries is best described in Shaw, 'Landholding and Land-Tax Revenues in Ottoman Egypt.'

10. Abd al-Rahim, *Al-Rīf al-Miṣrī*, p. 78.

11. Ibid., pp. 83–86.

12. In particular, Baer, 'The Development of Private Ownership of the Land.'

13. Abd al-Rahim, *Al-Rīf al-Miṣrī*, pp. 83–84.

14. Michel-Ange Lancret, 'Mémoire sur le système d'imposition territoriale et sur l'administration des provinces d'Egypte, dans les derniers années du gouvernement des Mamlouks,' *Description de l'Egypte, Etat moderne*, XI, 474–475 (hereafter cited as *DE*).

15. See Maxime Rodinson, *Islam and Capitalism* (Pantheon, 1973).

16. Blum, *The End of the Older Order*, pp. 19–20.

17. On sixteenth-century population and prices: Fernand Braudel, *The Mediterranean and the Mediterranean World of Philip II* (2 vols.; Harper Torchbooks, 1975), I, 402–410, 517–519. On eighteenth-century population in Europe: Blum, *The End of the Old Order*, p. 241. Given the evidence for a shared demographic experience in thc sixteenth century, Middle Eastern population may have begun to increase along with Europe's in the eighteenth. This possibility is also raised in Braudel's provocative discussion of the 'weight of numbers' in *Capitalism and Material Life 1400–1800* (2 vols.; Harper and Row, 1973), pp. 1–20. Egypt's population in 1800 has been underestimated by as much as one-third; see Justin A. McCarthy, 'Nineteenth-Century Egyptian Population,' *Middle East Studies*, 12, 3 (Oct. 1976), 1–39.

18. 'Between the 1730s and the first decade of the nineteenth century, cereal prices went up by 283 per cent in Denmark, 259 per cent in Austria, 210 per cent in Germany, and 163 per cent in France' (Blum, *The End of the Old Order*, p. 242; on land prices and speculation: pp. 17–20; 170;

241–242). In Cairo, the average prices of wheat, rice, and beans in 1791–1798 were approximately two and a half times what they were during 1680–1690 (see note 23 below).

19. For Europe: ibid., pp. 17–20.

20. Braudel, *The Mediterranean*, I, 584, 591–594; Robert Paris, *Histoire du commerce de Marseille de 1660 à 1789*, vol. 5, *Le Levant*, ed. Gaston Rambert (Paris, 1957), pp. 537–539.

21. The growth of French commerce in the eastern Mediterranean during the eighteenth century can be followed in Paris (ibid.: Paul Masson, *Histoire du commerce français dans le Levant au XVIIIe siècle* [Paris, 1896]). Textile production in parts of the eastern Mediterranean was expanding during this period, only partly in response to Europe's expansion. See Yahya Sadowski, 'Eighteenth-Century Syrian Social Revolution: 1720–1840,' paper read at the 1978 Middle East Studies Association conference, Ann Arbor, Mich. The Egyptian Delta silk-finishing industry was organized by Syrians who penetrated the Egyptian economy early in the century (M. P. S. Girard, 'Mémoire sur l'agriculture, l'industrie, et le commerce de l'Egypte,' *DE*. XVII, 208–209, 219–223; Albert Hourani, 'The Syrians in Egypt in the Eighteenth and Nineteenth Centuries,' *Colloque Internationale sur l'Histoire du Caire* (1969), pp. 222–224.

22. The economic history of the eastern Mediterranean in this period has yet to be approached with a region-wide perspective. The study of the Balkans is most advanced; see Peter F. Sugar, *Southeastern Europe under Ottoman Rule, 1354–1804* (Seattle and London, 1977), part 4. On the Lebanon: Iliya F. Harik, *Politics and Change in a Traditional Society: Lebanon 1711–1845* (Princeton, 1968); William R. Polk, *The Opening of South Lebanon, 1788–1845* (Harvard, 1963). On Palestine: Amnon Cohen, *Palestine in the 18th Century* (Jerusalem, 1973). For Egypt the best discussions of countrywide production and distribution are still to be found in various articles of the *Description de l'Egypte*, especially Girard, 'Mémoire sur l'agriculture, l'industrie, et le commerce de l'Egypte.' Production and trade in Cairo is discussed in André Raymond, *Artisans et commerçants au Caire au XVIIIe siècle* (2 vols.; Damascus, 1973).

23. Raymond, *Artisans et commerçants*, I, 53–65. Raymond stresses local conditions and events as determining fluctuations in the prices of basic commodities. Yet the century-long rise in commodity prices is roughly in accord with that of contemporary Europe. See note 18, above, and Fernand Braudel and Ernest Labrousse, eds. *Histoire economique et sociale de la France* (2 vols.; Paris, 1970), I, 383–391.

24. Paris, *Histoire du commerce de Marseille*, p. 523.

25. Bistra Cvetkova,'Quelques problèmes du féodalisme ottoman a l'époque du XVIe siècle au XVIIIe siècle,' *Actes du premier congrès international des études balcaniques et sud-est européenes*, Sofia, 1966 (5 vols.; Sofia, 1966–1970), III, 709–720.

26. Trian Stoianovich, 'Land Tenure and Related Sectors of the Balkan Economy,' *Journal of Economic History*, 13 (Fall, 1953), 402–403.

27. Deena R. Sadat, 'Rumeli Ayanlari: The Eighteenth Century,' *Journal of Modern History* 44 (Sept. 1972), 346–363. The literature discussing this has been summarized in Sugar, *Southeastern Europe under Ottoman Rule*, pp. 211–221.

28. Dominique Chevallier, 'Aspects sociaux de la question d'Orient,' *Annales*, 14 (1959) 35–64; Harik, *Politics and Change*, on waqf, pp. 83–85, 93–95.

29. Cohen, *Palestine in the 18th Century*, passim.

30. Cvetkova 'Quelques problèmes du féodalism,' pp. 717–718.

31. Stanford Shaw, *History of the Ottoman Empire and Modern Turkey* (2 vols.; Cambridge, 1976), I, 232, 238.

32. Ibid., pp. 246–247, 256–257.

33. Abd al-Rahim, *Al-Rīf al-Miṣrī*, pp. 83–84.

34. Raymond, *Artisans et commerçants*, II, 721.

35. Ibid., pp. 721–722; Abd al-Rahim, *Al-Rīf al-Miṣrī*, pp. 113–114.

36. Terence Walz, *The Trade between Egypt and Bilād al-Sudān 1700–1820* (Cairo, 1978), pp. 110–112, 115.

37. Abd al-Rahim, *Al-Rīf al-Miṣrī*, p. 95.

38. Raymond, *Artisans et commerçants*, II, 722–726, and I, 292.

39. Afaf Marsot, 'Political and Economic Functions of the Ulama in the 18th Century,' *Journal of the Economic and Social History of the Orient*, 16 (Dec. 1973), 130–154; idem, 'The Ulama of Cairo in the Eighteenth and Nineteenth Centuries,' in Nikki R. Keddie, ed., *Scholars, Saints and Sufis*

(California, 1972), pp. 149–166; idem, 'The Wealth of the Ulama in Late Eighteenth Century Cairo,' in Thomas Naff and Roger Owen, eds, *Studies in Eighteenth Century Islamic History* (Southern Illinois, 1977), pp. 205–216.

40. Raymond, *Artisans et commerçants*, I, 79–80.

41. Abd al-Rahim, *Al-Rīf al-Miṣrī*, pp. 87–91.

42. Ibid., pp. 87–91.

43. Ibid., p. 80. Cf. Blum, *The End of the Old Order*, pp. 206–207.

44. Lancret, 'Mémoire sur le système d'imposition territoriale,' pp. 474–475, 483.

45. Abd al-Rahman al-Jabarti, *Merveilles biographiques et historiques ou chroniques du Cheikh Abd-el-Rahman el-Djabarti* (Cairo, 1888–1896), VIII, 320–321: using Jacotin's figures (see table).

46. Ibid., VIII, 95–96.

47. Sadat, 'Rumeli Ayanlari,' p. 348.

48. MM. Dubois-Aymé and Jollois, 'Voyage dans l'intérieur du Delta, contenant des recherches géographiques sur quelques villes anciennes, et des observations sur les moeurs et les usages des Égyptians modernes,' *DE*, XII, 188–189.

49. The existence of production for the market should not be taken as abandonment of subsistence-oriented agriculture. Peasants satisfied subsistence needs first. Some cash cropping and household industry may well have been necessary to maintain the family's subsistence and to pay taxes.

50. On the village shaykh in general, see Gabriel Baer, 'The Village Shaykh 1800–1950,' in *Studies*, pp. 30–61; on the shaykh, khūlī and other village officials: Abd al-Rahim, *Al-Rīf al-Miṣrī*, pp. 18–36.

51. Lancret, 'Mémoire sur le système d'imposition territoriale,' pp. 477–483.

52. Abd al-Rahim, *Al-Rīf al-Miṣrī*, p. 111; Lancret, 'Memoire sur la systeme d'imposition territoriale,' pp. 469–470.

53. F. Mengin, *Histoire de l'Egypte sous le gouvernement de Mohammed-Aly* (2 vols.; Paris, 1823), II, 338.

54. Egyptian peasants at various times had recourse to violence in defense of their interests. What makes these cases remarkable is their degree of success. See Gabriel Baer, 'Submissiveness and Revolt of the Fallah,' in *Studies*, pp. 93–108.

55. Le Citoyen Shulkowski, 'Description de la route du Kaire à Salehhyéh,' *La décade égyptienne*, Vol. 1 (Cairo, Year VII), p. 25.

56. Ibid., pp. 23–26; Le Général Anderossy, 'Memoire sur le lac Menzaléh,' *La décade égyptienne*, Vol. 1 (Cairo, Year VII [1798–99]), p. 193.

57. Le Citoyen Malus, 'Mémoire sur un voyage fait à la fin de frimaire sur la Branche Tantique du Nil,' *La décade égyptienne*, Vol. 1 (Cairo, Year VII), pp. 136–137, 138–139; Shulkowski, 'Description,' p. 24; Général Reynier, *Mémoires du général Reynier sur les operations de l'armée d'orient, ou de l'Egypte après la bataille d'Héliopolis* (Paris, 1827), pp. 50–52.

58. Ibid., Shulkowski, 'Description,' pp. 26, 28.

59. E. Jomard, 'Observations sur les Arabes de l'Égypte moyenne,' *DE*, XII, 269–272, 278–280.

60. Lancret, 'Mémoire sur le système d'imposition territoriale,' p. 491.

61. Jomard, 'Observations,' p. 280.

62. See Abd al-Rahim, *Al-Rīf al-Miṣrī*, pp. 80, 113; and Ali Barakat, *Taṭawwur al-Milkiyya al-Zirā'iyya fi Miṣr wa Atharuh 'alā al-Ḥaraka al-Siyāsiyya 1813–1914* (Cairo, 1977), p. 15.

63. Girard, 'Mémoire sur l'agriculture, l'industrie, et le commerce de l'Egypte,' pp. 117, 172 ff.; idem, 'Notice sur l'aménagement et le produit des terres de la province de Damietta,' *La décade égyptienne*, Vol. 1 (Cairo, Year VII), pp. 229–245.

64. Stanford Shaw, trans. and ed., *Ottoman Egypt in the Age of the French Revolution* (Cambridge, Mass., 1964), p. 123. For a survey of the politics of the seventeenth and eighteenth centuries, see Raymond, *Artisans et commerçants*, I, 1–16; P. M. Holt, 'The Pattern of Egyptian Political History from 1517 to 1798,' in *Political and Social Change in Modern Egypt*, pp. 79–90.

65. J. W. Livingstone, 'Ali Bey al-Kabir and the Jews,' *Middle East Studies*, 7 (1971), 221–228.

66. Shaw, *Financial and Administrative Organization*, p. 78.

67. Shaw, *Ottoman Egypt in the Age of the French Revolution*, pp. 145–146, 157–158.

68. Shaw, *Financial and Administrative Organization*, pp. 7–8.

69. Abd al-Rahim, *Al-Rīf al-Miṣrī*, pp. 117–119; Jabarti, *Merveilles*, VIII, 206–207; Ibrahim el-

Mouelhy, 'L'Enregistrement de la propriété en Égypte durant l'occupation française (1798–1801),' *Bulletin de l'Institut d'Égypte*, 30 (1947–1948), 197–228.

70. Girard, 'Mémoire sur l'agriculture, l'industrie, et le commerce de l'Egypte,' p. 368; Le Compte Estève, 'Mémoire sur les finances de l'Égypte, depuis sa conquète par le sultan Selym 1er, jusqu'à celle du général en chef Bonaparte,' *DE*, XII, 148.

71. Edouard Driault, *Mohamed Aly et Napoléon* (*1807–1814*). *Correspondence des consuls de France en Egypte* (Cairo, 1925), pp. 59, 73, 97, 132–133, 227; Jabarti, *Merveilles*, VIII, 297; Mengin, *Histoire*, II, 397–398.

72. Driault, *Mohamed Aly et Napoléon*, pp. 8, 12–13, 25, 32–33, 54–55, 59, 69–71, 81–82.

73. Jabarti, *Merveilles*, VIII, 313.

74. Ibid., pp. 129–130, 132, 148–149, 176–178. Whether a significant number were relocated to Buhayra is unknown.

75. Ibid., pp. 206–215, 277–279.

76. Ibid., pp. 244–245, 320–323, 347–348.

77. Ibid., IX, 92.

78. Yacoub Artin, *La propriété foncière en Egypte* (Cairo, 1883), pp. 311–312, 89; Jabarti, *Merveilles*, IX, 91.

79. Artin, *Propriété foncière*, p. 89; Helen Rivlin, *The Agricultural Policy of Muhammad Ali in Egypt* (Cambridge, Mass., 1961), pp. 89 ff.

80. Jabarti, *Merveilles*, IX, 87–93.

81. Ibid., pp. 137–138; Mengin, *Histoire*, II, 49–55.

82. Jabarti, *Merveilles*, IX, 90–93, 122–123; Rivlin, *Agricultural Policy*, pp. 57, 121; Amin Sami, *Taqwīm al-Nīl* (4 vols.; Cairo, 1915–1936), II, 266–270.

83. Rivlin, *Agricultural Policy*, p. 59.

84. Abd al-Rahim, *Al-Rīf al-Miṣrī*, pp. 71–73; Shaw, *Financial and Administrative Organization*, pp. 1–7; idem, 'Landholding and Land-Tax Revenues,' pp. 93–94.

85. Levon Marashlian, 'The Armenian Boghos Bey Yusufian in the Viceregency of Muhammad Ali Pasha,' forthcoming in *Armenian Review*.

86. For example, Raymond describes how Cairo's beys engaged in commercial activities: *Artisans et commerçants*, II, 717–719. Cavalla itself was an entrepot to the rich region of cotton, rice, tobacco, and silk farming dominated by the commercial center of Salonica. During Muhammad Ali's thirty years there the area saw the rapid development of çiftlik cotton farming (Stoianovich, 'Land Tenure and Related Sectors of the Balkan Economy,' pp. 402–404).

87. Descriptions of this fleet and its activities before the 1820s show its function to be primarily commercial-diplomatic: Georges Durand-Viel, *Les campagnes navales de Mohammad-Aly et d'Ibrahim* (2 vols.; Paris, 1935), I, 100–102, 152, 155–157, 210; Driault, *Mohammad Aly et Napoléon*, pp. 132–133, 136, 188; idem, *La formation de l'empire de Mohamed Aly de l'Arabie au Soudan* (*1814–1823*) (Cairo, 1927), pp. 104–105.

88. Rubin Adalian, 'The Armenian Colony in Egypt during the Reign of Muhammad Ali,' paper read at the Middle East Studies Association conference, 1978, Ann Arbor, Mich.; A. G. Politis, *L'Héllenisme et l'Egypte moderne* (2 vols.: Paris, 1928), I, 179–180, 189, 194: Auriant, 'Mehemet-Ali et les grecs,' *Arcopole*, I (Jan.-March 1927), 24–43—all give some examples. No systematic treatment of Egyptian commerce in this period exists, and references to non-European merchants' roles are scattered. This picture of commerce under state patronage has emerged from work still in progress.

89. Moustafa Fahmy, *La révolution de l'industrie en Egypte et ses conséquences sociales* (Leiden, 1954), pp. 23–25.

90. John Bowring, 'Report on Egypt and Candia,' Parliamentary Papers 1840, XXI, pp. 23, 24; Georges Douin, *La mission du Baron de Boislecomte. L'Egypte et la Syrie en 1833* (Cairo, 1927), p. 85; Driault, *Formation de l'empire*, pp. 60, 63, 89, 99.

91. Bowring, 'Report on Egypt and Candia,' p. 25; Artin, *Propriété foncière*, pp. 26–27, 181–182, 195, 257–259.

92. Jabarti, *Merveilles*, IX, 198–199, 233–234, 305–306, 310. Rivlin conjectures that the total cultivated area declined is untenable (*Agricultural Policy*, p. 270).

93. Jabarti, *Merveilles*, p. 185.

94. Ibid., p. 191; Mengin, *Histoire sommaire de l'Egypte sous le gouvernement de Mohamad Ali* (*1823–1838*) (Paris, 1839), pp. 119–121.

95. Douin, *La mission de Baron de Boislecomte*, p. 111.

96. Artin, *Propriété foncière*, pp. 254, 256; Baer, *Landownership*, pp. 16–17; Rivlin, *Agricultural Policy*, p. 62: E. R. J. Owen. *Cotton and the Egyptian Economy 1820–1914* (Oxford, 1969). p. 61; Barakat, *Taṭawwur al-Milkiyya*, pp. 33–34.

97. Ibid., pp. 34–38.

98. Artin, *Propriété foncière*, pp. 261–262.

99. Ibid., pp. 263–264; idem, 'Essai sur les causes de renchérissement de la vie materielle au Caire dans le courant de XIX siècle,' *Memoires présentées à l'Institut Egyptien*, V, 2, (Cairo, 1907), 71–72: Ra'uf Abbas Hamid, *Al-Niẓām al-Ijtimā'ī fī Miṣr fī Ẓill al-Milkiyyāt al-Zirā'iyya al-Kabīra 1837–1914* (Cairo, 1973), p. 68.

100. Jabarti, *Merveilles*, VII, 352: Bowring, 'Report on Egypt and Candia,' p. 26.

101. See Baer, 'The Village Shaykh,' passim.

102. Sami, *Taqwīm al-Nīl*, II, 245.

103. Jabarti, *Merveilles*, IX, 316. Others have implied that masmūḥ was granted in Lower Egypt during the first cadaster, but there is no evidence for this. The Royal Council's register, *Sijill al-Dīiwān al-Khidīwī*, written at some time after the grants in question were made and quoted by Barakat, contains a contradictory account. First, it mentions 440,127 faddans in Lower Egypt not taxed in 1815–1816, and 1,775,611 faddans in Upper Egypt not taxed in 1820–1821, 'because it was *būr* [meaning either fallow or waste land] at that time.' Then, in summing up, it states, 'The total of the land of Upper and Lower Egypt upon which no tax was assessed, then, was 2,215,738 faddans, including ib'ādiyyas, the multazims' ūsya, masmūḥ al-mashaikh, ... masmūḥ al-masṭaba, ... and būr ...' (Barakat, *Taṭawwur al-Milkiyya*, pp. 27–31).

104. Jabarti, *Merveilles*, IX, 316: Barakat, *Taṭ*awwur al-Milkiyya, p. 31.

105. Artin, *Propriété foncière*, p. 293.

106. Baer, 'The Village Shaykh,' pp. 37–46.

107. Artin, *Propriété foncière*, pp. 100–102.

108. Mengin, *Histoire sommaire*, pp. 100–102.

109. P. N. Hamont, *L'Egypte sous Méhémet-Ali* (2 vols.; Paris, 1843), I, 103–104.

110. René Cattaui Bey, *La règne de Mohamed Aly d'après les archives russes en Egypte* (4 vols.; Cairo and Rome, 1931–1936), II, part 2, 373.

111. See Rivlin, *Agricultural Policy*, pp. 117–118.

112. McCarthy, 'Nineteenth-Century Egyptian Population,' pp. 28–29.

113. Jabarti, *Merveilles*, IX, 115, 224–227, 229, 231–232.

114. Bowring, 'Report on Egypt and Candia,' pp. 28 ff.; Edward Lane, *Manners and Customs of the Modern Egyptians* (London, 1966 ed.) pp. 133–134; Bayle St John, *Village Life in Egypt, with Sketches of the Said* (2 vol.; London, 1852), I, xvii; Rivlin, *Agricultural Policy*, p. 205; Baer, 'Submissiveness and Revolt of the Fallah,' passim.

115. See Barrington Moore's remarks in *Social Origins of Dictatorship and Democracy* (Boston, 1966), pp. 453 ff., esp. pp. 471–475.

116. Natural disasters were not decisive, however, as they occurred both earlier and later without producing crises of these proportions.

117. Artin, *Propriété foncière*, p. 129.

118. Ibid., pp. 129–130; Rivlin, *Agricultural Policy*, p. 64; Baer, *Landownership*, pp. 13–14.

119. Owen, *Cotton*, p. 62.

120. Barakat, *Taṭawwur al-Milkiyya*, p. 94.

121. Rivlin, *Agricultural Policy*, pp. 68–69.

122. Barakat, *Taṭawwur al-Milkiyya*, pp. 85–94. The Balta Liman tariffs were not actually put into effect in Egypt until after the retreat from Syria in the spring of 1841, and various delaying tactics.

123. Ibid., p. 106.

124. Ibid., pp. 106–107.

125. Ibid., pp. 85–94. The evidence for court factionalism has been uncovered by Dr. Afaf Marsot in the course of current research.

126. See Baer, *Landownership*, p. 17.

127. Artin, *Propriété foncière*, pp. 333–336.

128. Ibid., p. 100; Baer, *Landownership*, p. 7.

129. See John W. Livingstone, 'Ali Bey al-Kabir and the Mamluk Renaissance in Egypt, 1760–1772,' unpublished Ph.D. diss., Princeton, 1968. chap. 4.

130. Note the role of the Mouelhy family, soldiers and silk merchants established in the Hijaz and in Cairo, in Muhammad Ali's early campaigns in Arabia: Ibrahim el-Mouelhy, 'Ibrahim el-Mouelhy Pacha. Les Mouelhy en Egypte,' *Cahiers d'histoire égyptienne*, 2, 2–3 (Feb. 1950), 313–328.

131. 'Uhdas: Artin, *Propriété foncière*, p. 131. Bedouin ib'ādiyyas: idem, 'Essai,' pp. 71–72. Monopolies: Angelo Sammarco, *Précis de l'histoire d'Egypte*, vol. 4. *Les règnes de Abbas de Said et d'Ismaịl (1848–1879)* (Rome, 1935), pp. 10–11.

132. Barakat, *Taṭawwur al-Milkiyya*, pp. 97 ff.

133. Export price of wheat:

1850 50 P. T./ardebb
1852 66 P. T./ardebb
1859 74 P. T./ardebb

Source: Owen, *Cotton*, p. 80.

Export price of cotton:

average, 1851–1855 9.85 dollars/qantar
average, 1856–1860 13.45 dollars/qantar

Source: Mahmoud el Darwish, 'Note on the Movement of Prices of Egyptian Cotton, 1820–1899,' in Charles Issawi, ed., *The Economic History of the Middle East 1800–1914* (Chicago, 1975), p. 448.

134. Artin, *Propriété foncière*, pp. 280–281, 283, 287.

135. Baer, 'The Development of Private Ownership of Land,' p. 68.

136. Artin, *Propriété foncière*, p. 161.

137. Baer, 'The Village Shaykh, pp. 40–41.

Decline of the Family Economy in Mid-Nineteenth-Century Egypt

JUDITH TUCKER

In predominantly rural precapitalist society the peasant family constituted the basic unit of production. This family group slept under the same roof and shared the activities of production and consumption. Its internal logic was not toward maximization of profit, but rather the achievement of a balance between family demands for consumption and the drudgery of the labor required for additional consumption.[1] Those who worked and consumed were bounded with those members whose age or health limited them to consumption only. The family knew no division between home and workplace; the house and land constituted a single field of activity. Specialization of labor by age and sex was the rule. A hierarchical differentiation of duties was minimal; specialization took place along horizontal rather than vertical lines since there was no rigid separation between the economic and social aspects of life. Family members were united in the goal of providing goods and shelter for direct consumption of the family unit.

These models of a 'peasant economy' or a 'domestic mode of production,' in their exclusive focus on the working of the peasant family itself, fail to situate the peasant producer within a wider context. They suggest that the peasant unit remains static and unchanging, to be eventually bypassed or totally annihilated by the rise of capitalism.[2]

In precapitalist Egypt, the internal organization and control of the family was influenced by forms of exploitation. The peasant family not only fed and maintained itself, but it also produced a certain surplus to meet the demands of the state or landed officials in the form of taxes which were the lifeblood of a political system based on landed wealth. While the peasant family might maintain control of the organization of its production and consumption, the level of production, over and above that of its own needs, did not remain simply a question of whether or not to increase the level of family consumption. In facing the demands of the state and its officials, the peasant household was forced to organize its labor and cultivation so that the taxes could be paid and the produce delivered. Peasant labor was also expropriated in the form of corvée labor on state irrigation projects and the land of state officials. But beyond these demands for surplus produce and extra labor, the state and its officials had little interest in the regulation of peasant households. The family remained the basic economic unit; corvée labor was usually performed locally so that family life and work was not disrupted by the absence of able-bodied members.[3] While the peasant family exercised little real control over the use of its surplus product and extra labor, it retained autonomy in the organization of subsistence production and consumption.

During the first half of the nineteenth century, however, basic changes in the state structure and the economy as a whole, influenced by the penetration of capitalism, touched the peasant family. In the European context, where capitalism had more or less indigenous roots, capitalist development tended to socialize the processes of commodity production, that is, to remove the organization of labor and production from the locus and control of individual families and villages, and centralize it in large-scale corporate units. Material production was split between the socialized forms, commodity production, and private labor performed in the household. Although women and children occupied a central place in the early proletariat, the nineteenth century saw the progressive elimination of child labor and the transformation of women into a marginal labor force.[4] Men assumed the role of commodity producers, while women produced use-values through domestic labor. The family, no longer an integrated producer-consumer unit, became instead the realm of women and children where material production, although present, was devalued. The horizontal sexual division of labor in the precapitalist family, which may indeed have involved male dominance, gave way to the institutionalization of male supremacy; the male as wage earner and worker in the public sphere came to play a distinct role central to family subsistence. In the early stages of this transformation, families resisted the new forms of social organization and the loss of control over their production and labor time.[5]

In Egypt, as the growth of state power and the commercialization of agriculture began to undermine the family economic unit in favor of the state and a rising landlord class, there was resistance and a peasant defense of the family as a producer-consumer unit. The incursions of the state and the dispossession of peasant land were not accepted with ease or silence; violent resistance and flight were combined with a subtler use of existing institutions to thwart the new order. Women were particularly vocal as the erosion of the peasant family threatened their economic role and status.

The extent, focus and strategies of peasant resistance are intimately related to the nature of the economic and political changes of the period, as well as the existing cultural traditions and institutions. Any account of the transformation of the peasant family and patterns of resistance must therefore be given within the context of the sweeping social and economic changes of the first half of the nineteenth century.

I

The characterization of the Egyptian countryside and, indeed, the Egyptian economy and society as a whole at mid-century remains a subject of much debate. The ongoing integration of the Egyptian economy into a global economic system in this period is acknowledged by most writers, but there is little agreement on the nature and pace of this integration or its effects on the society. On the one hand, Egyptian society is perceived as basically static and unchanging: social institutions and the vast majority of the population were left untouched and intact throughout the course of the nineteenth century. This view is 'connected with the fact that during that period Egypt was not transformed from an agrarian into an industrial society'.[6]

A divergent view perceives the rise of an export-oriented economy, revolving around the cultivation and export of cotton, as the motor force of social change. Issawi asserts that:

> The transition from a subsistence to an export-oriented economy is accompanied by the breakdown of traditional feudal, communal, or tribal structures. The ties binding the individual to the village or tribe are gradually loosened or violently snapped, and labor becomes a mobile marketable commodity.[7]

The idea that integration into the world economy involved internal change of some magnitude rings true, but Issawi's interpretation remains incomplete. There is no analysis of the actual dynamic of capitalist penetration, as it comes into contact with internal realities. The resulting social transformation merely 'accompanies' economic change. Lack of attention to the specific character of capitalist penetration in Egypt assumes a certain passivity on the part of Egyptian society. Social transformations are wrought willy-nilly by economic developments: Egyptian social classes, especially the peasants (*fellahin*), apparently succumb to the new order with barely a whimper. The idea that internal class structure and even *fellah* resistance might shape the history of capitalist penetration is precluded.

Other writers have examined the impact of capitalist penetration on the indigenous society. The move toward cotton cultivation for export, beginning in the 1840s, invariably affected rural society. But what were the dominant features of the emerging system of agricultural production? The nineteenth century saw the growing commercialization of Egyptian agriculture, increasing differentiation among the peasantry according to the amount of land they controlled, and the rise of a wage-labor class, all of which might suggest capitalist organization. On the other hand, certain pecularities, most notably that this was a 'capitalism without local agricultural capitalists,'[8] have led to the characterization of Egyptian agriculture as 'backward colonial capitalism.'[9] 'The role of the state in the early process of capital accumulation and direct state invervention into relations of production in the countryside, which entailed primarily political rather than economic coercion, distinguishes this sort of 'retarded' capitalism. Capitalism transforms the precapitalist relations of production in the countryside, but the central role of the state and the persistence of many precapitalist forms of exploitation inhibited the transition to a fully capitalist system.

The role of the state in the transformation of the Egyptian countryside commenced in the first half of the nineteenth century. The peasant family unit gradually lost control over the organization of its production and consumption as the central government interfered directly in peasant life through a system of agricultural monopolies, corvée labor, military impressment, and the confiscation of peasant land.

Muhammad 'Ali officially became viceroy (*wali*) of Egypt in 1805. By 1812 he had annihilated his political opponents and embarked on an ambitious program of increasing state revenue to the end of gaining strength and independence for Egypt, still *de jure* under the suzereignty of the Ottoman Empire.[10] European demand for agricultural produce, stimulated by the disruptions of the Napoleonic Wars, led him to seize direct control of Egypt's grain production. In 1812, the entire grain crop of Upper Egypt was appropriated by the state and shipped to Lower Egypt for state sale to European traders. The rice crop of Lower Egypt was similarly monopolized, and by 1816, flax, sesame, safflower, safflower seeds, indigo, cotton, beans and barley came under total state control. The government advanced seeds and animals to the *fellahin* who in turn had to cultivate and transport the crop to a local depot. The state assigned crop prices, and, after the deduction of advances and employees' salaries, the *fellah* received a voucher for the balance. The peasants thus lost all control over marketing. They were forced to sell their crops to the state at a low fixed price: the state then charged greatly increased prices to foreign and local traders. Since the peasants were forbidden to hold back any produce, they suffered the additional burden of buying back grain, at higher prices than they had sold it, for their own consumption.[11]

The state also asserted control over cultivation. It dictated to each village official (the *sheikh al-balad*) the required amount and mix of crops, seeking not only to control the export trade, but also to be able to respond to foreign demands for increased amounts of certain crops, particularly cotton. Muhammad 'Ali sought political and economic leverage through the reorganization of Egypt as his own private farm. In a conversation with the British consul in 1830, he estimated the year's cotton crop at 200,000 quintals, adding: 'I did not think it proper this year to plant more but if England and I went hand in hand, and in the event of an American war, she should call on me for a quantity sufficient to supply all her manufactories, she should have it *exclusively*. Mention that.'[12]

Bravado soon changed to chagrin as agricultural production faltered in the mid-1830s and food and labor shortages plagued the countryside. The various monopolies were gradually dismantled and control of agricultural production was decentralized. It seems unlikely, however, that the *fellahin* were able to reassert their control over production. Although they were allowed to sell their wheat, corn, beans and barley on the local market in 1831, the government still designated the crops to be grown and fixed prices. It also insisted that the peasants pay their taxes in kind or sell their produce at government prices.[13] The state did cede direct management of the crop mix, although certain areas near the Nile, which included some of the best agricultural land, were reserved for the cultivation of cotton, indigo, opium and flax which remained state monopolies up until 1842.[14]

In the face of declining revenue and pressure from the European community, codified in the Anglo-Turkish Convention of 1838, the Egyptian government revised the monopoly system. At the same time, however, Muhammad 'Ali's redistribution of land preserved state control of production through indirect means. By 1844, nearly one-half of the agricultural land, and certainly the best land, had been granted by the state to royal family members, Turkish officials and village sheikhs.[15] The cultivation and sale of produce was directed by the new grantees under strong state influence. The French consul noted that such land grants constituted a total evasion of the free-trade stipulations of the 1838 Convention, and made little difference in the actual organization of production in the countryside:

> ... if the Pasha had executed the treaty of 1838 to the letter, the fellah, thanks to the suppression pure and simple of the monopolies, would produce and sell, and the traders would enter into direct communication with the great mass of peasants; this, one sees, is not the current situation; by virtue of his total power, the Pasha, while abolishing the monopolies, gave the land to landholders ... and he has created, thus, an intermediary class between agriculture and the trader, few in number, foreign to the mass of the population, but to which he has given free disposition of the crops, and which, therefore, on the one hand is by itself in a singular relationship with the fellah concerning all that pertains to the cultivation of the land, and, at the same time, on the other hand, is likewise in a singular relationship with European trade for the sale of products.[16]

The central bureacracy no longer told the peasant family what to produce, but state officials-*cum*-landlords controlled peasant activity on their estates; the erosion of peasant control of production continued.

Incursions of the state also affected peasant control of their labor power. The policies of Muhammad ʿAli necessitated the widespread use of corvée labor for public works and agriculture. The introduction of long-staple cotton, demanded by European industry, required the building of extensive irrigation works: the new canals and dams essential for summer cultivation. While corvée labor had been used on irrigation projects before the appearance of long-staple cotton, the scope and duration of forced labor now dramatically increased. As many as 400,000 peasants could be called to work each year for an average period of four months.[17] The Mahmudiyyah canal was built by the forced labor of approximately 315,000 peasants who were supplied by village sheikhs from seven different provinces. Peasants had to supply their own food and shelter during an enforced period of absence from home. Men, women and children, laboring without proper food, lodging or tools, led to a death toll on the project of anywhere from 12,000 to 23,000 in a ten-month period in 1819.[18] Corvée labor on irrigation projects occupied some 300,000 men in 1841, roughly one-sixth of the total population.[19] In the late 1840s, conditions improved slightly in an attempt to correct the acute shortage of agricultural labor. A levy of 58,000 men to excavate three large canals in Lower Egypt was subject to new conditions: 'They are only to be compelled to work 100 days at the excavations, the said period to commence as soon as possible after the harvest is completed, and to terminate at the autumnal season for sowing and preparing winter crops.'[20] In 1851, under ʿAbbas, the laborers reportedly were supplied with food and paid a daily wage of 20 paras.[21] Ironically, most of these state irrigation projects brought no benefit to peasant lands, but rather enabled the large estates to undertake cotton cultivation.

Military recruitment was another drain on the peasant family's control of its labor power. Muhammad ʿAli's political ambitions dictated the fielding of a sizeable army. After attempts to raise an army of slave and Sudanese recruits failed, he started a massive program of peasant recruitment.[22] By 1830, having directed provincial and village officials to supply set quotas of men, the Egyptian standing army and navy numbered about 53,000, supplemented by from 15,000 to 24,000 Bedouin irregulars.[23] By that year, however, the supply of able-bodied men had dried up; the levy of 1830 'produced such a small number of men suitable for military service that one is tempted to believe that it is the last the exhausted population can supply.'[24] The following year's recruits included boys of twelve and thirteen years, for 'men are needed at any price, and children become improvised soldiers.'[25] When the countryside could no longer satisfy recruitment needs, the state turned to Cairo itself, levying some 10,000 men in 1832, most of whom were reportedly Nubians or menial workers of other origins.[26]

The peasant population was subjected to a new round of levies during Ibrahim Pasha's brief reign in 1848. Soldiers and sailors who had formed the backbone of the labor force in the Nile dam project were returned to active military service and new corvée levies dragooned *fellahin* to take their places; 14,000 new soldiers were also conscripted from the provinces.[27] Although the military force was subsequently reduced under 'Abbas, the cuts were most often made by dismissing the more experienced semi-professional soldiers and retaining peasant recruits.[28] The early 1850s brought more waves of conscription: the countryside and cities as well as minority communities were called upon to provide recruits: the goal was a standing army of 100,000 men.[29]

If not caught in the net of corvée labor for irrigation projects or military service, the peasant was still subject to forced labor in state industries and mines. Muhammad 'Ali's industrialization scheme created some 40,000 factory workers, but it is not clear how many of these were *fellahin* as opposed to displaced craftsmen.[30] The closing of many factories in the 1830s did not spell the end of forced labor in industry; in 1842, for example, approximately 1,000 men were drafted for work in the state arsenal and dockyard.[31] State mines condemned unwilling workers to be 'bereaved of their wives and children, compelled to severe labor and food such as might be eaten during periods of dearth.'[32] The state continued to draft peasant labor for the mines when it entered into joint ventures with European companies: the contract between the Terranova Society and the Egyptian government for joint exploitation of sulfur mines in Upper Egypt included clauses stipulating that the state would furnish all manual workers.[33]

Exemption from forced labor and impressment sometimes was granted to peasants working on the large estates controlled by Muhammad 'Ali, his family members and officials. Peasant recruitment for labor on nearby estates seems scarcely distinguishable from other forms of corvée labor. Wages, such as they were, were usually in arrears and sometimes paid in unmarketable products. Ibrahim Pasha, for example, was said to have paid all workers on one of his estates in molasses produced by his sugar factory in Upper Egypt.[34] Others were not paid and relied on their village for food.[35]

The policies of forced labor and military impressment created a severe labor shortage in the countryside. Agricultural production suffered as the rural village population came to be composed chiefly of women, children, and the old and infirm.[36] Bowring estimated the entire Egyptian population in 1839 at 2 to 2.5 million, with a disproportionately high number of females, officially figured at 135 females to every 100 males, but, in his opinion, probably much higher.[37] The observations of foreign residents are confirmed by letters from district (*khutt*) sheikhs to the state's official gazette in 1829–30, reporting critical labor shortages in the lower and middle Egyptian areas of

Fuwwah, Kafr al-Sheikh, Tanta and Fayyum.[38] At mid-century, the situation had apparently been ameliorated, and the theme of rural desolation was not so prevalent, but labor shortages could still arise at harvest time.[39]

II

The dispossession of peasant land proceeded apace in the first half of the nineteenth century. The central government first increased its direct control of the land, and, when this policy failed, the state promoted the rise to power of local officials and a new landlord class. Like the loss of peasant control over its labor power, this had a grave impact on the structures and functions of the peasant family.

To gain direct and immediate control of the agricultural surplus, Muhammad ʿAli had to weaken, and then eliminate, the *multazims*, the holders of *iltizam* land. Originally developed as a form of tax-farm, the *iltizam* system had evolved during the seventeenth and eighteenth centuries into quasi-private ownership of land. The *multazims* were, in theory, responsible for collecting and delivering the *miri* (land tax) to the central government which owned all *iltizam* land. Their own income came from the retention of the difference between the *faʿiz* (what they could extract from the peasants) and the true amount of the tax. In addition, they were assigned a certain portion of the *iltizam* (*usya* land) for cultivation on their own account, using corvée or wage labor.[40] By the early nineteenth century, they were a class of absentee landlords who depended on local sheikhs and other retainers to watch over peasant production. *Iltizam* land, formerly held for a year or two, had become heritable and alienable property, and the *multazims* formed a distinct group with considerable political power.

In addition to *iltizam* land, some 600,000 feddans in Upper Egypt and the Cairo vicinity were held as agricultural *waqf* land, created by land grants made by former Sultans or by *multazims* out of their *usya* holdings. *Waqf* land, free of land tax in the seventeenth and eighteenth centuries, was taxed at very low rates in the early nineteenth century.[41]

Between 1806 and 1815, Muhammad ʿAli moved to wrest control of the land and tax collection from the *multazims* and *nazirs* (trustees of *waqf* land). The state first demanded half of the *faʿiz* and raised taxes on the *usya* land. In 1811, a cadastral survey in Upper Egypt resulted in the confiscation of all *iltizam* land with tax arrears or no positive proof of title. An 1814 survey of Lower Egypt followed, with the result that most *multazims* in the country were removed from their holdings with or without compensation. *Waqf* land was similarly taken over by the state. By 1815, the state had assumed control of most of the agricultural land in Egypt.[42]

The replacement of the *iltizam* by the *ihtikar* (state monopoly) system changed the organization of peasant production. Under *multazims*, peasant families had been free to organize their labor and production as they chose. In Lower Egypt, the peasant-held land had been divided into fixed portions (*athar*), farmed and passed down within the family group. In Upper Egypt, where uneven flooding changed the area of cultivatable land from one year to the next, each family had received a certain proportion of the available land each year.[43] In both cases, the role of the village sheikh and community had been central: the village as a whole was responsible for its assigned taxes and corvée labor was allocated by the local sheikhs.[44] Under the *ihtikar* system most of the land continued to remain in the possession of peasant families, but taxes were collected directly by state officials who also told the peasants what and when to plant. An intricate hierarchy of officials exercised broad powers which included the direct supervision of agricultural organization and production.[45]

In the 1830s, however, the combination of economic crisis and foreign pressure ushered in changes in policy; the Egyptian state abandoned most of its monopoly practices and tempered its direct control. Muhammad ʿAli began to grant sizeable portions of land to various officials and royal family members. These grants took three forms: *ʿuhdahs, abʿadiyahs* and *chifliks*. *ʿUhdah* grants resembled *iltizam* insofar as the holders were responsible for tax collection and were entitled to a certain portion of land which they might farm for themselves by employing day labor or a system of sharecropping.[46] They differed in that the grantee had to deliver the estate's produce to the state at fixed prices and heed the state's guidelines on land use. In theory the peasants retained their *athar* land, but the erosion of their control of the land continued.

Abʿadiyah grants conferred greater powers on their holders. Uncultivated land was granted tax-free on the condition that it be brought into cultivation; the grantees gradually acquired rights tantamount to full private ownership.[47] The grantees had to encourage peasants to come and settle from other regions, to work as wage laborers or sharecroppers.

Chifliks, the very large estates controlled by Muhammad ʿAli and his family, enjoyed advantages not available to *abʿadiyah* estates in that control was centralized and the connection to the state was close enough to assure first access to state irrigation works and financing. The peasants on *chifliks* lost all rights to the usufruct and were reduced to day laborers working for a percentage of the cereal harvest. They might be given, in addition, a small plot for subsistence cultivation. Peasant flight posed the problem of labor shortage and *chiflik* managers were known to commandeer *ʿuhdah* peasants for work on their estates.[48]

Between 1820 and 1844, the area of cultivated land held in various forms of estate grants rose from 10 per cent to 44 per cent of all cultivatable land, and, by mid-century, the best Delta land had passed entirely into the hands of the new grantees.[49] The area of *athar* land decreased. State policies of taxation, which fixed taxes on peasant land way above taxes on estate land, further hastened peasant dispossession through flight and bankruptcy.[50] Peasant land loss through outright state seizure for land grants, failure to pay taxes, foreclosures for non-payment of private debts and flight to escape the corvée and conscription had transformed the face of the Egyptian countryside by 1850. The Egyptian peasant family, formerly a semiautonomous producer with usufructory land rights and substantial control of labor time and production, was increasingly supervised and subject to widespread control of its land and labor.

III

The picture of peasant dislocation and dispersion must be balanced by an appreciation of peasant resistance to state encroachment and dispossession of land. Responses of revolt and flight went hand with a steady reassertion of the old forms of family existence.

Throughout the first half of the nineteenth century, peasant revolts against conscription, the corvée, taxes and growing state control sporadically rocked the countryside. The history of these revolts constitutes a convincing refutation of the theory of the 'submissiveness of the Egyptian *fellah*.'[51] Muhammad 'Ali's seizure of the grain crop in 1812 precipitated the first major revolt, a peasant rebellion in Upper Egypt which was violently suppressed.[52] In 1820–21, some 400,000 peasants in the province of Qina rallied behind Sheikh Ahmad and established an independent government until a military expedition crushed them two months later.[53]

The most serious revolt of the era broke out in the same area of Upper Egypt in 1822–23 under the leadership of another Sheikh Ahmad, who called for the overthrow of Muhammad 'Ali. Sheikh Ahmad declared that 'he had been sent by God and His Prophet to end the vexations from which the Egyptian people suffered and to punish Muhammad 'Ali for introducing innovations which ran contrary to the dogma of Islam.' The rebellion extended from Isna to Aswan and lasted for over six weeks. Many of the *fellah* soldiers sent to quell the revolt instead deserted to the rebels, so that the government had to use Turkish and Bedouin troops to calm the area.[54] The following years brought revolts in al-Minufiyah and al-Sharqiyah. Sporadic revolts against conscription policies occurred throughout the 1830s.[55] Disorders stemming from resistance to conscription were reported in Upper Egypt in 1848, and the governor of the region, Salim Pasha, was assassinated, although it is not clear whether personal affairs or opposition to conscription and a 'general hatred for his governorship' served as the motive.[56]

Individual resistance also occurred. In 1850–51, the heirs of al-Sayid ʿAmr ʿAmr from the village of Kafr Zein accused a man named Hawas of shooting ʿAmr to death because he was a military recruiter. The heirs were unable to find witnesses willing to testify on their behalf, probably because of the peasants' approval of Hawas' extralegal action, so that the village as a whole had to assume responsibility for the *diya* ('blood money').[57] In Qalyub the local military recruiter beat a woman to death when she refused to hand her son over for military service.[58] Individual resistance and wide-scale revolts were both fairly easily repressed, however, given the centralization and military might of the government but forms of peasant resistance continued throughout the period. After ʿAbbas revoked many of the *ʿuhdah* grants in 1849, he was forced to send army units to many villages to collect the taxes from recalcitrant peasants.[59]

Many peasant families, faced with the futility of direct resistance, chose instead to flee. Syria was one refuge. By 1830, an estimated 5,000 to 6,000 peasants from the province of al-Sharqiyah had moved to Syria where ʿAbd-allah Pasha of ʿAkka granted them land and temporary tax exemptions. Muhammad ʿAli, concerned by the shortage of agricultural laborers, in vain demanded their return.[60] Others swelled the populations of Alexandria and Cairo. Some 6,000 to 7,000 men, women and children squatted in three- to four-foot-high mud huts on the outskirts of Alexandria, living off the sale of garden produce or casual labor.[61] Flight to neighboring villages in order to escape tax payments and conscription was also common.

Faced with severe depopulation of the rural areas, the state responded with draconian measures. In 1828–29, Muhammad ʿAli, noting that: 'some of the indolent fellahin had left their villages, homelands and fields, and had taken up residence in Cairo and its environs, and were becoming beggars,' instructed the director of the Ministry of the Interior to find the missing peasants and return them at once to their natal villages.[62] Refugees in Cairo were seized and forcibly returned to their villages or taken in chains to work on state-controlled lands.[63] In Alexandria, government troops encircled the peasant shantytown and herded its inhabitants onto boats which would transport them home. Blows from whips and sticks hastened the evacuation of men, women, children and the aged.[64] The state also instructed the *maʿmurs* (provincial officials) to '... gather up the peasants who have fled with efficiency and dispatch, and return them to their place of origin ... if this cannot be done [efficiently], then jail the children of the missing *fellah* or those who are taking care of his property until the *fellah* returns.'[65] These measures were not entirely successful. In 1845 the state was still sending government troops into the provinces to round up all peasants who were not resident in their place of origin and march them back to their villages.[66]

Despite the dislocation inevitably produced by flight, it did constitute one way of preserving the family structure. Peasants usually fled in family groups. In Syria they could continue family production. The move to other Egyptian villages provided some continuity for the family as an economic unit. Flight to the towns, by removing the family from the land, destroyed the physical basis of the family unit and often transformed individual members into casual laborers. Even in the latter case, however, we see no evidence of large numbers of unattached men or women. The shantytowns in Alexandria, for example, replicated the village community. Flight did not remove male members from the family, thus enabling the family to retain a minimal control of their labor.

The corvée and military impressment had potentially more far-reaching effects on family structure. Corvée recruitment, however, was not limited to adult males. Many observers remarked, often with horror, on the numbers of women and children engaged in forced labor on irrigation projects to carry away the earth dug by the men.[67] 'Abbas Pasha, in a conversation with Hekekyan, recalled his opposition to Muhammad 'Ali's policy of utilizing forced female labor:

> One day in Shoobra His Highness [Muhammad 'Ali] said to me. 'Abbas, we must make the women work,' and I replied boldly, for I could not contain myself, 'I have seen women delivered on the dykes and forced the following day to recommence their work of carrying earth and mud clods. The men are made to work by us—without remuneration—who will then cook for them and make their bread?'[68]

After he assumed power, 'Abbas issued a decree in 1851 forbidding the corvée recruitment of pregnant women or those with children less than three years old, children under age eight, men and women over age seventy, and anyone with a dangerous infirmity. Stiff penalties were prescribed for any sheikh or official who recruited from one of the forbidden categories.[69] Although some of the excesses of the corvée system may have been eliminated, women and children still worked long hours on public works at little or no pay in the early 1850s.[70]

Most observers suggest that whole families were recruited for corvée labor. Hekekyan described the process of recruitment in one village where the sheikhs organized a body of 600 men, women and children for work on a transverse dike, opting to recruit families and leave behind able-bodied men.[71] A French overseer claimed that his canal project utilized family labor primarily at the request of the husbands and fathers themselves who didn't want to leave their families unattended at home.[72]

Joint family work under the corvée and the preservation of the family structure served the interests of both the peasants and the state. The family continued to live and work together, producing for its own subsistence in the periods of relief from forced labor. The corvée impoverished the family but did not sever the bonds of shared production and consumption. It fell to the family to provide for its non-producing members, even during the absence from home. Corvée labor could be extracted by the state precisely because the family remained more or less intact, carrying on the functions of production for subsistence, provision of shelter, care for the young, old, and sick, and social regulation. Peasant protests against the excessive use of female labor and state reform of the corvée system spoke to the need to preserve family structure in lieu of any real assumption by the state of the family's diverse functions. The reduction of family labor time available for subsistence production, however, inevitably taxed family resources and burdened productive members to the point where traditional social responsibilities and structures were modified.

Military impressment had more dramatic effects. The women who remained in the villages assumed new roles in agriculture. Hamont describes a village, stripped of men, where all the heavy labor was done by women.[73] Certain tasks previously reserved for men, such as operating the shadoof or climbing date palms to pollinate the flowers, became women's work.[74] The shortage of draft animals even led women to harness themselves in place of water buffaloes in order to turn millstones.[75] These new demands provoked distress and resistance. Weeping women and children would follow the recruiting party taking their men off to the army until they were forced to return to their village.[76] The British consul commented on the response to recruitment:

> Men are raised from villages by an arbitrary conscription, which is extremely obnoxious to the feelings of the people: and always creates a momentary insurrection among female inhabitants, when they are doomed to witness the affecting sight of their relatives carried off in irons.[77]

Whenever possible, as long as the man was not posted abroad, wives and children would follow the drafted male from garrison to garrison, setting up housekeeping in a nearby shantytown and living as best as they could, sharing the soldier's ration.[78] An estimated 22,000 women and children camped outside the Hankah garrison.[79] The large numbers and wretched conditions of army, navy and arsenal workers' families in Alexandria caused consternation as epidemics of plague swept the city in the late 1830s and early 1840s. Some 30,000 women and children were living near the military barracks in tiny huts, cisterns and catacombs where the plague was taking a heavy toll.[80]

Some evidence exists that the state undertook to provide subsistence to these families. Bowring stated that the arsenal workers and their families received food rations but that the actual wages of the men were very low and usually in arrears.[81] Another report claimed that Muhammad 'Ali, recognizing that the ration and pay of the soldier could not stretch to feed his family, assigned every soldier's male child an equal ration, thereby covering the food needs of the entire family. In the late 1840s, some 14,000 male children were supposedly receiving these rations.[82] The state thought of providing shelter as well, but a housing plan for the families of sailors and arsenal workers in Alexandria apparently was never implemented.[83]

Partial accommodation to the presence of soldiers' families was discontinued under Ibrahim. In 1848, the families of the 14,000 new conscripts were forbidden to follow their menfolk.[84] In the following year, under 'Abbas, the practice of providing rations for male children was abruptly terminated.[85] Despite such measures, the state was unable to keep soldiers' families in the countryside. Over ten years later, the Egyptian army retained its familial character:

> When the soldiers are camped, a camp of women is established at some distance; when they are in the barracks, a village of women is constructed as quickly as the barracks of the men; finally, in the cities, the families live in the houses closest to the barracks . . . always I have seen the women arrive at any destination at about the same time as the men.[86]

Troop movement abroad deprived the military families of support altogether. Some observers cite the presence of soldiers' families on campaigns abroad, even in Arabia and Greece, but it seems more likely that posting abroad, especially overseas, meant leaving the family in Egypt.[87] The wives might receive small sums from the state or directly from their husbands, but soldiers were paid little if at all. War widows continually crowded the doors of the War Ministry, asking for their absent husbands' pay.[88] Faced with total impoverishment, women were thrown back on their own or their extended families' resources; some turned to prostitution in order to feed their families.[89]

Despite the migration of women and children in the wake of drafted husbands in a conscious attempt to maintain the family unit, conscription made inroads on traditional structures. The military family was a nuclear family; the man, wife and children were removed from their village community and, more importantly, from the extended family which had formed their social and economic environment. A network of economic relations and social responsibilities bound them to their parents, brothers and sisters, and relatives by marriage. The formation of a nuclear family unit at some distance away weakened these ties. If the woman remained without her husband in the village, the man's absence affected patterns of material support and the division of tasks. Lastly, military impressment and the corvée brought in their train a loss of labor power and general impoverishment which adversely affected the ability, and therefore the willingness, of productive family members to support those who could not produce.

IV

The Egyptian *fellahin* had recourse to the Islamic legal system. The *shari'a* courts, whose jurisdiction extended to matters of property and family law, stood apart from the institutions of the central government, even though a degree of state influence cannot be precluded. The peasants' appeal against state encroachment and social dislocation could be made to the religious officials whose connection with the state was, at least, not overt, and whose authority was based on a higher sanction. Islamic law, as it came to be practiced in Egypt, embodied some of the traditional practices and patterns of the Egyptian family.

An examination of the minutes of court proceedings from the province of al-Mansurah and the *fatawa* (decisions) of the Hanafi *mufti* in Cairo on cases referred to him, illustrates the problems arising in family relations and the responses of the *fellahin* in the mid-nineteenth century. I have chosen to deal with the reactions of women with the understanding that female family members, beginning from a position of less privilege and power, were more directly affected by the erosion of family structures and functions. Peasant women and their relatives came in person to make appeals and complaints to the judge of the local *shari'a* court. Their problems focused around three major aspects of mid-century social life: the absence of husbands and other male relations for long periods of time, the erosion of material support formerly given by the extended family, and the interference of the *sheikh al-balad* (the village head who became a local government official under Muhammad 'Ali) in personal affairs.

The absence of the male head of the family called for clarification of the male role in social regulation. In a society where females inherited set portions of property, marriage arrangements were an economic as well as social matter which often served to consolidate property and bind two families together. The male household head, as the overseer of the family's land and possessions, could be expected to retain the ultimate power of decision over the giving of women in marriage. Islamic law as practiced in Egypt, while it modified the father's control in some regards by, for instance, allowing girls of legally major age to give themselves in marriage to men of the same social standing who paid the legally required *mahr* (nuptial gift), vested most marriage decisions in the adult males on the father's side. Any marriage arrangements involving a legally minor girl, a husband of a different social standing, or a *mahr* other than that considered legally 'fair,' were the prerogative of the family's adult males.

In 1848–49, the Hanafi *mufti* reviewed a case which posed the problems arising when the entire male line had left the village. A maternal grandmother wanted to marry her ten-year-old granddaughter to a man of equal social standing who offered a 'fair' *mahr*, but the girl's father had been missing for some time and her uncle, the father's brother, was serving in the military in Alexandria. The *mufti* ruled that the mother or grandmother could give the girl in marriage when the male adults were absent only if the suitor and the *mahr* were indeed proper. Marriage arrangements made by the women or the mother's family alone would, in any other circumstances, be of questionable legality.[90] Thus, although female relatives did not, in the absence of males, acquire identical powers as *walis* (guardians) in marriage arrangements, they were empowered by the court to assume a role previously relegated solely to male relations.[91]

A husband's absence meant not only a critical reduction in the production of the family unit, but also might jeopardize the wife's position in her husband's extended family. Many of the peasants who brought their cases to court were living and working in a unit composed of several brothers and their wives and children who shared the goods, land and livestock left by the deceased father. The brothers, viewed under law as a partnership (*shirka*), contributed more or less equal amounts of labor time to family production and held equal shares of the inheritance. The absence of one brother, however, might lead to a dispute over the proper division of the fruits of family production and the assignment of family responsibilities.

One peasant family quarreled bitterly in 1849–50 over the division of their joint property when the need arose (perhaps when their children were of age) to divide the patrimony and establish separate households. One of the brothers had served in the army, faithfully sending home his pay for the support of his wife and children. The quarrel revolved around what precisely should be considered part of the shared inheritance, and thus divided among them, and what belonged to each individual brother. The *mufti* ruled that the inheritance of the father and its increase should be divided equally, but what each brother earned during the others' absence 'through his own work and effort is his alone.' The money sent by the soldier was specifically for the support of his wife and children, and thus formed no part of the inheritance: indeed, if the other brothers used any part of it for other purposes, they were to refund this sum.[92] It appears that even though the soldier's wife and children remained a part of the wider family economic unit in his absence, the fact of absence itself modified the pattern of joint production and consumption. The wife and children formed a part of the peasant household only through their relationship with the husband and father. If the soldier had not sent home his pay, they might well have had to leave the family hearth.

The vulnerability of the peasant woman left without a husband often led her to attempt remarriage. In some cases, the woman could obtain a divorce on the grounds that her absent husband was not providing for her.[93] Frequently she had to wait for a report of her husband's death during military service, often many years in coming, before petitioning the court to declare her husband legally dead so that she might remarry. A not atypical case is that of one woman who waited in her village for 15 years until two men returned to inform her of her husband's death; she then asked the court if she could remarry.[94]

Hardships caused by the absence of the husband were exacerbated by a general breakdown of patterns of support within the family. One woman came to court on behalf of her two young daughters, pleading dire poverty and requesting the court to order the father of her dead husband to support his grandchildren.[95] Another woman, incapable of supporting herself, demanded maintenance by her brother.[96] The *mufti* always responded favorably, stressing the responsibility of male relatives to support any of the females in need. But the very fact that the women had recourse to the court with such matters seems to underline the breakdown of support patterns.

Court decisions showed less sympathy for the plight of the divorced or widowed woman who, in the absence of maintenance from her own family, was forced to work outside the family unit to support her children. The right of the mother to the care of the child until the male child reached age seven or nine and until the female child came of age was affirmed under Hanafi law. In the mid-nineteenth century, however, the number of disputes over child custody rose, most likely because the divorced or widowed woman, having lost her position in her husband's family, was not reintegrated into her parents' household. The woman lost her rights to the child if she had no means of support. The divorced husband could be asked to pay a certain sum toward the support of the child, but, should he plead poverty, he had the right, in lieu of payment, to entrust the care of the child to another female relative. A widow, left nothing by her impecunious husband, could also lose her custody rights in favor of her husband's family.[97]

If a woman turned to outside work to support herself and her children, she ran the risk of being declared an unfit mother. One woman, having obtained a divorce by agreeing to waive her rights to the return of her *mahr* (a common practice by which the wife might redeem herself from marriage), was left with no means of support except a small monthly sum from the husband for the care of their three-year-old son. Unable to maintain her own household, she went to work as a servant in her sister's house. The child's father claimed that, by working, she had neglected the child and negated her claim to monthly support payments and child custody. The *mufti* agreed: the mother could keep her son only if she left her sister's employ. Another woman lost custody of her three young girls by taking a job as a domestic servant in a nearby village.[98]

Peasant women who engaged in petty production and trade could also be deprived of custody. A man accused his divorced wife of buying and selling goods in the local market, thus winning custody of their six-year-old daughter. A woman who earned her living by making pancakes at home and selling them in the market was likewise declared unfit. Husbands and other relatives were also wont to deprive the woman of custody by accusing her of indecent behavior and prostitution.[99]

Many women remarried promptly, thereby integrating themselves into another family unit. Remarriage, however, usually involved forfeiting custody rights. Young children were forbidden by law to live in the same household as a 'foreigner' (*ajnabi*), that is, a person who was not a close relative.

The vast quantity of custody cases in this period, and the overwhelming number of judgments in favor of the father, suggest that the legal and customary rights of the peasant woman were weakening. Her plight speaks to the erosion of familial patterns of support in a period of social dislocation. The court, by basing its judgments of what constituted a fit mother on an ideal type, refused to come to terms with a changing reality.

Women turned to the court with more success when the issue of state interference in family affairs arose. The heavy-handed rule of the local sheikhs provoked protest, especially when the sheikhs tried to force women to marry against their will. In one case, a village sheikh took advantage of the fact that a young woman was working as a servant in his village, at some distance from her own home and family, to marry her under duress to one of his slaves. The court ruled such a marriage legally defective, citing the use of force and the unsuitability of the match.[100] Even when the woman was still within the family unit, the sheikh might force her male relatives to agree to a marriage using beatings or imprisonment to secure their consent.[101] The court firmly opposed any such interference, affirming the authority of the family's male *wali* and the woman's right of refusal.

V

In the realm of property relations, the records and role of the court illustrate the effect of, and the peasant response to, land expropriation as a force which undermined the family production unit. Peasant tenure in the mid-nineteenth century must be set in the context of the regulations and practices governing *miri* land. All peasant land holdings were *miri*; full ownership was vested in the state, and peasant holders enjoyed only usufruct rights. By custom the usufruct passed from father to son although the *multazim* reserved the right to appoint a successor of his choosing. With the destruction of the *iltizam* system, a local official, usually the *hakim*, acquired some powers of appointment.[102] *Miri* land, since it was not held outright by the *fellahin*, was not subject to the Islamic laws of inheritance which specified the portions to be given each heir. The courts at mid-century asserted two sometimes contradictory principles upon the death of the usufruct holder: (1) the sons or male relatives of the deceased, if capable of farming the land and paying the taxes, should inherit the usufruct, and (2) the local officials had the right to invest whomsoever they wished.[103]

In practice, the sons, unless they specifically ceded their rights to female family members, inherited the usufruct. Cases abound of daughters, wives and sisters asking for a share as part of their inheritance. Daughters were told by the court that the usufruct goes solely to the sons as long as they are working the land and paying the taxes. When a man died, leaving only his sister and his brother's sons, the court refused to consider the sister's request for a share. In another case a man was survived by his sister, two daughters and a nephew; the usufruct in its entirety went to the nephew.[104] Although female heirs rarely succeeded in overriding the customary male right to *miri* land, they appear to have been emboldened to contest those rights because of the extension of the *hakim*'s decision powers and the weakening of customary rights. Women did succeed in laying claim to the produce of the land as well as a share in money owed to the husband or father for the use of his land before his death.[105]

Under certain circumstances, women could obtain usufruct rights. If a father ceded part of his land to his daughter during his lifetime, the daughter had a strong claim to the retention of the land. In one case, the *mufti* forbade the dead man's sons to take *miri* land away from their sisters on the grounds that the women had cultivated it for a number of years before and after their father's death.[106] In the absence of male children, daughters sometimes managed to acquire rights at the expense of other male heirs. In the case of a widow with two young daughters who continued to cultivate her husband's *miri* land for five years after his death, the court denied the husband's brothers any right to the land.[107]

The most common female claim rested on the initial consent of male heirs. If male relatives ceded part of the land to female heirs upon the death of the holder, any of their later claims were void. The fact that they had waived their rights deserved mention in most court decisions, but the past performance of the females in meeting their tax responsibilities often had equal weight. The court was also quick to assert that the final right belonged to whomever the *hakim* invested, although there was some question as to what powers of discretion the *hakim* could exercise in the presence of male children.[108]

Rights to *miri* thus rested partly on custom and partly on the will of local officials. *Miri* land usually remained intact in the hands of one or more sons.

The exclusions of *miri* land from the sway of Islamic inheritance laws prevented land fragmentation. Peasant families tried to avoid fragmentation of the inheritable property as well. The rights of women to specific shares of the inheritance were sometimes unilaterally abrogated by their male relatives. In some cases, the sons of the deceased simply divided the father's inheritable property among themselves with no regard for the rights of their mother and sisters.[109] The *mufti*, in such cases, strongly upheld the rules of Islamic inheritance, insisting that the widow was entitled to one-eighth of her husband's estate, and the female children to one-half that of the males.

Males were expectedly loath to see family property pass into female hands, given the kinship nature of the family productive unit. Many peasant households, as the court records tell us, were a partnership of brothers, who, with their wives and children, shared the *miri* land left by their father as well as the inheritable property. Their sisters, who married into other households, removed their share of the inheritable property from the paternal household. Evidence exists that the sisters, upon the death of their father, sometimes ceded their share of the property to their brothers for a consideration.[110]

The legal division of inheritable property often took place some time after the father's death. The determination of whether or not the female heirs should share in any augmentation of the inheritable property was apparently related to the position of women within the family productive unit. As long as sisters and brothers remained under the same roof, working together, they formed an association. The sisters could make a legal claim to share in any increase in the estate acquired after the death of the father.[111] Quarrels often pitted females against their brothers. Sisters outside of the household might claim that their brother had purchased goods as the father's agent and therefore those goods were part of the father's estate. But the overall trend was to limit the female share to the minimum required by Islamic law or even to subvert legal injunctions by denying females part of their inheritance. These tactics strengthened the family productive unit at the expense of females who married outside of the household. Women were forced to appeal to the court; the court sided with them in case of flagrant violations, but may not have been able to insure implementation of its decisions.

When the rights of females in the paternal household were undermined, the husband's household offered little refuge. The married woman often found herself left with nothing should her husband die before his father. The court repeatedly ruled that as long as a son was living and working with his father, all family property was vested solely in the father. Widows often asked their father-in-law for payment of the *mahr* and a share of their husband's inheritance; if the woman had been living with her husband's family, her claims were invariably denied.[112]

As previously noted, in a household composed of brothers, the wife of any one brother had a much stronger claim. Women often complained, however, that their rights were whittled away by false claims of association on the part of their husbands' brothers, for example, a false claim to property which had been individually owned by the woman or by the woman's deceased husband.[113] In addition, the rights of partnership might be denied by the surviving brothers for other reasons. In one case, the children of a blind man, who had been living together with their father's brother, asked for a share in their uncle's property on the grounds that their father had been his associate.[114] The decision of the court, denying their claim, suggests that a non-productive household member and his dependants could not establish property rights over the fruits of household production.

In conclusion, legal struggles over inheritance show a trend of consolidation of family property at the expense of female members. Women were legitimate members of the production/consumption family unit as judged by the fact that they could make claims on family property not only through kinship, but also on the basis of their role in the family unit. In the mid-nineteenth century, however, the desire for consolidation led to increasing limitation of female rights. While women had never inherited *miri* land, they now faced contestation of their rights under Islamic law to other forms of property. Male relatives often tried to ignore or bypass the woman's legal rights. Insofar as they honored female claims, it was often done strictly within the letter of the law. The structure of the peasant household, in which several brothers shared hearth and labor, had not been radically transformed, but the many legal disputes over the division of property suggest that, in a period of scarcity and social dislocation, it was subject to strain. The courts, by defining the peasant family unit as an association (*shirka*) formed by the partnership of the original heirs who continued living together, may well have abetted the process of female disinheritance.

The court strongly defended family rights against the arbitrary incursions of the local sheikhs, whose appropriations of land and other property were often made at the expense of women and their heirs. In cases where sheikhs wrested houses, trees or goods from their female owners, the court issued clear injunctions.[115] The religious legal system usually sided with the peasants in their struggles with state officials, but at the same time it reaffirmed the legality of the political power. The court did champion women insofar as the violation of their rights to support and property constituted an attack on law or custom. Its willingness to accommodate its rulings to a new social reality was limited, but, nevertheless, it remained an institution to which women turned to raise their complaints concerning the encroachments on family life as they knew it.

VI

By mid-century the Egyptian family economy had experienced an onslaught of social and economic pressures. The state policies of the Muhammad 'Ali period, formulated in concert with the demands of capitalist penetration, had produced social dislocation in the countryside by siphoning off peasant labor and dispossessing the peasant family of land. Vast population movements, land loss and impoverishment had weakened the ability of the peasant family to continue producing as a unit and supporting its non-productive members. Although all members of the family had owed their status and security to their position in the household unit, women, in a patriarchal society, were more vulnerable and subject to greater limitation of their rights and privileges as the family unit faltered.

The continued survival of the peasant family during this period of extreme dislocation can be attributed to two factors. First, the state revised its policies. It eliminated the most disruptive forms of corvée and military recruitment and thus lessened the drain on peasant labor. Those policies had been counterproductive in that they had been destroying the basis of social and economic organization without providing alternative structures. Insofar as the state could not assume the traditional family functions, eg. providing for non-productive members, the survival of the family economy remained essential. Furthermore, a distinctive feature of the agricultural relations of production in this period, that is, the political rather than purely economic coercion of peasants in the process of capitalization, allowed for the preservation of the precapitalist family structure. It is only with the rise of a fully capitalist agricultural sector that the family as a cohesive production/consumption unit becomes obsolete.

The court records illuminate the second factor. Faced with the erosion of the family economy, peasant families themselves clung to former patterns of economic and social sharing, often turning to the court to reaffirm customary family relations. As these relations were being gradually modified by the new demands made on peasant production and labor, peasants reacted by shoring up patterns of family support. The drive for consolidation of family property, however, often took place at the expense of those family members whose legal and customary rights were weakest. It is within this context that women experienced a shrinking of their position in the family unit. It appears that the decline of the family, as a semiautonomous unit, may well have contributed to a loss of status and security among the female population. The common assumption that women stood to benefit with the impact of the West and the rise of 'modern' society should be re-examined in this light.

This article is reprinted from the *Arab Studies Quarterly*, vol. 1, no. 3 (1979), pp. 245–271. Reprinted by permission of the *Arab Studies Quarterly*.

NOTES

1. Basile Kerblay, 'Chayanov and the Theory of Peasantry as a Specific Type of Economy,' in Teodor Shanin, *Peasants and Peasant Societies* (Baltimore, 1971), p. 159. As Kerblay points out, Chayanov's theory of the 'peasant economy' works better for thinly populated areas where peasants can buy or take in more land, thus making the decision to expand labor a meaningful one. In the Egyptian context, periods of agricultural labor shortage, such as the early nineteenth

century, might give the peasant a similar choice as long as there was not competition for the land from other quarters.

2. The concept of a 'peasant economy' as proposed by Daniel Thorner. 'Peasant Economy as a Category in Economic History,' in Shanin, *Peasants*, allows for the existence of larger economic units—landlords' demesnes, haciendas employing peasants, and even capitalist farms—'alongside peasant producers.' The model proposed is reminiscent of a dual economy, in which various sectors in the society exist alongside one another without effective links of mutual transformation. Claude Meillassoux, *Femmes, Greniers et Capitaux* (Paris, 1975), argues, on the contrary, that the 'domestic mode of production,' which shares the focus of the 'peasant economy' model on the peasant producer/consumer unit, ceases to exist as such with the rise of exploitation by a dominant class.

3. Helen Rivlin, *The Agricultural Policy of Muhammad 'Ali in Egypt* (Cambridge, MA., 1971). p. 29. When the *multazim* had the right to use forced labor, the peasants who worked the land were drawn from the local village.

4. Eli Zaretsky, *Capitalism, the Family, and Personal Life* (Winnipeg, 1974), p. 29 and Evelyne Sullerot. *Histoire et Sociologie du Travail Feminin* (Paris, 1968), chap. 2, argue that the return of women to the home was functional for capitalism in that it served changing needs in quality and quantity of labor, and secured social stability. See Jane Humphries, 'The Working Class Family, Women's Liberation and Class Struggle: The Case of Nineteenth Century British History' in the *Review of Radical Political Economics* 9, no. 3 (Fall. 1977): 34, for an alternative explanation, whereby the working class itself defended the family structure because it acted as an obstacle to the cheapening of the value of labor power.

5. See E. P. Thompson, *The Making of the English Working Class* (New York, 1966). chap. 6.

6. Gabriel Baer, *Studies in the Social History of Modern Egypt* (Chicago, 1969). p. 212. Although Baer freely acknowledges that changes occurred in the socioeconomic structure of Egypt, and that there was 'considerable economic development,' as the former 'subsistence economy' was replaced by an 'export-oriented economy,' he remains firmly convinced that basic social institutions, including the family, were not affected. This thesis is difficult to reconcile with his own discussion of changes in rural society: peasant land expropriation, the rise of a class of landless peasants, the emergence of a market economy, and the growth of social differentiation among the village population. How peasant social and productive relations, especially within the family, remained totally unaltered by such sweeping developments is difficult to fathom.

7. Charles Issawi, 'Egypt since 1800: A Study in Lopsided Development,' in *The Economic History of the Middle East, 1800–1914* (Chicago, 1966), p. 36.

8. Roger Owen, 'The Management of Large Estates in Nineteenth Century Egypt,' n.p., n.d., p. 15.

9. Anouar Abdel-Malek, *Egypt: Military Society* (New York, 1968), p. 401. The concept of 'backward colonial capitalism,' first applied to developments in Egyptian agriculture by Abdel-Malek, has been further discussed by Owen. 'The Management of Large Estates,' and Richards. 'Primitive Accumulation in Egypt,' *Review* 1. no. 1 (summer, 1977).

10. Muhammad 'Ali's policies and goals have been variously interpreted. See Moustafa Fahmy, *La révolution de l'industrie en Egypte et ses conséquences sociales au 19ᵉsiècle* (Leiden, 1954); 'Abd al-Rahman al-Rafi'i, *'Asr Muhammad 'Ali* (Cairo, 1951); and Rivlin, *Agricultural Policy*, for three divergent views.

11. See Rivlin, *Agricultural Policy*, pp. 112–13. Rivlin describes yet other hardships of the system of agricultural monopolies: the peasants received tax credits (which were calculated in undervalued paper currency) instead of payment for the crop; they had to pay the cost of transport to the local depot; they were often cheated out of the little they were entitled to by corrupt government officials.

12. FO 142/3. Barker to Earl of Aberdeen, 8 March 1830, p. 119.

13. Rivlin. *Agricultural Policy*. pp. 114–15.

14. FO 78/381. Bowring Report, March 1839.

15. Richards, 'Primitive Accumulation.' p. 25.

16. MAE, Turquie: Alex, et Caire: 17. Barrot à Ministre, 10 January 1845.

17. Ibrahim *'Amr, Al-ard w'al-fellah* (Cairo, 1958), p. 81.

18. James Augustus St. John, *Egypt and Mohammed Ali* (London, 1834) II, p. 349: 'Abd al-Rahman

al-Rafi'i, *Tarikh al-Harakah al-Qawmiyyah fi Misr min Fajr al-Tarikh ila al-Fath al-'Arabi* (Cairo, 1963) III, p. 573.

19. MAE, Correspond, Politique des Consuls, Turquie: Alex et Caire Labot à Ministre, 29 Dec. 1841.

20. FO 142/15, Murray to Wellesley, 13 May 1847.

21. FO 142/16, Murray to Palmerston, 5 May 1849.

22. See Rivlin *Agricultural Policy*, p. 201. Rivlin also suggests that the move to peasant recruitment was influenced by the new conscription policy introduced into France at the time of the Revolution.

23. MAE. Correspond. Pol. des Consuls. Turquie: Alex et Caire: I, 'Notes sur les barbareques,' September 1829, gives the following figures according to Drovetti's estimates: Regular troops: 53,000: Irregulars: 15,000: Total 68,000. MAE, Correspond. Polit. des Consuls, Turquie: Alex et Caire. I. Huder Report, March 1830, revised the figures upwards: Regular troops: 54,000: Irregulars: 24,000; Navy: 9,400; Total: 87,500.

24. MAE, Correspond. Polit. des Consuls. Turq.: Alex et Caire: I, Mimaut à Ministre, 3 April 1830.

25. *Ibid.*, II. Mimaut à Ministre, 20 Feb. 1831.

26. *Ibid.*, II. Mimaut à Secretaire, 18 June 1832.

27. See MAE:, Correspond. Con. et Com., Alex: 32, Barrot à Ministre, 28 April 1848; also Correspond. Polit des Consuls, Turq: Alex et Caire: XX, Barrot à Ministre, 16 May 1848.

28. FO 142/16, Murray to Palmerston, 5 May 1849.

29. MAE, Correspond. Polit. des Consuls: Turq.: Alex et Caire: XXV. Sabatier à Ministre, 16 March 1854.

30. Rivlin, *Agricultural Policy*, p. 199.

31. FO 142/13. Barnett to For. Sec., 17 August 1842.

32. British Museum, London, MSS division, the *Hekekyan Papers*, vol. 2, 37449. p. 391, 1844.

33. MAE. Correspond. Con. et Com., Caire; XXIX, Delaporte à Ministre, 16 June 1851.

34. MAE, Correspond. Polit des Consuls: Turq: Alex et Caire, XVI. Lavalette à Ministre, 6 May 1844.

35. *Hekekyan Papers*, vol. 7. 37454, p. 347. 1855.

36. FO 78/257, Campbell to Duke of Wellington, 15 April 1835. Campbell discounts a state official's claim that there is no population deficiency in Upper Egypt, noting that: 'This is contrary to the reports generally given by all the travellers with whom I have conversed on the subject.' See also: FO 78/282, Campbell to Palmerston, 24 January 1836, for similar information on Lower Egypt.

37. FO 78/381, Bowring Report, March 1838, p. 6.

38. *al-Waqa'i' al-Misriyah*, 1245, n. v., n.d.

39. FO 142/16, Murray to Palmerston, 1 June 1848.

40. See Rivlin. *Agricultural Policy*, chap. 2 for a discussion of the *iltizam* system: see also Gabriel Baer, *A History of Land Ownership in Modern Egypt* (London, 1962), pp. 1–2.

41. Baer, *A History*, p. 3.

42. Rivlin, *Agricultural Policy*, pp. 47–55, 58.

43. *Ibid.*, p. 23.

44. See Richards. 'Primitive Accumulation.'

45. See Rivlin, *Agricultural Policy*, chap. 5.

46. Richards, 'Primitive Accumulation,' p. 23.

47. Baer, *A History*. p. 17.

48. Owen. 'The Management of Large Estates,' p. 10. It was proposed that the peasants working on *chifliks* farm a few *feddans* on their own account, using animals belonging to the estate, to supplement their income. We cannot be sure, however, if this proposal was ever implemented.

49. Richards. 'Primitive Accumulation,' p. 25; and Rivlin, *Agricultural Policy*, p. 236.

50. Baer, *A History*, p.29.

51. Gabriel Baer, *Studies in the Social History of Modern Egypt* (Chicago, 1969). p. 95. see all of chap. 6 for the history of peasant revolts from 1778 to 1951.

52. Richards, 'Primitive Accumulation,' p. 22.

53. Baer, *Studies*, p. 96.

54. Rivlin, *Agricultural Policy*, pp. 201–2.

55. Richards, 'Primitive Accumulation,' p. 22.

56. MAE, Correspond. Polit. des Consuls: Turq.: Alex et Caire: XX. Barrot à Ministre. 16 May 1848.

57. al-'Abasi al-Mahdi, *al-Fatawa*, vol. 5, 16 Rajab 1267, p. 426.

58. *Ibid.*, vol. 5. 30 Dhu al-Hijja, 1267, p. 429.

59. MAE, Correspond. Polit. des Consuls: Turq: Alex et Caire: XXI, Benedetti à Ministre 8 January 1850.

60. MAE, Correspond. Polit. des Consuls: Turq: Alex et Caire: I, Mimaut à Ministre, 26 April 1830.

61. MAE, Correspond. Con. et Com.: Alex.: XXIV, Mimaut à Ministre, 1 August 1831.

62. *al-Waqa'i' al-Misriyah*, no. 34, 6 Dhu al-Hijja, 1244.

63. *Hekekyan Papers*, vol. 2, 37449, p. 130.

64. MAE, Correspond. Con. et Com.: Alex, XXIV, Mimaut à Ministre, 1 August, 1831.

65. *al'Waqa'i' al-Misriyah*, n.v., n.d., 1245.

66. FO 142/13, Barnett to Secretary, 16 March 1845.

67. See Gérard de Nerval, *Scènes de la vie oriental* (Paris, 1848); also, *Hekekyan Papers*, vol. 3, 37450, and vol. 5, 37452.

68. *Hekekyan Papers*, vol. 3, 37450, p. 85.

69. MAE, Correspond. Polit. des Consuls: Turq.: Alex et Caire: XXIII, LeMoyne à Ministre, 28 April 1851.

70. See *Hekekyan Papers*, vol. 5, 37452, p. 413, and vol. 7, 37454, p. 365.

71. *Hekekyan*. vol. 7, 37454, p. 365.

72. Nerval, *Scènes*, p. 87.

73. P. N. Hamont, *L'Egypte sous Mehemet-Ali* (Paris, 1843), I, pp. 109–10; see also C. Rochfort Scott, *Rambles in Egypt and Candia* (London, 1837), II, p. 221.

74. St John, *Egypt*. I, p. 158; R. R. Madden, *Egypt and Mohamed Ali* (London, 1841). p. 32.

75. Hamont, *L'Egypte*, I, pp. 109–10; and *Hekekyan*, vol. 3, 37450.

76. St John, *Egypt*, I, p. 276.

77. FO 78/184, Barker to Malcolm, 8 July 1829.

78. Hamont, *L'Egypte*, II, pp. 19–20; see also EMAT, MR1678, 'Situation de l'armée régulière Egyptienne,' par Mathieu de Faviers, 30 May 1831.

79. Scott, *Rambles*, II, p. 216.

80. MAE, Correspond. Con. et Com.: Alex: XXVII, de Lessups à Ministre, 5 March 1837; Correspond. Polit. des Consuls: Turq.: Alex et Caire: XV, Gallice à See. 6 June 1843.

81. FO 78/381. Bowring Report, March 1838. p. 100.

82. MAE, Correspond. Polit. des Consuls: Turq.: Alex et Caire; XXI, Benedetti à Ministre, 5 December 1849.

83. MAE, Correspond. Con. et Com.: Alex: XXVII, de Lessups à Ministre, 5 March 1837; FO 78/381, Bowring Report, March 1839, p. 100.

84. MAE, Correspond. Polit. des Consuls: Turq.: Alex et Caire: XX, Barrot à Ministre, 19 June 1848.

85. *Ibid.*, XXI, Benedetti à Ministre, 5 December 1849.

86. EMAT, MR 1678, 'L'armée Egyptienne' par Motel, 27 June 1861.

87. MAE. Correspond. Con. et Com.: Alex XXIX, Benedetti à Ministre, 29 May 1841; Correspond. Polit. des Consuls: Turq.: Alex et Caire: XX, Barrot à Ministre, 19 June 1848.

88. Hamont. *L'Egypte*. II, p. 57.

89. MAE, Correspond. Con. et Com.: Alex: XXXIII, Benedetti à Ministre, 18 April 1849: Hamont. *L'Egypte*. II, pp. 19–20; St John, *Egypt*, II, p. 176.

90. al-'Abasi al Mahdi, *al Fatawa*. I, 5 Sha'ban, 1265, p. 21.

91. See Joseph Schacht, *An Introduction to Islamic Law* (Oxford, 1964), p. 120, on the exclusive male right to act as *wali* in the Hanafi tradition.

92. al-'Abasi al-Mahdi, *al-Fatawa*, II, 12 Sha'ban 1266, p. 306.

93. *Ibid.*, I, 8 Dhu al-Qa'da, p. 22.

94. *Ibid.*, I, 11 Rabi' II, 1265, p. 243.

95. *Ibid.*, I, Sha'ban 1266, p. 389.

96. *Ibid.*, I, 4 Dhu al-Hijja 1264, p. 378.
97. *Ibid.*, I, 16 Sha'ban 1269, p. 302: and I, 25 Jumada II 1267, p. 283.
98. *Ibid.*, I, 2 Safar 1267, p. 283: and I, 13 Rabi' II 1265, p. 264.
99. *Ibid.*, I, 5 Jumada II 1265, p. 266; I, 7 Jumada II 1268, p. 293; I, 9 Jumada II 1265, p. 266: I, 30 Shawwal 1266, p. 279.
100. *Ibid.*, I, 8 Rabi' I 1268, p. 38.
101. *Ibid.*, I, 4 Jumada I 1265, p. 18; and I, 19 Rabi' II 1265, p. 18.
102. Baer, *A History*, pp. 6–7.
103. See al'Abasi al-Mahdi, *al-Fatawa*, II, 23 Jumada II 1267, p. 91; II, 27 Sha'ban 1265, p. 49; II, 9 Dhu al-Hijja 1269, p. 168; II, 14 Safar 1268, p. 109.
104. Ibid., II, 18 Dhu al-Qa'da 1264, p. 33; II, 12 Sha'ban 1265, p. 48; and II. 17 Ramadan 1265, p. 50.
105. *Ibid.*, V, 12 Rajab 1268, p. 236; V, 8 Shawwal 1268, p. 343.
106. *Ibid.*, II. 18 Dhu al-Qa'da 1264. p. 33.
107. *Ibid.*, II. 9 Dhu al-Hijja 1269. p. 168.
108. *Ibid.*, II. 1 Dhu al-Qa'da 1267. p.98.
109. *Ibid.*, V. 28 Rajab 1266. p. 230; V. 12 Shawwal 1268, p. 238.
110. *Ibid.*, V. I Jumada I 1266, p. 229; II, 6 Dhu al-Hijja 1264, p. 35.
111. *Ibid.*, II, II Rajab 1265, p. 293.
112. See *Ibid.*, II, 22 Jumada I 1268, p. 329; I, 18 Dhu al-Hijja 1269, p. 109; II, 27 Rabi' II 1266, p. 303.
113. *Ibid.*, II, 21 Safar 1267, p. 313.
114. *Ibid.*, II, 25 Rabi' II 1266, p. 303.
115. *Ibid.*, II, 17 Dhu al-Qa'da 1269, p. 170.

Ottoman Women, Households, and Textile Manufacturing, 1800–1914

DONALD QUATAERT

In spite of their central place in Ottoman social and economic life, we know little about nineteenth-century Ottoman manufacturing women, the households in which they lived and worked, their economic activities, and changes in these pursuits over time. Women and their households mediated the process of growing Ottoman participation in the world economy, and changes in household processes of production and the household division of labor should be understood as adaptations to changing market opportunities, both domestic and international. Thus, I believe, there are relations between changes in Ottoman household economies and the regional and world economies of the nineteenth-century. But to view the evolution of nineteenth-century Ottoman household economies as merely a story of transformation from subsistence to market production would be too simplistic. Many Ottoman households already were committed to manufacturing for the market, at varying levels, well before 1800. As a famous example, in the town of Ambelakia in Ottoman Thessaly, the manufacture of red yarn was a family business in the eighteenth century. 'Every arm, even those of the children, is employed in the factories; whilst the men dye the cotton, the women prepare and spin it.'[1]

Vigorous and vibrant putting-out systems interlaced the Ottoman Empire, exchanging raw materials and semi-processed goods among its European, Anatolian, and Arab provinces. Women and men in north Anatolian towns such as Zile and Merzifon, for example, received raw cotton from the Mediterranean south and spun it into thread. Some of the newly made thread was exported to the Ottoman Crimea, and local weavers used some to make a coarse calico for regional use and for export.[2] Other Ottoman households were subsistence producers as of 1800 and, in declining numbers, remained so throughout the period. Also, as I will show, the nature of Ottoman household economies varied by region, as did changes in those economies.

A focus on households and women's work is a key to properly understanding the history of Ottoman manufacturing in the nineteenth century. It is widely held that Ottoman manufacture 'declined' in the age of the European Industrial Revolution. But what is meant by decline? Perhaps there was no decrease in gross Ottoman industrial output between 1800 and 1900. After all, the domestic Ottoman market as well as the export market for select Ottoman manufactures was much larger at the beginning of the twentieth century than before (see below).[3] The oft-cited Ottoman industrial decline may in fact reflect a decrease in the output generated by organized guild *male* labor. It thus is critical to examine the household division of labor by gender. Manufacturing output by urban guilds, which were male dominated, did fall off sharply in many areas. But, as I will demonstrate, manufacturing production by females working at home did not merely continue but sharply expanded in some regions and textile handicraft sectors. In addition, factory labor increased, particularly after 1880, and the majority of the textile workers were girls and women.

Rural households accounted for at least 80 per cent of the Ottoman population and usually consisted of the nuclear family, that is, a husband and wife (usually one) and their children. Rural households in the Black Sea coastal areas of Anatolia averaged 6.5 persons and as few as 5.3 persons elsewhere, figures that place Anatolia just above the average for preindustrial Europe. Multiple-family households in rural Anatolia did not account for more than 30 per cent of the total, whereas simple, or nuclear, households made up 50 to 60 per cent.[4] In the capital city of Istanbul, similarly, very good data reveal that the extended family made up only 16 per cent of all households counted. Upper-class Istanbul households averaged 5.7 persons, and those further down the social ladder averaged 4.5 persons. Polygyny was rare in the capital, involving only 2 per cent of all married Muslim men. In the Arab town of Nablus, the polygyny rate was higher, 16 per cent of the men enumerated.[5] It must be stressed that in both urban and rural households, the males often were absent, engaged in wage-earning labor at sites some distance from their homes. Migratory labor, involving work in other rural areas as well as in both remote and nearby urban centers, was a normal condition of existence for Ottoman families. Finally, a considerable amount of time in the average Ottoman rural household was devoted to manufacturing activities, sometimes for family use and at other times for sale. That manufacturing was an everyday part of Ottoman rural (and urban) life has been overlooked almost completely in the literature on both Ottoman manufacturing and Ottoman agriculture. Scholars of manufacturing have focused on urban male guilds, whereas researchers of the countryside usually have considered only crop growing and animal husbandry. Rural households were not simply agricultural producers. Instead, they were engaged in a mix of economic activities, for example, crop growing, mining, manufacturing, and fishing, the composition of which changed according to region, season, and opportunity. If crop prospects were poor, then the family would devote increased attention to manufacturing for sale to earn cash for purchasing foodstuffs.

Information on the nineteenth-century Bursa silk industry offers powerful hints but frustratingly little concrete data concerning the impact of female labor on changes in the gender division of household labor. For centuries, the town of Bursa and its environs had been renowned for rich brocades and fabrics. The gender division of labor in the industry varied according to its rural or urban location. Village families, both male and female members, provided the raw silk, unraveled in a single length from the cocoon. In the town itself, however, silk spinning may have been an exclusively female occupation as the century opened, as it was in the city of Damascus, located in a Syrian province of the Ottoman Empire. At Bursa, as in Damascus, male weavers, organized into guilds, wove almost all the silk cloth produced, although a few female workers were engaged as well. The involvement of the guildsmen weavers in the Bursa silk industry fell as silk cloth production plummeted after 1830. For several decades, redundant male weavers may have found work in the expanding industry of raw silk, which at that time was spun largely by hand. In 1812, total production of raw silk at Bursa, all of it manually reeled by both men and women, averaged 150,000 pounds.[6] Subsequently, thanks to rising foreign demand and new technology, output soared. The new technology came in the form of steam-powered machinery, housed in factories, that spun the raw silk from cocoons. In 1850 such spinning mills produced 10 per cent of total raw silk. By 1860, when Bursa raw silk output equaled 1.5 million pounds, 98 per cent of it was reeled in a factory setting—in nearly fifty mills that employed at least 4,200 persons.

In the Bursa factories, the labor force was entirely female, both girls and women, except for male superintendents and mechanics tending the engines. The same gender distribution simultaneously came to prevail in the silk-spinning mills being established in the Lebanon region, similarly founded to meet mounting European demand. In the first days of these mills, entrepreneurs at Bursa and in the Lebanon struggled with a labor source reluctant to enter a factory, and in both regions they employed a variety of methods, sometimes remarkably similar, to overcome impediments to labor recruitment. Both sets of entrepreneurs brought in women from France and

Switzerland, experienced in silk reeling, to instruct in the new technology and to demonstrate by example that women could work safely in such factories.[7] These entrepreneurs also found allies in religion, both Christianity and Islam. Around the 1860s, the Roman Catholic pope issued a decree permitting Bursa area girls of Armenian background to work in the mills, and in Lebanon local ulama as well as the Christian clergy played key roles in persuading local girls to work under foreign women supervisors in foreign-owned silk-reeling mills.[8] Appealing to the workers' more worldly needs, Bursa factory owners also offered high wages; a reeler in the mid-1850s earned five times as much as she needed for her daily bread. But wages quickly dropped. Labor supplies were augmented as urban Turks from Bursa and village girls from surrounding areas became available; silk reelers soon were among the most poorly paid factory workers in Ottoman manufacturing. The 'lowest daily wages were paid in the silk (and tobacco) factories in which mainly women worked.'[9] Married Turkish women in the city provided at least some of the labor. According to one European observer in the late 1860s, this wage labor enhanced the women's status in the eyes of their husbands since it increased family income. And, he approvingly noted, since the women dutifully returned to the women's quarters on coming home from work, wage labor had brought only advantages to the Ottoman Turkish family at Bursa.[10] Bursa entrepreneurs also turned to labor supplies outside the city. They recruited 'very' young girls from surrounding rural areas and housed them in dormitories built adjacent to the mills. These village girls, who began as apprentices as early as ten years of age, arrived in caravans for the labor-intensive reeling season. When the season ended, the girls and young women, who won a certain local fame for their purchases of fashionable clothing, as did the Lebanon reelers, returned home with 'practically all' of their wages. Once married, they generally quit the factory and usually did not return unless widowed.[11] But beyond their clothing purchases, we know little about how the wages were used—whether the girls retained the money and brought it into their marriages or turned it over to their parents. A tidbit of information from the 1850s implies that the young women helped to support their families, but we cannot generalize from that. There are other uncertainties. It is not totally clear if there was a net increase in the use of female labor in the silk industry or simply a continuation, in mechanized form, of established patterns and levels. Nor is it known if this work represented the entry for most families into wage labor or their shift from one wage-earning activity to another. The rise of mechanized silk reeling does coincide exactly with the sharp decline in cotton spinning in the Bursa area during the pre-1850 period; the availability of (temporarily) high-paying jobs in silk reeling might well have accelerated the decline of local cotton spinning.

The overwhelming predominance of female labor in the Ottoman silk-spinning industry can be explained by several factors. The Ottoman economy generally was labor scarce, and employing women solved the serious problem for factory owners of finding cheap labor. Also, the mills did not provide a reliable source of full-time income for their workers. After the great burst of factory building, the industry suffered from overcapacity and spinning factories were consistently underutilized. In the 1850s, the 1870s, the 1890s, and the early twentieth century, we are told, they typically operated not more than 200 days per year. The mills thus offered a kind of part-time labor that corresponded well with Ottoman society's view of female labor as supplemental. Such an activity also fit nicely with the time demands that raising silkworms placed on Ottoman families. Given the prevailing labor scarcities around Bursa, for example, it is hardly coincidental that cocoon raisers devised a method for feeding the silkworms that reduced the labor input by 70 per cent, compared with methods in France and Italy. Part-time factory work also was compatible with the demands of agricultural and domestic tasks on the workers. Mechanized silk reeling, as it evolved in the Ottoman lands, interfered minimally with the pre-existing division of labor within the household, whether rural or urban. For the factory owner, the arrangement had only one long-term disadvantage. Throughout the entire period, most factories operated well below capacity, although they often could have spun profitably the year round.[12]

Girls and women played an essential role in three arenas of textile production. They made yarn and cloth at home for immediate use by household members, they produced at home for the market, and they labored in workshops, away from the home setting.[13] Until the second quarter of the nineteenth century, a large proportion of female labor in textile production had been involved with spinning, with either the wheel or the distaff. But the import of European-manufactured factory-spun cotton yarn then rose incredibly, dramatically affecting the economic and social status of Ottoman women. Annual Ottoman imports of cotton yarn, a mere 150 tons in the early 1820s, rose to some 7,750 tons in the 1870s. The impact of this increase must have varied considerably, depending on whether the women had been spinning primarily for the marketplace or for domestic use. For most commercially oriented female spinners, the foreign yarn meant, in the long run, the loss of their spinning jobs and, in the short term, sharply declining wages as they accepted lower wages to compete with the cheap and strong imported product. To the extent that commercial cotton spinning was a preserve of women, the use of imported thread contributed to the displacement of these females from the workplace. And if the unemployed women did not find wage employ in the weaving of cloth from the imported yarn, the workforce might have become more gender homogeneous over time, that is, more exclusively male. This last assumption, however, is questionable. One of the major trends in nineteenth-century Ottoman manufacturing was the shift from guild to nonguild labor, quite probably accompanied by a rise in the importance of female labor in the overall production of cotton cloth and other textiles. If the rising imports of yarn had a negative or mixed impact on commercial yarn spinners, the effect on women spinning for home use was much more certain and definitely more positive. The hand spinning of yarn required to provide the average Ottoman family's clothing needs consumed a vast amount of time, an estimated one-twelfth of the woman's total labor output.[14] This household division of labor began to change in the second quarter of the nineteenth century when imports of machine-made European yarn began flooding into the Ottoman Empire. Purchase of imported yarn must have been attractive to hand spinners, who thus were relieved of a time-consuming and quite unremunerative task. Between 1820 and 1870 yarn imports freed an estimated 160,000 Ottoman women (calculated on the basis of full-time job equivalents) from the onerous and unprofitable task of spinning cotton.[15] The release of these women dramatically affected their households' distribution of labor through a combination of increased leisure time, increased cloth production for family consumption, and increased market production of agricultural commodities and cloth to pay for the purchased yarn.

In spite of the advantages, however, poverty kept many Ottoman women spinning cotton yarn at home both for domestic consumption and for sale. Since many families did not assign monetary value to the time spent spinning, the homespun yarn could undersell the European product. Though not necessarily yarn of comparable quality, it was usable for making lower-grade cloths. As the price of imported yarn and textiles fell steadily over the course of the century, so did the remuneration of spinners producing for the market. In the winter of 1857, 'all' the Kurdish women in the districts surrounding Diyarbakir occupied themselves by spinning for men in the town who wove *bez* cloth. These women were too poor to buy the raw cotton for spinning, much less imported yarn. Instead the women gathered and picked cotton and in return retained a small percentage of it. A woman would spin six pounds of cotton into yarn and then exchange it in town for nine pounds of raw cotton. She kept at this cycle until she had enough twist, 'which the husband converts into cloth, using for his family what is necessary and selling the rest.'[16] Hand spinning persisted through at least the 1860s around Erzurum, and in the Sivas region it was commonplace during the late 1880s. 'What goods are manufactured such as carpets, rough woollen cloth, yarn, leather, is done by the people (mostly the women) at their homes . . . Great quantities of yarn are used. It is now all made by the people (mostly the women) at home on the rudest kind of spinning wheels.'[17]

In the early twentieth century, at the great cloth-manufacturing center of

Aleppo, women working at home annually spun an estimated 100,000 kilograms of cotton yarn used for making the coarser cloths.[18] At nearby Maras, spinning yarn did 'not constitute a profession properly speaking.' Nonetheless, women 'in all the poor homes—that is, among nearly all families . . . during their spare moments' annually spun 90–100,000 kilograms of cotton yarn.[19]

Ottoman girls and women dominated the cotton and wool yarn spinning work force in the steam-powered mills that emerged late in the nineteenth century. These were concentrated in Salonika and inland Macedonia as well as in Izmir, Adana, and Istanbul. Young girls formed the bulk of the labor force and, in common with their European and American (and Bursa) sisters, did not remain long enough to acquire skills, much to the irritation of the owners.[20] Jewish girls in the Salonika mills, for example, worked until they married, as early as age fifteen, or until they had accumulated the necessary dowry.[21] One mill, in the Yedikule district of Istanbul, employed some 300 women and children to make 500,000 packets of yarn per year. In the Adana region of southeast Anatolia, one mill with 2,700 spindles employed 300 women and children, who annually produced 1 million kilograms of yarn. A nearby mill employed 550 persons, usually children and women, who worked twelve hours a day.[22] Around 1880 one of the mills in the European provinces of Salonika employed altogether 250 young women and 50 males. In the city of Salonika in the 1890s, mills employed 480 girls, twelve to eighteen years of age, and 160 men and boys. The men received two or three times the boys' wages, whereas girls' starting pay was half that of the boys. Approximately 75 per cent of the 1,500 workers in the Macedonian spinning mills were females, usually girls, some as young as six years of age. In the 1890s they worked fifteen hours a day in summer and ten in winter, with a thirty-five-minute break for dinner but none at all for breakfast. Women working in inland mills, for example at Karaferia and Niausta, were in a worse position than their Salonika counterparts. In early-twentieth-century Salonika, the combination of a booming tobacco-processing industry that competed for relatively scarce labor and an active workers' movement escalated wages in the cotton mills. (Women also dominated the workforce of the tobacco-processing factories.) But the inland mill workers had few wage-earning options.[23]

The weaving of cloth by women also remained commonplace throughout the period, long after indigenous cloth manufacture supposedly had disappeared from the Ottoman lands. Around Bursa in the 1860s, 'the peasantry find an economy in the women weaving at home stout articles for common wear.'[24] At Trabzon, similarly, the 'countrywomen' both worked in agriculture and spun woolen cloth for family members' outer garments.[25] At about this time, nearly 12,000 hand looms in the east Anatolian provinces of Diyarbakir and Erzurum employed that many men in addition to 6,000 youths under sixteen years of age. Two-thirds of these looms were used to weave cotton cloth and were located in the countryside, not in the towns. These rural weavers obtained the twist from women villagers, who in exchange received an equal weight in cloth.[26] We do not presently know the rural weaver's contribution to total family income, but only that other members of the family engaged in agriculture. In the towns of the region—Bitlis, Diyarbakir, Mardin, and Harput—the male weavers provided most of the family's cash and the wife earned about one-seventh of the total.[27]

At the end of the century, 'almost every family' in Asia Minor still owned a hand loom. 'They can make their own cloths while vast numbers would be unable to earn the money with which to purchase foreign cloth.'[28] This tenacious retention of looms well into the era of massive Ottoman imports of European cloth hints at the Ottoman household's flexible responses to changing market opportunities. In years of strong demand for agricultural products, the looms might be neglected, but in times of famine or weak demand for agricultural goods, cloth again might be made for the family or the market. Women in the province of Sivas in the 1890s used both locally spun and British yarn to weave a coarse cloth for men's trousers and other garments. These female weavers worked on as many as 10,000 looms in the province. In the district (*kaza*) of Davas in Aydin Province, about 185 looms were employed in weaving various cotton and linen textiles for sale, and girls and women operated a full three-quarters of them.[29] In the province as a whole, some 10,000 hand looms wove striped cloth (*alaca*) for home consumption and for sale.[30] These households simultaneously engaged in agriculture and manufacturing oriented toward the marketplace. Weaving output fluctuated with the harvest, another example of household labor ebbing and flowing with income opportunities and requirements, from agriculture to manufacturing and back again. During the 1870s rural artisans who manufactured goods for sale to their neighbors earned two-thirds of their income from agricultural sources and one-third from handicraft activities.[31]

As these examples demonstrate, female participation in the wage-earning manufacturing labor force was predicated on very low wages. Late in the nineteenth century, imported yarn created thousands of new jobs for women in the Istanbul area. Working at home in their newly found employment, these women used foreign yarn to crochet lace for export, earning piecework wages that were extremely low by Ottoman standards of the time, approximately 1.5 piasters per day. Similarly cheap female labor, earning no more than 1.5 piasters per day, permitted Ottoman hand-printed textiles to remain competitive with the mechanical imprints of European factories.[32] The significance of such wages can be illustrated if we assume that a family of six persons purchased all its bread needs. Around 1900 such a family would have required 35 to 40 piasters per week merely for its minimum bread requirements, exclusive of the monies needed for other foodstuffs, for housing, and for clothing. A lacemaker or a hand printer earned on the average 20 per cent of the sum needed to keep the family just in bread. Put another way, each woman's wages provided the bread she needed to survive plus a fraction of the bread needed by one other member of her family.

As an example outside of textiles, shoemaking in Istanbul demonstrates, together with Bursa silk reeling, that low wages were not confined to home industries and provides another indirect glimpse into the household division of labor. At the end of the century as many as fifty men and women labored together in shoemaking workshops. Male operators of sewing machines made half-shoes and earned up to 1.25 piasters per day. With an average urban family of five, if he worked seven days a week he could earn 25 per cent of his family's weekly bread. The sewing machine operator's wife, if employed in the shop, would finish buttonholes or sew on buttons. But she earned, again assuming a seven-day work week, only 10 to 15 per cent of the sum needed to buy the family's total bread. Labor from the children, which was quite common in nineteenth-century Ottoman manufacturing, clearly was necessary to meet the minimum subsistence requirements of the family.[33]

Women also were actively involved in the famed mohair industry of Ankara, a participation that dated back to the mid-eighteenth century, when they spun the lower-quality grades, and probably earlier. In the 1830s and 1840s, the mohair-weaving guild, struggling to meet European competition, implemented what was hailed as an innovation in the industry. Previously the guild sheikh had bought raw mohair at fixed prices and given it to the spinners (both female and male). But now the guild made contracts with 'poor women' who bought mohair in the local markets, spun it, and then sold it to the guild for whatever price they could command. As the guild sought to compete with the 'cheap price' of the European producers, the women supplemented rather than replaced the earlier method of obtaining yarn.[34] A free female labor force thus coexisted with the male spinning guild, a pattern also encountered in the Bursa silk industry, as well as in furniture and shoemaking in Istanbul and textile production at Aleppo. Similarly, in the area of the southern Balkan mountains, male braidmakers belonged to the guild (*gaitanci esnafi*), but the women who spun the wool yarn for them did not.[35]

The carpetmaking industry offers a good example of how the gender distribution of labor in a particular industry varied regionally. This variation indicates the absence of a uniform Middle Eastern or Islamic value system regarding the participation of women in the workforce. In the Middle East generally the carpet industry boomed in the late nineteenth century. In western and central Anatolia, for example, soaring output after 1850 employed perhaps 60,000 persons by World War I, most of them girls and women. In certain areas of Anatolia, women historically had been engaged in all phases of carpetmaking—that is, in the spinning and dyeing of the wool and the knotting of the rugs. From Sivas in 1888 we have this description. 'The dy[e]ing, spinning, weaving etc. are all conducted unitedly, the women of each family engaged in the business doing all the work from the spinning of the yarn by hand, dyeing it with vegetable dyes, to the weaving and completion of the carpet.'[36] In this case a single (female) individual carried out all the steps involved in making a rug. But elsewhere divisions of labor were common and apparently were proportionate to an area's involvement in commercial carpet production. In the late nineteenth century, for example, men at the great production center of Usak washed and bleached the wool and women spun it into yarn. This division of labor changed in the final three decades of the nineteenth century as the production of rugs tripled but the number of carpet looms only doubled. To accomplish this feat, Usak rugmaking families rearranged their lives so that the women could spend more time at the looms: for a brief period in the late 1890s, Usak men took over the task of spinning the wool yarn. Steam-powered spinning factories then were built in the town. Similarly, in one area of modern Iran, as women's commercial rug knotting became more valuable, men assumed such traditionally female tasks as carrying water. (In this case, there was no accompanying ideological shift in gender roles.)[37] At Usak, the division of labor changed in other ways as well: the early-nineteenth-century practice of women dyeing the yarn had given way to male dyeing by the 1880s. But at the important export center of nearby Kula, different divisions of labor prevailed. There women continued to dye the yarn until the century's end. Again, by way of contrast, men as well as women knotted commercial carpets at Gördes and Kula. In Qajar Iran during the same era tribal males usually did not work in carpet knotting but the women did. In some areas of Iran at this time, however, men played an active role in the industry. At Meshed and other major urban centers, males regularly worked as rug knotters; in cities such as Tabriz they worked together with women on the same looms. But in other Iranian cities, such as Kerman, only women knotted.[38]

These examples demonstrate the absence of clear-cut patterns of gender division of labor in nineteenth-century Middle Eastern manufacturing, at least in rugmaking. Ottoman (and Qajar) men and women readily interchanged productive roles to maintain family livelihoods. The presence of male and female rug knotters at Kula and Gördes and in several cities of Qajar Iran reflects a gender sharing of Middle Eastern jobs that popular stereotypes hold to be the monopoly of women. These Anatolian and Iranian examples also show that the division was not characterized by male domination of those activities that were heavily committed to market production; in all the highly commercialized production centers, both males and females knotted rugs.

The presence of male and female workers in the shoemaking shops of Istanbul, for its part, seems to suggest an easier set of gender relations than stereotypes would permit. In these situations the rigid barriers that are presumed to have existed between the sexes and in the gender division of labor simply were not present. That is, our assumptions about such divisions are incorrect, at least some of the time.

But the patterns of gender sharing in carpetmaking tasks at Usak and other long-established commercially oriented production centers were not universal in the industry. As Western demand for carpets mounted, Izmir and Istanbul merchants established new workshops in many regions. Similarly, a European merchant founded a new knotting center in 1912 in the Iranian town of Hamadan. Only girls and women knotted at these workshops, where unlike in the traditional centers they worked away from the home.[39] Thus in the late nineteenth century tens of thousands of girls and women were employed outside the home for the first time. Again, we have no data on consequent changes in the status of the female workers within the family or on the distribution of domestic and agricultural tasks within the household.

We do not know the causes of this exclusion of male knotters from the workshops founded in late-nineteenth-century Anatolia (and at Hamadan). Whether it resulted from the decisions of the families or of the West European merchants who organized the workshops is uncertain. The contemporary rugmaking industry of the late twentieth century is significant in this context. One of the largest firms presently organizing the hand knotting of rugs in the Middle and Far East employs female knotters at one location, males at another, and females at yet a third. To this company, gender is irrelevant; clearly, the firm has adjusted to prevailing local practices that make both groups available for knotting rugs.

The nineteenth-century growth in the three most important export industries—silk reeling, lacemaking, and carpetmaking—was fueled by European demand and, it seems important to repeat, sustained by a workforce that was overwhelmingly female and poorly paid.

In the textile industries generally, men previously had formed the vast majority of the urban guild weavers. As European competition mounted, these men continued to weave, but for declining wages, contributing relatively less to overall family income through their manufacturing tasks. In many of the industries that were either newly born, or expanding, or successfully adapting to changing conditions, female labor was dominant. This was true of the hand-spun yarn produced in the home and the machine-made yarn produced in factories, of carpet, lace, and raw silk production, and of linen and silk weaving in some areas. The importation of foreign yarn, for its part, relieved many women of spinning tasks and freed them to use this newly available time in more lucrative forms of manufacturing activity. But men as well as women wove, both for the market and for subsistence needs.

The situations examined here seem to support several conclusions concerning Ottoman women, households, and manufacturing. First, as should be obvious by now, women played an integral role in the textile-manufacturing life of the Ottoman Empire, both in the home and in the workshop. Many worked outside the home—Muslim, Christian, and Jewish Ottoman women and girls alike. Certainly this changes our view of day-to-day life in the Ottoman Empire. But does it not also speak to the issue of industrialization itself? Most of the activities recorded here took place not in mechanized factories but rather in small workshops and in households. By tracing women's work back into their homes, we have discovered a universe of manufacturing activity that simply is lost when the focus is on the factory. At the same time, by seeing the (apparently) rising incidence of women's work outside the home, we begin to understand more clearly the magnitude of the nineteenth-century changes. That female labor occupied the very bottom of the wage scale, receiving fractions of their male counterparts' pay, hardly was coincidental. From the poor wages they received we must conclude that women's work was considered supplementary and nonprofessional. But this work was absolutely essential to the survival of the Ottoman textile industries in the nineteenth century, when costs and prices fell steadily. Western market demands may have enhanced the economic importance of the female members of Ottoman households engaged in manufacturing. Finally, many nineteenth-century Ottoman households demonstrated considerable flexibility in the gender division of labor.

In several respects, the conclusions of this chapter have been corroborated by ethnographic research in the modern-day Middle East. A number of recent studies unambiguously demonstrate the vital importance of female labor in the economic survival of the contemporary Turkish village household and so make important links with the Ottoman past. Several of these studies, however, did not find the gender sharing of jobs that seems to have been common in the nineteenth century. Research focusing on villages in the Konya region of central Anatolia, for example, reveals no such sharing today. In general, this group of scholars argues that tasks are rigidly defined as male or female. Further, they observe that women assume new manufacturing responsibilities, men not only allow them to work harder and longer than before but also refuse to assume any additional tasks at home. Nor do these researchers find any enhanced power or status within the household resulting from the increased wage work of modern Turkish women.[40] These conclusions, however, are flatly contradicted by another researcher working on carpetmakers near Ayvalik, in western Anatolia. These workers became involved in carpet production quite recently, as part of a Turkish university's effort to restore the use of natural dyestuffs in the industry. The women and men freely interchange carpetmaking and household-maintenance tasks.[41] Thus places that are physically near to one another differ fundamentally in the gender division of labor. The difference simply may be a matter of variation by location, a phenomenon encountered often enough in the research presented here. Or perhaps ideology is shaping what researchers observe in the contemporary work sites and households. That is, the respective researchers find the gender sharing or gender division of work tasks that they are looking for.

The role of the historical past in transforming the status of contemporary manufacturing women remains uncertain. Is there more or less gender sharing of manufacturing tasks in the Middle East of the 1980s than during the preceding century? The question posed is difficult to address using the historical sources. What was the impact of rising nineteenth-century manufacturing for the marketplace on the status of wage-earning Middle Eastern women and on their family relationships? Did it spark a social reaction whereby men perversely imposed tighter social controls over women whose economic importance was being enhanced? We should expect to see considerable change in the role and status of these manufacturing women over time. After all, during the 1980s the popular classes veiled and secluded women much more than formerly. But whether such trends produced a stricter gender division of labor has not been determined.

This article is reprinted from Nikki R. Keddie and Beth Baron (eds), *Women in Middle Eastern History* (New Haven, 1991), pp. 161–176. Reprinted with permission of Yale University Press.

NOTES

1. David Urquhart, *Turkey and Its Resources* (London: Saunders and Otley, 1833), 47–51, 24.

2. Halil Inalcik, 'Osmanli pamuklu pazari, Hindistan ve Ingiltere: Pazar rekabetinde emek maliyetinin rölü,' *Middle East Technical University, Studies in Development 1979–80*, special issue, 1–65; Public Record Office (London), Foreign Office (hereafter FO) 78, various reports by Brant at Trabzon in the 1830s.

3. Over the period, the population increased at an annual rate of 0.8 per cent; the territorial base of the state, however, steadily shrank. Charles Issawi, ed., *The Economic History of Turkey, 1800–1914* (Chicago: University of Chicago Press, 1980), 11.

4. Justin McCarthy, 'Age, Family and Migration in the Black Sea Provinces of the Ottoman Empire,' *International Journal of Middle East Studies* 10 (1979): 309–23; McCarthy, *Muslims and Minorities: The Population of Anatolia and the End of the Empire* (New York: New York University Press, 1983), 110–11; FO, *Further Reports from Her Majesty's Diplomatic and Consular Agents Abroad Respecting the Condition of the Industrial Classes and Purchasing Power of Money in Foreign Countries* (London: Harrison and Sons, 1871).

5. Alan Duben, 'Turkish Families and Households in Historical Perspective,' *Journal of Family History* 10 (Spring 1985): 75–97; Duben, 'Muslim Households in Late Ottoman Istanbul'

(unpublished paper, 1986); Judith E. Tucker, 'Marriage and Family in Nablus, 1720–1856: Toward a History of Arab Marriage,' *Journal of Family History* 13, no. 2 (1988): 165–79; Tucker in Nikki R. Keddie and Beth Baron (eds.), *Women in Middle Eastern History* (New Haven: Yale University Press, 1991).

6. Halil Inalcik, 'Bursa,' *Encyclopaedia of Islam*, 2d ed. (Leiden: E. J. Brill, 1960), 1:1333–36; Hatt-i hümayun no. 16757, 1225/1810, Başbakanlik Arşivi (hereafter BBA).

7. Consular Reports of the United States, Department of State, National Archives, Washington, D.C. (hereafter CRUS), reel TI94R. no. 2, Schwaabe at Brousse 1 Oct. 1847; Régis Delbeuf, *Une excursion à Brousse et à Nicée* (Istanbul, 1906), 140 note 1, 142, 166–69; author's interview with Rana Akdiş Akay at Bursa, June 1986; cf. wages and prices cited in Issawi, ed., *Economic History*, 44–45, and FO 78/905, Sandison at Bursa, 6 Aug. 1852. For a fuller account, see Donald Quataert, 'The Silk Industry of Bursa, 1880–1914,' *Collection Turcica III: Contribution à l'histoire économique et sociale de l'Empire Ottoman* (Paris: Peeters, 1983), 481–503.

8. Akay 1986 interview; Edward C. Clark, 'The Emergence of Textile Manufacturing Entrepreneurs in Turkey, 1804–1968' (Ph.D. diss., Princeton University, 1969), 34; Roger Owen, 'The Silk-Reeling Industry of Mount Lebanon, 1840–1914,' in *The Ottoman Empire and the World Economy*, ed. Huri Islamoglu-Iran (Cambridge: Cambridge University Press, 1987), 276–77.

9. Quotation is from A. Gündüz Ökçün, trans., *Osmanli sanayii, 1913, 1915 yillari sanayi istatistiki* (Ankara: Ankara Universitesi Sosyal Bilimlez Fakulultesi Yayinlari, 1970), 22; also see CRUS, reel T194R. no. 2, Schwaabe at Bursa, 1 Oct. 1847.

10. Alexander Treshon von Warsberg, *Ein sommer im Orient* (Wien: C. Gerold's Sohn, 1869), 146.

11. See sources cited in note 5, above.

12. See sources in note 5, above. Also see Hüdavendigâr Vilayeti Salnamesi (hereafter VS) 1324/1906, 278; CRUS, reel T194; FO 195/299, Sandison at Bursa, 24 May 1851, 195/393, Sandison at Bursa, 13 Aug. 1855. To reduce labor costs, much of the industry moved out of the city altogether; at the turn of the century, 75 per cent of the mills' productive capacity was situated in towns and villages outside of Bursa. *La revue commerciale du Levant: Bulletin de la chambre de commerce française de Constantinople*, 30 Nov. 1909.

13. The documents consulted for this study often were unhelpful or misleading on the gender identity of the workforce. English- and Turkish-language sources usually refer to *worker* or *isci* without elaboration, only occasionally noting the person's gender. French- and German-language sources designate workers generally as *ouvrier* or *Arbeiter* and sometimes use these masculine forms to refer to workers who, I knew from other sources, were female.

14. Urquhart, *Turkey*, 149–50.

15. Sevket Pamuk, 'The Decline and Resistance of Ottoman Cotton Textiles, 1820–1913,' *Explorations in Economic History* 23 (1986): 205–25.

16. FO 195/459, Holmes at Diyarbakir, 14 Apr. 1857.

17. CRUS, 26 May 1887.

18. Germany, Reichsamt des Innern, *Berichte über Handel und Industrie* (Berlin: Carl Hermanns), I, Heft 9, 10 Aug. 1907.

19. *La revue*, 31 Mar. 1904, Lettre de marache, 30 Mar. 1904.

20. Great Britain, Parliamentary Papers, Accounts and Papers (hereafter A & P), 1899, 103, 6241, Sarell on Constantinople, 1893–97.

21. A&P, 1893–94, 5581, Salonica for 1891–92 (Blunt, 30 Sept. 1893).

22. Austria-Hungary, *Berichte der K. u. K. Österr.-Ung. Konsularämter über das Jahr 1901* (Vienna: Handelsmuseum) (hereafter KK), 1901, vol. 19, p. 1, and for 1902 and 1903; Ministère du Commerce, *Rapports commerciaux des agents diplomatiques et consulaires de France* (Paris, 1883–1914) (hereafter RCC), no. 109 (Mersin for 1892); *Berichte*, 1, Heft 9, 20 Aug, 1907.

23. RCC, no. 76, reel 33, Salonique for 1900, reel 35, Salonique for 1902; *Bulletin du Comité de l'Asie française*, Salonique, 25 juillet 1883. See also A & P, 1893–94, 97, 5581, Salonica for 1891–92 (Blunt, 30 Sept. 1893), 1908, 7253, 17, Salonica for 1907, 7472, 103, Salonica for 1910; *Berichte*, XIX, Heft 6, 18 Apr. 1913; and KK, 1905, vol. 2, p. 6, Salonich.

24. FO 195/774, Sandison at Bursa, 28 May 1864.

25. A & P, 1878–79, Biliotti at Trabzon for 1877–78.

26. FO, *Further Reports*, 797.

27. Ibid., 795.

28. CRUS, reel T681, Jewett at Sivas, 30 June 1893.

29. VS (Aydin) 1307/1891.

30. *Berichte*, Bd. VII, Heft 4, 19 Juli 1904, 300; CRUS, reel T681, Jewett at Sivas, 26 May 1893.

31. FO, *Further Reports*, 743.

32. *Berichte*, Bd. VII, Heft 4, 19 Juli 1904, 274, 301, 306–8. See also A & P, 1878–79, Biliotti at Trabzon for 1877–78.

33. This assumes a *per capita* consumption of 1.8 lbs./0.83 kgs per day at an average price of 1.0 kurus/okke of bread. Donald Quataert, 'Limited Revolution: The Impact of the Anatolian Railway on Turkish Transport and the Provisioning of Istabul, 1890–1908,' *Business History Review* 51, no. 2 (1977): 139–60, *Berichte*, Bd. VII, Heft 4, 19 Juli 1904, 306–8. See, for example, VS (Adana) 1318/1902, S. 188.

34. Cevdet Iktisat no. 52, 6 Za 1241/July 1826, no. 31, 3B 1244/January 1829, no. 694, 6 Za 1244/June 1829, BBA; Mesail-i mühimme Ankara eyaletine dair no. 2073, 1261/1845, BBA.

35. Nikolai Todorov, *The Balkan City, 1500–1900* (Seattle: University of Washington Press, 1983), 228; Salaheddin Bey, *La Turquie à l'exposition universelle 1867* (Paris: Hachette et Cie, 1867), 129; Michael R. Palairet, The Decline of the Old Balkan Woolen Industries, *c.* 1870–1914,' *Vierteljährschrift für Sozial und Wirtschaftsgeschichte* 70 (1983): 331–62.

36. CRUS, reel T681, Jewett at Sivas, 22 July 1888.

37. Nikki Keddie to author, 4 Oct. 1988.

38. *Uşak il yïllïğï* (Istanbul, 1968), 269; A. Cecil Edwards, *The Persian Carpet: A Survey of the Carpet-Making Industry of Persia* (London: G. Duckworth, 1953), 28, 59–60, 201. Further east, in the mid-twentieth century, Indian men also were commonly employed as knotters of commercially made rugs.

39. For a fuller account of the carpet industry, see Donald Quataert, 'Machine Breaking and the Changing Carpet Industry of Western Anatolia, 1860–1908,' *Journal of Social History* 11 (Spring 1986): 473–89, and sources therein; and Edwards, *Persian Carpet*, 90–91.

40. Günseli Berik, 'From "Enemy of the Spoon" to Factory: Women's Labor in the Carpet Weaving Industry in Rural Turkey' (paper presented at the annual meeting of the Middle East Studies Association, New Orleans, La., 22–26 Nov. 1985); Berik, 'Invisible Carpet Weavers: Women's Income Contribution in Rural Turkey,' Nilufer Isvan-Hayat, 'Rural Household Production and the Sexual Division of Labor: A Research Framework,' and E. Miné Çinar, 'Disguised Employment—The Case of Female Family Labor in Agriculture and Small Scale Manufacturing in Developing Countries; the Case of Turkey' (papers presented at the annual meeting of the Middle East Studies Association, Boston, 20–23 Nov. 1986).

41. Josephine Powell, 'The Role of Women' (paper presented at a symposium on village life and village rugs in modern Turkey, Georgetown University, Washington, D.C., 1987. Similarly, there is considerably disagreement among European historians concerning gender roles in rural manufacturing. See the works by Gay Gullikson, Hans Medick, and Jean Quataert.

Said Bey—The Everyday Life of an Istanbul Townsman at the Beginning of the Twentieth Century

P. DUMONT

We have but scanty information on the *curriculum vitae* of Said Bey. We do not know when he was born. We know that his father, Hakki Pasha, was Minister of the privy purse of the Sultan.[1] We also know that he had completed his secondary education at the Imperial College of Galatasaray, that his knowledge of French was perfect and that at the beginning of the twentieth century he was a member of the Superior Health Council at Istanbul and acted as a Palace translator, one of his functions being to turn detective stories into Turkish for Abdulhamid II. We are aware that he taught commercial French at the School of Commerce and—a final string to his bow—that he lectured on the art of translation at Galatasaray. Such are the only indications we have on his career and they are confirmed by the data provided by the official yearbooks of the Ottoman Empire.[2] His descendants, when questioned, could give us no further details.

But strangely enough, while we have practically no information about the broad outline of this man's life, we do know a great deal about the large and small events that constituted the everyday texture of his existence in the first years of the present century. As a matter of fact, the descendants of Said Bey have preserved six blue almanacs, published by Hachette, corresponding to the years 1901, 1902, 1904, 1906, 1908 and 1909, in which their owner noted day by day, on pages reserved for this purpose, everything that he considered to be of significance: meals taken at a restaurant, walks, meetings with friends, hours spent at the office, etc. He also jotted down his various daily expenses.

Thus, for instance, Said Bey gives the following account of the way he spent Wednesday, January 1902:

> Ticaret Mektebine. Nezleyim. Kalpakçılar başında ta'âm. Ma'ârife. Sirri ve Celal Beylerle. Bizim çocuklarla Fen Mektebi için mülakat. Nigârzade Feridun Beyle yayan indik Sıhhiye'ye. On bir buçuk Galata'da Arif Bey ve Zitterer Efendi ile rakı. Unkapanı Köprüsünden yayan. Eve kira beygiri ile birde. Hanım sinirlerinden muztarib. Gündüz Hanım Semiramis'la tramvayla Beyoğluna gitmişler. (At the School of Commerce. I have a cold. Lunch at Kalpakçılar başı. To the Directorate of Education. With Sirri Bey and Celal Bey. Conversation with our young people about the School of Sciences. Went on foot with Nigârzade Feridun Bey to the Health Directorate. At 11.30, rakı in Galata with Arif Bey and Mr Zitterer. On foot across the bridge of Unkapan. At one o'clock, home on a hired horse. Madame suffers from nerves. During the day, Madame went with Semiramis by tram to Beyoğlu.)

Then follows the list of daily expenses:

4 / kuruş /	masarif-i rahiyye
5	ta'am
20	Gardiyan Halil Ağaya
12	Konsomasyon
40	Lûgat Fransizcadan Türkçeye
10	Çocuklara şeker
12	Hanımın masarif-i rahiyyesine
4	Çocuklara bebek
5	Ekmek

(4/piastres/	Transport
5	Lunch
20	to the guardian Halil Aga
12	drinks
40	Dictionary, French-Turkish
10	Sweets for children
12	Transport expenses for Madame
4	Doll for the children
5	Bread)

This example, taken absolutely at random, shows that the document in question is in no way a diary or a text with a claim to literary merits. All Said Bey wanted to do was to mark down in his notebook, day by day, in a brief telegraphic style, various items that he came across, his object being simply to remember the occupations that filled his time. The diary contains no philosophical dissertations, no colourful descriptions of people or social groups with which our man was in constant contact, not a single comment on political events that were hitting the headlines. Said Bey's almanacs contain only bare enumerations of everyday facts and an inventory of daily expenses. Nevertheless, in spite of their curtness, these notebooks are of exceptional interest. First of all, there is no doubt that by meticulously keeping track of all family expenses—from the daily purchase of bread for some 3 or 4 piastres to the cost of repairs to his house, with mention, in passing, of the amounts paid for the setting in shape of his fez, for purchases of candy for his children, for his wife's slippers, for a nut-cracker, a bottle of cognac and a revolving bookcase, without forgetting the everyday expenses for food and transport—Said Bey provides us with very precise knowledge of an Istanbul household budget and enables us to analyse its structure and to follow its fluctuations throughout a period of seven years. But his agendas have also the merit of informing us with just as great a precision on the way of life of an Ottoman official at the beginning of the century. Said Bey wanted to preserve not only the recollection of his peregrinations through the town (which permits us to acquire an idea of the daily geography of a man in his position) but also of his professional occupations, of moments spent with his family and, especially, of his spare-time activities, for he certainly possessed—like many Istanbul dwellers of the bygone and present days—a great sense of conviviality. As a result, we find in his almanacs information that exists nowhere else except maybe in some realistic novels of the end of the nineteenth century.

There will be no mention in this paper of the data concerning Said Bey's family budget, for that aspect has been already presented and analysed by François Georgeon (with whom we have collaborated with regard to the present study) at the CIEPO symposium held in Tunis in September 1982.[3] We will therefore dwell here only on the 'everyday' topics. Our aim is not to describe in detail the day-by-day existence of an Ottoman official but to try and detect by means of Said Bey's notes (we have taken into consideration only those bearing on the year 1902, which he kept with particular regularity) some of the general characteristics of the way of life of this man who seems to have represented well enough a certain social stratum.

1 THE TIMETABLE

When looking through Said Bey's notes, one is impressed by the meticulousness with which he accounts for the use he makes of the time at his disposal. We might be led to think that we are dealing with a real maniac of the clock. Said Bey notes practically every day, hour by hour, the exact time when he leaves the house, when he arrives at the office or school, when he goes out to lunch. Neither does he forget to note the time when he comes home, when he goes out for a drink of rakı with his friends or the time when he goes to the theatre.

Sure enough, it is a lucky obsession, common to those who are tempted to fix on paper the flitting time. It gives us the possibility of figuring out precisely enough the way in which Said Bey spent his days and hours.

Let us first examine the time devoted to his professional life. As stated

	School of Commerce	Galatasaray Lyceum	Health Council
Monday	2 hours		2 hours
Tuesday		2 hours	2 hours
Wednesday	3 hours		2 hours
Thursday		3 hours	2 hours
Friday			
Saturday			3½ hours
Sunday			

above, Said Bey was engaged in activities belonging to three types. In the first place, he was a member of the Superior Health Council—an institution created in 1838 by order of Mahmud II. Its task was to organize throughout the country struggle against and prevention of infectious disease.[4] It is from the Directorate of Sanitary Affairs that Said Bey drew the main bulk of his salary. But he was also a Palace translator and taught French and the art of translation at the Imperial College of Galatasaray and at the School of Commerce.

It would not seem that his function as Sultan's translator occupied much of Said Bey's time. There is no mention of it in his notes of 1902: we merely see that he goes from time to time to the Yıldız Palace to receive his salary. As to the rest of the time devoted to professional duties, we know, thanks to his agenda, how it was scheduled. The table above summarizes the information at our disposal for autumn and winter.

As we see, Said Bey devoted ten hours a week to teaching. They were all morning hours, grouped on Monday, Tuesday, Wednesday and Thursday. In the afternoon, he went to the Superior Health Council where he spent about eleven and a half hours a week.

Consequently, Said Bey assigned about 21 to 22 hours to his professional life. To this should be added eventually the hours taken up by translations for the Palace, by preparation for lessons and by correction of students' papers. But there is no trace of such tasks in the agenda.

As to the time spent at the Superior Health Council, it is difficult to ascertain whether it involved really active work, or merely hours of attendance. The commission of which Said Bey was a member met only from time to time, when an epidemic broke out in some region of the Empire or if there was some urgent problem at hand.[5] It is probable enough that Said Bey merely put in an appearance at the Directorate of Sanitary Affairs. As a matter of fact, his notes often mention conversations or discussions with one or another of his friends during the office hours. This goes to prove that he probably did not spend much time doing actual work.

After an inventory of the everyday activities of Said Bey, undeniably one gets the impression that his job at the Sanitary Directorate was but a sinecure. There is also reason to believe that his tasks as teacher were not too cumbersome. As a matter of fact, we feel that we are dealing with one of those idle officials whom one often meets in the Turkish literature of the second half of the nineteenth century and the beginning of the twentieth, who, if novelists are to be believed, spent days on end drinking tea, sharpening pencils and conversing with their friends and colleagues at the office. When reading Said Bey's notes we cannot refrain from thinking of Mansur, the hero of *Turfanda mı, yoksa Turfa mı?* ('The new or the strange?'), who, like Said Bey, combined teaching jobs with a post in one of Istanbul's ministries and who suffered greatly from the sense of idleness in his professional life.[6] Said Bey also reminds us greatly of Bihruz Bey, a young bureaucrat sketched by Recaizade Mahmut Ekrem in *Araba Sevdası* ('Love of carriage') who seemed to spend much more time riding in a carriage than doing paperwork in some office or other.

Are we to believe then, on the basis of Said Bey's case, that the Ottoman bureaucracy was dedicated only to drinking tea throughout office hours and engaging in light conversation?

It would certainly be inaccurate to draw so general a conclusion from, as sole basis, the notes made by one man. Nevertheless, it is rather significant that Said Bey should resemble so greatly the profile sketched by literary authors. This type of bureaucrat must have recurred often enough to make the novelists' creations credible.

Let us now examine how the hours free from work are being made use of. It is clear enough that such hours occupy a significant part in Said Bey's life. Since his occupations—teaching and office—did not take up much of his time, Said Bey was in a position to reserve a good part of the day to leisure, contacts with friends, and conviviality.

We give below an example of the main activities filling up his leisure hours according to the notes going from 11 to 17 February. It should be noted that the period in question is particularly slack as far as social and festive events are concerned. Other parts of the year—in particular the month of Ramazan and summer-time—are much better provided for in this respect.

Monday, 11 February	– Midday meal at the bazaar
	– Muhallebi
	– Narghile at Direkler Arası
	– Visit to neighbours in the evening
	– Show of Meddah
Tuesday, 12 February	– Midday meal at Yani's
	– Rakı at Sirkeci
Wednesday, 13 February	– Midday meal at Tokatlıyan
	– Visit to neighbours in the evening

Thursday, 14 February	– Midday meal at Yani's
	– In the evening, Karagöz show
Friday, 15 February	– Çalgılı Gazino (café-concert)
Saturday, 16 February	– Confectioner's at Pera
	– Rakı at Tokatlıyan
	– Rakı again
	– Visit to Seyfeddin Bey
	– Greek carnival at Beyoğlu
Sunday, 17 February	– Arifiye kıraathanesi
	– Arab Çalgısı (Arab music)
	– Karagöz show in the evening

The above is but a small sample range in which we find however the enumeration of most of the entertainments with which Said Bey filled his idle hours.

First and foremost there are meals, at midday and in the evening, taken generally either at Yani's—a fashionable restaurant in Beyoğlu—or at the Tokatlıyan hotel which, with the Pera Palas, counted as one of the most select hotels of the time.[7]

It must be underlined that these meals were not aimed merely at the satisfaction of hunger. We note that Said Bey was accompanied on these occasions by one or several friends so that mealtime was also a time of relaxation and entertainment.

Another constant element in Said Bey's schedule is a glass of rakı either in a meyhane in Galata—a favoured district for spare-time activities at the beginning of the twentieth century—or in the vicinity of Sirkeci station, or else again at the Tokatlıyan hotel, as well as somewhere else in town. The daily drink before returning home provides Said Bey with another opportunity for meeting his friends, all of them men. It is clear that segregation by sexes is as yet strongly implanted in twentieth-century Turkey. True, from time to time Said Bey goes out with his wife and children but his hours of freedom are mainly devoted to meetings with men friends and his intense conviviality is exercised practically always in exclusively male company.

Other frequent activities of Said Bey are visits to the confectioner's, generally of the Western style (he goes there either with his friends or with members of his family) and—within a completely different context—sessions with the Narghile [water pipe], generally in the Direkler arası district, another leisure haunt of Istanbul, situated in the neighbourhood of Şehzadebaşı, where there was an impressive concentration of tearooms (çayhane) and 'reading rooms' (kıraathane) where men could relax and smoke the narghile.

Besides these virtually daily manifestations of conviviality—meals with friends, drinks of rakı, narghile—the notes of Said Bey dwell on other ways of whiling away idle hours: visits to neighbours, mostly after the evening meal, invitations to dinner, periodical sessions at the hairdresser's (a preferred spot for random conversation), walks through shopping streets often with the intention of buying clothes and—above all—rides in a carriage. The first almanacs at our disposal constantly refer to the carriage, and it is evident that this means of conveyance—which allows one to exhibit oneself in public and is a sign of a certain social standing—gives Said Bey the same thrill as to Bihruz Bey, the hero of *Araba Sevdası*. When financial difficulties will force Said Bey to sell his carriage, this will be a sure sign of his social decline.

Finally, there is the immense sector of all kinds of shows. In a single week—our specimen indicated above (11–17 February)—Said Bey lists five evenings devoted to show going: on Monday he saw a meddah (a narrator executing what we now would call a 'one-man show'), on Thursday he attended the Karagöz (shadow theatre), on Friday he went to a café-concert (Çalgılı gazino), on Saturday he saw a Greek carnival in the streets of Beyoğlu and finally, on Sunday, he went to a hall which seems to have specialized in Arab music (arab çalgısı). The week of 11–17 February is in no way an exceptional one. It would seem that the rhythm of Said Bey's outings is practically the same, week in week out. Besides the meddah, the karagöz and the Turkish café-concerts, he diligently attends the orta oyunu, a kind of improvised theatre, approaching in its technique the commedia dell'arte but typically Turkish in inspiration. He also goes to the theatre to see plays of Western type. From time to time, his notes mention opera and balls.

All in all, in view of the important role played in his life by spare-time activities, Said Bey reminds us more than once of the idlers and connoisseurs of social events whom one often meets in Turkish literature at the end of the last century. Fashionably dressed, a diligent visitor to the hairdresser, spending much of his time in rides through the town in a carriage, in attending show-rooms and café-concerts, in eating and drinking, we might say that he has a semblance of an Ottoman-style dandy. His bow lacks but one string: gambling. In 1902, cards are never mentioned in his notes. But a little later he speaks several times of his losses at cards. This completes the perfect profile of a man-about-town.

It should be noted that novels usually describe Ottoman dandies as completely westernized: they speak only French and attend assiduously French and Italian theatres of Beyoğlu as well as Embassy balls. Said Bey possesses all these characteristics. He speaks and reads French fluently, haunts all the auditoriums of Beyoğlu and has many members of ambassadorial staff among his acquaintances. But the remarkable thing is that his tastes remain, notwithstanding all this, genuinely Ottoman. The Karagöz, the meddah and the orta oyunu are mentioned more frequently in his notes than the Western-style plays. It is also evident that he prefers the çayhane and places where he can smoke the narghile to the confectioner's shops where he puts in an appearance from time to time. Turkish music (the so-called çalgı and şarkı) appeals to him more than Western concerts. It is interesting to note in this respect that he had among his friends some of the great Turkish composers of the beginning of the twentieth century—the famous Lemʿi Bey among them.

Thus, with regard to the use he makes of his free time, Said Bey appears as a man of synthesis. He is Western-orientated where fashion and certain customs are concerned, but remains nevertheless attached to the many specific features of his own culture. In other words, he appears as a perfect native of Istanbul. A citizen of an urban bridge between East and West, he has been nurtured in two cultures and passes to and fro, from the one to the other according to the whims of the moment and his peregrinations through the sprawling city.

2 SEASONAL VARIATIONS

As already stated, the week 11–17 February corresponds in the life of Said Bey to a rather slack period. His agendas allow us to detect clear-cut variations in the use he made of his time according to different seasons of the year.

In particular, Said Bey and the other members of his family spend considerable time buying new clothes at certain moments. These periodical purchases are generally made either a few days before the principal religious holidays—the Kurban Bayramı (Feast of the Sacrifice) and the Şeker Bayramı (Feast of Sweetmeats)—or at the approach of a new season. The beginning of spring, of summer and of winter are the periods when Said Bey's family proceeds to massive purchases, with no expense spared.

As an example, we are giving below a list of clothes purchases preceding the Feast of Sacrifice in 1902, indicating also the various activities pertaining to these acquisitions.

Friday, 1 March	– purchase of cloth for an overcoat
	– visit to the tailor
Saturday, 2 March	– purchase of neckties
	– clothes brush
	– sewing needles
Sunday, 3 March	– trying on the overcoat
Monday, 4 March	– trying on the overcoat
	– cloth for çarşaf
	– lining
	– ribbons
	– clothes for children
	– festoons
	– silk lining
Tuesday, 5 March	– veil for Said Bey's daughter
	– ribbons for children

Thursday, 7 March	– men's gloves
Friday, 8 March	– umbrella (or parasol)
	– aprons for children
	– hair buckles
	– cloth for children's coats
	– cloth (present)
	– neckties

After this date, vestimentary purchases stop and will be taken up again with redoubled energy at the end of March and beginning of April: aprons, handkerchiefs, shoes, cloth, suits, scarves, dresses, ribbons, shirts, socks, etc.

But even more than these purchases and other seasonal activities of the same type, it is the transfer to a summer resort that influences the rhythm of Said Bey's existence.

Said Bey is one of these fortunate people who have the possibility to leave the town every year and go to a summer resort situated nearby. He is not rich enough to have his own summer köşk and therefore rents a place, either at the Princes' Islands (Büyükada), or on the Asian shore of the Bosphorus, or else in the regions of Moda and Fenerbahçe.

In 1902, Said Bey moves to his summer resort on 12 April and returns from there on 14 October, which means that his sojourn there had lasted six whole months. It is not a simple holiday move as is practised now, but a real departure to the resort, with part of the furniture moved from the winter house and all the domestic staff following in the wake of the master.

The summer migration is distinguished mainly by the expansion of time allocated to leisure and convivial activities. From the beginning of June, the Galatasaray College and the School of Commerce have closed their doors for the whole summer season so that Said Bey no longer has teaching tasks to perform. All that remains for him is to attend—more rarely than in winter—his office at the Sanitary Directorate.

Under the circumstances, he can devote even more time than in winter to drinks of rakı, to meetings with his friends, to the Karagöz and orta oyunu, to the theatre and music. Furthermore, he pursues typically seasonal activities: he takes frequent sea-baths, sails in a boat, and from time to time goes for day-long excursions to some other place. Occasionally, his agenda mentions some 'curious' activity such as bicycle riding. But above all we find in his summer notes descriptions of real Istanbul and Mediterranean pastimes. Thus, he states that several times at nightfall, he and his family enjoy the cool of the evening at their doorstep, adding the sensations of the fresh night air to all the olfactory, auditory and visual pleasures of the summer resort darkness. On full-moon nights these simple nocturnal outings become more sophisticated: Said Bey takes his family for walks along the shore or they make excursions in a boat the better to enjoy the reflection of the sky in the murmuring sea waters.

As already stated, the summer/winter break was the most important one in the annual cycle of Said Bey's life. However, one cannot fail to notice how profoundly the rhythm of our man's life was also affected by the religious calendar. Doubtless Said Bey was not a very pious man. In 1902, while he scrupulously notes all his rakı sessions, never once does he mention a visit to a mosque. Nevertheless, both he and his family scrupulously observed all the religious holidays and also, incidentally, certain public holidays, such as the anniversary of the Sultan's accession to the throne and, after 1908, the anniversary of the advent of the Young-Turk regime.

Thus, for instance, his family—as becomes people belonging to a relatively high stratum of society—never failed to prepare the aşure on the tenth day of the month of Muharrem, commemorating both the creation of man by God and the death of Hüseyin, one of the Prophet's descendants.

Likewise, Said Bey and his family regularly took part in the festivity of the Hıdırellez, a half-Muslim and half-pagan holiday, at the beginning of May, celebrating the advent of spring and the triumph over death of everything that grows and lives.

We have also seen the important part played by the Kurban Bayramı in the life of the family. Not only did Said Bey prepare the celebration of this feast by bulk purchases of clothes but he dealt also with the great business of the moment: the purchase of animals to be sacrificed, the negotiations with a butcher who was to effect the sacrifice and, finally, the distribution of meat to the poor.

But naturally, the element of the religious calendar that had the most spectacular impact on the life of Said Bey was the month of Ramazan, with its sumptuous nocturnal meals, its *ad hoc* shows and all kinds of festivities. All through the month, we find in Said Bey's accounts the mention of 'night expenses' (gece masarifi), with amounts rising to 40 piastres. Very often we see there mention made of the meal at the end of the fast (iftar) in which Said Bey was sometimes joined by up to ten friends. And there are also traditional Karagöz theatre shows, showmen, meddah, sessions of songs and dances in cafés, etc. As outlined by the notes of Said Bey, the atmosphere of the month of Ramazan at the beginning of the twentieth century seems to have been (at least for Said Bey and his friends and relatives) rather similar to what travellers such as Gérard de Nerval had described with amusement and surprise some sixty years earlier.

It can finally be said that, just as Said Bey had a way of life typical of an Istanbul dweller, so he also conformed strictly enough to local customs in the organization of annual cycles. True, not everybody in Istanbul could afford six months at a summer resort with boating excursions by moonlight. Also at the Feast of the Sacrifice there were those who could sacrifice animals and those who could only eat the meat that was offered to them. As to the

Ramazan festivities, while everybody awaited with impatience the evening meal, there were few who could invite ten friends practically every night to their table. The schedule of Said Bey, such as it appears in his almanacs, is certainly a 'typical' one—but typical of only a certain social stratum, that of reasonably rich families.

3 THE FEMININE PATTERN OF TIME

The notes taken by Said Bey bear essentially, as one might expect, on his own activities. As he spent most of his time outside, he could not be sure of what his wife and children were doing in his absence. Nevertheless, Said Bey was a very attentive—if not a jealous—husband. He frequently indicates in his agenda—probably after having consulted his wife—the most important events of the day where other members of his family were concerned. Thanks to his curiosity, we are informed well enough about his wife's activities.

It must first of all be pointed out that she could not have devoted much time to housekeeping because she was assisted by several servants. It would seem that at home she took part only in works that needed a special know-how, as for instance the cooking of aşure. Her occupations consisted mainly of supervising the work of the cook, of the maid and of other servants. That is to say that she had a lot of free time on her hands—even more so than Said Bey. And if Said Bey seems to be modelled on the heroes of social novels from the end of the nineteenth century, his wife closely resembles the idle heroines described by most of the authors of the time (in particular by Mehmet Rauf and Hüseyin Rahmi Gürpınar).

Rare are the days when she does not go out for some visit or other convivial activity, unless she receives visitors herself. Here for instance is her schedule for the week of 14–20 January 1902:

Monday, 14 January	– Visit to the konak of Ahmed Hikmet Bey
Tuesday, 15 January	– Visit to the house of Mazhar Bey
Wednesday, 16 January	– Visit to the candy confectioner, Muhiddin Efendi
Thursday, 17 January	– Wedding in the district of Fatih
Friday, 18 January	– Walk in Beyoğlu with family. Purchases at 'Bon Marché' In the afternoon a second walk in Beyoğlu, visits
Saturday, 19 January	– Outing to Çamlıca. Visit to a friend's köşk Theatre at Şehzadebaşı
Sunday, 20 January	– Visit to Hakkı Bey's house in the Pangalti district

We see that Said Bey's wife had a very busy social life. If Said Bey meets friends every day, she, on her side, takes advantage of every opportunity to leave the house and seek out some entertainment.

Her most frequent pastime (as noted by the enumeration of her activities in the week of 14–20 January 1902) consists of visits to other women, mostly neighbours, though sometimes this takes her further from her home, to different districts of the city.

Her other preferred activities—after the visits—are purchases in shops or simply strolls in front of shop-windows. It is generally in Beyoğlu, the most elegant commercial district of Istanbul, that she satisfies her craving for new finery and for all kinds of trinkets, probably conforming in this to the practice in use among her friends. We have seen that Said Bey's consumption of clothes was lavish but that of his wife and children is astounding: ribbons, scarves, silks, veils, taffetas, ornaments and cloth of every kind, without speaking of shoes adapted to the seasons. Doubtless one needed a lot of free time to be able to make all these purchases.

When not paying visits or patronizing shops, Said Bey's wife attended festive occasions, as a rule exclusively in feminine company. Following her husband's example, she rode in a carriage and at certain times of the year participated in out-of-door parties in places where it was 'good form' to be seen: the Çamlıca hill or the Kağıthane meadows. It is in this last resort that she celebrated in 1902 with her friends the Hıdırellez as prescribed by one of the most approved customs of Istanbul.

She sometimes attended theatre or Karagöz shows, but, either because there were but few plays fit for ladies or because she did not particularly relish this kind of entertainment, she devoted much less time than Said Bey to this recreation.

Naturally, as in the case of her husband, her timetable was subject to seasonal variations: in summer-time sea-baths (in a deniz hamamı for women), nocturnal walks and picnics gave a new zest to life. During this season we witness an extension of her convivial activities. Similarly, religious celebrations preceded by a very active phase of preparations—including purchases of clothes and the cooking of special dishes—were also marked by increasing contacts with neighbours and by festive events.

It is interesting to note that at times Said Bey participated in his wife's activities. Thus he sometimes accompanied her on her shopping expeditions of the more important kind. It also happened that he went with her when she was visiting. But more often one is under the impression of witnessing two lives that run on parallel rails and which crossed but accidentally and at certain hours of the day. As a matter of fact, Said Bey's notes draw the image of rather classical relations between opposite sexes in Ottoman society. Said Bey lived in an essentially masculine world and, if he happened to meet women, it was—if we are to believe his notes—only in the presence of his wife. As to the latter, she was confined in a purely feminine universe which she left only in her husband's company.

This was the usual situation at the time in most Istanbul families. It suffices to read some novels to measure the extent to which the segregation between the haremlık and the selamlık—that is between female and male societies—was an admitted state of affairs at the end of the nineteenth century. Doubtless Said Bey saw his wife and spoke to her every day, but it was rare for him to remain for a long time in her company and that of her friends. When this did happen, he spoke of it as of an exceptional event: hanımlarla haremde oturdum ('I sat with the ladies in the harem').

Naturally, some people revolted against this state of things. The most renowned case is that of Halide Edip who strove energetically for equality of the sexes and the emancipation of women at the time when Said Bey was writing his notes. But Halide Edip and the other feminists represent but a very small minority movement which only the intellectuals considered as something serious.

What probably contributed more efficiently at the time to the suppression of the barrier between the world of women and that of men was the gradual introduction into society of vestimentary preferences and of social behaviour imported from the West: the progressive disappearance of a thick veil (replaced by a much lighter one in some cases), visits to the theatre and friends with the wife accompanying the husband, balls (even though the wife danced only with her husband), rides in a carriage in which the wife sat side by side with the husband, purchases made together in department stores—all these were novelties that insidiously made for the advent of a mixed society.

4 THE HOUSE—THE HOUSEHOLD

This extraordinary blend of acceptance of the Western way of life and of attachment to the customs and habits of old appears in the furniture and equipment of Said Bey's house, which represents indisputably a symbol of synthesis that was being enacted.

It is hard to determine the location of Said Bey's home. A careful study of his trips throughout the town points to the fact that the house was situated in the district of Aksaray, where there remain even in our days some very attractive specimens of Ottoman domestic architecture constructed either in wood or in stone.

We have no information whatsoever as to the dimensions of the house or the number of its rooms. On the other hand, we do know that it had a garden and an interior yard, with a stable in one of the corners. We can deduce from this that the house itself was rather big. We also have reason to believe that rooms were distributed in conformity to the classical model of an Istanbul house: haremlık on one side, selamlık on the other. Said Bey mentions on several occasions the harem where he went to meet his wife and, eventually, her friends.

In any case, there is no doubt whatsoever that the house was supplied with all the equipment of modern comfort. At regular intervals Said Bey paid the invoices for water distribution and city gas which served for cooking as well as for the large chandeliers that lit the rooms. After 1908, Said Bey also had dealings with the Electricity Company, and his house was probably among the first in Istanbul to have electric lighting.

Thanks to the indications on the cost of furniture, we get a more or less precise idea as to what his house contained. According to various data in our possession, we can conclude that the modern and occidental was intimately intermingled in it with the traditional furniture of a Turkish house. For instance, in 1902, Said Bey was in the process of paying for a blue stoneware stove, probably imported from France. But at the same time we note that he is purchasing a brazier (mangal) and a kind of little charcoal stove (maltız). We also know that his house contained a mass of Turkish-style sofas, but simultaneously we find among the purchases made by Said Bey several large *canapés*, armchairs, chairs, a pier-table, a European bed (karyola), and also a sewing machine, a phonograph, a telescope, and many other objects such as cases, chandeliers, etc., all aiming to give the house a European style.

The most prestigious piece of furniture of the family, purchased in 1902, was a piano, a perfect symbol of adherence to Western values. This piano was destined for Said Bey's eldest daughter, Semiramis. In the very year when her parents purchased this piano for her, she was also offered her first çarşaf and a whole set of veils. We do not know whether Semiramis ultimately became a good musician, but we see from Said Bey's notes that he was greatly interested in the instrument that had just invaded his home. Everything pertaining to the piano is carefully jotted down: repairs, visits of the tuner, weekly lessons given by a certain Madame Soulier.

It is finally noteworthy that Said Bey's home resembles closely the Turkish house such as it is described in 1902 by the volume of the *Guides-Joanne* devoted to Turkey and which runs as follows:

> All Turkish houses are divided into two distinctive parts: the apartment of men—the selamlık—and that of women—the haremlık. It is in the former only that a Muslim receives visitors, and he is the only man to penetrate into the latter. ... The sector reserved to men is separated from that of women by a long corridor. The first part is furnished only with a few low sofas permanently placed along the walls. In the second are accumulated all the luxuries of the house. For a few years now, European furniture has

> found favour in the richest harems of the capital and the inevitable piano appears already among the obligatory furniture of any person who wants to deserve respect. Cunning forerunner of a social revolution, it has already paved the way of old teachers of music even in the ladies' apartments.[8]

We find in this description all we know about the house of Said Bey: the division of the domestic space into two sectors, if not exclusive to each other then at least accessible to members of the opposite sex only under certain conditions; the double character of the furniture—a sign of a certain cultural duality—and finally, the piano—a most eloquent symbol of aspiration to a bourgeois style of life copied from the Western model. To better mark his adherence to European civilization, Said Bey went so far as to paper some rooms in his house, thus forsaking Turkish customs in matters of wall decoration. Nevertheless, he did not suppress his harem. Whilst eager to lead a European mode of life, on this particularly important element he clung to old Islamic tradition.

Six people—without counting the servants—lived in this house of which we know the principal characteristics: Said Bey, his wife and their children: Vehbi, Semiramis, Seniye and Ferdan. At the end of August 1902, Said Bey notes that Seniye died, apparently of an infection of the tonsils (unless it was diphtheria). A little later a new child, Hakkı, was born. This means that the family dwelling in this house formed a rather modest nucleus. We are very far here from the often-described traditional model of an Ottoman family, uniting several generations under the same roof and admitting polygamy. The notes of Said Bey do mention from time to time a mother-in-law, but the latter lived elsewhere, and every month Said Bey paid the rent of the place where she dwelt. This rather unusual situation must surely be explained by personal reasons of which we are unable to know anything. But in this case also we are entitled to think that, besides these personal reasons, there was simply the influence of the Western family model, the material and moral advantages of which had already been discussed for several generations in Turkish novels, plays and literary magazines.

Although Said Bey's family was of a modest dimension, it had at its disposal an important domestic staff. In the agendas of Said Bey appear regularly: a coachman (arabacı), a cook, an apprentice—functions unknown (çırak)—and a gardener. It also mentions from time to time a lady who must have been dealing with the children's education (hoca hanım) and a Miss (matmazel) who looked after them, a servant (hizmetçı) and a footman (uşak). In the budget of 1904 there is also a wet-nurse (sütnine) and two girls (kız). It is difficult to say whether all this staff was permanently serving the family, but we are led to believe that this family could always count on the presence of three or four servants. This profusion is explained by the fact that in many cases these people worked practically free of charge and were content with food and a little pocket-money. For instance, the two kız that figure in the yearbook of 1904 received 20 piastres per month, that is, barely equivalent to four drinks of rakı. This is doubtless an exceptionally low salary. But the matmazel, the best-paid member of the staff, received only 216 piastres. This means that her income was 54 times less than that of Said Bey.

It would seem that these underpaid servants were of a very poor quality, with no particular qualification. That must be the reason why Said Bey changed them often. Thus, hired on 21 March 1902, Mademoiselle Antoinette will be fired on the 24th of the same month, that is three days later. Coachmen, chosen in the Greek community, and (especially) cooks did not satisfy their master any better. In 1902, within a few months Said Bey changed his cooks ten times without our knowing the reason, but probably simply because they could not cook.

This great quantity of servants—be they of poor quality—allowed Said Bey to keep his position with dignity within the good society of Istanbul. The number of people surrounding him indicated to others his social status. This role was played also by the piano, the carriage and the many other emblems which decorated his life and whose object was to make him appear in the eyes of his circle a worthy son of his class.

Is Said Bey a typical personality or are his notes but a reflection of a purely individual experience? This problem was the guideline of our study. We believe we have definitely solved it. Such as he appears in the light of his court notes, Said Bey is certainly an ideal representative of a certain stratum of Istanbul society. His tastes, the background of his life, his views on family relations, his way of making use of his leisure hours are all constituent elements of a profile that verges on a caricature. He is not only an Istanbul official among others but the very prototype of an official, as though he had stepped out of some nineteenth-century novel.

But there is no reason to doubt that, in common with all men, Said Bey was also endowed with a personality of his own which distinguished him from his brethren. To enable us to detect the personal elements in what we know of Said Bey, we should have had the opportunity to compare his notes with those of others belonging to the same class. Did all officials of his rank fire their cook after he had burnt the food? Did they all possess a telescope in their house? Did they all purchase so many toys for their children? These and many other questions will be answered after we have been given the opportunity to examine agendas, almanacs, diaries, and other old documents, thousands of which are surely preserved in the attics of Istanbul, at the bottom of some trunk, among snapshots yellowed by age and which no one knows whom they are meant to portray.

This article is reprinted from Hans Georg Majer (ed.), *Osmanistische Studien zur Wirtschafts- und Sozialgeschichte. In Memoriam Vančo Boškov* (Wiesbaden, 1986), pp. 1–16. Reprinted with permission of Otto Harrassowitz.

NOTES

1. According to Semih Mümtaz S. Soysal, 'Ramazan Hatıraları', *Akşam*, 31 July 1947, 4.

2. *Salname-i Devlet-i Aliye-i Osmaniye*, 1318 (1902), 74; *Salname-i Maarif*, 1319 (1903), 101.

3. 'Le journal d'un bourgeois d'Istanbul au début du XXe siècle. II. Le budget', paper presented to the 5th symposium of CIEPO, Tunis, 13–18 Sept. 1982.

4. On this institution, see Carter V. Findley, *Bureaucratic Reform in the Ottoman Empire. The Sublime Porte 1789–1922*, Princeton, 1980, 261–262.

5. Daniel Panzac, 'La Peste dans l'Empire Ottoman,' thesis, Aix-en-Provence 1983, 641–660, gives a detailed description of the functioning of this institution.

6. The novel of Mizanci Murad Bey, *Turfanda mı, Yoksa Turfa mı?*, had been published in 1890.

7. See Said Naum-Duhani, Eski *İnsanlar, Eski Evler. XIX. Yüzyılda Beyoğlu'nun Sosyal* Topografyası, Istanbul 1982.

8. *Collection des Guides-Joanne, De Paris à Constantinople*, Paris 1902, 163–164.

The Crowd in the Persian Revolution[1]

ERVAND ABRAHAMIAN

INTRODUCTION

The Constitutional Revolution of 1905–9 was a major watershed in Persian history. It ended the traditional system of government in which the Shah, as the Shadow of God on Earth, ruled his people without any legal and institutional limitations. And it introduced the constitutional system of government in which 'the people' were sovereign, and their elected representatives made and unmade ministers, laws, budgets, concessions and foreign treaties. In this revolution the political crowd played a prominent role.[2] An organized procession in April 1905 raised the issue whether the Shah could freely choose his administrators. A larger assembly, nine months later, initiated the demand to limit the monarch's arbitrary powers by creating a 'House of Justice.' Spontaneous riots in June 1906, and the killing of demonstrators, poured a stream of blood into the wide gap between the government (*dawlat*) and the nation (*millat*). A general strike in July, and the exodus of 15,000 from Tehran into the British Legation, forced the court to grant the country a written constitution with an elected House of Parliament. And mass meetings throughout the next three years, accompanied by demonstrations of force in the streets, helped preserve the constitution from conservatives determined to re-establish royal despotism. As a French contemporary, in discussing the advantages of the Anarchist theory of revolution, argued: 'Events in Persia prove that the general strike and mass action in the streets can produce a successful revolution.'[3]

Although crowds have been important in Persia throughout the ages they have received scant attention from either historians, sociologists, or political scientists. Sympathetic observers have invariably glorified them as 'the people' in action, fighting for country, freedom, and justice.[4] Unsympathetic observers have metamorphosed them into 'mad mobs' hired by foreigners or subversives, and composed of 'vagrants,' 'thugs,' 'riff-raff,' 'professional beggars,' and 'the social scum.'[5] European journalists have often portrayed them as 'xenophobic monsters' hurling insults and bricks at Western embassies. And witty novelists have enjoyed describing them as fickle and humorous swarms making and unmaking politicians.[6] For all the crowd has been an abstraction, whether worthy of praise, fear, disgust, or wit, but not a subject of study.

The aim of this article is to study the political crowd in the Persian Revolution, to outline its role, to see whether it displayed a mentality that was 'singularly inferior,' 'murderous,' 'irrational,' 'destructive,' and 'intolerant,' as Gustave Le Bon's *The Crowd* would have us believe,[7] or whether it was 'remarkably single-minded,' and 'not fickle, peculiarly irrational, or generally given to bloody attacks on persons' as George Rudé's *The Crowd in History* has found to be true for England and France,[8] and to examine its social composition, defining, as far as possible, the different classes and groups that participated in various demonstrations, meetings, riots, and public disturbances. It is hoped that this will throw some light on the social basis of the constitutional movement.

CITIES ON THE EVE OF THE REVOLUTION

In traditional Persia urban life centered around the bazaar. It was there that landowners sold their crops, craftsmen manufactured their goods, tradesmen marketed their wares, borrowers raised loans, and philanthropic businessmen endowed mosques and *maktabs* (traditional schools). The bazaar was, in fact, the granary, the workshop, the marketplace, the bank, the religious nucleus, and the educational center of the whole society. Moreover, each craft, trade, and occupation was tightly structured into *asnaf* (guilds), with their own separate organization, hierarchy, traditions, ceremonies, and sometimes even their own secret dialects. A survey undertaken by the tax collector of Isfahan in 1877 lists two hundred independent guilds.[9] Skilled craftsmen, such as silversmiths, bookbinders, and tailors, numbered half the total. Tradesmen, like grocers, money-landers, and shopkeepers, formed fifty of them. And unskilled workers—laborers, coolies, and bath attendents—made up another fifty.

The political structure of the cities comprised an intricate balance of power between the monarch and the bazaar. Whenever the monarch was powerful, he nominated the guild *kadkhudas* (heads) and his appointees—such as the *Shaykh al-Islams* (the highest religious authority in the cities), the *Imam Jum'ahs* (the minister of the Friday mosques), the *kalantars* (the overseer of the guilds), and the *mushtasibs* (the officer in charge of weights and measures, prices, and the general affairs of the bazaar)—dominated urban life. Whenever he was weak, the guild masters elected their own elders, and the *Mujtahids*—religious authorities with no ties to the government but with close ties to the business community—exerted their independence and functioned as rivals of the political establishment.

In this balance of power, each side had one main weapon: the tribes and the streets. The monarch, having no police, bureaucracy, and standing army, could terrorize the bazaar community only by using the threat of hired tribesmen invading and plundering the city. And the bazaar community, having no legal channels, could safeguard its interests only by petitions, demonstrations, and the taking of *bast* (sanctuary) in holy places, royal lands, and foreign grounds immune from the local authorities. Thus, negotiations between the government and the bazaar often took the form of bargaining by assembly.

By the end of the nineteenth century, the balance of power had swung far in favor of the bazaar. The guilds were choosing their own *kadkhudas*. The *kalantar* had lost much of his importance. And the *muhtasib* had disappeared in many cities. Moreover, the impact of the West further widened the gulf between the monarch and the bazaar. The Qajar dynasty, crushed repeatedly in foreign wars, lost its legitimacy as the protector of all Shi'ahs. Deprived of crown lands by the Russians, it could no longer hire tribesmen at will. In dire need of loans, it turned to European creditors and in return granted unpopular monopolies, concessions, and capitulations. Forced to accept some programs of Westernization to survive in the age of imperialism, the court, on the one hand, alienated the conservative religious authorities and, on the other hand, unconsciously permitted the subversive doctrine of 'Divine Rights of Man' to undermine the accepted 'Divine Right of Kings.' And unable to defend home industries from the onslaught of imported manufacturers, it lost its aura as the protector of the people and appeared as a corrupt family partaking in the plunder and destruction of the country.

By the beginning of the twentieth century, the Qajars had become Oriental despots with high claims but with feet of clay. A bad harvest, and a small trade crisis, caused by the distant Russian–Japanese War, was enough to expose the basic weakness of the regime and to bring it crashing down.

THE CONSTITUTIONAL CROWD, APRIL 1905–JUNE 1907

Inflation struck in early 1905. *Habl al-Matin* (The Firm Clarion), a newspaper published in Calcutta but popular among merchants and liberals in Tehran, claimed that the price of wheat rose by 90 per cent, and that of sugar by 33 per cent.[10] It put the blame entirely on Monsieur Naus, the Belgian who had been appointed Director of Tariffs.

The first crowd of the Constitutional Revolution appeared in April 1905. It took the form of an orderly procession of money-lenders and cloth-merchants delivering a letter of protest to the government. The money-lenders sought payment on the loans they had advanced to the State Treasury two years earlier. The merchants objected that the new trade policies were favoring Russian traders against Persians, and demanded the immediate removal of Naus. One of the demonstrators gave the views of his group to the correspondent of *Habl al-Matin*: 'The government must encourage home industries, even if their products are not as good as foreign manufactures. Otherwise, the present policy of helping Russian traders will inevitably lead to the utter destruction of our industry and commerce.'[11] Receiving no satisfaction from the government, the petitioners closed their shops in the bazaar, distributed a photograph of Naus masquerading as a mulla at a fancy-dress party; and, led by a prominent shopkeeper and a wealthy scarf-dealer, took sanctuary in 'Abd al-'Azim Mosque outside Tehran. They remained there for five days, until the Crown Prince, Muhammad 'Ali Mirza, promised that Naus would be dismissed as soon as Muzaffar al-Din Shah returned from his European tour.

The monarch conveniently forgot this promise when he returned. As a compromise he appointed a committee of fifteen merchants with the vague responsibility of 'advising' the Trade Ministry on major decisions of policy.[12]

The streets remained quiet until the religious month of Ramazan. An eloquent and vehement preacher, speaking to a mass audience in the Tehran bazaar, took the occasion to attack by name the Russian Discount and Loan Bank, which had recently bought a religious school and a cemetery nearby and was preparing to expand its premises. He stressed that the Russians were planning not only the destruction of Muslim trade and finance, but also of Muslim schools and cemeteries. One eye-witness claims that an angry crowd of a few thousand demolished the bank before the preacher finished his sermon.[13] The merchants competing against foreign rivals, and the *'ulama'* (religious leaders) preaching against the heathen, had found common enemies: the Russians and their royalist collaborators.

These two groups took to the streets again in December, when the Governor of Tehran tried to lower the price of sugar by bastinadoing two prominent merchants, one of whom had built three mosques in Tehran. The victims in vain pleaded that the Russian–Japanese War had caused a shortage of sugar.[14] An observer wrote that the news of the beatings 'flashed like lightning into the arcades and the bazaars.'[15] A group of merchants closed their shops and took refuge in Masjid Shah Mosque at the side of the bazaar. There they were joined by Sayyid Jamal al-Din Isfahani, an eloquent and liberal preacher, and by three well-respected religious leaders: Sayyid 'Abdullah Bihbihani, Sayyid Muhammad Tabataba'i, and Shaykh Fazlallah. The following day, Jamal al-Din, speaking from the pulpit, asked the Shah to prove his religious sincerity by cooperating with the *'ulama'*. At this point, the *Imam Jum'ah* interrupted, denounced him as a Babi, and ordered his servants to clear the pulpit. The meeting broke up in commotion. Some of the religious leaders retired to Sayyid Bihbihani's home, where he warned that if they continued their protest within the city 'the common people' would identify them too closely with the sugar merchants.[16] He recommended the taking of sanctuary in 'Abd al-'Azim mosque. Seven of the leading *'ulama'*, together with their families, students, and servants, totaling two thousand, took his advice. Although they permitted only a handful of merchants to join them, the bazaar organized a general strike and demonstrated in front of the monarch's carriage, demanding the return of their religious leaders. From 'Abd al-'Azim they sent the government an eight-point proposal. The chief demands were: the formation of a 'House of Justice'; the enforcement of religious laws; the removal of Naus; and the dismissal of the Governor. They remained in sanctuary a whole month, until the Shah acceded to their demands. When they returned to Tehran they were greeted by large crowds lining the streets shouting 'Long live the Nation of Iran.' One participant commented that this was the first public mention of 'the nation'.[17]

Again the promises were made only to be broken. Again calm returned to the streets of Tehran. And again the calm was broken by a sudden storm, this time more violent and effective than before. In July, the government, feeling confident, ordered the immediate but quiet arrest of a prominent anti-court preacher. A passerby noticed the unannounced arrest, reported it to a school in the bazaar, and the students rushed to rescue the prisoner.[18] The officer in custody of the jail ordered his men to shoot. When they refused, he himself fired, killing one student. This turned the demonstration into a riot. The students charged the building, fought with the soldiers, routed them, and freed the prisoner. The riot then subsided into an orderly procession, carrying the body to an adjacent mosque. The bazaars closed. The leading *'ulama'*, with their large following, took sanctuary in the same mosque and demanded the dismissal of the chief minister. And the streets of the bazaar 'filled' with men wearing winding-sheets, to show that they were ready to fight to the death.[19] The government met, rejected the demand made by the *Mujtahids*, and decided to use force. So the following day, when a procession of mullas, students, and tradesmen, carrying a pole with the blood-stained shirt of the demonstrator, tried to make its way through the streets of the bazaar, the soldiers fired.[20] Although the number of casualties remained unknown, with some claiming that as many as 100 were wounded, only two bodies were rescued by the demonstrators, those of a preacher and a merchant. This use of force cleared the demonstrators off the streets but, at the same time, increased the resistance of the demonstrators in the mosque. They remained there four days without food and surrounded by troops, until they were permitted to retire to the holy city of Qum outside Tehran, on the condition that they were not to be accompanied by 'the people'. As they departed from the capital, they declared that the country would be left without religious guidance and legal transactions until the Shah dismissed his chief minister and introduced political reforms. The *'ulama'* had gone on strike.

The British Legation, in a detailed memorandum for the Foreign Office in London, described the events that followed:

> It appeared as if the Government had won the day. The town was in the hands of the troops. The popular leaders had fled. The bazaars were in the occupation of the soldiers. And there appeared to be no place of refuge. Under these circumstances the popular party had recourse to an expedient sanctified by old, and, indeed, immemorial custom—the rule of *bast*. It was resolved, failing all other resources, to adopt this expedient ... on 18 July, two persons called at the Legation at Gulahek, 7 miles from town, and asked whether, in case the people took *bast* in the British Legation, the Chargé d'Affaires would invoke the aid of the military to remove them. Mr Grant Duff expressed the hope that they would not have recourse to such an expedient, but he said it was not in his power, in view of the acknowledged custom in Persia and the immemorial right of *bast*, to use force to expel them if they came ... On the evening of the 19th, fifty Mullahs and merchants appeared in the Legation and took up their quarters for the night. Their numbers gradually increased, and soon there were 14,000 persons in the Legation garden.[21]

The crowd was formed predominantly of merchants, traders, craftsmen, apprentices, and journeymen. One participant described the scene: 'I saw more than 500 tents, for all the guilds, even the cobblers, walnut-sellers, and tinkers had at least one tent.'[22] The protest was led by *Anjuman-i Asnaf*, a recently formed association of guilds in the Tehran bazaar. Its elders prevented unauthorized persons from entering the garden, but permitted a few Westernized intellectuals, and some students from the Technical College, the Military Academy, and the Agricultural School to join their ranks. They enforced strict discipline to protect property, although, in the words of the British Legation, 'every semblance of a [flower] bed was trampled out of existence, and the trees still bear pious inscriptions cut in the bark.'[23] And they appointed a committee, composed mostly of liberal intellectuals, to negotiate with the court. This committee was not satisfied with royal promises and an ambiguous House of Justice. It demanded a written constitution and a House of Parliament. And it insisted that the demonstrators were willing to remain away from their work as long as it was necessary. Outside the garden walls, in the streets of Tehran, the wives of the protesters held periodic protest meetings; and in Qum, the religious leaders, whose group had increased to 1,000 mullas and theology students, staged their concurrent *bast*.

The court denounced the opposition as a bunch of traitors 'hired' by the

British.[24] But, faced by two mass demonstrations in Qum and the British Legation, a general strike in the Tehran bazaar, and the possibility of defections in the thin military ranks, it was forced to capitulate. The British Legation reported that the commander of the regiments in Tehran made 'the fatal announcement' that his men were unwilling to fight and that they were on the point of themselves joining the protestors.[25] On 5 August, 25 days after the flight of the 50 into the gardens, the Shah agreed to grant a constitution.

The merchants and money-lenders petitioning in April 1905 had jolted the foundation of the ancient regime. The religious leaders taking sanctuary in December 1905 had further weakened the old order. And the two groups, backed by the active participation of the bazaar masses in August 1906, had shaken the traditional system into ruin. The public remembered the words of the Prophet: 'The hand of God is with the multitude.'[26]

The constitutionalists had obtained their constitution, but had not yet secured it on firm foundations. The autocracy had been forced to give up its autocratic powers, but it had not yet resigned itself to the new order. The struggle between the two continued for the next three years. The court fought to regain what it had lost. The revolutionaries strived to preserve what they had gained. For both the streets were a vital battleground.

The monarch's procrastination over signing the regulations for parliamentary elections sparked off mass demonstrations in many cities and the opposition threatened to return to the British Legation. The Crown Prince's attempt to pacify the constitutionalists in Tabriz by lowering the price of bread incited the radicals to take to the streets shouting: 'We demand more than cheap bread. We demand a Constitution.'[27] The royalist refusal to accept the principle that the ministers should be responsible to the deputies led to mass rallies. A European observer commented: 'The Shah with his unarmed, unpaid, ragged, starving soldiers, what can he do in face of the menace of a general strike and riots?'[28] The monarch's stalling of the final draft of the Constitution fomented more demonstrations and protests throughout the country. In Tabriz armed volunteers prepared to fight, while a crowd of 20,000 vowed to 'remain away from work until the Fundamental Laws were signed.'[29] The strike lasted a whole month, until Muzaffar al-Din Shah, on his death-bed in December 1906, ratified the Constitution. When the new monarch, Muhammad 'Ali Shah, delayed sending a commissioner to Kirmanshah to endorse the parliamentary elections, the town went on strike. The British representative reported: 'The whole of the trades and employment of the bazaar, down to the porters, went into *bast* in the telegraph office.'[30] When some radical deputies accused the Prime Minister of plotting against parliament, the Tehran bazaar stopped work and demanded his resignation. And when he was murdered, a large crowd gathered to mourn the dead assassin and to pledge support to the revolution. One British reporter estimated the demonstration to number some 15,000 heads.[31] Another calculated it to be as many as 100,000.[32] Whatever the exact size, it succeeded in paralysing the counter-revolutionaries, at least for the time being.

The crowds of 1905, 1906, and early 1907 were all protesting against the court. In mid-1907, however, a new phenomenon made its appearance in the streets: the conservative crowd demonstrating for the court and against the constitution. It emerged first in Tabriz, then in Tehran, and finally in other provincial towns. By the end of 1907, the constitutionalists were seriously challenged on their home ground by the royalists. They had lost the monopoly of the streets.

THE CONSERVATIVE CROWD, JUNE 1907–JULY 1909

The revolution of August 1906 was an uprising of the urban masses. The craftsman and the journeyman, the wealthy merchant and the small tradesman, the wholesale dealer and the street vendor, the shopkeeper and the hired assistant, the *'ulama'* and the theology students, the Muslim and the non-Muslim, all joined together to batter down the court. If there was any section of the population that opposed or abstained from the uprising, it expressed itself neither in words nor in street actions. The Shah and his advisors were left isolated, facing a hostile country.

The political balance changed during 1907. In Tabriz, during the summer, rioters besieged the Town Council (*anjuman*) controlled by the radicals. By the end of the year, the city was sharply divided between the revolutionary citizens of the southern districts and the counter-revolutionary population of the northern precincts. In Tehran the royalists showed their strength in December, when they filled the expansive Cannon Square (*Maydan-i Tupkhanah*) and demanded the repeal of the Constitution. And in many other areas—in Yazd, Ardabil, Kirmanshah, Qazvin, Mashad, Shiraz, and Hamadan—demonstrators attacked and, at times, expelled the liberals from the city.

The revolution has been recorded mostly by its sympathizers: Edward Browne, the English admirer of the Persian liberals; Ahmad Kasravi, the ideologue of Persian nationalism who, as a youngster, observed the struggle in his home town, Tabriz; Mahdi Malikzadah, a participant of the revolution in Tehran whose father, a leading liberal, was murdered by the royalists; Ismail Amir-Khizi and Tahirzadeh-Bihzad, two armed volunteers in the civil war in Tabriz; Muhammad Hiravi, one of the intellectuals taking sanctuary in the British Legation; and reformist newspapers, such as *Habl al-Matin, Musavat* (Equality), and *Sur-i Israfil* (The Trumpet of Israfil). These sources, anxious to stress the popular legitimacy of the revolution, either ignored the royalist demonstrations or else dismissed them in derogatory terms. For example, Browne, Kasravi, Malikzadah, and *Sur-i Israfil*, in writing about the royalist rally in Cannon Square, describe the demonstrators as a bunch of 'hired hooligans,' 'gamblers,' 'blood-thirsty drunkards,' 'thugs,' and 'paid ruffians.' Of the many historians, only Malik al-Shuʿara Bahar has admitted, in passing, that the reactionaries had a following among the masses: 'During the revolution the upper class and the lower classes supported absolutism. Only the middle class advocated constitutionalism.'[33] However, he does not elaborate on the subject. He fails to explain which elements of 'the lower classes' participated in conservative crowds, what their motives were, and whether their behavior was rational and predictable.

Three separate elements can be identified in the royalist demonstrations: aristocrats, merchants, craftsmen and unskilled laborers tied to the palace economies as opposed to the bazaar economy; the conservative *ʿulama'* and their theology students; and, at times, the 'lower classes.'

The Qajars had no direct means of despotism, such as a state-wide bureaucracy or a standing army, but they controlled an extensive network of patronage and employment. They granted gifts and pensions to their favorite courtiers, fiefs and lucrative offices to their faithful administrators, and provided employment for thousands of household servants, clerks, craftsmen, journeymen, laborers, camel drivers and muleteers hired by the palace with its large harem, treasury, kitchens, storehouses, armory, workshops, and stables.[34] Moreover, the Crown Prince in Tabriz and the local magnates in the provincial capitals imitated, on a smaller scale, the royal way of life in Tehran. This element in the economy led Marx to the conclusion, somewhat exaggeratedly as far as Persia was concerned: 'In the Asiatic mode of production the large city, properly speaking, must be regarded merely as a princely camp, superimposed on the real economic structure.[35]

The liberals who drafted the constitutional demands in the British Legation were cautious enough to direct their grievances exclusively at the despotism of the court. The few radicals elected to the First Majlis sacrificed expediency in favor of principle. They spoke of human justice and social equality, and of the evil influences of both the political and the economic power of the court. The British representative remarked that the rich lived in 'apprehension' of having the wealth they had accumulated under the old regime expropriated by the new government.[36]

The reaction was predictable. When the Majlis, following the example of the British House of Commons after the Glorious Revolution, tried to establish a National Bank of Persia, many of the large landowners sabotaged the effort by refusing to contribute. When the deputies proposed a budget eliminating numerous court pensions and drastically reducing the income given to the monarch, the Household Treasury, which until then had made a special point of promptly meeting its commitments even when the State Treasury was in difficulties, informed its employees that their salaries and wages could not be paid because of the parliamentary budget.[37] The head of the finance commission argued in vain that he was reducing the 'unnecessary luxuries' of the court, not the wages and salaries of the palace employees.[38] Some of the small pensioners and the harem women protested inside the Majlis building, but received unfavorable answers. The pensioners were advised to persuade the monarch to sell his crown jewels.[39] Hasan Taqizadah, the leading liberal from Tabriz, announced that he had no interest in what happened to the Shah's wives.[40] And when the deputies pressed ahead with their budget, the employees of the palace first petitioned the Majlis,[41] and then took to the streets. They, together with court pensioners and their retainers, formed a noticeable segment of the royalist rally in Cannon Square. Malikzadah, in admitting that the budget hurt those employed by the palace, expressed no sympathy for their plight: 'In those days, a common method of abuse was to describe someone as having the "character of a groom," or the "mentality of a footman," for these lackeys had been so pampered by the court that they had become the most fanatical advocates of absolutism in the whole population of Tehran.'[42]

The same elements appeared in royalist disturbances in the provinces. In Tabriz, muleteers and camel-drivers employed by the court gained the reputation of being the most reactionary group in the city. In Shiraz, the retainers of a local magnate, Qavam al-Mulk, formed a counter-revolutionary society and fought the revolutionaries in the streets. And the British representative in Kirmanshah reported that the city was divided into 'the people's party,' and 'the aristocratic party'[43] composed of the local landowners with their hangers-on and servants.

The palace economies provided the royalist demonstrations with a guaranteed nucleus. The presence of religious personalities transformed these demonstrations from purely pro-Shah assemblies into 'Shah and Islam' rallies and riots. During the general strike of August 1906, the religious community was sharply but unevenly divided into two hostile camps: the few *Imam Jum'ahs* and *Shaykh al-Islams*, tied to the court and sympathetic to the Shah; and the popular *Mujtahids* and the numerous mullas, and the *maktab* teachers in the bazaar, allied to the liberals in the constitutional movement. This imbalance, however, swung into a balance as the revolution revealed its course and the liberals exposed their secular intentions: anti-clericalism, feminism, and egalitarianism between Shi'ites and non-Shi'ites, and Muslims and non-Muslims.

The year 1907 was a landmark in the religious history of Muslim Persia. It saw for the first time articles and pamphlets published within the country openly criticizing the clergy. *Sur-i Israfil*, in a satirical article on the clergy, made fun of the *'ulama'* who continually warned that religion was dying, and described mullas as ignorant, corrupt, and parasitical.[44] *Habl al-Matin*, commenting on the demands of the *'ulama'* to have a Supreme Court where they could judge the legitimacy of all legislation passed by the Majlis, remarked sarcastically: 'By the logic of this argument, the merchants also should have their own Supreme Court where they too, can pass judgment on the representatives of the people.'[45] And an anti-clerical tract distributed by the radicals in the bazaar caused a sharp reaction among the conservative deputies in the Majlis.[46]

Equally sharp reactions were produced by the issue of rights for the religious minorities, and by the question of women's role in society. When the Zoroastrian community petitioned the Majlis for equal treatment for all citizens, irrespective of creed, the conservatives took refuge in religion.[47] They argued that since the *shari'a* distinguished between Muslims and non-Muslims, and since the state had a sacred duty to enforce the *shari'a*, the distinctions should be retained in public life. One *Imam Jum'ah* claimed that he could not understand the Zoroastrians, for their community had been well treated in Persia for 1,300 years. He concluded that troublemakers must have incited them to make such an ungrateful and outrageous demand. The radicals rose to the challenge. They attested that years of oppression, not troublemakers, had forced the Zoroastrians to send in their request. And they supported the petition on the grounds that Muslim law advocated liberty and equality, not oppression and inequality. A similar crisis erupted when a group of women formed their own society.[48] The conservatives denounced the association as anti-Islamic. The radicals defended it with the argument that throughout the ages women in Islamic countries had been permitted to have their own organizations.

These controversial issues forced some of the *'ulama'* to forsake the dangerous road of constitutionalism for the safety of traditional despotism: 'No Absolutism, No Islam.' The defection was led by Hajji Mirza Hasan in Tabriz and Shaykh Fazlallah in Tehran. Hajji Mirza Hasan, the leading *Mujtahid* in the constitutional movement in Azarbayjan, broke with his radical allies in early 1908, formed his own royalist *Anjuman-i Islam* (Society of Islam) in the northern precincts of Tabriz, and challenged the authority of the liberals in the *Anjuman-i Shahr* (City Council). Shaykh Fazlallah, one of the triumvirate who led the religious demonstration of December 1905, split from the radicals in the summer of 1907 and took sanctuary in 'Abd al-'Azim Mosque with 500 of his followers. There they published a manifesto, opposing the introduction of non-Muslim laws legislated in Europe, and demanding the enforcement of the Muslim law found in the *shari'a*.[49] They also warned that the deputies who were modeling themselves after the French revolutionaries of the Paris Parlement in 1789 were encouraging 'anarchism,' 'nihilism,' 'socialism,' 'egalitarianism,' 'naturalism,' and, worst of all, 'Babism.'

Religious leaders, such as Shaykh Fazlallah and Hajji Mirza Hasan, influenced the behavior of three segments of society. First, they carried with them to the royalist side students, mullas, teachers, preachers, and retainers from their schools, mosques, and ecclesiastical foundations (*vaqfs*). This category formed most of the 500 who followed Shaykh Fazlallah to ʿAbd al-ʿAzim. After coming out of sanctuary, they proselytized, with some success, in the religious community. A Foreign Office observer reported to London that on the question of minorities 'a large body of the clergy' sympathized with the conservatives.[50] Second, they brought with them to the counter-revolutionary camp their *luti* clients. The *lutis* were religious-minded athletes in the bazaar, somewhat like the Hindu caste of 'thugs,' with strong ties to individual precincts, guilds, *zurkhanahs* (Houses of Strength), and members of the *ʿulama'*.[51] They played a significant role in the disturbances in Tabriz, and in the royalist rally of Cannon Square.

And thirdly, the religious leaders influenced the orthodox Shiʿite public, especially the poorer strata of the cities, such as the dyers, carpet-weavers, brick-layers, camel-drivers, muleteers, pedlars, bricklayers, bath-attendants, coolies, and laborers. The anti-clerical Kasravi commented briefly that Fazlallah's defection had a strong demoralizing effect on the radicals, for he and his entourage were highly 'respected by the population.'[52] Malikzadah, the proconstitutionalist historian, admitted that Fazlallah's agitation had some effect on the 'common people' (*mardum-i ʿavam*).[53] Another eyewitness confessed that the '*ʿavam-i bazaar*' (the common people of the bazaar) followed Fazlallah to the Cannon Square meeting.[54] And Amir-Khizi, commenting on the defection of some of the clergy in Tabriz, remarked: 'The common people (*mardum-i ʿavam*) genuinely believed the *ʿulama'* when they heard them denounce the radicals as irreligious, heretical, and anti-Islamic.'[55] Although these historians, in passing, admitted that the conservative clergy made inroads into the 'common people,' they continued to write as if the constitutionalists still represented 'the people.' Like the liberals in seventeenth-century England, they unconsciously ignored the propertyless lower classes and viewed the propertied middle class as 'the people.'

Besides religion, other factors helped draw the lower classes into the royalist ranks: down-to-earth factors such as the rising cost of bread, and the awareness that they had gained nothing from the revolution of the bourgeoisie.

In the early stages of the revolution, the rebels had successfully attracted the poor to their side by championing the demand for cheaper bread, and by persuasively arguing that the government was to blame for the high food prices. Thus, the petite bourgeoisie of the bazaar and the poor of the slums, the prosperous guilds of merchants and traders and the not-so-prosperous guilds of unskilled workers, had been able to demonstrate together against the Qajars. They parted company, however, as the regime changed and the prices continued to climb. The advocacy of a laissez-faire agricultural market by commercial interests on the liberal side further widened the breach.[56] In the summer of 1907, the Foreign Office representative in Tehran reported: 'The Majlis is attacked on several sides. The whole Court is hostile, and the population of the town discontented because bread is as dear as ever.'[57] Another observer wrote to London that the court was recruiting among 'the lower classes of the city.'[58] In Tabriz the conflict was sharper. The British Consul reported in June 1907 that a 'mob,' demanding bread, had besieged the City Council and had lynched one of its prominent members, a wealthy grain merchant who was suspected of cornering the market.[59] This was the first riot against the constitutionalists. Kasravi commented:

> In Tabriz during the Constitutional Revolution, as in Paris during the French Revolution, the sans-culottes and the propertyless poor reared their heads. The driving force of these men was toward anarchy. First to overthrow the despotic power of the court, and then to turn against the rich and the propertied classes. It was with the backing of such men that Danton and Robespierre rose to power. In Tabriz no Dantons and Robespierres appeared, but if they had we would also have had a 'reign of terror.'[60]

This danger threatened intermittently for the next two years in Tabriz. In early 1909, the British Consul again reported that the local constitutionalists feared 'a popular rising' because of the critical food shortage caused by the royalist blockade of the town.[61] One member of the City Council warned that serious riots were likely unless something was done to lower the price of wheat. Another reminded his audience that 'the mob' was 'no respecter of persons.' The Council executed a baker for selling flour above the fixed rate, but failed to win over the starving poor. Crowds of women assembled, threatened the liberals, and had to be dispersed by force. The British Consul commented: 'This was an ominous sign as women are always pushed forward to start bread riots.'

The less prosperous guilds suspected that they had nothing to gain from the revolution as early as the mass venture into the British Legation. Hiravi has written in his memoirs:

> I clearly remember the day when our Propaganda Section was warned that the reactionaries were sowing discontent among the junior carpenters and sawyers. The former were angry for having been taken away from their work and demanded to know what they had to gain from the whole venture. The latter were more unreasonable for they were illiterate and refused to accept any logic. If these two irresponsible groups had walked out of the Legation our whole movement would have collapsed, for there would have been open conflict among the various guilds. Fortunately, we succeeded in persuading them to vow that they would remain in sanctuary with the others.[62]

These suspicions turned out to be well founded when the Electoral Law was drawn up in September 1906.[63]

The electorate was divided into six estates (*tabaqat*): the princes and the Qajar tribe; the aristocracy and nobility; the *'ulama'* and their theology students; landowners and farmers; merchants; and the guilds. The following, however, were disenfranchised: landowners owning land worth less than 1,000 tumans; merchants without a definite place of business; shopkeepers who paid less rent than the local 'average'; and tradesmen, craftsmen, and workers who did not belong to a 'recognized guild.' Two months later, when a list of 105 guilds was drawn up, most of the trading and manufacturing associations were included, but many of the low-paid, unskilled occupations were excluded.[64] In the First Majlis, 60 per cent of the seats were taken by the *'ulama'* and the more prosperous members of the bazaar; and 40 per cent were occupied by landowners, civil servants, and a few professionals.[65] The 105 'recognized' guilds in Tehran were represented by 32 deputies, most of whom were from the commercial bourgeoisie: three merchants, three wholesale dealers, a secondhand dealer, two brokers, a tailor, a baker, and sellers of wheat, soap, books, lumber, thread, hats, iceboxes, tobacco, and silk. The propertied middle class, together with their religious allies, had gained control of the Majlis, and had effectively barred the propertyless lower classes from the corridors of power.

The victors, moreover, made no effort to gain the confidence of the disenfranchised. When a radical deputy proposed that more citizens should be brought into the electoral process, the majority responded that only countries with a large educated population could afford to abolish the estate system of voting.[66] And when the deputies were confronted by explosive issues, they cleared the public galleries and debated behind closed doors. The British Minister reported to London that as a result of this secrecy, the Majlis was losing 'public esteem' and becoming 'so discredited and unpopular that it may die a natural death.'[67] And to make matters worse, the constitutionalists made no attempt to help the poor by lowering certain taxes. When 2,000 peasants in Yazd petitioned against high taxation, and two of them committed suicide as an act of protest, some of the deputies claimed that the demonstrators were 'financed' by reactionary circles.[68] One sympathetic member reminded his colleagues that only recently, during the mass demonstration in the British Legation, they too had been accused of accepting money from dubious sources.

THE CONSTITUTIONALIST CROWD, JUNE 1907–JULY 1909

The constitutionalists lost the support of the poor, alienated some of the cautious religious leaders, and antagonized those employed in the palace economies. But they retained the allegiance of the bourgeoisie and the petite bourgeoisie in the bazaar: the merchants who gained most from the new order and who credited themselves with the destruction of the ancient regime;[69] the tradesmen and craftsmen who obtained an influential voice in the Majlis; their apprentices and journeymen who worked and lived with them as members of close-knit guilds; and the thousands in the bazaar who were independent of the insecurities of the daily food market because they could afford to buy annual supplies of necessities. The middle-class areas, therefore, remained hot-beds of revolution, and the lower-class slums turned into bulwarks of counter-revolution.

This division was sharply drawn in Tabriz, the first city to produce conservative demonstrations in the streets. The constitutionalists drew their adherents from the prosperous precincts of Amir-Khizi and Khiaban, inhabited by merchants, workshop owners, craftsmen, and tradesmen. Their rallies attracted the petite bourgeoisie, were invariably accompanied by bazaar strikes, and were protected by armed volunteers recruited from 'the educated classes.'[70] The royalists established their base in the impoverished districts of Davachi and Sarkhab, crowded with dyers, weavers, coolies, laborers, muleteers, and the unemployed. Their demonstrations often turned into bread riots and attacks on property owned by prominent liberals. At the height of the street fighting, the radicals sent a telegram to a group of Persian merchants residing in Istanbul, informing them that royalist mobs were 'on the verge of overthrowing the basic foundations of commerce.'[71] The historian Amir-Khizi, in his memoirs of the Civil War, separates the population of Tabriz into two categories: those prosperous enough to practice the habit of storing provisions to last them a whole year and make them independent of the market; and those dependent on the daily prices and directly harmed by the rising food prices.[72]

The conflict between the haves and the have-nots in Tabriz was intensified by religious factors. Since many of the bourgeoisie and petite bourgeoisie belonged to the unorthodox, Shaykhi sect, and most of the lower class adhered to the orthodox Mutashar'i faith, the conflict opened old sectarian wounds and turned the struggle into a religious war. Amir-Khizi has written that some of the poor fought the Civil War as if they were on a religious crusade against the heathen.[73] Their demonstrations were organized by the Mutashar'i *lutis* of Davachi and Sarkhab in their own precincts, and were spiritually inspired by the three Mutashar'i leaders: the *Imam Jum'ah*; Hajji Mirza Hasan, the *Mujtahid*; and Mir Hashim, a local preacher whose popularity in Davachi and Sarkhab had won him a parliamentary seat. The constitutionalist rallies, on the other hand, were supported by the head of the Shaykhi community, the *Shaykh al-Islam*, and were protected by his Shaykhi protégé, Sattar Khan, who was both a horse-dealer and the chief *luti* of the Amir-Khizi precinct.

The social basis of the constitutional movement in Tabriz can be seen in the backgrounds of the liberals executed by the Russians when they occupied the city, ostensibly to end the Civil War.[74] Among the 30 martyrs whose occupations are known, there were five merchants, three religious leaders, including the *Shaykh al-Islam*, three government employees, two shopkeepers, two arms dealers, two pharmacists, one carpenter, one tailor, a baker, a coffee-house keeper, a jeweler, one auctioneer, a musician, a journalist, a barber with his apprentice, a painter, a preacher, and a high school principal. Another four were hanged for being related to prominent revolutionaries: two of them were nephews of Sattar Khan; and another two were sons of a merchant who had organized the local cell of the Social Democratic Party.

In Tehran, where there was no Shaykhi-Mutasharʿi division, the struggle between the constitutionalists and conservatives was less bloody. But the diverging attitudes of the different strata of society were equally noticeable. This was most apparent during the Cannon Square rally, the first royalist demonstrations in the streets of the capital. One eye-witness wrote that some 10,000 monarchists massed into the square.[75] Another claimed that the area was so packed that he could not squeeze in.[76] In the crowd, there were the poor from the southern slums; conservative religious leaders, such as Shaykh Fazlallah, with their theology students and *luti* clients, claiming that the Majlis was threatening Islam; courtiers with their retainers, demanding the repeal of the budget; farm laborers from the royal stud-farm outside Tehran; and footmen, grooms, craftsmen, apprentices, journeymen and other employees of the palace and its stables, storehouses, and workshops. The radicals reacted sharply to this unexpected show of strength. They closed their stores and arcades, and 7,000 of them, all armed with rifles, took up positions around the Majlis Building to defend it in case of attack. The fact that they owned guns was proof enough that they belonged to the middle class. They were supported by the elders of the recognized guilds, who denounced the court and organized a general strike in the bazaar. The Shah was forced to back down: he asked his supporters to disperse; he agreed to dismiss from his employment those responsible for leading the rally; and he handed over to the ministries the control of some of the palace employees.

This, however, was only a tactical retreat. Seven months later, in June 1908, as soon as the Shah obtained a large loan from a wealthy aristocrat, he bought the allegiance of the Cossack Brigade, the only effective military force, and recruited volunteers from 'the lower classes of the city.'[77] And then he struck. The radicals reacted in their usual manner, closing the bazaar, assembling for rallies, and bringing out their guns. But this time they were faced not with rival demonstrators but with an army of soldiers willing to fight. The Cossack Brigade first bombarded the Majlis Building, and then a group of monarchists pillaged the Chamber. Some of the liberal leaders took sanctuary in the British Legation; others went into hiding; and a few were imprisoned and later murdered. Martial law was decreed, and all public meetings, even Passion plays, were prohibited. And to calm the bazaar, the Shah promised to reopen parliament in three months, purged not of patriotic constitutionalists but of irreligious revolutionaries. The day after the *coup d'état* the bazaar was open, although uneasy.

The conservatives had won in the capital, but the capital was not the whole of the country. In the provincial cities the struggle continued: protest demonstrations were organized, strikes were called, and arms were displayed in the streets. As soon as the news of the coup reached Tabriz, the internal struggle intensified and the bazaar struck for three days. In Rasht royalist troops tried to reopen the shops and arcades, and in the process killed three demonstrators. In Shiraz and Kirmanshah constitutionalists from the bazaars and retainers of local magnates continued to battle in the streets. And in Isfahan a crowd of 200 'small shopkeepers' tried to take refuge in the British Consulate.[78]

These signs of protest in the provinces could not overthrow the court, entrenched in the capital and defended by royalist troops. Only armed force could accomplish that task. Such forces materialized in early 1909. The Bakhtiyari *khans* joined the constitutionalists of the Isfahan bazaar, mobilized their tribesmen, and marched north toward Tehran. And a group of Caucasian revolutionaries, helped by the Social Democrats in Baku, made their way from the north, captured Rasht, and prepared to advance south to Tehran. These events transferred the struggle from the streets of the towns to the highways of the countryside, but they did not eradicate completely the importance of the bazaar. On the contrary, they encouraged the bourgeoisie in Tehran to revive their cause. A delegation from the bazaar reminded the Shah of his promise to reopen the Majlis within three months. Three hundred merchants and religious leaders took sanctuary in the Ottoman Embassy and demanded the re-establishment of the constitution. A group of shopkeepers went on strike in support of the revolutionaries in Rasht. When the monarch tried to terrorize them by bastinadoing four of the strikers, more stores closed down. They remained shut for a whole month. The British Minister reported that the customary religious ceremonies for Muharram had to be canceled for 'fear of disorders.'[79] And when the court tried to exact loans to pay its troops, the money-lenders refused. The Minister of War warned that the government could not answer for the behavior of its soldiers unless they received their arrears.[80] Faced again with an unreliable army and a hostile bazaar, the royalist cause collapsed as soon as the Bakhtyari tribesmen and the Caucasian fighters reached Tehran in July 1909. Muhammad 'Ali Shah was deposed, the throne was given to his twelve-year-old son, prominent reactionaries such as Shaykh Fazlallah and Mir Hashim were executed for 'hiring thugs to create public disturbances,'[81] and the Second Majlis was convened. The Civil War was over.

CONCLUSION

From this short sketch we can see that the political crowd played a major role in the Persian Revolution, but that its face and behavior had little resemblance to the 'monstrous mob' visualized by Gustave Le Bon. The vast majority of participants in rallies, demonstrations, and even riots were not criminals, hired thugs, and social riff-raff, but sober and even 'respectable' members of the community. They were merchants, religious authorities, shopkeepers, workshop owners, craftsmen, apprentices, journeymen, and students. The centers of revolutionary crowds were the bazaar and the middle-class precincts, not the slums.

By simply assembling in one place, the demonstrators did not reduce their collective mentality to the lowest level of 'destructiveness,' impulsiveness,' 'irrationality,' 'stupidity,' and 'fickleness.' On the contrary, they tended to be non-violent, except when shot at or suffering from starvation. On the rare occasions when they indulged in violence, they attacked property rather than human beings. Of course, their opponents exaggerated all incidents of destructive behavior into large-scale attacks on society and humanity. In June 1906, when radicals poured into the streets, the royalists cried in panic that the whole fabric of society was being undermined. And in December 1907, when the royalists rallied in Cannon Square and killed two would-be assassins who were trying to murder one of their preachers, the liberals claimed that 'drunken mobs' were running rampant in the capital, lynching all those wearing European-style hats.[82]

On the whole, demonstrators were both non-violent and remarkably rational, aiming for goals that were in their class and group interests. When the slogans ceased to represent their interests, they had no compunction in withdrawing and joining rival demonstrations. The defection of the poor from the side of the revolution into the camp of the reaction was not a sign of their inherent 'fickleness,' but a result of their dissatisfaction with the propertied middle class and its bourgeois revolution. And the fact that they expressed this dissatisfaction by joining the reactionaries was not a mark of their 'stupidity,' but an indication of the traditional and Islamic political culture of early-twentieth-century Persia.

This article is reprinted from *Iranian Studies*, vol. II, no. 4, Autumn 1969, pp. 128–150. Reprinted by permission of *Iranian Studies*.

NOTES

1. Parts of this article appeared in 'The Crowd in Iranian Politics 1905–53,' *Past and Present*, 41 (December 1968), pp. 184–210. I would like to thank the editors of the journal for permitting me to reprint those parts.

2. In this article the term 'crowd' is used to describe any large gathering whose behaviour is not regulated by formalized rules of conduct and whose aim is to impress its opponents either by collective action or by the show of group solidarity. This includes protest demonstrations indoors as well as hostile outbursts in the streets. But it excludes institutionalized gatherings, such as parliamentary assemblies, where laws of procedure structure the behaviour of individuals.

The qualifier 'political' is added to exclude religious disturbances with no political content and no political repercussions.

For more detailed definitions of 'crowd' see: G. Rudé, *The Crowd in History, 1730–1848* (New York, 1964), pp. 3–4, and L. Bernard, 'Crowd', *Encyclopaedia of Social Sciences* (New York, 1931), Vol. 4, pp. 612–13.

Descriptions of crowds have been obtained mostly from the following sources: I. Amir-Khizi, *Qiyam-i Azarbayjan va Sattar Khan* (The Revolution in Azarbayjan and Sattar Khan) (Tabriz, 1960); E.G. Browne, *The Persian Revolution of 1905–1909* (London, 1910); Y. Dawlatabadi, *Hayat-i Yahya* [*Yahya's Life*] [*Tehran, 1943*], Great Britain, *Correspondence Respecting the Affairs of Persia* (London, 1909), Vol. I, Nos. 1–2; Habl al-Matin; M.H. Hiravi-Khurasani, *Tarikh-i Paydayish-i Mashrutiyat-i Iran* (The History of the Genesis of the Persian Constitution) (Mashad, 1953); A. Kasravi, *Tarikh-i Mashrutah-i Iran* (History of the Persian Constitution) (Tehran, 1961); M. Malikzadah, *Tarikh-i Inqilab-i Mashrutiyat-i Iran* (History of the Constitutional Revolution in Persia) (Tehran, 1951), Vol. II-III, ii. 'A. Qudsi, *Kitab-i Khatirat-i Man* (The History of My Life) (Tehran, 1963); *Ruh-i Quds*; *Sur-i Israfil*; and K. Tahirzadah-Bihzad, *Qiyam-i Azarbayjan dar Inqilab-i Mashrutiyat-i Iran* (The Revolt of Azarbayjan in the Constitutional Revolution of Persia) (Tehran, 1953).

3. Quoted by H. Arsanjani, 'Anarshizm dar Iran,' (Anarchism in Iran), *Darya*, 17 July 1944.

4. Most of the histories of the Persian Revolution fit into this category.

5. E. Monroe, 'Key Force in the Middle East—The Mob,' *New York Times*, 30 August 1953, pp. 13–5: 'Provide Tehran with a political stir and out pour the mob from its slums and shanty towns no matter what the pretext for a demonstration ... Take a cluster of mean streets; fill with idle and semi-employed people; sprinkle with raw notions of social improvement; top with hunger or despair; add rising prices; stir and bring to a boil. Of the ingredients, the most important are the unemployed and the cramped quarters, for they insure that the rumor which sets men moving reaches the maximum of ears in the minimum of time. This applies in any continent—Europe, and America, as well as Asia and Africa. The years in which the historic Paris mob swayed policy were before Hausmann built the boulevards ... The Middle Eastern mob of today is so full of dumb resentfulness that it can change within seconds from a collection of separated beings into a mad thing, no longer out for simple ends such as loot or hire, but pouring into the bazaars, it will hack into stores and tear its booty to pieces.'

6. For a humorous story of the crowd see M. Jamalzadah's 'Rajal-i Siasi' (Politician) in his collection of essays entitled *Yiki Bud Yiki Nabud* (Once Upon A Time) (Tehran, 1941).

7. G. Le Bon, *The Crowd* (New York, 1966), pp. 35–59.

8. Rudé, *op. cit.*, pp. 237–257.

9. M. H. Tavildar-i Isfahan, *Joghrafiya-yi Isfahan* (The Geography of Isfahan) (Tehran, 1963).

10. *Habl al-Matin*, 9 and 23 March, 1905.

11. *Habl al-Matin*, 19 June, 1905.

12. *Habl al-Matin*, 17 August, 1905.

13. Qudsi, *op. cit.*, Vol. I, pp. 99–100.

14. *Ibid.*, p. 106.

15. Malikzadah, *op. cit.*, Vol. II, p. 41.

16. *Ibid.*, p. 47.

17. Qudsi, *op. cit.*, Vol. I, p. 112.

18. Kasravi, *op. cit.*, p. 95.

19. G.B., *op. cit.*, Number 1, pp. 3.

20. Malikzadah, *op. cit.*, Vol. II, p. 150.
21. G.B. *op. cit.*, Number 1, p. 3–4.
22. Quoted by Kasravi, *op. cit.*, p. 110.
23. G.B., *op. cit.*, Number 1, p. 4.
24. Recounted by Shaykh Yusif in the Majlis. Iranian Government, *Muzakirat-i Majlis* (Parliamentary Debates), First Majlis, p. 351.
25. G.B., *op. cit.*, Number 1, p. 4.
26. Quoted in Browne, *op. cit.*, p. 167.
27. Kasravi, op. cit., p. 159, and Malikzadah, *op. cit.*, Vol. II, p. 193.
28. Quoted by Browne, *op. cit.*, p. 137.
29. Quoted in Kasravi, *op. cit.*, p. 336.
30. G.B., *op. cit.*, Number 1, p. 27.
31. *Ibid.*, p. 60.
32. Cited by Browne, *op. cit.*, p. 153.
33. Malik al-Shuʿara Bahar, *Tarikh-i Ahzab-i Siasi-yi Iran* (History of Political Parties in Iran) (Tehran, 1944), p. 2.
34. For a detailed description of the palace economy see ʿA. Mustaufi, *Sharh-i Zindigani-yi Man* (My Life) (Tehran, 1945), Vol. I, pp. 524–64.
35. K. Marx, *Pre-Capitalist Economic Formations* (London, 1964), p. 178.
36. G.B., *op. cit.*, Number 1, p. 58.
37. Malikzadah, op. cit., Vol. III, p. 93, and Vol. IV, p. 59.
38. Parliamentary Debates, *op. cit.*, First Majlis, p. 385.
39. *Ibid.*, p. 400.
40. *Ibid.*, p. 400.
41. *Ibid.*, p. 383–85.
42. Malikzadah, *op. cit.*, Vol. IV, p. 59.
43. G.B., *op. cit.*, Number 1, p. 27.
44. *Sur-i Israfil*, 13 February 1907.
45. *Habl al-Matin*, 18 June 1907.
46. Parliamentary Debates, *op. cit.*, First Majlis, p. 229.
47. *Ibid.*, p. 188–90.
48. *Ibid.*, p. 484.
49. The text of the pamphlet published by the conservative *ʿulama'* is reprinted in Kasravi, *op. cit.*, pp. 415–23.
50. G.B., *op. cit.*, Number 1, p. 27.
51. For a description of the *lutis* see R. Arastah, 'The Character, Organization, and Social Role of Lutis in the Traditional Iranian Society of the Nineteenth Century,' *Journal of the Economic and Social History of the Orient*, Vol. IV (February 1961), pp. 47–52.
52. Kasravi; *op. cit.*, p. 376.
53. Malikzadah, *op. cit.*, Vol. III, p. 55.
54. Quoted by Hiravi, *op. cit.*, p. 126.
55. Amir-Khizi, *op. cit.*, p. 169.
56. *Habl al-Matin*, 23 September 1907.
57. G.B., *op. cit.*, Number 1, p. 27.
58. *Ibid.*, p. 141.
59. *Ibid.*, p. 35.
60. Kasravi, *op. cit.*, p. 355.
61. G.B., *op. cit.*, Number 2, pp. 97–9.
62. Hiravi, *op. cit.*, p. 50.
63. Electoral Law, Parliamentary Debates, *op. cit.*, First Majlis, pp. 6–7.
64. For the electoral results of the guilds see *Habl al-Matin*, 12 November 1906.
65. Z. Shajiʿi, *Namavandigan-i Majlis-i Shura-yi Milli dar Bist va Yik Dawrah-i Qanunguzari* (Members of Parliament in Twenty-one Sessions of the Lower House of Parliament) (Tehran, 1961), p. 176.
66. Parliamentary Debates, *op. cit.*, First Majlis, p. 348.
67. G.B., *op. cit.*, Number 1, p. 114.

68. Parliamentary Debates, *op. cit.*, First Majlis, p. 351.

69. *Habl al-Matin*, 2 October 1906: 'The merchant class played the leading role in the Constitutional Revolution. Without the merchants there would have been no revolution.'

70. Amir-Khizi, *op. cit.*, p. 410. I would like to thank Mr J. Habibune for giving me a description of the various parts of old Tabriz.

71. Quoted in *ibid.*, p. 163.

72. *Ibid.*, p. 320.

73. *Ibid.*, p. 177.

74. Bibliographical information obtained from: Malikzadah, *op. cit.*, Vol. V, pp. 184–222; Tahirzadah-Bihzad, *op. cit.*; and A. Kasravi, *Tarikh-i Hijdah Salah-i Azarbayjan* (An Eighteen Year History of Azarbayjan) (Tehran, 1961), pp. 297–422.

75. Quoted in Malikzadah, *op. cit.*, Vol. III, p. 142.

76. Qudsi, *op. cit.*, p. 158.

77. G.B., *op. cit.*, Number 1, p. 141.

78. *Ibid.*, Number 2. p. 46.

79. *Ibid.*, p. 60.

80. *Ibid.*, p. 107.

81. Quoted by Qudsi, *op. cit.*, p. 245.

82. *Sur-i Israfil*, 11 Zulhijja, 1325.

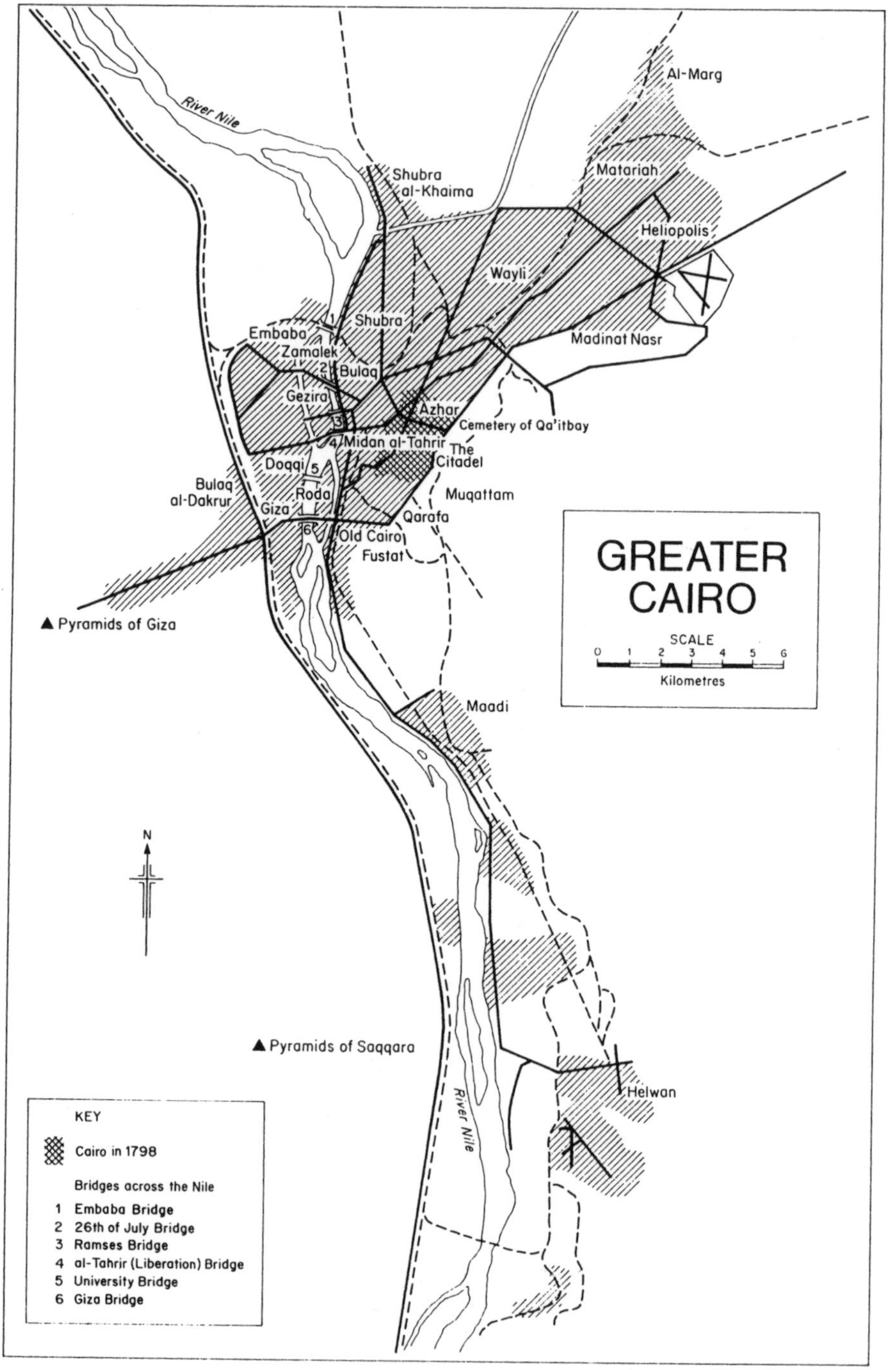

GREATER CAIRO
SCALE
0 1 2 3 4 5 6
Kilometres
River Nile
Al-Marg
Shubra al-Khaima
Matariah
Heliopolis
Wayli
Madinat Nasr
Shubra
Embaba
Zamalek
Bulaq
Gezira
Azhar
Cemetery of Qa'itbay
Midan al-Tahrir
The Citadel
Doqqi
Bulaq al-Dakrur
Roda
Muqattam
Giza
Qarafa
Old Cairo
Fustat
Pyramids of Giza
Maadi
N
Pyramids of Saqqara
River Nile
Helwan
KEY
Cairo in 1798
Bridges across the Nile
1 Embaba Bridge
2 26th of July Bridge
3 Ramses Bridge
4 al-Tahrir (Liberation) Bridge
5 University Bridge
6 Giza Bridge

Cairo

ANDRÉ RAYMOND

In a little less than a century (1863: arrival of Isma'il Pasha; 1956: masterplan of Cairo), the capital of Egypt moved on from its status as medieval town, neither much bigger nor much more populated than it had been five centuries earlier, to that of 'megalopolis' with nearly 10 million inhabitants.

Having entered the modern world shortly before 1880, in only a few decades Cairo underwent a metamorphosis which had begun almost three centuries earlier in the western European cities which served as its models. But scarcely had the rulers of Egypt begun to find answers to the problems posed by the simple 'modernization' of their city, than they came up against the almost inextricable difficulties faced by the vast cities of modern times.

The change was so brutal that it is useful to return to the recent past of Cairo in order to trace the origin of the urban landscapes which, juxtaposed, form the city of today.

THE ORIENTAL CITY (1798–1882)

> *From the heights of the Citadel, 'one sees . . . to the right and to the left, the expanse of the city, crossed by streets, dotted with squares, encumbered with mosques and large buildings, and in a hundred places decked out with flowers and gardens: it is not gay, it is not bizarre, it is not majestic in the ordinary sense of the word; in other words all symmetry is absent. But it is big, vast, full of air, life, warmth, freedom, and thus of beauty . . . Nothing here is perfectly straight: but in the absence of regularity, the general aspect is serious and noble, although varied, and power breathes here.*[1]

The city of 1798 as we know it from the works of the scholars of the French Expedition, and even the city of 1882, did not differ fundamentally from that of the Mamluk era, as described in minute detail for us by the great historian

Maqrizi (1364–1441). There is nothing easier than to follow the itineraries of Maqrizi on the maps of the *Description de l'Egypte*; the most basic features of the structure of the city were scarcely altered between the fifteenth and eighteenth centuries. The urban mass itself (the area and the population) did not change substantially: the noticeable progress during these four centuries (from 200,000 to 300,000 inhabitants) is moderate; and from 1798 to 1865 again the constancy of numbers is striking: 260,000 inhabitants according to the French scholars, 282,000 in 1865.

This permanence is evidence of a remarkable stability (one ought to say stagnation) of the modes of production and of the types of social organization from the heart of the Middle Ages right up to the dawn of the modern era. It is still perceptible today, to the traveller who takes the central artery of the Fatimid city (*qasaba*) between the gate of Bab al-Futuh and the area around Ibn Tulun. Despite the breaches which, at various times, have torn the urban fabric (New Road, Shari' al-Azhar, the road to the Citadel), despite the invasion of modernity which makes its mark in blind destruction and the proliferation of buildings cheap in style, Cairo astonishingly continues to conserve its monuments and ways of life.

1) Cairo in 1798

The Cairo of the *Description de l'Egypte* had nevertheless been profoundly marked by three centuries of Ottoman presence. The extension of the city southwards (in the direction of the Citadel and of the suburb, still distant then, of Old Cairo), and, above all, towards the west, beyond the Khalig canal which bordered the city on that side, and the probable growth in population between 1517 and 1798 (from around 200,000 to a little less than 300,000), should be seen in relation to the economic upsurge of the city in the sixteenth and seventeenth centuries: this upsurge is shown by the number and activity of its markets and caravanserais (220 mentioned in the *Description* as opposed to 58 in the time of Maqrizi). This development, for a long time obscured by tenacious anti-Ottoman prejudices, is easily explained. It is indeed true that in 1517 Cairo ceased to be the capital of a state that included Palestine, Syria and the Hijaz; but by the same token it became the principal provincial capital of a state which extended, without borders, from the Danube to Sudan, from the borders of Iran to the borders of Morocco, a state which was the most important, and the most enduring, political structure known in the West since the Roman Empire. Inside this empire, Egypt could attract the greatest profit from its privileged position on the route from the Orient, trade in coffee replacing that in spices from the end of the sixteenth century. Cairo did not translate this activity and this development into architectural embodiments comparable to those of the past; but a tour of what remains of Old Cairo is enough to show that the Ottoman imprint, in this domain as well, was not negligible, even if its embodiments are conceived on a more modest scale than those, clearly marvellous, of the Mamluk era.

In 1798, the city covered a total of 730 hectares (of which 660 were built up), which for a population of 263,000 represented a real density of around 400 persons per hectare. Careful examination reveals a fairly coherent structure. The heart of the town in 1798, as in the fourteenth century, lay in the part founded by the Fatimids, which continued to be called Qahira, especially in its main street, the Qasaba. The displacement of this initial centre came about as a result of urban growth which had been vigorous towards the south and west but weak towards the north and especially the east where the hills of debris had put a stop to all expansion. Here were the principal markets of the city, the international centres of commerce (which relied essentially on fabrics and coffee), between the Orfèvres bazaar and Khan al-Khalili and the great Azhar mosque, in the place where the oriental bazaar for tourists is still situated today. Around this centre, the city spread out following a radio-concentric pattern, keeping the most important activities near the centre and keeping at a distance secondary activities, or activities which would inconvenience the population because of noise or smells they might produce (blacksmiths, tanners, charcoal manufacturers). Secondary centres of activity formed nebulous areas in the intermediate zone alongside the residential districts of the bourgeoisie and the shaykhs (settled a short distance from their markets or their mosques) and the houses of the dominant Mamluk aristocracy. At the periphery of the city, different areas alternated: zones of 'industrial' activity; working-class districts (and shady ones: Bab al-Luk, today situated in the middle of the 'modern' city, was one of the centres of entertainment and prostitution); and finally to the west—in a less densely settled area—the rich residential districts; the prototype of these was Azbakiyya, on the edges of which Napoleon Bonaparte was to establish his headquarters in 1798, in the newly finished palace of a powerful Mamluk emir.

Although sometimes described with severity by travellers ('This city is abominable,' wrote the French officer Dupuis in 1798, 'the streets breathe out plague ... the people are frightful'), Cairo was not an anarchic city. Without doubt, it was somewhat neglected by the authorities, scarcely administered in the modern sense of the word (there were, so to speak, no urban 'functionaries') and totally deprived of municipal institutions. But urban functions were mainly undertaken by very varied collective organizations which encompassed individuals in a superimposed network of structures, leaving aside no aspect of their activities: trade guilds in the economic sphere, national and religious organizations, district communities in the geographic sphere. By using the shaykhs who led these communities (*ta'ifa*) as intermediaries, the rulers could control the population of Cairo. There were, moreover, specialized corporations which ensured, at the expense of the inhabitants, the functioning of 'public services': eight guilds of water-carriers transported drinking water from the Nile to the city and distributed it to the inhabitants; one guild of 'transporters of soil on donkeys' removed refuse to the hills of rubbish which surrounded Cairo in the east; three guilds of donkey and camel drivers likewise ensured urban transport, etc.

Despite an obvious urban decline, which did not begin perhaps before the last decades of the eighteenth century and was linked to a particularly unfavourable political, economic and social conjuncture, Cairo thus remained, at the end of the Ottoman epoch, an impressive city; the same Dupuis who judged the city and its inhabitants so unfavourably in 1798 did, however, add: 'I cannot yet find my way in this vast city, bigger than Paris.'

2) *Cairo from Bonaparte to Isma*'il (*1798–1863*)

The French occupation engendered only little visible change, caused by military operations and the repression of the revolts of 1798 and 1800 around the Azhar area, near Azbakiyya and at Bulaq, suburb and port of Cairo. By enlarging and regularizing them, the French improved some strategic routes: for example, the street linking Azbakiyya (General Headquarters of the Army) to the Muski bridge, or the route to Bulaq. But many improvements envisaged during the occupation did not get beyond the planning stage: for example, the banning of gates which allowed neighbourhoods to be closed, the destruction of benches put up outside shops which partly obstructed the streets, or again the removal of cemeteries which extended inside the city. Equally, it cannot be said that French efforts at improving lighting and cleaning of the city really bore any fruits. But some endeavours did, such as those aimed at improving the city's administration (establishment of a 'diwan', division of Cairo into eight wards, strengthening of administrative powers of shaykhs in their districts): even if these endeavours were short-lived, they were able to inspire, at least partially, the reforms undertaken in the following century. In a certain way, the French expedition thus marked for Cairo, as for Egypt, the beginning of a new era.

Between 1800 and 1860, Cairo hardly changed. Muhammad 'Ali, enterprising and innovative statesman in other areas, showed little interest in, and did little for, his capital. Several explanations can be given for a shirking of responsibility at first sight so surprising: distrust, perhaps, with regard to a city where so often formidable popular movements were born, which could explain his predilection for residences built outside the city (Roda, Shubra); preference for Alexandria, where development was on the contrary very rapid and which supplanted Cairo as a centre of international commerce. Whatever the reasons, for 30 years only relatively minor advances are evident: improvement of administrative structures (institution of a governorate, *muhafaza*), organization of districts and wards (*thumn*, an eighth, perhaps in imitation of French *arrondissements*), efforts to improve hygiene. Even the attempts to develop industry, and the first implementations at Bulaq (cloth mills and printing) and at Shubra (textile workshops) did not really alter the urban structure inherited from the Ottomans. The most pronounced efforts observable after 1830 were perhaps due to the influence of Ibrahim Pasha. All things considered, the achievements of Muhammad ʻAli in Cairo can be summed up in a few words: levelling of the accumulations of rubbish to the north and west of Cairo; drying some of the ponds (*birka*); drainage of Azbakiyya which was to become a garden; improvements in the road system (abolition of benches). A masterplan for the city was outlined (*tanzim* adopted in 1845): but the only achievement in this area was merely sketched; in 1845 the laying-out started of the New Road (*sikka al-gadida*, later Shariʻ Muski) which was meant to open the commercial quarter to the west. It was not finished until much later; also, it had not originally been conceived as allowing the passage of more than two loaded camels, which gives an idea of the modesty of the conception of urbanism in a city where, it is true, for a long time there had been only one horse-drawn vehicle, that of the pasha. In 1850, the city was similar to the one described by the French in 1798, and the (somewhat unreliable) census of 1846 gives a population of 256,000 inhabitants, a little fewer than 50 years earlier.

The next 15 years were hardly any more fruitful with regard to Cairo: there is hardly anything to point out other than the establishment, by ʻAbbas I in 1849, of barracks on the road to Matariah which were the distant point of departure from the ʻAbbasiyya quarter. At least these years saw the concrete realization of innovations which would later allow the development of the city: the completion, in 1854, of the railway from Cairo to Alexandria, which made Cairo very accessible from then on and soon turned it into a railway junction; the agreement to build the Suez Canal (in 1854) which produced, for the time being, no consequences, but which laid the way for the entry of Egypt into the world market, Cairo becoming again an important place of call on the main route to the East, an essential link in the network of world communications.

3) The temptation of the west

Credit must go to the reforming Khedive Ismaʻil for having conceived and begun to put into effect a considered plan for turning Cairo into a modern city. In his projects for the modernization of Egypt, which were not without some touch of megalomania, nor without a naivety which the European entrepreneurs and adventurers knew how to exploit at the expense of Egypt, the enlargement and embellishment of Cairo naturally occupied a choice place, the capital having to form a show-case for an effort which affected the whole country.

From the beginning of his reign, the Khedive displayed his taste for technical progress by putting into effect what had at times been projected by his predecessors: in 1865 a company with European capital and personnel was charged with proceeding with the supply of water into the city of Cairo, distribution of water beginning in 1875. At the same time, the Lebon Company obtained the concession for the provision of gas: lighting began in 1867 and, from 1882, 70 kilometres of streets and squares were lit by 2,459 lanterns. Simultaneously, the construction of the Suez Canal was undertaken and the deepening of the Isma'iliyya Canal (1864–66) made it possible to envisage the development of the city in new areas lying to the north and north-east of Cairo.

Isma'il's designs regarding Cairo were soon to take a grander turn. If it is probable that, long before his visit to France in 1867 (on the occasion of the '*Exposition Universelle*' or World Fair), the Khedive had dreamt of modernizing his capital, it is indisputably his stay in Paris and his contact with 'Hausmann-ism', then so triumphant, which gave his projects their definitive turn. Back in Cairo, thinking of transforming the inauguration of the Suez Canal in 1869 into an event which would excite world-wide interest, Isma'il decided to elevate his capital to the height of the image of Egypt which he wanted to present to the world, that of a modern country. The short time the Khedive allowed himself naturally did not permit him to consider remodelling the old city; what he could try, however, was to cover the western edge of the city with a façade capable of making a favourable impression on its European visitors. Thus the character, and the limits, of his enterprise were defined.

The two years Isma'il had at his disposal were filled with feverish activity. The person chosen to mastermind this enterprise was one of the most remarkable individuals of nineteenth-century Egypt, 'Ali Pasha Mubarak, who was also a remarkable Minister of Education and an eminent historian. The plan prepared for the whole city was directly inspired by Hausmann principles: a network of open streets connecting a dozen squares (*midan*), with the New Road continuing right to the desert, to the east of Cairo. But the effort was inevitably limited to a free area to the north-west of the old city, between the Bulaq road, the Old Cairo road (now Shari' Qasr al-'Aini), Bab al-Luk and the bank of the Nile, an area of about 250 hectares. Here the streets and pavements were planned, the land having been offered by the Khedive to possible builders. Once the network was drawn, actual building began, but at a rather slow pace: by the end of the reign only some hundreds of buildings had seen the light of day. At the same time, arrangements were under way to transform Azbakiyya (where an opera house had been hastily erected) into an 'English' park in the style of Parc Monceau, with little lakes, grottoes and bridges. In order to do this, Barillet-Deschamps, the creator of the Bois de Bologne, was brought from France; he also drew up plans for a big park on the island of Gezira and arranged shade on each side of the good road in the direction of the Pyramids, which had been improved. To facilitate access to the island and the left bank of the Nile, a metal bridge was constructed over the river, ending in the south of Gezira (1869). The main part of these works was completed in time for the opening of the canal.

After 1869, which was the peak of the reign, the pace of accomplishments slowed, the more so as Egypt began to experience serious financial difficulties, partly caused by the extravagances of the Khedive. However, from 1872, work was begun on Clot Bey Street (from the station to Azbakiyya) and above all on Muhammad ʿAli Avenue, which would link Azbakiyya to the Citadel over a length of two kilometres. This real progress was not without its drawbacks: among the 700 buildings destroyed were a number of important monuments; and the beautiful façades and arcades bordering the new avenue, which were cleaned three times a day, camouflaged filthy alleyways.

The major works of Ismaʿil in Cairo were not completed: the ruin of Egypt, and soon its subjection to foreign control, interrupted their implementation. Not everything was illusory, however, in a task which had been undertaken in haste ten years earlier. A movement had been set in motion and a new city was in the process of being born. This shows in the figures: that of population, which grew from 282,000 in 1866 to 375,000 in 1882, of whom 19,000 were foreigners; that of area, which reached 1,260 hectares, an increase of more than 50 per cent; the length of roadways, which quadrupled (from 58 to 208 kilometres). Although the development of the outlying areas to the north would have a great effect in the future, it was in its irresistible thrust to the west that the transformation of Cairo was apparent: the Ismaʿiliyya quarter—which would become the centre of Cairo, and remain so till the present, with its new streets still teeming with activity today (Qasr al-Nil, Sulayman Pasha, ʿImad al-Din)—is the legacy of the reforming Khedive to the twentieth century.

But the Cairo which Ismaʿil helped to create was distinguishable from the old city by a new characteristic which was just as important as this quantitative progress. Henceforth there would be two cities of Cairo juxtaposed. The former centre had been subjected to great modifications; but the wounds that had been inflicted on it had not modified the basic structure of the old city. On the other hand, another city, European in the organization of its structure and functions, already different in its population, strongly marked by the massive presence of foreigners, had been born in the west. These diverse traits characterized the 'colonial' cities of the nineteenth and twentieth centuries: even before Egypt succumbed to the blow of colonialism, colonization was establishing itself in the very heart of the country's structures. From 1882, the formula that inspired the inauguration of Shari' Muhammad 'Ali can be applied to Cairo thus divided: 'Cairo is like a cracked vase. The two parts will no longer join together.'[2]

THE COLONIAL CITY (1882–1936)

> *Foreigners [have made Cairo into] the centre of a capital from which Egyptians are excluded. There is no visible boundary between the Egyptian quarters and the others. We have crossed the smells of frying foods, as one crosses barbed wire, to reach those of Greek bakeries and Swiss cake shops.*[3]

The installation, avowedly provisional, of Great Britain in Egypt in 1882, changed progressively into a lasting presence which ended officially in 1936 (the date of the treaty recognizing the independence of Egypt) and in actual fact in 1954 (agreement on the evacuation of British forces). For 30 years British dominance, of which the political aspects are studied elsewhere, produced appreciable results in the field of economics: there was a real surge in Egyptian agriculture and the demographic development of a country which, until then, had been somewhat underpopulated was at first a positive element, available resources increasing faster than the number of mouths to feed.

The development of Cairo was paralleled throughout the whole country. Having become the capital of a state from then on practically independent of Turkey, a centre of colonial administration, seat of large foreign enterprises which were exploiting the country, Cairo added a whole range of new functions to the prestige which it traditionally drew from its cultural and religious role, and in a few decades it saw modernization and an accelerated growth whose harmful aspects would become apparent only later.

1) Increase in the population of Cairo

The most telling phenomenon during this period is naturally the rapid rise in the population of Cairo, which went from 375,000 in 1882 to 1,312,000 in 1937, an increase of 250 per cent in 55 years (the increase had been 51 per cent in the preceding 84 years).

In this movement of general growth, two phases should be distinguished. Between 1882 and 1917, the population of Cairo developed at the same pace as the demographic development of the whole of Egypt. During all this time, the population of Cairo remained at round about 6 per cent of the total population of the country: 5.5 per cent in 1882; 5.9 per cent in 1897; 5.8 per cent in 1907; 6.2 per cent in 1917 (791,000 out of 12,700,000 Egyptians altogether). The large-scale developments in the Nile Valley (repair of Delta

Dam in 1891, construction of the Aswan Dam in 1902), the generalization of permanent irrigation and the rise in the cultivation of cotton show that agricultural production had by then increased at an average rate of 1.6 per cent per annum, faster than the population. Average rural income rose around 1914 to E£ 30 a year. It is on this foundation of relative prosperity that the growth of Cairo developed. This period was also, as we shall see, the time when the great trappings of the urban environment were established. The properly Egyptian demographic increase was completed by a spectacular influx of foreigners (who in a few years numbered 75,000), personnel who were part of the colonial regime and entrepreneurs attracted by the Egyptian boom.

The war years (1914–18) saw a change of tempo in this increase: the population of Cairo began to grow at a speed faster than that of the whole Egyptian population. With 1,060,000 inhabitants in 1927 and 1,300,000 in 1937, Cairo represented 7.5 per cent and 8.2 per cent of the Egyptian population respectively. This accelerated movement towards urbanization which affected all Egypt (in 1897, 15 per cent of the population lived in towns with more than 20,000 inhabitants, of which there were 17; in 1947 the proportion was 30 per cent, in 57 towns) was evidently linked to the slowing of pace in the development of agricultural production; it increased at an average 0.4 per cent per annum between 1914 and 1947, which from then on became less than the pace of growth of population. Because of this, the average agricultural income went down: it was only E£ 26 in 1947. Economic pressure in the countryside, which had lessened before 1914, became much stronger; and this movement to towns chiefly affected Cairo, where migration accounted for more than half the increase in population: in 1927, out of a little more than 1,000,000 Cairenes, only 644,000 had been born in Cairo. The swelling of the population of Cairo was due less to the attraction of the city, where industrialization, little encouraged by the British occupiers, was developing at a very slow pace, than to the overpopulation of the countryside: Cairo thus helped absorb the overflow of rural population more than all the other urban areas.

In this overall growth, one element, which has already been pointed out, should be underlined: that of the importance of the foreign population, particularly the Europeans. The four principal foreign colonies comprised 59,460 people in 1927 (18,289 in 1882). During this time, the number of the British had increased tenfold (11,221 in 1927) and was now greater than that of the French. But the most numerous were the Greeks (20,115) and the Italians (18,575). The role played by foreigners in supplying official personnel in the administrative and economic domains explains this flood. Reasons of the same kind also explain the relatively high numbers of the minorities in Cairo: 94,000 Copts in 1927, almost 10 per cent of the population of the city;

34,103 Jews; also numerous Syrians who, because they were foreigners but Arab, were of intermediate status and who played an important economic and intellectual role.

2) *The Expansion of the city to the west and to the north*

Such a rapid numerical growth implies a considerable construction effort: the building industry in Cairo underwent a real boom between 1897 and 1907. Urbanizing enterprises achieved inside and around Cairo (filling-in of the last ponds, levelling of the hills, filling-in of the Khalig) allowed the growth of the receptive capacity of the old city whose quarters could absorb a significant portion of the newcomers: Gamaliyya had 44,788 more inhabitants between 1882 and 1927; Darb al-Ahmar had 52,544 more. But the old quarters were reaching saturation point and it was thus particularly to the west and north that were found the free spaces which would, in 30 years, be occupied by more than 500,000 new Cairenes.

The search for new ground was beset with difficulties of various kinds. In the west, the river was an obstacle to be cleared with difficulty and the amplitude of its floods made its banks rather inhospitable. Towards the north and the north-east, the two basic problems were those of distance from the centre of the city and aridity. These different problems were solved in only 20 years, between 1897 and 1917, and a 'second city'[4] of Cairo could thus come into being in the first decades of the twentieth century. A modern network of mass transportation was set up between 1894 (a concession was given to the Belgian financier Empain to establish a tram system) and 1917: at this date, Cairo had 30 tram lines which ensured internal communications (one line was built on the site of the former Khalig) and links with the suburbs (Bulaq, 'Abbasiyya, the Pyramids, Shubra, Old Cairo, Embaba); the 65 kilometres of lines, which formed almost the definitive network for Cairo, put the centre of Cairo only one hour away from its outermost parts. The filling-in of the Isma'iliyya Canal (in 1912) overcame the obstacle to the northward expansion of Cairo and provided a fast direct route in the direction of Heliopolis, which was then beginning to be developed. The construction of the Aswan Dam above all met the need to develop Egyptian agriculture; but the control of the Nile floods also allowed the stabilization of the ground at the edge of the river in Cairo, on both banks and on the islands (Gezira and Roda) and their use for the construction of new quarters to the west of the city. It also enabled the construction of the bridges which the city needed in order to expand westwards. Three bridges begun in 1902 and completed in 1907 were added to the Isma'il Bridge (the 'Abbas Bridge, linking Roda to Giza; a bridge between Roda and Old Cairo; the Muhammad 'Ali Bridge between Qasr al-'Aini and Roda) offering a way to the west from the south of the city. Once the bridge from Bulaq to the north of Gezira was built (1908–12) there were three routes to the left bank. The system of bridges did not need further modification until 1952.

These technical achievements and modern means of transport opened the way for the expansion of the city in other domains. Until 1900 the city changed only slowly, along the lines drawn up in the time of Isma'il: gradual urbanization of the Isma'iliyya quarter; establishment of administrative functions in the area to the east of Qasr al-'Aini; the peopling of the Faggala and Tawfiqiyya quarters betwen the old city and the Isma'iliyya Canal. It was from the beginning of the century that the great achievements in urbanization began. The area along the shore of the Nile, until then taken up by princely residences, was opened to urban development. In the Qasr al-Dubara area, division into lots followed the establishment of the British Consulate General (the 'Residence'): Garden City began in 1906 to strew its beautiful residences along the streets in curved lines, in the English manner. In Gezira, between 1905 and 1907, the Baehler Company bought and divided into lots, on a grid plan, the area which was to become the chic quarter of Cairo, Zamalek. Further south, the peopling of Roda began, while to the west of the Nile the occupation of Embaba and Giza was outlined.

To the north-east of Cairo, the almost desert plateau into which 'Abbasiyya extended was the object of an attempt at development which began in 1906, when a company directed by Baron Empain, whose activity in the field of transport we have seen, decided to create a satellite city there. The company acquired 2,500 and then 5,000 hectares of desert land at a derisory price and undertook its division into lots after building a tram line (the 'metro') which over a total length of 24 kilometres linked 'Heliopolis' to Cairo. Considerable amounts of European capital permitted the organization of the supply of water and electricity and the establishment of a network of sewers. The population developed rapidly; in 1910 there were only a thousand or so people in Heliopolis; but the number of inhabitants reached 28,544 in 1930 and 50,000 in 1947. For a long time an offshoot detached from the centre of Cairo, Heliopolis turned the focus of the development of the agglomeration towards the north-east to the point where, in the middle of the century, the growth of urban fabric had filled in the vast empty space which had originally separated the two.

The modernization and development of the city could take place only at the cost of a considerable outlay on equipment which very rapid urban growth would then render inadequate. The appearance in 1903 of a new type of vehicle, the automobile, hastened the transformation of the network of streets in the capital; macadamization had begun as early as pre-1882. The area of paved roads increased from 30,000 square metres in 1882 to 1,354,000 in 1900 and to 3,408,000 in 1927. But this modernization particularly affected the new city, where modern traffic was concentrated. In the old city the road system often remained archaic, and few major arteries were provided to ameliorate a clearly deficient network (the main ones being Shariʿ al-Khalig and Shariʿ al-Azhar). From 1909, the establishment of a network of sewers began in Cairo: planned for a million people, it reached its maximum capacity as early as 1930.

One of the great difficulties encountered by Cairo in its development was the absence of any municipal institution. At a time when Egyptian towns were being progressively endowed with municipalities, the capital was directly administered by the government or within the framework of the governorate of the province. The Tanzimat administration, created at the time of Muhammad ʿAli, enjoyed only limited power, and the control of certain departments escaped it entirely. This situation explains in part the obvious deficiencies in the organization of urban life. The diminished political status of Egypt, the seizure by foreigners of the administration, the privileges from which they benefited (their subjection to local taxes posed numerous problems), the concession of all public services to foreign companies, all this also helped make difficult the coordination of municipal action and its orientation towards the benefit of the main bulk of the population.

3) The two cities

The colonial period confirmed the tendency towards the establishment of two cities joined side by side, which had become apparent from as early as the time of Ismaʿil Pasha, but worsened later: if before 1882 the line of demarcation separated a 'traditional' sector and a 'modern' sector, after the colonization of Egypt the cleavage took on a national, social and economic character which accentuated its severity. From then on, one could legitimately speak of an 'indigenous' city and a 'European' city, just as in the case of the great colonial cities of North Africa. Two worlds, different in every way (even the appearance of the street system, anarchic in the east, regular in the west), faced each other on either side of a 'frontier' which ran from north to south, from Bab al-Hadid to Azbakiyya, to Abdin and to Sayyida Zainab. Instead of a progressive process of fusion, as could have been hoped for in the time of Ismaʿil, the differences became greater as the centre of gravity of the city inexorably moved towards the west, where power, activity and riches were accumulating.

Old Cairo covered only one part of the Ottoman city; the rectangle of the latter had been a little cut into, to the west of Shariʿ Khalig al-Masri, by the progress of modernism. Bulaq belonged to this sector. Some roads and the construction of modern buildings had in places introduced the appearance of progress. But, behind the alignments of 'European' façades, the old fabric continued to exist, becoming more and more dilapidated. This old city had been sacrificed to the European city, as early as the time of Isma'il, and this abandonment only worsened subsequently: the road system was neglected, there was insufficient rubbish collection, sewers were poor or non-existent, the water supply was incomplete. Nevertheless, the population in these quarters continued to grow at a rapid pace: between 1882 and 1927 the population of four of the divisions (*qism*) which formed the old city (Gamaliyya, Bab al-Sharaya, Muski, Darb al-Ahmar) rose from 122,411 to 259,535, an increase of 112 per cent; but, taking account of the even more rapid growth of the other areas of Cairo, the eastern city suffered a clear relative decline. The proportion of the population who lived there continually decreased: in 1897, 54.3 per cent of the total; in 1907, 51 per cent; in 1917, 47 per cent; in 1927, 40 per cent; and finally, in 1937, 34 per cent. Moreover, this population was particularly poor. The old city tended to become a refuge and to become proletarian; this could only precipitate a decline which was apparent in its external aspect—more and more abject—and in its activity—more and more reduced. The case of Gamaliyya[5] is absolutely typical from this point of view: this traditional quarter had been able to maintain itself with its artisanal and commercial activities until around 1914. But, after the war, prominent people had gradually deserted it and the decline of its economic activities contrasted with an ever more acute overpopulation, which led in turn to chronic unemployment. Modern economic activities had now been moved towards the west and the north, and this is where, indisputably, the present and the future of the city were to be found.

The western city, whose principal poles were the hotels and banks of the Isma'iliyya quarter, the royal palace of Abdin, the ministries and embassies of the Qasr al-'Aini quarter, appeared to converge on the two most ostentatious symbols of the foreign occupation: the British barracks in Qasr al-Nil and the Residence of the all-powerful representative of Great Britain. The business centre was still the town designed under Isma'il: the villas had disappeared and been replaced by large buildings. Here were concentrated the big shops, the boutiques, the banks, the best hotels (including the famous Shepheard's, rebuilt several times but which would finally disappear in the great fire in 1952). Here also the European population was concentrated; they held the levers of political decision and economic power. In several areas within the triangle whose top is the railway station and whose base is Shari' Khedive Isma'il, the foreign population (principally European) was in the majority in 1927 (for example, in Tawfiqiyya 62.3 per cent of the population were foreigners); altogether this area had 23,524 foreigners out of a total of 64,001 (37 per cent). The political centre was situated a little further south, along Qasr al-'Aini in a network of streets designed in a grid plan; here were most of the ministries and main government services. To the west, between the

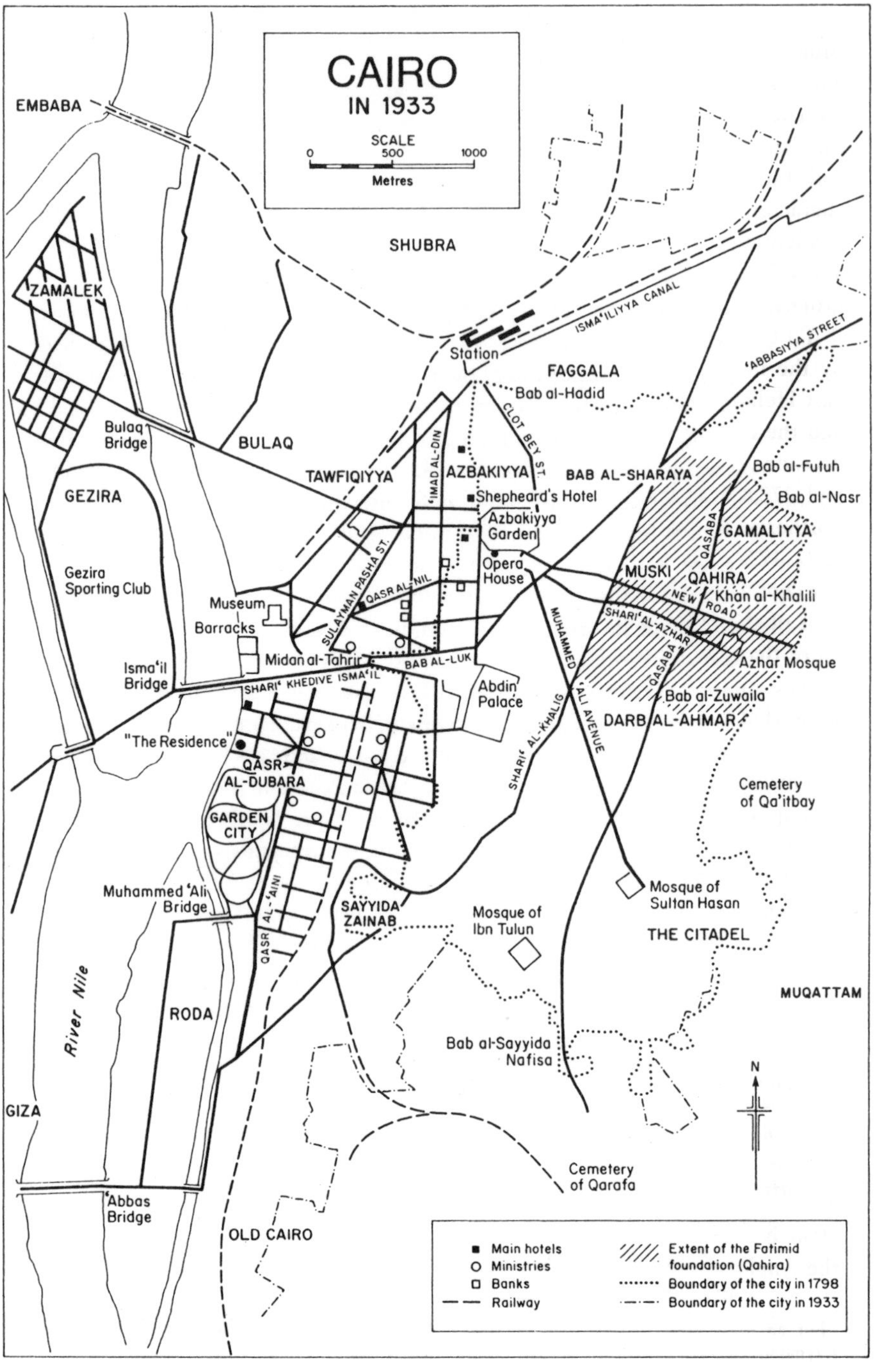

CAIRO
IN 1933
SCALE
0
500
1000
Metres
EMBABA
SHUBRA
ZAMALEK
Station
ISMA'ILIYYA CANAL
'ABBASIYYA STREET
FAGGALA
Bab al-Hadid
CLOT BEY ST.
Bulaq Bridge
BULAQ
'IMAD AL-DIN
TAWFIQIYYA
AZBAKIYYA
BAB AL-SHARAYA
Bab al-Futuh
Bab al-Nasr
GEZIRA
Shepheard's Hotel
Azbakiyya Garden
GAMALIYYA
QASABA
Opera House
MUSKI
QAHIRA
Khan al-Khalili
NEW ROAD
SHARI' AL-AZHAR
Gezira Sporting Club
Museum
SULAYMAN PASHA ST.
QASR AL-NIL
Barracks
Midan al-Tahrir
BAB AL-LUK
Azhar Mosque
Isma'il Bridge
SHARI' KHEDIVE ISMA'IL
Abdin Palace
MUHAMMED 'ALI AVENUE
Bab al-Zuwaila
DARB AL-AHMAR
"The Residence"
SHARI' AL-KHALIG
QASR AL-DUBARA
Cemetery of Qa'itbay
GARDEN CITY
Muhammed 'Ali Bridge
QASR AL-'AINI
SAYYIDA ZAINAB
Mosque of Ibn Tulun
Mosque of Sultan Hasan
THE CITADEL
River Nile
MUQATTAM
RODA
Bab al-Sayyida Nafisa
N
GIZA
Cemetery of Qarafa
'Abbas Bridge
OLD CAIRO
Main hotels
Ministries
Banks
Railway
Extent of the Fatimid foundation (Qahira)
Boundary of the city in 1798
Boundary of the city in 1933

Isma'il Bridge and Roda, the rich residential quarter, Garden City, stretched out. The beautiful quarters had crossed the Nile and spread themselves in Zamalek to the north of the gardens of the Gezira Sporting Club, created by the British for their physical pleasure and moral comfort. Further south, Roda and, further west, Giza had a clearly marked upper-middle-class residential character. The characteristics of the western city (business, well-to-do residential) explain why, despite the importance of its role, it gathered only 350,000 inhabitants (26.7 per cent of the total population of Cairo in 1937, a proportion which had scarcely changed since the beginning of the century).

To the north, a new city gradually took form, strongly marked in the west by the industrial development underway in Bulaq and Shubra, while in the east Heliopolis retained its character of a residential area for the bourgeoisie and the middle class, with a strong element of Egyptian minorities. The two divisions (*qism*) of Shubra and Wayli, which had 30,731 inhabitants in 1882, had 272,626 in 1927. The part of the population of all Cairo living in the northern area had not stopped growing since the beginning of the century: in 1897, 12.9 per cent; in 1907, 16.5 per cent; in 1917, 21.5 per cent; in 1927, 27.6 per cent. In 1937, the northern area had altogether 450,000 inhabitants (34 per cent of the total population of Cairo), more than the eastern city and much more than the western city. The development of transport enabled built-up areas even further away (southern suburbs of Maadi and Helwan) to advance somewhat, but they still did not muster more than a fairly limited population.

This 'fragmented' city was the image of a divided society, the image of a colonized country. In all the urban symbols the preponderance of foreigners was apparent, entrenched within their business and residential quarters. For the Egyptians, the dilemma was clear: to become resigned to the slow asphyxia of the old quarters or to accept assimilation into a way of life which had been brought to them from outside.

METROPOLITAN CAIRO (1936–76)*

> *Cairo at this time was seething with insolent activity ... Observers were struck with an impression of overwhelming size. The crowd had become terrifyingly huge ... The inequality of social strata, the split between their different ways of life and almost between their moral codes, the special characteristics of various districts are evidence of a fragmentation and a dispersal which should have made the city powerless. And yet the clamour that sometimes arose from this heterogeneous, jostling mass revealed a terrifying unity. The giant regrouped his shattered fragments and struck.*[6]

1936 is a political date without real significance for Egypt: the signing of the Anglo-Egyptian treaty put an end neither to the political preponderance

* For an up-to-date account of Cairo during this period, the reader should consult André Raymond, *Le Caire* (Paris: Fayard, 1993).

of the British, which could only end with the revolution of 1952, nor to the military occupation, whose last effects were swept away in 1956. But it is nonetheless true that, for Cairo, the period which began in 1936 marked the beginning of a new era. From then on the life and fortunes of Cairo were governed by a demographic evolution which underwent an abrupt change: until 1937, the population of Cairo grew at an annual rate of around 1.5 to 2 per cent (1897–1907: 1.4 per cent; 1927–37: 2.2 per cent). From then on the rate of growth moved on to more than 4 per cent: 1937–47, 4.8 per cent; 1947–60 and 1960–66, 4 per cent. The population of Cairo, which had doubled between 1882 and 1914 (32 years), doubled between 1917 and 1942 (25 years), and doubled again between 1947 and 1966 in only 19 years. As a result of this leap forward, the proportion of the Egyptian population represented by Cairo, which had risen gradually from 6 per cent to 8.2 per cent (in 1937), jumped the 10 per cent barrier in 1947 (10.8 per cent) and then grew rapidly to 12.8 per cent in 1960 and to 16 per cent in 1976. The slowing of growth shown by the 1976 census (annual growth of 1.8 per cent between 1966 and 1976) indicates a change of direction which will however alter these basic data only in the long term.

Because of this formidable demographic upsurge, a 'third city of Cairo' (P. Marthelot) can be seen to be coming into existence, one whose very amplitude and accelerated development justify its designation as 'metropolis', the first in Africa, one of the most important in the world, but with characteristics which make it a specifically Egyptian phenomenon.

1) A galloping demography[7]

When one approaches the demography of Egypt, and that of Cairo, of the present day, one handles figures which cause vertigo. The population of Cairo grew, from 1937 to 1947, from 1.3 million to 2 million inhabitants. In 1960 it was 3.3 million and, in 1976, 5.1 million. But at this last date, 'metropolitan' Cairo (including in particular the urbanized areas in the governorate of Giza, on the west bank of the Nile) had 6.7 million inhabitants (18.8 per cent of the population of Egypt) and 'Greater Cairo' had 8 million.

It is true that the whole of Egypt had been affected by a veritable demographic revolution, its annual growth increasing from an average of 1.2 per cent between 1927 and 1937, to 1.9 per cent between 1937 and 1947, and finally to 2.6 per cent from 1947.[8] But in Cairo two phenomena combined to accelerate growth beyond what anyone could have foreseen, to rates which, between 1947 and 1966, reached and passed 4 per cent. The natural rate of growth of the population of Cairo, which had for a long time been moderate, had overtaken the rate for Egypt. There are two consquences of this: first, the population of Cairo is very young (51 per cent of the population were under

20 in 1960); secondly, it is no longer possible to envisage stopping the growth of Cairo by simply limiting internal immigration. The growth of Cairo has become inevitable and must therefore be planned. The second phenomenon is the strength of internal immigration which sends an ever-increasing stream of people to Cairo from the rest of Egypt. This movement affected all the towns in Egypt, but Cairo more than any other: between 1960 and 1966 it absorbed almost 80 per cent of all migrant Egyptians and in 1960 it was estimated that 1,270,000 Cairenes (more than a third of the population of Cairo) had been born outside the city. The vigour of this internal migration is naturally linked to the strong demographic growth affecting all Egypt, to the rural pressure which has become explosive, and to the resulting endemic unemployment in the countryside. It is also due to a policy of industrialization followed energetically between 1956 and 1966 which attracted a considerable number of people to the areas around the industrial complexes created to the north and south of Cairo; the slowing of this effort is one of the reasons for the dip in the growth of Cairo after 1966. This migrant population, composed of individuals of a relatively low cultural level (45.6 per cent illiterate), little qualified professionally (42.6 per cent workers without qualifications) and having lower-than-average income at their disposal, palpably aggravate the various problems which Cairo faces. Recent immigrants are poor, they are hit heavily by unemployment and their needs, whether social (financial assistance, housing), economic (work) or cultural (education), are particularly pressing.

It is understandable that, in this rising whirlwind, the departure of some tens of thousands of foreigners, following the revolution of 1952 and particularly the Suez crisis (1956), was relatively imperceptible, even though among these foreigners had been a large number of high-level specialists and experts and also lower-grade technicians, whose emigration impoverished Egypt. In the political and social spheres, however, this departure was of great significance: it helped restore the capital to the Egyptians, in the same way that the policy of Nasser, whatever its gaps and failures, helped restore Egypt to its inhabitants, and it provoked a social and economic displacement which changed the face of the city.

Under the effect of such a strong demographic upsurge, the structure of the city was completely upset: between 1937 and 1947 the relative positions of the larger sectors of Cairo were inverted; the old city, the western city and the northern city changed in ten years from 34, 27 and 34 per cent of the total population respectively to 32, 25 and 38 per cent.[9] This trend has continued up to the present, so much so that the centre of gravity of the city, which for 60 years had been moving from the east to the west, tends to be fixed now in the northern area.

The relative decline of the 'oriental' city, already perceptible before 1937, has continued and accelerated since the war. The moderate increase in population figures of the six *qism* which make up this part of Cairo (in 1947, 574,051; in 1976, 773,053) corresponds, in percentage, with a progressive decline: in 1947 these six *qism* contained 28 per cent of the total population of Cairo; in 1960, 22.2 per cent; in 1976, 14.3 per cent. The old city has not, however, ceased to play an important role in the life of the Cairene conglomeration: it shelters a large proportion of the poorest among the population, in particular the new immigrants seeking asylum when they first arrive in Cairo. This is the role played by the colonial shanty-towns of North Africa. This situation also explains the considerable density (1,002 inhabitants per hectare in the whole of the Bab al-Sharaya *qism*, but densities exceeding 2,000 in certain quarters, for example that of al-'Utuf: 2,280). The limit of demographic saturation has been reached in this area, which explains why the slowing of overall growth in Cairo since 1966 has been particularly marked in the 'old quarters', where a decline in the population seems to have started. The crowding of the population explains a totally astonishing phenomenon: the peopling of the cemeteries of Cairo. Finding no space towards the east available for urban expansion, the human tide which has submerged the city has progressively colonized the cities of the dead of Qa'itbay and Qarafa, where the tombs were built like real houses, set out in an organized network of roads. From 1940, squatters in search of cheap housing invaded these cemeteries; the population living there is estimated at about 100,000, generally miserable, people.

The development of the western city, which has become the centre of the city because of the thrust beyond the Nile, has also slowed down: 575,788 inhabitants in 1947; 617,480 in 1976 in the five *qism* to the west. But this represents no more than a regularly decreasing proportion of the population of Cairo: 28.1 per cent in 1947; 19.6 per cent in 1960; 12.1 per cent in 1976. Its functions as the centre of administrative activities and services and its tendency to be a wealthy residential area, which did not allow great density, explain this stagnation. The expansion of the city further westwards continues now beyond the Nile: Giza and Embaba, which had 537,789 inhabitants in 1947, had reached 1,062,000 in 1965, an increase of 98 per cent, greater than the increase in the whole of Cairo taken together during the same period (96 per cent). In 1976, the governorate of Giza, of which a large part belongs to the urban mass of Cairo, had a population of 2,419,247.

But it is to the north of the city that the most spectacular changes have taken place. In 1947 there were 732,153 inhabitants there; 2,837,014 in 1976, an increase of 387 per cent. The northern area, which held 35.7 per cent of the total population of Cairo in 1947 and 46.5 per cent in 1960, today contains more than half this population (55.8 per cent in 1976) and the patches of urban development are now tending to merge. This growth is so vigorous that it seems as though the future of Cairo may well be taking shape there: the projects for a rapid north–south link (metropolitan)[10] and the industrialization of this area can but reinforce a movement which has the compelling appearance of a natural phenomenon, as if the capital of Egypt were resuming, in the middle of the twentieth century, a millenary movement to the north, the successive stages being Fustat (640), al-ʿAskar (750), al-Qata'iyah (870) and finally al-Qahira (969).

At the other end of Cairo, in the south, a similar movement of expansion is developing with comparable vigour, although somewhat later. If Old Cairo, just like the old quarters, is marking time relatively speaking (4.9 per cent of the total population in 1947; 5.4 per cent in 1976), while still gaining in numbers (from 100,904 to 273,670), the urban residential areas of Maadi and Helwan have been swept up in a frenetic process of growth: Maadi has grown from 42,994 in 1947 to 287,056 in 1976, Helwan from 24,028 to 316,190 people, a record growth of more than 1,200 per cent in 30 years, a growth linked to the rise of industry in this area. A new pole in Cairo has been created in the south, beyond the spaces which still remain to be conquered.

2) *Urban problems*

The figures which have just been cited are eloquent enough to presage the magnitude of the problems facing contemporary Cairo, where the trappings of urban development and the very life of the population are concerned. The daily existence of such a mass of humanity, distributed over an area of more than 20,000 hectares, is the source of innumerable difficulties, reminiscent of the kind which make the technicians of occidental metropolises grow pale, but in the economic and social environment of a country whose *per capita* income was estimated around 1972 at only $197.

Although perceptible progress has been made in this domain since the war, it cannot be said that the city of Cairo has at its disposal administrative structures which would enable it to organize its development. The creation in 1949 of the Cairo Municipality (*baladiyya*) and of a Ministry of Municipal and Rural Affairs marked, in this context, an important stage which was completed by the abolition of privileges for foreigners and the recovery by the Egyptians of the management of public utilities (end of concessions, from 1947; abolition of the Mixed Courts, 1948; nationalization of transport, 1956), and finally the abolition or tight control of *waqf* endowments. But the hesitations over what form to give the administration of Cairo and the tendency to manage the city from the top, in a bureaucratic manner, certainly impeded the planning of the development of the city almost as much as the lack of sufficient resources or the fact that the western part of the city depends on a separate administrative structure (the governorate of Giza). In total, except in limited sectors (Maadi, Heliopolis, Madinat Nasr, the Fatimid city), the attempt at regulation has been insufficient for a long time and, when an attempt at planning was made, it seemed to fall well short of meeting realities which could have been foreseen: the masterplan of 1965 set a ceiling of 3,500,000 inhabitants for Cairo. It might be thought that the High Committee, formed to supervise the development of Cairo, will be both more realistic and more efficacious.

One of the most difficult technical problems in Cairo is that of traffic. A considerable effort was made, after 1952, to extend and improve the streets of Cairo that were threatened with congestion by the volume of traffic. Among the most spectacular achievements (which were also of clear political significance) were the development of the central square, Midan al-Tahrir, relieved in 1946 of the encumbering presence of the British barracks, and the completion of the Nile Corniche, 50 kilometres long, the last barrier to which having been the garden of the British Residency which extended all the way to the river. Cairo is today hemmed in by a network of fast roads which outline its new shape. Communications towards the western part have been appreciably improved by the construction of the University Bridge (1958) and by the current construction of a bridge between the Bulaq Bridge and the Isma'il (now Qasr al-Nil) Bridge. This progress has not been enough to resolve the problems of traffic that the size of the city (roughly 50 kilometres north to south and 10 kilometres west to east) and the length of daily journeys of Cairenes (from the distant suburbs in the north, west and south to the centre) render particularly acute. Public transport is subjected to considerable strain; the spectacle of crammed buses and trains spilling forth hordes of travellers provides a daily illustration of this. The recent liberalization of the importation of private cars has helped make urban traffic congestion worse; this is particularly noticeable on the approaches to the Nile bridges. The sewage system and the pumping stations are also overworked and periodically threaten to give up the ghost: in 1965 the sewers overflowed, particularly in the most populated quarters, the least well equipped, to the point where, in the worst cases, a number of sewer vents were covered over with a thick layer of cement in order to avoid explosions and malodorous geysers. Upon one of these curious termite-hill-like excrescences, a ragamuffin in Sayyida Zainab wrote, with that so typically Cairene humour which is expressed in sometimes savage *nuktas* (jokes): *maqam Sidi Baladiyya* (the tomb of Mr Municipality). Exceptional measures undertaken during that year meant that the most urgent problems could be solved, but the low-lying places in the city remain, in winter, under threat of flood. Rubbish collection comes up against the same difficulties and is similarly inadequate.

More pressing for the people of Cairo are the problems of work and housing. We have already noted that one of the characteristics of urbanization in Egypt is that it has not been fundamentally linked to a process of industrialization, as was the case in Europe. Urbanization is first and foremost a rural exodus caused by insurmountable agrarian problems. It is not therefore surprising that unemployment should be very important in Cairo: according to the 1960 statistics, 66.8 per cent of the 'working' population have no specific work or are without a permanent job; 23.5 per cent work in public services; only 7.5 per cent work in industry. Industrialization is a vital necessity in Cairo but, despite the achievements in the northern part of Cairo and in Helwan, only a small part of the available workforce is in proper employment, and a great mass of people without a stable job must content themselves with a very low standard of living. This situation has inevitable repercussions on the problem of housing. The overall density of the city is made considerbly worse by the demographic upsurge: 79.6 people per hectare in 1937; 156 in 1960; 285 in 1976. It is particularly bad in the old quarters. The need for housing which is evidently considerable is even more difficult to satisfy, given that the worst affected people are also very poor. Matters deteriorate progressively because of the rapid degradation of the housing stock in the old quarters: it is estimated that every year 12,000 units become uninhabitable. According to a study undertaken in 1965, it would have been necessary to build 140,000 units of housing in five years, that is, 40,000 to cover the predicted growth in population, 30,000 to reduce the present density and 70,000 to replace the decrepit units. Since the number of units of housing actually built between 1965 and 1970 is estimated to be 75,000, it must be concluded that the situation perceptibly deteriorated during this period. The praiseworthy efforts to build social housing (working-class estates: in Embaba, 2,000 lodgings; in Helwan, 3,000) have fallen well short of needs: the density of housing by room, which had 2 people per room in 1947, increased to 2.3 in 1960 and seems to have risen perceptibly thereafter.

Aware of these problems, the planners envisaged creating satellite cities around Cairo, in the non-agricultural areas; this development would ease the human pressure which was overburdening the capital. Two big projects along these lines saw the light of day. The attempt to create a new town on the Muqattam Hills (in 1954–6) was a complete failure as a result of the difficulty of communications with Cairo, as well as the fairly harsh natural conditions on this desert plateau. The project to create a complete town, Madinat Nasr, to the east of Cairo, between the capital and Heliopolis, was more successful, doubtless thanks in part to massive support from the government which wanted to make this enterprise one of the outstanding achievements of the regime. The 'Town of Victory' was supposed to be built in 20 years or so in the arid area between ʿAbbasiyya and Heliopolis. It was forecast that 100,000 people would live there, 500,000 in the long term. It would comprise housing of varying types (from villas for high civil servants to working-class estates); there would be employment there (administrative, ministerial, industrial). The new town sprang out of the desert in a few years. But Madinat Nasr had

65,347 inhabitants in 1976, while from 1960 to 1976 the population of Cairo had grown by 1,735,000 people: to match the current pace of growth in Cairo, a dozen such towns should come forth from the desert in a fairly short time, in order that the past deficit and future excess can be absorbed. The Madinat Nasr undertaking was at too high a cost for such a hypothesis to be realistic.

3) *The faces of the city*

The history of Cairo and its various ruptures have helped juxtapose parts of the city which differ in their urban design as much as in their economic role and in the cultural and social level of their inhabitants: doubtless such contrasts have always existed; but between the slums of the peripheral and central quarters and the ultra-modern buildings along the Corniche, every day migrations of hundreds of thousands of Cairenes are set into motion, while the mass media in general (cinema and television) increase awareness of differences which, for that reason, become less and less tolerable. Here, without any doubt, lie the causes of the dramatic events in Cairo in January 1952 and January 1977: the ransacking of luxury shops and the places of amusement in the rich quarters is also the revenge of another Cairo which one could have passed through for years without knowing anything about it, other than some important tourist sites where the folklore furnishes a disguise suitable to misery.

Of the eastern city there remain only relics, in the old centre, in Bulaq and Old Cairo. Some strings of admirable monuments, some rare architectural combinations (in Qasaba the group of buildings of Qalawun, Nasir and Barquq, and in the vicinity of Bab al-Zuwaila, the great covered market and Darb al-Ahmar) still bear witness today to the thousand-year splendour of Cairo. But the overall impression here is one of misery aggravated by negligence of public services in this forgotten Cairo. Modern buildings replace ancient structures and swiftly become dilapidated, prematurely worn out by insufficient maintenance and over-dense occupation. The feverish agitation in the streets is an illusion: the traditional activities which assured the equilibrium of the old city (commerce and crafts) have declined, or only continued to exist in the Khan al-Khalili area as a kind of theme-park for tourists. In the western part of the old city, from the Port Said road (formerly Khalig/Cairo canal) a twin process of modernization (coming from the west) and decline (from the east) is tending to create a transitional zone where a fusion between the two cities is being worked out. These quarters are often the areas which were renovated at the end of the nineteenth century and the beginning of the twentieth century and are now becoming 'baladified'. The remains of the old city are more and more reduced here; modern slums predominate.

The modern city, to the west of Azbakiyya and the Abdin Palace, is progressively detaching itself from the old city. Business is still concentrated in the quarters conceived by Isma'il, and administrative life continues a little further south. Buildings dating from the turn of the century, frequently ill-maintained, do not wear at all well. But incessant activity still throbs in Talat Harb, Qasr al-Nil and Sharif Pasha, paralysing the traffic during rush hour. The traditional centre of the business quarter, Talat Harb Square (formerly Sulaiman Pasha) has taken on a slightly provincial air in comparison with the adjacent Liberation Square (Midan al-Tahrir) where the streams of vehicles which pour in from the whole conglomeration of Cairo converge. In order to allow pedestrians to move around, the square has been surrounded by elevated walkways where the incessant tramping inevitably evokes Fritz Lang's 'Metropolis'. Bus station, place of assembly for great popular rallies on days of gaiety, grief or anger, the Midan serves as the frontier between 'colonial' and 'metropolitan' Cairo, as shown by the high buildings which obstruct the view of the Nile (the Hilton Hotel, Shepheard's Hotel, the Mugamma administrative centre, the Arab League, the Municipality). It is here that in the plan for an urban 'metro', the north–south and west–east lines would cross.

In Garden City, large modern buildings are beginning to shoot up among the palaces and villas with their peeling façades amidst gardens left to run wild: the departure of foreigners and the decline of the old Egyptian elite has made way for a new bourgeoisie, less wealthy but more numerous. For tens of kilometres the Nile now flows between a double barrage of high buildings which show the measure of the change Egypt has undergone during the last 40 years: this 'Nile front', which grieves some town-planners, is the most spectacular and the most impressive aspect of Cairo in our time, running the length of a river which, hour after hour and season after season, has preserved all its magic, and whose nocturnal splendour was restored with the end of the black-out after the war with Israel. In order to allow the current of traffic bringing the inhabitants of the western quarters towards the centre to cross the majestic flow of the Nile, a sixth bridge has been built, an overpass over Gezira and its Sporting Club where the Egyptian bourgeoisie and the new ruling strata have replaced the colonizers. Round this central zone, the beautiful quarters of modern Cairo stretch out: Zamalek, the Corniche. Near here the great palaces rise up: Shepheard's, the Hilton, the Sheraton, the Meridien. No visible squalor spoils the fairyland quality of the Nile here: the old city is no more than a sumptuous and distant backcloth dotted with minarets, spread as far as the Citadel.

The west bank of the Nile is lined with lofty buildings and luxury villas, occasionally somewhat elderly-looking. The expansion of Cairo on this side has been so rapid that it seems to have ensnared some villages. From north to south, east to west, traditional rural houses alternate with brick huts of recent occupants and modern apartment blocks of all standards. The working-class and still very rural quarters of Embaba form an island of poor proletariat in the northern area, with working-class houses echoed by the rows of cheap housing on Sudan Avenue. Further south, Muhandisin shelters a middle-class population, while Doqqi has become one of the prime bourgeois residential quarters in Cairo. Seen from an aircraft, the urban tide comes up against the obstacle still presented by the Said railway: further on, the countryside is almost intact, and from the last buildings of the city, a few metres beyond the rails, the colourful spectacle of agricultural life in the Egyptian Delta can be seen following its thousand-year-old cycle. But not for long, doubtless, as, via Giza, the city progresses further west: in the middle of the villas strung along the Pyramids road, multi-storey buildings are now shooting up. Urbanization is gaining towards the north: a city of more than 300,000 inhabitants, poor and still rustic, Bulaq al-Dakrur is developing beyond the railway. The agricultural land of the governorate of Giza, until recently still a leisure reserve for city-dwellers, is the next objective of the wave which has been breaking over the left bank of the Nile for 30 years.

Towards the north, the urban thrust has developed along the link roads which radiate, like the fingers of a hand, from the area of Azbakiyya. This type of expansion explains the great variety of outlying parts and suburbs found in this area and the generally crude aspect of quarters which are ill-structured and badly linked one to another. The city progresses, at a pace of savage urbanization, within the agricultural land of the province of Qalyubiyya: the area of the Barrages, formerly separated from Cairo by about 30 kilometres of countryside, has now been integrated into the region of 'Greater Cairo'. In the northerly direction, along the Nile, the city has developed from the working-class districts of Bulaq and Shubra and constitutes a poor suburb right up to Shubra al-Khaima with fairly numerous industrial establishments. Outwards from the Corniche, the development of which entails modernization which is driving back the poor area of habitation further to the east and isolating it from the Nile, the urban plan is one of modern town-planning prematurely dilapidated. Towards the north-east, urbanization has spread along two principal axes, the modern road, which follows the line of the old Isma'iliyya Canal, and the Suez railway; the old villages are now hemmed in by a conglomeration which, by way of Wayli and Matariah, reaches al-Marg, the proposed terminus of the north–south metro line, 13 kilometres as the crow flies from Midan al-Tahrir. These suburbs, where semi-rural sectors alternate with 'modern' cheap estates and industrial areas, are inhabited by a working-class population, a medium-poor class and, on the fringes in the process of urbanization, a population recently arrived in town and progressively adapting to a new way of life.

In complete contrast with the less favoured quarters, the areas in the north-east and the east offer two examples of voluntary urbanization. Heliopolis has gained on the desert as it has fulfilled the design proposed, at the beginning of the century, by Baron Empain. Lots intended for individual villas, in the middle of which stand strange 'follies' from the beginning of the century (such as the replica of the Temple of Angkor built by the promoter) have now been invaded by buildings of four or five storeys. Linked, from its beginnings, to the city centre by a metro line, Heliopolis has become progressively more attached to the city through the expansion of Cairo on this side and just recently by the implantation of Madinat Nasr. Heliopolis was, after the western region of Cairo, the second bourgeois residential area where foreigners and the Coptic and Levantine middle class have for a long time set the fashion. Heliopolis has since been 'Islamized' and today there is a strong presence of army and administrative personnel living there, but the chic areas are still those in the centre, near the Nile. Now there is no longer a gap between Heliopolis and Madinat Nasr, as evidenced by the tall buildings along the eastern by-pass.

Towards the south, Old Cairo presents, like Bulaq to the north, an image of a historic Cairo on the road to rapid disappearance: Egypt of yesterday is still present in some quarters where vestiges of the Christian centuries remain and in the ruins at Fustat which bear witness to the beginnings of Islamization. Along the motorway which runs along the old aqueduct, from the Citadel to the Nile, the area between the Citadel and Old Cairo has been rapidly populated: low-quality buildings which have multiplied here are among the most deplorable examples of 'modern' working-class housing that can be found in Cairo; too close together and too quickly degraded, these buildings have taken the very worst from western town-planning.

Old Cairo was for a long time the southern limit of the conglomeration. Today, urbanization is pushing vigorously towards the south, along the Nile, in a narrow valley. Further away from Cairo, the rural sectors with their villages reappear, at some distance from the Nile. Maadi is no longer the calm residential area it once was, its luxurious villas lost in the midst of gardens and trees, but a town undergoing full expansion. Beyond, the urban fabric is tenuous along the road, but very soon one sees silhouetted against the horizon the plumes of smoke from the tall chimneys of the steel-works and factories of Helwan, near which enormous working-class estates stretch out, implanted in a desert and desolate countryside, far from the Nile. It would be easy to forget that Helwan was chosen as a second residence by the Khedive Tawfiq, and that its hot springs made it, in the first decades of the century, a peaceful spa town.

CONCLUSION

The suddenness of the change undergone by Cairo during the last century explains for the most part the incompleteness of the contemporary city; the irresistible expansion of the city produces, like so many boulders deposited by a glacier, fragments, glorious and miserable, of its past, distant and recent. From the Citadel, where Saladin installed himself, to Midan al-Tahrir, centre of gravity of the modern city, ten centuries of history file by, in disorder. It is not just the monuments, impressive relics of a thousand years of the past or witnesses of a more recent evolution, which are all visible together; there are also the astonishingly contrasting ways of life juxtaposed in a rich confusion of colour and sound: pockets of the medieval city and contemporary urban slums border, and sometimes surround, the modern quarters.

The forward sweep of Cairo, always further to the north, west and south, presents the town-planners with prodigiously complex difficulties; no solution can be envisaged except within the framework of a remodelling of the whole of Egypt. But, while awaiting the solutions on the horizon of the year 2000, it is the everyday existence of this prodigious city, both disturbing and fascinating in its contrasts, that must be assured, in its most physical aspects: housing, traffic, making public services work. The solution to these problems should not be deferred for very long; otherwise the Cairo that has for a long time played the role of safety-valve for the demographic expansion of Egypt will risk becoming the detonator of the Egypt of tomorrow.

This article has been translated by Margaret Owen especially for *The Modern Middle East: A Reader* from 'Le Caire' in *L'Egypte d'aujourd'hui: Permanence et changements 1805–1976* (Paris, 1977), pp. 214–241. With the permission of the Centre Nationale de la Recherche Scientifique and the author.

NOTES

1. Gobineau, *Trois ans en Asie* (Paris, 1983), vol. 2, p. 41.
2. J. Berque, *L'Egypte, Impérialisme et révolution* (Paris, 1967), p. 85
3. I. Fahri, *L'Egypte que j'aime* (Paris, 1972), p. 131
4. P. Marthelot, 'Le Caire, nouvelle métropole' in *Annales Islamologiques*, VIII, 1969, p. 189.
5. Expertly studied by J. Berque and M. Shakaa, 'La Gamaliyya depuis un siècle' in *Colloque international sur l'histoire du Caire* (RDA, 1972), especially pp. 75–6, 78–9, 80–2.
6. J. Berque, *Egypt: Imperialism and Revolution* (London, 1972), p. 604.
7. The expression belongs to Simonne and Jean Lacouture in their *Egypte en mouvement* (Paris, 1956).
8. See the article by D. Panzac in *L'Egypte d'aujourd'hui: permanence et changements 1805–1976* (Paris, 1977).
9. Following J. Abu-Lughod, *Cairo* (Princeton, 1971). In what follows, we will use the classification and figures given by the Statistics Service of the Cairo Administration, which will entail some modification of percentages.

10. The network studied by a subsidiary of R.A.T.P. comprises, in the first stage, a north–south line, al-Marg to Helwan, 42.5 kilometres long, to be crossed later by two other lines.

BIBLIOGRAPHY

ABU-LUGHOD (Janet), *Cairo*, Princeton, 1971.

ASKAR (Gamal), *A statement on the population of Egypt*, Cairo, 1976.

BERQUE (Jacques), *L'Egypte, Impérialisme et révolution*, Paris, 1967.

BERQUE (Jacques), et SHAKAA (Mustafa), *La Gamâliya depuis un siècle*, in *Colloque international sur l'histoire du Caire*, RDA, 1972.

CLERGET (Marcel), *Le Caire*, Cairo, 1934, 2 vols.

FARHI (Ibrahim) *et al.*, *L'Egypte que j'aime*, Paris, 1972.

HASSAN (Shafick S.), *Characteristics of Migrant Families*, in Cairo Demographic Centre, Research Monograph Series, no. 4, Cairo, 1973.

HASSAN (Shafick S.) and DAYEM (Mohamed A.), *Characteristics of Recent Migrants*, in Cairo Demographic Centre, Research Monograph Series, no. 4, Cairo, 1973.

JOMIER (Jacques), *al-Kāhira, la ville moderne, Encyclopedia of Islam*, 2nd edn., vol. IV.

LACOUTURE (Simonne), *Egypte*, Paris, 1963.

LACOUTURE (Simonne and Jean), *L'Egypte en mouvement*, Paris, 1956.

LANE (E.W.), *The Manners and Customs of Modern Egyptians*, London, 1954.

MABRO (Robert), *The Egyptian Economy 1952–1972*, Oxford, 1974.

MARTHELOT (Pierre), *Le Caire, nouvelle métropole* in *Annales Islamologiques*, viii, 1969.

MARTHELOT (Pierre), *Recherche d'identité et mutation urbaine: l'exemple du Caire*, in R.O.M.M. xviii, 1974.

NASSEF (Abdel Faiah), *Internal Migration and Urbanization in Egypt*, in Cairo Demographic Centre, Research Monograph Series, no. 4, Cairo, 1973.

NASSEF (A.) and ASKALANY (Ragaa), *Demographic Characteristics of Labour Force in Greater Cairo*, in Cairo Demographic Centre, Research Monograph Series, no. 3, 1972.

OWEN (Roger), 'The Cairo Building Industry', in *Colloque international sur l'histoire du Caire*, RDA, 1972.

RAYMOND (André), *Artisans et commerçants au Caire au XVIIIe siècle*, Damascus, 1974, 2 vols.

RAYMOND (André), 'Problèmes urbains et urbanisme au Caire', in *Colloque international sur l'histoire du Caire*, RDA, 1972.

RHONE (Arthur), *L'Egypte à petites journées*, Paris, 1919.

ROGERS (Michael), *al-Kāhira, Encyclopedia of Islam*, 2nd edn., vol. IV.

WIET (Gaston), *Cairo, City of Art and Commerce*, Oklahoma Press, 1964.

III

The Construction of Nationalist Ideologies and Politics to the 1950s

Introduction

MARY C. WILSON

The First World War brought the long nineteenth century to a crashing end. The Ottoman Empire was on the losing side and was punished in the peace settlement, along with the other major losers, Germany and Austro-Hungary. The price exacted from the empire was high, higher than that levied on the others; it was divided, first into its two major language areas, the Turkish-speaking areas in the north and the Arabic-speaking areas in the south, then those areas were divided into states, spheres of interest, and autonomous areas, according to the interests of Britain and France and their local proxies. In that manner, the empire which for four hundred years had provided the political framework for much of the Middle East disappeared from the map.

New borders signalled a new era in Middle East history. In the Turkish-speaking areas, as Feroz Ahmad has described in Part I, a Turkish national movement formed around Mustafa Kemal to defeat the planned partition of the northern portion of the Ottoman Empire. The Arabic-speaking areas were divided into new administrative divisions—states—and placed under British or French mandate.

The questions, who would define the political community and how, underlay the political struggles of the interwar period. Despite the apparent historical discontinuity represented by the creation of new states, the answers to these questions showed a remarkable degree of continuity with the Ottoman past. The completeness with which the idiom of Arab and Turkish nationalism came to dominate political life was new; the class that used nationalism and benefited from it was for the most part the same class that had served and benefited from the Ottoman order. All the articles in Part III are in some way concerned with nationalism and with the continuities and discontinuities of the new state system with the Ottoman past.

Şerif Mardin looks at the Republic of Turkey. The end point of his analysis is the laicism of the reforms that were carried out under the leadership of Mustafa Kemal. He sees the roots of this laicism in the secularizing reforms of the nineteenth century. By the 1870s, in his view, Islam figured in Ottoman politics solely in terms of its utility: did it provide 'a means of rallying the population of the empire'? The question which faced Mustafa Kemal fifty years later, therefore, was not about secularization. Rather, he faced the question of what was the best tool to mobilize people in the wake of the defeat and dismemberment of the Ottoman Empire. His answer was to discard Islam in favour of something that did not yet exist; he 'took up a non-existent, hypothetical entity, the Turkish nation, and breathed life into it'. Hence in Mardin's view the Turkish Republic is both the heir to nineteenth-century secularizing reforms and entirely new.

For Mardin the ability to conceptualize a Turkish nation was grounded in the prior secularization of Ottoman politics; for C. Ernest Dawn the origins of Arab nationalism lie elsewhere. Dawn finds the conceptualization of an Arab nation among intellectuals who viewed reform in terms of a return to true Islam. These intellectuals interpreted the disparity of power between Europe and the Ottoman Empire in the nineteenth century as a product of religious decline. They argued that 'True Islam was not incompatible with advanced civilization ... [but] true primitive Islam had been corrupted and, as a result, the Moslems had not been able to continue the remarkable progress of their early years.' Although this group remained staunchly loyal to the Ottoman Empire, their emphasis on 'true Islam' turned attention to the Arabs and the need to revive classical Arabic literary and religious studies. Carrying this thought to its end, others began to stress the primacy of the Arabs in the regeneration of Islam and of the Ottoman Empire. Thus, the theory of Arab nationhood and its role in history grew out of a particular diagnosis of Ottoman decline. Most Arabs were loyal to the Ottoman Empire until there was nothing left to be loyal to. Not until then, according to Dawn, did Arabism develop beyond the realm of ideology.

What carried Arabism into the centre of the political arena was the break-up of the Ottoman Empire and the imposition of European control over its constituent Arabic-speaking parts. At that time the language of nationalism became useful to some urban notables (see Albert Hourani's article in Part I) seeking to maintain or improve their political position. Nationalism was especially useful because it spoke to the interests of sectors of society other than the urban elite. Joel Beinin and Zachary Lockman approach nationalism from the point of view of the emerging working class in Egypt.

The Egyptian revolution of 1919, long studied as a nationalist uprising of countrywide scope and participation, also provided the opportunity for the emergence of a small but growing sector of organized labour. Tramway workers, railway men, sugar refinery workers, taxi and carriage drivers, government employees, utility workers—all went on strike to support nationalist objectives and to win their own labour demands. Their gains on the labour front cannot be understood except in the context of the massive 1919 uprising, as demonstrated by Lockman and Beinin. Thereafter, however, a pattern was set of 'dependence on bourgeois nationalists as leaders ... and on bourgeois nationalism as the dominant ideological framework.' This was useful to the urban elite which formed the nationalist leadership; but, to the labour movement in particular and to the working class in general, such dependence was in the end detrimental. In the chapter from their book *Workers on the Nile* included here, Beinin and Lockman describe the triumphal beginning of this partnership between bourgeois nationalism and organized labour during the 1919 revolution.

The birth of organized labour in Egypt is one of those signs that mark the interwar period as distinctly different from that which preceded it. For all the marks of discontinuity which follow World War I in the Middle East, there are yet significant continuities with the immediate Ottoman past. Philip Khoury addresses both continuities and disjunctures in his picture of urban politics in Syria in the interwar period.

Central to the picture of Damascene politics drawn by Khoury were the quarters of the city. And central to the political life of the quarter were its prominent families, the urban notables. Under Ottoman rule these notables were intermediaries between local society and Istanbul; in the mandate period they stood between local society and the French. In this latter position many of them found the language of nationalism useful. They also found useful a traditional figure of quarter life, the *qabaday*, to mobilize support for the anti-French demonstrations that punctuated the mandate period.

A hero of the commonfolk, the *qabaday* was a young man and a leader of young men. He was virtuous, generous, and the protector of the weak; he was also, in his youth and physical strength, threatening. His position, however, declined as Damascus grew, as Damascene politics became national politics, and as state institutions began to displace the centrality of the quarter in the network of social support during the interwar period. In the new state schools young men of different quarters met and mingled. Members of an incipient middle class, destined for careers outside the quarter, these youths no longer found the *qabaday* relevant. Their new leaders were the leaders of specially organized nationalist youth parties; their new horizons were national and regional; their new language of politics was ideological. Thus, as Khoury demonstrates, the politics of Damascus in the interwar period showed continuity with the past in its structure of personal clientele networks built around life in the quarter. He also shows that the structure of patronage based in the quarter was being eroded in the social and political context of the French mandate.

The march of new groups—workers and state school students—and old ones to the tune of nationalism played by the urban notables eventually destroyed the structure of notable politics. Ted Swedenburg adds one of these old groups, peasants, to the mix of forces and interests that came to be arrayed against the urban notables. In his telling, the end of the politics of notables was foreshadowed by the 1936–39 rebellion in Palestine when an 'alliance of peasants, workers, and radical elements of the middle class ... challenged *a'yan* (notable) leadership of the nationalist movement and threatened the bases of mercantile–landlord dominance'.

Swedenburg traces a pattern of increasing urban dominance over the economic and cultural lives of Palestinian peasants for a century before the rebellion, owing to changes emanating from the Ottoman state and to 'the conditions of peripheral capitalism'. This was accomplished in spite of peasant resistance: foot-dragging, banditry, and flight. Dominance, disguised by the ties of paternalism and patronage, characterized the relationship between urban notables and peasants into the period of the British mandate, of growing Jewish settlement under Britain's aegis, and of the rise of Arab nationalism.

During the mandate the failure of urban notables to achieve their own national goals undermined their position. The practices and interests of peasants—'the refusal to pay taxes, the moratorium on debts, the heavy contributions levied against the wealthy'—shaped the rebellion of 1936–39 and challenged the urban notables as it challenged British rule. It represented, in other words 'a congealing of nationalism, religious revivalism, and class consciousness'. The rebellion was eventually put down by a massive commitment of British troops. This bespeaks, in Swedenburg's analysis, not the failure of a 'backward' peasantry, but the success of a professional and technologically superior force.

The 1920 Iraqi rebellion also represented a congealing of a variety of resentments: religious, economic, and perhaps national insofar as the rebellion was anti-British. The development of national consciousness in Iraq, however, faced formidable obstacles as analysed by Hanna Batatu in Chapter 2 of his book, *The Old Social Classes and the Revolutionary Movements of Iraq*. Included here, this chapter explores the shifting identities of the peoples of Iraq in relationship to the creation of the state.

In Batatu's analysis the British occupation of Iraq during and after the First World War and the forty-day war between British forces and the Iraqi army in 1941 had profound effects on the development of national consciousness in Iraq. The first 'more than anything else helped the progress of the new sentiment...'. The second set nationalism on an anti-monarchical course which culminated in the 1958 revolution. Whether the monarchy tried to implement national cohesion or whether it feared the growth of a nationalism that was both anti-British and anti-monarchy, Batatu concludes that the 'monarchy, by choice or from necessity, directly or indirectly, through processes it initiated or through processes in which it became entangled, partly hindered the cohesion of Iraqis, but at the same time did much to prepare them for nationality'.

The same may be said of the late Ottoman Empire in relation to the development of Turkish and Arab nationalism. The nationalist ideologies that dominated the interwar politics of the successors of the empire became articulate in the conditions of the late nineteenth and early twentieth centuries. These conditions included the results both of a century of Ottoman reform and of more than a century of economic change tied to the spread of capitalism. Both helped inadvertently to create the new intelligentsia that began to articulate nationalist ideologies. In this sense the policies and historical processes of the late empire laid the groundwork for the rise of nationalisms amongst its constituent peoples. Nationalism did not, however, become politically meaningful until after the destruction of the Ottoman Empire. And even then, whether in Turkey or any of the Arab states, nationalist movements were never 'pure', but always represented a multiplicity of resentments and aspirations. Batatu perhaps puts this most clearly: 'Nationalism did not displace the old loyalties. Although it grew at their expense, it existed side by side with them....'

Religion and Secularism in Turkey

ŞERIF MARDIN

Few categorical assertions can be made in the social sciences, but certainly one of them is that social thought never starts with a clean slate. The contributions of social innovators, therefore, become fully meaningful only when their proposals are set in the framework of their institutional and intellectual inheritance.

This also holds true for a series of reforms which were carried out in Turkey in the 1920s and the 1930s, due in large measure to the single-minded drive and determination of Mustafa Kemal Atatürk, the architect of the Turkish Republic and its first president. These reforms established the principle of laicism—or secularism—as the foundation stone of Turkish constitutional theory and political life. The principle has endured to our day despite changes in régimes and constitutional renovation.

Laicism was a concept which emerged from French constitutional practice in the nineteenth century and referred to the necessity that the state refrain from lending its positive support to any one religious denomination. It was considered to have been fully achieved in France in 1905 with the definitive separation of Church and State. In Turkey, laicism amounted to more than the official disestablishment of religion, since Muslims did not dispose of an autonomous religious institution such as the Catholic Church which could carry its religious functions independently of the state. In France, religion and the state already operated on two distinct institutional registers and were eventually separated in the law of the land. In Turkey a limb of the state was torn out of its body when laicism became the state policy. This is the reason why Turkish secularization is considered a momentous achievement.

To say that Atatürk's policy is better understood when observed against his own background does not minimize this achievement, but it enables us to place this accomplishment in the frame of that celebrated meeting of East and West about which so much has been written. The historical context also brings out features which are crucial to an understanding of the future of laicism in Turkey. 'Cultural background' or 'historical context' as used here means not only the events of Atatürk's lifetime but the long-standing traditions and institutional arrangements in which he was rooted. It is these which provide the latent guidelines for the structuring of social relations in any society, even though they are also in constant flux.

Atatürk's secularizing reforms show at least two facts which had antecedents in Ottoman history, namely his opinions as to the functions of religion in society and the methods which he used to translate his ideas into policy. His ideas on religion bore the stamp of the empiricism of Ottoman secular officialdom, and the method that he used to implement his ideas—legislation—was foreshadowed by the policies of the nineteenth-century Ottoman modernizing statesmen.

OTTOMAN BUREAUCRACY AND MODERNIZATION

The Ottoman state, which emerged with its full outlines between the fourteenth and the sixteenth centuries, was an institutional achievement of major dimensions. As builders of an empire, the Ottomans confronted a number of obstacles which earlier Middle Eastern empires had only partly surmounted. One major task they faced was to establish effective government in a geographic setting which comprised a large variety of religious communities, ethnic groups and sub-cultures ensconced in ecological niches that were difficult of access. The Ottomans had to make nomads and city-dwellers contribute to a common purpose transcending their individual interests; they had to reconcile the requirements of imperial taxation with the autonomy of local magnates, who were often residual élites of earlier independent territories incorporated into the empire; and they had to find the means of integrating millions of Christians into a Muslim empire. In these tasks they seem to have succeeded better than their predecessors, an achievement which was, in great part, due to their ability to build a sultanic state. They created a class of military and administrative officials whose unstinting allegiance went to the Ottoman dynasty and sometimes even gave precedence to the state over the dynasty. They established a network of judicial and administrative positions staffed by district judges (*kadıs*) trained in Muslim law. They devised means of mobilizing the land resources of the empire, which were now integrated with a system of taxation and with military organization. They elaborated complex sets of regulations for commerce, and established control over a network of roads linking garrisoned cities. Subject populations such as the Christians, which the Ottomans had incorporated during their drive through the Balkans, were classified by their religious affiliation. The settlement of their civil concerns was delegated to their own ecclesiastical authorities—which the government used in order to secure access to their non-Muslim subjects.

Having added the Arab lands and Mecca and Medina to the empire in the sixteenth century, the Ottomans began to see themselves as heirs to the Islamic Caliphate, and the Ottoman sultan assumed the role of protector of the entire Muslim world.[1] In consequence, even though the Turks had been converted to Islam long before and had given a central place to Islamic institutions in their state, religion now acquired a new 'imperial' dimension. However, Islam was far from a unitary concern. A central Islamic tradition, which in its essentials showed great similarities, prevailed in cities throughout the Islamic world. But in the wider span of that world, as in many regions in the Ottoman empire proper, this unity disappeared, and heterodox doctrines, charismatic leaders and cults with deep local roots and only an Islamic veneer became items to reckon with. This religious heterogeneity was a source of deep worry for Ottoman statesmen—a pattern which, as I shall try to show, had changed very little even by the twentieth century.

One feature of Ottoman Islam was particularly galling to Ottoman officials. The Shiite form of Islam had been adopted in Iran in the sixteenth century by rulers who were engaged in a rivalry with the Ottomans for the mantle of leadership in West Asia. Ottoman Shiites were therefore considered by the Ottomans to be a dangerous fifth column working to undermine their hegemony. But quite apart from the dangers of Shiism, Ottoman officials evaluated the practice of Islam from a perspective which they shared as officials, namely the fear that the Ottoman empire, already made up of a mosaic of unwieldy components, would fragment. Faced, at the time when they were trying to consolidate the empire, by what amounted to a congerie of brotherhoods, sects and cults; confronted by a succession of millenarian movements; and, furthermore, pitted against potentially subversive magnates and what survived of erstwhile princely dynasties, Ottoman bureaucrats felt the need to get a grip over religion which would minimize the dangers that religious movements spelled out. To this end they used a number of policies. First, they tried to impose orthodox, Sunni Islam and were constantly on the lookout for traitorous Shii. Secondly, they deported to the far corners of the empire heterodox groups which they considered dangerous. Thirdly, and most important, they engaged in building a religious élite and an educational system controlled by this élite, both of which were in turn controlled by the state. The higher religious functionaries, the doctors of Islamic law (*ülema*) were, in effect, transformed into officials, for their livelihood was granted them by the state, and the path they travelled in their career was fixed by the state. The higher-ranking *ülema* also acquired an understanding of the conduct of Ottoman politics in positions which demanded that they participate in policy-making. For those at the top of the hierarchical pyramid, politics—as would be expected—was ubiquitous.

Because the rulers of Islamic societies had been designated heads of the community of believers, and because the law of the land in these societies was basically law drawn from the Koran, the Muslim religious hierarchy did, theoretically, have an organic connection with what may be termed the constitutional law of Islamic states. In the Ottoman empire, *ülema* were much more clearly integrated with the apparatus of the state. Through their control of education, of the judiciary and of the administrative network, they acted as agents of the state and thus indirectly ensured the state's control of social life.

Ottoman government was therefore both 'Islamic' and 'bureaucratic'. It was Islamic in the sense that Islam was the religion of the state and that the Sultan's primordial role was that of the leader of the Islamic community; it was 'bureaucratic' in the sense that working for the preservation of the state coloured the practice of Ottoman officials. Endangering the state was what—by definition—made a movement heretical. At times, such as during the seventeenth century, the style of government was more 'Islamic', but by the middle of the eighteenth century the pendulum had swung to a more bureaucratic style.

What I have described as the 'bureaucratic style' of government was the product of a special attitude among a group of secular officials who concentrated on the power dimension of social relations as the most important aspect of life. They were hard-headed, empirically minded and pragmatic. Their ideology was that of the 'reason of state'. This stance was in great part the result of their training, which differed from that of the *ülema.* The latter went through a three-tier *cursus honorum* in schools known as *medrese.* The preparatory classes of the *medrese* taught general subjects such as rhetoric and grammar, but as one proceeded to higher levels, religious studies predominated. Graduates of the *medrese* were expected to have specialized in one of the religious sciences. They were trained to draw out of religious texts knowledge that would be applicable to ritual, to the interpretation of legal problems, and—of primary interest for us—the conduct of social life. They showed considerable ingenuity in finding Islamic justification for many activities—such as the charging of interest—which were prohibited in the strict application of the law. There was, nevertheless, an idealistic aspect to their thinking, a feeling that the commands of religion came first and that human concerns had to be adapted to this pattern. Without letting the contrast run away with us, we may say that the reverse was true for the secular officials. The usual pattern here was that after elementary training at the tender age of eleven or twelve, the aspiring bureaucrat was apprenticed to a government 'bureau'. It was here that the real education of the bureaucrat would take place, and this feature becomes increasingly marked towards the end of the eighteenth and the beginning of the nineteenth century. It is this background which seems to have been the source of the primacy which the secular bureaucrat gave to realistic appraisals of power factors in society, relegating idealism to the background.

When the Ottoman empire began to decline, two divergent perceptions of the causes for this decline emerged among the bureaucrats and the *ülema*. For the doctors of Islamic law, the reason for the decline was religious: the Ottomans had neglected their duties as Muslims, and therefore they had lost the power they commanded when their faith had been strong. For the military and the central bureaucratic apparatus, the empire had declined because the machinery of the state had deteriorated: incompetents had been placed in positions of responsibility; prebends had been distributed to the undeserving; bribery had become common practice. Again, the contrast in attitudes does not appear with as clear an outline as I give it here, but in general such a dichotomy can be observed. It will be remembered that a third category of officials also existed: *ülema* who, by the very nature of the posts they occupied, had acquired a sophisticated knowledge of governmental affairs: these tended to give discreet support to the secular thesis.

To arrest the decline of the empire, the secular bureaucracy and the military officials undertook reforms which gave highest priority to military reorganization and the building of a new tax structure which would support it. At the beginning of the reform movement, some of the *ülema* sided with the reformists, and such an alliance was not unknown even in later years. Two reformist Sultans, Selim III (1789–1807) and Mahmud II (1807–39), were clearly out of the same mould that had established the tradition of *realpolitik* in the bureaucracy. They had little patience with arguments against the partial reform they were undertaking.

Although the body of Ottoman secular bureaucracy had shared the elaboration of policy with the higher *ülema*, they had long since disagreed with them on a number of issues. Now, at the beginning of the nineteenth century, they seized the initiation of change and embarked on a program which had the aim of introducing into Turkey administrative institutions and economic incentives which European enlightened despotism had used for some time. The changes thus brought about were eventually to undermine completely the prestige and position of the *ülema*: progressively eased out of the central processes of decision-making after the middle of the nineteenth century, they were eventually to be denied all but marginal roles in administration, the judiciary and the educational system.

Before the middle of the nineteenth century, in theory, the law of the land in the Ottoman empire was the *Şeriat*, the religious law based on the Koran.

Verses from the Koran, the tradition of the Prophet Muhammad and the rationalistic expostulations of the great Muslim jurists were the sources of this law. In fact, bureaucratic practice had created a fund of secular legislation which even the circuit judges—trained as they were in the *medrese*—had to take into account. This practice predisposed the architects of the reform movement (*Tanzimat*) to visualize statutory regulations as the lever which would ensure that their reforms would become part of the law of the state. The *Tanzimat* was therefore characterized by a flood of statutes, regulations, ordinances and by-laws. The practice was inaugurated by the proclamation by Sultan Abdulmecid of a basic charter, the so-called *Hatt-ı Hümayun* of Gülhane (1839). This document legitimized the entire enterprise of reform and outlined the direction it was to take. An already existing rift between statute law and religious law thus deepened during the *Tanzimat*.

The new regulations of the *Tanzimat* were, by their very nature, secular. They originated in the bureaux of the Porte and set very specific targets for the implementation of administrative, financial and educational policies. In the years which followed—known as the era of the *Tanzimat* (1839–76)—a new administrative law and a rationale for administration were gradually secreted in the interstices of change, a development Max Weber and Justice Holmes would have rightly appreciated. The religious underpinning of administrative practice was on its way out. Central to this transformation was the transfer of the functions of the circuit judge, trained in the *medrese*, to a new type of employee, the administrative official. A new school, the School of Administration (*Mülkiye*), was established in 1859 to train these cadres. Gradually, also, a system of secular courts came into being where the cases adjudicated were largely those which arose in relation to the new reform policy. A codification of commercial and criminal law was initiated. By the end of the nineteenth century, even religious law had been codified and systematized. But it was quite clear that the codification which had taken place was the product of a defensive move so that it could not be argued that the problems which could be solved under the *Code Napoléon* had no solution in Muslim law. This derived, mirror-image, nature of the new Muslim code, the *Mecelle*, did not show that Islamic law had triumphed but rather that it too had to bend to the exigencies of a Western European mode of posing legal problems.

The reform of public instruction followed the same course. It was placed in a new secular frame by the creation, in 1846, of a Ministry of Public Instruction.[2] In 1847 the state extended its direct grip on the educational process by replacing the system of neighbourhood schools financed by private support or by charitable grants by a system of state-financed primary schools.[3] In the 1850s and 1860s a system of post-primary education inaugurated by the state began to spread throughout Turkey. This major educational achievement of the *Tanzimat* was the *Rüşdiye*, the corner-stone of its policy for training cadres. The graduates were required to master advanced arithmetic, to learn from their courses on Turkish composition to write a clear report, and to be able to draw on their knowledge of world geography and history. The speed in the propagation of the *Rüşdiye* was not equalled by the next wave of educational development, the spread of *lycées* to the provinces; however, between 1882 and 1900 most provincial capitals acquired a *lycée*.[4] Secularization had started even earlier at the higher levels of education with the founding of the School of Medicine (1827)[5] and the Military Academy (1834, 1846).[6] A new, secular law school began to function in 1880.

All these developments were the consequence of the characteristic attitude of the Ottoman secular bureaucracy in matters which concerned the restoration of the power of the state: if Western institutions could rejuvenate the state, they would be adopted. It would be difficult otherwise to explain the ease with which Ottomans slid into westernizing reform. Again, it is in this light that we understand how, already in the 1880s, the Ottoman statesman Saffet Paşa (1814–83) could urge Turkey to adopt 'the civilization of Europe in its entirety, in short, to prove itself a civilized state'.[7] This statement was made privately, but Saffet Paşa also put himself on record publicly with similarly strong statements on the subject[8] and his statement is a fair summary of the thoughts of many of his colleagues. The distance travelled by Saffet Paşa in relation to his educational background should be noted since he had received a *medrese* education. But the reason for his eagerness to model the empire on Europe becomes clear when we isolate the formative influence of his youth; he acquired his values and world-view when, as a very young man, he was apprenticed to the Ministry of Foreign Affairs.

A more colourful picture of the way in which Ottoman bureaucrats of the *Tanzimat* could step out of what they considered to be the 'backwardness' of some Islamic practices may be found in a number of reports about Ahmad Vefik Paşa, an outstanding statesman of the era. Among his achievements Vefik Paşa could count the translation of Molière into Turkish. At one time he was the governor of Bursa province, the capital of which, the town of Bursa, was deeply imbued with religious traditions; undeterred, Vefik Paşa established a theatre in the town for the production of his translations of Molière and demanded that his employees buy season tickets. The local recorder of the Descendants of the Prophet, the *Nakib ul Eşraf* Asım Bey, claimed that he could not attend such lighthearted entertainment because of his exalted status as an Islamic official:[9] Vefik Paşa thereupon had Asım Bey's stables walled in by the municipality. On another occasion, during a tour of inspection, hearing that the lodge of a mystic order (*tekke*) was used as a refuge for brigands, he had the building torn down on the spot. During his renovation of Bursa he found that to implement his plans he had to demolish the tomb of a saint known as the 'walking saint'. Vefik Paşa went to the tomb, called three times, 'O Saint, walk away!' and then had the sanctuary demolished, remarking, 'He must have walked away by now.'[10]

The institutional secularization achieved by the men of the *Tanzimat* was paralleled by their favourable attitude towards the practical applications of modern science. This was one of the reasons why military medicine had such an early start in the empire. Medicine for civilian purposes was also placed at the head of their priorities, and when 'positivism' and 'materialism' began to influence Ottoman intellectuals at the end of the nineteenth century, it was through the channel of medicine and biology. Students of Claude Bernard brought back ideas derived from his *Introduction to the Study of Experimental Medicine*, and in the 1890s Büchner's *Kraft und Stoff* became an influential source of 'materialistic' ideas. A Turkish journalist, who was associated with the growth of a periodical publication which acted as a channel for the transmission of late nineteenth-century bourgeois optimism to Turkish audiences, recounts how his own scientific world-view was shaped in the years when he was a student at the School of Public Administration; the course on botany given by the imperial physician Salih Efendi 'cleansed' his mind and the minds of the other students of 'superstitions' through crystal-clear explanations of the life of plants.[11] I shall try to show below that this new pattern for learning, which had to emphasize clarity and internal consistency, was to have a striking effect in changing the attitudes of the new generation of bureaucrats which graduated from higher schools in the 1890s.

Secular as they would be, the architects of the *Tanzimat* could not escape the impingement upon their policies of an aspect of the religious structure of the Ottoman empire. They still were not taken in by the religion-oriented theory of the decline of the Ottoman empire. This in itself may be considered an achievement, since the old theory emerged in a much more sophisticated version, one which seemed much more reasonable than the earlier explanation. This new viewpoint, which took shape in the 1860s, stated that every society was kept from disintegrating by the strength of its moral fibre; what kept moral fibre strong was a society's culture. Islam was the culture of the Ottoman empire and Ottomans only neglected this culture at their peril. This theory, which was stolen from the arsenal of Western romanticism, did not meet with much approval on the part of the *Tanzimat* statesmen, even though it was beginning to find supporters among constitutional liberals. With one exception, leading to the codification of Muslim 'civil' law, the statesmen dismissed such arguments. What the statesmen of the *Tanzimat* could not dismiss so easily was the old Ottoman classification of populations on the basis of religious affiliation.

Like a number of Middle Eastern empires before them, the Ottomans had a system of administration which was two-headed. In one respect it was territorial—the Ottoman empire was divided into provinces—but in another respect the system was based on religious distinctions. According to this classification non-Muslims were dealt with on the basis not of ethnicity or language but of their religious affiliation. Thus, for instance, one basic Ottoman administrative unit was the Orthodox church through which Ottomans had access to a large number of their Christian subjects. The state left the internal administration of persons belonging to the Orthodox church to the Orthodox patriarchate.[12] Armenian Gregorians and Jews were also governed in their civil affairs by their highest religious dignitaries. In this sense, the Muslim community too was conceptualized as one unit, even though it incorporated Arabs, Turks, Albanians, Kurds and Circassians.

During the nineteenth century, the European great powers increased their influence in a role they had assumed for some time, that of the protectors of the various Christian populations of the Ottoman empire. This was a political manoeuvre aimed at gaining a foothold on the territory of the 'sick man of Europe'. The states which actively participated in this policy were seeking a share in the division of spoils which would follow the sick man's demise. Beginning with the middle of the nineteenth century, internal developments in the religious communities in the empire changed the structure of their internal administration. The laity increased its power, and lay assemblies took over many of the functions which till then had devolved upon the ecclesiastical hierarchy. One by one, also, the communities obtained the recognition of their new 'civil constitutions' by the Ottoman state.'[13] These communities were granted corporate personality in the law of the *Tanzimat.* The underlining of community boundaries in this fashion gave a new relief to the religious heterogeneity of the Ottoman empire. The *Tanzimat* statesmen were hoping that they could arrest this process, which set religious communities in a harder mould and which became the source of ideas demanding separation of these communities from the Ottoman empire. Indeed some of the states carved from Ottoman territory at the beginning of the nineteenth century such as Greece and Serbia had such antecedents.

The very process of community cohesion led a number of Ottomans to think of their own future in terms of a more cohesive Muslim community. We now encounter a third variant of the Muslim attitude towards the decline of the Ottoman empire. This was the idea that Ottoman Muslims should begin to look after their own interests *qua* Muslims. Such a policy might provide the 'cement' that would at least keep the Muslims of the empire unified; together, Muslims might keep the empire from further disintegration. By the year 1871, and the death of the Grand Vizier Ali Paşa, two factions had already formed among statesmen, one supporting the continuation of the institutional modernization of the Ottoman empire as a means of providing the allegiance of all Ottomans towards an Ottoman state, the second ready to use Islam as a new political formula.

From then on—and this is crucial for an understanding of Atatürk's attitude towards Islam—Islam was to be judged by men belonging to either faction as viable to the extent that it provided an effective political formula, a means of rallying the population of the empire. Atatürk rejected this option in the second decade of the twentieth century because he believed that attempts to implement it had proved a mirage. Part of his reaction had to do with the dissonance between his own conception of time span and that of the Islamists. He thought in terms of decades—Muslim propagandists were thinking in terms of millennia. This sensitivity to a time dimension is one of the aspects of the thinking of his generation which places it in a different category from the reformism of the early *Tanzimat.* I shall have more to offer on this subject below. What could and what could not be done with Islam as a political formula was demonstrated during the reign of Sultan Abdülhamid II (1876–1909).

By the time the Treaty of Berlin had been signed in 1878, more territory had been whittled away from the Ottoman empire. In the remaining territories, the Muslims constituted a clearer majority than before. Faced with this demographic pattern and the growing antagonism of the Muslim and Christian populations, the Sultan decided to steer a middle course among the contending formulas for the empire's salvation. He continued the work of the *Tanzimat* statesmen for the rationalization and the modernization of the state apparatus. He lent his support to the expansion of the system of secular courts and secular education. He left the *medrese* to stagnate: by the end of his reign they were poorly staffed, poorly financed institutions which served as a refuge for draft-dodgers.

Abdülhamid also believed in science and its practical applications, but he opted for the use of Islam as a lever which would instil some consciousness of a collective goal into his subjects. He realized that a modern state could not function with the tacit allegiance which had been sufficient to get the machinery of the state to function in the time of his predecessors. To raise agricultural productivity—to provide only one example—was one of his targets, but he realized that this could only be achieved by a series of measures comprising railroad expansion, agricultural training and the participation of the peasant in the scheme. But more important even than participation was to forge some identity among the rural masses which would enable them to give meaning to their own allegiance to the distant figure of the Caliph. To this end the Sultan implemented an extremely intelligent policy, establishing contacts with sheikhs and dervishes, using propaganda to mobilize the town populations—here the building of a railroad to the Hidjaz occupied a strategic place—and trying to reconcile the Arab population to an Ottoman identity. At least in the Anatolian peninsula, the policy did have some results, as is attested by a number of contemporary observers. What the Sultan was grappling with were two characteristics of the rural personality of his realm: the lack of autonomy of individuals and the absence of a conception of a unit transcending the village or the hamlet. Millions of Ottomans fell into this category, and the extent to which they were bereft of collective identity was to be observed much later, during the First World War, by a young officer. This is the way he describes his first experiences in training Anatolian recruits:

> At that time, as far as I was able to understand, our soldiers rather than being persons whom one could deal with as individuals, were better conceptualized as cogs in a community, as components of a group. In a community and in a group they could easily follow everything that was required of them. But whenever one of them would stray from the group and become isolated, he would be unable to determine an independent course of action for himself, of his own volition. Also, in collective undertakings, he would always look for someone to become dependent on or to follow. This often affected the conduct of war by my unit. A group of soldiers which had lost its sergeant or officer or directing agent would quite easily come apart. In moments of danger, a unit, instead of dispersing carefully at a moment's notice, would tend on the contrary to bunch up, to fall upon each other, and always in the direction of the centre of command.
>
> As for danger, its resonance was for them non-existent. They did not need any preparation to go to sleep. They could go to sleep within a minute, possibly within a second. They would even be asleep at the time we thought them to be awake. At a time when you thought everything was perfectly ordered, a sentinel you trusted, standing in his trench, with his weapon at the ready, his eyes looking ahead, could have fallen into a deep sleep. That a person from whom you could demand everything at a time when he was subject to a unified command and in a group could become so remote from any form of social responsibility was something which left one gasping.

The same author describes the responses he received when he began asking his men questions relating to their religion:

> When I asked the question 'What is our religion?' 'What is the religion which we follow?' I thought the answer I would receive would be 'Praised be the Lord, we are Muslims.' But this was not the responses I received. Some said 'We are of the religion of the Great Imam.' Others said 'We are the followers of the Prophet Ali.' Some could not solve this problem. Some did, indeed, say 'We are Muslims' but when the question was asked 'Who is our prophet?', they too became confused. Names of prophets that would never come to one's mind were mentioned. One said 'Our prophet is Enver Paşa.' Again when the question was asked of the few who had identified the Prophet, 'Is our Prophet alive or dead?', the matter once more became insoluble. Some said he was alive, some that he was dead . . .

The young officer who could not disguise the anguish he felt at the quality of the human material with which he was asked to conduct a war knew one thing: despite their crass ignorance of Islam, religion was still one of the ways by which they could acquire an 'internal gyroscope', a conception of the self which at the same time could be used to relate their selves to a national purpose. In contemporary Latin American usage, we would refer to what both the Sultan and the officer were seeking as *conscientización* or consciousness-building. What the Sultan did not realize was that the political message of Islam was not sufficiently focused to keep the many Muslims who made up his empire united around a common purpose, even though he did succeed in building some sense of Muslim identity and even of Ottoman identity among some of his subjects. Islam had thus been found to have a diffuse effect in building a social identity of sorts, and a solidarity of sorts, among the more isolated areas of the Ottoman empire. But even today the nature of the Islamic bond as a form of proto-nationalism is not understood. Nevertheless, it is a sign of the hardiness of the idea of consciousness-building through Islamization that the Young Turks who dethroned Sultan Abdülhamid did not entirely abandon experimentation with this formula, although their scepticism as to its effectiveness was growing.

Neither did the Sultan realize that the second part of his program, his continued support for institutional modernization and the upgrading of institutions for professional training, would run into trouble. In the end these educational reforms gave rise to new, unanticipated attitudes which encouraged the radicalization of persons trained in these institutions. These new tendencies were to take Turkey into laicism, for the new generation which emerged from the educational structure sponsored by the Sultan were marked by an uncompromising opposition to what they saw as the useless remnants of the *ancien régime.* The hardening of attitudes appeared both in the demand that reality should be made to fit an abstract plan or theory, and in the view that the time-span for a project was 'now'. This attitude differed fundamentally from that of the officials of the *Tanzimat*, ready as the latter were to live with compromises, half-measures, hybrid systems and conflicting values. From now on the word 'fossil' (or 'residue'—*müstahase*) was to appear with increasing frequency in the vocabulary of Ottoman progressive intellectuals. It is this sense of unease in operating with a system which was a mixture of the old and the new which appears most clearly in the ideas of Kemal Atatürk.

THE REFORM OF HIGHER EDUCATIONAL INSTITUTIONS AND SULTAN ABDÜLHAMID II

It may come as a surprise to discover that the first years of Sultan Abdülhamid's reign were marked by outstanding achievements in education. In particular, beginning with the 1880s a system of military schools which took in boarding students immediately after primary education was inaugurated. These schools, the military *Rüşdiye*, could lead all the way to the military academy for those who had decided on a military career. The system had been promoted by one of the Sultan's greatest enemies, his director of military education, Süleyman Paşa, who had engineered the deposition of Sultan Abdülaziz in 1876. Sultan Abdülhamid, who succeeded to the throne shortly afterwards, had Süleyman Paşa court-martialled but this did not prevent him from implementing the system of education devised by the general. In 1895 there were twenty-eight of these military middle schools functioning in the empire, eight in the capital and twenty in the provinces.[14] The total number of students in these schools was 6,000 and by 1898 it had reached 8,000. There also existed seven military preparatory schools of *lycée* level which prepared students for entrance into the military academy or the military medical school. The same pattern of preparatory school was available for students who desired to enter the school of administration.

The educational standards of the military *Rüşdiye* were high. Many of the students who opted for a military career came from families of low socio-economic background and their profession was necessarily the focus for their self-image. As they moved upward in the system of military education they acquired a view of the world which stressed the positive sciences. The students were also constantly reminded that the fate of the empire depended on their own contributions to its salvation. It was through an understanding of the forces that had made the Western states powerful that they would save the empire. There was therefore a continuity between the student's world-view and that of the bureaucrats who a few generations back had started reform. But there was also an outstanding difference: the new generation not only knew more geography, more modern history and more mathematics than their predecessors, but they also acquired a new vision of reality from their knowledge. The most talented among them developed a conception of the ways in which one could shape society which made the action of the *Tanzimat* statesmen appear dated and over-hesitant.

The new impatience of the graduates of the Ottoman *grandes écoles*—both military and civilian—becomes apparent when one contrasts the type of pedagogy prevailing in the traditional system with the new system of book learning and classroom studies. If the term 'apprenticeship' provides the key to the old education, the conception of 'utopian mentality' explains the hidden spring of the new system and the stamp with which it marked the graduates.

In the traditional system, knowledge was a limited thing: the basic outlines of Islamic knowledge had been established once and for all. This fund of knowledge was transmitted, like that of a form of artisanship, through a mastery of known techniques. The new knowledge—geography, physics, chemistry, biology—was an expanding body with its own momentum which one had to keep up with in order to be well informed. Techniques for its use were constantly changing. Thus, change came in at the beginning as a datum of Western positive science. In this light, the *ülema* who had not kept up with the expansion of the intellectual horizons came increasingly to be seen as ignorant charlatans rather than as repositories of ancient wisdom. This was one of the factors which propelled the students into a clear confrontation with religion. In the future, references to the need for change and to the way that religion was an obstruction to progress was to become a *leitmotif* in Atatürk's writings.

In the traditional system, initiation into the world of knowledge through the guidance of a mentor was central. In the bureau, the mentor had been the sponsor of the new employee, or the experienced official who took an interest in his career. In the *medrese*, the mentor was the tutor to whom the student was assigned for the duration of his studies. Personalities, thus established, together with the idea that knowledge was a limited fund which could only be approached through known techniques, limited the extent to which the initiate could go off at a tangent and dare to make new interpretations of matters already explored by his predecessors. In the new system, books which were distributed to the entire class were the foundation of knowledge; they became the reference-points for learning, and those published in France allowed one to be in advance even of one's teachers, who had gone to France only at an earlier stage.

Another, possibly more important, feature of the new learning was that the book, the classroom and the school now operated as what Erving Goffman terms a 'total institution'.[15] Each school was a self-contained universe in which students were segregated from Ottoman everyday life. In the training system of the bureau, students had culled their knowledge from actual official transactions. They were immersed in a complex skein of knowledge, practice, intrigue and planning. The new generation of officials was cut off from all this; they were studying principles and laws which were abstractions from reality, and had an artificial internal consistency. It was as if the generation of the 1890s thought that life as described in books was more real than life itself.

Here again, we get a better sense of what was involved in the change if we go back to the textbooks the students were using. The textbooks of geography, physics, mathematics and military science represented the systematization of knowledge as applied to a given field. This systematization proceeded by abstracting certain phenomena from the undifferentiated mass of impressions which made up the 'stuff' of everyday life. A model of the interaction between certain of these phenomena, selected as 'significant', was built and finally the model was made to run faster than reality. Science then appeared to the students in the form of abstract models of reality, a characteristic also emphasized by the lack of experimentation and the parlous state of laboratories. It was through an assimilation of theory that science was gaining a foothold among them.

By means of a similarly schematic presentation, students acquired their image of Western societies. Internally consistent systems, neat models and blueprints thus acquired a great importance in the minds of the generation of the 1890s. Thus it is no surprise to find out that the earliest protests of the Young Turks were concerned with what they considered the lack of consistency of their own system of education. For the most talented and idealistic, an interlocking of smoothly integrated parts became an obsession. What did not fit this interlocking pattern could be thrown out as irrelevant or harmful. Ottoman society with its trams operating in the midst of crumbling houses, newspapers which had to heed strange rules imposed by an ignorant censorship and regiments where graduates of the military academy took orders from officers promoted from the ranks, exemplified the type of dissonance that was most galling to the students. The ideal slowly began to emerge that it was either one or the other of the systems which had to emerge, not a mixture or a rickety compromise.

To 'run' a model of social reality faster than reality itself, one had to project oneself into a hypothetical future. The model of social reality constructed from the school vision of the world had, therefore, an additional element: that of a hypothetical future which could be shaped at will. This was also new compared to the ideas of the *Tanzimat* statesmen. The reformist of the *Tanzimat* was an activist, but he saw himself primarily as shaping the present, albeit for future use. The idea of a structured historical future developing out of the present with new features due to human intervention was not a datum of *Tanzimat* thinking. By contrast, the generation of the 1890s began to think of society in terms of both an abstract model and a blueprint for the future, albeit in the direction of 'progress'. Social 'projects' now became an intellectual exercise. A striking example of the centrality of hypothetical situations and of projects may be seen in a prefiguration of modern Turkey by the Young Turk, Abdullah Cevdet, entitled 'A Very Wakeful Sleep'.[16]

While the outline of a new type of social thinking began to emerge with the generation of the 1890s, the generation of the Young Turks, it does not become effective until the Young Turk revolution of 1908. Even then we see the Young Turks impelled to work with the familiar pieces of the Ottoman mosaic: various ethnic and religious groups, and Islam as the thin thread keeping the populations of the Ottoman empire together. As to the second use of the Islamic formula, its role as a 'raiser of consciousness', we see them become increasingly sceptical of this approach. It is because of this scepticism that the Young Turks—in keeping with their 'scientific-utopian' world-view—entrusted one of their colleagues, Ziya Gökalp, with research carried out to find an alternative formula to Islam. The Young Turks were thereby doing something the *Tanzimat* statesmen had never dreamed of: they had initiated a search for a systematic, internally consistent theory of reform.

Ziya Gökalp's investigations made him focus on two ideas, that of the 'nation' and that of 'civilization'. According to him, 'civilization' consisted of the technological and cultural implements which a number of societies could share. Modern western civilization, for instance, marked by industrialization and a number of new social institutions, was shared by many Western nations. Nationality was another component of the Western system of states, and this Ziya Gökalp linked to the concept of 'culture'. A 'culture' was the latent pattern of values, beliefs and institutions, which defined a people. Whenever such a people had been incorporated within a multi-ethnic, plural state, its values had remained in the background. A modern state was a state which coalesced around one of these peoples and boldly made use of its characteristic institutions. Turks were such a group whose specific cultural values had receded into the background when they had established the Ottoman empire. As to Islam, Gökalp indicated that a number of items which were accepted as integral aspects of religion—particularly the commands associated with the proper Islamic organisation of society—were in fact aspects of Arabic culture which had nothing to do with 'pristine' Islam.[17] Islam, therefore, was a religion that demanded of its followers 'faith', and it did not confine its followers to any form of social organization. Ziya Gökalp's blueprint for the future—which never emerged as a completed proposal—was to draw out the latent Turkish culture of the Turkish nation, to establish a Turkish state based on it, to accept Western civilization and to make Islam a matter of conscience, a private belief. A memorandum Ziya Gökalp had written for the Young Turks in 1916 concerning the role of Islam in Turkey was implemented by the Young Turks.[18] It led to the exclusion of the *Şeyhülislam*—the highest religious functionary in the Ottoman empire—from the cabinet, the separation of the religious courts from the Şeyhülislamate and their attachment to the ministry of justice; the placing of the administration of pious foundations under the authority of a member of the Cabinet; and the separation of the *medrese* from the Şeyhülislamate and their administration by the ministry of education.

With the defeat of the Ottoman empire in the First World War and the loss of the Arab lands a new situation arose. For all practical purposes Turkey now consisted of the Anatolian peninsula. Part one of the Islamic formula—its function as a link between Turks and Arabs—could now be jettisoned. It is remarkable, however, that Mustafa Kemal did not immediately dispose of this formula when he was organizing resistance against the terms of the treaty that were about to be imposed on Turkey. During the years when he was leading this resistance movement, between 1919 and 1922, he was dependent on the sympathies of Muslims outside Turkey, and often used the theme of the unity of Islam. He also made use of it to mobilize the feelings of Anatolian religious notables against an Ottoman administration which continued to function in the capital as a virtual prisoner of the Allies. He took advantage of the prestige of the Caliphate at the time when, paradoxically, he was about to suppress it. But in both cases he had made up his mind very early concerning the Turkey he visualized in the future.

THE TURKISH REPUBLIC AND THE NEW NATION

Atatürk's contributions are usually analysed in terms of his unique ability to bring about needed reforms. In this appraisal, he figures as the instrument of a great wave of progress leading to some predestined point. This image is thoroughly teleological, for it depicts him as outstanding not only in having been able to negotiate successfully a number of difficult passages to his own consciously set goals, but also because he 'fulfilled the requirements' of enlightenment thought. I believe this particular judgement to be somewhat simplistic but the appraisal also hinders us from placing Atatürk in a more 'sociological' context. The view which characterizes Atatürk as a servant of progress is derived from a primitive picture of the inevitability of progress. It does not help us to locate him in the major social upheavals which have shaken the world in the last four centuries and which continue to do so with increasing violence. The full meaning of Atatürk's contribution emerges only when we relate his work to that of two key processes which subsume the momentous changes which marked post-feudal society, namely the multifarious new patterns of collective integration and the changing dimensions of the individual's personal integrative systems.

A NEW INTEGRATIVE SYSTEM FOR THE COLLECTIVE

Most Turkish and foreign scholars see the foundation of the Turkish Republic as the reorganization—albeit a radical reorganization—of a remnant of the Ottoman empire. In fact, the watershed appears not only in the radicalization of the attitudes of the founding fathers of the Republic but also in the very conception of the Turkish Republic as a nation-state. What happened was that Mustafa Kemal took up a non-existent, hypothetical entity, the Turkish nation, and breathed life into it. It is this ability to work for something which did not exist as if it existed, and to make it exist, which gives us the true dimensions of the project on which he had set out and which brings out the utopian quality of his thinking. Neither the Turkish nation as the fountainhead of a 'general will' nor the Turkish nation as a source of national identity existed at the time he set out on this task. He was distinguished from his more cautious collaborators by such a vision of the future and the will to make it materialize. 'Nation' and 'Western civilization' were the two fundamental code words which provided the latent rationale for his project, and his attitude towards religion assumes coherence when we evaluate it from that vantage-point. The determination he showed in pursuit of an ideal of society is not contradicted by his great talent for temporizing: what gives meaning to his tactical reversals is the project on which his mind was focused.

The sequence of events which eventually led to the secularization of Turkey is well known and does not need to be related in detail. However, one characteristic of the way in which Mustafa Kemal tackled the issue from the very beginning shows the depth of his political talent and should not be overlooked as a foreshadowing of his policy of secularization. We find this prefiguration of his political genius in his use of the concept of a 'grand' National Assembly as the source of political legitimation for the resistance movement. The Sultan-Caliph was theoretically invested with his power because he was the leader of that Muslim community—the Ottoman community—which held the most effective power in the Muslim world. Since the person occupying the position of Sultan-Caliph was now a prisoner of the Allied forces, he could no longer act as a free agent. The *millet*, the concept which originally referred to the various religious subdivisions of the empire, but in this particular case to the Muslim community, would re-establish its sovereign rights as the fountainhead of legitimacy. In fact, since the end of the nineteenth century *millet* had been used with increasing frequency to translate the word 'nation'. Its meaning was therefore ambiguous. It is as a consequence of this ambiguity that the body which had been assembled in Ankara as a representative assembly, and which had a strong clerical representation in it, passed Article 1 of the Provisional Constitution proposed in 1920 without any objections (20 January 1920). This article stated that sovereignty belonged without reservation to the *millet*. The ambiguity of the term allowed clerics to believe that what had been invoked were the rights of the community, whereas for Atatürk it was a preparation for invoking the sovereignty of the nation.[19] The Assembly had accepted the reestablishment of the primitive rights of the Muslim community, but by the same token it had accepted that the Assembly could legislate in matters both secular and religious in the absence of a Sultan-Caliph. Mustafa Kemal made sure that no one bearing these double attributes would ever emerge again.

From the image of the Sultan-Caliph as a prisoner of the Allies, the Ankara regime moved on to a new constitutional system where temporal power was effectively severed from the Sultanate.[20] This was followed by the abolition of the Sultanate on 1 November 1922, the proclamation of the Republic on 29 October 1923, and finally the momentous laws of 3 March 1924: this series of laws, all passed on the same day, abolished the Caliphate, made all education a monopoly of the state, and abolished the *medrese.* Religious affairs and the administration of pious foundations were thereafter to be directed by directorates attached to the office of the prime minister. In April 1924, religious courts were abolished. In 1925, mystic orders (*tarikat*) were outlawed. In 1926, the Swiss Civil Code was adopted, and the link between the *Şeriat* and criminal law was severed. In 1928, the constitutional provision which still mentioned Islam as the religion of the state was abrogated. The same year the Latin alphabet was adopted.

Whenever a rationale was invoked for these moves, the reason given was that of 'the requirements of contemporary civilization'. This may be followed in a number of speeches Mustafa Kemal made in the 1920s. One of the most concise statements of this rationale is found in the 1931 statutes of the Republican People's Party. The new regime had, from the start, rallied its supporters by establishing a political party within the Grand National Assembly, the Republican People's Party. This party eventually emerged as the only legitimate organ of political articulation in the Republic and the centre where the official ideology of the new republican regime was elaborated. The 1931 statutes of the Party stated that it stood for the principle of 'laicism', defined as a condition in which the state took no role in religious life since religion was 'a matter of conscience'. The text stated: 'The Party has accepted the principle that all laws, regulations and procedures used in the administration of the state should be prepared and implemented in order to meet the needs of this world and in accordance with the foundations of and the forms provided by science and technology in modern times.'[21] Party leaders later underlined the idea that they did not consider laicism to be synonymous with atheism (*dinsizlik*), since the performance of religious ritual (*ibadet*) was protected by the Constitution. In 1937 the principle of laicism was introduced into the Constitution, together with five other guiding principles of the Party—republicanism, nationalism, étatism, populism and reformism.

The history of laicism in Turkey and of its application is, of course, much more complex than this synopsis can suggest, but the meaning of laicism as a project is best highlighted not by a description of its practice but by its relation to the primordial goals of the republican regime. One of these was the need to find a principle of social cohesion for Turkish society and to devise a means of raising social consciousness among the Turks (*conscientización*). Insofar as Islam had been found wanting in both these respects, it had been rejected. As Islam no longer served these purposes, it had indeed become a matter for the 'private' consciences of Turks.

The consciousness of the new Turks was to be rooted in science ('Western civilization') which Atatürk repeatedly mentioned as the source of all valid knowledge and behaviour. But then the matter was not so simple, because 'consciousness raising' aimed to elicit a set of characteristics which one expected the citizens of the new republic to possess. 'Science', as such, had no answer to questions regarding the building of national identity; nor did it tackle the issue of social identity, the orientation of the individual towards social ideals.

Two ideologies emerged in the 1930s which were expected to promote national identity: the so-called 'Turkish history thesis' and the 'sun-language' theory.

The 'Turkish history thesis' was built on the idea that Turks had contributed to civilization long before they had been incorporated into the Ottoman empire. They had originated an urban civilization in Central Asia from which many other civilizations had sprung. They had maintained their cultural identity even after becoming a minority in a multi-national empire. It was from this fund that an identity could be drawn for the citizens of republican Turkey. To a limited extent this thesis achieved its goal; Turks began to feel a new sense of their accomplishments as Turks, and pride in being a Turk did indeed develop whereas only five decades earlier the term Turk was still used as a synonym of nomad or peasant by denizens of the Ottoman empire.

The 'sun-language' theory was an attempt to rationalize a development which had been taking place in Ottoman literature since the middle of the nineteenth century, namely the increasing use of the vernacular instead of the flowery and allusive language of the Ottoman officials. The vernacular contained few of the Arabic and Persian roots that prevailed in 'officialese'. It was now proposed that 'pure' Turkish (i.e. Turkish which had not been infiltrated by the vocabulary and the grammar of other Middle Eastern civilizations) was an ancient language of central importance in the history of languages. It was claimed that many other languages had been built on this foundation and that one could find guidance for the reform of linguistic usage if one studied this early Turkish language. This was a difficult theory to sustain in the light of linguistic research; nevertheless, the practice of trying to reconstitute 'pure' Turkish did fire a number of Turkish intellectuals who devoted enormous energy to this task. To support linguistic reform became enshrined as an aspect of Kemalist radicalism, and this somewhat bizarre association between linguistic purism and republican radicalism continued to our day when it was picked up by marxism. It is part of the means available to modern Turks to build for themselves a Turkish identity.

In retrospect, however, the most solid foundation for building a republican-Turkish identity seems to have been another, more solid theory of society which provided a social ideology of Kemalism. This theory was solidarism, the official ideology of the French Third Republic. Solidaristic theorizing had reached Turkey through Durkheim and through Ziya Gökalp, one of Durkheim's admirers. The theory was based on the thesis that there was no necessary conflict between classes in modern society. What was important was the way social institutions and the contributions of all professional groups made society a going concern. Industrial society could be kept in equilibrium by propagating a social ethic focused on the contribution of individuals and groups to society. In addition, Turkish solidarism offered a social program which envisaged that 'capital accumulated through the appropriation of surplus values on behalf of society' would be invested in 'industrial plants and large farms to be established for the benefit of society'.[22] Kemalist education propounded a theory of citizenship based on these principles. It was the businessman, the schoolmaster and the politician who, working together under the shield of solidaristic redistribution, were to make up an integrated Turkish nation. In more recent years, Kemalism may have lost much of its momentum, but its dream of a non-conflictual and at the same time redistributive society has continued to mark Turkish social thinking. This pattern has also appeared in the diffuse aspirations of its newly mobilized population. It is also such an image of society which emerges from the thinking of the military group which tried in 1960 to re-establish a 'truly' Kemalist system.

THE NEW TURKEY AND THE INDIVIDUAL

One of the key words in the ideological vocabulary of Atatürk was *istiklâl* (independence), but at the individual level this emphasis was paralleled by his use of *müstakil* (autonomous, free).[23] I have tried to show how the attempt to replace the traditional system—en bloc, so to speak—by a new one is a tendency which one observes in the generation which preceded that of Atatürk. I have also pointed out that Atatürk's policies of reform concentrated on the building of a new collective identity in the make-up of which religion was denied a role. But then, there also exists another basic aspect of his secularizing reforms which aims to broaden the autonomy of the individual in society. Here Atatürk was working to liberate the individual from what he may have agreed to call the 'idiocy of traditional, community-oriented life'. Once again he was going well beyond the reforms of the *Tanzimat* statesmen. In view of the solid support which community culture found in Turkey, it may be said that he showed even greater courage in this field than in his actions within a more political context.

I believe that the drive that compelled him towards this goal was also a product of the dissonance created by his educational background. The peculiar form that this dissonance took was his disgust with the forms of social control which sprang from Ottoman folk culture. To provide an understanding of my use of such an explanatory model we must first consider the influence of Western political and social ideas on Atatürk.

Atatürk travelled outside the Ottoman empire a total of three times, once to observe military manoeuvres in France, the second time as military attaché in Sofia, and the third time during the First World War in Germany. His knowledge of Europe was not limited to these contacts, but was nevertheless acquired primarily from the Turkish press, which kept closely in touch with world events and which also followed scientific and cultural developments. A limited number of translations of the works of persons who were political theorizers of the era were also available to him. Atatürk read French and understood it well. In his library, preserved near his mausoleum, works of thinkers such as Rousseau do figure, and some have marginal annotations, but these probably date from the last years of his life. The consensus is that at the time he carried out his main secularizing reforms he had a general knowledge of Western political systems, but that he was also dependent on the information he received from his colleagues (such as the minister of justice, Mahmut Esat Bozkurt) who had studied abroad.

How, then, can one explain the consistency of his secularizing reforms? What gives us the feeling that there is a latent pattern around which they are unified? In particular, why does one feel this concerning his reforms dealing with the mystic orders, the rights of women, 'secularization' of dress, and state control of education?

A hypothesis I would like to propose is that these secularizing reforms are linked by the underlying common denominator of the liberation of the individual from the collective constraints of the Muslim community. To understand this, we have to look at the smallest operative unit of the community in the Ottoman empire, the *mahalle* or city quarter. In those times the *mahalle* was more than an administrative unit with somewhat arbitrarily drawn boundaries; it was a compact *gemeinschaft* with its boundaries protected by its own toughs and faithful dogs, and a setting within which much of the normal life of an average Ottoman citizen was shaped. It is here that primary education was undertaken, births were celebrated, marriages were arranged, and the last rites were performed for the dying. It was here that the mosque operated as a social institution bringing all inhabitants to hear what was expected of them. It was against the background of the *mahalle* that the authority of the paterfamilias was exercised and supported. And it was here that sometimes blood-money was paid; that the Islamic institution of morals-control wormed its way into drinking parties and gambling dens, and organized posses to surprise careless lovers; that the café—a communications centre—operated; that the first stamp was affixed by the prayer leader on a petition that was to travel on to higher authorities; and that local saints' tombs could be visited and living holy men dispensed their own kind of influence and justice. *Mahalle* rules were in fact quite flexible, but the flexibility operated behind a mask of decorum. It was quite inflexible with regard to overt mixing of sexes. Atatürk's reforms have an aspect which tried to replace the personalistic ties and the hypocrisy that pervaded the *mahalle* morals-control by a set of rules which tried to obviate control and replace it by a system of regulations that gave the individual responsibility for his actions.

Atatürk's determination to wrest the individual away from folk control had an origin which, once more, is found in the new educational system. *Mahalle* norms were not particularly galling to some one who had spent his entire lifetime there; but for students who spent most of their time at school as boarders, school directives became more important. School directives, however, stressed a completely different type of control; the rationality of bureaucracy took over, and what had to be achieved was the revitalization of the empire which was now dependent upon new virtues. *Mahalle* virtues were linked to the preservation of small groups. There was no use for them in the building of the nation-state. Religious morality was replaced by intellectual and military disciplines and once more Islamic ethics and commands related to the good of the community rose up as irrational restrictions with no purpose except the snuffing out of personality.

The school setting was not the only context in which community control and the specific values which came with it were being devalued. The devaluation of the *mahalle* was a cumulative process in which the rise of new ways of thinking about society also had a part. One of the indirect ways in which the *mahalle* ethos was devalued was that a new focus for the citizen's allegiance, 'society' (*cemiyet-i beşeriye*), began to appear in the writings of modernist intellectuals. This was a concept which differed from *devlet* (the state) insofar as it took in a number of social processes that were not subsumed under the heading of policy, power, coercion, rule and prestige, these being the primordial components of the concept of *devlet.* The family and the individual, both subjects of *mahalle* control, were sub-units comprised within the concept of 'society', and persons who wanted to reform 'society' also wanted to reform the family. 'Society' operated on the basis of free exchange of goods or services, and it therefore immediately condemned domestic slavery. The *mahalle*, on the other hand, accepted domestic slavery as a fact of life. Society was based on contract, and the *mahalle* operated on ascriptive bases; thus the *mahalle* began to appear as a fund of traditional values which were hampering the expansion of human personality.

At about the same time there began to emerge a rejection of the dress characteristic of the *mahalle.* Bihruz Bey, a super-westernized hero in one of the earliest Turkish novels, takes a walk in the park, sees his lower-class compatriots in baggy pants, and complains: '*Qu'est-ce que c'est que ça? Est-ce que le carnaval est arrivé?*' But the revulsion against folk culture which was building up is best expressed by the writer Yakup Kadri Karaosmanoğlu, who was to join Mustafa Kemal in Ankara. One of Yakup Kadri's stories concerns a westernized Turk who is beaten up by *mahalle* toughs because he dares to wear a hat. On one occasion he describes the oppressiveness of folk culture as follows:

> In this stagnant air, none of the atoms of which is moved by a melodious sound, in these squares, none of which is adorned by a figure, in these streets, the dust and the mud of which we daily brave, in the face of these people whose ears are deaf to any pleasantness, whose eyes are blind to any beauty, who squat at night in coffee houses with their coloured printed nightgowns listening to the tube of a gramophone vomit belly-dance tunes, I find the seeds of their sickness.

Yakup Kadri's complaint was that the *mahalle* ethos and intellectual climate killed creativity in Turkish writers. The same connection between *mahalle* as an amalgam of Islamic and folk culture and lack of creativity seems to have been made by Atatürk. Atatürk was very much of the opinion that baggy pants and the *fez* were part of a 'carnival'. Not only was his aesthetic sense offended but these clothes symbolized the stranglehold of a folk culture where final legitimation had always to be obtained in terms of religious values, and where both religion and man were therefore debased and corrupted. Western society, which received its legitimation from science, was much more open and therefore more inventive. It was only with a set of rules that would enable the individual to escape from the suffocating folk values that creativeness could be encouraged. Two policies were devised by Atatürk to this end: first, his secularizing measures, where the specific target was to destroy control, and secondly, his program of cultural westernization for the Republic.

THE INDIVIDUAL IN ATATÜRK'S SECULARIST REFORMS

The first view we get of Mustafa Kemal's attempt to liberate the individual from community norms is the law of 3 March 1924 on the 'Unification of Education'. Not only did this law take education once and for all out of the hands of the *ülema* but it opened the doors for co-education and thus a completely new integration of the sexes from the school years onwards. In fact, Ataürk's thrust to establish women's rights may be conceptualized as a concentrated effort to smash what to him appeared as the most stifling and dark aspect of the *mahalle* ethos, namely the restrictions it placed on contacts between men and women in the day-to-day routine of life. A large area of the changes brought about by the adoption of the Swiss Civil Code was concerned with the transformation of women's legal status. Among these were monogamous marriages, equality of status between men and women as heirs, and a number of provisions concerning property management. This was followed in 1930 by the granting of rights to women to vote and stand for election in local contests (Municipality Law of 14 April 1930)[24] and by the right to vote and stand for election in national elections in 1934.

Atatürk's many references to women working side by side with men in the Turkish Republic created the climate that enabled many Turkish women who had received education to enter professional life. As a result, Turkey today has an enviable proportion of its professional cadres filled by women. The 'lifting of the veil', which was never placed into a statute, followed from this development.

Once again, Atatürk's attitude towards the mystic orders (*tarikat*) is related to his attack against stifling *gemeinschaft*. When one reads the law of 1925 abolishing these orders, it is clear that what Atatürk had in mind was to disallow the influence of local charismatic leaders, who were either notables with local political power or appeared as ignorant and cunning figures exploiting the lower classes. Turks would in future be ruled not by corrupt sheikhs but according to the way set out by science. Their personality would not be determined by the counsel of a religious mentor but by immersion in Western culture.

ATATÜRK AND WESTERN CULTURE

To provide Turkish citizens with a new view of the world which would replace that of religion and religious culture, Atatürk sponsored a movement of cultural westernization which he equated with civilization. The alphabet was latinized partly to enable an easier access to works in Western languages. For a time, the performance of oriental music in public was banned. A conservatory was established in Ankara, where opera, ballet and Western polyphonic music were taught. Western-style painting was encouraged by the government, which also subsidized the publication of a number of cultural periodicals in which the products of modern Turkish painting were presented. In 1926 a statue of Kemal Atatürk was unveiled in Istanbul: in a country where the interdict against reproducing the human figure had been publicly enforced, this called for considerable courage. Statues now appeared all over Turkey. Folk culture was rescued by making it a subject of study in the 'People's Houses' (community centres established in the 1930s with the aim of propagating culture in a Western mould), and including its motifs in the subjects taught there: Turkish culture was thus brought back to the fore without its outer rind of *mahalle* Islam. And although, in a general sense, the experiment in the westernization of Turkish culture has had great success since the 1930s, this is the very point where a note of pessimism has to be introduced.

In the years following the death of Atatürk, and particularly after the institution of multi-party democracy in 1950, laicism was challenged by a number of groups. In fact, the principle had rooted itself sufficiently firmly never to be removed from Turkish constitutional practice. Even the Demokrat Party, which was often accused of having undermined laicism, kept the principle in operation. Nevertheless, the military intervention of 1960 was caused in part by fear that that party was encouraging religious obscurantism which would endanger the constitutional foundations of the Republic. Since 1960 religious currents have not abated; if anything they have become stronger, but the constitutional principle of laicism, upheld by a large segment of the Turkish intelligentsia, is still the foundation of Turkish constitutional law. What, then, is happening in Turkey? What is the meaning of the flood of Islamic publications, of the resurgence of *tarikat* and the growth of new sects, of the rise of a clerical party in parliament and of the muted streets during the month of Ramadan?

There is, first, a social context for the revival of Islam. Part of this is demographic: the population of Turkey is growing very fast, with enormous cohorts in the adolescent age groups for which ideology is so vital. In that sense Islam competes with marxism. But more important than the demography is 'social mobilization', the ability of a much larger proportion of Turkey's population—due to the influence of the mass media—to change their environment or propel themselves into other roles. This is accompanied by a severing of traditional roots, leaving a vacuum to be filled. In this situation some of the limitations of the Kemalist experiment begin to emerge.

Mustafa Kemal's ideas about the society which he imagined as emerging on the ruins of the Ottoman empire were focused on the collectivity, and acquired their particular strength from this. They were also focused on the individual's liberation from the stifling *gemeinschaft* of the Muslim community. But a new 'collective conscience' and liberation from community influences were only two aspects of what Mustafa Kemal really wanted to achieve, namely the forging of a new identity for Turks. For this identity to crystallize around the new symbols of the Republic, the latter had to have a 'sensory component' with the ability to 'arouse feelings'.[25]

What we observe is that the symbols of Kemalism assumed this function for only a limited number of Turks. But, in addition, Kemalism did not understand the role played by Islam for Turks in the building of personal identity. After all, Islam had an aspect which addressed itself to man's being-in-this-world, to his basic ontological insecurity, which enabled it to fasten itself on to psychological drives. It is a truism, but still one worth emphasizing, that Islam has become stronger in Turkey because social mobilization had not decreased but on the contrary increased the insecurity of the men who have been projected out of their traditional setting. This insecurity is sometimes 'cognitive' and appears as a search for a convincing political leadership or a bountiful economic system. Here Islam assumes an ideological guise and competes with marxism. In many cases, the insecurity is deeper, more truly ontological, and Islam appears in its aspect of a cosmology and an eschatology.

The revitalization of Islam in modern Turkey is a very complex occurrence, part of which is structured at the personal level, part of which relates to the attempt to bring back the full glory of Islam, and part of which is political. It is a pity that positivism, which played such a large part in the elaboration of Kemalism, did not choose in its Turkish version to remember Auguste Comte's warning: '*L'Humanité se substitute définitivement à Dieu, sans oublier jamais ses services provisoires.*'[26]

This article is reprinted from Ali Kazancigil and Ergun Özbundun (eds), *Atatürk: Founder of a Modern State* (London, 1981), pp. 191–219. Reprinted by permission of C. Hurst and Co.

NOTES

1. Halil Inalcik, *The Ottoman Empire X: the Classical Age 1300–1600*, London, Weidenfeld and Nicolson, 1973, 34.
2. Faik Reşit Unat, *Türkiye'de Egitim Sisteminin Gelişmesine Tarihi bir Bakiş*, Ankara, Milli Eğitim Basimevi, 1964, 19.
3. ibid., 38.
4. ibid., 45.
5. ibid., 14.
6. ibid., 65.
7. Niyazi Berkes, *The Development of Secularism in Turkey*, Montreal, McGill University Press, 1964, 185.
8. Niyazi Berkes, *Türkiyede Çağddaşlaşma Istanbul*, Doğu-Batı Yayinlari, 1978, 234.
9. Abdurrahman Şeref, *Tarih Konuşmaları*, 1923; ed. Eşref Eşrefoğlu, 1978, Istanbul, Kavram Yayinlari, 158–9.
10. ibid., 160.
11. Ahmed Ihsan (Tokgöz), *Matbuat Hatiralarim I 1888–1923, 1. Meşrutiyetin, Ilânına Kadar 1889–1908*, Istanbul, Ahmet Ihsan, 1930, 28–30.
12. Roderic H. Davison, *Reform in the Ottoman Empire 1856–1876*, Princeton University Press, 1963, 13–14.
13. *op. cit.*, 125 ff.
14. M.A. Griffiths, 'The Reorganization of the Ottoman Army under Abdulhamid II, 1880–1897', unpublished Ph.D. dissertation, University of California, Los Angeles, 1966, 94.
15. Erving Goffman, *Asylums*, London, Pelican Books, (1968) 1978, 17.
16. Bernard Lewis, *The Emergence of Modern Turkey*, 2nd edn, London, Oxford University Press, X 1968, 236.
17. Berkes, *Türkiyede Çagdaşlaşma, op. cit.*, 435.
18. *ibid.*, 451.
19. *ibid.*, 493.
20. G. Jaschke, *Yeni Türkiye'de Islâm* (transl. H. Örs), Ankara, Bilgi, Yayınevi, 20.
21. *ibid.*, 96.
22. Niyazi Berkes (ed.), *Turkish Nationalism and Western Civilization: Selected Essays of Ziya Gökalp*, London, Geo. Allen and Unwin, 1959, 312.

23. For a text, see Ş.S. Aydemir, *Tek Adam: Mustafa Kemal*, vol. 3, Istanbul, Remzi Kitabevi, 1966, 473.

24. B.N. Sehsuvaroğlu, 'Atatürk Ilkeleri Işığında ve Bugünkü Türkiye'de Kadın Hakları' in *Atatürk Devrimleri I. Milletlerarası Sempozyumu Bildirileri*, 1974, 422.

25. Victor Turner, *The Forest of Symbols*, Ithaca, NY, Cornell University Press, 1967, 28.

26. Auguste Comte, *Catechisme Positiviste*, 2 edn, Paris, 1874, 378.

From Ottomanism to Arabism: The Origin of an Ideology

C. ERNEST DAWN

Since 1918 the doctrine that the Arabs are a nation and that nationality is the basis of politics has come to be accepted by a very large majority of Arab political leaders and of at least the lay intellectuals. The espousal of this doctrine by a people who are predominantly Muslim in religion is a development of revolutionary significance, since for many centuries Muslims viewed the state in terms of religion and dynasty. Muslims have recognized the existence of distinct peoples or nations since the time of Muhammad. Indeed, Islam in its first century or so was the peculiar religion of the Arab nation, and to become a Muslim was to join the Arab nation as a dependent person. This system proved unworkable, however, and in the end Islam became the supreme bond which superseded nationality.[1]

The state in Muslim theory existed to enforce the *sharīʿah*, the law which God had sent to man through His messenger, Muhammad. Originally, it was held, the totality of the Muslims constituted a congregation, who ought to be joined together under the rule of one monarch, the caliph, or successor to the Prophet Muhammad, who was God's first viceroy on earth under Islam. After some centuries during which actuality was close to theory, the caliphate broke up, leaving the Muslims governed by a variety of dynasts or sultans. In theory, the *sharīʿah* remained to give unity to the Muslim congregation, and any ruler who enforced the *sharīʿah* was a legitimate ruler, regardless of how he had attained power.

Such was the nature (in theory) of the Ottoman Empire, the state sovereign in most of the Arab lands after 1517. The Arabs of southwestern Asia and of Egypt accepted the rule of the Turkish Ottomans, at least nominally, for four centuries. But by the end of the nineteenth century a few Ottoman Arab intellectuals had put forward theories which denied the right of Turks to rule Arabs. These intellectuals created a new ideology, Arabism, and offered it as a solution to the problems of the day. One might simply assume that the antique Arab consciousness was revivifying itself, that these Arabs were returning to the ways of their ancestors in reasserting the primacy of their nationhood. Such an assumption, however, would leave unanswered the question of why the Arab national consciousness was reactivated after a millennial slumber.

Interest in nationality as a political principle was rekindled among the Muslim peoples by contact with the West. At the turn of the nineteenth century, a few Turks and Egyptian Arabs who had resided in Europe began to become aware of the European ideas of fatherland and nation. By the middle of the new century, terms for these and related concepts existed in both Turkish and Arabic.[2] One of the most influential persons in spreading the new ideas was an Egyptian, Rifā'ah Rāfi' al-Ṭahṭāwi, who spent the years 1826–31 in France and described his experiences in a book published in 1834. This book enjoyed great popularity among both Arabs and Turks, it was reissued in 1848, and in 1840 a Turkish translation appeared.[3] The importance of European ideas in stimulating the thinking of these men is shown by their concern with the idea of patriotism. Love of one's place of birth or of one's homeland was a well-established virtue among the Muslims, but they did not give it political significance. Nor did the Muslims consider nationality to be connected with territoriality. Ṭahṭāwi and his contemporaries did. Ṭahṭāwi spoke frequently of nations and countries and made it clear that a nation was intimately bound to a specific country. To him Egypt was a country and the Egyptians a nation which should love its fatherland.[4] After he returned to Egypt, in the course of a long career as educator and author, he explicitly introduced the new concepts in poetry.[5]

Ṭahṭāwi and his Turkish counterparts of the early nineteenth century were not mere mimics who copied for the sake of imitation. The European notions had no obviously necessary application to the Ottoman situation. Different men, in fact, applied the general idea in different ways. While Ṭahṭāwi talked of Egyptian patriotism, the Ottoman reformers sought to create a sense of Ottoman patriotism.[6] None of these men went deeply into the European theories of nationalism. They accepted without question the traditional Islamic dynastic state. They rendered the new concepts with Arabo-Turkish words which had long since been used in both Arabic and Turkish with meanings not far removed from their new significations.[7]

Of course, contact with strange ways is never a guarantee that the strange ways will be imitated. At the beginning of the nineteenth century, the peoples of the Ottoman Empire had a long history of close contact with Europe, throughout which they had shown no desire to imitate Frankish customs.

Instead, even at the beginning of the nineteenth century most Ottomans regarded the ways of the Franks with repugnance.[8] As good Muslims, the Ottomans regarded Muhammad as the final, the perfect, and the best of the messengers whom God had sent to make His will known to man. The Muhammadan revelation contained all that man needed to know for this life and the next. The Muslim *sharī'ah*, or law, was perfect and unchangeable. The Muslims, then, were the best of peoples and had no need to learn from the infidels.

Yet Ṭahṭāwi and the Ottoman *tanẓīmāt* reformers, despite their having been nurtured by traditional Muslim Ottoman culture, obviously were interested in European patriotism and sought to apply the notion to their own country. When the Turks noted the zeal of patriotic Frenchmen in battle and their fidelity to the French state, they doubtless recognized the usefulness of such patriotism to the Ottoman state. Perhaps they also shared the impression which Ṭahṭāwi stated clearly when he attributed the remarkable progress and well-being of France to patriotism. In describing the wonders of Paris, he remarked, 'Without the astronomy [i.e. science] of the people of Paris, their wisdom, their accomplishments, their good administration, and their concern with the interests of their land, their city would be nothing at all.' He went on to describe their efforts and said, 'If Egypt took care and the tools of civilization were applied copiously there, then it would be the sultan of cities and the chief country of the world.' Ṭahṭāwi then presented a long patriotic poem about Egypt, probably the first poem of this new type in the Near Eastern languages.[9]

To men like Ṭahṭāwi and his Turkish counterparts of the early nineteenth century, patriotism was just another element of Frankish civilization which appeared to be useful to the Muslims. These men were acutely aware that the East had something to learn from the West. To understand what they, and their successors, meant by patriotism and nationalism and what value they believed it to possess for the inhabitants of the Ottoman Empire, one must comprehend their views on the value of the West to Islam.

The traditional Ottoman view of Europe was shaken by the unbroken string of military defeats which the Ottomans suffered throughout the eighteenth century and the first half of the nineteenth. The French expedition to Egypt made Ottomans even more aware of European progress. Quite naturally those in charge of the Ottoman state came to realize the importance of borrowing from the West in order to defend the Empire. Just as naturally the same men saw that their personal positions within the Empire could be bolstered by using the techniques of the West. Thus the Ottoman statesmen and Mehmed Ali, the governor-general of Egypt, began to carry out military and administrative reforms. In order to implement the reforms, Turks and Egyptians had to be sent to Europe in increasingly larger numbers. In Europe these young men became acutely conscious of the differences between the East and the West. As a result, a new element was added to their thinking: aware of the progress of the West, they began to desire progress for its own sake, not merely for the sake of defending the Empire from the advances of the Christians. To this second generation of Ottoman Westernizers belonged Ṭahṭāwi and the Ottoman *tanẓīmāt* reformers such as Reshid, Âli, and Fuad.

The overwhelming majority of the Ottoman people saw no need to imitate the West. The Islam of their fathers was good enough for them. Theologically and culturally most Ottoman Muslims remained conservatives. The early reforms were pressed through only by ruthless measures on the part of the rulers against the stubborn opposition of vested interest and Muslim conservatism. For the new situation created deep disturbance in the minds of Ottoman Muslims, the depth of which is indicated by the fact that the early Ottoman Westernizers, including those of the *tanẓīmāt* period, were in basic outlook just as conservative as the anti-Western majority.

Ṭahṭāwi and the *tanẓīmāt* reformers knew that in some ways the West had surpassed the East. At the same time, they felt that Islam and the Ottoman way of life were fundamentally sound. All that was necessary, they thought, was to borrow certain things from the West and the gap could be closed.[10] 'In the time of the caliphs,' Ṭahṭāwi wrote, 'we were more perfect than the other lands, because the caliphs used to appoint learned men and masters of the arts, etc.,' but then the Muslims declined and the Franks made progress.[11] 'The lands of the Franks,' he said, 'have reached the highest stage of excellence in mathematics and the natural and physical sciences . . .' On the other hand, Ṭahṭāwi was confident that Islam was still sound, far superior to Christianity. The Franks, for all their progress in the arts and sciences, he wrote, 'have not been guided to the straight path, and they have not followed the course of salvation at all. Just as the Islamic lands have excelled in the sciences and application of the *sharī'ah* and in the rational sciences and have neglected the wisdom sciences entirely . . . so the Franks . . . admit that we were their teachers in the other sciences and our precedence over them . . .' (p. 8). God was with the faithful, thought Ṭahṭāwi, for 'if Islam had not been succored by the decree of God . . . then there would have been nothing to compare to their [the Franks'] power, multitudes, wealth, and excellence' (p. 9). Accordingly, although the Muslims have 'neglected the wisdom sciences entirely, and thus need the Western lands to acquire what they do not know' (p. 8), Ṭahṭāwi did 'not approve of [borrowing] anything except what does not contradict the text of the Muhammadan *sharī'ah*' (p. 5).

The Westernizing conservatives like Ṭahṭāwi and the Turkish *tanẓīmāt* reformers recognized the necessity of reforming on the European model. At the same time, they retained the traditional Muslim's calm assurance that Islam and Eastern culture were inherently superior to Christianity and

Europe and were in no need of reformation in fundamentals. The Muslims and the East, they admitted, were in danger and had lost some of their previous greatness and glory, but this lamentable situation could be treated simply by borrowing whatever was necessary of the practical wisdom of the Europeans. By the middle of the nineteenth century, this comfortable self-assurance had been shaken. Thereafter the situation grew progressively more intolerable to the proud and sensitive Muslim who knew something of the world.

Although the Near East made material progress throughout the nineteenth century (even striking progress in some areas), by the middle of the century it had been far outdistanced by the astounding progress of Europe, and by the end of the century left far behind. At the same time, the progress of Europe was made manifest to a much larger number of Ottoman subjects than ever before. Many more young men spent some time in Europe. Western teachers in state and missionary schools made others acquainted with the world outside the Empire. That the ways of the infidel were attractive to Muslims was obvious. The upper classes aped Frankish dress and manners. Rulers borrowed large sums of money from Europeans to spend, in part at least, on public improvements *à la française.* Worst of all in the eyes of the orthodox was the attraction that study in Europe and in the infidel missionary schools held for the youth.

It was equally obvious that the infidels held the basic precepts and institutions of Islam and the Ottoman state in disdain. Alien and infidel courts, operating outside the *sharīʿah*, favored the Christian over the faithful. When Christian subjects engaged in disorderly or treasonable conduct (so the Muslim Ottomans believed), the European powers used pressure, even armed force, to insure special privileges and sometimes independence for the rebellious Christians. Perhaps worst of all were the charges of Christian missionaries and the belittling remarks of Europeans about Eastern civilization. Even learned European Orientalists passed judgements that, when stripped of subtle nuances of phrasing, reduced in the Muslim's view to Lord Cromer's 'reformed Islam is Islam no longer.'

With the new situation there was a change in the thinking of Ottoman intellectuals. Gone was the old calm confidence that Islam was inherently superior to other religions and Muslim Ottoman civilization basically sounder than European. Whereas the older intellectuals had merely asserted Muslim and Ottoman superiority, the new ones made impassioned defenses of the true faith and vehement refutations of the false. The defense of Islam and of the East became the overriding concern of Ottoman intellectuals. All were obsessed with the denial that Islam and the East were inferior to Christianity and Europe. In mode of denial, however, the Ottoman intellectuals differed from each other. Some simply denied that in their day Islam and the Ottoman lands were behind the West. Others admitted it, but explained it away.

Some (probably most) Ottoman intellectuals remained conservative and merely reaffirmed with renewed vigor the traditional belief that Islam was the best of all possible ways of life. The production of apologetics and polemics in both Arabic and Turkish became notable after 1860.[12] The most popular and widely read of them was the book *Iẓhār al-Ḥaqq* by the Indian Muslim Raḥmatullāh al-Hindi, which was published in Arabic at Constantinople in 1867 and soon translated into Turkish.[13] In all this there was nothing new. Islam was affirmed and Christianity attacked with the traditional arguments of early Islam. The remarkable thing is the great increase in quantity after 1860. Similarly newspapers in both Turkish and Arabic took up the defense of Islam and the East. There were many, but the most notable was the Arabic *al-Jawā'ib*, which was published in Constantinople following 1860 by Ahmad Fāris al-Shidyāq.[14]

Some of these men were concerned with more than the defense of a religion, Islam. They also took upon themselves the defense of a civilization. They compared European society unfavorably to Ottoman. Shidyāq, who had lived in England and France, was willing to admit that the West was superior in material wealth. But in words suggestive of Western attacks on the monotony and materialism of modern industrialism, he insisted that the East still was superior in insuring true happiness, culture, and morality to man.[15] He summed up his attitude with the remark (p. 603), 'Without doubt, the peasants of our country are more fortunate than those people.' He was outraged by the assertion of a European Orientalist that the Europeans 'had all necessary knowledge of the Eastern languages' and that European scholars had 'become the professors of the Persians and the teachers of the Arabs.' Shidyāq applied eighteen synonyms for 'lie' to this assertion and made a violent assault on the errors and vanities of Orientalists.[16] Shidyāq, and those like him, were strong defenders and advocates of the Ottoman Empire. We may refer to them as Ottoman conservatives.

In the minds of other Ottoman intellectuals, the traditional apologetics and polemics were not adequate for the defense of Islam. These intellectuals, unlike the conservatives, admitted that in their day Islam was in a deplorable state. They agreed with the conservatives, however, that Islam and the East were inherently superior to other religions and to the West. True Islam, they argued, was not incompatible with advanced civilization like that of Europe. The Muslims were in such a sad condition because true primitive Islam had been corrupted and, as a result, the Muslims had not been able to continue the remarkable progress of their early years. The remedy was simply to restore Islam to its pristine purity so that the Muslims, by adopting and adapting the necessary elements of modern civilization, might regain their former greatness. We may therefore designate them modernists, in contrast to the conservatives, and since they, like the conservatives, were advocates of a strong Ottoman state, as Ottoman modernists. Among the Turkish element of the Empire, the point of view is exemplified in the New Ottomans who became active in the 1860s. This group now explicitly adopted the ideas of Ottoman patriotism and the Ottoman fatherland.[17] During the 1870s, very similar ideas became widespread in Egypt as a result of the activities of Jamāl al-Dīn al-Afghāni.[18] Primitive Islam, said Afghāni (pp. 165–7), required its followers to exercise reason and examine the bases of their faith. Quoting Guizot, he argued that European progress was the result of the appearance in Europe of a similar theology, Protestantism.

Although most of the modernists were Ottomanists, a few Syrian Christians who shared the general ideas of the modernists advanced a quasi-secular Arab nationalism. American and French missionary schools in Lebanon brought many Syrians, mostly Christians, into close contact with the West. By the 1860s these Arabs had contributed greatly to a revival of classical Arabic literature and to the diffusion of modern knowledge. One of the most important spokesmen for the group was Ibrāhīm al-Yāziji, who in 1868 called for an Arab national revival. He agreed with the Ottoman modernists that in his day the East was in a deplorable condition, even though it was the home of civilization. His concern, however, was with the Arabs alone. He recalled vividly the glory and greatness of the Arabs in the past. To him, the Arabs were the most remarkable of nations, because they had achieved more in a short period of time than any other people. The Europeans made their rapid progress only because they had been able to borrow directly from the Arabs. The Arabs had declined after the non-Arab (Turk) came to dominate them and reduced learning to the religious sciences and religion to bigotry and fanaticism. To Yāziji, the means for the Arabs to regain their rightful glory was for the Arab nation to cast off the foreigner and to rid itself of bigotry and fanaticism. Then the old vigor of the Arab nation would return and the Arabs would resume their former progress in civilization.[19]

The Christian version of Arabism was not to the liking of the Syrian Muslim Arabs. In fact, the Muslim Arabs of Syria were outraged at the spectacle of Christians assuming the air of masters of Arab learning. Attacks on the pretensions of Yāziji and other Christian Arab literary men were popular. The Muslim Arabs of Syria adopted the battle cry, 'Arabic shall not be Christianized.'[20] Yāziji's secular Arabism found few followers, and Ottomanism, whether conservative or modernist, remained the dominant ideology within the Ottoman lands until 1914.

Ironically, the outlines of a Muslim theory of Arab nationalism were propounded by the greatest of the Arab Ottoman modernists, the Egyptian Muḥammad 'Abduh, whose primary goal was the revival of Islam and who was himself, during his political phases, an advocate of the Ottoman state.

'Abduh reaffirmed the essential superiority of Islam. He recalled the past glories of Islam, its rapid spread, great empire, and splendid civilization.[21] Islam is the perfect religion because it is based on reason and demands that its followers exercise their rational faculties and know the bases of their belief. This is the cause of the great Muslim progress in the past (pp. 6–10, 194–223). Other religions are inferior to Islam. 'Abduh developed Afghāni's use of Guizot and declared that Europe did not begin its amazing progress in civilization until the Europeans began to learn from the Muslims, and, having adopted a creed 'which is in concord with Islam, except for the recognition of Muhammad's mission,' 'organized their lives in a fashion analogous to the precepts of Islam' (pp. 109, 131–2). The Muslims declined when Islam was perverted by intermixing science and religion, which ought to be kept separate, so that in the end the Muslims ceased to exercise reason (pp. 13–19).

'Abduh thus maintained the intrinsic adequacy and superiority of Islam as a way of life. The sad condition of the Muslims in his day was the result of deviation from pristine Islam. 'The Muslims have spent an age in inflicting harm on their souls, they have passed the time in chipping away the mortar of their faith,' he wrote in 1887, 'and they have injured the bonds of their conviction, because of the shadows of ignorance of the roots of their faith which have covered them.' He went on to attribute the decline in Muslim political fortunes to the corruption of true Islam:

> Weakness has followed corruption in morals, lapses in behavior, and the abasement of souls, so that most of the populace resembles cattle, whose only ambition is to live to the end of their days, eating, drinking, and reproducing, contending with each other in bestiality. After that it was all the same to them whether majesty was with God, His prophet, and His caliph or with whoever else was lord over them.[22]

'Abduh's prescription for the ills of Islam was the rejection of Western civilization and the return to pure Islam. He warned against sending Muslims to the schools of the missionaries, who were 'foreign devils,' whose 'satanical whisperings' had 'deceived a number which is not small.' Primitive, uncorrupted Islam, not the teachings of the missionaries, was 'Abduh's remedy. 'In acquiring this vital knowledge,' he wrote in 1886,

> we have no need to seek benefits from those who are foreign to us. Rather, it is sufficient for us to return to what we have abandoned and to purify what we have corrupted. This consists of our religious and humanistic books, which contain more than enough of what we seek, and there is nothing in books other than ours which adds anything to them except that which we do not need.[23]

Religious revival, 'Abduh believed, was the only way for the Muslims to regain their political greatness. In 1887 he wrote:

> Anyone of Islamic faith who has a heart believes that the preservation of the high Ottoman state is the third article of faith after faith in God and His prophet, for it alone is the preserver of the dominion of religion, the guarantor of its possessions, and the religion [of Islam] has no government [sultān] except it [the Ottoman state].

He went on to say:

> The Islamic caliphate has fortresses and walls, and whatever strengthens confidence in it and zeal to defend it in the hearts of the faithful strengthens its walls. Nothing instills confidence and kindles zeal in the hearts of the Muslims except what the religion [of Islam] sends to them. If anyone believes that the name of the fatherland, the interest of the country and other such resounding words can take the place of religion in raising ambitions and pressing on their realization, then he has strayed onto an evil path.[24]

Although ʿAbduh, during his days as a political activist in the 1880s, was a strong advocate of Ottomanism, his belief in the necessity of returning to Islam led him to formulate an idea which was implicitly contrary to Ottomanism. The cure for the disease of the Muslims was the restoration of the true, original Islam, and that meant the Islam of the Arabs. 'The Koran is the source of the success of the Muslims,' he wrote in 1887,

> and there is no power capable of reforming their affairs except returning to it . . . The Koran must be taken in its strictest aspects in accordance with the rules of the Arabic language, so as to respond to it as did the shepherds and camel-drivers to whom and in whose language the Koran descended. The Koran is close to its student when he knows the Arabic language, the practices of the Arabs in disputation, their history, and their customs in the days of the revelation, and knowledge of these is the most excellent way to understand it.

ʿAbduh then went on to urge, as the basis of the necessary religious revival, the intensive revival of the classical Arabic literary and religious studies.[25]

ʿAbduh in his later years gave up the political activism of his middle years, but he never gave up his basic ideas. When Christians, Arab and European, charged that Islam was inherently inadequate to the problems of the modern world, ʿAbduh in vigorous replies reaffirmed that Islam was the perfect system and, if restored to its full vigor, completely sufficient for modern life. Having given up political activism, he stressed religious reform even more. And to the end he held that fundamental religious reform required a revival of Arabic studies.[26]

ʿAbduh's ideas were taken up by a close associate and devoted pupil, the Syrian Muḥammad Rashīd Riḍa, who, after March 1898, spread them through his journal, *al-Manār.* Rashīd Riḍa also was concerned with the question of how Islam and the East were to regain their rightful glory. His answer was the same as ʿAbduh's: 'Have we said ... "Is it possible to restore the glory of the East through the strength of Islam?" Yes! a thousand times yes!' He continued: 'The roots of the Islamic religion and its true teachings and humanistic learning united the tribes of the Arabs, advanced them from the depths of barbarism to the apex of excellences, honored them over the states of the world with sovereignty and suzerainty, and guided them to the sciences and the arts.' Echoing ʿAbduh, he declared that in Islam, God had sent 'a true *sharīʿah* ... through which the kingdoms of Europe became glorious and mighty, which Europe acquired only from Islam.' The diagnosis and prescription was the same as ʿAbduh's:

> It is beyond dispute that the deviation of the Muslims from its highway robbed them of their achievements and that returning to it will bind their hearts together, unite them, and return to them their sovereignty ... If ... [the Muslim men of learning] set the Koran before themselves and revive its meanings intelligently ... then the spirit of union will fall on the [Muslim] congregation from Heaven, and the Easterners and Westerners [of the congregation] will be united and they will return to the East its glory.[27]

Rashīd Riḍa, like ʿAbduh, was led by his doctrine of primitive Islam to stress the priority of the Arabs. The return to primitive Islam inevitably stressed an Arab revival. Rashīd Riḍa's reform was to be carried out by the Ottoman sultan, as caliph, following the advice of a society of learned men which had its seat in Mecca. One of the specific proposed reforms was the revival of Arabic studies, which was indeed at the root of the matter. 'It is necessary to spread the Arabic language rather than Turkish,' said Rashīd Riḍa, 'since it [Arabic] is the language of religion, and so its revivification is the revivification of it [religion] and its [Arabic's] spreading is the means of spreading it [religion] and of understanding it.'[28] Rashīd Riḍa soon went on to make it even clearer that an Arab revival was the only way to restore Islam.

> To be filled with passion for the history of the Arabs, to strive to revive their glory, is the same as working for Islamic union, which in the past was achieved only through the Arabs and which will not be regained in this century except through them ... The basis of this union is Islam itself, and Islam is nothing but the Book of the Omnipotent and the *sunnah* of His prophet ... Both are in Arabic; no one can understand Islam if he does not understand them both correctly, and no one can understand them correctly if he does not understand their noble language.

From this, it was an easy step to glorifying the Arabs: 'The greatest glory for the Muslim conquests belongs to the Arabs and ... the religion grew and became great because of them. Their foundations are the most solid, their light is the clearest, they are in truth the best nation born into the world.'[29]

Rashīd Riḍa thus developed to completion ʿAbduh's emphasis on the necessity of Arab revival as the foundation for a general Muslim revival. At the same time, Rashīd Riḍa made explicit the notion that the Arabs were the best of the Muslims. Nevertheless, for a long time he retained his hope that his reform would be carried out under the patronage of the Ottoman sultan and his loyalty to the Ottoman state. It remained for another Syrian Arab, an associate of Rashīd Riḍa, to add political content to the theory. This was done by ʿAbd al-Raḥmān al-Kawākibi, who came to Cairo in 1898.

Kawākibi believed that in his time 'confusion and weakness had encompassed all the Muslims.'[30] He still took pride, however, in the past greatness of Islam and maintained its superiority to other ways of life. The non-Muslims had excelled the Muslims only in the 'empirical sciences and arts' (p. 9). Islam remained 'a straight, firm, correct, well-founded religion which is not surpassed, and not [even] approached by any other religion in wisdom, in order, and in solidity of structure' (p. 15; cf. p. 67). In fact, the Christians did not make progress in the arts and sciences until Protestantism, which is similar to true Islam, appeared, after which Orthodoxy and Catholicism remained 'favored by the masses, but dwindled away entirely among the educated, because science and Christianity do not agree at all.' The one who follows true pure Islam, however, increases his faith whenever he increases his science or exercises thought, for ... he will not find in it [true Islam] anything which reason rejects or scientific investigation refutes' (p. 124; cf. pp. 92–4).

Accordingly, Kawākibi rejected blind imitation of the West. He vehemently criticized the Muslim upper classes as 'weaklings' who saw 'perfection in foreigners, as children see perfection in their fathers.' The foreigners deceived the Muslims and made them falsely ashamed of their religion and their customs (p. 160). Kawākibi's diagnosis of the disease was that of the Ottoman modernists. 'Is there still anyone who doubts,' he wrote, 'that the existing religion ... is not the religion by which our ancestors were distinguished over the worlds? Nay, unfortunate changes have fallen upon the religion which have changed its foundation' (p. 60). Thus, 'the cause of the languor [of the Muslims] is religious defectiveness' (p. 200). The remedy was also the same:

> We should rely upon our knowledge of the clear [word] of the Book, the sound [parts] of the *sunnah* [the customary usage of Muhammad], and the confirmed [provisions] of the *ijmāʿ* [the consensus of the early congregation] ... for the creed of the ancestors is the source which the congregation will not discard, nor will it reject returning to it (p. 12; cf. p. 67).

Kawākibi, like ʿAbduh and Rashīd Riḍa, was led by his diagnosis of the ills of Islam to underline the pre-eminence of the Arabs and their unique role in the revival of Islam. A return to true Islam meant a revivification of Arab Islam, for the Koran and the *sunnah* could be understood only through knowledge of 'the Arabic language, which is the language of the Koran ...' (p. 71; cf. pp. 95, 170). Like Rashīd Riḍa, Kawākibi made much of the pre-eminence of the Arabs in Islam (pp. 195–8), and concluded that '... the Arabs are the sole medium for religious unification—Nay! for Eastern unification' (p. 198). Kawākibi went beyond his predecessors in singling out the Arabs of Arabia as the best of the Arabs because they were the closest to the original Muslims (pp. 12, 193–5). He also made political proposals. He respected the Ottoman Empire as 'the greatest state, whose affairs concern the generality of the Muslims' (p. 142) and made proposals to reform its administration (pp. 142–8). He loved 'the Ottomans [sultans] for the kindness of their dispositions and their elevation of religious rites' (p. 210). On the other hand, he believed that 'every nation within the population of Turkey should attain administrative autonomy' (p. 143, n.). Moreover, he criticized the opportunism of Ottoman policy toward the Muslims and their caliphate policy (pp. 211, 201–7). Finally, Kawākibi proposed the establishment of an Arab 'caliphate' in Mecca, not as a successor to the historical caliphate, but as a means of facilitating the reform of Islam and the formation of a great pan-Islamic federation (pp. 207–10).[31]

The theory of Arab nationalism thus grew out of the modernist diagnosis of Muslim decline and prescription for Muslim revival. The Arab nationalist theorists were Arabist modernists in distinction to their close relatives, the Ottomanist modernists. Both varieties of modernists shared one characteristic with the conservatives. All were unwilling to admit that the East was inferior to Europe; instead, all maintained that Islam and the culture of the East were intrinsically superior to Christianity and Western civilization. The conservatives simply denied inferiority and reaffirmed superiority. The modernists, both Ottomanist and Arabist, admitted inferiority in their day but explained it away by making their backwardness the result of deviation from true Islam, which was inherently the perfect system. This might be interpreted as simple religious bigotry. Yet these Muslim intellectuals were defending a civilization as much as a religion. Their attitude, moreover, was shared by many Christian intellectuals who, like their Muslim brethen, were unwilling to admit the inferiority of the East to the West.

Some Christian Arabs, such as Ibrāhīm al-Yāziji, put forward a theory which implicitly advocated a secular nationalism. As the Muslims could not accept the separation of Islam from Arabism, it is doubtful that Yāziji's ideas had much influence on the course of Arab nationalist thought. The subject remains to be investigated, but it seems likely that ideas such as Yāziji's contributed to the development of regional nationalisms among the Christians of Syria and Lebanon.[32]

Yet Yāziji agreed with the Ottoman modernists on one point. The Easterners, or at least the Arabs, instead of being inferior to the Europeans, were the most remarkable of people, a people who had civilized the West. Yāziji, like the Ottoman modernists, was seeking a way to restore the past glory of the Arabs. He found it in a return to the true spirit of the Arab nation.

Other Christian Arab intellectuals shared Yāziji's desire to restore the greatness of the East but, unlike him, saw the East in broader terms. One was Adīb Isḥaq, a contemporary of Yāziji in Beirut and then an associate of Afghāni and 'Abduh in Cairo during the late 1870s. Isḥaq maintained that the East was the 'home of the seeds of the religious and political movements which changed the form of the earth and the conditions of man.'[33] Isḥaq was ontraged by the aspersions which Westerners cast on the East, which had taught civilization to the West (pp. 198–199; cf. p. 200). Yet Isḥaq admitted that in his day there had been a decline: the East is 'the older brother of the West, which nursed it as an infant, fed it as a boy, supported it as a youth, and needs it as a mature man' (p. 473). The contrast between Eastern and Western civilization Isḥaq explained as the result of the casting aside of the true *sharī'ah* of the East and the consequent decline in spirit and learning (pp. 54, III–12, 201–2). The East would revive, not through the efforts of foreigners, who had selfish designs of their own (p. 113–14), but through the efforts of sincere Eastern patriots who, after they had been moved to 'reverence for the ancient glory and outrage with the new abasement, so that the fire of ambition and zeal will burn in [their] hearts' (pp. 174–5), would 'expunge the shameful innovations and purify the true *sharī'ah*' (p. 202) and lead the East to the restoration of its past greatness (pp. 112, 202–3).

Isḥaq was led by the great problem of his day to identify himself with the 'East,' which was his favorite term for his 'homeland.' Specifically, however, he was an Ottomanist (pp. 96–7, 111–13, 128–9, 132, 382–4). He was proud of being an Arab, but his pride in the Arabs was subordinate to his Ottomanism and Easternism (pp. 149–50, 200).

Other Christian Arabs identified themselves with the civilization of the East even more closely than did Isḥaq. The outstanding case was that of Aḥmad Fāris al-Shidyāq, who was born a Christian but converted to Islam shortly before 1860 and became one of the most famous of the Ottoman conservatives. Yāziji and Isḥaq, when confronted with the contrast between the East and the West, found hope in the past greatness of the East. In doing this, they necessarily recalled the past greatness of Muslims, not Christians. Shidyāq, even before his conversion to Islam, made this explicit by identifying Eastern civilization with Islam. In reply to the belittling remarks of a European Orientalist, he wrote, 'Those [European] professors have not taken learning from its *shaykhs*, i.e., from Shaykh Muḥammad, Mulla Ḥasan, and *Ustādh* Sa'di [i.e., Muslim scholars]; no, they have been parasites on it and have taken unfair hold [of it]. Whoever [of the Europeans] is educated at all in it is only educated by Priest Ḥanna, Monk Tūma, and Priest Matta. Then he puts his head in nightmares, and the nightmares enter his head, and he thinks that he knows something, but he is ignorant.'[34] Other Christian Arabs were to follow Shidyāq, but without renouncing the religion of their birth.

By 1914, some Christian Arabs had gone a long way toward accepting the theory of Arabism which Rashīd Riḍa and Kawākibi had advanced. One was Nadrah Maṭrān, a Lebanese by origin. His nationalism had a racial basis. 'Racial pride is a fundamental virtue,' he said in 1913, 'and I do not know a nation more strongly affected by its influences than the Arab nation.' Nevertheless, he was willing to admit that Islam was one of the glories of the Arab nation. He described how, when the 'Arab Muslim armies' were advancing against Damascus, the Arab Christian Ghassanids, 'instead of fighting the Muslims and standing in their faces, were stirred by the sentiment of brotherhood and abandoned the religious bond and the political tie which made them the clients of the Romans and contracted friendship with and fidelity to the speakers of their language, the sons of their father.' It was good for the Christian Arabs of Syria to submit to the rule of the Muslims, for the latter 'were Arabs who ruled an Arab country which had a right to glory in them and to pride themselves in their works and their conquests . . .' Maṭrān went on to make the glory of Islam virtually equivalent to the glory of the Arabs.

> Religious fellow-feeling had become predominant with all the nations without exception, and so it was with the Muslims, and it is not strange if we saw them [the Muslim Arabs] submitting to the rule of the Seljuks, the suzerainty of the Ayyubids, and the dominion of the Ottomans, since they believed them capable of supporting the glory of Islam and of raising the banner of the caliphate . . .[35]

It was good for the Christian Arabs to join the Muslims, because that brought glory to the Arabs. It was equally good for the Arabs to submit to the rule of non-Arab Muslims, because that maintained the glory of Islam. Muslim and Christian Arab ideas on Arabism had converged. The Arabs, said the Muslims, are the best of nations because God chose them to receive the perfect religion, Islam. Islam, said the Christians, is dear to all Arabs, because it made them great. A Syrian Christian contemporary of Maṭrān put the matter neatly: 'Let everyone of us say I am Arab . . . and if being Arab is only possible through being Muslim, then let him say I am an Arab and a Muslim . . .'[36]

Arabism, then, grew out of modernist Ottomanism and in response to the same stimulus. Both theories were primarily concerned with denying that Eastern culture was inferior to that of the West. They shared this trait with Ottoman conservatism. Something of the emotional make-up of all the theorists is revealed by Adīb Isḥaq, who admitted that he had 'made love of the self the source of love of the fatherland and of the nation.' In another place he explained: 'Belonging to the fatherland connects it and the inhabitant with a firm bond of personal honor, and he [the inhabitant] is jealous of it and defends it, just as he defends his father who has begotten him, even if he is very angry with him.' The abasement of Isḥaq's fatherland in comparison to the West thus humiliated Isḥaq personally. His great goal, like that of the other modernists, both Ottomanist and Arabist, was to deliver the East from its humiliation. 'We have composed a history of the French Revolution,' he wrote,

> only to make us remember it is an example and a lesson to a nation which remembers and reflects. And to instruct those who suffer tyranny, those who yearn for deliverance from humiliation, how people before them achieved this goal, and changed from weakness to strength, from humiliation to mightiness, from slavery to freedom, and raised their heads, and rejoiced their souls . . .[37]

The gap between the general advancement of the Islamic East and that of the Christian West was the great innovator in Ottoman intellectual and political activity during the nineteenth century. That some of the ways of the alien and infidel West must be imitated was obvious to a minority of significant magnitude. The majority, perhaps, remained firmly orthodox and either opposed all innovations or left the great matters where they belonged, in the hands of the Omnipotent, but those who influenced and directed state policy were forced to look to the West. The necessity of imitating the infidel alien, however, was a heavy blow to their pride and self-esteem. Consequently, their advocacy of Westernization was mingled with the defense of Islam and of the East.

In the beginning, when the gap between East and West did not appear unbridgeable, the apologetics of the Westernizers were moderate and restrained. As the gap grew wider, the Westernizers came more and more to be primarily apologists until the advocacy of Westernization was all but submerged in a flood of self-justification and anti-Westernism. Men who set out to show how the Islamic East could overtake the Christian West ended by devoting most of their energies to explaining that the East was really superior. Some, the conservatives, were content with showing the falsity of Christianity by means of the orthodox apologetics and polemics and with emphasizing the unpleasant aspects of European life. Others, the modernists, went on to show that the Europeans actually owed their progress to their having absorbed something of the true spirit of Islam, which the Muslims, alas, had forsaken.

Interest in patriotism and nationalism was one of the results of the Ottoman preoccupation with the humiliating differential between East and West and with means of erasing it. National patriotism, the Westernizing Ottomans believed, was one of the sources of European strength and progress and should therefore be adopted by the Ottomans just as military and administrative techniques should be adopted. This belief led to the appearance of a generalized Islamic Ottomanism within the Turkish element of the

Empire and of a local Islamic Egyptian nationalism with Ottomanist overtones in Egypt. In general, the conservatives, like the *tanẓīmāt* reformers and Aḥmad Fāris al Shidyāq, agreed with the modernists, like the New Ottomans, Afghāni, and the young Muḥammad ʿAbduh, in posing as the supreme interest the defense of the Ottoman Empire and of the Islamic East against the Christian West.

The modernist justification of the Islamic East created the basis of Arab nationalist theory. To show how the East could catch up with the West and to prove that the East was in fact superior to the West, the modernists dwelt on the perfect system, uncorrupted original Islam. To the modernists, the return to pure Islam was the answer to the problems of their day. But, as Muḥammad ʿAbduh was the first to note, emphasis on early Islam heightened the importance of the Arabs, their language, and their past to the defense and revival of Islam and the East.

Islam was as much the center of Arabism as it was of Ottomanism. Yet Arabism and Ottomanism were something more than recrudescences of religious bigotry and fanaticism. Both were defenses against the West, not against Christianity alone. Both were justifications of a civilization, the East, the worth and adequacy of which had been questioned by the progress of the West. Some Christian Ottomans, at least among the Arabs, shared the Muslim's sense of personal dishonor in the existence of the gap between Islamic East and Christian West. They joined in the defense of the East against the West, and they took pride in the past greatness of Islam.[38]

Arabism, like Ottomanism, was the result of preoccupation with the problem which the general progress of Europe posed for the inhabitants of the Ottoman Empire. This preoccupation led to the giving of political content to nationality in a region where religion and dynasty had been the twin pillars of the state. Nationality was incidental to a scheme of thought which was directed chiefly at expounding a plan for progress and at vindicating the worth of a way of life. The Ottomanists attempted to make a single nationality of the diverse ethnic elements which peopled the Ottoman Empire. The Arabists raised a single people, the Arabs, to a position of pre-eminence. The aim of both, however, was to defend the East and to further the glory of Islam in the face of the West. The common goal of Arabism and Ottomanism expressed the sentiment of identity which was shared by most Ottomans in a world dominated by European civilization. However much they disagreed, in moments of crisis all closed ranks around the fundamental necessity of maintaining their cultural identity and self-dignity.

But disagree they did. For though Arabism and Ottomanism, both conservative and modernist, were very similar responses to the same problem, the differences between the answers are significant. The question arises of how different people of similar background in the same situation came to give divergent answers to the same problem. The question cannot be answered by anything in the content or the technical structure of the ideas under consideration. A modernist might be Ottomanist or Arabist, an Ottomanist either conservative or modernist. The ethnic sentiment of the Arabs is of little help as a clue, for, despite the obvious value of Arabist theory in bolstering Arab pride, most Arabs remained Ottomanists until 1918. The search for a complete explanation of the emergence of Arabism from Ottomanism must extend beyond the realm of ideologies. However, that poses a new problem which cannot be dealt with here. One conclusion can be proposed: Arabism developed from modernist Ottomanism and, like modernist and conservative Ottomanism, was a reaction against the failure of the Ottoman civilization to keep pace with Europe.

This article is reprinted from C. Ernest Dawn, *From Ottomanism to Arabism: Essays on the Origins of Arab Nationalism* (Urbana, 1973), pp. 122–147. Reprinted by permission of the University of Illinois Press.

NOTES

1. A. N. Poliak, 'L'Arabisation de l'Orient sémitique,' *Revue des Etudes Islamiques*, 1938, pp. 37–40; Ignaz Goldziher, *Muhammedanische Studien*, 2 vols. (Halle, 1889–1890), I, 101–176.

2. Bernard Lewis, The Impact of the French Revolution on Turkey', *Journal of World History*, I (July 1953), 107–108.

3. J. Heyworth-Dunne, 'Rifā'ah Badawi Rāfi' aṭ-Ṭahṭāwi: The Egyptian Revivalist,' *Bulletin of the School of Oriental and African Studies* (London University), IX (1939), 961–967; X (1940), 400–401. The long-standing need for a systematic and comprehensive treatment of modern Arab intellectual history has now been satisfied by Albert II. Hourani's masterful *Arabic Thought in the Liberal Age*, 1798–1939 (London: Oxford University Press, 1962; rpt, Oxford Paperback, 1970).

4. Rāfi' al-Ṭahṭāwi, *Kitāb talkhīṣ al-ibrīz ila talkhīṣ bārīz* [*The Book of the Distillation of Pure Gold, Even the Distillation of Paris*] (Cairo, 1323II/1905), pp. 5, 7, 14, 19, 20–21, 55–58, 258, 260, 262.

5. Walther Braune, 'Beiträge zur Geschichte des neuarabischen Schrifttums,' *Mitteilungen des Seminars für Orientalischen Sprachen zu Berlin*, XXXVI (1933), 119–123; Heyworth-Dunne, *BSOS*, X (1939), 399–400, 403, 404. For examples of his patriotic poems, see 'Abd al-Rahmān al-Rāfi'i, *Shu'arā' al-waṭaniyah* (*The Poets of Patriotism*) (Cairo: Maktabah al-Nahḍah al-Miṣrīyah, 1373II/1954), pp. 8–12.

6. Roderic H. Davison, 'Turkish Attitudes Concerning Christian-Muslim Equality in the Nineteenth Century,' *American Historical Review*, LIX (1954), 852. For more recent scholarship, see below, note 17.

7. The same was true of much later writers on nationalism; see Sylvia G. Haim, 'Islam and the Theory of Arab Nationalism,' *Die Welt des Islams*, n.s., IV (1955), 127–140 and above, pp. 77–85.

8. For an example, see Lewis, p. 118, note 35.

9. Ṭahṭāwi, pp. 54–55.

10. For suggestive remarks, see Niyazi Berkes, 'Historical Background of Turkish Secularism,' *Islam and the West*, ed. Richard N. Fiye (The Hague: Mouton and Co., 1957), pp. 48–62, and Davison, pp. 849–853. For more recent works, see below, note 17.

11. Ṭahṭāwi, p. 9. In this paragraph, other references to this work will be given in the text.

12. *Journal Asiatique*, 7th ser., XIX (1882), 169–170; 8th ser., V (1885), 244; IX (1887), 360.

13. Ignaz Goldziher, 'Ueber Muhammedanische Polimik gegen alli al kitab,' *Zeitschrift der Deutschen Morgenländischen Gesellschaft*, XXXII (1878), 343–344; C. Snouck Hurgronje, *Mekka in the Latter Part of the Nineteenth Century*, trans. J. H. Monahan (Leiden: E.J. Brill, and London: Luzac and Co., 1931), p. 173.

14. C. Brockelmann, 'Fāris al-Shidyāḳ Aḥmad b. Yūsuf.' *Encyclopaedia of Islâm*, [1st ed.], II, 67–68; M. Hartmann, 'Djarīda,' *ibid.*, I, 1019.

15. Ahmad Fāris al-Shidyāq (Faris El-Chidiac), *Kitāb al-sāq 'ala al-sāq fi-ma huwa al-faryāq* (*La Vie et les aventures de Fariac*) (Paris, 1855), pp. 597–605, 641–644, 659–660, esp. pp. 603–605, 659 for denial of true civilization to the Europeans.

16. *Ibid.*, appendix, pp. 1–2. The contrast between the new conservatives like Shidyāq and the older ones is well illustrated by the contrast between this appendix and the remarks of Ṭahṭāwi (pp. 68–75) concerning Orientalists.

17. T. Menzel, 'Kemāl Mehmed Nāmik,' *Encyclopaedia of Islam*, [1st ed.], II, 849–850; Davison, 861–864; Niyazi Berkes, 'Ziya Gökalp: His Contribution to Turkish Nationalism,' *Middle East Journal*, VIII (1954), 379–480; Ettore Rossi, 'Dall Impero Ottomano alla Repubblica di Turchia,' *Oriente Moderno*, XXIII (1943), 364–366, 367–368, 369. Since the first publication of this essay, a number of major studies relating to nineteenth-century Turkish Ottoman intellectual history have appeared: Bernard Lewis, *The Emergence of Modern Turkey*, 1st ed. (London: Oxford University Press, 1961; 2nd ed., 1968); Şerif Mardin, *The Genesis of Young Ottoman Thought* (Princeton, N.J.: Princeton University Press, 1962); Roderic H. Davison, *Reform in the Ottoman Empire, 1856–1876* (Princeton, N.J.: Princeton University Press, 1963); Niyazi Berkes, *The Development of Secularism in Turkey* (Montreal: McGill University Press, 1964).

18. Jamāl al-Dīn al-Afghāni, *Réfutation des Matérialistes*, trans. A. M. Goichon (Paris: Paul Geuthner, 1942), pp. 121–130, 133–134, 152–171. Cf. Charles C. Adams, *Islam and Modernism in Egypt* (London: Oxford University Press, 1933), pp. 15–16. Afghāni has subsequently received new attention. Elie Kedourie, *Afghani and 'Abduh: An Essay on Religious Unbelief and Political Activism in Modern Islam* (New York: The Humanities Press, 1966), primarily on the basis of the political activities of Afghāni and 'Abduh, convicts both of unbelief, cynical opportunism, and the deliberate subversion of Islam. Nikki R. Keddie, *An Islamic Response to Imperialism: Political and Religious Writings of Sayyid Jamāl ad-Dīn 'al-Afghāni'* (Berkeley and Los Angeles: University of California Press, 1968), concentrating the analysis on Afghāni's writings, handles the problem with care and subtlety. She concludes that Afghāni was 'some kind of "Islamic deist," a believer in a creator who set the world in motion and made it operate according to natural law' (p. 96), who followed the old philosophical tradition of the Islamic world by which the Islam of the *'ulama'* was regarded as an instrument for managing the masses which, being a lower truth if not false, was both needless for and unworthy of the elite. Albert H. Hourani, reviewing Keddie in *International Journal of Middle East Studies*, I (1970), 90–91, 189, convincingly counters the more recent arguments and reaffirms the view presented in his *Arabic Thought in the Liberal Age*, rpt., pp. 107–129, which had already drawn attention to the complexities of Afghāni's career as political revolutionary, religious reformer, and believing Muslim.

19. See Ibrāhīm al-Yāziji's essay, 'al-'Ulūm 'inda al-'arab [The Sciences among the Arabs],' and his poem 'Tanabbahu wa istafīqu [Awake! Awake!].' in 'Isa Mikhā'il Sāba, *al-Shaykh Ibrāhīm al-Yāziji, 1847–1906*, Nawābigh al-fikr al-'arabi, 14 (Cairo: Dār al-Ma'arif, 1955), pp. 49–50, 71–74.

20. Ignaz Goldziher, *ZDMG*, XXVIII (1874), 167–168.

21. Mohammed Abdou, *Rissalat al Tawhid: Exposé de la religion musulmane*, trans. B. Michel and Moustapha Abdel Razik (Paris: Paul Guethner, 1925), pp. 123–130. In this paragraph, subsequent references to this work are given parenthetically in the text. This work, which was first published in 1897, is a reworking of lectures delivered in Beirut in 1885–1888.

22. Muḥammad Rashīd Riḍa, *Ta'rikh al-Ustādh al-Imām al-Shaykh Muḥammad 'Abduh*, 2nd ed. (Cairo: al-Manār, 134411/1925–26), II, 506.

23. *Ibid.*, pp. 507, 353.

24. *Ibid.*, p. 506.

25. *Ibid.*, pp. 515–516.

26. See 'Abduh's *al-Islām wa al-nasrānīyah ma' al-'ilm wa al-madanīyah* [*Islam and Christianity Compared with Respect to Science and Civilization*], ed. Muḥammad Rashīd Riḍa, 7th ed. (Cairo: al-

Manār, 1367II/1947–48), esp. pp. 62-64 (for Islam as the final and perfect religion), and pp. 81, 119–121, 151–154 (for Arab revival as the foundation of Islamic revival). This book, which was first published in 1902, is a compilation of articles which had previously been published in periodicals.

27. *Al-Manār,* I, no. 40 (I Sha'bān 1316/Dec. 24, 1898, 2nd printing 1327II/1909), 799, 800, 800–801, 885. Rashīd Riḍa had already expounded these ideas at length in a series of articles: *ibid.*, 606–610, 628–633, 649–655, 670–679, 696–704, 722–730.

28. *Al-Manār,* I, 764–771, 788–793 (quotation on 770).

29. Quoted in Sylvia G. Haim, 'Intorno alle origini della teoria del panarabismo,' *Oriente Moderno,* XXXVI (1956), 415, 416. The passages were published in May and July, 1900.

30. 'Abd al-Raḥmān al-Kawākibi, *Umm al-qura* [*The Mother of Villages* (one of the names for Mecca)] (Cairo: al-Maṭba'ah al-Miṣrīyah bi-al-Azhar, 1350II/1931), p. 3. Subsequent references to this book in this and the following paragraphs will be given in the text.

31. For a discussion of al-Kawākibi's Arab caliphate, see Sylvia G. Haim, 'Blunt and al-Kawākibi,' *Oriente Moderno,* XXXV (1955), 132–143.

32. Relatively few Christians actually participated in the Arab political movement of the early twentieth century. They worked instead for Lebanese or Syrian nationalism. Al-Yāziji himself exhibits traces of Syrian nationalism in his essay, 'Syria': Sāba, pp. 93–95.

33. Adib Isḥaq, *Al-Durar* [The Pearls], ed. 'Awni Isḥaq (Beirut): al-Maṭba'ah al-Adabiyah, 1909), p. 105. In this and the succeeding paragraphs, further references to this work will be given in the text.

34. Shidyāq, Appendix, p. 2; see also pp. 703–704.

35. Text of Maṭrān's speech in *al-Mu'tamar al-'arabi al-awwal* [The First Arab Congress] (Cairo: al-Lajnah al-'Ulya li-Ḥizb al-Lāmarkaziyah, 133111/1913), pp. 58, 55, 56.

36. Sylvia G. Haim, 'The Arab Awakening': A Source for the Historian? *Die Welt des Islams,* n.s., II (1953), p. 249, n. 1. For a later (1930) expression of the same idea, see *Oriente Moderno,* X (1930), 57.

37. Isḥaq, pp. 102, 454, 165.

38. Additional evidence of Christian Arab Ottomanism and resentment of the West, including Protestant missionary activity, is contained in A.L. Tibawi, *British Interests in Palestine, 1800–1901: A Study of Religious and Educational Enterprise* (New York: Oxford University Press, 1961), pp. 9–12, 21–28, 89–116, 175–177, and the same author's 'The American Missionaries in Beirut and Butrus al-Bustānī,' *St Anthony's Papers,* no. 16 (Carbondale: Southern Illinois University Press, 1963), pp. 166, 170–173. See also Hourani, rpt., pp. 99–102, on Bustānī's thought.

1919: Labor Upsurge and National Revolution

JOEL BEININ AND ZACHARY LOCKMAN

The Egyptian working class was quiescent during the early years of the First World War, and the nationalist movement that had provided it with much of its leadership had apparently been suppressed. A more direct form of British rule was imposed on Egypt in 1914, and colonial planners looked forward with confidence to the country's smooth postwar integration into the empire. But in Egypt as in so many other countries, from the heartland of Europe to the colonies of Asia, the war and its turbulent aftermath were to mark one of the great turning points of modern history. While the old order crumbled in much of the European metropole, many of the peoples subject to colonial domination rose up in militant and sometimes violent struggles for independence. Egypt in 1919 was part of the great wave of nationalist upsurge that engulfed India, China, Ireland, Turkey, and the Arab East. The political, social, and economic conditions that characterized the Egypt that emerged from the war were the tinder the spark of nationalist agitation ignited, producing the popular uprising against British rule that came to be known as the 1919 revolution.

In the course of that revolution, and during the protracted period of unrest and nationalist struggle that followed it, working-class activism and organization became significant and permanent features of the country's economic and political life. The year 1919 thus witnessed not only the rebirth of the nationalist movement and the involvement of broad sections of the indigenous population in the struggle for Egypt's independence, but also the birth of a labor movement which, despite defeats and long periods of weakness, would make its presence increasingly felt during the interwar years. The emergence of this movement at a time of nationalist upsurge was no coincidence. Given

Table 1 Wholesale Prices of Basic Food Items, Cairo (1 January 1913–31 July 1914 = 100)

	Local wheat	*Sa'idi beans*	*Shami maize*	*Sugar*	*Wheat flour*
Avg. 1915	112	82	77	132	116
Avg. 1916	123	111	91	144	135
Jan. 1917	172	165	102	152	182
July 1917	204	192	167	160	229
Avg. 1917	199	162	138	179	211
Jan. 1918	266	145	138	248	277
July 1918	225	174	170	250	248
Avg. 1918	242	165	164	271	265
Jan. 1919	221	170	166	294	248
March 1919	221	170	166	294	248
Avg. 1919	257	247	189	294	239

SOURCE: *Annuaire Statistique 1923/1924*, pp. 212–15.

Egypt's semicolonial status and the form of capitalist development it had experienced, the national question could not be easily separated from the social and economic grievances felt and expressed by working people. For this reason the 1919 revolution also marked the first full articulation of the special labor–nationalist relationship which had already been foreshadowed by the Nationalist party's prewar role in labor affairs and would significantly shape the Egyptian union movement in the following decades.

THE REVIVAL OF LABOR ACTIVITY

By the end of the First World War, nearly every segment of Egyptian society had reason to resent British rule and be receptive to renewed nationalist agitation. The war had disrupted the country's economy. Although large landowners had generally benefited from high cotton prices, they resented official agricultural policies designed to serve British interests rather than their own. The bulk of the peasantry suffered from the requisitioning of their animals and their grain and, later in the war, from being drafted by the hundreds of thousands for forced labor with the Allied armies in the Middle East and Europe. The temporary weakening of ties with the European economy stimulated significant growth in those industries that produced substitutes for imports unavailable during the war or which catered to the needs of wealthy Egyptians as well as the very large Allied forces stationed in Egypt. Total industrial employment increased substantially, though some industries—cigarettes, for example—were hard hit by the loss of export markets and sources of raw materials, and laid off many workers.[1]

Onions	*Oil*	*Eggs*	*Lentils*	*Weighted avg.*
108	96	103	109	103
94	119	133	125	128
114	136	130	131	150
111	207	136	167	193
149	165	159	139	176
228	171	209	127	208
70	196	192	169	206
101	232	210	158	211
87	296	231	167	215
90	314	215	167	216
129	318	178	230	239

Any gains in employment or wages made by the urban working population, in particular by the growing working class, were soon eroded by two interrelated factors that defined the context for the rising tide of labor discontent in 1917–1918 and set the stage for the social explosion of 1919. The first of these factors was the appearance of severe food shortages, especially in the large cities. Heavy demand by the Allied forces, the cut-off of foreign supplies, and an increase in the area planted in cotton when restrictions were lifted led to serious shortfalls in the food supply by the end of 1917. This gave rise to and was compounded by the second factor, a high rate of inflation. The prices of many food items had been rising slowly but steadily through 1915 and 1916, after which they began to skyrocket, as Table 1 shows. Retail prices rose even faster than wholesale prices, while government measures to set maximum prices for basic commodities and to import wheat from Australia, to be distributed below cost as bread, were ineffective. The combined impact of shortages and inflation was devastating to the standard of living of wage workers and salaried employees, many of whom were driven to the very edge of subsistence. The British authorities calculated for example that the monthly expenses for food of a typical Cairo family 'of the poorest class' rose from 109 piastres a month in February 1914 to 305 piastres in 1919.[2] The rapid decline in the real wages of many Egyptian workers, which produced widespread suffering, largely accounts for the revival of labor activism during the last year of the war.

Under conditions of martial law, Egyptian workers had been able to voice their grievances only by means of petitions to the authorities. Their complaints were similar to those heard before the war: low wages, long hours of work, abusive treatment, and unjust dismissals. The humble, indeed, self-effacing and obsequious tone of some of these petitions, however, reflected the debilitating effects of wartime repression.[3] But as the battle front receded eastward, away from Egypt's borders, and the regime relaxed its grip somewhat, workers began to resume organized activity and confront their employers more forcefully. The threat of repression seemed less serious, while the accelerating inflationary spiral made action imperative.

The first group of workers to take the initiative were the original pioneers of the labor movement, the cigarette workers. Their already precarious situation before 1914 had been made even more difficult by wartime dislocation because wages were cut and unemployment rose. As early as August 1917 a strike broke out at the Coutarelli factory in Alexandria, and the following February a series of larger strikes began in both Alexandria and Cairo. The cigarette workers in Alexandria were able to win a modest wage increase because of their high level of organization and discipline, and the sympathy of the press, whereas the strikers in Cairo were less united and faced vigorous police repression. T.R. Russell, then assistant commandant of the Cairo police, reported in a letter to a friend:

> I've been having a busy four days with some cigarette-rollers on strike. We've got very strict laws of course on illegal assemblies and this morning about five hundred of the strikers refused to accept the very good terms the Governor [of Cairo] had got for them out of the Company. They came here *en masse* and I told them off, but they then announced their intention of marching on the Abdin Palace. I let them start and then sent word after them that I would see them again. They all came back to Headquarters and when I got them all in the yard I locked the gate and put a strong guard over them, searched and listed the lot of them, read them the riot act and then let them go. I hear they have accepted the terms since.[4]

In fact, the Cairo strike was finally broken with the help of the police only after violent clashes and numerous arrests.

The fact that it was the cigarette rollers who were the first to resume open and militant activity after three years of silence is not surprising. These workers had remained part of the elite of the working class—highly paid, relatively well-educated, and with a high proportion of foreigners among them. Their long history of struggle and organization made it possible for them to move quickly from the limited and largely unsuccessful stoppages of 1917 to the more general and fruitful strikes of 1918. They were able with little difficulty to revive the unions they had first established more than a decade earlier. Indeed, this step was a vital necessity for them because they were threatened not only by conjunctural unemployment and declining real wages, but also by the looming threat of mechanization. Within a few months other groups of workers cautiously began to become more active. Among these were the Cairo tramwaymen, who by December 1918 had begun to raise many of the same demands for which they had fought in 1908–1911. At this point they still lacked any form of union organization, and limited themselves to petitioning management because a strike would certainly have led to an immediate confrontation with the authorities which the workers were in no position to win. By the beginning of 1919, however, it was apparent that the union movement had begun to revive, and signs of life and movement were visible among workers in many trades.

One of these signs was the reappearance of the Manual Trades Workers' Union (MTWU) in Alexandria, henceforth its main base of support. This organization was revived by unionists who had been active in the local branch before the war and with the cooperation of the Nationalist party, which was also slowly coming back to life. As before, the MTWU sought to unite all Egyptian workers and artisans, regardless of trade or relationship to ownership of the means of production, into one citywide organization. This was in contrast to the industrial and craft unions which were at this time being re-established or being newly formed by Egyptian and foreign workers. The MTWU was well aware of this contrast and insisted that its model was the most appropriate one for the labor movement. A statement it issued several days after its formal re-establishment at the beginning of March 1919 argued:

> The Union in Alexandria calls on all workers outside its ranks to join, because this would bring unity and strengthen the Union in its course. We warn the workers against those who are infiltrating among them in order to agitate for the creation of a new union, which would destroy their unity. There is no need for the existence of several unions in a single city like Alexandria.[5]

This warning certainly reflected the desire of the MTWU and its Nationalist party patrons to monopolize the organization of the Egyptian working class of Alexandria, though the warning also reflected a form of consciousness still rooted in the social milieu of petty-commodity production and in the low level of differentiation between wage workers on the one hand and artisans, small proprietors and their employees on the other hand. This perspective blurred real and potential differences among these groups by subsuming all of them in the ideological category of 'workers in the manual trades.' Although the Nationalist party and the labor organizations under its influence were to remain loyal to this perspective for some years, it became increasingly less appropriate to the realities of the postwar working-class and labor movement. Yet in 1919 the MTWU in Alexandria was quite successful in its efforts to organize among railway workers—its traditional base of support among workers in modern industry. The MTWU was the first organization to reappear on the local labor scene; it had an established labor record and solid political credentials; and its leadership was in the course of that eventful year assumed by Dr Mahjub Thabit, a veteran of the prewar labor-nationalist upsurge and a popular figure among the workers.

EGYPTIAN WORKERS AND EGYPTIAN NATIONALISM

The revival of the labor movement at the end of 1918, and especially during the first two months of 1919, must be seen in the context of political developments. The war had come to an end in November 1918, and the question of Egypt's future status immediately came to the fore. A group of nationalist politicians and notables, most of them large landowners, formed a delegation (*wafd*) under the leadership of Sa'd Zaghlul Pasha which demanded the right to put forward Egypt's claim to full independence at the Peace Conference. The British authorities, however, refused to recognize the Wafd or permit it to travel to Europe to press its case. The Wafd responded by launching a campaign to gather the signatures of former elected officials, notables, and other members of the upper and middle classes deputizing it to act as the sole legitimate representative of the nation in striving peacefully for complete independence. Two representatives of the Nationalist party—chosen not by the party but by Zaghlul, who was emerging as the forceful and popular leader of the new nationalist movement—were added to the Wafd, together with representatives of the Coptic community. The growing popularity of the Wafd and the spreading agitation associated with it led to the resignation of the Egyptian government, which unlike the Wafd was not opposed in principle to protectorate status, and had thereby lost its credibility as spokesman for the nation. In an effort to resolve the ensuing political crisis and squelch the nationalist upsurge, the British arrested Zaghlul and three of his colleagues on March 8, 1919, and deported them to Malta.[6]

There is no evidence of any direct connection between the Wafd's political agitation at the beginning of 1919 and the rising tide of labor unrest. The members of the Wafd leadership had little interest in the problems of the urban working class, or indeed in social issues in general. Rather they were seeking, at least initially, to mobilize upper- and middle-class opinion for a peaceful campaign for Egyptian independence—a struggle to compel the British to transfer power to the indigenous elite. The Wafd's activists and organizers were, to be sure, drawn from the same *effendiyya* strata which had been attracted to the Nationalist party before the war. That party, however, though much weakened by wartime repression, held to its uncompromising demand for immediate and unconditional independence, and had shown an interest in social problems. The Wafd by contrast was initially quite uninterested in, or at best conservative on, social issues. Its leaders were committed to legal methods of struggle, and before March 1919 had no expectation of, and no desire to encourage, mass popular agitation, much less a revolution.

If the leadership of the postwar Egyptian nationalist movement was generally upper-class and conservative—even by comparison with other contemporary nationalist movements, for example the Indian National

Congress or the Kuomintang—this is not to say that its demands did not represent the interests of other classes as well, at least up to a point. The vast majority of the country's population responded to the Wafd's appeal in 1919 for a variety of reasons. The struggle against the foreign occupier and the goal of that struggle (complete independence) meant different things to different segments of Egyptian society.

The sources of urban working-class support for the national cause in 1919 were essentially those that underlay the labor–Nationalist party link in 1908–1911. For most Egyptian workers, class divisions coincided with ethnic or national divisions in the workplace. The poor conditions of labor and the abusive treatment at the hands of foreign employers and foremen which they experienced were quite naturally linked to foreign domination of the economy and to British rule. The occupation regime protected the power and privileges of the foreigners who controlled their working life and whose arbitrary and high-handed behavior was so bitterly resented. When workers sought to organize and improve their lot, the role of the British-controlled police in strikebreaking and repression was certainly evident enough. It was therefore inevitable that the sense of oppression felt by workers subject to deteriorating working and living conditions at the hands of foreign employers or a foreign-controlled government would converge with these same workers' sense of humiliation as Egyptians subject to foreign rule in their own land. There were thus concrete reasons for Egyptian workers to wholeheartedly support a nationalist movement aimed at ending British rule (itself a desirable goal) but which might, by restoring Egypt's sovereignty, also create more favorable conditions in which to seek a better life for themselves. Segments of the Egyptian bourgeoisie had their own reasons and projected advantage for wanting to end foreign domination of the country's economy, so that the nationalism of the upper and middle classes possessed an economic component with which Egyptian workers could identify. Nearly all classes shared, up to a point, a common set of enemies and goals, such that the young working class supported and participated in the national cause and accepted its bourgeois leadership.

Labor activity was already on the rise before March 1919, stimulated by inflation, rising unemployment resulting from the postwar contraction of industry, and accumulated wartime grievances. But under the martial law regime it remained quite difficult for workers to organize and especially to strike with much hope of success, as the experience of the Cairo cigarette rollers had shown. The popular nationalist revolution that was to erupt in March–April 1919 shook the occupation regime to its foundations and created political conditions in which workers, whose numbers had increased during the war, could quickly organize themselves and launch strikes for economic demands which blended completely into the national struggle. The popular uprising, spontaneous and massive, incorporated and sustained this new social movement, and made possible its rapid growth and quick victories. In this period of political and social turbulence the tramway and railway workers were once again in the vanguard of the labor movement. An examination of their involvement in the first phase of the 1919 revolution, in a sense the formative experience of the Egyptian workers' movement, will illustrate that interaction of class and national dimensions so crucial in much of subsequent Egyptian labor history.

THE CAIRO TRAMWAY WORKERS IN THE REVOLUTION

The workforce that operated the tramway system of Egypt's capital consisted of just over 2,000 workers in 1918, a decline of about 10 per cent from the prewar level. In that same period, however, ridership had gone up by over 30 per cent. Overall fewer workers were conveying many more passengers in more crowded cars running on a reduced schedule, all of which pointed to a speed-up by management and a deterioration in working conditions.[7] The demands the workers formulated and presented to the company at the end of 1918 included an eight-hour workday, a substantial wage increase (drivers and conductors earned ten to fifteen piastres for a ten to twelve-hour day, a rate essentially unchanged since 1908), paid days of rest, better treatment by supervisors, a more rational and equitable system of disciplinary penalties, severance pay based on length of service, and free uniforms.[8] These demands were similar to those raised before the war, and indicated the absence of any improvement in relations between workers and supervisors, but they also reflected the impact of the war-related drop in real wages and intensified exploitation on the job. Cairo Tramway Company (CTC) failed to accede to the demands, and in the first months of 1919 the tram workers began to organize. When the revolution broke out, they were ready to seize the opportunity.

Zaghlul and his three colleagues were arrested on March 8. The following day saw peaceful protest demonstrations by students, and by the 10th, all of the capital's students, including those of al-Azhar, the great mosque and center of Islamic learning, were on strike. On that day a large demonstration clashed with security forces, causing the first casualties of the revolution. The following days and weeks witnessed a veritable explosion of popular protest with almost daily demonstrations in the streets of Egypt's cities and bloody clashes with British military forces. This was accompanied throughout the country by attacks on British installations and personnel, the cutting of railway lines, and other forms of popular revolutionary violence.

One of those forms was the destruction of tram cars—from this time forward a standard feature of outbreaks of popular protest. Overturning and wrecking tram cars was an effective means of paralysing mass transit in the capital as well as a way of venting popular anger at a very visible symbol of foreign economic power. This anger may also have been stimulated by the fact that with even second-class fares at five milliemes (one-half piastre), a tram ride was still too expensive for many poor Egyptians. By March 11, the Cairo tram system was no longer functioning, and the public at first supposed that the company had suspended operations to protect its vulnerable property from the demonstrators. It soon became clear, however, that though the demonstrations and attacks may have disrupted service, the tramways of Cairo had stopped running altogether because the tram workers had gone out on strike. The taxi drivers also stopped work, and within a few days other forms of public transport such as hackney cabs and mule-drawn omnibuses had virtually ceased to circulate.[9]

The British authorities were certainly soon aware of the tramway workers' strike, because on March 12 the High Commissioner received a telegram from one Yusuf Khalil announcing the strike and demanding on behalf of the tramwaymen that the British authorities intervene with the CTC. The Residency, however, was not interested in playing the role of mediator. Indeed, one official commented that the workers were adequately paid and worked reasonable hours, and another that 'as things stand—a foreign company with no labour clauses in their contract [that is, the concession agreement]—Eg[yptian] Govt. could only really interfere if the Co. appealed for assistance in settlement of difficulties with their employees'.[10]

The legal niceties of the situation were quite beside the point, however. In reality the British authorities were in no position to intervene as decisively as they had in 1908 and 1911. The revolutionary situation that prevailed in March–April 1919 made it very difficult for them to attempt to break the strike. Army and police forces in the capital and elsewhere in Egypt were stretched thin in trying to contain the more immediate and dangerous threats to British authority and the established order. At the same time, the tram workers' strike enjoyed widespread public support. The indigenous population of Cairo perceived the strike as an important part of the national struggle and displayed sympathy and support for the workers as fellow Egyptians oppressed by foreign bosses. Even when the tram company was able to run a few cars under heavy British guard, a general boycott left them empty. As the weeks passed, other means were employed to keep the transport system shut down. The London press reported early in April that non-striking tramway and railway personnel and shopkeepers had been attacked with sulfuric acid by unknown assailants, presumably striking workers or members of one of the secret nationalist organizations. The use or threat of violence must certainly have intimidated the company and those loyal to it, and a martial law decree promulgated on April 16 made such acts punishable by death.[11]

The Wafd opposed these attacks and, in the midst of a popular revolution, publicly denounced all forms of violence. Although some of its leaders had secret links with the underground terrorist organizations, most of the prominent Wafdists were genuinely fearful of popular violence and worried that, once unleashed, the masses might threaten property and social order. In a statement issued on March 24, the Wafd leadership in Egypt warned the people that

> the Military Authorities have issued a warning that they will employ the most harsh military means as punishment in dealing with attacks on means of transport and public property. It is obvious to everyone that attacks on persons or on property are forbidden by divine law and by positive law, and that sabotage of the means of transport clearly harms the people of our country ... Therefore the undersigned see it as their sacred national duty to refrain from any attack and ask that no one violate the law, so as not to obstruct the path of all those who serve the nation by legal means.

This appeal was in response to official proclamations imposing the death penalty on anyone found guilty by a British military court of interfering in any way with the normal operation of the railway, telegraph, or telephone systems. Precisely this kind of sabotage by peasants was widespread in the countryside. Although the Wafd's appeal was signed by a host of pashas as well as by Muslim and Christian religious leaders, it did little to stem the tide of popular violence. That would require severe measures of repression, including the burning and aerial bombardment of villages, and eventually political concessions by the British.[12]

The Cairo tram strike continued through March and into April while the workers and the CTC negotiated but failed to reach a settlement. Under pressure from a British Residency anxious to end the dispute and return the capital to normalcy, the company did make some concessions. On March 28, for example, management announced the creation of an investigations panel to examine charges brought against workers by their supervisors. But the workers believed that such a body would be a creature of management unless worker representatives participated on an equal basis, and the company's offers were rejected. It was only in mid-April, after the new Prime Minister Husayn Rushdi Pasha took an active role in the talks, that an agreement was reached on all but one of the issues in dispute. The main features of the settlement were a workday of eight-and-a-quarter hours, a general and permanent raise of one piastre a day as well as the incorporation of the two piastre wartime cost of living allowance into the regular wage, half-pay for sick workers, one paid day of rest every twelve days, and the establishment of an investigations panel to resolve differences between workers and inspectors over penalties. The one major issue left unresolved was that of severance pay. The workers still insisted on compensation of at least one month's pay per year of service as a deterrent to arbitrary or mass firings and as a cushion against the vicissitudes of unemployment. The two sides agreed to defer the issue while the CTC director in Cairo consulted with the head office in Brussels, but the prime minister promised that the question would be resolved to the workers' satisfaction.[13]

The settlement of the Cairo tramway strike was part of a general subsidence of the revolutionary upsurge in late April. Rushdi Pasha, whose resignation on March 1 had precipitated the political crisis that had led to the arrest of Zaghlul, had resumed the post of prime minister on April 9 after the British agreed to release the Wafd leaders and allow them to travel to Europe. This was seen as a great defeat for the occupation regime and a victory for the Wafd. The Residency made these political concessions in order to restore calm and public order, and the settlement of the tram strike should be seen as a step in the same direction. The Rushdi government was, however, brought down twelve days later by a political strike of government employees which marked the culmination of the much broader strike wave in which the tramwaymen had participated. The end of the government employees' strike on April 23 was followed by the return to work of many other groups of strikers, including the tram workers, and the wave of popular protest and violence finally petered out. The very end of April thus witnessed the end of the first, militant phase of the 1919 revolution, and in the months that followed the focus of the struggle for independence shifted from the streets and countryside of Egypt to the ministries and conference rooms of Europe.

The tram workers owed the major gains they won in April 1919 to their own militancy and solidarity, but more to the extraordinary political conditions of that turbulent spring. The state had found itself temporarily unable to intervene forcefully and break the strike, the workers had enjoyed broad public support, and the Egyptian government, backed by the British authorities, had for political reasons been willing to pressure the CTC to make concessions. Motivated by a desperate economic situation and by their solidarity with the national cause, the tramwaymen were able to take advantage of the unique situation that prevailed in March–April 1919 to win many of their demands. This unprecedented victory was achieved in the absence of a union, but there must have been informal structures, such as mass meetings, through which the workers chose delegates to negotiate with management and heard their reports. Still, the gains achieved in April were not entirely secure. Without a union recognized by the company and the government as the workers' representative and empowered to monitor implementation of the agreement, it was likely that in more favorable circumstances the CTC would regain the upper hand. The high rate of inflation persisted, and a number of issues were still not definitively or satisfactorily resolved. It was therefore not surprising that labor relations at the Cairo Tramway Company remained unsettled in the following months, and 1919 would see still further instances of industrial conflict in this key enterprise.

RAILWAY WORKERS IN THE REVOLUTION

Unrest had been growing among the railway workers too in the early months of 1919. This was especially true at the ʿAnabir in Bulaq, where some 4,000 workers were now employed, and at the Jabal al-Zaytun repair shops at al-Qabbari in Alexandria. The ʿAnabir had of course been the scene of industrial conflict before the war, and both workshops were strongholds of nationalist sentiment. Indeed, the MTWU was busily recruiting among the Jabal al-Zaytun workers before March 1919. In February the Jabal al-Zaytun workers, represented by a MTWU lawyer named Husayn al-ʿArarji, sent a petition to Brigadier General Macauley, director of railway traffic, demanding a doubling of wages, an end to arbitrary dismissals and fines, leaves of absence for the *hajj*, and time off for Friday prayer. As with the tramwaymen and many other Egyptian workers, low wages and maltreatment by foremen were central issues.

Macauley himself considered the pay issue as most important, and though he recognized that some of the workers had not had a raise in a long time, a doubling of wages was simply out of the question. In any event, he saw the pay demand as a symptom of a peculiarly 'Oriental' attitude toward work and wages.

> The native way of looking at such matters differs entirely from the European; the native considers that he is entitled to pay in proportion to his expenses, whatever these latter may happen to be; and the European expects to give and receive pay according to his skill and efficiency. These two views can never be reconciled.[14]

Macauley's analysis reflected a belief widespread among British colonial officials and others that non-Western peoples were incapable of rational thought, the opposite of Europeans in all respects, and not only backward but incomprehensible.[15] Yet workers' insistence that they are entitled to a living wage is not a particularly 'Oriental' phenomenon, and it is clear that the railway workers who petitioned Macauley really were suffering from a sharp decline in real wages. In this same period output per worker was reported to have dropped sharply because of widespread malnourishment in the workforce.[16] In truth, the workers' demands about wages and other issues must be understood as rational responses to concrete circumstances, and not as the product of some inherent defect of the 'native mind.'

In any event Egyptian State Railways, Telegraphs, and Telephones (ESR) management regarded the discontent as potentially dangerous and responded by transferring seven workers allegedly active in the agitation. Workers loyal to management had already claimed in a counterpetition that the troublemakers were a small group of 'notorious men known for their revolutionary ideas arising from reading newspapers & their inclination to Bolshevist principles.' Despite the failure of MTWU lawyer al-'Ararji to get the seven reinstated, the organization continued to recruit at Jabal al-Zaytun and elsewhere in Alexandria.[17]

The demands raised by the 'Anabir workers in Cairo in these months also focused on higher pay, but included shorter hours and other issues as well. One grievance unique to the 'Anabir was the stationing of a contingent of British soldiers in the workshops, ostensibly to acquire industrial skills. The workers feared that management was preparing to replace them with soldiers. On March 15, as the revolution erupted in full force, the 'Anabir workers went on strike, and this brought most maintenance and repair work on the ESR's locomotives to a halt. The workers also destroyed switches and cut the railway lines near Imbaba, which prevented trains from leaving for Upper Egypt. These acts of sabotage, coming just two days after the imposition of the death penalty for such offenses, indicate that alongside their grievances in the workplace the 'Anabir workers were motivated by support for the revolution and saw their strike as an integral part of the struggle for independence. In fact, throughout the country peasants were taking identical steps to sabotage rail transport as well as the communications system.

The British authorities responded by dispatching army units to occupy the 'Anabir and the surrounding neighborhood in force, and they also sought to seal the Bulaq district off in order to prevent contact between the large, staunchly nationalist populace of one of the country's oldest and most important industrial zones and the mass demonstrations and clashes taking place elsewhere in the city. Prevented from participating *en masse* in the huge demonstration at al-Azhar on March 17, the railway workers planned their own march for the following day in order to break the blockade of their neighborhood. Joined by the striking workers of the Government Press and many residents of Bulaq, they marched, carrying banners, toward the center of the city. Near the Abu al-'Ala bridge British troops opened fire on the crowd and dispersed it, killing and wounding many.[18]

The railway workshop workers (Jabal al-Zaytun had been struck on March 16) were joined by many traffic department workers and remained on strike well into April. As with the tramwaymen, intimidation was used to prevent employees loyal to management from returning to their jobs. Twenty-six ESR employees were said to have been the victims of acid attacks by mid-April, but there can be no question that the great majority of workers supported the strike and the national struggle to which it contributed.[19] With the aid of soldiers and loyal staff, the British were ultimately able to restore railway operations, though on a much-reduced scale, and it was only after the release of Zaghlul and his colleagues that the railway workers slowly returned to work. In a sense their strike petered out rather than ended, and this reflected the general downturn in mass mobilization, though there was no immediate resumption of normal service. Slowdowns and brief stoppages persisted, and the ESR clerical staff struck in mid-month as part of the general strike of government employees. Citing their 'bad records,' management did not permit some 155 strikers to return to their jobs, and unrest continued at Bulaq and elsewhere into May.[20]

The railway workers had won at least some of their demands, the most important of which was a substantial increase in wages, but these gains were achieved through the decrees of ESR officials rather than through any form of collective bargaining, another indication of the difficulty which even the militant 'Anabir workers were to experience in creating their own stable and independent organizations. Apart from the MTWU in Alexandria, there is no evidence that the railway workers established or participated in any union in the course of March–April 1919, though they did have links with the nationalist movement led by the Wafd—links which were to form the basis for a long-lasting and important relationship.

PATTERNS OF PARTICIPATION AND LEADERSHIP

Tramway and railway workshop workers were not the only ones to strike during the spring of 1919. The workers at the ESR printing press, the Government Press, the Arsenal and the government workshops, the Alexandria tramways, the Hilwan electric railways, the Cairo electric company, postal, port, lighthouse and customs employees, taxi and carriage drivers—these and others also went on strike within days of the outbreak of the revolution. Peasants working in industry were also involved. On the night of March 15/16, for example, a large band of 'pillagers' (probably local peasants) attacked the railroad station near the Hawamdiyya sugar refinery on the western bank of the Nile just south of Cairo. Many of the refinery's 1,800 workers (recruited from local villages) left to join the rioters who threatened to attack the refinery itself. Local police and notables reinforced by Australian troops prevented this, but the refinery was idle through April because most of its workers were absent.[21] Many workers who did not actually strike in this period seized the opportunity to begin organizing themselves, present their demands to their employers, and prepare for future action. These demands almost always included higher wages to offset inflation, the eight-hour day, improvements in oppressive working conditions (especially abuse by foreign supervisors), and compensation for illness and dismissal. Few workers actually realized any of these demands in March and April 1919, and none achieved nearly as much as the tramwaymen or even the railway workers. Nonetheless, these months saw a wave of strikes and industrial unrest involving many thousands of Egyptian workers that was unprecedented in Egyptian history.

The great majority of the strikers were employed either by the government or by the foreign-owned public utilities, the most heavily Egyptian sectors of the labor force and ones that included the greatest concentrations of workers. Their combined ethnic identity and concentrated force were stimuli to these workers' collective experience and action in both class and nationalist dimensions. For them as for a general population supportive of the national cause, strikes that raised economic demands were regarded as an integral part of the broader struggle of the Egyptian people for independence and dignity. The workers were Egyptians, their oppressive bosses were foreigners, and the work stoppages contributed materially to the campaign against the occupational regime. This explains the public support for the strikers manifested in the boycott of the Cairo tramways, and also explains both why the Wafd's leaders acclaimed the strikers as patriots and the secret nationalist groups were ready to use violence against strikebreakers.

The massive strike wave was sparked off by, and can be understood only in the context of, the even more massive explosion of popular protest against British rule. The contribution of the working class in the 1919 revolution was none the less significant in its own right, despite the limited size and social weight of this social group. It should not be overestimated—labor activism never reached the point of a coordinated nationwide general strike, for instance—but neither should it be underestimated. The disruption caused by the strikes and the participation of workers in demonstrations certainly gave added force to the national struggle and increased the pressure on the occupation regime. Without the paralysis of key government institutions and of the country's transportation systems, largely the result of strikes, the events of 1919 would have had far less impact and been much easier for the British to contain.

In this upsurge of mass mobilization, wage workers in large enterprises were only one of several groups to stop work, motivated at least partly by solidarity with the national cause. Students, lawyers, shopkeepers, and even the normally docile government employees went on strike in March–April, and members of nearly every class marched in demonstrations demanding the release of Zaghlul Pasha and complete independence. This wave of popular action was accompanied by a wave of organization in which many sectors of the population participated. Students, lawyers, teachers, *'ulama*, and others created new organizations or mobilized existing ones in support of the national struggle. The term *niqaba*, generally used by this time for labor unions, was also widely used by nonworkers to denote their own organizations; even large landowners referred to their organization, established in 1921, as a *niqaba*. This flexible usage reflected the perception of workers as just another occupationally differentiated section of the Egyptian nation rather than as a distinct class. The labor strikes and unionization were thus only part of a nationwide upsurge of militancy and association in which many different groups organized themselves by trade. In this process the sectional interests of the workers were seen as identical to the national interest, whereas the Wafd, until this time a small group of wealthy notables making extravagant claims to speak for Egypt, really did come to be perceived as the embodiment of the national cause.

In these same months the first organizational links were forged between workers and nationalist activists. Where workers had already established ties with the Nationalist party or the MTWU before the war, persons associated with that party emerged as leaders of or spokesmen for the new unions or pre-union formations. This was the case in Alexandria where Dr Mahjub Thabit came to lead the MTWU, whose base was among the railway workers. Ahmed Bey Lutfi, who had served as a leader of the Nationalist party, the MTWU, and the Cairo tramway workers before the war, now re-emerged as counsellor to the Heliopolis tram workers. Muhammad Kamil Husayn and Muhammad Zaki ʻAli, both lawyers linked to the Nationalist party, led the Cairo tramwaymen at different times. The ease with which these men assumed leading roles in labor affairs was the result of the Nationalist party's long history of involvement in this sphere and the contacts they had established before the war. Another contributing factor was the relative absence of rivalry between the Nationalist party and the Wafd in the first months of the revolution. In March and April all factions in the national movement were united in rejecting protectorate status or anything less than complete independence, and it was not felt to be important that some of the activists who were organizing workers in the national cause were linked to the Nationalist party rather than to the newer and broader Wafd. Furthermore, the Wafd had neither the organizational infrastructure nor sufficient cadre of its own to involve itself directly in labor affairs as a distinct political tendency. The Wafd only gradually transformed itself into an organized movement complete with a central staff, effective methods of developing and maintaining ties with its various constituencies and a nationwide network of local committees. In later years, having been eclipsed and reduced to a politically marginal position by the vast popularity of Zaghlul and his movement, the Nationalist party would become the Wafd's bitter rival. But in 1919 the two were part of the same revolutionary tide, and the Wafd functioned as more of a national front than a party.

Most workers had, however, no prewar connection with a middleclass nationalist leader that could serve as the basis for a new relationship, and it was in the heat of the revolutionary upsurge itself that these links were forged. A group of militant workers might approach a lawyer or notable known for his nationalist activism, and possibly also his interest in labor affairs, or alternatively, such a figure might seek out and cultivate contacts among a particular group of workers. In either case he would then lend his skills, connections, and prestige to the workers and their emerging union as part of his nationalist activism.

The framework in which these first links were often forged, where workers and the lawyers who would help them create and lead their unions made initial contact, was the mass meeting or rally frequently held in one of the larger mosques. Before the Wafd formalized its organization and developed institutionalized links with the masses, especially during the stormy first weeks of the revolution, the mass meeting was a key instrument of communication and mobilization for the urban population. Thousands or even tens of thousands of people, including workers, artisans, shopkeepers, students, and professionals, would gather almost daily to hear speeches and reports from the Wafd's leaders, exchange information, and coordinate the national struggle. On special occasions, such as the April 16 rally in support of the striking government employees, a crowd of 80,000 could jam the precincts of the al-Azhar mosque complex and the surrounding streets.[22] From these meetings demonstrations would depart to wend their way through the city's streets, to be dispersed eventually by British gunfire. The great mosques had for centuries been vital centers of civil society, and as enclosed sanctuaries were relatively safe from the incursions of British forces. Usually situated in the older, less Europeanized sections of the cities, the mosques served as great social and cultural symbols of Egypt's distinct identity and nationhood, and together with the palatial homes of the members of the Wafd were the nerve centers of the revolutionary movement.

This is not to suggest that the primary motivation of those who gathered at al-Azhar was some antiforeign or anti-Christian fervor supposedly inherent in Islam. Both the crowds and the orators at al-Azhar and elsewhere included Copts as well as Muslims, and the whole tone of the 1919 revolution was resolutely secular. The Wafd consistently propounded a purely ethnic Egyptian identity, and denounced all forms of sectarianism as harmful to the cause of national independence. Religion was regarded as a private matter to be entirely separated from public affairs and the political struggle, though, of course, not all Egyptians may have drawn these distinctions as finely as the bourgeois and rather Europeanized nationalist leaders. Some Muslims may indeed have seen the struggle for Egypt's independence as a campaign for the defense of Islam, and the removal of oppressive Christian rule over a Muslim land, but for the great majority the central issue was self-rule for an Egypt in which all Egyptians regardless of their faith could live together in peace and share in a common culture and destiny. It is a fundamental misreading of modern Egyptian history to attribute mass support for the national movement of 1919 to an Islamic xenophobia allegedly ingrained in the belief system of Egypt's Muslim majority. The absence of any evidence of sectarian strife in

1919 disproves this interpretation, as do the instances of class conflict among Muslims—attacks by Muslim peasants on the estates of Muslim large landowners, for example—that occurred in March–April 1919 and terrified the upper class. In Egypt's large industrial and transport enterprises, where Muslims and Copts worked side by side and went on strike with apparently total unanimity, religious differences played no role in this period.

Once initial contact had been made between workers and their bourgeois patrons, more tangible links quickly developed. There is some evidence, based on British intelligence reports, that some nationalist activists were distributing, or promising to distribute, money to striking workers from funds raised by the Wafd's extensive canvassing campaign among the country's prosperous strata. On April 26, for example, a tailor named Ahmad Bahnasi, claiming to be on the run from the British because he had incited the people of his home village to destroy the railway line, spoke to a crowd at the ibn Tulun mosque in Cairo. He said that the nationalist lawyer Muhammad Kamil Husayn 'had asked him to ask the strikers to go and take strike money from him' and gave out slips of paper with Husayn's name and address. A British intelligence report of early May stated that the railway workers at the Anabir, at Zagazig and at the Tanta locomotive works were disgusted with strikes because they had received many promises from Wafdist agitators but no strike pay. To survive during the strikes of March–April the railwaymen had had to sell their wives' jewelry, gold ornaments given as wedding presents which were poor people's only store of wealth, and even their families' clothing in order to buy bread. They were not about to strike again unless they received some tangible support beforehand.[23]

It is likely that there is more involved here than an effort by British intelligence to attribute the militancy of the workers to bribery by outside agitators. It is quite plausible that some money was paid out or at least promised to workers because it was certainly in the interests of the nationalist leadership to provide workers with the means to endure lengthy strikes or even to initiate strikes in sectors that the leadership wished to have paralysed for political reasons. With no strike fund or savings, the workers themselves might have felt that the sacrifices they were making for the national cause entitled them to some material support from wealthier compatriots, though this is not to say that the workers who participated in the events of March–April 1919 did so because they were 'bought' by the Wafd. Any material or moral support extended to the workers by the Wafd came only after the workers had already gone on strike, motivated by both economic and political grievances. In any event the amounts of money involved were probably not large and can have been small recompense for the sacrifices of the strikers, very few of whom received any money at all.

After the first phase of the revolution had come to an end and the strike wave had subsided, a period characterized by consolidation and organization rather than conflict ensued. In May and June 1919, many groups of workers formally established unions, often with the support or under the leadership of nationalist notables. The Cairo tramway workers, for example, formed their union on June 15, some two months after their strike had been settled. Many of these new organizations were industrial unions made up of all those employed for wages at a particular large enterprise. But there was also a wave of unionization among craft workers as well as employees in retail shops, restaurants, cafés, and other small establishments. The Wafd leadership in Egypt—Sa'd Zaghlul and other top leaders were still in Europe at the time—was very supportive of this development, and regarded the new unions of Egyptian workers as an important asset of the national cause. In the fall of 1919 'Abd al-Rahman Fahmi described the emergence of a labor movement in Egypt in a secret report sent to Zaghlul:

> I will explain to you the results of the efforts made to spread unions (*ta'mim al-niqabat*) throughout the length and breadth of the land. These efforts have, praise be to God, borne fruit: a union has been formed for every craft (*hirfa*), and there remains in Egypt no craft or trade (*san'a*) without a union. It is true that the government has not recognized these unions up to now, and it is not anticipated that it will recognize them in the present circumstances. But they are in any case very useful to the nationalist movement and a powerful weapon which should not be underestimated. In time of calamity they will respond to the call of patriotism as quickly as possible.[24]

In many of these new unions, bourgeois lawyers or notables played leading roles and constituted the link between the labor movement and the nationalist movement. The relationship between unionized workers and these middle- or upper-class personalities could take various forms. Where there was a membership with extensive experience of unionism, and was militant, independent, or relatively well educated, the outsider holding a high union post—generally that of honorary president, president, counsellor (*mustashar*) or treasurer—might be merely a respected figurehead or some combination of advisor, patron, negotiator, and link to the national movement. In these cases it was the members of the executive board and the union's officers, elected at regular general meetings of all paid-up members, who actually ran the organization on a day-to-day basis, though outsiders may have had significant influence on major policy decisions. In other unions, however, the lawyer or notable made the decisions himself and ran the union, by acting through a coterie of worker activists loyal to him. This was especially true where a small or weak union depended on the leader and his party connections for organizational continuity, money, and protection from harassment by employers or the police. Even in such cases, however, the potential for conflict existed between the workers and their counsellors, which indicated that union members were not passive when they felt their interests were being neglected or harmed.

The reasons that induced many Egyptian workers to seek or accept leadership from members of the middle and upper classes were in general still at work in 1919 and later years. For many unions, there were concrete practical benefits to be derived from a relationship with a politically influential or legally talented patron, though such relationships reflected, and in later years would tend to perpetuate, the relative weakness and dependent status of the young working-class and labor movement. The country's subjection to foreign rule was also a crucial factor in subordinating the union movement to the bourgeois-led national movement. The key issue of Egyptian political life from 1919 until 1956 was British domination and the struggle for complete independence, and as a result the central dynamic governing labor's political role was for much of this period its relation to the national movement. The control of many unions by outsiders, usually lawyers linked to the Wafd, was in this sense a manifestation of their incorporation into the national movement. On the other hand these professionals and notables were accepted as leaders at least in part because the unions thereby became a integral component of the broader struggle for Egypt's independence and dignity. The events of 1919 had fused national and class consciousness into one composite world-outlook for most Egyptian workers, an alloy which was to be reinforced by the course of political and economic life in subsequent years.

The complex patron–client relationship between the Wafd and the labor movement was based on a degree of common interest in opposing imperialism and the foreign interests it protected. This relationship operated on both the practical-organizational level (skills, resources, publicity, popular support, control of unions) and the ideological level (the conception of the workers' movement as lacking legitimate goals and interests of its own, as essentially one component of the national movement embodied in the self-proclaimed representative of the entire nation, the Wafd). In the interwar period this special relationship developed and changed in form and content, though nationalism continued to play a central role in shaping the workers' movement. Indeed, the subsumption of labor's own interests in a national struggle whose tone was set by other social strata would have profound and long-lasting effects.

The British authorities had ultimately been able to contain the popular uprising of March–April 1919, but only at the price of releasing Zaghlul and allowing him to make his case. In the following months the Wafd enhanced its prestige and consolidated its support among the masses. Although the Peace Conference rejected Egyptian demands for independence and recognized the British protectorate, the Wafd's success in mobilizing the people in demonstrations and the near-total boycott of the Milner Mission proved its growing strength. Although nationalist agitation and British repression continued through 1919, this was a period of political rather than violent struggle, of unionization among workers in the aftermath of the firestorms of March and April, and of a decline in the level of industrial conflict. The relative calm of late spring and early summer, however, was broken by an important strike at the Suez Canal which indicated that even foreign workers in Egypt had been deeply affected by the local and global upheavals that characterized the immediate postwar period.

RADICALISM AND NATIONALISM AT THE SUEZ CANAL

The work force of the Suez Canal Company (SCC) was divided into two segments of unequal size. One was made up of a small number of mainly foreign workers, relatively well-paid and permanently employed. The other was much larger and consisted of workers, mostly Egyptian, employed provisionally or indirectly at lower wages and lacking any job security. Wartime inflation and other grievances had led to unrest among both foreign and Egyptian workers at the SCC and the other foreign-owned firms serving the waterway before March 1919. Greek workers, who constituted the largest single ethnic group among the SCC's permanent cadre, formed the core of a new union in Port Said early in 1919, and were led by a lawyer named Zizinia. In its petition to the canal company the union, known as Le Phénix, asked for the eight-hour day, the permanent addition of all temporary wartime raises to the official wage scale, extra pay for work on Sundays and holidays, and the automatic granting of permanent status to all workers after a certain number of years' service.[25]

This last demand was especially important to the many SCC workers who despite years of employment were still considered provisional employees, were paid less for the same work, and enjoyed no benefits. That the cadre workers took up this issue is very significant, for it constituted an effort by the most privileged segment of the workforce to reach across ethnic lines to their disadvantaged Egyptian fellow workers. The Greek workers may have been motivated not only by abstract principles of class solidarity but perhaps also by a recognition that their own status and jobs were vulnerable as long as the company was allowed to maintain a large reserve of cheap Egyptian labor. Rather than seeking to exclude the nonpermanent workers and fight to defend their own privileges, the organizers of Le Phénix resolved to compel the Suez Canal Company to treat all its workers equally.

The new union did not call a strike during March–April 1919, though, once the situation grew more settled, the union stepped up its organizing efforts and attracted many of the SCC's Egyptian workers. 'Ali Bey Lahayta, a local nationalist notable who had been arrested earlier for fomenting a strike, cooperated with Zizinia behind the scenes, and gave Le Phénix the seal of approval of the nationalist movement. A hitherto separate organization of Italian workers also merged with Le Phénix, which grew rapidly among the canal workers in Port Said and, to a lesser extent, in Suez and Ismailia. The Italians in particular had a well-deserved reputation for militancy, perhaps because of their relatively longer industrial experience and their exposure to trade unionism and socialist or anarchist politics in Italy.

There was another factor, however, that in 1919 helped create what might seem a rather unlikely alliance between Italians in Egypt and the Egyptian nationalist movement. An Italian of radical convictions would presumably be opposed to British rule in Egypt on grounds of anti-imperialist principle, but many other Italians felt great resentment after the war toward what they believed had been Britain's treacherous refusal to allow Italy the rewards of her wartime sacrifices. In particular the British had upheld Greek over Italian territorial claims, and this had engendered Italian hostility toward both the Greeks and the British—attitudes shared by many Egyptians. Indeed Italian workers and radicals in Egypt would play a key role in the labor movement in the summer of 1919, prompting General Allenby, the British High Commissioner in Egypt, to assert that the union movement 'commands the support of the natives, who however do not appear to appreciate its real meaning, and of the Italians in Egypt, who, in this movement, are making common cause with the Egyptians against the present regime, which they hope to embarrass in this way.'[26]

By May 1919 Le Phénix felt strong enough to risk a confrontation with the powerful Suez Canal Company. Having failed to get a satisfactory response to its demands, the union called a general strike of all canal workers, and on May 13 work stopped at the SCC and all shipping companies. The next day the coalheavers also stopped work, and the strike spread slowly throughout the Suez Canal region, affecting even cigarette and electric company workers. The striking workers were led by a committee composed of three Greeks, two Italians, a Frenchman, and an Egyptian, and enjoyed considerable public support. Large sums were contributed to aid the strikers, mainly by European residents of the canal cities. French intelligence sources claimed that the donations were made by wealthy persons in order to forestall the emergence of Bolshevism among the workers, whereas the British asserted that Egyptian merchants were promoting the strike as a means of taking over the positions and profits of the local labor contractors. Neither of these allegations is supported by the evidence. The grievances of the Suez Canal Company's workers were unquestionably authentic, and the coalheavers and other area workers simply seized the opportunity offered by Le Phénix's strike to improve their own wages and working conditions. The coalheavers returned to work by June 1 after the contractors had agreed to supplement their piece rate out of their own pockets, but the other strikers remained out.[27]

Nonetheless, the Suez Canal continued to function in late May and early June despite the strike because British naval personnel took over key positions. The French government, pressured by SCC officials and shareholders in Paris, grew increasingly nervous, and demanded that the British authorities take action to break the strike. Allenby refused because (according to the French) he was worried that 'once drawn into such affairs he might find himself much more involved than he would have wished; every step on his part must be well-considered if he wishes to avoid compromising his authority.' The French Minister in Egypt insisted that the strike was political in character, because it had been fomented by foreigners and was supported by the nationalists, and the protectorate must therefore intervene. The French were quite disturbed by what they regarded as the reluctance or inability of their ostensible ally to protect their investments and interests in Egypt forcefully. Still, Allenby continued to reject French demands, and argued that the strikers were not disturbing public order and the canal was functioning. The British authorities had enough problems elsewhere and were not anxious to dispatch military forces to break a popular strike at a delicate political juncture.[28]

Because British intervention was not forthcoming and the strikers remained united, the SCC was eventually forced to make concessions. The cadre workers won some of their principal demands, including the eight-hour day and a fortnight's paid leave with passage to and from Europe so that foreign workers could visit their homelands, and returned to work on June 10. It is not clear what if anything the non-cadre SCC workers, and those employed at other companies, won as a result of the strike. Certainly such practices as maintaining a reserve of nonpermanent workers and contracting work out were not abolished at this time, and yet the partial success of the strike was to provide the impetus for the emergence of the International Workers' Union of the Isthmus of Suez in the following months. Led by the radical Greek Dr Skouphopoulos, this union sought to unite all those who worked at Canal-related enterprises into one organization around a core of SCC workers.

The Suez Canal workers' four-week strike was characterized by an unprecedented degree of unity between foreign and indigenous workers, and this unity resulted from the convergence of the militancy (and in some cases political radicalism) of the European workers and the nationalism of the Egyptian workers. This kind of organization across ethnic lines and common struggle had been rare in Egypt, and was facilitated by the fact that the Suez Canal area labor force included Europeans influenced by left-wing ideas and leaders and unsympathetic to the occupation regime. Their willingness to take risks in order to help their Egyptian co-workers opened the way to cooperation with local nationalist leaders and the formation of a strong union of all Suez Canal Company workers.

The summer of 1919 marked the limit of cooperation between Egyptian and foreign (especially Italian) workers elsewhere in Egypt as well, though it did not always take the form of joint organization. The strike wave of March–April had largely involved Egyptian workers and been inextricably linked with the nationalist upsurge. During the following three months the young labor movement began to emerge in its own right, and appear as a distinct phenomenon. Egyptian nationalism was of course a key factor in this process, but foreign workers became much more active and militant as well, often in cooperation with indigenous workers. It was this unprecedented development that led General Allenby to comment in July 1919 that 'the foreign and native working classes have apparently identified in their own minds the Syndicalist [that is, trade union] movement and the Extremist [that is, nationalist] agitation.'[29] In that sense the Suez Canal strike in May–June foreshadowed another explosion of industrial conflict in the summer. That explosion unavoidably had a nationalist dimension, but its class dimension was more crucial and more pronounced than that of any previous upsurge of the Egyptian labor movement. If the spring of 1919 had seen the birth of a workers' movement in the midst of national revolution, then the summer of that year saw the working class find its own distinctive voice and come out fighting for its own demands.

AUGUST 1919: 'IL PLEUT DES SYNDICATS!'

As early as June there had been signs of increasing unrest in many sectors of the working class. There were real reasons for labor dissatisfaction. Whatever wage gains had been made in the spring were rapidly being eroded by renewed inflation as prices began to leap upward again after March (see Table 1, above). In addition, specific groups of workers had their own particular grievances. The tramway workers, for example, wanted higher wages, but they also felt that the CTC was reneging on the concessions it had made in the spring. The panel the company had created to investigate sanctions against workers was composed of white-collar employees loyal to management and approved whatever punishments supervisors imposed. Promised pay raises had not been implemented, the issue of severance pay remained unresolved, and other company obligations provided for in the April agreement had not been fulfilled. Early in August the tram workers presented the CTC with a list of demands to definitively settle these issues. The workers also insisted that the company formally recognize the new union as their bargaining agent. The head of the union was the nationalist lawyer Muhammad Kamil Husayn, recently released from internment and once again in the thick of labor affairs.[30] On all sides, Egyptian and foreign workers (many of them now unionized) began pressing their demands.

The first week of August saw a brief strike by dockworkers at the port of

Alexandria, but what really set off the explosion was the sudden strike on August 10 of the Cairo tramway workers. Apparently fearing that the company was about to fire a large number of workers in order to pre-empt a strike, the union chose to act first. The tram system was completely shut down, and negotiations began under government auspices. The bold action of the tramwaymen, who had in the past often set the pace for the entire workers' movement, broke the dike of passivity. Within a few days many of the Egyptian and foreign workers of Cairo and Alexandria were on strike. The great strike wave of August 1919 included the tramways of Cairo, Heliopolis, and Alexandria, omnibus drivers, the ʿAnabir and Jabal al-Zaytun railway workers, numerous cigarette factories, the ʿAbu Qirqas sugar mill, the Hawamdiyya refinery, waiters and kitchen workers in the major cafés, restaurants, and pâtisseries of Cairo and Alexandria, shop and bank employees, bakery workers, the Maʿasara quarrymen, the Candida engineering works in Alexandria, Bonded Stores warehouses and the Spathis soda factory. There were also strikes in Suez, Tanta, and Mansura. The strike wave was accompanied by a wave of unionization which largely though not exclusively affected relatively skilled or educated foreign workers and white-collar employees. During these weeks, for example, new unions were established by bank, hotel, and shop employees, journalists, tailors, carpenters, electricians (foreign and native), lithographers, bakery workers, waiters, chauffeurs, automobile mechanics, lawyers' clerks, cab drivers, painters, and hairdressers. It was the sudden mushrooming of labor unions that prompted the daily newspaper *La Bourse Egyptienne* to proclaim in its headline of August 21: '*Il pleut des syndicats!*'

The spread of strike fever from the Cairo tramwaymen to other workers was apparently not entirely spontaneous. When the tram strike first began, British intelligence reported rumors that certain nationalists and European workers were trying to bring other public utility workers out on strike as well. These rumors had some basis in fact, for a group of Italian radicals, with the tacit support of the Wafd, was indeed trying to generalize the strike wave and encourage the formation of unions. Two individuals played important parts in this agitation. One was Max di Collalto, proprietor of the Italian-language Cairene daily *Roma* and leader of the Société Internationale des Employés du Caire, which claimed over 1,000 members. His role was mainly that of propagandist. A second Italian, Giuseppe Pizzuto, was more directly active in labor struggles. An Italian subject born in Egypt, Pizzuto had served in the Italian army during the war, then returned to become president of the printers' union. Although his precise political affiliations cannot be determined, he was certainly a revolutionary socialist and much affected by the radical upsurge then taking place in Italy. He took his internationalist principles seriously, for he convinced the printers' union (hitherto an exclusively European preserve) to accept Egyptians as members on equal terms. Workers in the printing trades were for a time among the most radical segments of the working class, a phenomenon found in many countries.[31]

Pizzuto went into action at the earliest opportunity. He attended the first meeting of the striking tramwaymen accompanied by 60 Italian workers to express support for their struggle, and broached the idea of a government takeover of the tramways. On their way home the Italians were reported to have shouted 'Long Live Bolshevism!' Shortly thereafter Pizzuto established a 'Bourse de Travail' in Cairo and served as its secretary. The Bourse functioned during August as a sort of trade union center, sponsoring the formation of new unions (most of them craft unions of skilled foreign workers), assisting in talks with employers, and issuing almost daily bulletins to the press about strikes, disputes, demands, and union activities. The Bourse claimed that it had 15,000 members in twelve affiliated unions, but this seems an exaggeration.

The August strike wave had two distinct but overlapping components. The predominantly Egyptian workers in the transport sector and a few other large enterprises touched off and constituted the core of the upsurge of class conflict. At the same time, the mainly foreign workers in the skilled and service trades also went on strike or at least formed unions, and in these sectors the struggles were coordinated by the Bourse de Travail set up by the Italian radicals. Unity seems to have been strong across ethnic, national, and religious lines with no reports of internal conflicts among the strikers. Within a few weeks, however, the strike wave among the foreign workers subsided, for many of them had won substantial gains from the small proprietors who employed them, their unions were firmly established, and they returned to work. The British authorities also moved against the Bourse de Travail which they saw as a dangerous center for radical agitation linked to the nationalist movement. Allenby sought to have Collalto deported to Italy, but was initially unsuccessful. When the pro-occupation *Egyptian Mail* launched a press campaign against the Bourse and its leader Pizzuto, the linotypists at the newspaper agreed not to set in print any article hostile to the organization of which their own union was an affiliate. It was only at the end of September that Collalto and Pizzuto were deported, a step that offended public opinion and prompted a brief protest strike by Cairo printing workers.[32] The removal of the two Italian activists from the scene resulted in the demise of the short-lived but influential Bourse de Travail.

DÉNOUEMENT: THE CAIRO TRAM STRIKE

Even while the Bourse had been active, the main focus of both official and public concern were the tram strikes in Cairo, Alexandria and Heliopolis. The strikes involving foreign workers had in general been brief and most of the stoppages involving Egyptian workers had ended in August, but the tram strikes continued. In Cairo it had become evident shortly after the strike began that the central issue was that of union recognition. The CTC claimed to be willing to negotiate with its workers, but it adamantly refused to negotiate with Muhammad Kamil Husayn or anyone else as the representative of a tramway workers' union. The tramwaymen were quite determined that their union be recognized, as they demonstrated at a meeting of nearly 2,000 strikers—essentially the entire workforce—on August 15, five days after the strike began. Muhammad Kamil Husayn chaired this meeting as president of the union, and rank-and-file workers were represented in the leadership by delegates elected from the various branches of the company. These delegates represented a fair cross-section of the CTC workforce: those elected by the drivers and conductors in the three depots were mainly Egyptian Muslims; the two representatives of the inspectors and station chiefs were foreigners; and the delegates from the workshops consisted of a Jew, an Italian, an Egyptian Muslim, and a Syrian Christian. The nonsectarian character of the union and the strike was further demonstrated when the opening benediction was given by a priest, Father Zakhari al-Antuni, who spoke of the benefits of unity and concord. At this meeting the workers voted (with only one dissenting ballot) to reject a proposal by the prime minister that the president and delegates of the union agree to negotiate with the tram company not as representatives of the union but as representatives of the company's employees.[33]

Another mass meeting held three days later at the American Cosmograph movie theater reaffirmed this decision and also adopted a new and unprecedented tactic devised by the union's president. In order to compel the company to recognize the union, the workers agreed to assign the union all back wages still owed to them from before the strike, and they signed forms requesting the company to deposit their wages in the union's account at the Banco di Roma. Not surprisingly the CTC refused to cooperate, and the workers refused to draw their wages directly from the company. The stalemate was broken after the governor of Cairo stepped in to mediate and the workers backed down, but the tactic was one Muhammad Kamil Husayn would employ again.[34]

The nationalist press was of course strongly supportive of the strike, and the British believed that the Wafdist central committee was distributing large sums of money to the tramway workers in the capital. The nationalists were also said to have imposed a special levy of fifteen piastres a day on every cab driver in Cairo for the benefit of the strikers.[35] Support for the tram workers and criticism of the Cairo Tramway Company also came from circles beyond those with a purely political interest in undermining British authority. Muhammad Tal 'at Harb, for example, the apostle of Egypt's economic independence and later the founder of Bank Misr, was motivated by the long strike to write a series of articles in September 1919 on the question of the tramways. Critical of foreign domination of Egypt's economy and anxious to promote indigenous capitalist development, Harb sharply attacked the tram company's corporate structure and the easy concession terms granted it by the Egyptian government. The CTC was now claiming that it could not afford to raise its workers' wages unless it was allowed a fare increase, but Harb argued that an increase would only benefit the company's founders and directors. Harb's articles were sympathetic to the workers, and epitomized the convergence of the interests of the young working class and a nascent Egyptian industrial bourgeoisie, both fighting the power of foreign capital in their country.[36]

Much of the middle-class European and Levantine tram-riding public also expressed resentment toward the CTC and sympathy for the workers. Their viewpoint was represented by Emile Boulad, a lawyer of Syrian origin who practiced in both the Mixed and National Courts. His pamphlet *Les Tramways du Caire en 1919* was published during the strike, for which Boulad held the company to blame. Boulad believed that by granting a minimum wage of fifteen piastres, free uniforms, a workday of eight or nine hours, reasonable provision for days of rest, severance pay, and sick pay the company's labor troubles would end. He also criticized management for poor service, dirty and overcrowded cars, a shortage of first-class seats, and untrained workers. Boulad denounced the company's plan to raise fares, and advocated special trams at half-fare for workers during certain times of the day. This last proposal, however, seems to have been due less to a concern for the plight of poor workers than a desire to segregate them from the middle classes. In order to protect the public interest and prevent continual labor strife, Boulad proposed that an independent and impartial lawyer be appointed to the company's departments that handled the recruitment and disciplining of workers. His proposals were submitted to a public meeting of tram passengers held at the Cinema Obelisk on September 28. Four delegates were chosen to help mediate the strike which by that time had gone on for more than seven weeks.

The British authorities did not intervene directly to break the strike—an indication of how much the revolution had weakened their grip on Egypt—but they were quite concerned about the dangerous political implications of the simultaneous tramway strikes in Cairo, Alexandria, and Heliopolis. One official wrote:

> If the strikers should succeed in enforcing all their demands, their success would not only be considered as a triumph for them, but would also be looked upon by the natives as a defeat of both the employers and the Authorities, a fact which will probably encourage the mass of the population to make trouble.[37]

Therefore, two measures were taken in late August to quell the strike wave spearheaded by the Cairo tramwaymen. First, Muhammad Kamil Husayn was arrested, allegedly for trying to organize the 'Anabir workers and bring them out on strike. The railway workshop workers had struck briefly in mid-August, but then returned to work, and were not heard from again until the autumn. Despite Husayn's arrest the tramwaymen's union continued to function and the workers stayed out on strike.[38]

The other measure was more far-reaching in its consequences. Until this time there had existed no institutionalized system of mediating labor disputes. If a dispute or strike were significant enough, the governor of the city concerned or even the prime minister might bring the two parties together, and try to resolve the conflict. This informal system was overwhelmed and collapsed during the August strike wave, and so the government of Muhammad Sa'id Pasha, with General Allenby's encouragement, announced the creation of a Labor Conciliation Board (LCB) on August 19. This body was to investigate disputes between workers and employers, appoint mediators to convene negotiations, propose measures to resolve disputes, and participate in the development of representation for workers and employers. The first president of the LCB was Dr Alexander Granville, who was also serving at that time as president of the Quarantine Board, vice-president of the Alexandria Municipal Commission, and head of the Red Cross. Its other members were Rafla Tadrus Bey, a government official; Muhammad Sadiq Bey, chief of the Alexandria prosecutor's office; and William Hornblower, a British official who soon resigned.[39]

The establishment of this specialized body to deal with labor disputes is a clear indication of how seriously British colonial officials and the Egyptian government took the new phenomenon of class conflict. Clearly, the time had come to develop some means of lessening the impact of industrial strife which might boil over and threaten the political stability of the occupation regime and the interests of foreign capital. Yet in keeping with the principles of classical liberalism, the LCB was granted only very limited powers, for it could not impose binding arbitration, or enforce compliance with agreements reached under its auspices, but merely report its findings and make recommendations. Furthermore, given the scale of industrial unrest, the Board was incapable of handling every dispute, and once again the job of mediation generally devolved on the local governors. Nonetheless, the creation of the Labor Conciliation Board was a significant first step by the Egyptian state in recognizing the importance of the working-class and labor movement, and in deploying methods of control other than the police.

British officials had considered going even further that autumn. Sir Miles Cheetham, who replaced Allenby during the latter's absence in England, discussed with the Foreign Office a draft decree officially recognizing trade unions for workers other than white-collar civil servants, subject to approval in each case by the minister of the interior.

The Egyptian government was desperate to enhance its popularity, and reportedly favored the idea. The power to deny formal legal status to unions whose charters the government did not approve would constitute a powerful means of control, while the courts could dissolve any union whose conduct contravened public policy. But the Residency was worried about the public perception of such a step at a time of widespread labor militancy and nationalist agitation. Cheetham cabled Curzon that

> Government recognition would give impetus to [the trade union movement] and be regarded as a victory of Extremists, and it is doubtful if, in present circumstances, Government policy, as proposed, would be immediately effective ... I think that law may be interpreted as a sign of weakness at present moment and increase influence of Extremists.[40]

In the end the proposal was shelved, and many years were to pass before legal recognition of unions won a serious place on the government's agenda. In 1919 the British officials who directed Egypt's affairs were not surprisingly too fearful that the new unions would be an instrument with which the Wafd, and perhaps radical elements as well, could mobilize the working class to take this step. The creation of a mediation board with limited powers was the furthest they were willing to go in confronting the emergence of an active Egyptian workers' movement.

The first major task of the new Labor Conciliation Board was the settlement of the Cairo tram strike, which remained difficult. The company claimed it could not afford to make any substantial concessions unless tram fares were increased, though the government's accountants who examined the CTC's books ultimately rejected this contention. It was only at the beginning of October that an agreement was finally achieved, and tram service was resumed on October 5 after fifty-six days. The October agreement gave the drivers and conductors a wage increase that brought their pay scale to between sixteen and twenty-one piastres a day when counting the supplement for inflation. The other CTC workers also won increases. The company agreed to rehire all the strikers and not oppose union activity, though it continued to refuse to actually recognize or deal with the union. All penalties imposed by inspectors had to be approved by the head of the traffic department after consultation with the investigations panel, which was to include an Arabic-speaking representative of management, a clerical employee to act as recorder, and a worker appointed by the company. Also important was the company's promise to publish (in both French and Arabic) and distribute copies of its work rules and conditions of service (*la'ihat al-khidma*) to the workers. The strikes on the Heliopolis and Alexandria tram systems also came to an end on the basis of agreements similar to that reached in

Cairo. In Alexandria, however, the strike was settled only after the Municipal Commission, exasperated by the tram company's intransigence and its plans to double fares, threatened to buy out the tram concession and run the system itself.[41]

The settlement of the tram strikes marked the end of the great strike wave that had erupted in mid-August. Unrest among the 'Anabir workers had fluctuated during the summer and fall, and a strike had seemed imminent in late October. But in the end the railwaymen contented themselves with a twelve-hour protest strike for higher wages, and on the whole the 'Anabir workers were only marginally involved in the labor militancy of the second half of 1919.[42] It was the tram workers, especially those of Cairo, who had touched off the explosion of industrial unrest, and it was they who stayed out on strike long after the many Egyptian and foreign workers who had initially followed their lead returned to work. The agreement of October 1919 which ended the Cairo tram strike embodied substantial gains for the workers, especially with regard to wages, but it also involved compromises. The workers did not win recognition for their union or severance pay, and the composition of the investigations panel still did not give them the strong protection against managerial abuse they had sought. Nonetheless the bargain was seen as a victory for the workers, and the agreement of October 1919 served as a point of reference in numerous struggles in the following years. It is a measure of the degree to which favorable political circumstances allowed the Cairo tramwaymen to win important gains in 1919 that decades would pass before the promise of the October agreement would be fully realized.

The strike wave of August 1919 was made possible by the popular uprising of the preceding spring. The national revolution against British rule opened the floodgates of labor organization and militant action. while the persistence of high inflation rates ensured that worker activism would continue. In 1919 a specific conjuncture of political, social, and economic factors not only propelled workers in large industrial and transport enterprises into action but won their struggles popular legitimacy and material support. Workers' efforts to improve their lot were seen as an integral part of the struggle of the whole Egyptian nation to free itself of foreign domination. This identification continued to earn the workers popular sympathy on into the summer and fall, even while they were fighting to achieve more purely economic demands. Those demands were also taken up by foreign workers in Egypt who took advantage of the opportunities opened up by the weakening of the colonial regime to form new unions and confront their employers. Many of the foreign workers were influenced by the Italian socialists who, along with their internationalism and anti-imperialism, stressed a new and radical notion of class identity and unity across ethnic and occupational lines. It may seem paradoxical that it was just when Egyptian nationalism was at its most militant and vigorous that foreign workers joined with their indigenous co-workers in common struggle against their employers, though in fact it was the resurgence of nationalism that facilitated the emergence of a workers' movement that could temporarily encompass workers of many nationalities. In a period of political struggle involving the broad masses of the population, common ground was established on which Egyptian workers motivated both by their own grievances in the workplace and by patriotic sentiment could cooperate on a relatively equal basis with their foreign counterparts.

By the end of 1919 there were an estimated twenty-one unions functioning in Cairo, seventeen in Alexandria, and others in the Suez Canal cities, the Delta towns, and elsewhere.[43] This momentous year had witnessed the birth of an Egyptian workers' movement closely linked to the simultaneous upsurge of nationalism. That movement would bear marks of the circumstances of its birth for a long time in the form of a special relationship with the Egyptian nationalist movement. This is not to say that the subsequent history of Egyptian labor was already determined in 1919, but in many ways the 1919 revolution was the formative experience of the Egyptian union movement—an experience that played a large part in molding the ideological perspective and organizational practice of both unionized workers and bourgeois nationalists active in labor affairs. The 'lessons' learned in 1919 would be reinforced by the daily experiences and struggles of Egyptian workers inside and outside the workplace. This helped foster continued dependence on bourgeois nationalists as leaders or patrons and on bourgeois nationalism as the dominant ideological framework. Countervailing tendencies were of course also at work which would in time lead Egyptian workers to see the disadvantages and contradictions in the labor–nationalist relationship and increasingly question it. But in 1919 this was all far in the future. In the course of a few stormy months the indigenous working class had emerged, forcefully and irrevocably, onto the stage of history with its own forms of organization and struggle. Egypt would never again be without a union movement which, however weak and divided at times, would nevertheless retain strong roots among the workers, and remain a significant factor in industrial and political life.

This article is reprinted from Joel Beinin and Zachary Lockman, *Workers on the Nile* (Princeton, 1988), pp. 83–120. Reprinted by permission of Princeton University Press.

NOTES

1. On the war's impact on various classes, see ʻAbd al-ʻAzim Ramadan, *Tatawwur al-haraka al-wataniyya al-misriyya min sanat 1918 ila sanat 1936* (Cairo, n.d.), pp. 66–82, and the classic nationalist account of the revolution, ʻAbd al-Rahman al-Rafiʻi, *Thawrat 1919* (Cairo, n.d.: Third Printing), I, pp. 40–44.

2. Great Britain, Foreign Office, Archives in the Public Record Office, London, FO 407/186/325. According to Issawi, war-related malnutrition had a major impact on the death rate in Egypt as the total number of deaths per year rose from 300,000 before the war to 500,000 by 1918. Charles Issawi, *Egypt at Mid-Century* (London, 1954), p. 41.

3. See for example Egypt, Mahfuzat majlis al-wuzara', nizarat al-ashghal, maslahat al-sikka al-hadid, carton marked '2 January 1882–22 December 1918', 'Iltimas kalimat haqq awhat bi-nashriha 'awatif al-ikhlas' and 'Sadan iltimas kumsariyyat al-sikka al-hadid', two pamphlets published anonymously by railway workers sometime between November 1916 and October 1917.

4. Quoted in Ronald Seth, *Russell Pasha* (London, 1966), p. 130. See also Amin 'Izz al-Din, *Ta'rikh al-tabaqa al-'amila al-misriyya mundhu nash'atiha hatta thawrat 1919* (Cairo, 1967), pp. 161–74.

5. *al-Muqattam*, March 6, 1919, quoted in 'Izz al-Din (1967), p. 184.

6. For a more detailed account of these events see al-Rafi'i, *1919*, Ramadan, *Tatawwur*, or Marius Deeb, *Party Politics in Egypt: the Wafd and Its Rivals, 1919–1936* (London, 1979), ch. 2.

7. *Egypte, Ministère des Finances, Annuaire Statistique 1914*, pp. 218–19; *Egypte, Ministère des Finances, Annuaire Statistique 1919*, pp. 138–40.

8. Muhammad Zaki 'Ali, *Taqrir 'an halat 'ummal al-tram bi'l-qahira* (Cairo, 1920); Amin 'Izz al-Din, *Ta'rikh al-tabaqa al-'amila al-misriyya, 1919–1929* (Cairo, 1970), p. 16.

9. al-Rafi'i, *1919*, I, pp. 117–19; *al-Watan*, March 14, 1919, quoted in 'Izz al-Din (1970), p. 16. On the poor public reputation of the tramway company, see Emile Boulad, *Les Tramways du Caire en 1919* (Cairo, 1919), pp. 14–19.

10. FO 141/748/8839/1, notes by Thomas and Moesworth.

11. al-Rafi'i, *1919*, I, p. 126; Michael Messeri, 'Tnu'at hapo'alim bazira hapolitit bemitzrayyim, 1919–1936—I: Tza'adim rishonim', *Hamizrah Hehadash* 21 (1971): 148; Seth, *Russell Pasha*, p. 146.

12. al-Rafi'i, *1919*, pp. 168–9. On the links between the secret groups and certain key Wafdists, notably 'Abd al-Rahman Fahmi, who was then general secretary of the Wafdist central committee in Cairo, see Muhammad Anis, *Dirasat fi watha'iq thawrat 1919, I: al-murasalat al-sirriyya bayna Sa'd Zaqhlul wa-'Abd al-Rahman Fahmi* (Cairo, 1963); and Ramadan, *Tatawwur*, pp. 158–75.

13. Muhammad Zaki 'Ali, *Taqrir 'an halat 'ummal al-tram bi'l-qahira ma'a kalima 'an al-'ummal* (Cairo, 1945), p. 12; 'Izz al-Din (1970), pp. 26–7.

14. FO 141/687/8705/2.

15. See for example the Earl of Cromer, *Modern Egypt* (London, 1908), I, ch. 1, II, chs. 34, 61–2. This book was standard reading for British officials in Egypt and was taken as gospel, a distillation of the wisdom and experience of Egypt's de facto ruler for over two decades.

16. Messiri, 'Tnu'at hapo'alim', I, p. 145.

17. FO 141/687/8705/3, 4.

18. FO 141/687/8705/28, Blakeney to Cheetham, October 23, 1919; al-Rafi'i, *1919*, I, pp. 125–6, 131–2, 141; memoirs of 'Abd al-Rahman Fahmi Pasha (at the Dar al-Watha'iq, Cairo), p. 122.

19. FO 141/687/8705/8, Macauley to General Officer Commanding Forces in Egypt, March 22, 1919.

20. FO 141/781/8915, General Staff Intelligence, April 10, 28, 1919; FO 141/687/8705/14; FO 407/184, Allenby to Curzon, no. 277, May 1–2, 1919.

21. France, Archives of the French Embassy in Cairo (hereafter F)/512, Henri Naus (general director of the sugar company) to the French minister in Cairo, April 30, 1919.

22. al-Rafi'i, *1919*, pp. 138–9.

23. FO 141/781/8915, Reports of April 28, May 7, July 8, 1919.

24. Quoted in Anis, *Dirasat*, p. 154.

25. F/510, Services des Informations de la Marine dans le Levant (hereafter SIML), no. 198-CE, Port Said, March 30, 1919, 'Rapport de l'agent D.'; FO 141/487/7392/7–9.

26. FO 407/185/27, Allenby to Curzon, July 1, 1919; FO 407/185/36, Allenby to Curzon, July 12, 1919; F/512, SIML, no. 210-CE, May 6, 1919. Within Le Phénix Greek and Italian workers cooperated closely, except for Greeks from the Dodecanese Islands (then under Italian rule) who were hostile toward their Italian co-workers.

27. FO 141/781/8915, May 14, 26, June 4, 1919; FO 141/487/7392/2, 3, 4, 5; F/510, SIML, no. 213-CE (May 17, 1919) and no. 214-CE (May 22, 1919).

28. F/39, P. Lefevre-Pontalis to S. Pichon, Minister of Foreign Affairs, June 5, 1919. See also FO 141/487/7392/23, June 23, 1919.

29. FO 407/185/57, Allenby to Curzon, July 22, 1919.

30. FO 141/781/8915, June 3, 1919; FO 141/748/8839/12, Dr Granville, 'Note on the Strike of the Cairo Electric Tramways', October 6, 1919; 'Ali, *Taqrir*, p. 12; al-Rafi'i, *1919*, II, p. 29.

31. FO 141/748/8839, Department of Public Security/Military Intelligence, August 10, 1919; FO 407/185/57, Allenby to Curzon, July 22, 1919; FO 407/185/171, Cheetham to Curzon, September 8, 1919; FO 141/779/9065/12.

32. *La Bourse Egyptienne*, August 21, 1919; FO 407/185/137, 171, 215; FO 141/781/8915; F/39, Alexandria, September 20, 1919.

33. *La Bourse Egyptienne*, August 18, 1919.

34. *La Bourse Egyptienne*, August 19, 27, 1919; FO 141/748/8839/3a, August 19, 1919. The Banco di Roma seems to have served as a repository and conduit for nationalist and labor funds, a manifestation of the special relationship between some segments of the Italian community in Egypt and the independence movement. British and tramway company officials were of course well aware of the bank's role; see for example FO 141/748/8839/7, Secretary of State for Foreign Affairs to the High Commissioner, September 5, 1919, which includes a copy of a letter on this matter from Gaston Ithier, director of the CTC's parent company in Brussels.

35. FO 407/185/205, Cheetham to Curzon, August 18, 1919; FO 141/781/8915, August 26, September 6, 1919.

36. These articles originally appeared in *al-Ahram* ending on September 17, 1919, and were also published in Hafiz Mahmud et al., *Tal'at Harb* (Cairo, 1936), pp. 74–82. On Tal'at Harb and the early history of Bank Misr, see Eric Davis, *Challenging Colonialism: Bank Misr and Egyptian Industrialization, 1920–1941* (Princeton: Princeton University Press, 1983).

37. FO 141/781/8915, August 18, 1919.

38. *Ibid.*, August 25, 1919.

39. *La Bourse Egyptienne*, August 19, 1919.

40. FO 407/185/181, 202, 208, Cheetham to Curzon, September 25, 26, October 6, 1919; /219, Curzon to Cheetham, October 13, 1919.

41. FO 141/748/8839/12, Granville, 'Note', October 6, 1919; Belgium, Ministère des Affaires Etrangères, N. Leysbeth (consul in Alexandria) to Paul Hymans, Foreign Minister, September 22, October 10, 1919; *La Bourse Egyptienne*, August–October 1919, passim.

42. FO 141/687/8705/17, Macauley to the Residency, September 1, 1919; /27, Major Courtney, Intelligence, to the Residency, October 22, 1919; /28, Blakeney (ESR general manager) to Cheetham, October 23, 1919; FO 407/186/325; FO 141/781/8915, Intelligence, October 27, 1919. The passivity of the 'Anabir workers may be explained by such measures of intimidation as the arrest of M.K. Husayn and government threats to militarize the railways as well as by the fact that they had already won substantial wage increases earlier in the year.

43. A.A.I. El-Gritly, 'The Structure of Modern Industry in Egypt', *L'Egypte Contemporaine*, no. 241–2 (November–December 1947).

Syrian Urban Politics in Transition: the Quarters of Damascus during the French Mandate

PHILIP S. KHOURY

For urban politics in Syria, the interwar years were pivotal. The country was in a transitional phase, uncomfortably suspended between four centuries of Ottoman rule and national independence. Although the Empire had collapsed and new forms of social and political organization were available, there remained a distinctive Ottoman cast to Syria's urban elites. Meanwhile, France had occupied the country, but was ruling clumsily and with a growing measure of uncertainty. The Mandate system itself dictated that the French could not remain in Syria indefinitely and Arab nationalism, however inconsistent and inarticulate, had become the reigning political idea of the age. The cry of independence rang across much of Syria, and nowhere more loudly and clearly than in her cities, the traditional centers of political life.

As late as the French Mandate, the Syrian city retained several of its important medieval focal points: a congregational mosque, a citadel, a central marketplace, and a complex of ancient residential quarters. It was still characterized by deep cleavages between different religious sects and ethnic groups, between the rich and the poor, between the various trades, and between long-settled urbanites and recent in-migrants from the countryside. Artisans remained loosely organized in corporations (*aṣnāf*), each craft grouped together, often on a single street or alley. The religious minorities, Christians and Jews, were also clustered in their own quarters with their own places of worship. 'Except for a very small number of educated [and wealthy] people ... [quarter residents] were pretty much absorbed in the narrowness of their life, and seldom if ever thought of the community at large or of its interests ...' In some senses, the most acute cleavages were those between the different quarters, which were separated from one another by walls and gates, locked tight at dusk by watchmen. This physical separation had come about for many reasons, but was above all 'an expression of the innate impulse for protection through unity.[1]

Even though the quarters[2] retained their distinctiveness and purpose in the early twentieth century, their cohesiveness had already begun to be eroded by new social forces. This was a direct consequence of the structural changes that had been sweeping the Middle East since the early nineteenth century—changes in administration and law; in commerce, industry and agriculture; in the movement of goods, peoples and ideas; and, most notably, in the Ottoman state's relations with Europe. Not only did a shift occur in the relative importance of Syria's cities away from the interior and toward the coast but there were also shifts in the relative importance of different sections of the city and changes in their primary economic and administrative functions.

The integration of the Middle East into the world economy meant that, with different speeds and rhythms, old local economies decayed as pastoral and subsistence agriculture 'gave way' to settled, market-oriented farming. Meanwhile, an economic and legal framework became established for the appropriation and extreme concentration of property, and cities were able to extend an influence far beyond the countryside in their immediate vicinity, creating larger, more fully integrated regional economic and political units.[3] New landholding patterns uprooted peasants and encouraged increased migration to the cities. New patterns of trade and production hastened the impoverishment of some quarters and the enrichment of others. New concentrations of wealth coupled with the spread of modern education accelerated the process of class differentiation. In-migrants moved into quarters vacated by the recently rich and educated, or the state settled refugee populations in those areas. Other in-migrants and refugees settled on the outskirts of the city, creating poor suburban quarters.

Population movement in and out of Syrian cities was also affected by new and cheaper means of travel, and by World War I, which stimulated emigration to neighboring lands and to the West. The growth of a market economy gradually served to lower the barriers between quarters and between ethnic and religious communities, and hence encouraged higher forms of social integration and organization in the city at large. Supporting this process was a reinvigorated and modernized state, which became increasingly able to assert its authority in ways which had never been felt before.

However, although the winds of change in Syria intensified after World War I, their impact on urban politics should not be exaggerated. For instance, the exercise of local political power was marked by a remarkable degree of continuity, which was not disrupted by the dissolution of the Ottoman Empire and its replacement by the French Mandate. For the most part, the men who were important in local affairs under the Ottomans were the same men, or the sons of the same men, who wielded political influence under the French. Political leaders continued to organize their personal support systems as they had in late Ottoman times. Urban leadership remained the basic building block of political influence in Syria. And near the heart of urban politics were the quarters, the traditional domain in which political leadership operated and from which it derived much of its support.

Yet, despite the continuity of aims, of personnel, and even of organizational methods, political leaders under the Mandate were obliged to broaden the range of their operations in order to retain independent power and influence. Their relations with an openly hostile Christian and imperial power were never as smooth as they had been with the Ottomans. The French were perceived to be an illegitimate authority. Fortunately for urban leaders, the forces of change had made available new methods, mechanisms, institutions, and classes to which they could turn to consolidate their positions and supplement their power. New loyalties to the city, the state, and ultimately to nationalism began to corrode traditional ties to the quarter, family, clan, and confessional group. Nationalism produced movements and organizations of greater complexity and territorial scale.[4]

The older quarters—marked by their mosques, fountains and baths, small shops, and cafés—could not remain untouched by the changing circumstances. Some maintained a certain stability but many others did not. Ironically, as their inhabitants attained their highest levels of political consciousness and organization, they also experienced a steady erosion of control over urban politics and the active forces of society. Outside the quarters, modern institutions and classes claimed greater amounts of the urban leadership's attention and time, becoming in the process new and dynamic focal points for nationalist resistance. Although the quarters remained one of the crucial foundations of urban politics, during the French Mandate the center of political gravity in Syrian cities began to shift irreversibly.

THE QUARTERS OF DAMASCUS

There is no more important or suitable city in which to examine the changing character of Syrian urban politics than Damascus. In its capacity as the premier metropolis, capital, and center of the national independence struggle against the French, Damascus embodied, shaped, and reflected nearly all the major political trends of the period. In terms of the erosion of old urban patterns and the formation of new ones the experience of Damascus is representative of the experience of other major Syrian cities during the interwar years.[5]

By the 1930s, Damascus contained nearly forty identifiable quarters (see Map 1 and Table 1), although several were no more than neighbourhoods

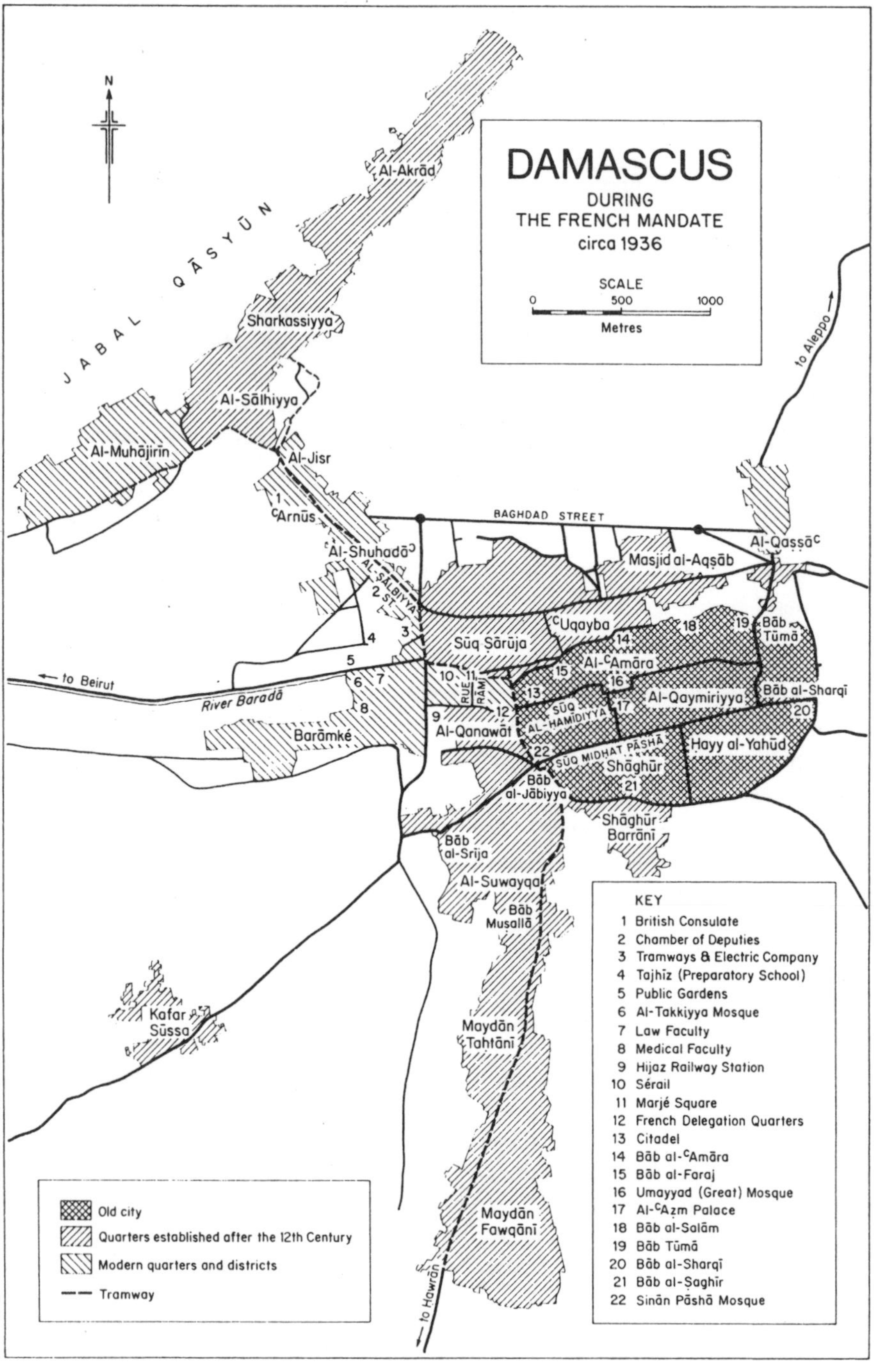
DAMASCUS
DURING
THE FRENCH MANDATE
circa 1936
SCALE
0
500
1000
Metres
N
JABAL QĀSYŪN
Al-Akrād
Sharkassiyya
Al-Sālhiyya
Al-Muhājirīn
Al-Jisr
ᶜArnūs
Al-Shuhadāᶜ
AL-SALHIYYA ST.
BAGHDAD STREET
Masjid al-Aqsāb
Al-Qassāᶜ
to Aleppo
ᶜUqayba
Bāb Tūmā
Sūq Sārūja
Al-ᶜAmāra
to Beirut
River Baradā
RUE RAMI
Al-Qaymiriyya
Bāb al-Sharqī
SŪQ AL-HAMIDIYYA
Al-Qanawāt
Barāmké
SŪQ MIDHAT PĀSHĀ
Hayy al-Yahūd
Shāghūr
Bāb al-Jābiyya
Shāghūr Barrānī
Bāb al-Srīja
Al-Suwayqa
Bāb Musallā
Kafar Sūssa
Maydān Tahtānī
Maydān Fawqānī
to Hawrān
Old city
Quarters established after the 12th Century
Modern quarters and districts
Tramway
KEY
1 British Consulate
2 Chamber of Deputies
3 Tramways & Electric Company
4 Tajhīz (Preparatory School)
5 Public Gardens
6 Al-Takkiyya Mosque
7 Law Faculty
8 Medical Faculty
9 Hijaz Railway Station
10 Sérail
11 Marjé Square
12 French Delegation Quarters
13 Citadel
14 Bāb al-ᶜAmāra
15 Bāb al-Faraj
16 Umayyad (Great) Mosque
17 Al-ᶜAzm Palace
18 Bāb al-Salām
19 Bāb Tūmā
20 Bāb al-Sharqī
21 Bāb al-Saghīr
22 Sinān Pāshā Mosque

TABLE 1 *The quarters of Damascus and their population by religious community, circa 1936*

Quarter	*Muslims*	*Christians*	*Jews*	*Total*
Group 1				
al-Qaymariyya	5,817	241		6,058
Bāb Tūmā [Bāb Sharqī]		6,750		6,750
Ḥayy al-Yahūd			9,706	9,706
al-Kharāb	1,849			1,849
Madhnat al-Shaḥm	7,750			7,750
al-Jūrra	1,378	591		1,969
Bāb al-Barīd	1,715			1,715
Bāb al-Salām	1,599			1,599
ʿAmāra Jawāniyya	4,044			4,044
Shāghūr Jawānī	6,383			6,383
Group 2				
Sūq Sārūja	6,868			6,868
ʿUqayba	5,095			5,095
Baḥṣa Sanjaqdār	2,655	310		2,965
al-Qaṣṣāʿ		1,872		1,872
ʿAmāra Barrāniyya	7,980			7,980
Masjid al-Aqṣāb	6,900			6,900
Shāghūr Barrānī	12,332			12,332
al-Qanawāt	8,625			8,625
Bāb al-Jābiyya	1,933			1,933
Bāb al-Srīja	12,000			12,000
Qabr ʿĀtaka	8,027			8,027
Birka Ḥaṭṭāb	2,020			2,020
al-Suwayqa	5,620			5,620
Tayāmna	—	—	—	—
Group 3				
Mūṣallī	2,826			2,826
Sūq al-Maydān	7,015			7,015
al-Haqla	1,493			1,493
Maydān Fawqānī	10,595			10,595
Maydān Taḥtānī	1,730			1,730
al-Qāʿa	3,400			3,400
al-Sāḥa	3,040			3,040
Bāb Muṣalla	5,279	1,217		6,496
Group 4				
al-Akrād	6,650			6,650
Sharkasiyya	9,610			9,610
Abū Jarash	9,600			9,600
al-Ṣālḥiyya	2,622	182	10	2,814
al-Muhājirīn	3,442			3,442
Total	177,892	11,163	9,716	198,771

Source: René Danger, Paul Danger, and M. Ecochard, *Damas: Rapport d'enquête monographique sur la ville 1936* (unpublished), adapted from Table 13. These population figures are derived from a cadastral survey which the French High Commission conducted in the mid-1930s. They do not necessarily correspond to the exact boundaries of the quarters but they do reflect approximate population sizes of quarters.

within larger quarters of the city's northwest and south. Most quarters and much of the town population were located on the southern bank of the Barada, a river which conditioned the very history of Damascus as it irrigated the gardens (known as al-Ghūṭa) to the city's east and west.[6] For the sake of convenience, however, the city can be divided into four sections or districts.

The first section is old Damascus (see Table 1, Group 1), a maze of ten quarters encircled by the ancient wall. Some quarters (like ʿAmara and Shāghūr) were subdivided, part of each falling inside the wall and part lying just outside.[7] The residents of the Muslim quarters were active in the traditional religious, political, and commercial life of the city, to which the neighboring Great (Umayyad) Mosque, Citadel, and suqs of al-Hamīdiyya and Midḥat Pāshā (also known as Sūq al-Tawīl or The Street Called Straight) were central. Because quarters were almost exclusively residential (they did contain nonspecialized shops and markets [*suwayqa*] and some limited craft production) many of their male inhabitants were employed elsewhere, usually nearby in the old commercial district. This was also true for the two quarters containing the ancient religious minorities of Damascus: Bāb Tūmā, which housed 60 per cent of the Christian community of the city, and the Jewish Quarter (Ḥayy al-Yahūd), in which nearly all Jews resided during the Mandate (see Table 1, Group 1). The central bazaars, in addition to including their prosperous shopkeepers and traders, comprised a vast array of productive activities—mostly handicrafts such as clothing, household goods, metal wares, and jewelry—grouped into tens of corporations, each located along a single street or alley.[8] It is not clear whether these corporations ever provided a sense of solidarity and organization strong enough to allow them to be used for political purposes in the Mandate era. A number of them had already disappeared under the impact of the European commercial invasion, and many others had seen better days. Moreover, most had come under direct state supervision in the last decades of the Ottoman Empire, a situation that French Mandatory authorities sought to reinforce. The great bazaars frequently went on strike during the Mandate era, but whether they did so under their own volition or because the nationalist leadership forced them to is a question worthy of further investigation.[9]

Some quarters had a significantly higher concentration of wealthy residents than did others—in particular, ʿAmāra (home of the local religious aristocracy) and al-Qaymariyya (known for its wealthy merchants)—and several displayed a certain economic homogeneity, although this was not true of the Christian and Jewish quarters. Residents of some exclusively Muslim quarters seem to have formed communities because of their involvement in similar occupations or trades. However, these individuals did not necessarily belong to the same ethnic group or come from the same place of origin. Their fairly high level of collective consciousness and purpose resulted from occupational and kinship ties that had developed over long periods of permanent residence in the quarter. Ties of descent and residence encouraged neighborhood and even quarter-wide solidarity and disposed local residents toward collective action.

The quarters of the old city are characterized by their walls, narrow and crooked streets, and inward-looking houses built around courtyards.[10] By the mid-1930s, the old city contained about one-fourth of the Damascene population. But with rapid demographic growth in the interwar period, and the city's physical expansion to the northwest, old Damascus's share of the city's total population diminished considerably.

The second section of Damascus (Table 1, Group 2) includes the quarters and subquarters on the northern, western, and southern peripheries of the old city, which lay just outside the ancient wall. This section contained 40 per cent of the city's population in the mid-1930s. Most of its quarters were outgrowths of the old city which had begun to take shape in the later Middle Ages and eventually came to be fully integrated into the life of the town. Several were exclusively residential and catered to the wealthy classes. Sūq Sārūja dated from the fourteenth century and in the nineteenth became known as 'Little Istanbul,' owing to its popularity with the class of Ottoman functionaries; al-Qanawāt was established as early as the sixteenth century but assumed its cosmopolitan ambience in the nineteenth century. Both quarters housed prominent political leaders of the late Ottoman and Mandate periods. Others, like ʿUqayba, which was north of the old city and became in the 1930s one of the centers of modern industry, were less exclusive.[11] Al-Qaṣṣāʿ, to the northeast, became an appendage of Bāb Tūmā's in the early twentieth century, housing wealthier Christian families who had found life in Bāb Tūmā's crowded ancient dwellings increasingly difficult.[12] The greater security provided by the Ottoman state after the 1860 massacres in Damascus, which the European powers reinforced, certainly contributed to the development of this new quarter beyond the old fortified walls of Bāb Tūmā.

The third section of Damascus (Table 1, Group 3), popularly referred to as al-Maydān, took its shape as a suburb after the Ottoman conquest of Syria in the sixteenth century.[13] It is actually a long, narrow series of quarters and subquarters extending southwards into the grain-producing Hawran. Al-Maydān did not have as high a population density as did those quarters closer to the old city, and its commercial and residential buildings were rarely more than one storey high. Its population in the mid-1930s, which constituted nearly a fifth of the city's total, was the most socially heterogeneous in Damascus: it was filled with Hawrani peasants, Druze highlanders, Arab tribes in winter, and a small Christian community of artisans and merchant-moneylenders (in Bāb Muṣalla), all living a rather rudimentary lifestyle. It also housed a wealthy community of Muslim grain and livestock merchant-moneylenders which had grown out of the local janissary forces (*yerliyye*) that dominated the Maydān until the nineteenth century. As the wholesale provisions market of the city, the Maydān contained few bazaars or industries. Rather, it featured a significant number of storehouses (*ḥawāṣil*) that handled the grain and livestock trade that came from the Hawran and Palestine and for provisioning the annual pilgrimage to Mecca which originated in Damascus.[14] Beginning in the nineteenth century, al-Maydān became slowly integrated into Damascus as the forces of agrarian commercialization in Syria developed, but during the Mandate it was still characterized by sharp social conflicts and a high crime rate. Because its largely immigrant population was poor, came from ethnically and geographically diverse origins, and were forced to settle in al-Maydān where land and dwelling rents were among the lowest in Damascus, the quarter was unable to develop a single collective consciousness, let alone a single identifiable political leadership. Certain communities in al-Maydān actively participated in nationalist resistance efforts during the Mandate, but it was virtually impossible to organize for collective action.

The fourth section of Damascus (Table 1, Group 4) was also its most sparsely and most recently settled section. In the mid-1930s its quarters lying to the northwest of the old city up to the slopes of Jabal Qāṣyūn housed only 15 per cent of the city's population. Several quarters within the section deserve special mention because each had its own distinctive characteristics. The closest to old Damascus in its physical and social features was al-Ṣālḥiyya. Originally a medieval village, it enjoyed a renaissance in the late nineteenth century. Here could be found the typical array of pious foundations, mosques, and *madrasas* (religious schools) common in the older quarters across the Barada.[15] Between al-Ṣālḥiyya and old Damascus arose during the Mandate several modern garden districts (the best known being al-Shuhadā', 'Arnūs, and al-Jisr) which housed French officials and other members of the town's small European community in addition to a growing number of wealthy Muslim families. Built in this area were new government schools, the parliament, European-style hotels and social clubs, and a burgeoning modern commercial district along the now-famous al-Ṣālḥiyya street. Closest to the old city were Marjé Square and the various buildings housing the French administration, including the Sérail. This new center of urban life was well laid out with paved roads; the absence of walls created a sense of openness and security.

Further up the hill lay al-Muhājirīn, a distant suburb settled by Muslim refugees from Crete in the late nineteenth century.[16] The other significant quarter in section four was the Ḥayy al-Akrād, which was originally a village established by Kurdish settlers during the reign of Saladin and which became a refuge in the nineteenth century for immigrant Kurds who were not especially welcome further inside Damascus. There, on uncultivated terrain, they built their quarter and organized their own paramilitary forces. In contrast to the well-planned al-Muhājirīn with its prosperous inhabitants and its streets laid out at right angles, the Kurdish quarter was generally poor and its streets were a maze for protective purposes. In time the Kurds, who engaged in farming and the livestock trade, lost many of their particular customs and even their language as they became more fully a part of Arab Damascus. Their clan structure, however, was not as easily dissolved. Clan heads continued to exercise much local influence in the quarter even after some moved further inside the city into wealthier residential quarters like Sūq Sārūja in the last half of the nineteenth century.[17]

URBAN LEADERSHIP

The older quarters remained important focal points of social and political organization, despite various external pressures which broke through their self-contained and isolated structures. Moreover, each quarter tried to preserve its own personality during the Mandate. A typical older quarter had its own local leaders, including a *mukhtār* (headman, called *āghā* in some quarters), the *imāms* (prayer leaders) of the local mosque, and the *wujahā'* (notables) who were usually the quarter's wealthy landowners and merchants. Together they sat on the council of the quarter (*majlis al-ḥayy*) which acted as a mini-government to protect quarter residents from excessive state interference, to represent the quarter in disputes with other quarters, and to mediate internal conflicts. Often one of these traditional leaders could be found on the Municipal Council (*majlis al-baladī*) of Damascus. At the lower end of the quarter's social scale, community life revolved around kinship groups, religious associations, and street gangs.[18]

Protection from government agents was one of the most important services that secular and religious dignitaries rendered their neighbors, friends, and clients. During the Mandate, when tax collectors in Damascus made their rounds to investigate individuals who had not paid their head or property taxes, they were not only accompanied by a police officer but also by the *mukhtār* and the *imām* of the quarter. In fact, in certain quarters tax collectors were not allowed to conduct their investigations unless they secured the agreement of the *majlis al-ḥayy* or its leading notable beforehand. In the case of Sūq Midḥat Pāshā, which received protection from the militant Shāghūr quarter, custom dictated that tax collectors had to go to the home of the notable to request ('often beg for') a written introduction before entering the sūq. Without this document, the tax collector could conduct no official business there.[19]

During the Mandate, the older quarters also maintained informal *dīwāns* (councils) where local dignitaries met with delegations from all classes, communities, and interest groups to discuss the critical issues of the day. These *dīwāns* were usually held in the outer salons (*maḍāfa* or *salāmlik*) of the great residences of the quarter belonging to its wealthy landowning-bureaucratic and mercantile families. Such gatherings contributed far more than newspapers and other media to the formation and reinforcement of public opinion. Since the Mandate authorities frequently censored or suspended publication of newspapers and magazines, the *dīwān* served as a great storehouse of much fresher and more confidential information. Public political consciousness in the cities was advanced far beyond the level of education of the common people, who were largely illiterate and thus had little direct need for newspapers.[20]

The contribution of prominent families in the quarter to the political life of the city was considerable. They were instrumental in mobilizing local forces to protest and resist or to support the government. They organized public gatherings in squares, cafés, theaters, and gardens; circulated petitions; boycotted elections and also foreign concessions and goods; shut down the great bazaars; raised funds; disseminated political information; and gauged the pulse of the city for the 'beys' [*bēgawāt*] (the appellation given the nationalist leadership during the Mandate).[21] These notable families had traditionally played the role of patron and broker, intervening on behalf of their clients with the government or mediating their personal disputes. By offering services to their neighbors and friends, they guaranteed loyalty and support and, in return, created for themselves an advantageous stability in the quarter. Their access to the state depended on their ability and willingness to maintain the social peace, which in turn depended on the degree of their independent influence in local society. Patronage was the source of this independent influence.[22]

Because the population of Damascus nearly doubled in the two decades following the French occupation of Syria in 1920, the older quarters began to lose their intimacy and warmth, and their emotional support systems broke down. They became crowded and increasingly impersonal, owing to an unprecedented in-migration of peasants and tribes from outlying areas and to improved health conditions and facilities which lowered infant mortality rates.[23] The delicate balance of forces in the quarters and the positions of influence of the notable families was upset by the pressure of increased population. The great families found it increasingly difficult to absorb the growing number of newcomers to Damascus into their personal networks. Patronage became a more complex and competitive operation, which a number of the notable families could no longer manage satisfactorily. Feeling increasingly claustrophobic and threatened by the changing character of their quarters, especially their growing facelessness, some of the wealthier families in the old quarters left for the new garden suburbs to the town's northwest.[24]

Contributing to this flight during the Mandate was the widening social and cultural gulf between the modern educated and European-clad upper and upper-middle classes, which produced the urban leadership, and the largely unlettered and tradition-bound masses. The sweeping structural changes, initiated in the nineteenth century, helped to erode patronage systems, promoting instead an increasingly differentiated class structure. As class distinctions became more obvious, the wealthier and Europeanized classes found reason to distance themselves from the popular classes. One simple way was to move out of their ancestral quarters into the cleaner, safer, and more spacious areas on the outskirts of Damascus. Muslim notable families who linked their interests to the Mandate authorities or to European commercial enterprises were among the very first to leave. They could do so conveniently since their political influence was no longer dependent on building and maintaining patronage networks in the popular quarters.

A related factor precipitating this flight was the growing inadequacy of the ancestral courtyard house in the old quarter.[25] It became in time less able to accommodate the changes taking place in the structure and orientation of the upper-class family. In the course of two or three generations (that is, by the early twentieth century), the extended family or clan had developed its own distinct economic branches. Within the extended family, a hierarchy of power and influence became established and rival branches emerged.[26] Members of the wealthier branches preferred to move into their own homes, designed along European lines and reflecting the new patterns of social relations between the sexes and the generations. The availability of space in the gardens to the northwest of the city proved to be ideally suited to their needs. Moreover, improved technology brought new advantages for the privileged, such as running water and other sanitary devices which could not easily be installed in older homes. At the same time, paved roads and motorized vehicles brought the city-center within reasonable reach of outlying areas.

Not all wealthy families found it convenient to make such a move. The landed families who already owned the garden districts, which were to become modern Damascus, had a distinct advantage and interest in doing so. But an important determinant was the source of a family's wealth. Many could meet the financial demands of moving but were unable to leave because of the source of their livelihood. For instance, merchants whose enterprises depended on their daily presence in the city-center could not risk such a move. By contrast, families who lived off of farm or urban real estate rents (and who thus had much less of a need to be in daily contact with the old commercial center of the city) could more easily afford the comforts of suburban life. Merchants in traditional businesses not directly linked to European commercial interests also tended to be those who had not acquired a modern education, Ottoman trappings, or European tastes, and who therefore were set apart from the absentee landowning-bureaucratic families that had served the Ottoman state as a provincial aristocracy of service.[27] Muslim merchant families tended to be more tradition-bound and, hence, more quarter-bound. Meanwhile, a cosmopolitan, landed upper crust, with a new attitude toward property relations, and newly acquired European tastes in dress and creature comforts, encouraged intimate social relations only with the wealthiest and most sophisticated merchant families, and increasingly with members of a rising educated middle class. The exclusive social and cultural proclivities of the members of this class encouraged them to live together at a distance from the rest of urban society.[28]

By the mid-1930s, not only had several of the great families in regular collaboration with the French moved out of their ancestral quarters but eight of the ten principal nationalist leaders had also done so. Most had moved to the northwestern suburbs. Jamīl Mardam, the architect of nationalist strategy in the 1930s, had left the Sūq al-Ḥamīdiyya area where the Mardam-Beg palace was situated; Shukrī al-Quwwatlī and the only merchant in the Bloc leadership, Luṭfī al-Ḥaffār, had moved out of the popular Shāghūr quarter. Only Fakhrī al-Bārūdī and Nasīb al-Bakrī continued to be permanent fixtures in their quarters: Bārūdī in al-Qanawāt, which was still a very comfortable residential quarter and conveniently located for his many political and economic enterprises, and Bakrī in the old city, to better service his personal network, which consisted of popular quarter bosses and veterans of the Great Revolt of 1925.[29]

Unlike those notables who collaborated with the French, the most influential nationalist leaders were careful not to sever ties with the popular quarters. They retained large personal followings which cut across class and even confessional lines. However, their actual physical presence became more infrequent. At election time, on feasts, and at other commemorative occasions, such as the annual Maysalūn memorial or the Prophet's birthday, Jamīl Mardam and Shukrī al-Quwwatlī could always be seen amongst the common people in the old quarters, where they opened the outer salons of their spacious family residences to supporters and well-wishers. Nationalist chiefs always listed their ancestral quarters as permanent residences and in election primaries they ran on their quarter's list. Because their new suburban houses were inconveniently and sometimes inaccessibly located, it was necessary to maintain their traditional homes for social and political purposes.[30] On lesser occasions, nationalist chiefs were rarely present. Surprisingly, the task of organizing strikes, demonstrations, and nationalist rallies did not require their presence.

During the Mandate period, a growing division of labor developed within the independence movement, particularly after the failure of the Great Revolt, which was followed by the nationalist elite's decision to adopt the different but clearly more comfortable strategy of 'honorable cooperation' with the French. This strategy placed a greater emphasis on diplomacy, supported by carefully orchestrated strikes, boycotts, and demonstrations which aimed to discredit rival factions of notables collaborating with the French High Commission and to convince the French that the nationalists alone should be invited to form a national government in Syria.

The collapse of the Great Revolt had discredited revolutionary armed struggle as a viable strategy. It not only heavily damaged the material interests of the nationalist elite but it caused massive hemorrhaging in the ranks. Afterwards, the nationalist leadership no longer sought immediately to overturn the French-controlled system of rule, but something rather less: the modification of the existing system and the gradual relaxation of French control. To survive, nationalists had to pursue more delicate relationships with the French. Meanwhile, the French High Commission, under pressure from Paris to develop a more consistent and hence less offensive imperial policy in Syria, welcomed and encouraged this new strategy.[31]

After the suppression of the Great Revolt in 1927, nationalist leaders in Syria's major cities organized themselves into a new political organization, the National Bloc (*al-Kutla al-Waṭaniyya*). In each town, the Bloc was not a unified or well-integrated political party but rather was an alliance of like-minded urban political leaders, each heading an autonomous machine which was used in the common cause of national independence.[32] During the Mandate, a combination of elements drawn from the traditional and modern sectors of urban society powered these political machines. Although the lines between the traditional and modern sectors were often blurred because urban society was still evolving gradually and unevenly, one distinction was clear: the support of the traditional sectors of society stemmed less from ideological considerations than did the support of the modern sectors. In his own quarter, the Bloc chief built and reinforced his personal network by using his inherited wealth and family connections to funnel crucial benefits and services to a broad array of individuals from classes beneath his own. Despite an ongoing process of class polarization and hence an increased opportunity for class conflict, society in the popular quarters was still organized according to relations of personal dependence. At the top of the social pyramid stood the great urban-absentee landowning families, such as Mardam-Beg, Al-Quwwatlī, Al-Bārūdī, Al-Bakrī, and Al-Ghazzī, from which the nationalist leadership of Damascus emerged and, in particular, the National Bloc, the most effective political alliance of the Mandate era.

As National Bloc chiefs became increasingly preoccupied with diplomatic bargaining at the summit of politics, they were obliged to leave the day-to-day task of organizing and maintaining their patronage systems to members of their families, personal secretaries, and other prominent personalities in their political orbit. In other words, as Bloc leaders began to distance themselves socially and physically from the city-center, they turned to other intermediaries who could more conveniently maintain face-to-face contacts and purvey the material benefits and services which buttressed each leader's personal network. Prominent merchants and religious leaders in the quarters were two such natural intermediaries.

Merchants and *imāms* in the popular quarters supported the National Bloc for a variety of reasons, but mainly because they perceived foreign rule as the primary cause of their seemingly endless misfortunes. The French-imposed banking and tax systems were inimical to the financial interests of the Muslim commercial bourgeoisie. The partition of greater Syria severely damaged commerce and industry, and the French were either unwilling or unable to permit merchants and industrialists to have access to foreign capital, giving them few investment outlets. Many, although by no means all,[33] saw the French as robbers of Syria's national wealth and the major obstacle to economic development. At the same time, the upper layers of the Muslim commercial bourgeoisie were closely intertwined with the absentee landowning class in the Syrian capital from which the major National Bloc leaders emerged. They maintained social and financial relations through marriage and joint ventures. Merchants provided loans to landowners and often handled the distribution of their crops. They generally responded promptly to the Bloc's call for strikes and boycotts. The new strategy developed by the Bloc in the wake of the Great Revolt, with its emphasis on patient diplomacy, appealed to a commercial bourgeoisie that had suffered considerable financial misfortune during the Revolt and therefore feared continued political instability. The merchant classes had reason to support the Bloc's new tactics. The Bloc would not resort to violent confrontations or full-scale rebellion again, unless the French proved completely intransigent and purposely closed off all access to the High Commission. However, although merchant families supported the National Bloc with funds and their own personal networks of artisans, small shopowners, and peddlers in the quarters and bazaars, rarely did they become official members of the Bloc or of any other nationalist organization. Their participation in nationalist politics came about through their personal association with individual nationalist leaders.[34]

Muslim religious leaders in Damascus, a number of whom belonged to mercantile families, were also of invaluable service to the nationalist movement. In general, the religious establishment's interests and influence had been declining for several generations, owing to increased government control over their institutions and a much altered intellectual climate. Traditional ideas—historically the monopoly of the *'ulamā'*—began to lose their influence with the educated elites, and the traditional activities of the *'ulamā'*, as interpreters of the law, educators, and heads of the mystic orders, declined in social value. Less and less significance came to be attached to posts in the religious institutions whereas greater wealth, power, and status accrued to those individuals in the new, modern branches of administration, and from large-scale landownership. This is not to suggest that religious solidarity among the Arabs had vanished; it still existed alongside other loyalties to family, tribe, ethnic and confessional group, neighborhood, and village. But all these ties had been challenged by the rise of new loyalties, such as the rise of secular nationalism, that had accompanied the general structural changes begun in the nineteenth century.[35] Religious leaders suffered further humiliations under the French, who, as a Christian power, tried to impose direct supervision over such religious institutions as the *awqāf* (pious trusts), which often provided a major portion of their incomes. Equally damaging to their interests was the French effort to denigrate the influence of Islam by relegating it to the status of one religion among many. A beleaguered religious establishment, ranging from ranking legal scholars and judges to preachers in the local mosques, supported the resistance to foreign hegemony in Syria.

Although the influence of religion and the status of religious leaders had declined, these individuals had not lost their ability to shape public opinion among the illiterate and the uneducated in the popular quarters. For most urbanites, the mosque and *masjid* continued to be the central institution in their lives, giving preachers the opportunity to argue for resistance to the French and defense of traditional society in religious terms. To the common people, nationalism was still only a code word for the defense of Islam against foreign aggression, despite ongoing efforts by secular nationalists, including the National Bloc leadership, to dilute the Islamic content of nationalist ideology. As long as Islam had a grip on the minds of the common people, religious leaders were able to reinforce their own positions as guardians of the faith and the culture, if not of the nation.[36]

Although wealthy merchants and *imāms* recruited clients, financed various nationalist activities, and helped to organize their quarters and the bazaars on a political footing, neither group was able to pose a challenge to the National Bloc's control over nationalism or its domination of local politics during the Mandate. Whereas merchants and *imāms* remained bound up in the closeness of quarter life, the marketplace, and the mosque, having little or no opportunity to break out of this restrictive environment, the nationalist leadership was able to devote its undivided attention to politics on a grander scale. Because many nationalist chiefs could live off land rents collected by their families, they had little need to seek full-time employment. It was during the Mandate that a class of professional politicians arose in Damascus and other Syrian towns. Hailing from affluent families, with a long history of administrative service and with a common upbringing, education, and set of political experiences, the nationalist elite was eminently (and almost exclusively) qualified to represent Damascus at the summit of politics. Therefore, as long as urban society continued to regard these individuals as the 'natural' leaders of the opposition to the French, they could expect the continued support of merchants and the religious establishment.

Merchants and *imāms* enhanced their personal status by associating with nationalist chiefs. But this enhancement alone was not sufficient to ensure their long-term loyalty. It was also expected that once a nationalist leader reached the heights of government, he would reward his followers. Hence, allegiance might be offered with the knowledge that returns in the form of government contracts, licenses, jobs in the central administration and municipality, new mosques, paved roads, sewage systems, and other facilities might be in the offing in the long run.

There was fierce competition among nationalists for access to the French. Only this access would give a leader control of government offices and services—the most valuable form of patronage. Competition for clientele networks was equally fierce, for only those networks could prove a leader's local power and indispensability to the French. Competition in both arenas was closely intertwined; success in one depended on success in the other.

QABAḌĀYĀT

One figure in the quarters who could give the nationalist leader a decisive edge in competition for clientele during the Mandate was the local gang leader, the *qabaḍāy* (pl. *qabaḍāyāt*), or, in the patois of Damascus, the *zgritī*.[37]

Probably no individual with independent influence in the quarters was closer to the common man than was the *qabaḍāy*. He was something akin to an institution. Each quarter had its own set of historical figures who were glorified from one generation to the next. In time, an ideal type was formed, one that characterized the *qabaḍāy* as strong, honorable, the protector of the feeble and the poor as well as of the religious minorities, the upholder of Arab traditions and customs, and the guardian of popular culture. He was hospitable to strangers, always pious, and a clean liver.[38] This image placed far less emphasis on the *qabaḍāy*'s darker side, his shady dealings, his preference for physical coercion, and even his 'mortal' crimes for personal gain. The common people clearly differentiated between the *qabaḍāyāt* and the *zuʿrān* or hoodlums who ran protection rackets (*khūwa*) in the quarters and bazaars, although in reality such distinctions were hazy.[39]

A *qabaḍāy* might eventually become fairly well-to-do, but what distinguished him from the dignitaries of the quarter were his significantly lower social origins, his general want of formal education, his outspoken preference for traditional attire and customs, and the much narrower range of his interests and contacts, all of which accorded him a less exalted status than that enjoyed by merchants or religious leaders.[40] He survived best in the traditional milieu of the self-contained quarter with its inwardness and narrowly defined interests. There he was needed to provide physical protection from hostile external forces and extra-legal mechanisms for settling personal disputes. But, by the time of the Mandate, the *qabaḍāy* had begun to feel threatened by the pressures of change created by rapid urbanization, the growth of a market-oriented economy, and the rise of new classes and institutions outside the popular quarters. This period was a transitional phase in the life of the Syrian city, and in the organization and functions of its quarters; the *qabaḍāy* survived it, although not without difficulty.

A *qabaḍāy* might rise to leadership in the quarter by several different paths, and it is difficult to separate myth from reality when tracing the emergence of any particular strongman. It is, however, possible to trace the career of at least one prominent *qabaḍāy* of the Mandate period in Damascus, his links to the National Bloc, and his contribution to the independence movement.

Abū ʿAlī al-Kilāwī [al-Gilāwī][41] claims to have been born in 1897, in Bāb al-Jābiyya, an old popular quarter situated near the entrance to Sūq Midḥat Pāshā and which included the charming Mosque of Sinān Pāshā. The origins of the Kilāwī family are obscure. They seem to have first settled in al-Maydān some time in the early nineteenth century where they were engaged in the transport of wheat from their native Hawran to flour mills in al-Maydān. They may have belonged to one of the tributaries of the Rwala Beduin who roamed with the Rwala chieftains of Al-Shaʿlān before the Mandate.[42] The Kilāwīs also claimed descent from Abū Bakr, the Prophet's companion and first Caliph, and billed themselves as members of the *ashrāf* (descendants of the Prophet), although the great religious families of Damascus did not recognize their claim. According to Abū ʿAlī, the family's surname had originally been al-Bakrī until the end of the nineteenth century. When his father died unexpectedly, the family dropped al-Bakrī for some inexplicable reason and adopted instead the surname of Abū ʿAli's maternal grandfather. During the Mandate, the Kilāwīs were not regarded as members of the aristocratic al-Bakrī family of Damascus; however, they were very partial to the Bakrīs and especially close to Nasīb Bey of the National Bloc.[43]

Abū ʿAlī had two older brothers. He happened to be much closer to the oldest, Abū Ḥasan, who assumed the leadership of the family upon their father's death, and under whose wing Abū ʿAlī grew up learning the ways of the quarter. Abū ʿAlī attributes his rise to the status of a *qabaḍāy* to several factors, all of which suggest that he did not inherit the title. One factor was his own physical strength, which he displayed early in life despite his slight build. The youth of Bāb al-Jābiyya and other quarters engaged in different forms of informal competition which helped lay the groundwork for the rise of a *qabaḍāy*. Abū ʿAlī, for example, excelled in wrestling (*muṣāraʿa*). To the beat of two drums, the youth of the quarter would congregate in an open field or garden where wrestling matches were staged between boys dressed in leather shorts worn above britches. By the age of sixteen, Abū ʿAlī was reputed to be the best wrestler in his quarter.[44]

By this age, the youth of the quarter had already begun to practise the martial arts and in particular swordsmanship. Wielding a long, silver-handled sword in one hand and a small metal shield (*turs*) in the other, two young men would face each other, twirling their swords through different orbits over and around their heads while interspersing blows against their own shields and those of their opponents in a complicated cadence.[45] The boy who could handle his sword most adeptly and innovatively advanced in the competition, and the best five or six contestants were asked to form a troupe. This troupe would then have the honor of performing on all festive occasions in the quarter, such as weddings and the Prophet's birthday.[46] In his day, Abū ʿAlī was the leader of such a troupe of swordsmen and from it he began to build his own personal following.

Horsemanship was Abū ʿAlī's other forte. After their father's death, his brother, Abū Ḥasan, used his family's relations with the beduin tribes south of Damascus to convert the Kilāwī transport business into a horse-breeding and trading concern. The center for their new activities was a small stud farm which the family owned just south of al-Maydān. In time, the Kilāwīs became renowned horse-dealers throughout the Arab East, purveying purebred show animals and racehorses to the royal families of Transjordan and Saudi Arabia, and to other Arab dignitaries. By the time he was twenty, Abū ʿAlī was considered to be the best horseman in his quarter, a reputation which soon spread throughout Damascus and the rest of Syria. By the mid-1930s, the Kilāwī stable of show horses had become an attraction at all national parades, and Abū ʿAlī always rode at the head.[47]

Successful business enterprises helped to vault the Kilāwī family into the social limelight of Bāb al-Jābiyya. Neighbors began to ask for favors or assistance and in no time they built up a solid core of followers and clients from among the poorer elements of the quarter, some of whom were personally loyal to Abū ʿAlī. The result was that Abū ʿAlī was able to put together his own gang, composed mainly of unemployed youth and casual laborers.

In the early 1920s, as the Kilāwīs began to accumulate capital, they were able to purchase a fairly large apartment in the heart of their quarter, one with a special salon for entertaining. This salon also was used as an informal courtroom where the Kilāwīs, now much trusted in Bāb al-Jābiyya, served as administrators of extra-legal justice, arbitrating or mediating disputes between individuals and families who for one reason or another were not comfortable going before the religious or civil courts. The Kilāwīs also lent their salon to poorer families for wedding parties and other social functions, and it eventually became one of the meeting places of the roving *dīwān*. Abū 'Alī claimed that he and his brothers never asked for money or other material rewards for their hospitality and services. But they did expect personal loyalty to the family, which they acquired as the Kilāwī network grew and the family name came to be mentioned with both reverence and fear.

One of the most prominent features of urban life in Damascus was the *'arāda* or traditional parades held in the quarters to celebrate some religious event such as a circumcision, the return of the pilgrimage, or the Prophet's birthday. These occasions allowed the youth of one quarter to compete with the youth of neighboring quarters in wrestling matches, sword games, horseracing, and the like. The honor of the quarter was always at stake in these events, as were specific controversies over turf and freedom of movement. Certain quarters were known to be long-standing rivals, most notably Sūq Sārūja and al-Ṣālhiyya,[48] and Shāghūr and Bāb al-Jābiyya. Yet another way in which Abū 'Alī al-Kilāwī reinforced his status in the quarter was to lead his stalwarts in street fights against rival gangs of Shāghūr.

By the early twentieth century, however, the parades had begun to assume secular dimensions as they came to mark political events such as the election of a deputy, the return of an exile, the Young Turk revolt of 1908, or the Italian invasion of Libya in 1911.[49] This politicization accelerated during the Mandate, and acts of defiance against the French and their collaborators highlighted the continued independence of life in the quarters. But, equally important, as political consciousness rose in the quarters, the fierce rivalries between them were transformed into an alliance of quarters against the French. The narrowness and insularity of quarter life began to break down as the scope for political activity widened.

The Great Revolt of 1925 hastened the erosion of many of the traditional social and political barriers and rivalries between quarters and helped to bind them together in a common front against the French. There is little doubt that the many stories of individual heroism which quickly became part of the local history and mythology of the Revolt helped many a young man to enhance his reputation in the popular quarters of the city, enabling him to achieve the status of *qabaḍāy*. In fact, there was a noticeable turnover of *qabaḍāyāt* at this time, owing to the emergence of new heroes during the Revolt who replaced those who had been killed. Probably the most respected and esteemed *qabaḍāy* of his day was Ḥasan al-Kharrāṭ, the nightwatchman of Shāghūr, who led a rebel attack on French positions in the Syrian capital and was later killed by French troops.[50] His elimination permitted another rising star of the Revolt, Maḥmūd Khaddām al-Srīja, to assert himself as the undisputed strongman of Shāghūr.

Abū ʿAlī al-Kilāwī frankly admitted fifty years after his own participation in the Great Revolt that it also enabled his family to consolidate their position as the *qabaḍāyāt* par excellence of Bāb al-Jābiyya.[51] When the Revolt erupted, the Kilāwīs and their armed gang prepared their quarter for insurrection against the French. Abū ʿAlī joined the rebel band of Nasīb al-Bakrī, whose family had patronized the Kilāwīs for some time. After the French regained control of most of Damascus in October, Abū ʿAlī followed Bakrī's forces into the gardens around the Syrian capital. One particular episode at this time contributed to his immortalization in the minds of future generations. Seriously wounded in a single-handed attempt to liberate his rebel comrades imprisoned in the Citadel of Damascus, he managed to flee on horseback, taking refuge among his traditional enemies in Shāghūr. Two days later, a weak but determined Abū ʿAlī al-Kilāwī recruited some young men of Shāghūr and rode back with them to Bāb al-Jābiyya, where he rounded up more followers and returned to the Ghūṭa to rejoin the Bakrī band.[52]

Like the great merchants and the *imāms* of the local mosques, the *qabaḍāyāt* rarely joined the National Bloc or any other political organization. Rather, their affiliation and loyalty was to one or another of the Bloc chiefs. Abū ʿAlī al-Kilāwī's allegiance was to Nasīb al-Bakrī not to the Bloc's executive council.

The *qabaḍāyāt* were typically more important to a nationalist leader's political machine in the quarters than were the merchants or religious figures. The Bloc chief's resources were limited, especially when in and out of jail or in temporary exile; therefore the recruitment and maintenance of his clientele required considerable finesse. He generally preferred to devote his personal attention to winning and sustaining followings among the wealthier families of the quarters; and, with these he made certain that he was able to maintain regular personal contacts at all times. When the National Bloc chief began to distance himself from his ancestral quarter, he had to depend more heavily on intermediaries to dispense favors and services to the larger mass of poorer residents with whom he probably never came into direct contact. Merchants, whose status was based on wealth, philanthropy, and religious piety, were among those intermediaries who assumed this function for the politicians. But as class differentiation evolved during the Mandate, merchants increasingly began to take less and less interest in the poor and their individual problems. They neither found ample time for, nor were they well-disposed toward, the poor. Philanthropy, after all, did not require regular contact with the lower classes. Some members of the Muslim religious establishment also placed a greater distance between themselves and the common people. Others, however, including preachers in the popular quarters, actually strengthened their influence among the destitute and the illiterate. Although leading religious dignitaries and lower-ranking *imāms* generally supported the nationalist chiefs, they also formed benevolent societies (*jam'iyyāt*) which assumed a militant anti-western and anti-secular political character by the mid-1930s and which eventually posed an unwelcome challenge to the authority of the nationalist leadership in the quarters.[53]

The *qabaḍāy*, in contrast, posed no such threat. He hailed from the common people, was under the protection of the *bey*, was often indebted to him for loans and services, and, in any case, lacked the education, status, and statesman-like qualities to reach the *bey*'s level of political leadership. Thus, while the National Bloc leader, assisted by his personal secretary and family, policed the core of his patronage network, the *qabaḍāy* looked after its periphery, servicing it directly whenever possible and guaranteeing its support when the *bey* required it.[54]

Although some *qabaḍāyāt* were able to attract their own personal followings by performing such services as the mediation of disputes, the protection of the neighborhood, and small philanthropic activities, they had neither direct control nor access to large material resource bases which might have allowed them to build their own independent patronage networks. In the final analysis, they were beholden to the politicians in many of the same ways that other clients were. The only significant difference was that the *qabaḍāy*'s apparatus for recruiting and policing his *bey*'s clientele gave him direct access to the *bey*'s immediate entourage, in particular to his personal secretary. In this way, the *qabaḍāy* could count on preferential treatment and a few more privileges than could the average client on the periphery of the *bey*'s network.[55] Although the scope for social mobility was not wide, a number of *qabaḍāyat* managed to enrich themselves through connections with their patrons.

At any given time the residents of a quarter might refer to several individuals as *qabaḍāyāt*. A quarter could support more than one strongman, although it was not uncommon to associate the *qabaḍāyāt* with a single family. Residents of Bāb al-Jābiyya referred to '*wilād* al-Kilāwī' (the sons of al-Kilāwī) as frequently as they did to any one member of the family. It was the family, through its connections, which provided protection and assistance to the quarter. Abū 'Alī did make a name for himself in particular as the family rabble-rouser, the gifted equestrian, and the local enforcer. But he frankly admitted that his oldest brother, who had some education, made the family's major decisions, ran its business, and dealt with the National Bloc politicians and their deputies. Abū 'Alī was in effect Abū Ḥasan's lieutenant, prepared to execute his commands. When Abū Ḥasan died, the leadership of the Kilāwī family passed to Abū 'Alī (his other brother was regarded as a high-liver and a playboy, which disqualified him), who had already begun to educate his eldest son to fill the role of family lieutenant.[56]

Part of the mythology surrounding the *qabaḍāy* was that he never took money from politicians or their secretaries, or from merchants in the quarter for carrying out various instructions, such as mobilizing the youth of the quarter to demonstrate or enforcing a strike or boycott. Abū ʿAlī admitted that the Bloc offered him money at various times and cited several attempts by merchants close to the Bloc to pay him to keep the General Strike of 1936 going.[57] Defending the ideal image of a *qabaḍāy*, he also claimed that to accept such offerings ran against his honor. He did not deny, however, that some *qabaḍāyāt* broke this code of personal honor and morality by accepting cash and other benefits for merely fulfilling their duties. For example, after the National Bloc took office in 1936, in the wake of the general strike and the Franco-Syrian treaty negotiations in Paris, Shukrī al-Quwwatlī, the Minister of Finance and the National Defense, saw to it that Maḥmūd Khaddām al-Srīja, probably the most renowned *qabaḍāy* of the 1930s in Damascus, received a regular stipend from a *waqf* originally designated for the poor in his native Shāghūr for services to al-Quwwatlī, the leading politician of that quarter.[58]

Given the combination of resources which fed any Bloc chief's political machine, the support that these leaders received from the quarters was uneven. A politician like Nasīb al-Bakrī was extremely well-connected to numerous *qabaḍāyāt* like the Kilāwīs, the Dīb al-Shaykh family of the ʿAmāra quarter, and to other veterans of the Great Revolt in which Bakrī featured so prominently. Bakrī, who cut a much more socially and religiously conservative figure than did his more cosmopolitan Bloc comrades, and who had the religious prestige of his family behind him, moved easily among the tradition-bound masses of the popular quarters. By contrast, Shukrī al-Quwwatlī, Jamīl Mardam, and Fakhrī al-Bārūdī (the other major Bloc figures in Damascus) were all extremely influential in their respective quarters and particularly with merchants, but could not claim large personal followings in other quarters, despite the respect they commanded. Unlike Bakrī, however, they serviced much more diversified political machines: each had a significant following in the modern sectors and institutions of Damascus, especially among the educated youth and emerging middle classes.[59]

No National Bloc chief could claim to have considerable influence in the two popular quarters on the periphery of Damascus, Ḥayy al-Akrād and al-Maydān. In the Kurdish quarter, where clan loyalties persisted, the great Kurdish families of Al-Yūsuf and Shamdīn still held sway. Although Arabized in the course of the nineteenth century, they were never particularly well-disposed toward Arab nationalism, which threatened to erode the ethnic and clan loyalties on which their influence was in part based. Furthermore, the role that Kurdish auxiliary troops had played in suppressing the Great Revolt strained relations between nationalists and the Kurds of Damascus for the duration of the Mandate.[60]

In the long, narrow, socially heterogeneous al-Maydān to the city's south, the Bloc's problems were of a different order and magnitude. There, the social tensions and dislocations produced by the unsettling effects of increasing in-migration kept political power fragmented. Although the Maydān, unlike Ḥayy al-Akrād, contributed heavily in blood and sweat to the cause of independence (the French bombarded it from the air twice during the Great Revolt, nearly destroying the entire quarter), those al-Maydānī families who could claim influence were never closely linked to the National Bloc. Some, like the great merchant *āghāwāt* of Sukkar and al-Mahaynī, assisted the Bloc only when they wanted to and were not intimately tied to any Bloc chief's political machine. Others, like the Ḥakīm family, opposed the National Bloc, supporting its major rival faction headed by Dr ʿAbd al-Raḥmān Shahbandar, the recognized leader of the Great Revolt.[61]

Although there is no single explanation for why the Maydān evaded the influence of the National Bloc, the Bloc was clearly ill-equipped to mitigate the Maydān's social contradictions, to ameliorate its poverty, general squalor, and unsettledness, and hence to integrate and organize its population for political action. This left the area vulnerable to politicization by more socially conscious forces, ranging from Muslim benevolent societies to modern radical political organizations like the Communist and Baʿth parties, which could better provide a suitable and effective framework for integration. In a wider context, the rapid pace of urbanization during the Mandate was not accompanied by the kind of industrialization that could have provided this growing pool of unskilled labor with jobs which would have brought it under some form of social and political control.[62]

BEYOND THE QUARTERS

Although the popular quarters remained important units of political and social organization as their internal structures and interrelations changed during the Mandate, their importance to the independence movement declined. The advancement of urban political life had produced new focal points outside the quarters. These were the modern institutions which, from their inception, were closely identified with the growth of a professional middle class whose fundamental interests lay beyond the quarters. The dominant sentiments of this class of lawyers, doctors, engineers, educators, journalists, and other members of the intelligentsia transcended the narrowness of quarter life; their primary loyalties were to the city, state, and the nation rather than to the family, clan, confessional group, or quarter.

The importance of the modern middle class to the development of the independence movement in Syria grew with time. Although it was intimately involved in the birth of the Arab nationalist movement in the last years of the

Ottoman Empire, and its members could be found in all secret nationalist societies before and during World War I, it really only began to have a significant impact on political life in the 1930s.[63] Many factors were behind its ascent at this time, all of which were connected to changes in the structure of Syrian society that had been occurring since late Ottoman times. But among the most important factors was the development of modern secular education, which only became available to social strata below the upper class during the Mandate period. The addition of the professional middle class to the ranks of the nationalist movement involved a generation of individuals who were younger than the leadership of the National Bloc. Moreover, this generation was not as tainted by the Ottoman experience and legacy, and it possessed a higher level of education than that of its elders in the Bloc.

The number of primary and secondary school students in government institutions nearly doubled between 1924 and 1934.[64] The Syrian University also expanded in this period, and opportunities opened for the brightest high school and university graduates to go to France on scholarships for advanced studies in a wide variety of fields (in particular, law, medicine, and teacher-training). All of these factors certainly played a role in broadening the horizons of the urban youth and in shifting the focus of their activities out of the quarters and into modern institutions and structures. This new focus, in turn, helped to supplant their traditional loyalties with new ones, most notably with nationalism. But although modern education paved the way for social mobility and afforded middle-class status, it did not necessarily guarantee middle-class incomes. Rising but unfulfilled expectations created a vast reservoir of frustration and antagonism which the Syrian nationalist leadership had to channel to its own ends. Otherwise, it stood to sacrifice its potential influence in what was rapidly becoming the most dynamic sector of Syrian society. The National Bloc also recognized that the new educated cadres were in need of leaders with whom they could identify socially, culturally, and intellectually. Traditionally educated and attired merchants and religious leaders, and the semi-literate *qabaḍāyāt* of the popular quarters, were bound to be ineffective as role models for the rising middle classes. A new set of leaders, more closely attuned to their needs and conscious of their aspirations, had to emerge to service the educated youth.

The National Bloc discovered early on that the major source of disaffected, educated youth in Damascus (and in other cities) was the expanding government school system. There, already grouped together, were thousands of students being inculcated daily with patriotic ideals by Syrian instructors and, as a result, drifting away from the influence of the traditional quarters with their increasingly archaic and outmoded social and cultural norms. School life temporarily freed these young people from the entanglements of family obligations and careers.[65] Their growing political awareness coupled with their youthful lack of inhibitions could be translated into major support for the National Bloc. All that was wanting was some force to harness their unbridled energy.

Not long after its establishment, the National Bloc began to turn its attention to developing a youth wing from among high school and university students. In 1929, such an organization was born—the Nationalist Youth (*al-Shabāb al-Waṭanī*). As was often the case with the more innovative National Bloc projects, the propelling force behind the Nationalist Youth was Fakhrī al-Bārūdī. His interest in the educated young stemmed from several sources. His own fairly broad intellectual interests in literature, the arts, and Arabic music enabled him to stay in close touch with the main intellectual currents and fashions that attracted the young between the wars. His personal inheritance, which included large revenues from his family's farms around Damascus, allowed him to offer patronage to young talented journalists, poets, and musicians whom he encouraged to frequent his large home in al-Qanawāt. It is not surprising that he preferred to spend much of his time cultivating the young, the educated, and the talented instead of building relations with *qabaḍāyāt* as did his cousin and major rival in the National Bloc, Nasīb al-Bakrī. Bārūdī was neither as conservative nor as rigid as Bakrī, and, although conscious of Arab traditions, he was much more discriminating in his choice of those he emphasized. He was clearly a politician with a vision of the future as well as one of the past.[66]

In addition, Bārūdī's immediate environment conditioned his decision to cultivate the educated youth. Al-Qanawāt was largely populated by upper- and upper-middle-class Muslim families like his own who afforded their children the best local education available in Arabic. It seems that Bārūdī was impressed by the youth of his quarter and especially by their social and political awareness. He held out great hope for the coming generation of leaders. But he also felt that it was incumbent upon his generation to develop the talents and direct the energies of the young and educated who were forced to grow up in a tension-ridden and unsettling era of foreign dominion. For Bārūdī, the National Bloc had a very important role to play alongside the educational system in developing and refining the national consciousness of Syrian youth.

Immediately after the Great Revolt, Bārūdī began to devote greater attention to the problem of forming a youth organization affiliated to the National Bloc. Meanwhile, efforts to mobilize students in the government schools were already underway, especially at the *tajhīz*, the major government preparatory school in Damascus.[67] The central figure in this activity was Maḥmūd al-Bayrūtī, a man in his late twenties who had already acquired a reputation in Damascus for leading several important demonstrations and strikes, always with a small personal following of elementary- and high-school students at his side.

Bayrūtī, the son of a low-ranking functionary in the Damascus municipality (*al-baladiyya*) from Sūq Sārūja, was born in 1903. He belonged to a new generation of nationalists. From an early age, he aspired to a military career and, on completing his primary education, he enrolled at the War College (*al-Kulliyya al-Ḥarbiyya*), graduating just before the French occupation in 1920. Although qualified to become a second lieutenant, Bayrūtī, was unwilling to cooperate with French military authorities. Instead, he joined a group of school chums in secret political activities against the French which were soon uncovered. To avoid arrest, Bayrūtī, took refuge in Amman, where he tried to become an officer in Amīr ʿAbdullah's army, only to discover that his political record in Damascus and his want of proper connections disqualified him. Fortunately, he was able to return home after the French granted their first general amnesty in 1921. By now, Bayrūtī, had developed a fairly high degree of political consciousness which he ascribed to his career setbacks and to the patriotic ideals instilled in him by his instructor at the War College, Nuzhat al-Mamlūk, an Istanbul-trained army officer who was to play a key role in organizing the National Bloc's paramilitary wing in the mid-1930s.[68]

Like other young men of his generation whose dreams had been shattered by the political convulsions rocking Syria, Maḥmūd al-Bayrūtī expressed deep disappointment over the lack of effective political leadership in Damascus. His hopes were temporarily raised by the founding of the nationalist Iron Hand Society in 1922, under the command of Dr Shahbandar. But these too were dashed later in the same year when the French broke up the Iron Hand organization and arrested and eventually exiled its leadership. He was among the many young men who spent the next two years interned with the nationalist leadership. After his release, Bayrūtī, decided to resume his education and enrolled at the Damascus Law Faculty, but the outbreak of the Great Revolt in 1925 disrupted his education. His participation in the Revolt led to a brief stint in prison. Disappointed by the outcome of the Revolt, he decided not to resume his studies and opted for a career in commerce. With a small family stake he established a novelties store on rue Rāmī in the immediate proximity of the Sérail (French High Commission headquarters) and Marjé Square. His store could not have been more conveniently located; most nationalist manifestations during the Mandate focused on the Sérail. To attract students, Bayrūtī added a small library on the second floor of his shop, and in no time it became a popular place in which to congregate. Its location beyond the quarters also afforded youngsters a certain degree of freedom from the watchful eye of the family, from traditional religious figures, and from *qabaḍāyāt*.

Eventually Bayrūtī began to encourage small groups of students to gather at his store after school where they met older students from the university, especially the Law Faculty. They listened to discussions of critical political issues, talked over common problems, and read newspapers and the regular decrees of the High Commissioner. At these gatherings and, under Bayrūtī's guidance, various courses of political action were plotted. By the late 1920s his shop had become a springboard for student demonstrations. With the Sérail nearby, protesters did not have to go far to make their opinions heard.

As his following increased with each political activity born on the rue Rāmī, Bayrūtī felt a greater need to offer his students some regimentation. Impressed by the *esprit de corps* of the one Boy Scout troop in Damascus, the Ghūṭa Scouts, but unhappy that its leaders refused to engage the troop in political activities, Bayrūtī and a young activist medical student from al-Maydān, Midḥat al-Bīṭār, formed their own Umayyad Scouts in early 1929. Many of the young visitors to his store became the troop's first members.

News of this development delighted Fakhrī al-Bārūdī, who had already begun to hear good things about Bayrūtī's activities with students; especially pleasing was Bayrūtī's willingness to politicize the Boy Scout movement. Soon thereafter, Bārūdī began to extend personal invitations to Bayrūtī and his followers through one of his minions, a young law student from al-Qanawāt, Khālid al-Shiliq. Bayrūtī quickly developed a warm relationship with Bārūdī and began to reap the benefits of his patronage. At Bārūdī's encouragement, Maḥmūd al-Bayrūtī, assisted by Khālid al-Shiliq, established the Nationalist Youth before the end of the decade, putting it under the direct responsibility of the National Bloc.[69]

Maḥmūd al-Bayrūtī, who visibly prospered through his National Bloc connection, virtually monopolized the leadership of the Nationalist Youth in Damascus until the mid-1930s, when his Bloc patrons decided that his organization desperately needed a new, more attractive face. Already, rival political organizations led by a rising generation of radical nationalists were bidding for the increasingly critical student population in Damascus and other towns. Bayrūtī was ill-equipped for the intensifying competition. He had performed an important service, but the National Bloc had to provide a more authentic role model for the educated youth if it intended to retain its grip on the independence movement, especially after the Bloc gained control of government in the late 1930s and was more subject to criticism from rival nationalist organizations.[70] It therefore became necessary to turn to a group of articulate, young, European-schooled lawyers, doctors, and engineers for the critical task ahead.

Despite his comparatively limited education, and a certain roughness around the edges, Maḥmūd al-Bayrūtī lived and operated in a social and political milieu more akin to that of the National Bloc leadership than that of a *qabaḍāy* like Abū ʿAlī al-Kilāwī. Clad in European clothes and proudly sporting the fez of the *effendi* class of politicians and bureaucrats, he was literate and ideologically motivated. With a political base outside the popular quarters among the young educated elites, Bayrūtī was an early representative of the forces of political modernization in Syria which had begun to shift the center of political life out of the popular quarters and into new, more sophisticated institutions and structures such as the government schools, the university, and various youth organizations. Unlike Abū ʿAlī and other *qabaḍāyāt*, Bayrūtī was a 'party man,' a title he revered but one that Abū ʿAlī clearly did not respect.

Both men held each other in low esteem. Bayrūtī saw Abū ʿAlī as a relic, an obstacle to progress, whereas Abū ʿAlī saw Bayrūtī as a party hack, a man whose highest commitment was to his organization, not to the common people.[71] Interestingly, as other youth leaders began to eclipse Bayrūtī in importance, he became more dependent on individual Bloc chiefs, especially Jamīl Mardam, for his patronage and, in this sense, began to resemble the *qabaḍāy*. Yet he remained closely linked to and identified by the Bloc organization which he continued to serve. Although his age and lower social origins prevented him from joining the Bloc's inner political circle or participating in critical strategy sessions, he nevertheless operated on a higher political level than did any *qabaḍāy* and was duly accorded greater recognition from his Bloc mentors. Like the *qabaḍāy*, he served as an intermediary, but more for the Bloc organization than for any single Bloc leader. Unlike the *qabaḍāy*, his base of operations was fundamentally outside the popular quarters among the educated elites. Consequently, he worked in a milieu that ultimately proved to be more important to the future of the Syrian national independence movement and to urban politics in general.

CONCLUSION: TOWARD THE END OF AN ERA

The Mandate years were a critical transitional phase for urban political life in Syria. Rapid population growth, an inflated cost of living, the spread of agrarian commercialization, the accelerated collapse of traditional industries and the retarded development of new ones, the growing polarization of class forces, and the shaping of a new intellectual climate contributed to a rearrangement of social and political forces in Damascus and in other cities. Physical and psychological barriers between the older residential quarters began to break down. In some instances, the walls separating the quarters literally came tumbling down, as during the Great Revolt, when the French bombarded a large area in the old city (al-Ḥarīqa) and large sections of al-Maydān.[72] The political realities of life under an 'illegitimate' and capricious foreign ruler elevated the political awareness of the common people. It also allowed the urban leadership of Damascus to divert the attention of the popular quarters away from their traditional rivalries and new class conflicts by channeling their competitive energies toward the goal of national independence. In aligning together, quarters contributed to the growing complexity and scale of urban politics.

The focus of political activity moved, however, outside the quarters altogether, to French High Commission headquarters and to other symbols of foreign control and influence, from the foreign-owned concessions to French cultural centers.[73] When individuals from the quarters marched they did so by quarter, chanting each quarter's traditional slogans and carrying its traditional banners, but they marched alongside men (and now women)[74] from other quarters, demonstrating for a common purpose. This was a new wrinkle in urban political life.

The *qabaḍāyāt* seemed to enjoy a new lease on life and a new importance in politics during the Mandate period. They remained an important component in the *beys*' political machines at a time when nationalist leaders required extraordinary support to remain in the political game orchestrated by the French. But, in fact, the *qabaḍāy* was merely enjoying a reprieve from political obsolescence. This could perhaps best be seen in the changing composition of the active forces demonstrating against the French and their local collaborators in the 1930s. Greater numbers of young men, organized by Boy Scout troop or by political affiliation, could be found at the head of these manifestations. Everything about them seemed different, from their secular slogans denouncing French imperialism and invoking pan-Arab unity, national liberation, and (by the end of the Mandate) even socialism, to their European dress and modern uniforms.[75] More and more such individuals belonged to the rising middle classes and hailed from the wealthier or new quarters of Damascus. But even those who did not, when they marched did so under the banner of their youth organization or school, and not with their quarter. Although the national independence movement, headed by the National Bloc, formed a set of broad alliances which linked together different elites, classes, and confessional groups, the dynamic element in the movement had become by the 1930s the new modern educated classes whose base and activities were beyond the older popular quarters and even the ancient commercial district.

This emerging generation of young men, who belonged to the professional middle class and who came from mercantile backgrounds, the old aristocracy of officials, or, increasingly from lower social origins, were inspired by ideologically advanced political organizations, which a number of them had witnessed during their student days in Europe in the 1920s and 1930s. On returning to Damascus and other cities they quickly grew impatient with the manner in which the popular classes were politically organized. They found the old-fashioned merchants, *imāms*, and, above all, the *qabaḍāyāt* to be out of step with the changing times and hence to be obstacles to progress. But the more radical of these young men also became impatient with the loose and shifting associations of the absentee landowners and wealthy merchants who in alignment formed the effective leadership of the independence movement. They were disturbed by many facets of the National Bloc's organization: the clubby atmosphere and the panoply of family ties and personal relations binding it together; the maintenance of individual followings and the lack of subordination to party will and policy; and, by the 1930s, the lapse of the most critical principle of the movement—Arab unity. These young men were discouraged by the Bloc's narrowly focused strategy whose principal aim was not liberation but rather patient negotiations with the French in the hope of gradually relaxing their control over Syria, all without upsetting the political status quo.

In such circumstances, it was not long before the National Bloc leadership found its control over urban politics and the independence movement threatened by these rising elites. In order to survive, nationalist leaders had to stay in step with the times. This meant adjusting not only to the changes taking place in the older quarters, but even more particularly to the new institutions and organizations of urban political life that had arisen alongside the quarters, creating in the process a new balance of local power. By the end of the Mandate era, to maintain control of the independence movement and of the reigning idea of nationalism required, above all, a concentration of attention and resources in these new areas. The traditional style and methods of urban politics had reluctantly but clearly begun to give way.

This article is reprinted from the *International Journal of Middle East Studies* 16 (1984), pp. 507–540. Reprinted with permission of Cambridge University Press.

NOTES

Author's note: Hanna Batatu, Richard M. Douglas, Andrea Gordon, Roger Owen, Jean-Paul Pascual, André Raymond, Yasser Tabbaa, and Mary C. Wilson offered helpful criticisms and suggestions as I drafted this article. Alka Badshah of M.I.T. produced the map of Damascus. William L. Porter, Director of The Aga Khan Program for Islamic Architecture at M.I.T., and Richard M. Douglas, trustee of the I. Austin Kelly, III Fund at M.I.T., provided the funds for this project. I wish to thank all these individuals and institutions for their counsel and generous support.

1. Hanna Batatu, *The Old Social Classes and the Revolutionary Movements of Iraq* (Princeton, 1978), pp. 19–22. Scholars are not in agreement on the question of how much should be attributed to 'insecurity' as a factor in the creation of the walled quarter in the Arab or Islamic city. See T.H. Greenshields, '"Quarters" and Ethnicity, in G.H. Blake and R.I. Lawless, eds, *The Changing Middle Eastern City* (London, 1980), p. 124. Pre-modern quarters were often, but not always, separated by fortified walls and gates. They were characterized by a maze of narrow crooked streets. Off of an irregular series of dead-end streets and alleys were houses hidden behind high walls, and turned away from the street around internal courtyards. This achieved maximum privacy for the family. The traditional Arab courtyard house was designed to seclude family from family and to segregate women [in the *ḥarāmlik*] from men, though only the affluent were able to uphold this

ideal. It appears that these patterns reflected the quarter's desire for internal privacy and seclusion as much as it did its desire for protection from external forces. Recent scholarship by André Raymond, among others, suggests that pre-modern quarters were not irrationally (and hence inferiorly) organized, as an earlier generation argued, but conformed logically to the ideals and values of Islamic society regarding family and economic organization. These enforced a strict differentiation between residential areas and commercial areas. In contrast to residential quarters, commercial areas were more 'regular,' open, and accessible to the public, something that would be expected of a business district. See André Raymond, 'Remarques sur la voirie des grandes villes arabes,' in R. Hillenbrand, ed., *Proceedings du 10ème Congrès de l'UEAI* (Edinburgh, 1982), pp. 72–85. Eugen Wirth goes a step further by suggesting that many of the physical structures in the Arab and/or Islamic city, such as the courtyard home, existed previous to the appearance of Islam in the Middle East. Arab Muslim society adapted and reinforced these ancient patterns and structures but did not invent them. ['The Middle Eastern City: Islamic City? Oriental City? Arabian City? The specific characteristics of the cities of North Africa and Southwest Asia from the point of view of Geography,' lecture by Wirth, Center for Middle Eastern Studies, Harvard University, 1982.] On this subject also see Roberto Berardi, 'Espace et ville en pays d'Islam,' in Dominique Chevallier, ed., *L'Espace social de la ville Arabe* (Paris, 1979), pp. 99–123.

2. Scholars are far from agreement on a precise definition of the term 'quarter' in the Arab, Middle Eastern, or Islamic city. To start with, the Arabic equivalent of 'quarter' differs from city to city and region to region: *ḥāra* in Cairo and Damascus; *maḥalla* in Aleppo and in Baghdad; and *ḥawma* in much of North Africa [Raymond, 'Remarques', p. 74] including Algiers and Fez, but also *darb* in some parts of Morocco [see Dale F. Eickelman, 'Is There an Islamic City? The Making of a Quarter in a Moroccan Town,' *International Journal of Middle East Studies*, 5 (1974), 278]. I agree with Greenshields that the 'term has been used rather loosely ... as though a quarter is a readily identifiable unit, representative of a certain pattern of social organization, and possessing a certain structure and set of distinguishing characteristics which it shares with other quarters.' Greenshields, 'Quarters', p. 124.

3. For a penetrating analysis of the Ottoman Empire's (including Egypt's) commercial and financial encounter with Europe in the nineteenth and early twentieth centuries, see Roger Owen, *The Middle East in the World Economy 1800–1914* (London, 1981); also see Hanna Batatu. 'The Arab Countries from Crisis to Crisis: Some Basic Trends and Tentative Interpretations,' in American University of Beirut, *The Liberal Arts and the Future of Higher Education in the Middle East* (Beirut, 1979), pp. 3–7; and Philip S. Khoury, 'The Tribal Shaykh, French Tribal Policy, and the Nationalist Movement in Syria Between Two World Wars,' *Middle Eastern Studies*, 18 (April 1982), 180–193.

4. See Philip S. Khoury, 'A Reinterpretation of the Origins and Aims of the Great Syrian Revolt of 1925–27,' in George N. Atiyeh and Ibrahim M. Oweiss, eds, *Arab Civilization* (Albany, 1988), pp. 241–271.

5. On the structure of Damascus in different historical periods see the following: Samir Abdulac, 'Damas: les années Ecochard (1932–1982)', *Les cahiers de la recherche architecturale*, no. 10/11 (April 1982), 32–43; Karl K. Barbir, *Ottoman Rule in Damascus*, 1708–1758 (Princeton, 1980); G. Besnard, 'Damas, son oasis, ses habitants,' *L'Asie française*, 31 (1931), no. 292, 239–250; Anne-Marie Bianquis, 'Damas et la Ghouta,' in André Raymond, ed., *La Syrie d'aujourd'hui* (Paris, 1980), pp. 359–384; Dominique Chevallier, 'A Damas. Production et société à la fin du 19ᵉ siècle,' *Annales*. Economies, Sociétés, Civilizations, 11 (1964), 966–972; René Danger, 'L'urbanisme en Syrie: la ville de Damas,' *Urbanisme (Revue mensuelle)* (1937), 123–164; K. Dettmann, *Damaskus. Eine orientalische Stadt zwischen Tradition und Moderne* (Nürnberg, 1967); N. Elisséeff, 'Damas à la lumière des théories de Jean Sauvaget,' in A.H. Hourani and S.M. Stern, eds, *The Islamic City: A Colloquium* (Oxford, 1970) and 'Dimashq,' *Encyclopaedia of Islam* (new edition); Ṣafūḥ Khayr, *Madīnat Dimashq. Dirāsa fī jughrāfiyya al-mudun* (Damascus, 1969); Philip S. Khoury, *Urban Notables and Arab Nationalism. The Politics of Damascus 1860–1920* (Cambridge, 1983); A. von Kremer, *Mittelsyrien und Damaskus* (Wien, 1853); Irène Labeyrie et Muhammad Roumi, 'La grande traversée de Damas,' *Les cahiers de la recherche architecturale*, no. 10/11 (April 1982), 44–51; Ira M. Lapidus, *Muslim Cities in the Later Middle Ages* (Cambridge, Mass., 1967); Louis Massignon, 'La structure du travail à Damas en 1927,' *Cahiers Internationaux de sociologie*, 15 (1953), 34–52; J.M. Proust-Tournier, 'La population de Damas,' *Hanon. Revue Libanaise de Géographie*, 5 (1970), 129–145;

Muḥammad Saʿīd al-Qāsimī, *Qāmūs al-ṣināʿat al-shāmiyya*, ed. by Ẓāfir al-Qāsimī, 2 vols. (Paris, 1960); Abdul-Karim Rafeq. *The Province of Damascus, 1723–1783* (Beirut, 1966); 'Abd al-Qādir Rihāwi, *Madīnat Dimashq* (Damascus, 1969); Jean Sauvaget, 'Esquisse d'une histoire de la ville de Damas,' *Revue des Etudes Islamiques*, 8 (1934), 421-bis-480; J. Sauvaget and J. Weulersse, *Damas et la Syrie sud* (Paris, 1936); R. Thoumin, 'Damas. Note sur la répartition de la population par origine et par religion,' *Revue de Géographie Alpine*, 25 (1937), 633–697; Thoumin, 'Notes sur l'aménagement et la distribution des eaux à Damas et dans sa Ghouta,' *Bulletin d'études orientales*, 4 (1934), 1–26; Thoumin, 'Deux quartiers de Damas: Le quartier chrétien de Bab Musalla et le quartier kurde,' *Bulletin d'études orientales*, 1 (1931), 99–135; Jacques Weulersse, 'Damas. Etude de développement urbain,' *Bulletin de l'Association de Géographes français*, no. 107 (June–October 1937), 102–105; K. Wulzinger and C. Watzinger, *Damaskus*, 2 vols., (Berlin, 1921–1924).

6. Thoumin, 'Deux quartiers de Damas,' p. 99.

7. Referred to as 'Amāra Jawāniyya [inner] and 'Amāra Barrāniyya [outer], and Shāghūr Jawāniyya and Shāghūr Barrāniyya. See René Danger, Paul Danger, and M. Ecochard, *Damas: Rapport d'enquête monographique sur la ville 1936*, (unpublished), Table 13. I wish to thank Jean-Paul Pascual of the Institut Français d'Etudes Arabes in Damascus for making the Danger report available to me. It is an extremely important document for the study of interwar Damascus in nearly all its facets.

8. Scholars seem to agree that in the pre-modern cities, quarters varied widely in size, both in terms of space and population, and that the religious minorities (Christians and Jews in the Arab cities) inhabited their own separate quarters both because the state wanted to contain (and keep an eye on) them and because minorities naturally sought protection through clustering. Otherwise, scholars are still divided over the degree of social and economic homogeneity in the quarters. Their research suggests a wide variety of forms, depending on city and quarter. For example: (1) Although most quarters were not ethnically homogenous, there were important exceptions, such as the Kurdish quarter of Damascus. (2) The distribution of inhabitants in most pre-modern quarters seems to have been along a rich–poor axis, in the sense that the vast majority of quarters were inhabited by the poor and there were a small number of quarters in which the wealthier classes and strata resided. Yet, at the same time, there were quarters which contained different economic classes and strata. The poorest quarters were frequently on the city periphery and developed with the influx of migrants from the countryside and refugee populations from other regions or countries; where land prices and housing rents were cheapest; and where much of the city's noxious industries (furnaces, tanneries, slaughterhouses) were located. (3) An earlier generation of scholars has argued that quarters were homogeneous in the sense that their inhabitants belonged to the same or a related economic activity or profession. They even suggested a direct link between the guilds and certain residential quarters. Recent research by André Raymond on Cairo and Algiers and Jean-Claude David on Aleppo suggests quite the opposite: residential quarters were not grouped or unified by occupation or trade as previously thought, and their inhabitants worked in separate commercial areas, outside the quarters but often nearby them. Although all residential quarters had their nonspecialized shops (*suwayqa*), hawkers, pedlars, and small artisans, they did not constitute economic units as such; in other words, quarters were not organized along economic lines. See André Raymond, *Artisans et commerçants au Caire au XVIIIe siècle* (Damascus, 1973, 1974); 'Remarques,' pp. 73–77; 'The Residential Districts of Cairo During the Ottoman Period' in *The Arab City. Its Character and Islamic Heritage* (n. pl., 1980), pp. 100–110. 'Le Centre d'Alger en 1830,' *Revue de l'Occident Musulman et de la Méditerranée*, 31 (1981), 73–84; and J.C. David, 'Alep,' in André Raymond, ed., *La Syrie d'aujourd'hui* (Paris, 1980), pp. 385–406, and David, 'Alep, dégradation et tentatives actuelles de réadaptation des structures urbaines traditionnelles,' *Bulletin d'études orientales*, 28 (1975). In the case of Damascus, some of the quarters of the old city seem to have been economically and socially homogeneous, while others, including the Christian and Jewish quarters, were not. The more recently established quarters (between the fourteenth and the nineteenth centuries), which encircled the old city, were more easily identifiable by their major class component.

9. Information on the labor movement in Syria during the French Mandate can be found in 'Abdullah Ḥannā, *al-Haraka al-ʿummāliyya fī sūriyya wa lubnān 1900–1945* (Damascus, 1973) and Elisabeth Longuenesse, 'La classe ouvrière en Syrie. Une classe en formation,' 3ème cycle Dissertation. Ecole des Hautes Etudes en Sciences Sociales (Paris, 1977).

10. On the foundation of these quarters and their density during the Mandate see René Danger, 'L'urbanisme en Syrie: la ville de Damas.' *Urbanisme* (*Revue mensuelle*), (1937), 129, 136; Abdulac, 'Damas,' pp. 32–33.

11. Danger, 'L'urbanisme,' p. 143. Jean-Paul Pascual has pointed out to me that wealthy residents of Sūq Sārūja even constructed houses with facades which purposely resembled those found in Istanbul.

12. Greenshields writes that in Middle Eastern cities '. . . the partial or complete departure of an ethnic group [he includes religious communities in his definition of ethnic groups] from its original quarter ... leaves a vacuum which in many cities is filled by the invasion of new population elements, often of a different group, and results in an intermixing of populations . . .' '"Quarters" and Ethnicity,' p. 131. This process had begun to take place during the Mandate era in the Ḥayy al-Yahūd as Jews began to emigrate to Palestine or to the West. See Danger, 'L'urbanisme,' pp. 123–164.

13. Bianquis, 'Damas,' p. 362.

14. Danger, 'L'urbanisme,' pp. 136, 143. On the origins and adaptation of the *ḥawāṣil* and *khāns* (caravansérails) in Damascus see George Saba, Klaus Salzwedel, 'Typologie des caravansérails dans la vieille ville de Damas,' *Les cahiers de la recherche architecturale*, 10/11 (April 1982). 52–59.

15. See ibid., pp. 129, 136. Al-Ṣālḥiyya dates from the twelfth century.

16. See Sauvaget, 'Esquisse,' pp. 473–474; Greenshields, '"Quarters,"' p. 122; Bianquis, 'Damas,' p. 374.

17. Thoumin, 'Deux quartiers,' pp. 116–20, 131; Also see Khoury, *Urban Notables*, chapter 2.

18. Aḥmad Ḥilmī al-ʿAllāf, *Dimashq fī maṭlaʿ al-qarn al-ʿashrīn*, ed. by ʿAlī Jamīl Nuʿaysa (Damascus, 1976), pp. 41–43.

19. J. Grellet, 'La Fiscalité municipale en Syrie,' *Centre de Hautes Etudes Administratives sur l'Afrique et l'Asie Modernes* [*CHEAM*] (Paris) no. 331, n.d., pp. 31–32.

20. Conversation with the late Farīd Zayn al-Dīn (Damascus, 14 April 1976). According to Zayn al-Dīn, a radical nationalist leader during the Mandate, there was another informal council which met in the quarters. It was called *majlis al-shiyūkh* (*Council of Shaykhs*), composed of leading intellectuals who met in different homes to discuss political strategy. Occasionally, quarter notables would attend in order to learn how to explain to the common people what was going on at the summit of nationalist politics.

21. Zafer Kassemy [Zāfir al-Qāsimī], 'La participation des classes populaires aux mouvements nationaux d'indépendance aux XIXe et XXe siècles: Syrie,' in Commission Internationale d'histoire des mouvements sociaux et des structures sociales, ed., *Mouvements nationaux d'indépendance et classes populaires aux XIXe et XXe siècles en Occident et en Orient* (Paris, 1971), p. 348.

22. I have been deeply influenced by the theoretical and empirical studies on patron–client relations of James Scott and, in particular, his 'Patron–Client Politics and Political Change in Southeast Asia,' *American Political Science Review*, LXVI, no. 1, 91–113. More of Scott's work and that of a number of prominent social scientists can be found in the excellent collection: Ernest Gellner and John Waterbury, eds, *Patrons and Clients in Mediterranean Societies* (London, 1977). On the political and social behaviour of urban notables in the Middle East see Albert Hourani, 'The Islamic City in the Light of Recent Research,' in A.H. Hourani and S.M. Stern, eds, *The Islamic City* (Oxford, 1970), pp. 9–24; Hourani, 'Ottoman Reform and the Politics of Notables,' in W.R. Polk and R.L. Chambers, eds., *Beginnings of Modernization in the Middle East: The Nineteenth Century* (Chicago, 1968), pp. 41–68; and Khoury, *Urban Notables*, pp. 1–55.

23. The population of Damascus in 1922 (beginning of Mandate) was estimated at 169,000 [169,367]. In 1943 (end of the Mandate), it was estimated at 286,000 [286,310], meaning that the population increased 1.7 times in two decades. The increase in the 1930s was more rapid than it was in the 1920s. Similarly, the population of Aleppo doubled (2.05 times) in the same period. For statistical information and sources on the population of the cities (and countryside) in Syria during the French Mandate see Philip S. Khoury, *Syria and the French Mandate: the Politics of Arab Nationalism 1920–1945* (Princeton, 1987), pp. 11–12, 15–16, and 241–271.

24. See N. Elisséef, 'Dimashk,' *Encyclopaedia of Islam* (new edition), p. 290.

25. On the changing architectural style and social functions of houses in Syrian cities, see R. Thoumin, *La maison syrienne dans la plaine hauranaise, le bassin du Barada et sur les plateaux du Qalamoun* (Paris, 1932); A. Abdel-Nour, *Introduction à l'histoire urbaine de la Syrie Ottomane* (*XVIIe-*

XVIIIe siècle) (Beirut, 1982); Jean-Charles Depaule, 'Espaces lieux et mots,' *Les cahiers de la recherche architecturale*, 10/11 (April 1982), 94–101; and Jean-Claude David, Dominique Hubert, 'Maisons et immeubles du début du XXe siècle à Alep,' *Les cahiers de la recherche architecturale*, 10/11 (April 1982), 102–111.

26. See Khoury, *Urban Notables*, chapters 2 and 3.

27. Ibid., chapter 2.

28. This information and analysis is based on conversations with Wajīha al-Yūsuf (Beirut, 15 and 29 August 1975), and with 'Alī 'Abd al-Karīm al-Dandashī, Maḥmūd al-Bayrūtī, Fu'ād Sidawi, and George Sibā' (Damascus, 13 and 14 February 1976 and 9 and 10 March 1976). One of the most prized of the creature comforts found in the new homes constructed in the bourgeois suburbs of towns like Damascus or Aleppo was the modern (private) bathroom. Unlike the new suburban quarters for the poor (often filled with recently arrived in-migrants from the countryside) where public baths (*ḥammāmāt*) had to be constructed, the wealthy suburban quarters did not require public baths; indeed, their inhabitants did not want them. Another such creature comfort was the modern kitchen. See David and Hubert, 'Maisons,' pp. 64–65 and Muhammad Roumi, 'Le hammam domestique: nouvelles pratiques et transformations de l'espace,' *Le cahiers de la recherche architecturale*, 10/11 (April 1982), 74–79.

29. Fakhrī al-Bārūdī, Personal Papers, 'Al-Bārūdī File 1922–47,' in Markaz al-Watha'iq al-Tārīkhiyya [Damascus], *al-Qism al-Khāṣṣ*.

30. The first President of the Syrian Republic, Muhammad 'Alī al-'Abid saw to it during his tenure in office (1932–1936) that a tramway line connected the center of Damascus with the bourgeois suburb of al-Muhājirīn where the 'Abid family had moved during the Mandate, after leaving Sūq Sārūja. This enabled the 'Abids, one of the most prominent notable families and possibly the wealthiest family in Damascus, to service their original clientele in Sūq Sārūja in addition to the poorer residents of their new district, especially during the holy month of Ramadan, when they fed hundreds of people nightly at their al-Muhājirīn palace. Conversation with Naṣūḥ [Abū Muḥammad] al-Maḥayrī. (Damascus, 12 March 1976.)

31. See Philip S. Khoury, 'Factionalism Among Syrian Nationalists During the French Mandate. *International Journal of Middle East Studies*, 13 (November 1981), 462–469; and Khoury, 'A Reinterpretation.'

32. The National Bloc was the pre-eminent nationalist organization of the Mandate era. Its influence on political life in Syria can be compared to that of the Wafd Party in Egypt in the interwar period. For information on its organization, headquarters in Damascus and branches in Aleppo, Hama, Homs, and Latakia, rivalries with the French, with other nationalist organizations and within the Bloc itself, ties to the rest of the Arab world, and its ascent to government, see Khoury, *Syria and the French Mandate.*

33. Naturally, not all merchants were anti-French. Numerous merchants engaged in the import-export trade with Europe (many of whom belonged to the religious minorities) collaborated rather freely with the French. Furthermore, the structural constraints of colonial rule necessitated some degree of collaboration with the Mandatory authorities by nearly everyone engaged in commerce and industry. The question is: to what degree did merchants and industrialists collaborate? The answer is to be found in the character and orientation of the enterprises they ran. Similarly, there were, at times, serious disputes between merchants and industrialists over which commercial or financial policy they wished the French to pursue in Syria. The best example of such a split occurred in the early 1930s when Syrian merchants wanted easy access to cheap Japanese cloth as it sold so well locally, whereas industrialists wanted the French to put an end to what they claimed was 'dumping' by raising import duties on foreign cloth. Roger Owen has kindly reminded me of this example. Specific information on Japanese competition, which reached its height in 1934 (protective measures began to be introduced at the end of that year), can be found in PRO: *FO371/4188*, vol. 19023.

34. Conversations with 'Ali 'Abd al-Karīm al-Dandashī and Maḥmūd al-Bayrūtī (Damascus, 9 and 10 March 1976).

35. See Khoury, *Urban Notables*, chapter 3 and Conclusion.

36. Conversation with Ẓāfir al-Qāsimī (Beirut, 24 and 26 July 1975). Al-Qāsimī's father was the leading religious figure of Bāb al-Jābiyya. Also see Philip S. Khoury, 'Islamic Revivalism and the Crisis of the Secular State in the Arab World: an Historical Appraisal, in I. Ibrahim, ed., *Arab Resources: The Transformation of a Society* (Washington, D.C., 1983), pp. 213–236.

37. See al-ʿAllāf, *Dimashq*, pp. 244–247. According to the author, who wrote during the early Mandate, *al-zgritiyya* is a Turkish word referring to the 'courageous of the quarter.'

38. These characteristics have been isolated in an inspiring article on the power structure in Beirut's Muslim quarters in the early 1970s, and in particular the role of *qabaḍāyāt* in these quarters. See Michael Johnson, 'Political bosses and their gangs: Zuʿama and qabadayat in the Sunni Muslim quarters of Beirut,' in Ernest Gellner and John Waterbury, eds *Patrons and Clients in Mediterranean Societies* (London, 1977), pp. 207–224. Conversation with Fu'ad al-Sidawi, *qabaḍāy* of the Christian quarter of Bāb Tūmā during the Mandate (Damascus, 13 February 1976). A list of some nineteenth- and early-twentieth-century *qabaḍāyāt* of Damascus is provided by al-ʿAllāf, *Dimashq*, pp. 247–251.

39. *Zuʿrān* featured prominently in the medieval Muslim city [see Lapidus, *Muslim Cities*]; in Damascus during the Mandate [al-ʿAllāf, *Dimashq*, p. 244]; and in Beirut during the Lebanese civil war of the 1970s [based on my personal observations]. Also see Johnson, 'Political Bosses,' p. 212.

40. Conversations with Abū ʿAlī al-Kilāwī, ʿAlī ʿAbd al-Karīm al-Dandashī, and Maḥmūd al-Bayrūtī (Damascus, 3, 9, 10 March 1976).

41. The following information on the personal life and career of Abū ʿAlī al-Kilāwī is based on several days of conversations with him and with several other *qabaḍāyāt* of the Mandate and early independence eras whom I met at his home in Bāb al-Jābiyya (Damascus, 14 February, 3 and 15 March 1976).

42. On the Al-Shaʿlān, see Khoury, 'Tribal Shaykh,' pp. 183–185.

43. For the rise on the Bakrī family see Khoury, *Urban Notables*, pp. 34–35.

44. See al-ʿAllāf, *Dimashq*, pp. 242–243.

45. Ibid., pp. 240–243.

46 Al-Kilāwī was also an accomplished Arabic musician who played a three-stringed guitar and sang popular beduin ballads. His dialect reflected his long years of association with tribes south of Damascus.

47. As late as 1976, Abū ʿAlī was still riding and showing his horses in national parades in Damascus, despite his antipathy toward the current Syrian regime.

48. al-ʿAllāf, *Dimashq*, pp. 259–262.

49. On the transformation of *ʿarāḍa* into political manifestations in the twentieth century, see J. Lecerf and R. Tresse, 'Les ʿarāḍa de Damas,' *Bulletin d'études orientales*, 7/8 (1937–1938), pp. 237–264; and Ẓāfir al-Qāsimī, *Wathā'iq jadīda min al-thawra al-sūriyya al-kubrā* (Damascus, 1965), pp. 63–74; France, Ministère des Affaires Etrangères, *Syrie-Liban 1930–40*, de Martel to MAE, 5 July 1935, vol. 491, pp. 31–33.

50. On al-Kharrāt and other hero/martyrs of the Revolt, see Adham al-Jundī, *Tārīkh al-thawrāt al-sūriyya fī ʿahd al-intidāb al-faransī* (Damascus, 1960).

51. Besides the Kilāwīs, other noted *qabaḍāyāt* of the Mandate era were Abū Ghāssim ʿAbd al-Salām al-Ṭawīl (al-Qaymariyya quarter); Abū Rashīd Khūja (al-Kharāb); Abūl Haydar al-Mardīnī (Bāb al-Srīja), Maḥmūd Khaddām al-Srīja (Shāghūr); and Abū ʿAbdū Dīb al-Shaykh (ʿAmāra).

52. Information on the Great Revolt and Abū ʿAlī's role in it comes from his personal memoir which his eldest son, ʿAlī, had recorded, and which Abū ʿAlī kindly made available to me. The memoir is entitled: *Thawra ʿamma 1925. al-Faransiyyīn fī sūriyya* (n.pl., n.d.).

53. The *jamʿiyyāt* were the prototype for the Syrian Muslim Brotherhood (founded in the 1940s). See Johannes Reissner's groundbreaking study *Ideologie und Politik der Muslimbrüder Syriens* (Freiburg, 1980). In Damascus, their leaders included *shaykhs*, teachers, lawyers, and doctors. Their principal goals were the spread of Muslim education based on modernist and *salafiyya* ideas; the spread of Muslim ethics and morals and nationalist and anti-imperialist sentiments. They were especially involved in the affairs of Palestine at the time of the Arab revolt of 1936–1939. The earliest of the societies was the *jamʿiyyat al-Gharrā'* (founded in 1924). Others included *jamʿiyyat al-tamaddun al-Islāmī* (1932), *jamʿiyyat al-hidāya al-Islāmiyya* (1936), and *jamʿiyyat al-ʿulamā'* (1938). By the mid-1930s, they were leading violent campaigns against the influx of foreign goods and culture into Syria; the proliferation of cabarets serving alcohol, permitting gambling, and featuring female dancers; the increasingly liberal dress code adopted by bourgeois women (including the wives of National Bloc leaders); women frequenting public places, in particular cinemas; and the holding of lotteries. See Markaz al-Wathā'iq al-Tārīkhiyya [Damascus], *Dākhiliyya*, File. 33/5431–3098. Shaykh Hamdī al-Ṣafarjalānī to Minister of Interior

(Damascus): *niẓam nādī*, 5 May 1932; Jamīl Ibrāhīm Pāshā, *Mudhakkirāt Jamīl Ibrāhīm Pāshā* (Aleppo, 1959), pp. 78–79; *Oriente Moderno*, 14 (1934), p. 438; ibid., 15 (1935), p. 636; ibid., 18 (1938), pp. 532–533; *'Adil al-'Aẓma Papers* [Syria: Institute for Palestine Studies, Beirut], File 16/398, 7 February 1939 and File 16/398a, 9 February 1939.

54. See Johnson, 'Political Bosses,' pp. 214–220.

55. Ibid., pp. 218–220.

56. Conversation with Abū 'Alī al-Kilāwī (Damascus, 3 March 1976).

57. On the General Strike of 1936, which lasted nearly fifty days, and which led the French to open up direct negotiations in Paris with National Bloc leaders on the subject of a Franco-Syrian treaty, and which ultimately allowed the Bloc to get control of the Syrian government by the end of the year, see Khoury, 'Politics of Nationalism,' vol. 3, Epilogue-Conclusion.

58. Information on al-Srīja and his gang was found in Markaz al-Wathā'iq al-Tārīkhiyya [Damascus], *Registre correctionnel*, 5 October 1932–8 February 1934, pp. 216–218.

59. On the formation, composition, and operation of individual political machines in Damascus during the Mandate, and in particular those of Shukrī al-Quwwatlī and Jamīl Mardam, see Khoury, 'Politics of Nationalism,' vol. 3, chapters 12, 13, and Epilogue-Conclusion.

60. On the origins of the Kurdish notable families of Damascus in the nineteenth century see Khoury, *Urban Notables*, chapters 3 and 4. This information has been supplemented by conversations with Wajīha al-Yūsuf [Ibish], daughter of 'Abd al-Raḥmān Pāshā al-Yūsuf (the leading Kurdish notable of Damascus in the late nineteenth and early twentieth centuries) and wife of Ḥusayn Ibish (the leading Kurdish notable of the Mandate era, and the biggest landowner in the province of Damascus) (Beirut, 15 and 29 August 1975). Another political force to draw support from the Kurdish quarter by the late 1930s was the Syrian Communist Party. The Party rank and file in Damascus included a number of Arabized Kurds owing to the fact that its leader, Khālid Bakdāsh, was a Kurd from the quarter. See Batatu, *The Old Social Classes*, chapter 24.

61. See Khoury, 'Factionalism among Syrian Nationalists,' pp. 460–465.

62. This same phenomenon seems to have appeared in Palestine during the British mandate. The major difference, however, was that Jewish capital and the British administration were able to provide a framework and opportunities for in-migrants which the French administration in Syria could only provide on a much less developed scale. Therefore, in Damascus, those in-migrants who remained on the periphery of the city had to await the appearance of new forces: in the case of political integration, the Ba'th and Communist parties; in the case of economic integration, the development of industrialization on a significant scale which only occurred at the end of World War II. On developments in Palestine, see Joel S. Migdal, 'Urbanization and Political Change: The Impact of Foreign Rule,' *Comparative Studies in Society and History*, 19 (July 1979), 328–349. On French involvement in the Syrian economy, see Khoury, 'Politics of Nationalism,' vol. 1, chapter IV.

63. On the contribution of this class to the independence movement, see Khoury, *Syria and the French Mandate*, chapters 15 and 16.

64. 1.7 times. See Ministère des Affaires Etrangères, *Rapport à la Société des Nations sur la situation de la Syrie et du Liban 1924*, Appendix 4, p. 95; PRO: *FO 371/625, vol. 19022, MacKereth to F.O., 7 January 1935.*

65. Conversation with Qustantin Zurayq (Beirut, 10 January 1976).

66. On al-Bārūdī's upbringing and career see Fakhrī al-Bārūdī, *Mudhakkirāt al-Bārūdī*, 2 vols. (Damascus, 1951–1952); Nahāl Bahjat Ṣidqī, *Fakhrī al-Bārūdī* (Beirut, 1974); Aḥmad Qudāma, *Ma'ālim wa a'lām fī bilād al-'Arab* (Damascus, 1965), vol. 1. p. 10; George Fāris, *Man huwa fī sūriyya 1949* (Damascus, 1950), p. 54; Virginia Vacca, 'Notizie Biografische su Uomini Politici Ministri e Deputati Siriani,' *Oriente Moderno*, 17 (October 1937), p. 478; and Khoury, 'Politics of Nationalism,' vol. 2, pp. 664–667. More information comes from conversations with 'Alī 'Abd al-Karīm al-Dandashī and Maḥmūd al-Bayrūtī (Damascus, 9 and 10 March 1976).

67. On the contribution of the *tajhīz* of Damascus to the independence movement see Khoury, *Syria and the French Mandate*, , chapter 15.

68. Information on Bayrūtī's upbringing and career comes from a long conversation with him in Damascus on 10 March 1976; and conversations with other youth leaders of the Mandate era, including 'Alī 'Abd al-Karīm al-Dandashī. I have also depended on *al-Muḍḥik al-mubkī*, [Damascus weekly satirical magazine] no. 18 (1929), p. 12; and George Fāris, *Man huwa*, pp. 70–71. On Mamlūk's career, see ibid., p. 429.

69. Conversation with Maḥmūd al-Bayrūtī (Damascus, 10 March 1976); Fāris, *Man huwa*, pp. 70–71; *al-Muḍḥik al-mubkī*, no. 103 (21 November 1931), p. 14.

70. Conversation with Munīr al-ʿAjlānī (Beirut, 2 September 1975). On the development of the new 'nationalist youth' leadership, see Khoury, *Syria and the French Mandate*, chapters 15 and 16.

71. Conversation with Abū ʿAlī al-Kilāwī and Maḥmūd al-Bayrūtī (Damascus, 15 February and 10 March 1976).

72. See Khoury, 'Politics of Nationalism,' vol. 2, chapter 6.

73. The Franco-Belgian-owned Société des Tramways et d'Electricité was the most visible foreign concession visited by nationalist demonstrations during the Mandate. The cinemas, located in the modern districts, were another focal point. On the one hand, political organizations that wished to start a demonstration could find a ready-made crowd afternoons and evenings coming out of films. The Roxy cinema was used most frequently. On the other hand, some Muslim benevolent societies led demonstrations against cinemas which permitted the attendance of women. Most cinemas were Christian-owned. ʿAdil al-ʿAẓma Papers [Syria], File 16, no. 398, 7 February 1939 and File 16, no. 398a, 9 February 1939.

74. See R. Tresse, 'Manifestations féminines à Damas au XIXe et XXe siècles, in *Entretiens sur l'évolution des pays de civilization arabe*, III (Paris, 1939), pp. 115–125.

75. The Nationalist Youth was transformed into a paramilitary organization in 1936, called the Steel Shirts (*al-Qumṣān al-Ḥadīdiyya*), with nearly 5,000 members by the end of the year. Khoury, *Syria and the French Mandate*, chapters 16 and 17. It was around this time that the French-controlled Syrian army (*Troupes Spéciales*) began to attract young 'talented' nationalists and the civilian nationalist elite finally saw the importance of encouraging their sons and young men from the rising middle classes to enter the military academy at Homs. Since the early nineteenth century, the notable families of Damascus and other Syrian towns had actively discouraged their sons from pursuing military careers which they felt were beneath their dignity and standing in society. This traditional bias and the fact the military was under French sway helped to preserve this attitude, until the possibility of Syrian independence grew in the 1930s and nationalists began to think seriously about the institutional future of Syria. However, the military academy and the army itself, unlike the high schools and law faculty, were not important politicizing forces for Syrian youth before independence. For one thing, the French made concerted efforts to keep the military apolitical and most political agitation within the military seemed to focus on issues of promotion and pay scale and not on entering the political arena as such. Furthermore, it is likely that many of the young men who entered the military academy from the mid-1930s till the French left Syria in 1946 were already politicized in high school. In any case, the academy only graduated approximately 150 men between 1935 and 1946, a third of whom came from Damascus. The Syrian Army on independence was, itself, only 12,000 strong. Michael H. Van Dusen, 'Intra- and Inter-Generational Conflict in the Syrian Army' (Ph.D. dissertation, The Johns Hopkins University, 1971), pp. 45–46, 165–66, 382–89.

The Role of the Palestinian Peasantry in the Great Revolt (1936–1939)

TED SWEDENBURG

Between 1936 and 1939, a major anti-colonial rebellion known among Arabs as the Great Revolt shook the mandate territory of Palestine. The struggle pitted a poorly armed peasant movement against the might of the world's pre-eminent colonial power, Great Britain. Despite the militancy and duration of the revolt, scholarly work on this period tends to emphasize the shortcomings of the insurgent movement and, in particular, to discount the role of the peasantry. Dominant accounts generally define the fellahin as 'traditional, backward, and conservative,' as 'activated by tribal and religious loyalties,'[1] and as 'too isolated, ignorant and poor' to play a significant role in the national movement.[2] Because they consider the peasants to be completely dominated by the local ruling class, these scholars view them as incapable of political initiative. Moreover, they attribute the disintegration of the revolt to the traditional clannish, factional, and regional divisions among fellahin that prevented them from maintaining a unified movement. The rebellion's demise is thus seen as due to the peasantry's accession to leadership in the vacuum left by the urban elites. A parallel argument, which imposes a model derived from industrial capitalism upon an agrarian society, attributes the uprising's defeat to its failure to develop a strong leadership. Since only a revolutionary party could have provided the command structure and social program necessary for victory, the peasantry as a class is considered incapable of providing guidance. Such analyses not only dismiss the crucial role of the peasants, who made up 75 per cent of the population of Palestine,[3] but also ignore their legitimate social and political demands.

I propose, as an alternative, to read existing historical accounts 'against the grain' so as to bring the marginalized Palestinian peasantry to the center of my analysis.[4] I will argue that the peasantry's relation to the ruling notables was never simply one of complete subservience. As Gramsci notes, a dominant class's hegemony is never 'total or exclusive'; it is, rather, a process, a relation of dominance that has, as Raymond Williams says, 'continually to be renewed, recreated, defended and modified. It is also continually resisted, limited, altered, challenged by pressures not all its own.'[5] The Palestinian peasantry, therefore, while subordinated to the rule of the notables, nonetheless possessed a long tradition of opposition to their hegemony. It also possessed a history of challenging capitalist penetration and state formation. Such traditions of resistance were kept alive in popular memory and could be drawn upon as powerful tools of mobilization in moments of rupture. These 'folk' traditions were not isolated, however, from other influences. They did not exist in a state of pristine purity, but were affected and transformed both by the dominant ideologies of the notables, who led the nationalist movement, and by alternative discourses emanating from more radical factions of the educated middle class. Also the fellahin's 'common sense' notions[6] and their forms of political mobilization were jolted by the rapidly changing material conditions of the British mandate period. The Palestine peasantry, in short, was not simply an unchanging, backward social category.

During the course of the revolt, the rebels, who represented a broad alliance of peasants, workers, and radical elements of the middle class, developed an effective military force and began to implement social and political programs that challenged *a'yan* (notable) leadership of the nationalist movement and threatened the bases of mercantile-landlord dominance. The threat of a counter-hegemonic peasant leadership with a class-based program caused large numbers of wealthy urban Palestinians to flee the country. The movement also posed a serious threat to British strategy in the region and forced them to expend considerable military energies to crush the rebellion, which they succeeded in doing only after more than three years of struggle.

In order to recuperate and to assess the Palestinian peasants' historical achievements and traditions of resistance, I will trace the historical evolution of Palestinian society and its prevailing ideologies prior to the rebellion, going back to the period before capitalism was imposed as the dominant mode of production in Palestine. This will lay the foundation for a revised understanding of the pivotal role of the struggles of the Palestinian peasantry against the expansion of the Ottoman state, Zionist colonization, and British occupation that culminated in the Great Revolt.[7]

PALESTINE IN THE PRECAPITALIST ERA

In the period immediately prior to its occupation by Egypt's ruler Muhammad 'Ali in 1831, Palestine was only loosely controlled and integrated into the

Ottoman empire.[8] At best, Ottoman sway extended to Palestine's towns and their immediate environs. But even the towns, dominated by notables whose authority was based on religious or genealogically claimed 'noble' status, enjoyed substantial autonomy and frequently rebelled against Ottoman authority.[9] Towns along the coast had suffered a decline in the late eighteenth century due to the demise of the cotton trade with France and the ravages inflicted by the successive invasions of coastal Palestine by Egypt's 'Ali Bey (1770–71) and France's Napoleon Bonaparte (1799).[10] By the early nineteenth century the center of gravity had shifted to the towns of the interior highlands. While these urban centers in no way rivaled the great commercial emporia and textile-producing cities of northern Syria (Damascus, Homs, Hama), they were important centers of local and regional trade and artisanal production (particularly the olive oil of Nablus). In an era of weak imperial authority, these towns were generally dominated by the countryside. The population of the rural areas was concentrated in the central highlands of the Galilee, Jabal Nablus (Samaria), and Jabal al-Khalil (Judea). Here, clan-based coalitions organized along highly fluid 'tribal' lines (Qays and Yemen) competed over local resources and political power. A rudimentary class structure separated the shaykhs of the leading patrilineages (*hamulas*) and the district tax collectors (*shuyukh al-nawahi*) from the mass of peasant producers.[11] The shaykhs' obligations to the Ottoman state were to maintain security and to collect taxes, a portion of which they retained. In practice they only sporadically remitted taxes to the state; more frequently they defended their autonomy by raising rural confederations to fend off tax-foraging expeditions sent out by the Ottoman governors of Damascus and Sidon.[12] Local class antagonisms were thus somewhat mitigated by the benefits that the peasantry gained in supporting their local chieftains against direct Ottoman rule.

The lowlands of Palestine—the plains of the coast and the Jordan and Esdraelon valleys—functioned as a hinterland for the highlands. But they were not merely an empty zone. The plains were cultivated but sparsely populated. Villagers who resided permanently in the more secure and salubrious hills and foothills went down to the lowlands to work the nearby plains on a seasonal basis. In contrast to the highlands, where individual ownership (*mulk*) by the head of the extended family predominated and where orchard and vine cultivation was typical, the peasants of the plains participated in *musha* or 'communal' tenure and practiced extensive grain cultivation.

Unlike the highlands, in the lowlands agricultural practices interpenetrated with pastoralism, for both villagers and nomads used marginal and fallow lands to pasture their herds. The relation between peasants and nomads, usually represented as implacably hostile, was actually one of complexity and fluidity, characterized by moments both of cooperation and of struggle. Commentators who have described conditions on the plain as 'anarchic' and have singled out the Bedouin as the chief cause of desolation merely reproduce the viewpoint of the Ottoman state. In fact the lowlands were simply a zone where peasants, nomads, bandits (both of peasant and of nomadic stock), and the forces of the state vied for control, with no group able to take decisive command. Bedouin chiefs commonly ruled over certain areas and 'protected' peasants against the forces of the state (and against thieves and other nomadic tribes), in return for protection fees paid as a form of rent.

PRECAPITALIST IDEOLOGIES

Although the peasants of Palestine recognized the Ottoman sultans as successors to the Prophet and thus as legitimate rulers, in practice they exercised a great deal of independence from the state; Ottoman authority may have been legitimate but it scarcely intervened in everyday life. The local shaykhs served as mediators between the peasants and the state, but, given the balance of forces, they enjoyed virtual autonomy. Their own authority rested upon their imputed 'noble' descent. As is typical in precapitalist societies,[13] relations between the 'noble' shaykhs and their inferiors appeared highly personalized and intimate. This appearance in fact served to refract the underlying relations of exploitation, recasting them in terms consonant with the constitution of amicable interpersonal relations. Class antagonisms were also softened by the shared interests of shaykhs and peasants in defending highland villages from state intervention and in struggling against competing rural confederations. In addition, peasants were positioned in their productive relations through idioms of kinship,[14] while other relations based on village, regional, and 'tribal' ties also served to divide peasants internally.[15] These vertical cleavages were not insuperable, for the various confederations (including Bedouin) were able to unite under the leadership of the shaykhs to resist foreign invaders, as in the broad-based 1834 rebellion against Egyptian occupation.[16] The principles of these dynamics of division and unity are expressed in the famous proverb, 'I and my brother [unite to fight] against my cousin, but I and my cousin [unite to fight] against the stranger.'[17]

Lack of state control over rural areas was also reflected in the distinctly 'folk' character of peasant Islam. Mosques were virtually unknown in the villages, for rural religious practice centered instead on the worship of saints (*walis*) whose shrines (*maqams*) dotted the countryside. Nearly every village possessed at least one *maqam* where peasants went to plead for the *wali*'s intercession on their behalf.[18] A proliferation of shrines underlined the localized, particularistic nature of Palestinian folk Islam. However, other aspects of popular religion point equally to its socially unifying effects. For one thing, it was not *strictly* Islamic, for Muslim peasants visited many Christian churches and respected them as holy shrines.[19] Feasts (*mawsim*) celebrated in honor of various prophets also enhanced popular unity. For example, the *mawsim* of Nabi Rubin (Reuben), held south of Jaffa, attracted pilgrims from all the nearby towns and villages and lasted for a full lunar month.[20] The *mawsim* of Nabi Musa (Moses), celebrated near Jericho, was an even bigger event, attended by peasants, city-dwellers, and Bedouin from all over southern Palestine and Jabal Nablus.[21] Such feasts, joining peasants from a wide area together with town-dwellers, were important rituals of popular solidarity.

Despite localized folk practices, the peasants of Palestine remained part of the wider Ottoman Islamic community which owed its loyalty to the sultan in Istanbul. In theory at least, their broader sense of belonging involved diffuse notions of duties and obligations to the Ottoman state, including the duty to pay taxes. Although the prevailing balance of forces in practice diminished the effects of such sentiments of loyalty to imperial authority, they held the potential to override localized interests. As the Ottoman authorities increased their hold over the provinces, they could draw on such sentiments to impose their hegemony.

PALESTINE'S INTEGRATION INTO THE WORLD MARKET

During the course of the nineteenth century, Palestine, like most of the non-Western world, was integrated into the capitalist world market, which dramatically transformed its social structure. These changes were not a 'natural' evolutionary process, but required the sharp intervention of the Ottoman state under pressure from the European powers. Such developments began with the Egyptian invasion of Palestine and the rest of Syria, and Ibrahim Pasha's vigorous efforts to secure order there between 1831 and 1840. After the Egyptian exodus, the transformation proceeded more slowly as the Ottomans gradually subdued the towns and pacified the countryside, making the atmosphere safe for export agriculture and commerce.

The process involved a major shift in the local balance of forces. Ottoman authorities broke the power of the rural confederations and shifted control over local administration and tax collection from the independent-minded rural shaykhs to an emerging class of urban *a'yan* or notables, the Porte's local partners in its project of 'reform.' Their local power eroded, many rural shaykhs subsequently shifted their base of operations to the towns and merged with the urban notable class.

The *a'yan* took command over much of agricultural production, besides seizing political control over rural areas. Notable families and an emerging commercial bourgeoisie acquired vast properties in the wake of a series of new land laws beginning with the Ottoman Land Code of 1858. These new laws required individual registration of title to what was considered state or *miri* land and facilitated a massive land grab. The *a'yan*, who controlled the state apparatus administering the laws, were best positioned to profit from the situation. Many peasants failed to register their properties, some to avoid paying the registration fee, others to keep their names off government rolls and so escape conscription into the Ottoman army. Still others, rather than simply lose their lands in this fashion, registered their properties (sometimes a whole village) in the name of a powerful notable, who then served as their 'patron' in their relations with the state. Other forms of alienation occurred when the Ottoman government decreed that specific tracts of land, especially in the northern plains, were 'not permanently cultivated' or when it confiscated particular domains for 'security' reasons. Such properties were put up for sale, and the largest of them were often purchased by absentee owners residing in Beirut. Peasants who had customarily farmed these lands were transformed into sharecroppers working for large landowners; a similar change occurred among those who 'voluntarily' registered their lands in the names of notables. As cash gained in importance in the regional economy and as the Ottomans began to demand taxes in cash, numbers of fellahin fell into debt to usurers, either notables or commercial bourgeois members of the local ruling bloc. Many peasants foreclosed on their loans, lost title to their lands, and became sharecroppers. Others, who remained 'independent' small or middle peasants, often became deeply dependent on their creditors.

The effects of these transformations were uneven. Land alienation was concentrated in the central and northern plains of the coast and the Esdraelon valley, where Ottoman authorities were most concerned to establish permanent settlements and where the most profitable crops for export to Europe could be grown. The highlands, however, generally remained a stronghold of smallholdings but even there many peasants were forced to take out loans and thereby became dependent on moneylending notable 'patrons.'

The subordination of the local economy to the needs of the capitalist world economy paralleled the subjugation of the peasantry. Pacification of the countryside and the onset of landlord-merchant control over agrarian production created a dramatic rise in agricultural exports. As a cash economy gradually developed, peasants were increasingly forced to sell part of their product on the market. Already by the 1870s, Palestine exported significant amounts of wheat, barley, sesame, olive oil, and citrus to Europe and to regional markets.[22]

Such transformations were not motivated simply by external factors but were integrally linked to the rise of leading classes composed of two sectors: first, the notables, predominantly Muslim, who owned large tracts of land, engaged in moneylending, and dominated the increasingly centralized government and religious apparatuses; and, second, the commercial bourgeoisie, composed chiefly of Palestinian and Lebanese Christians, Jews, Europeans, and European protégés, who were representatives of banking and merchant capital but who also owned large tracts of land.[23] Muslim notables, allied with

Christian merchants, constituted the dominant sector, whose hegemony was organized under the form of what social scientists have termed 'patron-client' relations, or pyramid-shaped networks of notables and their peasant client-clans.

IDEOLOGIES OF NOTABLE DOMINANCE: PATRONS AND CLIENTS

Notable patrons used their power and influence to assist their peasant clients in dealing both with the state and with other groups (such as peasants belonging to other patronage networks and Bedouin). In return, peasants supported their patrons in political struggles. The notables also provided sharecroppers with their subsistence needs during the year and made regular advances to them on holidays. In addition, they carried over the sharecroppers' debts in case of a series of poor harvests.[24] Similar favors were accorded to their smallholding 'clients' as well as to farm laborers who worked for landlords on a seasonal basis. The hierarchical relation between notable and peasant appeared to involve a high degree of mutuality and reciprocity. On the basis of an empirical description of this system many observers have concluded that it is wrong to conceive of Palestinian society during this era in terms of social classes.[25]

What most observers have done is to accept, at face value, native conceptions (with a notable bias) about how politics and economics 'worked.' In fact, the patron-client system was simply the form that class relations assumed as Palestine was integrated into the capitalist world market as a dependency of the industrialized European powers. During this period landlords and usurers seized control over the countryside and manipulated existing precapitalist means of domination for their own interests.[26] The form that the relations between the fundamental classes took—'paternalism' in the sphere of production (cash advances by patrons to peasants) and 'patronage' in the sociopolitical sphere (an 'exchange' of favors)—tended to refract the fundamentally exploitative relations between landlord-usurers and peasants.[27] Politicoeconomic relations between them were represented as 'exchanges' between individuals unequal in status—notables whose superior birth and noble lineage qualified them to rule and to manage property, and peasants who had internalized their position of inferiority and who behaved deferentially toward their superiors. On the other hand, 'politics' in the larger sense of the 'affairs of state' appeared as a struggle among the notables themselves, in which peasant clients played only a supporting role. The notables acted as 'their' peasants' representatives to the government, a role acquired not through democratic elections but by ascribed superior status. The literature that characterizes political struggle in this period as 'factionalism' in fact disguises a high degree of class unity at the upper level. But on

there was a high degree of class unity at upper level

the lower levels, patron-client ideology largely reinforced and rigidified pre-existing vertical cleavages based on idioms of clan, village, and regional distinctions. The patron-client system did not assume the form of exchanges between 'free' individuals, as under full-blown capitalism. Instead, the system of exploitation required an extra-economic element, the force of status hierarchy, to justify the 'exchange' between persons of unequal position. Economic relations between patron and client were always expressed in such terms as 'honor,' gift-giving, kinship. Although paternalism and patronage provided the ideological basis for rule by the notables, their hegemony did not go unchallenged by the fellahin. There was room for struggle even on the basis of such an ideology. From the peasants' point of view, the system was designed to guarantee them the rights to a 'fair' and 'just' exchange. A notable could not charge too much rent without appearing to break his end of the bargain, without seeming to fail in his duty to uphold a standard of noblesse oblige. This meant that a landlord-usurer who charged peasants high interest on loans was simultaneously forced to advance them additional credit to maintain his labor force. In addition, the patron had to provide his client with the culturally regulated 'just' minimum of subsistence in order to neutralize potential class antagonisms. This level of subsistence was determined through similar struggles of a distinctly class character, for the peasant was able to use the notable's dependence on his labor as a wedge to demand adherence to the notion of 'fair' exchange. In the political realm, peasants (primarily the smallholder) could shift their allegiance if they received insufficient benefits from their patron. The patron-client alliances were thus far more fluid in composition than the model of a solid pyramidal structure purveyed by social scientists would suggest.[28]

Subordination of the political economy of Palestine to nineteenth-century Western industrial capitalism entailed, paradoxically, the reinforcement of precapitalist or 'feudal' ideologies. While peasants increasingly worked for capital, they did so under transformed precapitalist forms of productive relations and ideologies. In order to make these transformations, the notables had to 'work on' precapitalist ideologies of hierarchy, so as to reinforce the peasants' attitude of deference and to reproduce their sensibility of mutuality and exchange. The conditions of peripheral capitalism required a much more active ruling-class hegemony than had been needed in the precapitalist era. Ruling-class ideologies now had to penetrate deeply the cultural life of the peasantry,[29] including their religious 'common sense.' As a consequence folk practices were substantially transformed by notables in this period.

The organization of the feast of Nabi Musa exemplifies this process. In the latter half of the century, the Ottomans appointed the Husaynis—a rising notable clan from Jerusalem—as hosts of the Nabi Musa feast and custodians of the shrine.[30] Festivities were now launched at Jerusalem with a procession in which the banner of Nabi Musa was brought from the Husayni-owned Dar al-Kabira where it was housed. Notables led the procession followed by crowds from the city and the villages. At the site of the feast itself (near Jericho), the Husaynis and the Yunises, another Jerusalem notable family, served two public meals a day to all visitors.[31] Such rituals demonstrated notable generosity and claims to supremacy in powerful ways.

At the same time as unifying folk practices were subsumed under notable control, saint worship came under increasing attack by religious reformers, particularly from the Salafiya movement. Mosques, where state-backed Islamic orthodoxy was preached, replaced the *maqams* as village centers of worship. The chief reason for the suppression of saint worship was the localism it expressed.[32] Though such folk practices were not immediately wiped out, they were forced into regression as more and more peasants were 'educated' and came to regard such activities as 'un-Islamic.'

THE EMERGENCE OF ORGANIZED OPPOSITION

The piecemeal implementation of notable domination confined resistance against land transfers and growing state control to a localized, sporadic, and manageable level. No large-scale eruptions or even jacqueries occurred. However, opposition was still significant. For instance, many peasants demonstrated their opposition to the changing state of affairs by leaving their villages to settle as farmers in Transjordan or by migrating overseas. Others chose to join gangs of bandits, which continued to operate in the hills despite increasing pressure from security forces. Young men sought refuge with Bedouin tribes or even resorted to self-mutilation to avoid conscription into the army. Perhaps the major form of resistance in this period took place at the point of production. Palestinian peasants, particularly in the plains where sharecropping predominated, were often described at the time as 'lazy, thriftless and sullen.'[33] As James Scott has observed, 'footdragging and dissimulation' are a common form of resistance under unequal power relations.[34] While such resistance may not have posed a grave danger to the new system, it at least slowed the process of accumulation.

Peasant opposition to the colonization of Palestine by foreigners in fact presented the greatest threat to the hegemony of local notables. In 1878, Jewish settlers from Europe, with the backing of powerful capitalist financial interests, began to take advantage of the general land-grab in Palestine by acquiring lands and establishing agricultural colonies in the fertile coastal plains and the Esdraelon valley. By 1914, 12,000 Jews lived in such colonies, which produced valuable citrus and wine exports and encompassed over 162,500 acres of land concentrated in the richest agricultural regions. Most estates were purchased from absentee landowners in Beirut who had only

→ peasant opposition to colonization of Palestine → greatest threat to hegemony of notables

recently acquired them. As new colonies were set up, large numbers of peasant sharecroppers were forcibly removed from the lands they considered their birthright, although they may never have formally 'owned' them. Jewish settlers who established colonies even on 'marginal' lands were able to improve them due to their access to capital and advanced scientific techniques, and so denied nomads and peasants their customary-use rights to these common lands for grazing and gathering.

Palestinian notables were not at this stage implicated in any great degree in land sales to Jewish settlers. They protested Jewish immigration and land purchases as early as 1891, but their efforts were largely 'sporadic and nonsystematic' and limited to sending formal petitions of protest to Istanbul.[35] The advances made by urban Jews in commerce and industry were perceived as a greater threat to the interests of the Arab upper classes, particularly the commercial bourgeois sector, than were their purchases of agricultural properties.

In contrast, peasants whose livelihoods were directly threatened by Jewish colonies—especially those who cultivated and who pastured their herds in the northern and central plains—reacted in militant fashion. By 1883, displaced peasants and Bedouin were already attacking, raiding, robbing, and generally harassing the new Jewish settlements. Although spontaneous and fragmented, this violent opposition meant that the government was routinely forced to call out troops to drive fellahin off lands purchased by Jewish colonists. These activities eventually prompted the notables to protest the Zionist influx, albeit feebly.

The *a'yan*'s ineffectiveness in confronting the external threat began to undermine their own legitimacy (and that of the Ottoman state in general) in the eyes of many Palestinians. The disastrous experiences that befell dispossessed peasant sharecroppers in particular prompted them to question the usefulness of the patron-client system. Arab nationalism, emerging at the same moment, was able to tap these sentiments. As a nascent movement that advocated in its different versions either complete Arab independence from the Ottoman empire or greater autonomy, it became a significant social force in the wake of the ferment aroused by the Young Turk revolution (1908). Although the nationalist movement was less important in Southern Syria (Palestine) than in Lebanon and Northern Syria, and though it was dominated by notables and the commercial bourgeoisie, nonetheless there arose within it a radical wing composed of elements of the educated middle class. Opposition to Zionism was one of the Palestinian radical nationalists' chief themes, which they advanced through a new means of communication that had sprung up in this era of enhanced political freedom, namely newspapers. Although the early Arab nationalist movement is usually characterized as a strictly urban phenomenon, beginning in 1909 the political activities of its militant wing included helping to organize peasant attacks on Jewish settlements.[36] These raids increased in tempo in the years immediately preceding World War I, but this militant sector of the developing Arab national movement and its peasant connections assumed real prominence only during the years following the war.

THE BRITISH OCCUPATION OF PALESTINE AND THE MANDATE, 1918–29

Expectations for national independence rose sharply in Greater Syria as World War I and the privations it caused came to a close. These hopes intensified in 1918 with the establishment of an Arab government at Damascus under Prince Faysal. Many young Palestinian radicals from the educated middle class held prominent positions in the new Sharifian government. At the same time, their influence in Palestine began to outstrip that of the more moderate notables. Through organizations such as al-Nadi al-ʻArabi (the Arab Club) and al-Muntada al-Adabi (the Literary Club), the radicals pushed for a program of complete independence of Palestine from Britain and for its political unity with the rest of Syria. By contrast, the Palestinian notables who had organized Muslim-Christian Associations in all the towns favored a separate political autonomy for Palestine under British protection. The euphoria that followed the end of the war was dampened by the Balfour Declaration, which announced Britain's intention of establishing a 'national home for the Jewish people' in Palestine. This tarnished Britain's local reputation and helped win broad popular support for the militant nationalist program. Popular radicalism in turn pressured the notable *zuʻama* or 'chiefs' to adopt more combative positions themselves. The militants capitalized on the moment by pushing through a resolution advocating Palestine's political unity with Syria at the notable-dominated First Palestine Arab Congress.[37]

In this period the radicals not only organized effectively in the public arena but also secretly purchased arms and prepared for armed revolt in favor of Faysal.[38] So effective was the radicals' work among the peasantry that in December 1919, British Naval Intelligence reported with concern that fellahin were listening with keen interest to both Damascus and local newspapers advocating pan-Arabism and discussed the possibility of anti-Zionist actions.[39] Despite widespread illiteracy, 'advanced' pan-Arab and anti-Zionist ideas circulated among the peasantry and helped to mobilize them. At least one organized act of violence against the British occurred. In April 1920, Palestinian radicals (connected to the Arab government at Damascus) organized over 2,000 armed Bedouin from the Hawran (Syria) and the Baysan valley of Palestine in an attack on British military forces.[40] The countrywide anti-British upsurge that the radicals expected to ensue did not, however, come to fruition.

In the same month, soon after Faysal was crowned as king of Syria, radicals intervened in the Nabi Musa procession at Jerusalem. In 1919 the practice of delaying the procession for speeches had been introduced;[41] this year Musa Kazim al-Husayni, Jerusalem's mayor and a leading notable, praised Faysal in his speech, while young activists made 'inflammatory' declamations from the balcony of the Arab Club. The crowds, including peasants from the surrounding villages, responded by roaming the streets of the Old City, attacking Jewish residents.[42] This event transformed the *mawsim* of Nabi Musa from a folk festival into an annual nationalist demonstration.[43]

In May 1921, clashes between Arabs and Jews at Jaffa led to generalized fighting and attacks on Jewish settlements throughout the country. The British military quickly and violently restored order. Two months later King Faysal's troops at Damascus were defeated by the French, who dismantled the Arab government. The moment of crisis had ended. Great Britain, which now held a mandate to govern Palestine under the auspices of the League of Nations, strengthened its control. The threat of pan-Arab militants to *a'yan* hegemony and their ability to mobilize the peasantry subsided. The notables, who favored a policy of peaceful negotiations with the British authorities rather than mass mobilization as the means of achieving the nationalist goals, re-emerged as the dominant force within the national movement.

During the 1920s, the notables reasserted their hegemony over the Arab population of Palestine through a consolidation of their role as 'natural' leaders of the national movement. British authorities in turn absorbed members of notable families into important administrative positions in the mandate government.[44] As chief agents of state rule in the late Ottoman and mandate periods, they expected to emerge as the country's rulers once Great Britain granted Palestine its independence. Their principal means of organization, the Muslim-Christian Associations, were not mass-membership bodies but were composed of religious leaders, property owners, those who held positions in the Ottoman administration, and 'noble' families of rural origin—in short, the *a'yan* class. These associations periodically met in Palestine Arab Congresses and in 1920 set up an Arab Executive, chaired by Musa Kazim al-Husayni, to tend to the daily affairs of the national movement. At the same time, mandate authorities co-opted a young militant from a prominent notable family, Hajj Amin al-Husayni, making him first Grand Mufti (1921) and then president of the Supreme Muslim Council (SMC) in 1922. As 'Head of Islam in Palestine,' Hajj Amin gradually consolidated all Islamic affairs under his administration and began to compete with the more cautious Arab Executive for leadership of the nationalist movement.[45]

The notables continued to lead the Arab population of Palestine in the mandate period under the ideology of patronage. *A'yan* served as mediators between the people and the British authorities. Politics was strictly reserved for organizations (the Muslim-Christian Associations, the SMC) 'qualified' to lead. Once the radical pan-Arab threat had passed and Palestine was established as a territorial unit, notables were able to co-opt the growing popular self-awareness of 'Palestinian Arabness' that arose in response to the Zionist threat and to alien rule.[46] Furthermore, the British bolstered the *a'yan* position by ruling through their agency and by upholding their control over rural areas.[47]

In spite of the fact that the legitimacy of notable leadership was constructed on 'national-popular' sentiments, the notables themselves were caught in a fundamentally contradictory position, for while the *a'yan* posed as leaders of nationalist aspirations, they served as officials in the British mandate administration. Rifaat Abou-el-Haj sums up the predicament of Palestinian notables (characteristic of all Mashriq elites):

> [As the nationalist elite] actually began to collaborate with the new ruling powers, the [elite] cadre managed to portray itself in the 'vanguard' of resistance against outside domination—in some instances even taking a revolutionary posture. The other role it adopted for itself was that of realist-pragmatist mediator with which it defended its compatriots against the direct and therefore presumed odious rule of the foreigner.[48]

The British in Palestine depended in particular on erstwhile 'radical' Amin al-Husayni to act as such a mediator. The Mufti worked hard to prevent outbursts and to pacify the Muslim community, channeling nationalist energies (including those of his former comrades) into legal activities.[49]

The contradictory position of the Palestinian notables—at once servants of the British mandate and leaders of 'the nation'—was rendered even more unstable than that of Arab elites elsewhere, due to the competition of the Zionist movement. Since Zionists opposed the establishment of any legislative body in Palestine that would relegate the Jews to a minority position, they effectively blocked the development of national Palestinian institutions of self-rule. Had not the threat of Jewish immigration appeared somewhat limited due to internal problems of the Zionist movement, conditions might have been more unstable in the 1920s. But meanwhile, the Zionists were quietly building an infrastructure that served as the basis for expansion of the Jewish community in the 1930s and made the Yishuv virtually self-governing.[50]

The lack of progress in the creation of Palestinian institutions of self-rule began to undermine even the notables' own liberal self-image. Steeped in Western liberal ideas,[51] the *a'yan* expected the British to behave toward them according to the standards of justice that Great Britain preached. As it gradually became clear that the British authorities did not adhere in practice to the standards that the two groups supposedly shared, Palestinian liberal notables became disillusioned. Both notables and liberal intellectuals developed an ambivalent attitude toward the West and, in particular, Britain.[52]

Although the notables never entirely abandoned their affection for Britain since service in the mandate administration was still profitable, disaffection for British policies slowly undermined their confidence in diplomatic discussions between 'gentlemen' as the best means of resolving the national question.

Rapidly changing agrarian conditions during the 1920s were potentially more unsettling to *a'yan* hegemony. Land purchases by the Zionists continued apace, resulting in the dispossession of increasing numbers of peasants. The notables' appeals that the government halt the process were ineffectual. Moreover, by 1928, land sales to the Zionists by Palestinian landowners had eclipsed those by non-Palestinians.[53] A section of the notable class was thus enriching itself through land sales to Zionists and contributing directly to peasant landlessness, especially in the northern and central plains. This portion of the *a'yan*, clustered around the leadership of the Nashashibi clan, which opposed the Husayni dominance in the national movement, generally comprised its wealthier and commercial elements, who used their profits for urban construction and expansion of citrus production.

Small but growing numbers of peasant holders also sold their lands to Zionist developers, usually not for profit but to pay off debts. Peasant indebtedness to usurers who charged high rates of interest was exacerbated by the mandate government's rationalization of rural property taxes, now set at a fixed percentage based on the net productivity of the soil (that is, minus the cost of production). This meant that the capital-intensive Jewish agricultural enterprises paid lower rates because of higher 'labor costs.' Regressive indirect taxes added to the peasants' financial burden. The weight of taxation therefore fell disproportionately on poor Palestinian fellahin, whose contributions helped to finance industrial and agricultural development in the Jewish sector and to pay Britain's expenses in defending the Jewish 'national home.'[54] The British administration also ensured that taxes were more efficiently collected by enlisting the services of the village *mukhtars* (headmen) to maintain rural security and to pass on taxes and information to the government.[55]

As a consequence of such pressures, by 1930 some 30 per cent of all Palestinian villagers were totally landless, while as many as 75 to 80 per cent held insufficient land to meet their subsistence needs.[56] Some peasants made up this imbalance by renting additional farmlands, but most now depended on outside sources of income for survival. During peak periods of economic activity in the mandate, about one-half of the male fellahin workforce (over 100,000 persons) engaged in seasonal wage employment outside the village (on road or construction projects, in citrus harvesting and packing, and so forth). Often the entire male population of a village was recruited to work as a team on short-term construction projects.[57] Thus Palestinian rural villagers no longer filled a purely 'peasant' position in the economic structure; increasingly they assumed a dual economic role as peasants and as casual laborers.

So while notable landowners and moneylenders maintained economic dominance over the villages, particularly through client networks, the new experiences of peasants in the wider labor market altered their 'traditional' fellahin subjectivities and provided alternative sources of income.

Indebtedness and expropriation at the hands of Zionist colonies forced a significant sector of the peasantry to emigrate permanently to the rapidly growing metropolises of Haifa, Jaffa, and Jerusalem. There they worked mainly as casual laborers and as a 'scuffling petty bourgeoisie' in petty trading and services, a class situation typical of urban centers in underdeveloped colonial social formations.[58] Permanent wage work was difficult to come by in the face of competition from Jewish workers who monopolized positions in the more advanced Jewish economic sector. The work that Arab workers did obtain was extremely low-paying, due to an abundant labor supply and the difficulties inherent in organizing casual workers. As a consequence, the costs of Arab labor were never fully met by wages but were subsidized by the workers' access to subsistence agriculture and support networks at home in the village.[59]

These rural-to-urban migrants did not remain passive in the face of such conditions. On the contrary, they set up various associations based on village of origin which ignored the *hamula* distinctions that were so divisive at home.[60] They also joined semi-political organizations headed by artisans, enlisted in trade unions whenever possible, and came in contact with militant religious reformers like Shaykh 'Izz al-Din al-Qassam. Their entry into the urban wage workforce helped to weaken clan, village, and regional divisions; these new experiences also had an impact on the home villages, with which migrants maintained close contact. Thus the old cleavages that buttressed patron-client networks were slowly breaking down under the impact of capitalist development. The nationalist leadership tried to reverse the process by making frequent appeals to the British on behalf of the impoverished peasantry, but this had little effect on British policies or on economic conditions.[61] Furthermore, the fellahin were increasingly skeptical of the *a'yan*'s sincerity. By 1927, according to a British official, the notables were apprehensive that the peasantry 'show[ed] a growing tendency to distinguish between national and Effendi [notable] class interest.'[62]

The brewing crisis in agriculture, closely tied to steady Zionist progress in the 1920s (between 1919 and 1929 the Jewish population of Palestine had doubled, reaching 156,000 persons[63]), was a major factor in igniting the violence that erupted over expanded Zionist claims to the Wailing Wall at Jerusalem (known by Arabs as the Buraq, the western wall of the Haram al-Sharif, third holiest shrine in Islam). The Mufti as usual tried to settle the problem through the good offices of the British, at the same time attempting to allay the anger of the populace, who saw in Zionist 'religious' expansionism a condensed form of the general danger Zionism posed to Palestinian Arab

-lots of labor.

differnt class interests

sovereignty.[64] A series of provocative demonstrations at the wall by Zionist extremists took place during 1929. Finally, on 23 August, peasant villagers, influenced by the propaganda work of nationalist militants, arrived in Jerusalem for Friday prayers armed with knives and clubs. Hajj Amin made every effort to calm the crowds, but radical religious shaykhs made speeches inciting them to action.[65] Violence broke out against Jews in Jerusalem and quickly spread throughout the country; British forces restored order in brutal fashion.

The widespread nature of the violence demonstrated that the mass of the population was ready to take direct action against the Zionist threat, independently of the cautious notable leadership. Unfortunately they could also be incited to ugly sectarian violence, which assumed the dimensions of a pogrom at Hebron and Safad. One of the most important forms of organization to emerge from this outbreak was the guerrilla band known as the Green Hand Gang established by Ahmad Tafish in the Galilee hills in October 1929. Composed of men associated with radical circles who had taken part in the August uprising, the band launched several attacks on Zionist colonies and British forces in the north.[66] The band's organization probably resembled that of the gangs of peasant bandits who traditionally operated in the Palestine hills and who were a growing security problem in the 1920s.[67] But unlike them, Ahmad Tafish's band had an overt political purpose. Although quickly subdued, the Green Hand Gang aroused considerable sympathy among the peasantry who, the Shaw Commission concluded in 1930, were 'probably more politically minded than many of the people of Europe.'[68] This atmosphere of popular agitation provided new opportunities for alternative political forces within the national movement to challenge notable hegemony.

HARBINGERS OF REVOLT, 1930–35

The early 1930s were characterized by extremely unstable conditions, which the Palestinian *zu'ama* were incapable of controlling. Contradictions piled one on top of another, ushering in a series of crises that, by fits and starts, led to the explosion of 1936.

One major destabilizing factor was the global depression. Due chiefly to forces released by the worldwide economic downturn, Jewish immigration to Palestine jumped sharply in the early 1930s. Between 1931 and 1935 the Jewish community grew from 175,000 to 400,000 persons, or from 17 to 31 per cent of the total population of Palestine. The advance of anti-Semitism in Poland, the tightening of the US quota system in 1929, and the triumph of Nazism in Germany all contributed to the floodtide of immigration to Palestine.[69]

The effects of Jewish immigration upon Palestinian Arab society were uneven. Between the late 1920s and 1932, the country suffered a recession and a steep rise in Arab unemployment. But with the refugee influx, the economy expanded in the 1933–36 period, while the rest of the world (except the Soviet Union) languished in deep depression. As a result of an agreement, known as the Haʿavara, between the World Zionist Organization and the Nazis, Jews leaving Germany were able to import large amounts of capital into Palestine. Nearly 60 per cent of all capital invested in Palestine between August 1933 and September 1939 entered by means of the Haʿavara.[70] This capital inflow permitted wealthy Jews greatly to increase their investments in industry, building, and citriculture. In addition, rapid British development of Haifa as a strategic eastern Mediterranean port meant the construction of a new harbor, an oil pipeline (which began pumping oil from Iraq in 1935), refineries, and a railroad during the same period.[71] As a consequence, job opportunities for Arab workers expanded. The greatest share of jobs, however, went to Jewish workers, as Zionist leaders and especially the Histadrut (the Zionist labor federation) made sure that the burgeoning Jewish economic sector provided for the new Jewish immigrants. This caused resentment among Arab workers and led to clashes with Jews over access to jobs.[72] The economy suffered another recession from 1936 to 1939, which affected semi-proletarianized Arab workers much more deeply than largely unionized Jewish labor.

The capital influx accompanying Jewish immigration increased the pace of land purchases as well. Zionist acquisitions from large Palestinian owners and small peasants now assumed greater importance than in the 1920s.[73] An increasingly desperate economic situation constrained peasants to sell their lands, for by 1936 the average debt of a peasant family—25 to 35 pounds per year—equaled or surpassed their average annual income of 27 pounds.[74] The money peasants earned from land sales usually did little more than release them from debt and propel them toward the urban slums. Due to inflated real-estate prices, large Palestinian landowners, on the other hand, could make huge profits by selling their estates to the Zionists. Some owners arbitrarily raised rents to force their tenants off the land prior to concluding such a sale, in order to avoid paying compensation to the peasants.[75] A law, decreed in 1933, extending greater rights to tenants contributed to a noticeable increase in disputes between landlords and peasants over tenancy rights. Militant nationalists were involved in encouraging such conflicts.[76] By the mid-1930s the government was routinely forced to call out large numbers of police in order to evict sharecroppers from sold properties as, more and more frequently, peasants resisted dispossession through violent means.[77]

The bankruptcy of the notables' policies was therefore increasingly apparent: they had made no progress toward achieving national independence and were incapable of stemming the Zionist tide of increasing population, land settlement, and economic development. The *a'yan*'s inability to achieve successes threatened their hold over the national movement and made it difficult for them to claim the discourses of nationalism or even Islam as their exclusive property. Moreover, the notable front had splintered over disagreements on national strategy. Opposition to Husayni leadership crystallized around the Nashashibi clan, which represented the richest landowners, citrus growers, and entrepreneurs. More heavily involved than other notables in land sales to the Zionists, and the greatest beneficiaries of citrus exports to England, the Nashashibi-led groups of the notable-mercantile class opposed pan-Arab unity and was ready to accept less than total independence from Britain.[78] This group, which established the National Defense Party in 1934, had a certain base of support through its patron-client networks.[79]

The radical nationalists took advantage of the openings provided by the series of crises and by the swelling of their ranks with a new contingent of young men educated in mandate institutions. As Göran Therborn notes, the training of an intellectual stratum in colonial situations often generates revolutionary ideologies, due to the disparity between the nature of the training they receive, suitable for an advanced capitalist society, and the colonial form of subjection.[80] The mandate educational system in Palestine produced young men whose qualifications were not commensurate with the holy roles assigned to them, and so their discontent generated new and critical forms of subjectivity.

The 1930s witnessed an upsurge in Palestine of independent political organizing by the educated middle class, just as in the rest of the Arab world, where a new generation of radical nationalists were raising slogans of socio-economic justice and Arab unity and developing novel forms of political organization.[81] Palestinian radicals set up a variety of bodies such as the Young Men's Muslim Association, the Arab Youth Conferences, and the Arab Boy Scouts (independent of the international Baden-Powell movement). The most important organization was the Istiqlal (Independence) Party, established in 1932, whose roots lay in the old Istiqlal movement associated with the Sharifian government at Damascus.[82] Led by elements of the educated middle class and the disaffected offspring of notable families, it appealed to educated professionals and salaried officials: lawyers, doctors, teachers, government employees.[83] Unlike other Palestinian parties founded in the 1930s, it was organized not on the basis of family or clan loyalties but around a political program, and thus it was the first (excluding the Communist) to appeal to and construct a new and modern form of subjectivity. It also distinguished itself by centering its political actions on opposition to the British mandate government rather than aiming them at the Jewish community alone.

The Istiqlal took a 'populist' political stance representative of an aspiring national bourgeoisie.[84] Its adherents criticized the chronic unemployment besetting Arab workers, and the high taxes, rising prices, and unjust government treatment that the peasants suffered under. The Istiqlal advocated the establishment of a nationalist parliament and the abolition of 'feudal' titles, such as *pasha, bey*, and *effendi*, that were common among the notables. In 1933, Istiqlalists began to attack the notable leadership, asserting that, because it had remained abject in the face of Zionism and imperialism, Palestinian nationalism was not the cause of the *zu'ama* but, rather, that of the poor.[85] The Istiqlalists therefore attempted to mobilize the popular classes along the faultlines of class antagonisms by constructing a popular-democratic discourse that took advantage of fellahin disaffection from the notables and used it for 'national' purposes.[86]

In 1934, however, only a year and a half after its founding, the Istiqlal Party ceased to function effectively. Aided by the party's division into pro-Hashemite and pro-Saudi factions, Hajj Amin al-Husayni was able to sabotage it. Many Istiqlalists subsequently joined the Mufti's Palestine Arab Party, which, paradoxically, made it into something more than simply a clan-based grouping.[87] In addition, their entry pushed Hajj Amin to take a more militant stance. But even after their party's demise, Istiqlalists continued to be active as individuals, while other independent groupings stepped up their organizing efforts. The Arab Youth Congress attempted to prevent illegal Jewish immigration by organizing units to patrol the coasts.[88] Arab labor garrisons were set up at Jerusalem, Haifa, and Jaffa to defend Arab workers against attacks by Jewish workers trying to prevent Jewish capitalists from hiring Arabs.[89]

Efforts to mobilize the peasantry were even more consequential. Educated young men from the villages, who returned home to serve as teachers, spread radical nationalist notions among the fellahin, particularly in the northern foothills of Jabal Nablus (the region known as the Triangle, comprising the environs of Nablus, Janin, and Tulkarm) where villages had lost land to Zionist colonies on the coastal and Esdraelon plains.[90] Poetry was an especially significant vehicle for this dissemination of nationalist ideas and sentiments in the countryside. Written in simple language and style, nationalist poetry frequently criticized the notable leadership.[91] According to Ghassan Kanafani, it often took the form of 'almost direct political preaching.'[92] Poems and songs by artists like Ibrahim Tuqan, 'Abd al-Karim al-Karmi, and 'Abd al-Rahim Mahmud were well known in the countryside and recited at festive and public occasions. Peasants had access to newspapers (which began to appear daily after the 1929 riots) and magazines that printed nationalist poetry; the anthropologist Hilma Granqvist reports that fellahin from the village of Artas who went to Bethlehem for market heard newspapers read aloud in the coffee shops there.[93] Probably most villages had similar access to the printed word. Al-Baquri claims that the poetry of the nationalist bards 'rang out on the lips of the fighters and popular masses' during the 1936–39 revolt.[94]

this is what happened when nationalism started to centralize

The Palestine Communist Party should be mentioned in this context, even though its impact on events was minimal. Founded in 1922, the PCP remained primarily a Jewish organization until 1929, when the Comintern ordered it to undergo 'Arabization.'[95] At its Seventh Congress in 1930, it began to orient itself programmatically toward the peasantry. Asserting that in an agricultural country like Palestine it was 'the peasant revolution' that was 'the most significant,' it called for the confiscation of estates held by big Arab landowners, religious institutions, and Jewish colonies, and for their distribution to landless and land-poor peasants. The PCP urged peasants to refuse to pay taxes and debts and advocated armed rebellion. It also proposed conducting propaganda at the mosques on Fridays and at popular festivals like Nabi Musa, for 'it is during such mass celebrations that the fighting capacity of the fellahin is appreciably aroused.'[96] In addition, the PCP campaigned vigorously on behalf of Bedouin and peasants dispossessed by Zionist colonization.[97] But due to its paucity of Arab members, the fact that no cadre lived in villages, and widespread perceptions that it was chiefly a Jewish organization, the party's influence in the Palestinian Arab community remained circumscribed. In any case, after the onset of the Comintern's Popular Front strategy, the PCP dropped its call for agrarian revolution (typical of the world Communist movement's ultra-left 'Third Period') and began trying to build closer ties with middle-class nationalists. 'Abd al-Qadir Yasin asserts that the party's social demands were influential among workers and peasants by the mid-1930s,[98] but such claims are difficult to verify, since the PCP's ideas were not backed up by practices. At best, Communist notions may have influenced radical nationalist individuals with whom the party maintained contact.

A wave of renewed violence in 1933 further demonstrated the notables' tenuous hold over the nationalist movement. Violence rapidly spread through the urban centers (and some villages) of the country after an anti-British demonstration at Jaffa in October led to clashes with police. Unlike the situation in 1929, this violence was aimed specifically at the British mandate administration, which represented a significant shift in the movement's strategy and political awareness. The British leaned harder than ever on the Mufti to keep these disturbances from getting out of hand. In return for preventing the fellahin from following the 'extremists' and for restraining demonstrations, the British granted the Supreme Muslim Council complete control over *waqf* (religious endowment) finances.[99] But as tensions mounted, Hajj Amin's position as mediator became more precarious. He moved in two directions at once, trying both to maintain good relations with the British by reining in the national movement and to retain credibility with the populace by adopting a militant posture.

Hajj Amin's primary activities concerned land sales, a significant issue of public concern. The Palestinian Arab press frequently editorialized against land traffic with the Zionists, and in the early 1930s the Muslim-Christian Associations and the Arab Executive had sent agents out to the villages, urging peasants not to sell their land.[100] In the fall of 1934 the Mufti and the SMC initiated a more vigorous campaign, mobilizing the ideology and institutions of Islam to fight land sales (and to maintain Hajj Amin's influence with the peasantry). The Mufti toured areas where transactions were occurring, to explain the dangers they posed to the nation and condemn them as acts of sin and high treason.[101] In January 1935, he issued a *fatwa* (legal opinion) on the matter that forbade traffic in land with the Zionists and branded *simsars* (real estate brokers) as heretics (*mariq*).[102] But religious propaganda alone could not reverse the economic forces that led the peasants into indebtedness and forced them off the land. The dire agrarian situation was exacerbated by a series of crop failures between 1929 and 1936 and by competition from cheap agricultural imports, their prices depressed by the global economic downturn.[103] The Mufti recognized, in theory, the need for structural changes, and he called for (1) measures to protect peasants from big landowners; (2) the establishment of national industries; (3) aid to small farmers; and (4) a campaign of purchasing national products.[104] But the SMC's only concrete action was to put some tracts of land under *waqf* (mortmain) protection.

By the mid-1930s the political impasse in Palestine forced even the Mufti to realize that more drastic measures might be called for. Accordingly, in late 1933 a young associate of Hajj Amin's, 'Abd al-Qadir al-Husayni, organized a secret military group known as Munazzamat al-Jihad al-Muqaddas (Organization for Holy Struggle).[105] At the same time, various groupings of radicals were also preparing for military struggle. And in 1934, according to Palestine Communist Party propaganda, a popular bandit known as Abu Jilda was carrying out significant armed activity in the countryside. Abu Jilda's 'partisan detachments,' the Communists claimed, were pulling the country toward disorder and toward armed revolt against the colonial authorities.[106]

THE REVOLT OF AL-QASSAM

The spark that ignited the explosion came from an independent organization intimately connected to the peasantry and semi-proletariat created by the agrarian crisis. That organization was founded by radical Islamic reformer Shaykh 'Izz al-Din al-Qassam. A native of Jabla, Syria, and a key figure in the 1921 revolt against the French, al-Qassam took refuge in Haifa after fleeing Syria under sentence of death. A man of great religious learning who had studied at Cairo's al-Azhar, al-Qassam was associated with the Islamic reform (Salafiya) movement,[107] as well as with certain Sufi *turuq*.[108] He quickly achieved prominence in Haifa as a preacher and teacher. Unlike other political activists in Palestine, al-Qassam concentrated his efforts exclusively on the lower classes with whom he lived.[109] He set up a night school to combat illiteracy among the casual laborers (recent migrants from rural areas) of Haifa shantytowns and was a prominent member of the Young Men's Muslim Association. In 1929 al-Qassam was appointed marriage registrar of Haifa's Shari'a court. The duties of this office, which required that he tour northern villages, permitted him to extend his efforts to the peasantry, whom he encouraged to set up growing and distribution cooperatives.[110]

Using his religious position, al-Qassam began to recruit followers from among the fellahin and the laborers of Haifa, organizing them into clandestine cells of not more than five persons. By 1935 he had enlisted 200, perhaps even 800, men.[111] Many received military training, carried out after dark; all were imbued with al-Qassam's message of strict piety, of struggle and sacrifice, of patriotism, the necessity for unity, and the need to emulate early Islamic heroes.[112] In the 1920s, al-Qassam made a name for himself by attacking as un-Islamic certain folk religious practices still common in the Haifa area.[113] Such censure accorded with al-Qassam's Salafiya leanings and recalled the actions of 'Abd al-Karim, leader of the 1924–27 anti-Spanish rebellion in the Moroccan Rif. A Salafiya advocate like al-Qassam, 'Abd al-Karim had banned a number of traditional folk religious practices in the interests of promoting unity among the Rif rebels.[114] Al-Qassam's political activities also paralleled those of Hasan al-Banna, founder of the Muslim Brothers (al-Ikhwan al-Muslimin) in Egypt. Just as al-Banna recruited his first followers in the new towns of the Canal Zone, so al-Qassam recruited in the newly developing city of Haifa. But while al-Banna attracted the new Egyptian petty bourgeoisie, al-Qassam focused on the recently dispossessed peasants working as casual laborers in the slums.[115]

Al-Qassam's appeal to religious values was not simply a return to tradition or a retreat into the past, but instead represented a real transformation of traditional forms for revolutionary use in the present.[116] He seized on popular memories of the Assassins and the wars against the Crusaders by invoking the tradition of the *fida'iyin*, the notion of struggle that involved sacrifice. His clandestine organization resembled that of a Sufi order: his followers grew their beards 'wild' and called themselves shaykhs.[117] This was not as incongruous as it might seem, for, as Thomas Hodgkin argues, the Islamic worldview contains elements that can be articulated together to constitute a revolutionary tradition.[118] Al-Qassam's efforts represent just such an articulation and condensation of nationalist, religious 'revivalist' and class-conscious components in a movement of anti-colonial struggle.

Although his followers may have begun carrying out small armed attacks on Zionist settlements as early as 1931,[119] it was not until November 1935 that al-Qassam decided the moment was ripe for launching a full-scale revolt. Accompanied by a small detachment of followers, he set out from Haifa with the aim of raising the peasantry in rebellion. An accidental encounter with the police led to a premature battle with the British military, however, and al-Qassam died before his rebellion could get off the ground.

Nonetheless, his example electrified the country. Independent radical organizations eulogized al-Qassam and gained new inspiration from his revolutionary project. Al-Qassam rapidly achieved the status of a popular hero, and his gravesite became a place of pilgrimage.[120] His legacy also included the many Qassamites still at large and prepared for action, as well as militant nationalists who set up fresh political groupings in the towns and organized armed bands on the Qassam model. Urban radicals also redoubled their organizing in the villages in preparation for a new anti-British outbreak.[121] In such a highly charged atmosphere, only a small event was needed to trigger an explosion.

THE GREAT REVOLT (AL-THAWRA AL-KUBRA)

That incident occurred on 13 April 1936, when two Jews were murdered in the Nablus Mountains, perhaps by Qassamites. Following a wave of brutal reprisals and counter-reprisals, the government declared a state of emergency. In response, 'national committees' led by various militant organizations sprang up in the towns and declared a general strike. The notables followed along, trying to retake control of the unruly movement. On 25 April all the Palestinian parties (including the Nashashibi's National Defense Party) met with the national committees and set up a coordinating body known as the Higher Arab Committee (HAC), with Amin al-Husayni as its president. Although the HAC grew out of the notables' move to regain their dominant position, nonetheless, as a merging of the independent radical groupings with the traditional leadership it was more representative than the old Arab Executive had been.[122] The HAC quickly declared that the general strike would continue until the British government put an end to Jewish immigration to Palestine, and it restated the other basic national demands—the banning of land sales and the establishment of an independent national government.

Though it initially sprang up in the towns, the revolt's focus rapidly shifted to the countryside. A conference of rural national committees convened in May and elaborated a specific peasant agenda, including a call for nonpayment of taxes and the denunciation of the establishment of police stations in villages at fellahin expense.[123] In addition, Istiqlalists (still active as individuals) toured the countryside of the Triangle to mobilize support for the general strike, while both Qassamites and SMC preachers spread propaganda and attempted to organize among peasants.[124]

In mid-May, armed peasant bands in which Qassamites featured prominently appeared in the highlands. They were assisted by armed commandos in the towns and by peasant auxiliaries who fought part-time. Though connected to the urban national committees, in general these bands operated independently of the Mufti and the HAC.[125] From mountain hideouts they harassed British communications, attacked Zionist settlements, and even sabotaged the Iraq Petroleum Company oil pipelines to Haifa. This last activity posed a particular threat to British global hegemony, for in the 1930s Great Britain still controlled the bulk of Middle East oil, and the Haifa pipeline was crucial to imperial naval strategy in the Mediterranean.

The towns, in a state of semi-insurrection, were finally brought under control by the British in July, which left the countryside as the undisputed center of revolt.[126] In the following month Fawzi al-Qawuqji, hero of the Syrian Druze rebellion of 1925, resigned his commission in the Iraqi army and entered Palestine with an armed detachment of pan-Arab volunteers, declaring himself commander-in-chief of the revolt.[127] Although the military effectiveness of the rebel movement was improved and al-Qawuqji was hailed as a popular hero throughout the country, he never managed to unite all the diverse bands under his command.

While popular forces fought the British in the countryside, the notables of the HAC—only one of whom had been arrested—were negotiating with the enemy for a compromise to end the conflict. British authorities increased the pressure in late September by launching tough countermeasures—boosting their military force to 20,000, declaring martial law, and going on a new defensive. The HAC was also constrained by the onset of the agricultural season: peasants wanted to resume work, but, more important, harvest season started in September on the plantations of wealthy citrus-growers.[128] The HAC, preferring negotiations to mass mobilization, which threatened notable leadership, called off the six-month-old general strike on 10 October, with the understanding that the Arab rulers (of Iraq, Transjordan, and Saudi Arabia) would intercede with the British government on the Palestinians' behalf and that the government would act in good faith to work out new solutions. A long interim period ensued. While notables pinned their hopes on a Royal Commission of Inquiry, activists and rebel band leaders toured the villages and purchased weapons in preparation for a new round of fighting.

In July 1937, the British Peel Commission published its recommendations for the partition of Palestine into Arab and Jewish states. Arab reaction was universally hostile; even the Nashashibi faction which had defected from the HAC condemned the partition proposal. Feelings ran especially high in the Galilee, a highland region with few Jewish residents, which the plan of partition included in the proposed Jewish state.[129] In September, following the assassination of the British district commissioner for Galilee (possibly by

Qassamites), the second phase of the revolt erupted. British authorities responded by banning the HAC and deporting or arresting hundreds of activists. The Mufti managed to evade arrest by escaping to Lebanon in October. Shortly thereafter, fierce fighting broke out. With the notable leadership in exile or imprisoned, command now shifted decisively to the partisans in the countryside.

Rebel bands were most active in the Nablus and Galilee highlands, the areas of greatest popular resistance. The Jerusalem-Hebron region, where the Munazzamat al-Jihad al-Muqaddas operated, was also an important center. In these districts the various bands set up their own court system, administrative offices, and intelligence networks. While peasants and ex-peasant migrants to the towns composed the vast majority of band leaders and fighters, young urban militants played important roles as commanders, advisers, arms transporters, instructors, and judges.[130] Qassamites were particularly well represented at the leadership level. By taxing the peasantry, levying volunteers, and acquiring arms through the agency of experienced smugglers,[131] the bands were able to operate autonomously from the rebel headquarters-in-exile set up by the notable leadership at Damascus. A network of militants in the towns, particularly from among the semi-proletariat, collected contributions, gathered intelligence, and carried out acts of terror against the British, the Zionists, and Arab *simsars* and collaborators.[132]

In the summer and fall of 1938 the rebellion reached its peak. Some 10,000 persons had joined the insurgent bands, now sufficiently well organized for a handbook of instructions to be issued for their members.[133] Commanders of the largest bands established a Higher Council of Command to enhance military coordination. Most of the Palestinian highlands were in rebel hands, and by September government control over the urban areas had virtually ceased.

Once rebels gained the upper hand in the towns, the peasant character of the revolt expressed itself even more clearly. Rebel commanders ordered all townsmen to take off the urban headgear, the fez, and to don the peasant headcloth, the *kafiya*; urban women were commanded to veil. This action was both practical, in that it protected rebels from arrest by the British when they entered the towns, and symbolic, in that it signified the countryside's hegemony over the city. Insurgents also instructed urban residents not to use electric power, which was produced by an Anglo-Jewish company. Few dared disobey these orders. Large sums of money were extracted from wealthy city-dwellers as contributions to the revolt, and particularly large 'contributions' were demanded from the big orange-growers and merchants at Jaffa who supported the Nashashibi opposition.[134]

On 1 September, the joint rebel command issued a declaration that directly challenged the leading classes' dominance over the countryside. Although limited in scope, the declaration represented a social program which went beyond the merely 'national' goals of the *a'yan*. In it the commanders declared a moratorium on all debts (which had so impoverished the peasantry and by means of which notables controlled agricultural production) and warned both debt collectors and land agents not to visit the villages. Arab contractors, who hired work teams for the construction of police posts in the villages and roads to facilitate access to rebel strongholds, were also ordered to cease operations. In addition, the statement declared the cancellation of rents on urban apartments, which had risen to scandalously high levels. This item was particularly significant in that, by linking the needs of peasants and urban workers, it revealed the new class alliance underpinning the revolt.[135]

The rebels' interference with landlord-usurer control over the countryside and their demands for contributions from the wealthy constituted a 'revenge of the countryside,' which prompted thousands of wealthy Palestinians to abandon their homes for other Arab countries. Well-off Palestinians tended to view the rebels as little better than bandits. In part this charge was justified, for there were serious discipline problems within the rebel camp, despite the considerable advances the bands achieved in coordination and unity of purpose. For instance, clan or family loyalties occasionally interfered with the class or national interests of certain rebel commanders, who carried out petty blood-feuds under cover of nationalist activity.[136] Some peasants were alienated by the coercive manner employed by particular leaders to collect taxes and by their favoritism toward certain clans. Moreover, although class divisions among the peasants were not well developed, villagers were by no means homogeneous in their class interests. The assassination of a *mukhtar* who collaborated with the British, for example, was likely to alienate those members of his *hamula* who benefited from the *mukhtar*'s ties to outside forces.

Most accounts of the revolt stress the internal problems faced by the rebels. Although such criticisms are exaggerated and detract from the rebels' positive accomplishments, they cannot simply be dismissed. The British and the Nashashibis were able to exploit the contradictions within the rebel movement through such means as the formation of 'peace bands' in late 1938 to do battle with the rebels. Although representative primarily of the interests of landlords and rural notables, the 'peace bands' were manned by disaffected peasants.[137]

More important for British strategy than the 'peace bands' was the signing of the Munich Agreement on 30 September 1938. This allowed Britain to free one more army division for service in Palestine and to launch a military counteroffensive. Is it possible that British Prime Minister Chamberlain signed the Munich Agreement not merely to appease Hitler momentarily but also to protect Britain's oil supply in the Mediterranean from 'backward' but dangerous bands of peasants? It would be difficult to chart a clear cause–effect relation, but it is evident at least that, for the British chiefs of staff, Palestine was a crucial strategic buffer between the Suez Canal and potential enemies to the north (Germany, Soviet Union) and was an indispensable link in land communications. With war looming on the horizon in Europe, Britain was seeking desperately to end the disturbances in Palestine.[138]

In any event, the Munich Agreement had disastrous consequences not just for Czechoslovakia but for the rebellion in Palestine as well. By 1939 the rebels were fighting a British military force of 20,000 men as well as the RAF. In addition, Orde Wingate, a British officer, organized a counterinsurgency force of Jewish fighters known as the Special Night Squads to terrorize villagers and to guard the oil pipeline.[139] The British counteroffensive increased pressure on the rebels and prompted further internal problems, such as abuses in collecting taxes and contributions and an upsurge in political assassinations.

However, the intensified military offensive was still not enough to finish off the rebellion, so the British launched a diplomatic one as well. In March 1939 the government issued a White Paper declaring that it was opposed to Palestine becoming a Jewish state, that Jewish immigration would be limited to 75,000 over the next five years, that land sales would be strictly regulated, and that an independent Palestinian state would be set up in ten years with self-governing institutions to be established in the interim. Although both the notables and the rebels rejected the White Paper, the Palestinian populace responded to it more favorably.[140] Clearly, while it did not satisfy the maximum national demands, the White Paper represented a concession wrung from the British by armed resistance. Zionist reaction against the White Paper, by contrast, was much more virulent.

The revolt was gradually crushed by extreme external pressures and the resultant internal fracturing of the movement. After over three years of fighting, the intervention of substantial British military forces aided by the Zionists, and nearly 20,000 Arab casualties (5,032 dead, 14,760 wounded[141]), the rebellion was finally subdued. In July the last major rebel commander was captured; once the war with Germany began in September 1939, fighting ended altogether. An entirely new set of circumstances on the international scene were to determine subsequent events in Palestine.

CONCLUSION

I have tried to propose an alternative to the prevailing analyses of the Great Revolt in Palestine, which represent Palestinian society as so fractured by vertical cleavages that neither the class nor national unity necessary for success in the anti-colonial, anti-Zionist struggle could emerge. Given the prevailing social structure, so the argument goes, once the Palestinian peasantry took leadership of the revolt it could only act true to its inherently 'backward' character. Arnon-Ohanna's assessment is typical: 'The absence of cooperation and mutual responsibility, the deep-seated divisiveness of a society based on patriarchal lines and *hamulas*, the ancient inter-village and inter-*hamula* wrangles over stretches of land and water sources, over blood feuds, family honor and marital problems—these were simply transferred to the [guerrilla] bands movement.'[142] According to many of those who make such an argument, only one force could have ensured victory: a modern, revolutionary party.[143]

I have argued that the model of vertical cleavages was essentially ideological, in that it was the form through which the Palestinian ruling class maintained its political and economic hegemony. As an ideology of rule, it worked by refracting the underlying class structure of the society, making relations of exploitation appear as amicable 'exchanges' between persons of unequal status. In an effort to show that class antagonisms overdetermined this relation, I argue that peasants manipulated the dominant ideology in their struggle for a better life. Although peasants lived in a state of subordination, landlord-notable domination was never total but was resisted on the basis of the very *terms* of the dominant ideology, that is, the struggle for a 'just' exchange.

What is more, peasants possessed traditions of resistance, which they could call on in moments of crisis to forge a movement of opposition. I have charted a genealogy of these traditions of resistance prior to 1936. Despite its weak and often broken lines of descent, its vague and hidden traces, there are strong indications of such a tradition: a semi-autonomous existence prior to 1831, banditry and unorthodox religious practices, resistance to the expansion of the Ottoman state and to land registration in the late nineteenth century, and spontaneous struggles against new colonies of European Jews. Buried deeper within popular consciousness, moreover, were memories of earlier struggles, such as that of Salah al-Din's (Saladin) against those earlier European invaders, the Crusaders. Such traditions do not necessarily imply practices of a conservative or retrograde nature, for, as Raymond Williams has argued, the 'residual' can be an important source for progressive political practices even in advanced industrial societies.[144]

I have stressed too that the fellahin's folk heritage was not a pure, unblemished one. Their 'common sense' was penetrated and altered over time by dominant ideologies of the state during the resurgence of Ottoman power in the second half of the nineteenth century, and by the nationalist idioms of the notables in the mandate period. Peasant consciousness was influenced as well by radical ideas emanating from militants of the middle class. Older traditional notions came to be articulated with the newer discourses of the nation, democracy and reformist Islam. In some cases, as with al-Qassam's attack on folk Islamic practices, popular traditions were modified in order to enhance the unity of the popular movement. In other instances, traditional

there were lots of divisions which prevented unity 1800s

practices such as banditry were transformed into powerful modern vehicles of struggle.

My aim has also been to demonstrate that the Palestinian peasantry was not an unchanging 'backward' component of Palestinian society, but that it underwent constant change in the period under study. During the nineteenth century it was transformed from a class of relatively independent producers to one dominated by landowners and usurers, producing to a growing extent for the capitalist world market. A substantial number of peasants were displaced by Zionist colonization and indebtedness, forced out of agriculture altogether, and made into casual laborers. The fellahin were transformed further in the twentieth century, assuming a dual character as peasants and as casual workers. The partial integration of peasants into the wage circuit of 'free' labor socialized peasant-workers in new ways and contributed to the dissolution of the precapitalist institutions in the village. Although the notables and the British tried mightily to uphold the hierarchies of patron-client networks, the grounds on which they were established were destabilized by the advances of Zionism and the notables' own failure to achieve 'national' goals. Peasants totally abandoned by the system—dispossessed of their lands by Zionist colonies and driven into the towns as a subproletariat—eagerly embraced new ideas and practices that challenged notable dominance.

All these forces came into play during the Great Revolt. The peasant-led movement represented a congealing of nationalism, religious revivalism, and class consciousness, no element of which can be neatly disentangled from the others. Here I have underscored the emergence within the rebel movement of specific demands and practices of the peasantry as a class, in part because in other accounts this aspect is so underplayed. The refusal to pay taxes, the moratorium on debts, the heavy contributions levied against the wealthy: all these rebel practices aimed at addressing the needs of the peasants. In addition, the declared moratorium on rental payments for apartments indicates the movement's close linkage with the urban semi-proletariat. The campaign of terror launched against collaborators, land agents, *mukhtars*, and Arab police officers represented a serious attempt to deal with traitors whose activities had hurt peasants, even though by all accounts it was carried to unnecessary extremes. While such demands and actions on the part of the rebels did not, strictly speaking, constitute 'revolutionary' practice, they nonetheless posed a considerable threat to the political and economic hegemony of the notables. They also show that to claim that the rebels had *no* discernible, coherent social or political program is to oversimplify the issue considerably.[145]

We have seen how the rebels were able partially to overcome 'traditional' social divisions based on region and clan. The establishment of a council of command by the leading commanders was an important political step in this direction, as were the efforts of Qassamites who organized on the basis of an Islamic discourse colored by the interests of the popular classes. Such factors made crucial contributions to the remarkable degree of coherence that the rebellion was able to achieve.

Much has been made, in accounts of the rebellion, of the internal problems besetting the rebel forces. Indeed, misguided practice—such as regional, familial, and lineage loyalties which overrode fidelity to the movement, and the resort to assassination, brutality, and heavy-handed methods in extracting 'contributions' from peasants—posed real problems for the movement and undermined its ability to sustain broad popular support. It is difficult here to achieve a 'correct' analytical balance. But we should remember that throughout the world, unsavory practices have been common during moments of social upheaval. We should not therefore focus on them exclusively in order to discount an entire movement. Such problems would not necessarily have magically been transcended under the guidance of a 'revolutionary' party and leadership, for a party is no guarantee of a successful outcome for social struggle. To focus attention on the absence of a party, as many have done, is to belittle the militant, honest leadership and forms of organization that the peasantry and semi-proletariat were able to muster. While some commanders were given to self-aggrandizement and petty feuding, many others (most of whom remain anonymous) deserve to be remembered. Qassamites, who played a key leadership role, were particularly noted for their devoutness and honesty, and 'Abd al-Rahim al-Hajj Muhammad, the most respected commander, was renowned for his nationalist convictions, for his opposition to political assassination, and for his tirelessness as a fighter.[146]

If anything, it was the formidable strength of the enemy that was more crucial to the peasant rebels' defeat than their purported 'backwardness.' The British, determined to maintain control over this area of major strategic importance (particularly the harbor at Haifa, the oil pipeline, and communication routes to India), mustered a substantial military force to fight the rebels. In addition, the powerful Jewish community was enlisted to assist the British efforts. Jews were enrolled in the police and the constabulary; Jewish fighters were organized into special counterinsurgency squads by Orde Wingate. Zionist revisionists, without British approval, launched terrorist attacks against the Arab community. Moreover, the rebellion gave the Zionists the opportunity to build up their military capabilities. While by the end of the revolt the Arab community was substantially disarmed, the Zionists in the meantime had put 14,500 men, with advanced training and weaponry, under arms.[147] This military imbalance between the two communities, enhanced during World War II, was an extremely important factor in the disaster that befell the Palestinian Arabs in 1948.

I have tried, then, to develop a counterargument to the dominant analysis of the Great Revolt. The 'master narrative' of the rebellion tends to proceed by defining (and thereby diminishing) the peasants and casual laborers as 'traditional,' 'backward,' 'fanatical,' or even 'terrorists.' By presenting the peasantry as essentially unchanging, this approach also permits scholars to ignore the very real history of peasant resistance which preceded the rebellion. Other writers sympathetic to the revolt often disparage it for lacking a revolutionary party at its helm. Such arguments allow analysis to trivialize or ignore the accomplishments of the revolt and to concentrate on other questions, such as the role of the middle class, the treachery of the notables, or the Palestine Communist Party (which in fact was largely irrelevant to this affair[148]). What is at stake in such a dismissal is that the legitimate social and political desires of subaltern popular social movements have gone unheeded by the 'progressive' as well as the dominant commentaries. Scholarly work that would constitute a social history of the revolt, including an investigation of the cultural life of the peasantry, the economic organization of the countryside, traditions of resistance, and ideologies of domination and opposition, has therefore scarcely begun.[149]

For this reason, I have stressed in polemical fashion the positive accomplishments of the peasantry in the course of the Great Revolt—achievements which have so often been minimized. This should be seen, then, only as a tentative step toward the development of a complete analysis, which requires the investigation of both structures of dominance and movements of opposition in their complex historical relation.

NOTES

1. Musa Budeiri, *The Palestine Communist Party, 1919–1948: Arab and Jew in the Struggle for Internationalism* (London: Ithaca Press, 1979), pp. 46–47.

2. Ann Mosely Lesch, *Arab Politics in Palestine, 1917–1939: The Frustration of a Nationalist Movement* (Ithaca: Cornell University Press, 1979), p. 17.

3. Ibrahim Abu-Lughod, 'The Pitfalls of Palestiniology: A Review Essay,' *Arab Studies Quarterly* 3 (1981): 403–11.

4. Methodologically this requires a strategy of reading from the margins of existing works on the history of Palestine. This chapter does not pretend to be an exhaustive survey but is meant to suggest further avenues of research. A major problem is that the role of peasant women cannot be recovered through such a reading strategy; other means are required to develop an analysis of this important question.

5. Gramsci's notion of hegemony is summarized by Raymond Williams, *Marxism and Literature* (Oxford: Oxford University Press, 1977), pp. 112–13.

6. Antonio Gramsci, *Selections from the Prison Notebooks*, ed. and trans. Quintin Hoare and Geoffrey Nowell Smith (New York: International Publishers, 1971), pp. 323–26, 419–25.

7. The conclusions of the following four sections are based in part on my M.A. thesis: Theodore Swedenburg, 'The Development of Capitalism in Greater Syria, 1830–1914: An Historico-Geographical Approach,' University of Texas at Austin, 1980.

8. Palestine was only united as an administrative entity under the British mandate. In the Ottoman period, it was ruled from various cities such as Damascus, Sidon, Beirut, and Jerusalem. I am treating it here as a geographical unit.

9. Aref el-Aref, 'The Closing Phase of Ottoman Rule in Jerusalem,' Moshe Ma'oz, ed., *Studies on Palestine during the Ottoman Period* (Jerusalem: Magnes Press, 1975).

10. Constantin F. Volney, *Travels throughout Syria and Egypt in the Years 1783, 1784, and 1785*, vol. 2 (England: Gregg International Publishers, 1973).

11. This class structure is comparable to what Rey terms a 'hierarchical society': Pierre-Philippe Rey, 'Les formes de la décomposition des sociétés précapitalistes au Nord-Togo et le mécanisme des migrations vers les zones de capitalisme agraire,' in Emile le Bris et al., eds, *Capitalisme négrier* (Paris: Maspero, 1976), pp. 195–209.

12. Volney, *Travels*, pp. 252–53. A similar relationship among peasants, their overlords, and the state characterized conditions in Southeast Asia during the same period: Michael Adas, 'From Avoidance to Confrontation: Peasant Protest in Precolonial and Colonial Southeast Asia,' *Comparative Studies in Society and History* 23 (1981): 217–47.

13. Karl Marx, *Grundrisse*, trans. Martin Nicolaus (New York: Vintage Books, 1973).

14. Maurice Godelier, 'Infrastructures, Societies and History,' *Current Anthropology* 19 (1978): 63–68. Empires based on a tributary mode of production typically left economic systems based on kinship intact, only modifying them to ensure that tribute was rendered. See also Samir Amin, *The Arab Nation* (London: Zed Press, 1978), pp. 87–102.

15. The situation in Palestine resembled that of the Kabyle Mountains of Algeria, where during the same era 'league feuds channeled or drained off the energies of the peasants and diverted them from the social struggle ... Even though the leagues and alliances ... veiled social tensions and disjunctures, these were nonetheless manifest': René Gallissot, 'Pre-Colonial Algeria,' *Economy and Society* 4 (1975): 424–25.

16. Mordechai Abir, 'Local Leadership and Early Reforms in Palestine, 1800–1834,' in Ma'oz, ed., *Studies on Palestine*, pp. 284–310.

17. Taufik Canaan, *Mohammedan Saints and Sanctuaries in Palestine* (London: Luzac, 1927), p. 251. Such proverbs are typical of mountain peasants of the Arab world and of 'segmentary' Bedouin societies. (For Morocco, see David M. Hart, *The Aith Waryaghar of the Moroccan Rif* [Tucson: University of Arizona Press, 1976].) My own reading of this proverb diverges from the usual interpretation given by anthropologists, who see it exclusively in terms of kinship and alliance. I suggest a broader political interpretation.

18. Canaan, *Mohammedan Saints*.

19. Ibid., p. 98.

20. Ibid., pp. 215–16.

21. Ibid., p. 193.

22. Alexander Schölch, 'The Economic Development of Palestine, 1856–1882,' *Journal of Palestine Studies* 39 (1981): 35–58.

23. Alexander Schölch, 'European Penetration and the Economic Development of Palestine, 1956–85,' in Roger Owen, ed., *Studies in the Economic and Social History of Palestine in the Nineteenth and Twentieth Centuries* (Carbondale: Southern Illinois Press, 1982), pp. 10–87.

24. Ya'akov Firestone, 'Crop-sharing Economics in Mandatory Palestine,' *Middle Eastern Studies* 11 (1975): 10.

25. Lesch, *Arab Politics*, p. 89.

26. For criticisms by anthropologists of the patron-client model as applied to Mediterranean societies, see Michael Gilsenan, 'Against Patron-Client Relations,' in Ernest Gellner and John Waterbury, eds, *Patrons and Clients* (London: Duckworth, 1977), pp. 167–83; Luciano Li Causi, 'Anthropology and Ideology: The Case of "Patronage,"' *Critique of Anthropology 4/5* (1975): 90–109; and Paul Littlewood, 'Patronage, Ideology and Reproduction,' *Critique of Anthropology 15* (1980): 29–45.

27. Littlewood, 'Patronage,' pp. 37–38.

28. See David Seddon, *Moroccan Peasants* (Folkestone, Ky.: Dawson, 1981), p. 92, and Göran Therborn, *The Ideology of Power and the Power of Ideology* (London: New Left Books, 1980), pp. 56–57, 61–62, for discussions which support this line of argument.

29. Gramsci, *Selections*, p. 54.

30. J.C. Hurewitz, *The Struggle for Palestine* (New York: W.W. Norton, 1950), p. 54.

31. Canaan, *Mohammedan Saints*, pp. 197, 204–5.

32. Gilsenan, 'Against Patron-Client Relations,' pp. 53, 151–52; see also Albert Hourani, *Arabic Thought in the Liberal Age, 1798–1939* (London: Oxford University Press, 1962), p. 150.

33. Claude Regnier Conder, *Tent Work in Palestine* (New York: D. Appleton, 1878), p. 267.

34. James Scott, 'Hegemony and the Peasantry,' *Politics and Society* 7 (1977): 284.

35. Yehoshuah Porath, *The Emergence of the Palestinian-Arab National Movement, 1918–1929* (London: Frank Cass, 1974); Neville Mandel, *The Arabs and Zionism before World War I* (Berkeley and Los Angeles: University of California Press, 1975), pp. 70, 214–22.

36. Mandel, *Arabs and Zionism*, pp. 70, 214–22.

37. Porath, *Emergence*, pp. 7–8.

38. Abdul-Wahhab Kayyali, *Palestine: A Modern History* (London: Croom Helm, 1978), pp. 71–72; Porath, *Emergence*, pp. 129–30.

39. Kayyali, *Palestine*, p. 73.

40. Nathan Weinstock, *Le Sionisme contre Israel* (Paris: Maspero, 1969), p. 169.

41. Kayyali, *Palestine*, p. 75.

42. Lesch, *Arab Politics*, p. 89.

43. Hurewitz, *Struggle*, p. 54.

44. Ylana M. Miller, *Government and Society in Rural Palestine 1920–1948* (Austin: University of Texas Press, 1985), pp. 16–18.

45. Hurewitz, *Struggle*, pp. 52–53.

46. Miller, *Government*, pp. 27, 54–62.

47. Ibid.

48. Rifaat Abou-el-Haj, 'The Social Uses of the Past: Recent Arab Historiography of Ottoman Rule,' *IJMES* 14 (1982): 187.

49. Porath, *Emergence*, pp. 200–202.

50. Miller, *Government*, pp. 24–25, 47.

51. Hourani, *Arabic Thought*, passim. For an example of a liberal Palestinian mode of argument, see George Antonius, *The Arab Awakening* (London: Hamish Hamilton, 1938).

52. Walid Khalidi, ed., *From Haven to Conquest* (Beirut: Institute for Palestine Studies, 1961), p. 72.

53. Yehoshuah Porath, *The Palestinian Arab National Movement: From Riots to Rebellion, 1929–1939* (London: Frank Cass, 1977), pp. 83–84.

54. Talal Asad, 'Anthropological Texts and Ideological Problems: An Analysis of Cohen on Arab Villages in Israel,' *Review of Middle East Studies* I (1975): 1–40.

55. Gabriel Baer, 'The Office and Functions of the Village Mukhtar,' in J.S. Migdal, ed., *Palestinian Society and Politics* (Princeton: Princeton University Press, 1980), pp. 103–23.

56. Shulamit Carmi and Henry Rosenfeld, 'The Origins of the Process of Proletarianization and Urbanization of Arab Peasants in Palestine,' *Annals of the New York Academy of Sciences 220* (1974): 470.

57. Ibid., pp. 481–82.

58. Ken Post, *Arise Ye Starvelings: The Jamaican Labour Rebellion of 1938 and Its Aftermath* (The Hague: Martinus Nijhoff, 1978), pp. 133–36.

59. Sarah Graham-Brown, *Palestinians and Their Society, 1880–1946: A Photographic Essay* (London: Quartet Books, 1980), p. 150. For a theoretical analysis of this phenomenon in South Africa see Harold Wolpe, 'The Theory of Internal Colonialism: The South African Case,' in Ivar Oxall et al., eds, *Beyond the Sociology of Development* (London: Routledge & Kegan Paul, 1975), pp. 229–52.

60. Rachel Taqqu, 'Peasants into Workmen: Internal Labor Migration and the Arab Village Community under the Mandate,' in Migdal, *Palestinian Society*, p. 271.

61. Miller, *Government*, pp. 79–89.

62. Nels Johnson, *Islam and the Politics of Meaning in Palestinian Nationalism* (London: Routledge & Kegan Paul, 1982), p. 37.

63. David Hirst, *The Gun and the Olive Branch* (New York: D. Appleton, 1977), vol.2, p. 63.

64. Philip Mattar, 'The Role of the Mufti of Jerusalem in the Political Struggle over the Western Wall, 1928–29,' *Middle Eastern Studies* 19 (1983): 104–18.

65. Ibid., p. 114; Lesch, *Arab Politics*, pp. 210–11.

66. Kayyali, *Palestine*, p. 156; Shai Lachman, 'Arab Rebellion and Terrorism in Palestine 1929–1939: The Case of Sheikh Izz al-Din al-Qassam and His Movement,' in Elie Kedourie and Sylvia G. Haim, eds, *Zionism and Arabism in Palestine and Israel* (London: Frank Cass, 1982), p. 56.

67. Ivar Spector, *The Soviet Union and the Muslim World, 1917–1956* (Seattle: University of Washington Press, 1956), p. 100.

68. Ibid., p. 156. The Shaw Commission's statement reflects an ethnocentric and classist bias that assumes that the non-Western peasantry was inherently apolitical. In fact, movements of peasants have posed the greatest threat to imperialist rule in the underdeveloped world.

69. Porath, *Palestinian Arab*, p. 40.

70. Lenni Brenner, *Zionism in the Age of Dictators* (Highland Park, N.J.: Lawrence Hill, 1983), p. 65; Weinstock, *Sionisme*, pp. 135–36.

71. Carmi and Rosenfield, 'Origins,' p. 476.

72. Porath, *Palestinian Arab*, pp. 129–30.

73. Ibid., pp. 182–84.

74. Weinstock, *Sionisme*, p. 64.

75. Porath, *Palestinian Arab*, pp. 103, 105.

76. Kenneth Stein, 'Legal Protection and Circumvention of Rights for Cultivators in Mandatory Palestine,' in Migdal, ed., *Palestinian Society*, pp. 250–54.

77. Kayyali, *Palestine*, p. 179.

78. Porath, *Palestinian Arab*, p. 67.

79. Lesch, *Arab Politics*, pp. 110–11.

80. Therborn, *Ideology*, pp. 17, 46.

81. Philip S. Khoury, 'Islamic Revivalism and the Crisis of the Secular State in the Arab World: An Historical Reappraisal,' in I. Ibrahim, ed., *Arab Resources: The Transformations of a Society* (London: Croom Helm, 1983), pp. 219–20. Women's organizations emerged in Palestine as a new form of mobilization in this period, but those discussed in the literature were led by the wives of the notable leaders (Mrs Matiel E.T. Mogannam, *The Arab Woman and the Palestine Problem* [London: Herbert Joseph, 1937]) and were similar in form to the Muslim-Christian Associations. It is possible that their example inspired mobilization by women of the educated middle classes, but for now we can only conjecture.

82. Kayyali, *Palestine*, pp. 167–68.

83. 'Abd al-Qadir Yasin, *Kifah al-Sha'b al-Fisastini qabl al-'am 1948* (Beirut: PLO Research Center, 1975), pp. 125–26; Hurewitz, *Struggle*, p. 63.

84. Yasin, *Kifah al-Sha'b*, pp. 125–26. This national bourgeoisie existed, however, in embryo only.

85. Ibid., pp. 125–26; Kayyali, *Palestine*, pp. 167–68, 172.

86. For a discussion of populism see Ernesto Laclau, *Politics and Ideology in Marxist Theory* (London: New Left Books, 1977), especially p. 109.

87. Kayyali, *Palestine*, p. 187; Porath, *Palestinian Arab*, pp. 16–17.

88. Zvi Elpeleg, 'The 1936–39 Disturbances: Riot or Rebellion?' *Wiener Library Bulletin* 29 (1976): 41.

89. Kayyali, *Palestine*, p. 177.

90. Porath, *Palestinian Arab*, p. 181.

91. Adnan Abu-Ghazaleh, 'Arab Cultural Nationalism in Palestine during the British Mandate,' *Journal of Palestine Studies* 3 (1972): 48–49.

92. Ghassan Kanafani, *The 1936–39 Revolt in Palestine* (Committee for a Democratic Palestine, n.d.), p. 17.

93. Abu-Ghazaleh, 'Arab Cultural Nationalism,' p. 87; Hilma Granqvist, *Marriage Conditions in a Palestinian Village* (Helsingfors: Societas Scientarium Fennica, 1931), p. 99.

94. Abd al-'Al, al-Baquri, 'Al-thawra bayn barakat al-jamahir wa tadahun al-qiyadat,' *Tali'ah* 7, no. 4, p. 95.

95. Joel Beinin, 'The Palestine Communist Party, 1919–1948,' *MERIP Reports* 55 (1977): 8–9.

96. The resolutions of the Seventh Congress are reproduced in Spector, *Soviet Union*, pp. 91–104.

97. Beinin, 'Palestine Communist Party,' p. 12; Budeiri, *Palestine Communist Party*.

98. Yasin, *Kifah al-Shab*, p. 143.

99. Kayyali, *Palestine*, p. 175.

100. Porath, *Palestinian Arab*, pp. 92–93.

101. Ibid., pp. 96–97.

102. Yasin, *Kifah al-Shab*, pp. 147–48.

103. Firestone, 'Crop-sharing,' pp. 17–18.

104. Yasin, *Kifah al-Shab*, pp. 146–48.

105. Kayyali, *Palestine*, pp. 179–80.

106. Budeiri, *Palestine Communist Party*, p. 77.

107. It has been claimed that al-Qassam was a student of Muhammad 'Abduh's, but S. 'Abdullah Schleifer, in 'The Life and Thought of 'Izz-al-Din al-Qassam,' *Islamic Quarterly* 23 (1979): 61–81, asserts that 'Abduh's influence on al-Qassam was very limited.

108. Al-Qassam's grandfather and granduncle were prominent shaykhs of the Qadari order in his hometown of Jabla, and al-Qassam taught for a time in a school maintained by that *tariqa*. Al-Qassam is said to have belonged to the Tijaniyya and Naqshbandi *turuq*, the latter of which was involved in anti-colonial struggles in Syria during the nineteenth century: Schleifer, 'Life and Thought,' pp. 62–63, 69.

109. Lachman, 'Arab Rebellion,' p. 77.

110. Porath, *Palestinian Arab*, pp. 133–34; Kayyali, *Palestine*, p. 180; Schleifer, 'Life and Thought,' p. 47.

111. Kayyali, *Palestine*, p. 180; Porath, *Palestinian Arab*, p. 137.

112. Hirst, *Gun and Olive Branch*, p. 76.

113. Schleifer, 'Life and Thought,' p. 68; Lachman, 'Arab Rebellion,' p. 62.

114. Hart, *Aith Waryaghar*, pp. 170ff., 377ff.

115. Gilsenan, 'Against Patron-Client Relations,' pp. 217–28.

116. Laclau, *Politics and Ideology*, p. 157. Al-Qassam's practices recall Walter Benjamin's notion of the 'dialectical image,' a reconstellation of materials from the past in the revolutionary present: Susan Buck-Morss, 'Walter Benjamin—Revolutionary Writer (1),' *New Left Review* 128 (1981): 50–75. See also Williams's category of the 'residual': *Marxism*, pp. 121–27.

117. Lachman, 'Arab Rebellion,' p. 64.

118. Thomas Hodgkin, 'The Revolutionary Tradition in Islam,' *History Workshop* 10 (1980): 148–49.

119. Lachman, 'Arab Rebellion,' p. 65; Yasin, *Kifah al-Shab*, p. 154, maintains that armed action began only in 1933.

120. Lachman, 'Arab Rebellion,' p. 72.

121. Ibid., p. 74; Kayyali, *Palestine*, pp. 182–83.

122. James J. Zogby, 'The Palestinian Revolt of the 1930's,' in I. Abu-Lughod and B. Abu-Laban, eds., *Settler Regimes in Africa and the Arab World* (Wilmette, Ill.: Medina U.P.I., 1974), pp. 182–83.

123. Kayyali, *Palestine*, p. 192.

124. Lachman, 'Arab Rebellion,' p. 78; Porath, *Palestinian Arab*, pp. 179–82.

125. Porath, *Palestinian Arab*, pp. 192–93.

126. Ibid., pp. 179–82.

127. The Palestinians had shown solidarity with the rebellion of 1925, when the Mufti had headed an emergency committee to aid the Druze: Michael Assaf, *The Arab Movement in Palestine* (New York: Masada Youth Organization of America, 1937), p. 39.

128. Porath, *Palestinian Arab*, pp. 211–21; Kayyali, *Palestine*, p. 201.

129. Lesch, *Arab Politics*, p. 122.

130. Porath, *Palestinian Arab*, p. 261.

131. Tom Bowden, *The Breakdown of Public Security: The Case of Ireland 1916–1921 and Palestine 1936–1939* (Beverly Hills: Sage, 1977). Among the usual items the smugglers trafficked in was hashish.

132. Kayyali, *Palestine*, p. 212; Porath, *Palestinian Arab*, pp. 249–50; Lachman, 'Arab Rebellion,' p. 80.

133. Porath, *Palestinian Arab*, p. 247; Yuval Arnon-Ohanna, 'The Bands in the Palestinian Arab Revolt, 1936–39: Structure and Organization,' *Asian and African Studies* (Jerusalem) 15 (1981): 232. According to Arnon-Ohanna (p. 233), band membership was between 6,000 and 15,000.

134. Porath, *Palestinian Arab*, pp. 267–69.

135. Ibid., pp. 267–68; Kayyali, *Palestine*, p. 214.

136. Porath, *Palestinian Arab*, p. 269.

137. Ibid., pp. 251, 262, 269.

138. Gabriel Sheffer, 'Appeasement and the Problem of Palestine,' *IJMES* (1980): 377–99.

139. Christopher Sykes, *Cross Roads to Israel* (London: New English Library, 1967), p. 193.

140. Porath, *Palestinian Arab*, p. 293.

141. Walid Khalidi, ed., *From Haven to Conquest* (Beirut: Institute for Palestine Studies, 1971), pp. 848–49.

142. Arnon-Ohanna, 'Bands,' p. 247.

143. Those who advance the 'solution' of the revolutionary party are of various political persuasions and include Porath, *Palestinian Arab*, p. 269; Yasin, *Kifah al-Shab*, pp. 195–96; Budeiri, *Palestine Communist Party*, p. 107; Weinstock, *Sionisme*, p. 178; Tom Bowden, 'The Politics of Arab Rebellion in Palestine, 1936–39,' *Middle Eastern Studies* II (1975): 147–74; Kayyali, *Palestine*, p. 231.

144. Williams, *Marxism*, pp. 121–27.

145. This claim is made by, for instance, Graham-Brown, *Palestinians*, p. 171.

146. Porath, *Palestinian Arab*, p. 183; Elpeleg, '1936–39, Disturbances,' pp. 48–49; Lesch, *Arab Politics*, p. 223.

147. Hirst, *Gun and Olive Branch*, p. 104.

148. For instance, Samih Samara Samih, *Al-'amal al-shuyu'i fi filastin: al-tabaqa wa-al-sha'b fi mawajaha al-kuluniyaliya* (Beirut: Dar al-Farabi, 1979). Budeiri, *Palestine Communist Party*, Alain Greilsammer, *Les communistes israéliens* (Paris: Presses de la Fondation Nationale des Sciences Politiques, 1978). For a review of this growing body of literature, see Alexander Flores, 'The Palestine Communist Party during the Mandatory Period: An Account of Sources and Recent Research,' *Peuples méditerranéens* II (1987): 3–23, 175–94. Such studies touch only lightly on the 1936–39 rebellion and contain little socioeconomic analysis of the Palestinian social formation.

149. The work of Sarah Graham-Brown is a noteworthy exception. On this point, see Ibrahim Abu-Lughod, 'The Pitfalls of Palestiniology: A Review Essay,' *Arab Studies Quarterly* 3 (1981): 403–11.

Of the Diversity of Iraqis, the Incohesiveness of their Society, and their Progress in the Monarchic Period toward a Consolidated Political Structure

HANNA BATATU

At the turn of the century the Iraqis were not one people or one political community. This is not meant to refer simply to the presence of numerous racial and religious minorities in Iraq: Kurds, Turkomans, Persians, Assyrians, Armenians, Chaldeans, Jews, Yazīdīs, Sabeans, and others. The majority of the inhabitants of Iraq, the Arabs, though sharing common characteristics, were themselves in large measure a congeries of distinct, discordant, self-involved societies.

A wide chasm, to begin with, divided the main cities from the tribal country. Urban and tribal Arabs—except for dwellers in towns situated deep in the tribal domain or tribesmen living in the neighborhood of cities—belonged to two almost separate worlds. The links between them were primarily economic. But even in this regard their relationships could scarcely be said to have been vigorous. As late as the 1870s, in the districts that were remote from the main towns or from Shaṭṭ-al-'Arab and the Tigris—steamers traded only on these rivers, as the Euphrates could not be navigated with ease—wheat rotted in the granaries or, as there was no other means of turning it to account, was used as fuel, while from time to time the people at Baghdād suffered from scarcity of grain. Although in subsequent decades there was an increasing but slow advance in the direction of interdependence, economic disparateness remained only too real. Segments of the tribal domain unreached by river steamers continued to be largely self-sufficient, and even had market towns of their own. Similarly, the cities had their own countryside, which nestled close to them or was within reach of their protection. Here the lands on which townsmen directly depended were cultivated by peasants who, although by origin tribesmen, were now held together by a territorial connection. But most of the agricultural and pastoral lands of Iraq formed part of the tribal domain.

No less crucial was the social and psychological distance between the urban and tribal Arabs. In many ways they were very different from each other. The life of the urban Arabs was on the whole governed by Islamic and Ottoman laws, that of the tribal Arabs by Islamically tinged ancient tribal customs. Some of the urban Arabs, in particular the educated stratum, had come under the influence of Turkish—and in Shīʿī cities, Persian—culture; tribal Arabs, on the other hand, had escaped that influence altogether. Among urban Arabs class positions were somewhat strongly developed, among the more mobile of the tribesmen relations were still patriarchal in character. Many of the townsmen had, in the words of a nineteenth-century Iraqi historian, 'become habituated to submission and servility.'[1] The freer of the tribesmen were, by contrast, irrepressible. As far as they were concerned, government was a matter for contempt. As one Euphrates satirical *hawsah* or tribal chant expressed it: *Maldiyyah, wa mā min samm biha; taina, wa tchānat mahyūbah.*[2] (It is a flabby serpent and has no venom; we have come and have seen it, it is only in times past that it kept us in awe.) Again, the Arabs of the cities were very conscious of their Muslimness; with the tribal Arabs the feeling for Islam was not as intense. I am not oblivious of the power that the Shīʿī divines had over the Shīʿī tribes of the Euphrates, but even the latter never developed the passion for religion so characteristic of urban Muslims. It is significant that, in time of tribal levées, the chants of tribesmen had usually secular—tribal or Arab—themes, such as the old Arab motif, *al-murūʾ*ah, manliness, whereas the masses of the city rallied more naturally to religious cries. 'Ad-Dīn! Yā Muḥammad!'—'The Religion! O Muḥammad!'[3] was one of the more common slogans of the populace in Baghdād.[4] Of course, both tribal and town Arabs were conscious that they were Arabs, in particular when they were confronted, say, with a Turk or a Persian; but their Arab consciousness was in no way akin to that of the later Arab nationalists. That they were Arabs was to them a natural fact, a fact they may have taken pride in, but they did not feel at all impelled to do something about it. Theirs, in other words, was not a dynamic Arabism, nor did the nation as such form the focus of their sentiments or of their loyalty.

The contrast that we have drawn between urban and tribal Arabs should not be overemphasized. We cannot afford to forget that many townsmen were of relatively recent tribal origin. Even today a large number of the inhabitants of Baghdād, quite apart from the tribal immigrants of the last four decades, still remember the name of the tribe to which they once belonged. A glance at the accompanying table [Table 1] is enough to suggest that there must have been in past centuries some sort of a recurrent turnover of the town

TABLE 1 *The Calamities of Which We Have a Record and Which Overtook Baghdād in the 17th, 18th and 19th Centuries*

1621	Famine
1623	'Hundreds or thousands' of Sunnīs massacred and 'thousands' of others sold into slavery by Persians
1633	Flood
1635	Plague
1638	General slaughter by Turks: about 30,000 victims, mostly Persians
1656	Flood
1689	Famine and plague
1733	Persian siege: 'more than 100,000' died of starvation
	Pestilence
1777–8	Civil war in Baghdād
1786	Flood; failure of harvest; famine; civil strife
1802–3	Plague; 'most of the people of Iraq (?!)' annihilated
1822	Plague; flood
1831	Plague, flood, siege, famine. The population of Baghdād dwindled from about 80,000 to about 27,000 souls
1877–8	Plague; famine
1892	Flood
1895	Flood

Sources: Ibn Sanad al-Basrī al-Wā'ilī (1766–1834), *Maṭāli'-us-Su'ūd Biṭayyibī Akhbār al-Wālī Dāūd* ('Fortune's Preludes to the Happy Annals of the Governor Dāūd') as abridged in 1873 by Amīn b. Ḥasan al-Ḥalwānī al-Madanī (Cairo, 1951), pp. 39 and 87; Anthony N. Groves, *Journal of a Residence at Baghdād during the Years 1830 and 1831* (London, 1832), pp. 114, 135, and 236; S. H. Longrigg, *Four Centuries of Modern Iraq* (Oxford, 1925), pp. 53, 57, 68, 73–4, 93, 143, 184–185, 203, 212, and 265; and Aḥmad Sūsah, *Aṭlas Baghdād* ('Atlas of Baghdad') (Baghdad, 1952), pp. 31–32.

population. One is even tempted to say, in noting the succession of plagues, famines, floods, and other disasters that afflicted Baghdād, that the city was something like a deathtrap, a 'devourer' of people, and the tribal domain a replenisher, a population reservoir for the city, although there were possibly also other sources for the population inflow. In fact, it would appear that in the centuries preceding ours, when the flame of the riverine cities burnt low and tribal power was rampant, there was a process of tribalization of towns. At any rate, the tribal immigrants were in a way something of a link between the two disparate societies. Once in the city, however, they naturally gave in little by little to urbanizing influences.

The social division did not exist only between the cities and the tribal domain. The tribal domain itself was in fragments. The old tribal confederations had broken up. Baghdād Wilāyah[5] alone had 110 tribes,[6] and although these tribes observed similar rules and had similar institutions, their relationships were in no little degree dominated by raids or forays. The tribes were also divided into *filiḥ*, peasants; *ma'dān*, Marshdwellers; *shāwiyah*, People of the Sheep; and *ahl-il-ibl*, People of the Camel. The latter formed, in effect, the tribal aristocracy. They haughtily disdained all the other tribes and would not fraternize or intermarry with them.[7] Similarly, the spirited Euphrates tribesmen, who lived in intimate contiguity with the great ancestral deserts, scorned the more submissive and more quiescent tribesmen of the lower Tigris. 'Iraqi tribesmen are of two groups,' was later to affirm a well-known Euphrates shaikh,

> to the first group belong those who have to this day retained all the lofty qualities that distinguished their forefathers ... such as the love of liberty, the readiness to sacrifice for it, the loathing of injustice, self-respect and self-denial, and a bold and zealous spirit ... They are the tribesmen that live on the Euphrates and north of Baghdād. The second group are Arabs by race but, in view of their contact with the successive Arab and non-Arab governments of past centuries, their frequenting of cities, and their mingling with the riff-raff, have lost some of their Arab qualities and forgotten or feigned forgetfulness of their ancient dignity and noble customs ... They are the tribesmen that settled in some of the districts of the Tigris to the south of Baghdād.[8]

When we turn to the cities we find that the physical bonds between them were loose and tenuous. Apart from a faltering telegraphic service and iron steamers on irregular Tigris sailings, communications were primitive and uncertain. The journey from Baghdād to Baṣrah took a week, and traveling was in itself an adventure. Partly as a consequence of this, the cities differed in their economic orientation. The ties of Mosul were with Syria and Turkey, and those of Baghdād and the Shīʿī holy cities with Persia and the western and southwestern deserts. Baṣrah looked mainly to the sea and to India. The different schemes of weights and measures in the different towns of Iraq,[9] the wide variation in the prices of the same commodity by reason of the dissimilar marketing conditions,[10] and the extensive use of different currencies[11] attested to the latent economic disunity. All this tended to favor the growth of a strong spirit of localism. A Mosulite relates in his memoirs how, when in 1909 he was appointed by a governor of the new Young Turk government[12] to a judgeship in Baṣrah, a large number of its dignitaries signed a petition objecting to his appointment on the grounds that he was 'neither a Baṣrite nor of the *ashrāf*[13] or *mallāks*[14] of Baṣrah.'[15]

Of course, the more conscious of the townsmen thought of themselves as part of the realm of Islam, and Islam's ideals, though denuded of much of their old vigor, tended to rescue them to some extent from their localism and associate them with their brother Muslims within and beyond the confines of the Ottoman Empire. But Islam in Iraq was more a force of division than of integration. It split deeply Shīʿī and Sunnī Arabs. Socially they seldom mixed, and as a rule did not intermarry. In mixed cities they lived in separate quarters and led their own separate lives. To the strict Shīʿīs, the government of the day—the government of the Ottoman sultan that led Sunnī

Islam—was, in its essence, a usurpation. In their eyes, it had not the qualification to even execute the laws of Islam. They were, therefore, estranged from it, few caring to serve it or to attend its schools.

The Shīʿī–Sunnī division assumed a more acute form when it coincided with another type of social division: the class division. The interconnection between the sectarian and class cleavages is discussed elsewhere at some length.[16] Here it suffices to refer to its aggravating effect upon the feeling between the two sects and to add, by way of parenthesis, that the presence of this factor suggests that their mutual estrangement, if expressed religiously, had its roots, at least partly, in economic and social causes.

All the urban cleavages found an expression in one other phenomenon: that of the *maḥallah* or city quarter. In the towns of Iraq, in other words, the groups that belonged to different faiths, sects, or classes or that were of different ethnic or tribal origin tended to live in separate *maḥallahs*. For example, on Baghdād's main bank—the eastern bank—the Shīʿīs lived in ad-Dahhānah, Ṣabābīgh-il-Āl, al-Qushal,[17] Sūq-il-ʿAṭṭārīn, and other quarters; the Jews mostly in at-Tawrāt, Taḥt-it-Takyah, Abū Saifain, and Sūq Ḥannūn; the Christians in ʿAqd-in-Naṣārah and Ra's-il-Qaryah.[18] Much of the rest of the eastern side of the city was Sunnī, but subdivided on other lines. Thus al-Maydān was inhabited by the Turkish military, al-Ḥaydarkhānah by 'aristocratic' families and upper officials, Dukkān Shnāwah by lower officials, inner Bāb-ish-Shaikh by artisans,[19] and Bāb-ish-Shaikh's outer fringes by Baghdādī army officers of humble origins, and other elements. The large stratum of *kasabah*[20] also lived in Bāb-ish-Shaikh and Dukkān Shnāwah, as well as elsewhere.[21] The same phenomenon characterized Baghdād's suburbs: al-Kādhimiyyah, which contains the tombs of the seventh and ninth of the Shīʿī Imāms,[22] was exclusively Shīʿī and had a large concentration of Persians, while al-Aʿḍhamiyyah, which owes its origin to the tomb of Abū Ḥanīfah, a leading Sunnī legist and theologian of the eighth century, and which symbolically lies on the opposite shore of the Tigris, was exclusively Sunnī and inhabited for the most part by descendants of the Arab tribe of ʿUbaid.[23]

The members of each of the different crafts into which the artisans were divided, who were organized somewhat loosely in guilds or *aṣnāf*, tended also to reside together in single streets, and in some towns would appear to have been originally an extension of one and the same or of a few family groupings.[24]

As a rule, the inhabitants of the *maḥallah* existed in a world of their own. Except for a very small number of educated people, they were pretty much absorbed in the narrowness of their life, and seldom if ever took thought of the community at large or of its interests, or had even any real understanding of the concept of such a community. Moreover, those forming part of a *millah*,[25] as the Christians and the Jews, enjoyed autonomy in their personal and denominational affairs.

There is no lack of evidence in our sources of the strength of the *maḥallah* mentality at that time. When, for example, in April 1915 the people of Najaf rose against the Turks and expelled them from the city, each of Najaf's four quarters became independent, and continued to enjoy that status till the coming of the English in August 1917.[26] The constitution of one of the quarters, that of Burāq, has been preserved. In view of its significance and its reflection of the level of contemporary political thinking of some of the Iraqi townsmen, it is worthwhile reproducing a number of its paragraphs (the reader will also note how the social organization of the quarter in this city was still largely based on the tribe, which bears out the point previously made concerning the process of tribalization of towns; but at the same time it must be remembered that Najaf had closer relations with the tribal domain than with the main cities):

The 1915 Constitution of the Burāq Quarter of Najaf

In the name of God the Merciful, the Compassionate, and whose help we seek.

We write this document in order to secure unity and cohesion amongst ourselves, we the inhabitants of Burāq quarter, and our names are at the end of this document.

We have assembled ourselves and become united and of one blood, and follow one another should anything happen to our quarter from other quarters. We will rise together against an outsider who is not from us, whether the result be to our advantage or to our disadvantage, and the conditions of our union are as follows:

(1) If an outsider is killed, the murderer has to pay 5 līras [about £5 sterling] and the remainder of the blood money is to be paid by the whole tribe.

(2) If anybody from our union is killed, half of the *faṣl*[27] is for the murdered man's family and half for the union.

(3) If anyone kills anybody from his own tribe and the tribe has no responsible head, the murderer must leave the place for seven years and anybody who aids him is also to be dismissed for the same period. The *faṣl* is 30 līras in gold ... One-third is to be given to the union and two-thirds to the relatives ....

(7) Should harm befall one of us who steals, robs, loots, or fornicates, we are not only not responsible but also not his friends.

(8) If any one of us is arrested for our doings by the government, or imprisoned, all his expenses will be paid by us.

The above is for all of us. We are united with Kāḍhim,[28] whether he is in the town or not, and on this condition we all put our signatures ... and God is our witness.[29]

The tendency to split into independent *maḥallas* was by no means a peculiarity of Najaf. During World War I, the eastern quarter of the small Euphrates town of Samāwah sided with the British, while the western quarter preserved an overt neutrality.[30] The two quarters under their own autonomous shaikhs had been waging continual war against each other for the preceding twenty years.[31] At Mosul 'feeling between the different wards,' observed a British vice-consul in 1909, 'is often strong and bitter and not infrequently gives rise to quarrels . . . Barricades are erected and the arms used are clubs, maces, revolvers, knives, and stones. Only one such engagement took place last year, one man being killed and several wounded.'[32] Even in Baghdād the loyalty to the *maḥallah* was apt to assert itself in vigorous terms. From an account we have of a demonstration that took place in October 1911, and that was seemingly organized by the Turkish authorities to protest Italy's invasion of Tripoli, it appears that the people were grouped by *maḥallas*, and that a vehement scuffle occurred between the delegation of the quarter of Bāb-ish-Shaikh and that of Ḥaydarkhānah over the questions of precedence and who should march at the head of the demonstration.[33]

Thus far we have regarded the various loyalties in the Iraq of pre-World War I as if they were simply negative and divisive. In fact, from the standpoint of the individual involved in them, and insofar as they had not petrified or been drained of their substance, they fulfilled a positive need. The tribes, the *maḥallas*, and the *aṣnāf* were partly an expression of the innate impulse for protection through unity—a protection that the Ottoman government, by reason of its weakness, could not regularly provide. 'To depend on the tribe,' wrote in 1910 one of Baghdād's deputies to the Ottoman parliament, 'is a thousand times safer than depending on the government, for whereas the latter defers or neglects repression, the tribe, no matter how feeble it may be, as soon as it learns that an injustice has been committed against one of its members readies itself to exact vengeance on his behalf.'[34] That the *maḥallah* served a similar function is reflected in the already cited Constitution of the Burāq quarter of Najaf. The *aṣnāf* were also in a sense organizations for mutual support. One of their duties, as expressed in regulations dating from 1910, was to render assistance to those of their members who were 'ill or in want.'[35] The links within the tribes were particularly intimate, and helped to cultivate strong and exclusive sentiments. The individual belonging to them knew he was not alone and, having an anchor on which to lean in misfortune, seldom experienced the gloom of helplessness.

We may now once again profitably change our point of view. The various loyalties, of which we have spoken, have been hitherto treated by us largely as if they were in a static condition. As a matter of fact, they were already involved to a greater or lesser degree in a process of erosion, especially at

Baghdād and its environs, at Baṣrah, and in the tribal regions of Shaṭṭ-al-'Arab and the lower Tigris. This was the cumulative effect of the introduction of river steam navigation (1859), the appearance of the electric telegraph (1861), the attendant deepening of English economic penetration and tying of Iraq to the world of capitalism, the opening of state schools (since 1869), the development of the press (especially after 1908), and the repeated attempts by the Turkish governing authority between 1831 and 1914 to gather all the means of power into its hands, break the cohesion of the tribes, and Ottomanize the town population.

The ensuing penetration of money and of the idea of profit among some of the tribes, the passing of these tribes from a subsistence to a market-oriented economy, the transformation of their shaikhs from patriarchs into gain-seeking landlords, the Turkish policy of playing off tribal chief against tribal chief, the vying of the bigger of these chiefs against each other for peasants, and the consequent intermixture of tribesmen so changed the conditions of life in the affected regions as to attenuate the old tribal loyalties or render them by and large ineffectual.[36]

In the cities and towns the inflow of English goods affected adversely what had survived of the old crafts, in particular the weaving of cloths,[37] and thereby weakened the attachment to the *aṣnāf.* In Baghdād itself, however, much of the industrial decline must more appropriately be connected to the ravages of the plague and flood of 1831.

One further byproduct of the new processes was the coming into being of a new but as yet diminutive social force: the new intelligentsia, which in effect meant the birth of a new loyalty—nationalism.

Nationalism did not displace the old loyalties. Although it grew at their expense, it existed side by side with them, corroding them, yes, but at the same time absorbing some of their psychological elements and expressing itself within the emotional and conceptual patterns of the Islamic religion.

Many facts and influences assisted, directly or indirectly, the diffusion of the new national feeling: among others, the rise in the number of young Iraqis attending Turkish schools of higher learning, mainly the Military Academy at Isṭanbūl; the increasing exposure to European modes of thought; the growth of pan-Turkism, the heightened tempo of Ottomanization, and the relative insensitiveness of the Turks to local needs; the spread of books and newspapers; the more frequent inter-Arab contacts and the emergence of pan-Arab clubs and societies; the greater interest in Arab history and in the achievements of the past and the sensing of the poverty and dreariness of present conditions; and, of course, the pull of the common language and common ethnic origin of the majority of Iraqis. But what more than anything else helped the progress of the new sentiment was the English invasion of

1914–1918, or rather the resistance that it stirred and that reached its climactic point in the armed uprising of 1920. For the first time in many centuries, Shī'īs joined politically with Sunnīs, and townsmen from Baghdād and tribesmen from the Euphrates made common cause. Unprecedented joint Shī'ī–Sunnī celebrations, ostensibly religious but in reality political, were held in all the Shī'ī and Sunnī mosques in turn: special *mawlids*, Sunnī ceremonial observances in honor of the Prophet's birthday, were on occasions followed by *ta'ziyahs*, Shī'ī lamentations for the martyred Ḥusain,[38] the proceedings culminating in patriotic oratory and poetic thundering against the English.[39] The armed outbreak that this agitation precipitated could not be said to have been truly nationalist either in its temper or its hopes. It was essentially a tribal affair, and animated by a multitude of local passions and interests, but it became part of nationalist mythology and thus an important factor in the spread of national consciousness. Indeed, it would not be going too far to say that with the events of 1919–1920, and more particularly with the bond, however tender, that was created between Sunnīs and Shī'īs, a new process set in: the painful, now gradual, now spasmodic growth of an Iraqi national community.

Under the monarchy, which was established in 1921, it became by degrees clear that the advance of this process was not only contingent upon the integration of the Shī'īs into the body politic or the firm fastening of Shī'īs and Sunnīs to one another, the voluntary unifying of their wills—even their intermarrying—but also upon the successful resolution of another historic conflict which lay at the very basis of many of the divisions bedeviling Iraqi society: the twofold conflict between the tribes and the riverine cities, and among the tribes themselves over the food-producing flatlands of the Tigris and Euphrates.

Much of the premonarchic history of the country could be understood in terms of this conflict. In a sense, the life principles of the cities and tribes in Iraq's river valleys were mutually contradictory. To be more concrete, the existence of powerful tribes was, as a rule, a concomitance of weak cities. Inversely, the growth of the cities involved the decline of the tribes. Thus in the period between the thirteenth and eighteenth centuries, which witnessed the eclipse of the 'Abbāsid Caliphate; the depredations of the Il-Khānid Mongols; the well-nigh utter ruin of the ancient dikes; the invasions of the Jaylars, Black Sheep, and White Sheep Turkomans, Timūrid Mongols, Ṣafawids, and Ottomans; and the protracted but intermittent Turkish-Persian wars, one paramount fact recurrently asserted itself: the enfeeblement of the towns. The inevitable accompaniment of this was the advance of tribal power. But the new life and new ideas infused into Iraq in the second half of the nineteenth century—by dint of the new communications and the new links with the capitalist world, and through other factors already referred to—reversed the historical trend, leading to the recovery of the towns and the beginning of the decomposition of the tribal order.

In this conflict the reforming Ottoman sultans of the nineteenth century and the Young Turks, whom the 1908 Revolution raised to political ascendancy, could be said to have championed, in ways peculiar to them, the cause of the towns. The English, on the other hand, anxious as they were to avoid the costly maintenance of a large force of occupation, saw in the balancing of tribesmen against townsmen the surest guarantee of the continuance of their own power. They attempted not only to arrest the incipient process of detribalization, or vindicate the authority of the tribal chiefs, or keep at a minimum the interaction between townsmen and tribesmen, but also to solidify the existing cleavage by the consolidation and official recognition of tribal customs. The Tribal Disputes Regulations, issued by the English on July 27, 1918, as a proclamation having the force of law and, on English insistence, made law of the land in the monarchic period under Articles 113 and 114 of the Iraqi Constitution of 1925, excluded the countryside from the purview of the national law. Down to the July 1958 Revolution, Iraq would thus remain legally subject to two norms—one for the cities and one for the tribal countryside.

At the same time, the contributions of the English in the form of ideas or skills in the fields of administration, irrigation, agriculture, and other areas of life, though incidental to their pursuit of basic imperial interests, no doubt helped the progress of the Iraqis toward a viable state. In the 1920s the presence of the English may have also been decisive in keeping Iraq in one piece. If the RAF and the British alliance were to be withdrawn, wrote in that decade the British High Commissioner Henry Dobbs, 'the Government of Iraq would, I believe, in a few months, either vanish altogether or remain clinging desperately to a strip of territory along the Tigris between Sāmarrā' and Kūt, the whole of the rest of the country falling away.'[40] As the monarchy was as yet a delicate reed, its army deficient in strength, and the tribal domain 'crammed with arms,' it is difficult not to agree with Dobbs. On the other hand, the English did their best—the Iraqi nationalists complained—to overlook the needs of the royal army and to delay as long as possible the introduction of conscription which, in contrast to the principle of voluntary service then in force, would have, it was presumed, strengthened the monarchy militarily, and simultaneously reduced its financial burden.

Though a creation of the English, the Hashemite monarchy was, in the first two decades of its life, animated by a spirit inherently antithetical to theirs. Owing to the initial intimate interweaving of its dynastic interests with the fortunes of the pan-Arab movement, its basic instinct in the period 1921–1939 was to further—to the extent that its status of dependence permitted—

the work of nation-building in Iraq. With this in mind, but also in order to meet its administrative needs, it added greatly to the existing educational facilities,[41] thereby ultimately adding to the ranks of the new middle-class intelligentsia, the natural carrier of national sentiment. Consistently enough, the monarchy took pains in those years to nurture in the schools the passion of patriotism and a lively sympathy for the pan-Arab ideal. However, in the time of Faiṣal I (1921–1933), the chief accent of royal policy was on the urgent and yet exceedingly difficult task of cultivating among Iraq's diverse elements enduring ties of common feeling and common purpose. 'In Iraq,' Faiṣal maintained in a confidential memorandum,

> there is still—and I say this with a heart full of sorrow—no Iraqi people but unimaginable masses of human beings, devoid of any patriotic idea, imbued with religious traditions and absurdities, connected by no common tie, giving ear to evil, prone to anarchy, and perpetually ready to rise against any government whatever. Out of these masses we want to fashion a people which we would train, educate, and refine ... The circumstances, being what they are, the immenseness of the efforts needed for this [can be imagined].[42]

Realizing how much depended on the conciliation of the Shīʿīs, and clearly troubled by the half-truth that 'the taxes are on the Shīʿī, death is on the Shīʿī, and the posts are for the Sunnī'—which he heard 'thousands of times'—Faiṣal went out of his way to associate the Shīʿīs with the new state and to ease their admission into the government service; among other things, he put promising young members of this sect through an accelerated program of training, and afforded them the chance to rise rapidly to positions of responsibility.[43] He also saw to it that the Kurds received an appropriate quota of public appointments. At the same time he felt that there could be no solid progress toward genuine statehood without the strengthening of the army. As the government was 'far and away weaker than the people'—there were in 1933 in the country at large 'more than 100,000 rifles whereas the government possesses only 15,000'[44]—Faiṣal had doubts whether he could cope with two simultaneous armed outbreaks in widely separated regions.[45] It would be 'foolish,' he thought, to carry out important reforms or development projects without the assurance of an adequate protective force. For all these reasons he regarded the army as 'the spinal column for nation-forming.'[46] Accordingly, in 1933, the year in which Iraq gained undivided control over its internal affairs, Faiṣal raised the strength of the military establishment to 11,500 men[47] from the total of 7,500 at which it had remained fixed since 1925.[48]

In his efforts to refashion Iraq on national foundations, Faiṣal I proceeded with care and, keeping his eyes fastened not on what was purely desirable but on what could in practice be achieved, he avoided any step suggestive of adventurism. Of course, in this as in other relevant lines of policy, he was not actuated by sheer devotion to the interests of his people, for he was laying the base for the power of his own family, even as he was laying the base for a compact state.

Although under the young and inexperienced Ghāzī (1933–1939) the country fell a prey to tribal rebellions and military coups, and the personal influence of the monarch palpably declined, there was nevertheless no essential deviation from the prior trend of royal policy. Except during a brief period in 1936–1937, the pan-Arab character of the state became more pronounced. The army rose in strength to 800 officers and 19,500 men by 1936,[49] and to 1,426 officers and 26,345 men by 1939.[50] There had been few Iraqi officer pilots in 1933, but in 1936 they numbered 37 and were expected to add up to 127 at the end of the following year.[51] More than that, the standard-gauge line from Baghdād to Baijī, which was meant to form part of the strategic Berlin-Baghdād railway, but was left unfinished at the end of World War I, was now extended to Tall Kochek on the Syrian frontier,[52] which made possible a continuous haul from Mosul to the Gulf, and signified not only the advance of central state control but also progress toward the transformation of Iraq into a rationally organized economic unit. Over and above this, the elements that had stood nearest to Faiṣal I—the principal ex-Sharīfian officers[53]—and that had been fighting tooth and nail for an army based on conscription, gained their end in 1934, and thus facilitated the eventual turning of the military forces into an effective means for the intermingling of tribesmen with townsmen and the breaking down of the hard-and-fast line between the tribes—a necessary precondition for their integration in national life.

In brief, through the whole period of 1921–1939 the monarch, centered at Baghdād, had in effect a social meaning diametrically opposed to that of the tribal shaikhs, the then still virtual rulers of much of the countryside. The shaikh represented the principle of the fragmented or multiple community (many tribes), the monarch the ideal of an integral community (one Iraqi people, one Arab nation). Or to express the relationship differently, the shaikh was the defender of the divisive tribal ʻurf (tradition), the monarch the exponent of the unifying national law. In view of the presence of large non-Arab minorities in the country, there was, to be sure, some inherent contradiction between the ideal of one Iraqi people and that of one Arab nation, but the element of contradiction was mitigated by the fact that the aim of pan-Arab unity—as distinct from inter-Arab cooperation—was at no time actively pursued.

The social meaning of the monarchy changed in the time of Prince ʻAbd-ul-Ilāh, who ruled as regent during the minority of his nephew, Faiṣal II, that is from 1939 to 1953 and, after the coming of age and crowning of the young king, clung tenaciously to the reins of government until his destruction at the hands of the revolutionaries of 1958.

The change had its genesis in the period 1936–1941. In those years the principal ex-Sharīfian officers—Nūrī as-Saʿīd, the archpolitician-to-be of the monarchy, among others—saw wielded against them the weapon—the army—that they had helped to forge, and which had constituted the very anchor of royal policy. In a sense, the series of military coups in which they got enmeshed was a rebounding upon them of their own attempts to use the army for factious ends.[55] In another sense, the coups represented a successful, even if shortlived, break by the armed segment of the middle class[55] into the narrow circle of the ruling order: power had been before 1936 pretty much the preserve of the English, the king, the principal ex-Sharīfian officers,[56] and the upper stratum of the propertied classes. From this it should not be inferred that the coups were, narrowly speaking, class actions, or that in the instance of each and every officer who was involved in the coups there was a direct or conscious connection between his social origin and his political behavior. Of course, the coups were carried out on the initiative of a small number of individuals, and could partly be explained by the personal motives of the leading officers, or the intrigues of ambitious politicians, or the lure or example of the neighboring militarist regimes—those of Iran and Turkey—but the coups succeeded, if briefly, because they appealed to sentiments or manifested tendencies—reformism, or pan-Arabism, or neutralism, or intense opposition to English influence, or sheer discontent at the exclusion of all but a few from any effective role in the political life of the country—sentiments and tendencies that were shared by substantial portions of the officer corps and of the middle class from which the corps largely stemmed.

The coups were also very instructive. For one thing, their recurrence laid bare that the officer corps was afflicted with divisions. Quite apart from the self-seeking coteries that a politicized army tends to engender, three fundamental elements became distinguishable, one Kurdish, one pan-Arab, and one strictly Iraqi: the 1936 coup was led by Kurds and Iraqists; in the countercoups of 1937 and 1938 and in the movement of 1941 the critical role was played by pan-Arabs. The superior weight of the pan-Arab trend was the consequence, partly, of the monarchy's own initial pan-Arab predilection and, partly, of the fact that a very large number of the younger officers hailed from the northern Arab provinces, which leaned strongly toward pan-Arabism, inasmuch as they had been economically linked with Syria and Palestine before World War I and now still suffered from the partition of the Arab areas of the Ottoman Empire and the obstacles of the new frontiers.

Moreover, it became apparent from the coups how tenuous were the threads that held the life of the monarchy and how easily they could be snapped. Amongst the papers said to have been left behind by General Bakr Ṣidqī, the chief figure in the 1936 overturn, was a project for the forming of a dictatorship and the putting away of the king.[57] The leaders of the 1941 movement, for their part, did not hesitate to depose ʿAbd-ul-Ilāh when, rather than accept the independent course that they were steering, he identified himself with the English in World War II and, seeing the peril of his situation, made his escape to their base at Ḥabbāniyyah, and eventually to his uncle's feud in Transjordan.

But, from the perspective of broad political trends, the most significant thing about the whole interlude of military coups was its climactic and closing sequence of events: the Thirty-Day War of 1941, the use by the English of Transjordan's Arab Legion against the Iraqis, and their reimposition of ʿAbd-ul-Ilāh as regent by force of arms.

Time never effaced from the hearts of Iraqis the remembrance that in their hour of danger the Hashemite house stood on the side of their enemies. The War of 1941 was a great spur to their national feeling. They had not been of one mind about the intervention of the army in state affairs or the political tendencies of the leading officers, but when the war came, they quickly forgot their differences, save for a minority. In Baghdād and the other towns the sentiments of Shīʿī and Sunnī and Arab and Kurd merged for the moment and while the fighting lasted. Among men in humble life, in particular, such an accord of spirits reigned as had not been witnessed since the uprising of 1920. In this atmosphere ʿAbd-ul-Ilāh's every act appeared as a betrayal. At any rate, from this point onward nationalists and Hashemites moved on different planes of thought and feeling. The monarchy lost its nationalist physiognomy, and the nationalists became at heart antimonarchic.

In the years that followed, the entire orientation of royal policy changed. In the first place, the army, which had been the primary concern of the monarchy, and which by 1941 had risen to 1,745 officers and 44,217 men,[58] was in large measure broken up. In the year 1941/42 alone, 324 officers were pensioned off[59] and, by 1948, 1,095 other officers had been discharged from service before reaching retirement age.[60] The army as a whole was left in a lamentable state. In the words of British Colonel Gerald de Gaury:

> Its boots were [at the end of the Second World War] mostly unfit for wear in marching, its supply of clothes short, its leave long overdue, its pay meagre, and its rations had been reduced to a figure a thousand calories below the minimum considered necessary by European medical men for Eastern troops. Money for repair of barracks and camps had been stopped. The Police were forbidden to assist in tracing or arresting deserters and by the summer of 1943, out of an established strength of thirty thousand men, twenty thousand were deserters.[61]

Though restlessness in Kurdistan necessitated a partial retreat in 1944 from this injurious and vindictive course of conduct, the army was still in bad shape when four years later it had to fight a war in Palestine.[62] Ill-prepared, poorly led, inappropriately armed, suffering from an insufficiency of skilled personnel, and kept in short supply by the English as a matter of policy, it was unable to fulfill its task. Defeat gave a stimulus to changes in the direction of greater efficiency. But the monarchy's distrust of the military did not subside. Only once—in 1952—and after much hesitation did it venture to use the army as a repressive force inside Baghdād. Otherwise, it kept the striking units unammunitioned and far from the capital. However, after the capture of power by the army in Syria in 1949 and in Egypt in 1952, the government took pains to bind the military element to the throne by ties of material interest. Conditions of service for officers were ameliorated,[63] and various benefits—clothing and housing allowances, liberal pensions, and grants of land, among other things—were conferred upon them. But the rift dividing them from the Hashemites had grown too wide. Few, indeed, would be on the side of the royal family at the hour of its fall.

The failure to win back the loyalty of the officer corps was related to another aspect of the post-1941 monarchical policy. Alienated from the nationalists, the Crown had been tying its fortunes more and more intimately to those of the English and the tribal shaikhs, and thus had developed a living interest in the continuance not only of the English connection but also of the tribal order. Into this alliance the Crown had been driven further by a series of fierce urban mass uprisings—the *Wathbah* of 1948[64] and the *Intifāḍas* of 1952[65] and 1956[66]—and by the related drift toward the Left, in the towns, of large portions of the middle and laboring classes. The daily lives of these people had been deeply affected by the trend of rising prices and scarcity of supplies induced by World War II, by the inflationary currents let loose by the oil boom of the 1950s, and by the large-scale movement of peasants into the capital caused by the attractions of city life, the weak connection with the land of the once nomadic agricultural tribesmen, the oppressiveness of the shaikhly system, and the drying up of river branches in the lower Tigris due to the rapid pump development in the provinces of Kūt and Baghdād.[67]

The alliance with the English found ultimate expression in the Baghdad Pact of 1955, a commitment which, being out of accord with the general sentiment of the country and of other Arab lands, and prefaced by relentless proceedings against every movement of opposition or liberty of speech,[68] added in no little degree to the antipopular and antinational character of the monarchy.

The tie-up with the shaikhs, symbolized by the marriage in 1953 of Prince ʿAbd-ul-Ilāh to Hiyām, daughter of Muḥammad al-Ḥabīb al-Amīr, chief of the tribe of Rabīʿah, was reflected in the solicitude shown in the last seventeen years of the monarchy for the interests of the shaikhs, and in particular in the intensification of the practice of applying the land settlement laws in their favor. Vast expanses of customary tribal land and of the best state land were by this means allowed to pass into their exclusive possession. By thus increasing their essentially nonproductive grasp over agriculture, and at the same time keeping their villages barren of governmental controls, the monarchy enabled them to weigh more and more heavily on a peasantry now reduced in many regions to a status akin to serfdom. The shaikhs became an economic incubus and began to symbolize the extreme economic inequality that was by this time hindering, even more than tribalism—itself undermined by this very inequality—the integration of the community and the inclusion of the peasants within the purview of national life.

In other words, by its alliance with the shaikhs, the monarchy ceased, in effect, to play a unifying social role. Moreover, by its commitment to a rural social structure, which condemned the majority of the inhabitants of the country to depressed conditions and which, therefore, constituted a serious impediment to the progress of the Iraqi economy as a whole, the monarchy itself became, in a crucial sense, a retarding social factor.

On the other hand, by choice, or on account of pressures from below; or in the process of meeting security needs, or attending to urgent problems, or fulfilling the expectations of favored interests, or vying with the ascendant Nāṣirite wave in neighboring countries; or through involvement in the consequences of the economy's slow progress from subsistence to market conditions, or in other chains of events previously set in motion or externally activated, the monarchy added to the material factors making for a consolidated and more powerful state.

For one thing, the mileage of gravel or hard surfaced roads increased from probably about 500 in 1944[69] to about 1600 in 1955.[70] These roads were mostly to be found in the middle and northern parts of the country. They struck outwards from Baghdād and such centers as Mosul and Kirkūk. The south continued to be connected, by and large, by earthen roads that were exposed to churning and rutting after flood or rain. The areas of agricultural production also remained on the whole unlinked by feeder roads to the main road system.

For another thing, the administrative machine and security apparatus of the state grew larger. Government officials, excluding the employees of the port and the railways, numbered only 3,143 in 1920, but 9,740 in 1938, and 20,031 in 1958.[71] The officers and technical staff of the railways added up to 1,639 in 1927, 1,738 in 1937, and 3,872 in 1957.[72] Similarly, policemen increased from 2,470 in 1920 to 12,266 in 1941, and 23,383 in 1958.[73] The last figure included the 8,368 officers and men of the Mobile Force, which now served as the chief repressive instrument of the monarchy.

Again, to safeguard Baghdād and the south of Iraq against devastating floods and to provide a more regular supply of water for irrigation, dams and barrages were erected in the 1950s on the Diyālah, the Lesser Zāb, the upper Euphrates near Ramādī, and the upper Tigris near Sāmarrā'. Obviously, the benefit from the control of the environment was general, but these undertakings also afforded expectation of greater incomes for the already advantaged shaikhs and the other strata of the landed class. At the same time, the strengthening of the state's command of the rivers and the expansion of its potentially cultivable land increased, to a significant degree, its ability to enforce its will.

The building of dams and reservoirs had been made possible by an unprecedented flow of money into the country's treasury. Moved initially by the desire to punish Iran for its nationalization law of 1951, and afterwards by the hope of buttressing Iraq's monarchic regime, the oil companies had sharply stepped up production. The receipts of the state from oil rose from £1.5 million in 1941 to £5.2 million in 1950, £58.3 million in 1953, and £79.8 million in 1958.[74] This outpouring of capital, which had also been spurred by better terms of oil payments, greatly added to the financial power of the state. In consequence, and by reason of the special character of the oil companies—their foreign ownership, their extraneousness to the local economy, and their employment of only a tiny segment of the working population—the state became in large measure economically autonomous from society—which, as could be imagined, heightened its potential for despotism. Simultaneously, the overflow of royalties made the state, from the economic standpoint, dangerously dependent upon the oil companies; in 1954 its receipts from oil formed 65.7 per cent and in 1958 61.7 per cent of its total revenue.[75]

The growth of the material power of the state did not in the end help the monarchy. Its moral divorce from the mass of the politically conscious strata of the people was fatal. It could no longer be sure of the loyalty of the very elements—the officials, the army, and even the police—through whom it exercised its will upon the country.

Ironically, the monarchy continued to add to the ranks of the stratum that had become most hostile to its existence, that is to the ranks of the educated and semieducated class. It had really little choice. The process of expansion of the school system, begun in the 1920s, could not be reversed. No little prestige had come to be attached in the society to the earning, particularly, of a university degree. Once some Iraqis had received higher training, others, in ever larger numbers, pressed for similar opportunities. The government could not now plead lack of funds. The needs of a moving society had also to be met. Anyhow, the number of state college students increased from 99 in 1921/22 to 1,218 in 1940/41 and 8,568 in 1958/59, and the number of state

TABLE 2 *Population of Baghdād, Mosul, and Baṣrah (1908–1977)*

Year	*Baghdād*[a]	*Percentage increase*	*Mosul*	*Percentage increase*	*Baṣrah*	*Percentage increase*
1908[b]	150,000					
1922[c]	200,000		70,000		55,000	
1935[d]	350,000		100,000		60,000	
1947[e]	515,459		133,625		101,535	
1957[f]	793,183	53.9	178,222	33.4	164,905	62.4
1965[g]	1,490,756	87.9	264,146	48.2	310,950	88.6
1977[h]	2,600,000		450,000		550,000	

[a] Within limits of the jurisdiction of the mayor of the capital.
Sources:
[b] Estimate by Ḥabīb K. Chīha, *La Province de Bagdād* (1908), p. 165.
[c] Official estimate, *Al-ʿIraq Year Book* (*1922*), p. 44.
[d] Estimate, *Dalīl-ul-Mamlakat-il-ʿIrāqiyyah Lisanat 1935–1936* ('Directory of the Iraqi Kingdom for the Year 1935–1936'), p. 97.
[e] Official 1947 Census. Figures supplied to this writer by Dr. Fūād Massī of the Directorate General of Census.
[f] Official 1957 Census, Iraq, Ministry of Interior, Directorate General of Census, *Al-Majmūʿat-ul-'Iḥṣāiyyah Litasjīl ʿĀm 1957* ('Statistical Compilation Relating to the Census of 1957') *Provinces of Baghdād and Ramādī* (in Arabic), p. 168; *Provinces of ʿAmārah and Baṣrah*, p. 112; and *Provinces of Mosul and Arbīl*, p. 167.
[g] Official 1965 General Census, Iraq, Ministry of Planning, *Annual Abstract of Statistics, 1969*, pp. 44, 52, and 59.
[h] Rough estimate.

secondary school students from 229 to 13,969 and 73,911 in the same years.[76] Elementary education made similar progress. On the other hand, qualitatively the advance on all levels was not as impressive. Moreover, in 1958 more than six-sevenths of the population was still illiterate. One other factor has to be emphasized: the monarchy, by differentiating more and more Iraqiṣ from the unlettered mass, was giving them a middle-class status without, however, assuring them of a middle-class income. Here lay one of the sources of the agitation that was a recurrent feature of the cities and towns in the last decade of the monarchy.

Evidently, the continued enlargement of the educated class involved the continued erosion of traditional loyalties, but now not necessarily the continued growth of nationalist sentiments. This is because of the rise, as has already been intimated, of new ideological currents, and in particular of communism.

No less erosive of old loyalties and productive of new ties was another process that was at work in the period of the monarchy: the rapid advance of urban life. According to official census records (see Table 2), the population of Greater Baghdād, roughly estimated at about 200,000 in 1922, rose to 515,459 in 1947, and 793,183 in 1957. Basrah underwent, it would appear, similar demographic changes, but the rate of increase for Mosul was clearly lower. The counts made by the government may or may not have been thorough or competently carried out, but the rapid growth of the population in the capital and at Iraq's seaport is undoubted and, as noted elsewhere, largely explicable by unprecedented migrations of peasant-tribesmen from the countryside. These great internal movements produced, to be sure, tensions, conflicts, and unbalances, but simultaneously brought more and more Iraqis into closer association with each other.

Innumerable tangible and intangible ties were also woven among them by the development of communications, including automatic telephone exchanges at Baghdād and Baṣrah, a powerful wireless transmitting station at Abū Ghrayb, and a modern television station in the capital, not to mention the 'voices' broadcasting from abroad.

From all the foregoing, it should be clear that in the period 1921–1958 the monarchy, by choice or from necessity, directly or indirectly, through processes it initiated or through processes in which it became entangled, partly hindered the cohesion of Iraqis, but at the same time did much to prepare them for nationality.

However, it should be borne in mind that what is becoming the Iraqi community has also grown in crises, in moments of great danger and common suffering, in the tremors of agitated masses and their outbursts of anger: if this community in embryo will in the future hold together and maintain its separate identity, the Uprising of 1920, the War of 1941, the *Wathbah* of 1948, the *Intifāḍah* of 1952, and the Revolution of 1958, though not free of divisive aspects, will be seen as stages in the progress of Iraq toward national coherence.

Of course, the national or patriotic idea was in 1958 still very weak. Even now it is as yet beyond the comprehension of the masses of the peasants. Moreover, in the towns the influence of the old norms, if considerably reduced, nonetheless persists. Interestingly enough, some of the peasant tribes, which had broken with their shaikhs and migrated to Baghdād to start a new life, ignored urban laws and entered into written compacts binding themselves to regulate their conduct and settle their disputes in accordance with their ancient tribal customs. Obviously, the psychology and ways of the old order—the work of long centuries—are still embedded in the life of broad strata of the people, and will not easily wither away. But most crucial is the fact that the new national loyalty, while more in keeping with new conditions, is still hazy, uncertain of its direction (Iraqism? Pan-Arabism?), unacceptable to the Kurds, poorly assimilative of the Shīʿīs, and lacking the normative ethics, the warm intimacy, and the sustained emotional support once associated with the old loyalties.

This article is reprinted from Hanna Batatu, *The Old Social Classes and the Revolutionary Movements of Iraq*, 1978, pp. 13–36. Reprinted by permission of Princeton University Press.

NOTES

1. Sulaimān Fā'iq (an Ottoman provincial governor and father of Iraqi ex-Premier Hikmat Sulaimān), *Tārīkh Baghdād* ('The History of Baghdad'), trans. from the Turkish by Mūsa Kāḍhim Nawras (Baghdad, 1962), p. 174.

2. Isma'īl Ḥaqqī Bey Bābān Zādeh, 'From Isṭambūl to Baghdād' (1910). This book was translated at length by the *Revue du Monde Musulman*, XIV: 5 (May 1911), For the quoted verse, see p. 255.

3. 'Make the Religion Triumph! O Muḥammad!'

4. This is a clearly Sunnī slogan and was used, for example, by demonstrators on 6 October 1911, against Italy's invasion of Tripoli; *Lughat-ul-*'Arab, 9 October 1911, quoted by *Revue du Monde Musulman*, 6th Year, XVIII (February–March 1912), 223–224.

5. The *wilāyah* was an Ottoman administrative division.

6. See Hanna Batatu, *The Old Social Classes and the Revolutionary Movements of Iraq* (Princeton, 1978), p. 77.

7. *Ibid.*, p. 68.

8. Farīq al-Muzhir Al-Fir'aun, *Al-Ḥaqā'iq-un-Nāṣi'ah Fī-th-Thawrat-il-'Irāqiyyah Sanat 1920 wa Natāijuhā* ('Luminous Facts on the Iraqi Insurrection of 1920 and Its Results') (Baghdad, 1952), I, 22.

9. For example, the weights of Baghdād were: the *ṭghār* (2000 kilos), the *waznah* (100 kilos), the big *mann* (24 kilos), the small *mann* (12 kilos), and the *uqiyyah* (2 kilos). The weights of other towns, while bearing the same names, were of different amounts. Thus the *waznah* of Ḥillah equalled 102.565 kilos, and of Dīwāniyyah 108.835 kilos and not 100, as in Baghdād. Similarly, the *ṭghār* of Baṣrah equalled 1538 kilos and not 2000, as that of Baghdād. See *Dalīl-ul-Mamlakat-il-'Irāqiyyah* . . . ('The Directory of the Iraqi Kingdom for 1935–1936'), (Baghdad, 1935), pp. 59–60.

10. For example, even in 1921–1922 the tax conversion rates for wheat, i.e. the rates at which the tax in kind was converted into cash, and which reflected the prevalent prices, were 250, 384, and 400 rupees per ton at the province headquarters of Baghdād, Mosul, and Baṣrah, respectively. See Great Britain, *Report . . . on the Administration of Iraq for April 1922–March 1923* (London, 1924), p. 102.

11. Thus before World War I the Persian currency appears to have been more widely used than the Turkish currency in the Kurdish districts of Iraq. See Vital Cuinet, *La Turquie d'Asie* (Paris, 1894), III, 38–39. In Baṣrah, Indian and Persian coinage were in large use. See Great Britain, Foreign Office, Historical Section, *Arabia, Mesopotamia* . . . (London, 1919), pp. 119–120. The official currency was, of course, Turkish.

12. This government assumed power after the 1908 Revolution in Turkey.

13. The descendants of the Prophet.

14. Landlords.

15. Sulaimān Faiḍī, *Fī Ghamrat-in-Niḍāl* ('In the Throes of the Struggle') (Baghdad, 1952), p. 78. The objection obviously betrays also a class consciousness.

16. See Batatu, *The Old Social Classes*, Chapter 4.

17. A section of this quarter was inhabited by Jews.

18. Some Moslem families lived in these quarters. The Sunnī Pāchachīs, for example, had their residence in Ra's-il-Qaryah.

19. A number of well-known religious families had their homes here, such as the Gailānīs, who lived in Bāb-ish-Shaikh because the Qādiriyyah shrine, built in memory of their ancestor, Shaikh 'Abd-ul-Qādir al-Gailānī, was located in this quarter.

20. *Kasabah* is a general term applicable to humble people who have no regular employment and earn their livelihood by doing various odd jobs.

21. Conversations with Kāmel ach-Chādirchī, Qāsim Ḥasan, Jamīl Kubbah, and other Baghdādīs on various occasions.

22. Mūsa b. Ja'far al-Kāḍhim and Muḥammad b. 'Alī aj-Jawād. The *imāms* were, in the eyes of the Shī'īs, the only legitimate rulers and supreme pontiffs of Islam.

23. For the last point, see Maḥmūd Shukrī al-Alūsī, *Tārīkh Masājid Baghdād wa Athāriha* ('The History of the Mosques and Ancient Monuments of Baghdad') (Baghdad, 1927), p. 26, note.

24. Even as late as the 1930s there were such instances in Najaf. The large al-Bahhāsh family, for example, had a street of its own in the Mishrāq quarter of that city, and its members were mostly jewelers and moneychangers. See Ja'far b. Shaikh Bāqir Al-Maḥbūbah an-Najafī, *Māḍī-n-Najaf wa Ḥāḍiruhā* ('The Past of Najaf and Its Present') (Sidon, 1934), I, 201.

25. A *millah* was an officially recognized religious community.

26. Great Britain, *Reports of Administration for 1918 of Divisions and districts of the Occupied Territories of Mesopotamia* (1919), I, 68.

27. *Faṣl* literally means the deciding of disputes, but here refers to blood money, that is blood is paid for with money instead of with blood, and thus the blood feud is wiped out.

28. Kāḍhim Ṣubḥī was the shaikh or headman of the quarter.

29. For the text of the constitution, see Great Britain, *Reports of Administration for 1918*, I, 111.

30. Great Britain, (Confidential) *Personalities. Iraq* (*Exclusive of Baghdad and Kāḍhimain*) (1920), p. 121.

31. *Ibid.*, p. 101.

32. Great Britain, Foreign Office, FO 195/2308, Report by H.E. Wilkie Young, Mosul, accompanying dispatch of 28 January 1909. For text of report, see also *Middle Eastern Studies*, VII, No. 2 (May 1971), 229 ff.

33. *Lughat-ul-'Arab*, 9 October 1911, quoted by *Revue du Monde Musulman*, 6th Year, XVIII (February-March 1912), in its Review of the Arab Press section, p. 223, note.

34. Bābān, 'From Isṭambūl to Baghdād, p. 256.

35. The duties are summarized in the *Report by His Britannic Majesty's Government to the Council of the League of Nations on the Administration of Iraq for the Year 1926* (London, 1927), p. 37. The regulations were issued by the Ottoman government, which may have itself prescribed the duties in question. On the other hand, the regulations may have merely reflected practices habitually carried on by the *aṣnāf.*

36. See Batatu, *The Old Social Classes*, pp. 73 ff.

37. Ibid, p. 240.

38. Grandson of the Prophet.

39. 'Alī Al-Bāzirgān, *Al-Waqāi' ul-Haqīqiyyah fī-th-Thawrat-il-'Irāqiyyah* ('The Real Facts about the Iraqi Revolt') (Baghdad, 1954), pp. 90 and 94; and Great Britain, *Review of the Civil Administration of Mesopotamia* (London, 1920), p. 140.

40. Great Britain, Foreign Office, FO 406/63 E 862/6/93, Letter of 4 December 1928 from Sir H. Dobbs, Baghdād, to Mr. Amery, London.

41. The number of state elementary school students increased from 8001 in 1920–1921 to 89,482 in 1939–1940, and the number of state secondary school students from 110 to 13,959 in the same period: Iraq, Ministry of Education, *At-Taqrīr-us-Sanawī 'An Sayr-il-Ma'ārif*... ('Annual Report on the Progress of Education for the Year 1955–1956') (Baghdad, 1957), pp. 43 and 54.

42. For the text of the memorandum, which was written in March 1933, see 'Abd-ur-Razzāq al-Ḥasanī, *Tārīkh-ul-Wizārat-il-'Irāqiyyah* ('The History of the Iraqi Cabinets') (Sidon, 1953), III, 286–293. For the quoted statement, see p. 289.

43. For this point I am indebted to Kāmel ach-Chādirchī of the National Democratic party: conversation, February 1962.

44. Faiṣal I's confidential memorandum of March 1933, al-Ḥasanī, Tārīkh-ul-Wizārat, III, 288.

45. *Ibid.*, p. 289.

46. *Ibid.*, p. 290.

47. Stephen H. Longrigg, *Iraq 1900 to 1950. A Political, Social, and Economic History* (Oxford, 1953), p. 246.

48. *Ibid.*, p. 166.

49. Great Britain, Foreign Office, FO 371/20013/E 6797/1419/93, Minutes by J.G. Ward of 30 October 1936.

50. Great Britain, Foreign Office, FO 371/23217/E 2372/72/93, Quarterly Report No. 26 by the British Military Mission on the Iraqi Army and Royal Iraqi Air Force for the Quarter Ending 28 February 1939.

51. Great Britain, Foreign Office, FO 371/20796/E 44/14/93, Letter of 22 December 1936 from Sir A. Clark Kerr, Baghdād, to Anthony Eden, London.

52. Great Britain, Naval Intelligence Division, *Iraq and the Persian Gulf* (1944), pp. 581 and 583.

53. The ex-Sharīfian officers were the Iraqi officers in the Ottoman army who during World War I abandoned the Ottoman cause and attached themselves to the service of the family of Sharīf Ḥusain of Mecca, and especially of his son Faiṣal, then in active revolt against the Turks.

54. Nūrī as-Saʿīd and his brother-in-law, Jaʿfar al-ʿAskarī, who was also an ex-Sharīfian officer, had followers in the army since the 1920s, and used their position to combat the influence upon the military of Yasīn al-Hāshimī, another soldier-politician.

55. The term 'middle class,' as used in these pages, refers to that composite part of society which is plural in its functions but has in common a middling income or a middling status, and which includes merchants, tradesmen, landowners, army officers, students, members of professions, civil servants, and employees of private companies. It would be a mistake to make too sharp a distinction between one section of this class and another, say between army officers and tradesmen or landowners, for it must not be forgotten that the real unit of class is not the individual but the family, and that members of one middle-class family pursue different professions. Thus out of the fifteen members of the Supreme Committee of the Free Officers and the nine members of the Committee-in-Reserve of the Free Officers, who prepared for the coup of 14 July 1958, seven and six respectively were sons of merchants or middlemen, or small or middling landowners. Colonel Salāḥ-ud-Dīn aṣ-Ṣabbāgh, the moving spirit behind the politically minded military element in the years 1938–1941, was also the son of a merchant and landowner. See his *Fursān-ul- ʿUrūbah fīl ʿIrāq* ('The Knights of Arabism in Iraq') (Damascus, 1956), p. 21.

56. The ex-Sharīfian officers were by origin from the middle or humbler walks of life, but by this time many of them had become propertied and, though not yet fully accepted socially by the old families, formed part of the political elite.

57. Conversation of King Ghāzī with British ambassador, Great Britain, Foreign Office, FO 371/21846/E 172/45/93, Letter of 25 December 1937 from Sir A. Clark Kerr, Baghdād, to Anthony Eden, London.

58. For these figures, see Retired Staff Major Maḥmūd ad-Durrah's *Al-Ḥarb al-ʿIrāqiyyah al-Briṭāniyyah, 1941* ('The British–Iraqi War of 1941') (Beirut, 1969), p. 243.

59. Iraq, Ministry of Economics, *Statistical Abstract, 1943* (Baghdad, 1945), pp. 29–30.

60. Ad-Durrah, *Al-Ḥarb*, p. 420.

61. Colonel Gerald de Gaury, *Three Kings in Baghdād, 1921–1958* (London, 1961), p. 146.

62. Retired Staff General Ṣāliḥ Ṣāʿib aj-Jubūrī (ex-chief of staff of the Iraqi army), *Miḥnat-u-Filasṭīn wa Asrāruhā-s-Siyāsiyyah wa-l-ʿAskariyyah* ('The Misfortune of Palestine and Its Political and Military Secrets') (Beirut, 1970), pp. 142–144.

63. Consult Table 41–1 in Batatu, *The Old Social Classes*.

64. See Batatu, *The Old Social Classes*, Chapter 22.

65. *Ibid.*, Chapter 30.

66. *Ibid.*, Chapter 39.

67. *Ibid.*, pp. 132 ff., 142 ff., 150 ff., and 470 ff.

68. *Ibid.*, p. 680.

69. Great Britain, Naval Intelligence Division, *Iraq and the Persian Gulf*, p. 562.

70. Lord Salter, *The Development of Iraq. A Plan of Action* (Baghdād, 1955), p. 61.

71. For the 1920 figure, see Great Britain, *Review of the Civil Administration of Mesopotamia* (1920), p. 122. For the other figures, see Iraq, Ministry of Finance, *Budget of the Iraq Government for the Financial Year 1938*, Consolidated Statement Q, p. 14; and Iraq, *Al-Waqāiʿul-ʿIrāqiyyah*, No. 14122 of 29 March 1958, Schedule Q of General Budget Law for the Financial Year 1958. All figures include teachers, but exclude foreign personnel and Iraqi *mustakhdims*, i.e. holders of nonpensionable appointments.

72. These figures include foreign personnel, but exclude nontechnical employees, who numbered 4,633 in 1927, 6,800 in 1937, and 11,798 in 1957. The number of Iraqi and foreign officers, officials, and employees of the port was 427 in 1920, and 402 in 1930. No figures are

available for subsequent years. Great Britain, *Review of the Civil Administration*, p. 122; Great Britain, *Special Report ... on the Progress of Iraq during the Period 1920–1931* (London, 1931), pp. 168 and 176; Iraq, Ministry of Economics, *Statistical Abstract ... for the Years 1927/28–1937/38*, p. 111; and Iraq, Ministry of Planning, *Statistical Abstract, 1959*, p. 317.

73. Great Britain, *Review of the Civil Administration*, p. 122; and Iraq, Ministry of Economics, *Statistical Abstract*, 1943, p. 24, and *1958*, p. 170.

74. See Table 6–2 in Batatu, *The Old Social Classes.*

75. *Ibid.*

76. The number of Iraqis sent abroad for a higher education also increased from 9 in 1921/22 to 66 in 1938/39, and 859 in 1958/59. For all figures except those for 1958/59, see Iraq, Ministry of Education, *At-Taqrīr-us-Sanawī ... 1955–56* pp. 54, 68, 69, 75, and 175. For the 1958/59 figures, consult Table 17–5 in Batatu, *The Old Social Classes.*

IV

The Middle East Since the Second World War

Introduction

MARY C. WILSON

Despite the outward change to the political contours of the Middle East following the First World War, there was great continuity in social and political life. After the Second World War, however, internal and external pressures combined to shatter the political patterns and social structures established in the latter period of Ottoman rule and maintained in the interwar period. Internal social pressures, the reorientation of Middle Eastern states and societies in the changing constellation of global politics and economics, and new technologies spawned new ideologies and gave shape to a new politics.

The creation of Israel, a powerful catalyst to the new politics of the period, has been the subject of historical writing since 1948. Owing to popular criticism of Israeli goals and the means used to achieve these goals during and after the 1982 occupation of Lebanon, a new school of historical interpretation has emerged in Israel. These 'new historians' use Israeli archives to question Israel's official creation story. While challenges to the official story were not new, coming from Israeli historians they gained authority.

Avi Shlaim is one of the leading new historians. His article, which begins this section, puts Israel's victory in the 1948 war squarely into the realm of verifiable and comprehensible history. Simply put, Israel won because it had more fighters and superior weapons. Israel did not face an Arab world united to destroy it; it faced a system of Arab states, whose leadership was focused on survival within the state borders drawn after World War I.

Shlaim's approach is dispassionate, but his subject is highly emotive. Some are loath to consign Israel's beginnings to the mundane world of power politics, some reject the suggestion that fear was and by implication is manipulated for internal political ends, and some reject the notion that the Arabs were and by implication are not united in the desire to save the Palestinians. An equally dispassionate piece on Israel and the Palestinians by David McDowall begins where Shlaim ends. For Shlaim the outcome of the 1948 war was based in the military reality of more fighters and better arms; for McDowall, following Zionist ideology, the future of a Jewish state of Israel is based on maintaining a majority of Jewish citizens. He explores the demographic history of Israel since 1948 and asks by what means can the state of Israel maintain the Jewish majority necessary to the Zionist definition of Israel as a Jewish state.

McDowall wrote his article during the first *intifada* (1987-1993), which forced Israel and others to recognize that the Occupied Territories could no longer be left in limbo: neither part of Israel proper, nor a Palestinian state, nor a part of an existing Arab state. Through the direct negotiations between Israel and the PLO begun in Oslo in 1993, Israel managed temporarily to solve the dilemma posed by the large Palestinian population in the Occupied Territories. These negotiations outlined a Palestinian state in terms of highly concentrated Palestinian populations in non-contiguous urban centers, enabling Israel to retain territory in the Occupied Territories it deemed strategic while it divested itself of responsibility for a large non-Jewish population. With the breakdown of the Oslo agreements however, the Occupied Territories are back in limbo and in the midst of a second *intifada* against Israeli occupation. In 2003, Israel faces demographic problems similar to those that McDowall described ten years ago, and Israel's budgetary and economic problems are more severe. The Palestinian birthrate in Israel is currently 4.8 compared to 2.7 for Jews. In Israel and the Occupied Territories there are twice as many Palestinians born as Jewish Israelis. The Israeli Central Bureau of Statistics reported that immigration in 2002 was the lowest in thirteen years. The largest number of immigrants came from former Soviet republics, migration from Argentina tripled, fueled by severe economic troubles there, and migration from the United States increased by 23 percent. Although Israel counted its one millionth immigrant from the former Soviet Union in 2000, it is not public knowledge how many of these one million have stayed. Moreover, even if these or other Jewish Israelis maintain Israeli citizenship, Jewish Israelis need only visit Israel once every four years to be counted in the census. Both Labour Prime Minister Barak (1999-2001) and Likud Prime Minister Sharon (2001-) declared Israel capable of absorbing one million Jewish immigrants over ten years. Both refused to consider the repatriation of any Palestinians. Arnon Sofer of the University of Haifa estimates that in 2002 there were 5 million Jews and 5 million non-Jews in Israel and the Occupied Territories.

Israel is usually considered to have little in common with its neighbors. McDowall's work suggests that lines of analysis that are taken for granted as regards the Arab states, Iran, and Turkey are also pertinent to Israel. For example, Israel no less than its Arab neighbors is a country permanently at war, and the Israeli military encroaches on the political domain, even if not in so open a manner as in some Arab states. Hence posing the question of the role of the military in politics is as fitting for Israel as it is for some of its neighbors. Religious parties also influence the politics of the state and, as in the Arab states their presence and power have increased since 1967. The clash between Orthodox Jews in Israel and other Jews seems sharper than ten years ago with the strong showing of the Shinui Party (committed to decrease state subsidies to the Orthodox and abolish their military exemption) in the January 2003 elections. Finally, two related problems usually taken as endemic to other Middle Eastern politics are shown to be Israeli problems as well: the problems of minority rule and of ruling minorities.

The next two articles, by Stephen Humphreys and Joel Gordon respectively, address the topic of Arab nationalism. Humphreys joins a developing trend in history writing by putting himself into his text, "...when I arrived in Lebanon...," thus mitigating the authoritative, objective voice as anthropologists began to do some twenty years ago. Gordon explores film and memory to write about Nasser and Arab nationalism in the 1950s and today. By simultaneously looking at the past and how the past is rendered in the present, he too undermines the conventional authoritative voice of historical analysis.

Despite the prominence of Islam and Islamism in analyses of politics in the Middle East since the Iranian revolution, Humphreys makes a case that "of all the ideologies that have played on the Middle Eastern stage in this century ... none has had a greater impact ... than Arab Nationalism." Yet, he points out, even the dream of an Arab nationalism larger than the state is long gone as demonstrated by the lack of effective nationalist response to Israel's invasion of Lebanon in 1982 and the fissures in the Arab world revealed during the Gulf war of 1990-91. Hizbullah, which did succeed in getting Israeli forces to withdraw from southern Lebanon after a ten-year struggle, is not a nationalist party.

Arab ethnic identity exists but has not proven to be an effective framework for political action, as Avi Shlaim amply demonstrates in his article on the 1948 war. Humphreys offers some reasons why: first, Arab nationalism faced the complicated problem of conceiving an Arab nation separate from the Islamic *umma* and second, Arab nationalism focused on who is an Arab rather than on how Arabs might build the institutions of a common political life. Then there were the regional identities and politics at play that had been rearranged and exaggerated by the creation of new states after the First World War. Within those states non-Arab and non-Muslim minorities posed problems for the conception of a national identity. Indeed, the twentieth century may be viewed as a century where Arab nationalism competed with state interests, with the triumph at the end of the century of the state over the nation. If that triumph was suggested by the actions of the Arab states in the 1948 war, no Arab state abandoned rhetorical support for the Palestinians, the central plank of the Arab nationalist platform, until the 1990-1991 Gulf War. And yet, what Humphreys could not have foreseen, the al-Aqsa *intifada*, which began in 2000, has at least temporarily restored the rhetorical unity of Arab support for Palestinians.

In Egypt, Arab nationalism was embodied by Nasser, and during his lifetime he embodied Arab nationalism in the Arab world. Gordon looks at a 1996 movie that recreates the highlight of Nasser's political career: the nationalization of the Suez Canal in 1956. Public response demonstrates that Nasser's appeal and attraction, his Arab nationalism, still has legs in Egypt. Gordon joins a widening stream of history writing about how people remember and memorialize the past and what that says about the people who are present. The events of the Suez crisis are by now well known; how Egyptians construe them is a new and welcome subject.

Nikki Keddie, in the next article, takes a long view of the Iranian revolution. In an exercise in comparative history, she both looks at it in the context of previous upheavals in Iran and compares it to other world revolutions. Iranian anomalies include the importance of the orthodox clergy to the revolutionary process, the relative unimportance of the peasantry, and the permeability of Iranian cities to mass revolution. The most arresting internal contrast presented by Keddie is that between the 1905-11 constitutional revolution and the 1978-79 Islamic revolution. The constitutional revolution, despite the leading role played by the *'ulama*, had as its aim a Western-style constitution and resulted in greater secularization of law and government. The Islamic revolution, despite the greater Westernization of education, law, government, culture, and economy that had taken place in Iran by the 1970s, resulted in a self-styled Islamic republic.

The difference of form and result, Keddie finds, lies in historical context. In the first revolution, the enemy was the traditionalist Qajar dynasty. For most Iranians it was the weak government of the Qajars that had allowed Britain and Russia undue influence in Iranian affairs. Hence the constitutional revolution could aim both to curb European influence and to reform government along European lines so that a weak ruler would not necessarily mean a weak government. The second revolution aimed to curb Pahlavi rule that had used Westernization to increase its own power at the expense of all other social, cultural, economic, or political ties amongst the population. The dynasty was also perceived to be much more deeply involved with foreign (Western) powers than the Qajars, to the detriment of Iran and Iranians. Hence the 1978-79 revolution took on the language and symbolism of Shi'i Islam, which rejected both the Pahlavis and the West. Finally Keddie makes the important point that the Islamic revolution was a revolution in Shi'i practice as much as a revolution in the form, symbols, and social location of power in Iran: 'Khomeini's notion of direct *'ulama* rule is new to Shi'ism.' In the years since the overthrow of the shah and the writing of this article, it is this latter revolution that has sparked increasing controversy in Iran among the laity and the *'ulama* alike.

Olivier Roy addresses this 'crisis of religious legitimacy.' Ayatollah Khomeini was regarded as both a learned cleric of the highest order and a political leader. He therefore embodied religious and political leadership. But as Roy points out, even during his time, 1979-1989, as leader of Iran and of the Islamic revolution, the political needs of the state trumped the *shari'a*. 'The official reason for subordinating *shari'a* to the State law is to achieve the higher interest of the Islamic State and hence of Islam. But here again it is the political instance which decides what is essentially Islamic...' The problem of combining political and religious leadership was made plain with the appointment of Ayatollah Khomeini's successor. The deeper crisis of religious legitimacy is that as religious figures have taken over the political leadership of the state, their religious autonomy has been sacrificed to the political needs of the state, what Roy calls the 'statization' of religion. Instead of religion dominating the state, the reverse has occurred. Along with this process, Shi'ism in Iran has also become nationalized. The Shi'i leadership in Iran is now a state hierarchy; the concerns of this hierarchy are no longer universal to all Shi'is, but are now largely limited to Iran. While the process of the state subordinating religion is different from what is happening in the Arab states where the state has subordinated Arab nationalism, in Iran as in the Arab states individual state interests have the upper hand over the broader interests of religion or nation writ large.

In the structure of power in Saudi Arabia, Mamoun Fandy sees the dominance of state over religion as well: the 'interaction between state and religion brought about certain adjustments to islamic [sic] practice rather than the other way around.' Thus the Wahhabi *Ikhwan*, who were essential to establishing the territorial reach of the Al-Saud, were suppressed once the *Ikhwan* began to attack British controlled territory in the 1920s because conflict with Britain would have jeopardized the fledgling state. *Raison d'état* trumped the religious ideology of the state then and since, though never again in such an open confrontation. In 1990, the government sought and got a *fatwa* from the Council of Higher *'Ulama* justifying the participation of American (non-Muslim) troops in defense of the realm. Following the Gulf War there has been increased criticism of the official organs of religious rectitude from the margins of the *'ulama*, made up largely of *'ulama* from the margins of Saudi society.

Fandy uses two analytical tools to describe Saudi society. He argues that Saudi social/political structure is built not on religious ties but on secular ties of *'a'iliyya* (familialism) and *qaraba* (social nearness/distance). Put simply the five thousand or so members of the royal family are more privileged than non-royals, and those who are close to the royal family are more privileged than those who are not. The social margins of Saudi society are those who have least contact with any member of the royal family.

The state's enforcement of the strict practices of Wahhabism serves to legitimize the Saudi government, but it is a two-edged sword. While the council of Higher *'Ulama* issued a *fatwa* justifying the American presence on Saudi soil in 1990, junior *'ulama* issued *fatwas* against seeking the help of non-Muslims in war against Muslims. Even a conservative Islamist government can attract the attention of Islamist critics: 'Saudi islamists [sic] felt that if the Americans stayed longer, they would further erode the authority of islam [sic] in the kingdom.' Although the government did not change its external policies, it did accommodate Islamists' wishes in its internal policies.

The articles of Part IV do not cover every important subject or include every important category of analysis for the study of the post war Middle East. The editors believe, however, that those articles we have been able to put before you illuminate their subjects and provide new ways of seeing and thinking about subjects that have not been covered.

Israel and the Arab Coalition in 1948

AVI SHLAIM

"A nation," said the French philosopher Ernest Renan, "is a group of people united by a mistaken view about the past and a hatred of their neighbors." Throughout the ages, the use of myths about the past has been a potent instrument of forging a nation. The Zionist movement is not unique in propagating a simplified and varnished version of the past in the process of nation-building. But it does provide a strikingly successful example of the use of myths for the dual purpose of promoting internal unity and enlisting international sympathy and support for the state of Israel.

The traditional Zionist version of the Arab–Israeli conflict places the responsibility on the Arab side. Israel is portrayed as the innocent victim of unremitting Arab hostility and Arab aggression. In this respect, traditional Zionist accounts of the emergence of Israel form a natural sequel to the history of the Jewish people, with its emphasis on the weakness, vulnerability, and numerical inferiority of the Jews in relation to their adversaries. The American Jewish historian Salo Baron once referred to this as the lachrymose view of Jewish history. This view tends to present Jewish history as a long series of trials and tribulations culminating in the Holocaust.

The War of Independence constituted a glorious contrast to the centuries of powerlessness, persecution, and humiliation. Yet the traditional Zionist narrative of the events surrounding the birth of the state of Israel was still constructed around the notion of the Jews as the victims. This narrative presents the 1948 war as a simple, bipolar no-holds-barred struggle between a monolithic and malevolent Arab adversary and a tiny peace-loving Jewish community. The biblical image of David and Goliath is frequently evoked in this narrative. Little Israel is portrayed as fighting with its back to the wall against a huge, well-armed and overbearing Arab adversary. Israel's victory in this war is treated as verging on the miraculous, and as resulting from the determination and heroism of the Jewish fighters rather than from disunity and disarray on the Arab side. This heroic version of the War of Independence has proved so enduring and resistant to revision precisely because it corresponds to the collective memory of the generation of 1948. It is also the version of history that Israeli children are taught at school. Consequently, few ideas are as deeply ingrained in the mind of the Israeli public as that summed up by the Hebrew phrase, *me'atim mul rabim*, or "the few against the many."

One of the most persistent myths surrounding the birth of the State of Israel is that in 1948 the newly-born state faced a monolithic and implacably hostile Arab coalition. This coalition was believed to be united behind one central aim: the destruction of the infant Jewish state. As there is no commonly accepted term for the liquidation of a state, Yehoshafat Harkabi, a leading Israeli student of the Arab–Israeli conflict, proposed calling it "politicide" – the murder of the *politeia*, the political entity. The aim of the Arabs, Harkabi asserted, was politicidal. Linked to this aim, according to Harkabi, was a second aim, that of genocide – "to throw the Jews into the sea" as the popular phrase put it.[1] Harkabi's view is just one example of the widely held belief that in 1948 the Yishuv, the pre-state Jewish community in Palestine, faced not just verbal threats but a real danger of annihilation from the regular armies of the neighboring Arab states. The true story of the first Arab–Israeli war, as the "new historians" who emerged on the scene in the late 1980s tried to show, was considerably more complicated.[2]

The argument advanced in this chapter, in a nutshell, is that the Arab coalition facing Israel in 1947–49 was far from monolithic; that within this coalition there was no agreement on war aims; that the inability of the Arabs to coordinate their diplomatic and military moves was partly responsible for their defeat; that throughout the conflict Israel had the military edge over its Arab adversaries; and, finally, and most importantly, that Israel's leaders were aware of the divisions inside the Arab coalition and that they exploited these divisions to the full in waging the war and in extending the borders of their state.

THE MILITARY BALANCE

As far as the military balance is concerned, it was always assumed that the Arabs enjoyed overwhelming numerical superiority. The war was accordingly depicted as one between the few against the many, as a desperate, tenacious, and heroic struggle for survival against horrifyingly heavy odds. The desperate plight and the heroism of the Jewish fighters are not in question. Nor is the fact that they had inferior military hardware at their disposal, at least until the first truce, when illicit arms supplies from Czechoslovakia decisively tipped the scales in their favor. But in mid-May 1948 the total number of Arab troops, both regular and irregular, operating in the Palestine theater was under 25,000, whereas the Israel Defense Force (IDF) fielded over 35,000 troops. By mid-July the IDF mobilized 65,000 men under arms, and by December its numbers had reached a peak of 96,441. The Arab states also reinforced their armies, but they could not match this rate of increase. Thus, at each stage of the war, the IDF outnumbered all the Arab forces arrayed against it, and, after the first round of fighting, it outgunned them too. The final outcome of the war was therefore not a miracle but a faithful reflection of the underlying military balance in the Palestine theater. In this war, as in most wars, the stronger side prevailed.[3]

The Arab forces, both regular and irregular, mobilized to do battle against the emergent Jewish state were nowhere as powerful or united as they appeared to be in Arab and Jewish propaganda. In the first phase of the conflict, from the passage of the United Nations partition resolution on 29 November 1947 until the proclamation of statehood on 14 May 1948, the Yishuv had to defend itself against attacks from Palestinian irregulars and volunteers from the Arab world. Following the proclamation of the state of Israel, however, the neighboring Arab states and Iraq committed their regular armies to the battle against the Jewish state. Contact with regular armies undoubtedly came as a shock to the Haganah, the paramilitary organization of the Yishuv which was in the process of being transformed into the IDF. Yet, the Jewish propaganda machine greatly exaggerated the size and quality of the invading forces. A typical account of the war of independence, by a prominent Israeli diplomat, goes as follows: "Five Arab armies and contingents from two more, equipped with modern tanks, artillery, and warplanes ... invaded Israel from north, east, and south. Total war was forced on the Yishuv under the most difficult conditions."[4]

The five Arab states who joined in the invasion of Palestine were Egypt, Transjordan, Syria, Lebanon, and Iraq; while the two contingents came from Saudi Arabia and Yemen. All these states, however, only sent an expeditionary force to Palestine, keeping the bulk of their army at home. The expeditionary forces were hampered by long lines of communication, the absence of reliable intelligence about their enemy, poor leadership, poor coordination, and very poor planning for the campaign that lay ahead of them. The Palestinian irregulars, known as the Holy War Army, were led by Hasan Salama and 'Abd al-Qadir al-Husayni. The Arab Liberation Army consisted of around 4,000 Arab volunteers for the Holy War in Palestine. They were funded by the Arab League, trained in bases in southern Syria, and led by the Syrian adventurer Fawzi al-Qawuqji. Qawuqji's strong points were politics and public relations rather than military leadership. The Arab politicians who appointed him valued him more as a known enemy and therefore potential counter-weight to the grand mufti, Hajj Amin al-Husayni, than as the most promising military leader to lead the fight against the Jews. The *mufti* certainly saw this appointment as an attempt by his rivals in the League to undermine his influence over the future of Palestine.[5]

The Arab coalition was beset by profound internal political differences. The Arab League, since its foundation in 1945, was the highest forum for the making of pan-Arab policy on Palestine. But the Arab League was divided between a Hashemite bloc consisting of Transjordan and Iraq and an anti-Hashemite bloc led by Egypt and Saudi Arabia. Dynastic rivalries played a major part in shaping Arab approaches to Palestine. King ʿAbdullah of Transjordan was driven by a long-standing ambition to make himself the master of Greater Syria which included, in addition to Transjordan, Syria, Lebanon, and Palestine. King Faruq saw ʿAbdullah's ambition as a direct threat to Egypt's leadership in the Arab world. The rulers of Syria and Lebanon saw in King ʿAbdullah a threat to the independence of their countries and they also suspected him of being in cahoots with the enemy. Each Arab state was moved by its own dynastic or national interests. Arab rulers were as concerned with curbing each other as they were in fighting the common enemy. Under these circumstances it was virtually impossible to reach any real consensus on the means and ends of the Arab intervention in Palestine. Consequently, far from confronting a single enemy with a clear purpose and a clear plan of action, the Yishuv faced a loose coalition consisting of the Arab League, independent Arab states, irregular Palestinian forces, and an assortment of volunteers. The Arab coalition was one of the most divided, disorganized, and ramshackle coalitions in the entire history of warfare.

Separate and conflicting national interests were hidden behind the fig-leaf of securing Palestine for the Palestinians. The Palestine problem was the first major test of the Arab League and the Arab League failed it miserably. The actions of the League were taken ostensibly in support of the Palestinian claim for independence in the whole of Palestine. But the League remained curiously unwilling to allow the Palestinians to assume control over their own destiny. For ʿAbd al-Rahman ʿAzzam, the secretary-general of the Arab League, the *mufti* was "the Menachem Begin of the Arabs." ʿAzzam Pasha told a British journalist (who relayed it to a Jewish official), that the Arab League's policy "was intended to squeeze the *mufti* out."[6]

At Arab League meetings, the *mufti* argued against intervention in Palestine by the regular Arab armies, but his pleas were ignored.[7] All the *mufti* asked for was financial support and arms and these were promised to him but delivered only in negligible quantities. It is misleading, therefore, to claim that all the resources of the Arab League were placed at the disposal of the Palestinians. On the contrary, the Arab League let the Palestinians down in their hour of greatest need. As Yezid Sayigh, the distinguished historian of the Palestinian armed struggle, put it: "Reluctance to commit major resources to the conflict and mutual distrust provoked constant disputes over diplomacy and strategy, leading to incessant behind-the-scenes manoeuvring, half-hearted and poorly conceived military intervention, and, ultimately, defeat on the battlefield."[8]

THE HASHEMITE CONNECTION

The weakest link in the chain of hostile Arab states that surrounded the Yishuv on all sides was Transjordan. Ever since the creation of the Amirate of Transjordan by Britain in 1921, the Jewish Agency strove to cultivate friendly relations with its Hashemite ruler, 'Abdullah ibn Husayn. The irreconcilable conflict between the Jewish and Arab national movements in Palestine provided the setting for the emergence of the special relations between the Zionists and 'Abdullah, who became king in 1946 when Transjordan gained formal independence. Failure to reach an understanding with their Palestinian neighbors spurred the Zionist leaders to seek a counterweight to local hostility in better relations with the neighboring Arab countries. Indeed, the attempt to bypass the Palestine Arabs and forge links with the rulers of the Arab states became a central feature of Zionist diplomacy in the 1930s and 1940s.

The friendship between the Hashemite ruler and the Zionist movement was cemented by a common enemy in the shape of the grand mufti, Hajj Amin al-Husayni, the leader of the Palestinian national movement. For the *mufti* had not only put his forces on a collision course with the Jews; he was also 'Abdullah's principal rival for control over Palestine. Both sides perceived Palestinian nationalism as a threat and therefore had a common interest in suppressing it.[9] From the Zionist point of view, 'Abdullah was an immensely valuable ally. First and foremost, he was the only Arab ruler who was prepared to accept the partition of Palestine and to live in peace with a Jewish state after the conflict had been settled. Second, his small army, the Arab Legion, was the best trained and most professional of the armies of the Arab states. Third, 'Abdullah and his aides and agents were a source of information about the other Arab countries involved in the Palestine problem. Last but not least, through 'Abdullah the Zionists could generate mistrust, foment rivalry, and leak poison to weaken the coalition of their Arab adversaries.

In 1947, as the conflict over Palestine entered the crucial stage, the contacts between the Jewish side and King 'Abdullah intensified. Golda Meir of the Jewish Agency had a secret meeting with 'Abdullah in Naharayim on 17 November 1947. At this meeting they reached a preliminary agreement to co-ordinate their diplomatic and military strategies, to forestall the *mufti*, and to endeavor to prevent the other Arab states from intervening directly in Palestine.[10] Twelve days later, on 29 November, the United Nations pronounced its verdict in favor of dividing the area of the British mandate into two states, one Jewish and one Arab. This made it possible to firm up the tentative understanding reached at Naharayim. In return for 'Abdullah's promise not to enter the area assigned by the UN to the Jewish state, the Jewish Agency agreed to the annexation by Transjordan of most of the area earmarked for the Arab state. Precise borders were not drawn and Jerusalem was not even discussed as under the UN plan it was to remain a *corpus separatum* under international control. Nor was the agreement ever put down in writing. The Jewish Agency tried to tie ʿAbdullah down to a written agreement but he was evasive. Yet, according to Yaacov Shimoni, a senior official in the Political Department of the Jewish Agency, despite ʿAbdullah's evasions, the understanding with him was:

> entirely clear in its general spirit. We would agree to the conquest of the Arab part of Palestine by ʿAbdullah. We would not stand in his way. We would not help him, would not seize it and hand it over to him. He would have to take it by his own means and stratagems but we would not disturb him. He, for his part, would not prevent us from establishing the state of Israel, from dividing the country, taking our share and establishing a state in it. Now his vagueness, his ambiguity, consisted of declining to write anything, to draft anything which would bind him. To this he did not agree. But to the end, until the last minute, he always said again and again: "perhaps you would settle for less than complete independence and statehood, for full autonomy, or a Jewish canton under the roof of the Hashemite crown." He did try to raise this idea every now and again and, of course, always met with a blank wall. We told him we were talking about complete, full, and total independence and are not prepared to discuss anything else. And to this he seemed resigned but without ever saying: "OK, an independent state." He did not say that, he did not commit himself, he was not precise. But such was the spirit of the agreement and it was totally unambiguous.
>
> Incidentally, the agreement included a provision that if ʿAbdullah succeeded in capturing Syria, and realized his dream of Greater Syria – something we did not think he had the power to do – we would not disturb him. We did not believe either in the strength of his faction in Syria. But the agreement included a provision that if he did accomplish it, we would not stand in his way. But regarding the Arab part of Palestine, we did think it was serious and that he had every chance of taking it, all the more so since the Arabs of Palestine, with their official leadership, did not want to establish a state at all. That meant that we were not interfering with anybody. It was they who refused. Had they accepted a state, we might not have entered into the conspiracy. I do not know. But the fact was that they refused, so there was a complete power vacuum here and we agreed that he will go in and take the Arab part, provided he consented to the establishment of our state and to a joint declaration that there will be peaceful relations between us and him after the dust settles. That was the spirit of the agreement. A text did not exist.[11]

NEUTRALIZING THE ARAB LIBERATION ARMY

King ʿAbdullah was the Zionists' principal vehicle for fomenting further tension and antagonism within the ranks of the conflict-ridden Arab coalition, but he was not the only one. Fawzi al-Qawuqji, the commander of the Arab Liberation Army, was another weak link in the chain of hostile Arab forces. The first companies of the ALA started infiltrating into Palestine in January 1948 while Qawuqji himself did not arrive until March. Qawuqji's anti-Husayni political orientation provided an opportunity for a dialogue across the battle lines that were rapidly taking shape in Palestine as the British mandate was approaching its inglorious end.

Yehoshua ("Josh") Palmon was one of the Haganah's ablest intelligence officers and a fluent Arabic speaker. From close observation of factional Arab politics, Palmon was aware of the bitter grudge which Qawuqji bore the *mufti*. In 1947 Palmon discovered wartime German documents bearing on this feud and he passed them on to Qawuqji. These documents confirmed Qawuqji's suspicion that it was the *mufti* who had instigated his arrest and incarceration by the German authorities. Qawuqji expressed a desire to meet Palmon but, on being appointed to command the ALA, he dropped the idea. From officers who arrived in Palestine before their chief, however, Palmon learnt that Qawuqji was not hell-bent on fighting the Jews. He apparently realized that such a war would be neither short nor easy and he was said to be open to suggestions for averting it.[12]

David Ben-Gurion, the chairman of the Jewish Agency Executive, approved Palmon's plan for a secret meeting to try and persuade Qawuqji to keep out of the fight between the Haganah and the *mufti*'s forces provided no promises were made to limit their own freedom of action to retaliate against any armed gangs.[13] Palmon went to see Qawuqji at the latter's headquarters in the village of Nur al-Shams on 1 April. After a great deal of beating about the bush, Palmon got down to the real business of the meeting which was to turn inter-Arab rivalries to the advantage of his side. A solution could have been found to the problem of Palestine, he said, had it not been for the *mufti*. Qawuqji launched into a diatribe against the *mufti*'s wicked ambitions, violent methods, and selfish lieutenants. When Palmon mentioned 'Abd al-Qadir al-Husayni, the *mufti*'s cousin, and Hasan Salama, Qawuqji interjected that they could not count on any help from him and, indeed, he hoped that the Jews would teach them a good lesson. Palmon then suggested that the Haganah and the ALA should refrain from attacking each other and plan instead to negotiate, following the departure of the British. Qawuqji agreed but explained frankly that he needed to score one military victory in order to establish his credentials. Palmon could not promise to hand him a victory on a silver plate. If Jews were attacked, he said, they would fight back. Nevertheless, he went away with a clear impression that Qawuqji would remain neutral in the event of a Jewish attack on the *mufti*'s forces in Palestine.[14]

The extent of Palmon's success in neutralizing the ALA became clear only as events unfolded. On 4 April the Haganah launched Operation Nahshon to open the Tel Aviv-Jerusalem road which had been blocked by the Palestinian irregulars. First, Hasan Salama's headquarters in Ramla was blown up. Although an ALA contingent with heavy guns was present in the neighborhood, it did not go to the rescue. Qawuqji was as good (or as bad) as his word to Palmon. Next was the battle for the Qastal, a strategic point overlooking the road to Jerusalem, which changed hands several times amid fierce fighting. ʿAbd al-Qadir al-Husayni telephoned Qawuqji to ask for an urgent supply of arms and ammunition to beat off the Jewish offensive. Thanks to the Arab League, Qawuqji had large stocks of war material but, according to the Haganah listening post which monitored the call, he replied that he had none.[15] ʿAbd al-Qadir al-Husayni himself was killed in the battle for Qastal on 9 April. He was by far the ablest and most charismatic of the *mufti*'s military commanders and his death marked the collapse of the Husayni forces in Palestine.

THE ROAD TO WAR

The tide now turned decisively in favor of the Jewish forces. The mixed towns of Tiberias, Haifa, Safad and Jaffa fell into Jewish hands in rapid succession and the first waves of Palestinian refugees were set in motion. With the collapse of Palestinian resistance, the Arab governments, and especially that of Transjordan, were subjected to mounting popular pressure to send their armies to Palestine to check the Jewish military offensive. King ʿAbdullah was unable to withstand this pressure. The flood of refugees reaching Transjordan pushed the Arab Legion toward greater participation in the affairs of Palestine. The tacit agreement that ʿAbdullah had reached with the Jewish Agency enabled him to pose as the protector of the Arabs in Palestine while keeping his army out of the areas that the UN had earmarked for the Jewish state. This balancing act, however, became increasingly difficult to maintain. Suspecting ʿAbdullah of collaboration with the Zionists, the anti-Hashemite states in the Arab League began to lean towards intervention with regular armies in Palestine, if only to curb ʿAbdullah's territorial ambition and stall his bid for hegemony in the region. On 30 April the Political Committee of the Arab League decided that all the Arab states must prepare their armies for the invasion of Palestine on 15 May, the day after expiry of the British mandate. Under pressure from Transjordan and Iraq, King ʿAbdullah was appointed as commander-in-chief of the invading forces.[16]

To the Jewish leaders it looked as if ʿAbdullah was about to throw in his lot with the rest of the Arab world. So Golda Meir was sent on 10 May on a secret mission to Amman to warn the king against doing that. ʿAbdullah looked depressed and nervous. Meir flatly rejected his offer of autonomy for the Jewish parts under his crown and insisted that they adhere to their original plan for an independent Jewish state and the annexation of the Arab part to Transjordan. ʿAbdullah did not deny that this was the agreement but the situation in Palestine had changed radically, he explained, and now he was one of five; he had no choice but to join with the other Arab states in the invasion of Palestine. Meir was adamant: if ʿAbdullah was going back on their agreement and if he wanted war, then they would meet after the war and after the Jewish state had been established. The meeting ended on a frosty note but ʿAbdullah's parting words to Ezra Danin, who accompanied and translated for Golda Meir, were a plea not to break off contact, come what may. It was nearly midnight when Mrs. Meir and her escort set off on the dangerous journey back home to report the failure of her mission and the inevitability of an invasion.[17]

In Zionist historiography the meeting of 10 May is usually presented as proof of the unreliability of Israel's only friend among the Arabs and as confirmation that Israel stood alone against an all-out offensive by a united Arab world. Golda Meir herself helped to propagate the view that King 'Abdullah broke his word to her; that the meeting ended in total disagreement; and that they parted as enemies.[18] The king's explanation of the constraints that forced him to intervene were seized upon as evidence of treachery and betrayal on his part. In essence, the Zionist charge against 'Abdullah is that when the moment of truth arrived, he revoked his pledge not to attack the Jewish state and threw in his lot with the rest of the Arab world.[19] This charge helped to sustain the legend that grew up around the outbreak of war as a carefully orchestrated all-Arab invasion plan directed at strangling the Jewish state at birth.

The truth about the second 'Abdullah-Golda meeting is rather more nuanced than this self-serving Zionist account would have us believe. A more balanced assessment of 'Abdullah's position was presented by Yaacov Shimoni at the meeting of the Arab Section of the Political Department of the Jewish Agency on 13 May in Jerusalem: "His Majesty has not entirely betrayed the agreement, nor is he entirely loyal to it, but something in the middle."[20] Even Meir's own account of her mission, given to her colleagues on the Provisional State Council shortly after her return from Amman, was nowhere as unsympathetic or unflattering as the account she included much later in her memoirs. From her own contemporary report on her mission, a number of important, but frequently overlooked points, emerge. First, 'Abdullah did not go back on his word; he only stressed that circumstances had changed. Second, 'Abdullah did not say he wanted war: it was Golda Meir who threatened him with dire consequences in the event of war. Third, they did not part as enemies. On the contrary, 'Abdullah seemed anxious to maintain contact with the Jewish side even after the outbreak of hostilities. 'Abdullah needed to send his army across the River Jordan in order to gain control over the Arab part of Palestine contiguous with his kingdom. He did not say anything about attacking the Jewish forces in their own territory. The distinction was a subtle one and Golda Meir was not renowned for her subtlety.

Part of the problem was that 'Abdullah had to pretend to be going along with the other members of the Arab League who had unanimously rejected the UN partition plan and were bitterly opposed to the establishment of a Jewish state. What is more, the military experts of the Arab League had worked out a unified plan for invasion. This plan was all the more dangerous because it was geared to the real capabilities of the regular Arab armies rather than to the wild rhetoric about throwing the Jews into the sea. But the forces actually made available by the Arab states for the campaign in Palestine were well below the level demanded by the Military Committee of the Arab League. Moreover, King ʿAbdullah wrecked the invasion plan by making last-minute changes. His objective in ordering his army across the River Jordan was not to prevent the establishment of a Jewish state but to make himself master of the Arab part of Palestine. ʿAbdullah never wanted the other Arab armies to intervene in Palestine. Their plan was to prevent partition; his plan was to effect partition. His plan assumed and even required a Jewish presence in Palestine although his preference was for Jewish autonomy under his crown. By concentrating his forces on the West Bank, ʿAbdullah intended to eliminate once and for all any possibility of an independent Palestinian state and to present his Arab partners with annexation as a *fait accompli.*

As the troops marched into Palestine, the politicians of the Arab League continued their backstage manoeuvers, labyrinthine intrigues, and sordid attempts to stab each other in the back – all in the name of the highest pan-Arab ideals. Politics did not end when the war started but was inextricably mixed with it from the moment the first shot was fired until the guns finally fell silent and beyond.[21] On 15 May, the day of the invasion, an event took place which presaged much of what was to follow and exposed the lengths to which the Arab politicians were prepared to go in their attempts to outwit their partners. Syrian President Shukri al-Quwwatli sent a message to King ʿAbdullah saying it was necessary to halt the advance into Palestine and to provide the Palestinians instead with all possible arms and funds. ʿAbdullah suspected that this was a ploy to find out his true intentions. His answer was a flat rejection of this proposal.[22] His army had already been given its marching orders. The die was cast.

If King ʿAbdullah's relations with his fellow Arab leaders had sunk to one of their lowest points, his contact with the Jewish Agency had been severed altogether. The momentum generated by popular Arab pressure for the liberation of Palestine was unstoppable. The Jews were in a similarly truculent and uncompromising mood: they had proclaimed their state and they were determined to fight for it, whatever the cost. It was an ultimatum that Mrs. Meir had gone to give King ʿAbdullah, not sympathy or help in dealing with his inter-Arab problems. The Hashemite-Zionist accord, which had been thirty years in the making, looked about to unravel amid bitter recriminations. Five Arab armies were on the move, dashing the hope of a peaceful partition of Palestine that lay at the heart of this accord. As the soldiers took charge on both sides, the prospects of salvaging anything from the ruins of the Zionist-Hashemite accord looked at best uncertain.

THE INVASION

The first round of fighting, from 15 May until 11 June, was a critical period during which the fate of the newly born Jewish state seemed to hang in the balance. During this period the Jewish community suffered heavy casualties, civilian as well as military; it reeled from the shock of contact with regular Arab armies; and it suffered an ordeal which left indelible marks on the national psyche. For the people who lived through this ordeal, the sense of being *me'atim mul rabin*, the few against the many, could not have been more real. During this period, the IDF was locked in a battle on all fronts, against the five invading armies. The IDF had numerical superiority in manpower over all the Arab expeditionary forces put together, but it suffered from a chronic weakness in firepower, a weakness that was not rectified until the arrival of illicit arms shipments from the Eastern bloc during the first truce. The sense of isolation and vulnerability was overwhelming. And it was during this relatively brief but deeply traumatic period that the collective Israeli memory of the 1948 War was formed.[23]

Israel's political and military leaders, however, had a more realistic picture of the intentions and capabilities of their adversaries. David Ben-Gurion, who became prime minister and defense minister after independence, expected 'Abdullah to take over the Arab part of Palestine in accordance with the tacit agreement that Golda Meir had reached with him in November 1947. So he could not have been altogether surprised to learn from Mrs. Meir in May 1948 that 'Abdullah intended to invade Palestine. The real question was whether 'Abdullah's bid to capture Arab Palestine would involve him in an armed clash with the Israeli forces.

Ben-Gurion did not have to wait long for an answer to this question. No sooner had the Arab armies marched into Palestine, when the Arab Legion and the IDF came to blows. Some of the fiercest battles of the entire war were fought between these two armies in and around Jerusalem. Even before the end of the British mandate, an incident took place which cast a long shadow over relations between the Yishuv and Transjordan. An Arab Legion detachment launched an all-out attack, with armored cars and canons, on Gush Etzion, a bloc of four Jewish settlements astride the Jerusalem–Hebron road. After the defenders surrendered, some were massacred by Arab villagers from the Hebron area and the rest were taken captive by the Arab Legion.[24] The Etzion bloc was an enclave in the middle of a purely Arab area which had been assigned to the Arab state by the UN. Nevertheless, this ferocious assault could not be easily reconciled with 'Abdullah's earlier protestations of friendship or professed desire to avert military hostilities.

In Jerusalem the initiative was seized by the Jewish side. As soon as the British evacuated the city, a vigorous offensive was launched to capture the Arab and mixed quarters of the city and form a solid area going all the way to the Old City walls. Glubb Pasha, the British commander of the Arab Legion, adopted a defensive strategy which was intended to avert a head-on collision with the Jewish forces. According to his account, the Arab Legion crossed the Jordan on 15 May to help the Arabs defend the area of Judea and Samaria allocated to them. They were strictly forbidden to enter Jerusalem or to enter any area allotted to the Jewish state in the partition plan. But on 16 May the Jewish forces tried to break into the Old City, prompting urgent calls for help from the Arab defenders. On 17 May, King ʿAbdullah ordered Glubb Pasha to send a force to defend the Old City.[25] Fierce fighting ensued. The legionnaires inflicted very heavy damage and civilian casualties by shelling the New City, the Jewish quarters of Jerusalem. On 28 May, the Jewish Quarter inside the Old City finally surrendered to the Arab Legion.

After the Jewish offensive in Jerusalem had been halted, the focal point of the battle moved to Latrun, a hill spur with fortifications, that dominated the main route from Tel Aviv to Jerusalem. Like Gush Etzion, Latrun lay in the area allotted by the UN to the Arab state. But Latrun's strategic importance was such that Ben-Gurion was determined to capture it. Against the advice of his generals, he ordered three frontal attacks on Latrun, on 25 and 30 May and on 9 June. The Arab Legion beat off all these attacks and inflicted very heavy losses on the hastily improvized and ill-equipped Jewish forces.

Any lingering hope that Transjordan would act differently to the rest of the Arab countries went up in smoke as a result of the costly clashes in and around Jerusalem. Yigael Yadin, the IDF chief of operations, roundly rejected the claim that there had ever been any collusion between the Jewish Agency and the ruler of Transjordan, let alone collusion during the 1948 War:

> Contrary to the view of many historians, I do not believe that there was an agreement or even an understanding between Ben-Gurion and ʿAbdullah. He may have had wishful thoughts... but until 15 May 1948, he did not build on it and did not assume that an agreement with ʿAbdullah would neutralize the Arab Legion. On the contrary, his estimate was that the clash with the Legion was inevitable. Even if Ben-Gurion had an understanding or hopes, they evaporated the moment ʿAbdullah marched on Jerusalem. First there was the assault on Kfar Etzion, then the capture of positions in Latrun in order to dominate the road to Jerusalem, and then there was the entry into Jerusalem. From these moves it was clear that ʿAbdullah intended to capture Jerusalem.[26]

Yadin's testimony cannot be dismissed lightly for it reflected the unanimous view of the IDF General Staff that the link with Transjordan had no influence on Israel's military conduct during the War of Independence. As Major-General Moshe Carmel, the commander of the northern front, put it: "All of us felt that *à la guerre come* [sic] *à la guerre* and that we had to act against all the Arab forces that had invaded the country."[27] What may be questioned is the assumption of Israel's military leaders that ʿAbdullah intended to capture Jerusalem.

One of the many paradoxes of the 1948 War was that the greatest understanding – that between Israel and Transjordan – was followed upon the outbreak of war by the bloodiest battles. One explanation of this paradox is that within the context of the tacit understanding between the two sides, there was plenty of scope for misunderstandings. Jerusalem was the most likely area for misunderstandings to arise both because of its symbolic and strategic importance, and because the fact that it was to form a separate enclave under an international regime permitted both sides to keep their fears and their hopes to themselves. In the first round of fighting, which ended when the UN-decreed truce took effect on 11 June, Transjordan and Israel looked like the worst of enemies. During the rest of the war, however, they were, in the apt phrase of one Israeli writer, "the best of enemies."[28]

The other Arab armies were not as effective as the Arab Legion in the first round of fighting. There was little coordination between the invading armies and virtually no cooperation. Although there was one headquarters for all the invading armies, headed by an Iraqi general, Nur al-Din Mahmud, it had no effective control over those armies, and the military operations did not follow the agreed plan. Having accomplished the initial thrust into Palestine, each army feared that it would be cut off by the enemy from the rear. Consequently, one after the other, the Arab armies took up defensive positions. The Egyptian army sent two columns from their forward bases in Sinai. One advanced north along the coastal road in the direction of Tel Aviv. Its advance was slowed down by its attempts, mostly abortive, to capture Jewish settlements scattered in the northern Negev. It continued its advance, bypassing these settlements, until it was stopped on 29 May by the Negev Brigade in Ashdod, 20 miles from Tel Aviv. The second column, which included volunteers from the Muslim Brotherhood, proceeded towards Jerusalem through Beersheba, Hebron, and Bethlehem. It was stopped at Kibbutz Ramat Rahel at the southern edge of Jerusalem on 24 May. An Arab Legion unit was stationed nearby but it extended no assistance to the Egyptian fighters. Thus, after only 10 days of fighting, the Egyptian advance was halted.

The Iraqi army, despite considerable logistical difficulties, managed to assemble a sizeable force, with tanks and artillery, for the invasion of Palestine. In the first three days following the end of the mandate, the Iraqi army launched attacks on three Jewish settlements, all of which were repulsed. Having given up the attempt to capture Jewish settlements, the Iraqi army retreated, regrouped, and took up defensive positions in "the triangle" defined by the large Arab cities of Jenin, Nablus, and Tulkarem. When attacked by IDF units, in Jenin for example, it held its ground. It also launched occasional forays into Jewish territory, but none of them lasted more than a few hours. Although its westernmost point was less than 10 miles from the Mediterranean, the Iraqi army made no attempt to push to the sea and cut Israel in two. One reason for the relative passivity of the Iraqi military leaders was the fear of being cut off by the enemy.

Another reason was their mistrust of the Arab Legion or, more precisely, of its foreign commander Glubb Pasha. Salih Sa'ib al-Jubury, the Iraqi chief of staff, claimed that it was the failure of the Arab Legion to carry out the mission assigned to it in the overall invasion plan that exposed his own army to attacks from the Israelis and prevented it from achieving its aims. According to al-Jubury, the Legion acted independently throughout, with terrible results for the general Arab war effort.[29]

In the north, the Syrians crossed into Israel just south of the Sea of Galilee and captured Zemah, Sha'ar ha-Golan, and Massadah before being stopped at Degania. They retreated, regrouped, and launched another offensive a week later north of the Sea of Galilee. This time they captured Mishmar Hayardem, establishing a foothold on the Israeli side of the Jordan river, from which the IDF was unable to dislodge them. While the Syrians were fighting in the Jordan Valley, the Lebanese forces broke through the eastern gateway from Lebanon to Israel and captured Malkiya and Kadesh. IDF operations behind the lines and against villages inside Lebanon succeeded in halting the Lebanese offensive. By the end of May the IDF had recaptured Malkiya and Kadesh and forced the Lebanese army on the defensive.

All in all, the combined and simultaneous Arab invasion turned out to be less well-coordinated, less determined, and less effective than Israel's leaders had feared. Success in withstanding the Arab invasion greatly enhanced Israel's self-confidence. Ben-Gurion was particularly anxious to exploit the IDF's initial successes in order to move on to the offensive and go beyond the UN partition lines. On 24 May, only ten days after the declaration of independence, Ben-Gurion asked the General Staff to prepare an offensive directed at crushing Lebanon, Transjordan, and Syria. In his diary he wrote:

> The weak link in the Arab coalition is Lebanon. Muslim rule is artificial and easy to undermine. A Christian state should be established whose southern border would be the Litani. We shall sign a treaty with it. By breaking the power of the Legion and bombing Amman, we shall also finish off Transjordan and then Syria will fall. If Egypt still dares to fight – we shall bomb Port Said, Alexandria and Cairo.[30]

These plans were overambitious. By the end of the first week in June a clear stalemate had developed on the central front and a similarly inconclusive situation prevailed on all the other fronts. The UN truce came into force on 11 June. To the Israelis it came, in Moshe Carmel's words, like dew from heaven. Though they had succeeded in halting the Arab invasion, their fighting forces were stretched to the limit and badly needed a respite to rest, reorganize, and train new recruits. On the Israeli side, the four weeks' truce was also used to bring in large shipments of arms from abroad in contravention of the UN embargo – tanks, armored cars, artillery, and aircraft. On the Arab side, the truce was largely wasted. No serious preparations were made by any of the Arab countries to reorganize and re-equip their armies so that they would be better placed in the event of hostilities being resumed. The UN arms embargo applied in theory to all the combatants but in practice it hurt the Arabs and helped Israel because the Western powers observed it whereas the Soviet bloc did not.[31] Consequently, the first truce was a turning-point in the history of the war. It witnessed a decisive shift in the balance of forces in favor of Israel.

THE SECOND ROUND OF FIGHTING

Inter-Arab rivalries re-emerged with renewed vigor during the truce. As far as King ʿAbdullah was concerned, the war was over. He began to lobby in the Arab world for the incorporation of what was left of Arab Palestine into his kingdom. He made no secret of his view that the resumption of the war would be disastrous to the Arabs. His solution, however, was unacceptable to any of the other members of the Arab coalition. Syria and Lebanon saw ʿAbdullah as a permanent threat to their independence, while King Faruq saw him as a growing menace to Egypt's hegemony in the Arab world. Count Folke Bernadotte, the UN mediator, omitted all reference to the UN partition plan, and proposed the partition of mandatory Palestine between Israel and Transjordan. ʿAbdullah could have hardly asked for more but since the Arab League and Israel rejected Bernadotte's proposals out of hand, he saw no point in going out on a limb by publicly accepting them.

Having failed to promote a settlement of the Palestine problem, Bernadotte proposed the extension of the truce that was due to expire on 9 July. Once again, Transjordan found itself in a minority of one in the Arab League. All the Arab military leaders pointed to the gravity of their supply positions but the politicians voted not to renew the truce. To deal with the difficulty of resuming hostilities when their arsenals were depleted, the Arab politicians settled on a defensive strategy of holding on to existing positions. ʿAbdullah suspected that the decision was taken with the sinister intention of undermining his diplomatic strategy and embroiling his army in a potentially disastrous war with the Israelis. He therefore summoned Count Bernadotte to Amman to express his extreme unease at the prospect of war breaking out afresh and to urge him to use the full power of the UN to bring about a reversal of the Arab League's warlike decision.[32] But the Egyptians pre-empted by attacking on 8 July, thereby ending the truce and committing the Arab side irreversibly to a second round of fighting.

If ʿAbdullah was against a second round of fighting, Glubb Pasha was even more reluctant to be drawn in as his army had only four contact days' worth of ammunition and no replenishments in sight. Indeed, in the second round, the Arab Legion only reacted when it was attacked. When hostilities were resumed, the IDF quickly seized the initiative on the central front with Operation Danny.

In the first phase the objective was to capture Lydda and Ramla; in the second it was to open a wide corridor to Jerusalem by capturing Latrun and Ramallah. All these towns had been assigned to the Arab state and fell within the perimeter held by the Arab Legion. On 12 July, Israeli forces captured Lydda and Ramla and forced their inhabitants to flee eastwards. In Latrun, on the other hand, the Israeli offensive was repulsed as was the last minute attempt to capture the Old City of Jerusalem.

The ALA, the Egyptian, Iraqi, Syrian, and Lebanese armies all suffered some reverses in the course of the second round of fighting. The IDF offensive in the north culminated in the capture of Nazareth and in freeing the entire Lower Galilee from enemy forces. On the other hand, the attempt to eject the Syrians from the salient at Mishmar Hayarden was not successful and the fighting ended in stalemate. Israel's overall position improved appreciably as a result of the ten days' fighting. Israel seized the initiative and was to retain it until the end of the war.

The second UN truce came into force on 18 July and, unlike the first truce, it was of indefinite duration. As soon as the guns fell silent, Arab politicians resumed the war of words against one another. The line that the Arab Legion was being prevented from using its full strength against the Jews, both through the treachery of the British officers and the withholding of supplies by the British government, was actively propagated by the Syrian and Iraqi officers and by 'Azzam Pasha. The Iraqi army officers operating in Transjordan were particularly hostile to the British who served in the Arab Legion.[33] The suspicion that Glubb was secretly working to impose on the Arabs London's policy of partition accounted for the virtual breakdown of the relations between the two Hashemite armies and for the Iraqi branch jealously guarding its freedom of action.[34]

LULL IN THE STORM

During the lull in the storm 'Abdullah kept flirting with the idea of bilateral negotiations with Israel to settle the Palestine problem. Though it did not go as planned, the war had served its basic purpose in enabling him to occupy the central areas of Arab Palestine. Not only was there nothing else to be gained from an appeal to arms, but such an appeal could jeopardize both his territorial gains and his army, the mainstay of his regime and his only defense against his Arab opponents. Accordingly, he shifted his attention from the military to the political arena.

The Israelis had their own reason for wanting to resume direct contact with their old friend. Disunity in the Arab camp gave them considerable room for manoeuver. The Arabs had marched into Palestine together but as they sustained military reverses, each country looked increasingly to its own needs. Each country was licking its wounds and was in no position and in no mood to help the others or to subordinate its interests to the common cause. Under these circumstances, anyone looking for cracks in the wall of Arab unity could easily find them. Israel, with the memory of its military victories still fresh in everybody's mind, was well placed to play off the Arabs against one another.[35] This was the background of the renewal of contact with King 'Abdullah's emissaries in September 1948.

Rumors that 'Abdullah was once again in contact with the Jewish leaders further damaged his standing in the Arab world. His many critics suggested that he was prepared to compromise the Arab claim to the whole of Palestine as long as he could acquire part of Palestine for himself. "The internecine struggles of the Arabs," reported Glubb, "are more in the minds of the Arab politicians than the struggle against the Jews. 'Azzam Pasha, the *mufti* and the Syrian government would sooner see the Jews get the whole of Palestine than that King 'Abdullah should benefit."[36]

To thwart 'Abdullah's ambition, the other members of the Arab League, led by Egypt, decided in Alexandria on 6 September to approve the establishment of an Arab government for the whole of Palestine with a seat in Gaza. This was too little and too late. The desire to placate public opinion, critical of the Arab governments for failing to protect the Palestinians, was a major consideration. The decision to form the Government of All-Palestine in Gaza, and the feeble attempt to create armed forces under its control, furnished the members of the Arab League with the means of divesting themselves of direct responsibility for the prosecution of the war and of withdrawing their armies from Palestine with some protection against popular outcry. Whatever the long-term future of the Arab government of Palestine, its immediate purpose, as conceived by its Egyptian sponsors, was to provide a focal point of opposition to 'Abdullah and serve as an instrument for frustrating his ambition to federate the Arab regions with Transjordan.

But the contrast between the pretensions of the All-Palestine Government and its capability quickly reduced it to the level of farce. It claimed jurisdiction over the whole of Palestine, yet it had no administration, no civil service, no money, and no real army of its own. Even in the small enclave around the town of Gaza its writ ran only by the grace of the Egyptian authorities. Taking advantage of the new government's dependence on them for funds and protection, the Egyptian paymasters manipulated it to undermine 'Abdullah's claim to represent the Palestinians in the Arab League and in international forums. Ostensibly the embryo for an independent Palestinian state, the new government, from the moment of its inception, was thus reduced to the unhappy role of a shuttlecock in the ongoing power struggle between Cairo and Amman.[37]

Israel was content to see the rift develop inside the Arab League but prudently refrained from expressing any opinion in public for or against the All-Palestine Government. Before the Provisional State Council, on 23 September

1948, foreign minister Moshe Sharett described what remained of Arab Palestine as a "geographical expression" rather than a political entity. There were two candidates for ruling this part of Palestine: the *mufti* and King 'Abdullah. In principle, said Sharett, Israel had to prefer a separate government in the Arab part to a merger with Transjordan; in practice, they preferred a merger with Transjordan though their public posture was one of neutrality.[38] In practice, Israel also took advantage of the renewed contacts with 'Abdullah in order to thwart the establishment of a Palestinian state and expand the territory of the Jewish state. As Yaacov Shimoni, the deputy head of the Middle East department in the foreign ministry, candidly confessed:

> Sharett knew that we had agreed with 'Abdullah that he will take and annex the Arab part of Palestine and Sharett could not support this ludicrous, impotent, and abortive attempt made by the Egyptians against 'Abdullah. This attempt had nothing to do with us. It was a tactical move by 'Abdullah's enemies to interject something against his creeping annexation. At that time there was no annexation. Formal annexation only occurred in April 1950. But he had started taking and preparing for annexation. So they tried, without any success, to build a countervailing force.
>
> The second point is that at that time Sharett and our men knew what the powerful State of Israel has forgotten in recent years. He understood the meaning of diplomacy and knew how to conduct it. Sharett was definitely aware that publicly we were obliged to accept the Palestinian Arab state and could not say that we were opposed to the establishment of such a state. In the first place, we had accepted the UN resolution which included a Palestinian Arab state. Secondly, this was the right, fair, and decent course and we were obliged to agree to it. The fact that below the surface, behind the curtain, by diplomatic efforts, we reached an agreement with 'Abdullah – an agreement which had not been uncovered but was kept secret at that time – was entirely legitimate but we did not have to talk about it. Sharett knew that our official line had to be in favour of a Palestinian state if the Palestinians could create it. We could not create it for them. But if they could create it, certainly, by all means, we would agree. The fact that he made a deal with 'Abdullah on the side to prevent the creation of such a state, that is diplomacy, that is alright. Sharett behaved in accordance with the rules of diplomacy and politics that are accepted throughout the world.[39]

THE WAR AGAINST EGYPT

The rivalries among the Arab states that gave rise to the so-called Government of All-Palestine complicated Israel's diplomacy but simplified its strategy. David Ben-Gurion, the man in charge of grand strategy, was constantly on the look-out for divisions and fissures in the enemy camp that might be used to extend Israel's territorial gains. Arab disunity provided the strategic luxury of fighting a war on only one front at a time and the front Ben-Gurion chose to renew the war was the southern front. In early October he asked the General Staff to concentrate the bulk of its forces in the south and to prepare a major offensive to expel the Egyptian army from the Negev. In view of the worsening relations between Egypt and 'Abdullah, he thought it unlikely that the Arab Legion would intervene in such a war.[40]

On 15 October, the IDF broke the truce and launched Operation Yoav to expel the Egyptian forces from the Negev. In a week of fighting, the Israelis captured Beersheba and Bayt Jibrin, and surrounded an Egyptian brigade (which included Major Gamal 'Abd al-Nasir) in Faluja. As Ben-Gurion expected, Transjordan remained neutral in the war between Israel and Egypt. The Arab Legion was in a position to intervene to help the Egyptian brigade trapped in the Faluja pocket but it was directed instead to take Bethlehem and Hebron, which had previously been occupied by the Egyptians. 'Abdullah and Glubb were apparently happy to see the Egyptian army defeated and humiliated.

The formation of the Government of All-Palestine revived the *mufti*'s Holy War Army – *Jaysh al-Jihad al-Muqaddas*. This irregular army endangered Transjordan's control in Arab Palestine. The Transjordan government therefore decided to nip in the bud the challenge posed by this army to its authority. On 3 October, the minister of defense laid down that all armed bodies operating in the areas controlled by the Arab Legion were either to be under its orders or disbanded.[41] Glubb carried out this order promptly and ruthlessly. Suspecting that Arab officers would balk at performing such an unpatriotic task, he sent British officers to surround and forcibly disband the Holy War Army. The operation brought the Arabs to the brink of internecine war when they were supposed to be cooperating against the common enemy. But it effectively neutralized the military power of 'Abdullah's Palestinian rivals. Against this background, the Israeli attack on the Egyptian army was not altogether unwelcome. Glubb privately expressed the hope that the Jewish offensive "may finally knock out the Gaza government and give the gyppies [*sic*] a lesson!" In a letter to Colonel Desmond Goldie, the British commander of the First Brigade, Glubb explained that "if the Jews are going to have a private war with the Egyptians and the Gaza government, we do not want to get involved. The gyppies and the Gaza government are almost as hostile to us as the Jews!"[42]

The Israelis followed up their "private war" in the south by launching a major offensive in the north. Israel's enemies were now being picked off one by one. On 29 October, Operation Hiram unfolded, resulting in the capture of central Galilee and in the displacement of many more Arabs. The "cleansing of the Galilee" was the result of high-level policy rather than a random by-product of the war. Central Galilee contained a large number of Arab residents, including refugees from western and eastern Galilee. On 26 September, Ben-Gurion had told the cabinet that, should the fighting be renewed in the north, the Galilee would become "clean" and "empty" of Arabs.[43] In the event, it was Israel that renewed the fighting, and it was the IDF that carried out the expulsions. Four brigades were concentrated in the north for Operation Hiram. In four days of

Zionist forces actually go out of Egypt

fighting they pushed the Syrians further east, caught Qawuqji's Arab Liberation Army in a pincer movement and knocked it out of the fight, and banished the Lebanese army from the Galilee. In hot pursuit of the retreating forces, the Carmeli Brigade crossed into Lebanon and captured fourteen villages which were later relinquished when the armistice agreement was signed. Thus, on the northern front, too, the tide turned dramatically and menacingly against the Arabs.

The third UN truce came into force on 31 October. On 22 December Israel once again broke the truce by launching a second offensive in the south. The objective of Operation Horev was to complete the destruction of the Egyptian forces, to drive them out of Palestine, and to compel the Egyptian government to negotiate an armistice. Conflict between the Arab states and lack of coordination between their armies in Palestine gave Israel the freedom to choose the time and place of the second offensive. Egypt appealed to its Arab allies for help but its appeals fell on deaf ears. Lebanon, Saudi Arabia, and the Yemen all promised assistance but failed to honor their promises. The Iraqis shelled a few Israeli villages near their front line as a token of solidarity with their embattled ally. Without exception the Arab states were either afraid to intervene or did not wish to intervene. The Israeli troops surged forward, expelled the Egyptians from the south-western flank of the Negev, and penetrated into Sinai to the outskirts of El-Arish. Operation Horev succeeded in compelling Egypt, the strongest Arab state with the best claim to lead the others, to open armistice negotiations with the State of Israel and thus to bring the war to an end. On 7 January 1949, the UN-decreed cease-fire went into force marking the formal end of the first Arab–Israeli war.

CONCLUSION

This survey of Israel's strategy and tactics in dealing with the Arab coalition in 1948 is not intended to belittle Israel's victory but to place it in its proper political and military context. And when one probes the politics of the war and not merely the military operations, the picture that emerges is not the familiar one of Israel standing alone against the combined might of the entire Arab world but rather one of a remarkable convergence between the interests of Israel and those of Transjordan against the other members of the Arab coalition, and especially against the Palestinians.

My purpose in writing this survey was not to pass moral judgment on Israel's conduct in 1948 or to delegitimize Zionism but to suggest that the traditional Zionist narrative of the birth of Israel and the first Arab–Israeli war is deeply flawed. The Zionist narrative, like all nationalist versions of history, is a curious mixture of fact and fiction. The new historiography has been denounced by its critics for being driven not by the scholarly search for truth about the past but by an anti-Israeli political agenda. Despite these criticisms, which are themselves politically inspired, the new historiography is essentially a cool attempt to use official documents in order to expose some of the fictions that have come to surround the birth of Israel. It offers a different perspective, an alternative way of looking at the momentous events of 1948. History is a process of demystification and the new historiography helps to demystify the birth of Israel, to give a fuller, more nuanced, and more complex picture of what is undoubtedly one of the great success stories of the twentieth century. That the debate between the traditional, pro-Zionist and the "new historians" should be so heated is hardly surprising. For the debate about the 1948 War cuts to the very core of Israel's image of itself.

NOTES

1. Yehoshafat Harkabi, *Arab Attitudes to Israel* (Jerusalem, 1972), pp. 37–38.
2. See Avi Shlaim, "The Debate about 1948," *IJMES* 27 (1995) 287–304.
3. Walid Khalidi, *From Haven to Conquest: Readings in Zionism and the Palestine Problem Until 1948* (Beirut, 1971), pp. 858–71; Simha Flapan, *The Birth of Israel: Myths and Realities* (London, 1987), pp. 187–99; and Benny Morris, *1948 and After: Israel and the Palestinians* (Oxford, 1994), pp. 13–16.
4. Jacob Tsur, *Zionism: The Saga of a National Liberation Movement* (New York, 1977), pp. 88–89.
5. Zvi Elpeleg, *The Grand Mufti: Hajj Amin al-Hussaini, Founder of the Palestinian National Movement* (London, 1993), p. 86.
6. Flapan, *The Birth of Israel*, p. 130, quoting from a report by Michael Comay of a conversation with the British journalist Claire Hollingworth.
7. Muhammad Amin al-Husayni, *Haqa'iq 'an qadiyyat filastin* [Facts about the Palestine Question] (Cairo, 1956), p. 22.
8. Yezid Sayigh, *Armed Struggle and the Search for State: The Palestinian National Movement, 1949–1993* (Oxford, 1997), p. 14.
9. On the relations between 'Abdullah and the Zionists see Mary C. Wilson, *King 'Abdullah, Britain and the Making of Jordan* (Cambridge, 1987); Joseph Nevo, *King 'Abdullah and Palestine: A Territorial Ambition* (London, 1996); Yoav Gelber, *Jewish–Transjordan Relations, 1921–1948* (London, 1997); and Avi Shlaim, *Collusion across the Jordan: King 'Abdullah, the Zionist Movement, and the Partition of Palestine* (Oxford, 1988).
10. Ezra Danin, "Talk with 'Abdullah, 17 November 1947," S25/4004, and Elias Sasson to Moshe Shertok, 20 November 1947, S25/1699, Central Zionist Archives (CZA), Jerusalem. See also Shlaim, *Collusion across the Jordan*, pp. 110–117.
11. Interview with Yaacov Shimoni, 26 August 1982, Jerusalem.
12. Unsigned report, 16 March 1948, S25/3569, CZA.
13. David Ben-Gurion, *Yoman Ha-milhama, 1948–1949* [War Diary: The War of Independence, 1948–1949], 3 vols., Gershon Rivlin and Elhanan Orren, eds. (Tel Aviv, 1982), vol. 1, p. 330.
14. Interview with Yehoshua Palmon, 31 May 1982, Jerusalem. See also Dan Kurzman, *Genesis 1948: The First Arab–Israeli War* (London, 1972), pp. 67–69; and Larry Collins and Dominique Lapierre, *O Jerusalem* (New York, 1972), pp. 269–270.
15. Kurzman, *Genesis 1948*, p. 137.
16. Government of Iraq, *Taqrir lajnat al-tahqiq al-niyabiyya fi qadiyyat filastin* [Report of the Parliamentary Committee of Enquiry into the Palestine Question] (Baghdad, 1949).

17. Golda Meir's verbal report to the thirteen-member Provisional State Council. Israel State Archives, *Provisional State Council: Protocols, 18 April–13 May 1948* (Jerusalem, 1978), pp. 40–44. See also Shlaim, *Collusion across the Jordan*, pp. 205–14.

18. Golda Meir, *My Life* (London, 1975), pp. 176–80.

19. For a comprehensive review of the literature and the debate see Avraham Sela, "Transjordan, Israel and the 1948 War: Myth, Historiography and Reality," *Middle Eastern Studies* 28 (1992) 623–88.

20. State of Israel, *Political and Diplomatic Documents, December 1947–May 1948* (Jerusalem, 1979), pp. 789–91.

21. Among the more revealing Arabic sources on the discord and deception inside the Arab coalition are Iraqi Parliament, *Taqrir Lajnat al-Tahqiq*; 'Abdullah al-Tall, *Karithat filastin* [The Catastrophe of Palestine] (Cairo, 1959); Salih Sa'ib al-Jubury, *Mihnat filastin wa-asraruha al-siyasiyya wa al-askariyya* [The Palestine Disaster and its Political and Military Secrets] (Beirut, 1970); and Muhammad Hasanayn Haykal, *Al-'Urush wa'l-juyush: kadhalik infajara al-sira'a fi filastin* [Thrones and Armies: Thus Erupted the Struggle for Palestine] (Cairo, 1998). For two excellent reviews of Arabic sources and Arab historiography on the 1948 War, see Walid Khalidi, "The Arab Perspective," in Wm. Roger Louis and Robert W. Stookey, eds., *The End of the Palestine Mandate* (London, 1986), pp. 104–36: and Avraham Sela, "Arab Historiography of the 1948 War: The Quest for Legitimacy," in Laurence J. Silberstein, ed., *New Perspectives on Israeli History: The Early Years of the State* (New York, 1991), pp. 124–54.

22. King 'Abdullah of Jordan, *My Memoirs Completed: "Al-Takmilah,"* translated from the Arabic by Harold W. Glidden (London, 1978), pp. 20–21.

23. Anita Shapira, "Politics and Collective Memory: The Debate over the 'New Historians' in Israel," *History and Memory* 7 (1995) 9–40.

24. Major 'Abdullah al-Tall, who led the attack, reveals in his memoirs that he tricked Glubb Pasha into allowing him to rush reinforcements to another unit which was falsely reported to have fallen into a Jewish ambush in Kfar Etzion. See Tall, *Karithat filastin*, pp. 31–34.

25. John Bagot Glubb, *A Soldier with the Arabs* (London, 1957), p. 110.

26. Interview with Lieutenant-General Yigael Yadin, 19 August 1982, Jerusalem.

27. Interview with Major-General Moshe Carmel, 1 September 1983, Tel Aviv.

28. Uri Bar-Joseph, *The Best of Enemies: Israel and Transjordan in the War of 1948* (London, 1987).

29. Jubury, *Mihnat filastin*, pp. 189–90.

30. Ben-Gurion, *Yoman Ha-milhama*, vol. II, pp. 453–54.

31. Amitzur Ilan, *The Origins of the Arab–Israeli Arms Race: Arms, Embargo, Military Power and Decision in the 1948 Palestine War* (Basingstoke, 1996); and Robert Danin, "The Rise and Fall of Arms Control in the Middle East, 1947–1955: Great Power Consultation, Coordination, and Competition" (D.Phil, thesis, University of Oxford, 1999).

32. Folke Bernadotte, *To Jerusalem*, trans, Joan Bulman (London, 1951), pp. 163–64; 'Arif al-'Arif *al-Nakba* [The Catastrophe] 6 vols. (Beirut and Sidon, 1956–60), vol. III, p. 593; PRO, C. M. Pirie-Gordon to B. A. B. Burrows, 25 July 1948, FO 371/68822.

33. PRO, Sir Alec Kirkbride to FO, 6 August 1948, FO 371/68830.

34. Muhammad Mahdi Kubba, *Mudhakkirati* [My Memoirs] (Beirut, 1965), pp. 261–67.

35. Interview with Yehoshua Palmon, 31 May 1982, Jerusalem.

36. PRO, Glubb to Burrows, Secret and Personal, 22 September 1948, FO 371/68861.

37. Avi Shlaim, "The Rise and Fall of the All-Palestine Government in Gaza," *Journal of Palestine Studies* 20/1 (1990) 37–53.

38. Moshe Sharett, *Besha'ar Ha-umot, 1946–1949* [At the Gate of the Nations, 1946–1949] (Tel Aviv, 1958), pp. 307–9.

39. Interview with Yaacov Shimoni, 26 August 1982, Jerusalem.

40. Ben-Gurion, *Yoman Ha-milhama*, vol. III, p. 737, diary entry for 7 October 1948.

41. Glubb, *Soldier with the Arabs*, p. 192.

42. Glubb to Goldie, 16 October 1948. I am grateful to Colonel Goldie for giving me access to this letter.

43. Benny Morris, *The Birth of the Palestinian Refugee Problem, 1947–1949* (Cambridge, 1987), p. 218.

Dilemmas of the Jewish State

DAVID McDOWALL

The Uprising in December 1987 brought into sharper focus problems of great magnitude and complexity now facing the State of Israel. By comparison, the problems the Palestinian people face may be great but they are comparatively simple. They desire self-determination for those already in Palestine, and the opportunity to return for those who live outside. They must either persuade Israel to yield to their demands or they must abandon their own identity. Having little to concede, the choice is straightforward. In his book *The New Diplomacy* (London, 1983) Abba Eban placed responsibility for the fate of the occupied territories firmly in the Palestinian lap. 'In the final resort,' he wrote, 'the Arab cause in the West Bank and Gaza will stand or fall by the decision of the Palestinian Arabs.'[1] In view of the actual circumstances now facing Israel, such a verdict must be in doubt It is Israel which must now decide what to do on account of its refusal to talk with the Palestine Liberation Organisation (PLO) and its continued retention of the occupied territories.

Today's Jewish Israelis no longer enjoy the simple verities that carried them forward in 1948, and which carry the Palestinians of the territories forward today. They are painfully circumscribed by the contradictions between Zionist ideology and growing realities, and by the fundamental choices that they must make to determine the fate of Palestine and its inhabitants. It is an unenviable position. No decisions can be made concerning the Palestinian Arabs which are not also to do with Israel's self-perception and the future of Zionism.

Zionism was the driving force of Israel's creation, the belief that the return of the Jews from the Diaspora would rescue them from the perils of Gentile rule, anti-semitism and assimilation, and that it would provide the opportunity to create for the first time in 2,000 years a society which was wholly Jewish in ethos and characteristics. The critical push factor had been the pogroms and anti-semitic policies of tsarist Russia, which caused three million Jews to migrate westwards during the years 1882–1914. Most of these went to the New World, some went to central or western Europe, and only a tiny fraction went to Palestine. Those who opted to build the Yishuv were secularists, motivated not by Judaism but by the climate of nineteenth-century European nationalism, fulfilling 'the quest for self-determination and liberation under the modern conditions of secularisation and liberalism.'[2]

Early Zionists believed that the Jewish nation should be based upon solidarity rather than territory, but the pogroms of 1881 changed such thinking into ambitions for a Jewish state in Palestine.[3] This was the dream of Theodor Herzl, the 'father' of modern Zionism, whose great achievement was to make the Zionist dream central to Jewish political thought.

It was inevitable that the vision of building a new all-Jewish society, which would wipe away the odious caricatures associated with the Jews of Europe, attracted Jewish socialists of various hues, all of whom broadly subscribed to the idea of emancipation through labour. For some socialist thinkers, for example those who shared the views of Ber Borochov,[4] this was in part a matter of class war. For others, like the visionary Ahad Ha'am, it was more a matter of universal socialist redemption, but for most Labour Zionists it was 'an attempt to create an economic infrastructure for a Jewish community in Palestine founded on the Jews' own labour'.[5] The greatest practitioner of this outlook was David Ben Gurion, who saw Jewish economic independence as the essential precondition to political independence. The Zionist Labour movement dramatically achieved this precondition in Palestine during the Mandate period, 1920–48.

THE NEED FOR A JEWISH MAJORITY

From the outset Zionism was predicated upon certain principles, of which the idea of creating a Jewish majority in Palestine was among the most important.[6] As a minority in Palestine the Jewish community would lose its meaning and be like Jewish communities in the Diaspora. The achievement of a majority was politically necessary—'the establishment of a Jewish community large enough to give the Arabs a permanent feeling of respect', as Ben Gurion's colleague, Moshe Sharett, put it.[7] Virtually all Zionists considered a Jewish majority 'an absolute prerequisite to Zionism,'[8] regardless of differences over how to deal with the Arab presence in Eretz Israel.

Today, however, in spite of the dramatic influx of Jews from the CIS and Ethiopia in 1990 and 1991, the achievement of this majority remains in doubt.

Immigration remains insufficient so far to head off Arab population growth. The higher Arab birth rate has been a matter for recurrent comment and discussion in Zionist circles for over half a century, especially at times of low *aliyah*, or immigration. As early as 1924 Chaim Weizmann recognized the enormity of the challenge it posed. 'Only today,' he wrote to a friend, 'I received the health statistics from Palestine. The natural increase in the Arab population amounts to about 15,000 a year. The Jews brought in last year 10,000. How can people possibly speak of ever forming a majority ... if they don't throw [in] every ounce of energy which they possess... to give us a proper position in Palestine?'[9] As the fate of Palestine approached the moment of crisis, in 1943, Ben Gurion called on parents to fulfil their 'demographic duty', stressing that 2.2 children per family was insufficient and that the Jewish population in Palestine was in a state of demographic decay.[10]

After the 1948 war, with the departure of almost all the Arabs and with massive immigration, the problem of the birth rate seemed less acute. Even so, Ben Gurion initiated an award scheme in 1949 for mothers bearing their tenth child. This was terminated ten years later since the object was contradicted by the number of Palestinian mothers claiming the award.[11] In the 1950s and early 1960s there were renewed concerns over natality rates. In 1966 Professor Roberto Bacchi reported to the cabinet that by the end of the century there would be 4.2 million Jews and 1.6 million Arabs in Israel. Partly as a result of his report, a government demographic centre was established in 1967 because 'an increase in natality in Israel is crucial for the future of the whole Jewish people.'[12]

This increase has not come about, despite repeated calls by politicians and the worry expressed, for example, by Golda Meir over the number of Arab babies born in Eretz Israel. During the years of intense immigration, 1950–3, the Jewish birth rate was 3.5 per cent, but by the early 1970s it had declined to 3 per cent and by the end of the 1970s it had fallen to 2.8 per cent. This level is substantially higher than the rate of 2.2 per cent in Western industrialized countries, but it did not compare with Arab birth rates of just over 4 per cent. At the end of 1985 the Likud Knesset Member (MK) Meir Cohen Avidor called for a year of internal *aliyah*, a euphemism for more babies: 'we should aim at 100,000 additional births in Israel next year,' he said, 'that would be more than the number of *olim* (immigrants) in a decade.'[13]

Exhortations to breed more babies are not confined to Israel's Right. On 11 May 1986 the National Unity Government met specifically to discuss the demographic situation. By that time 60,000 Palestinian Arab babies were being born annually in Palestine/Eretz Israel as against 50,000 Jewish ones. Speaking on Israel Radio, Prime Minister Peres appealed to mothers to have at least four children, and reiterated the essential imperative for Jews to remain a majority.[14]

The alternative and primary source of Jews for the Jewish State has been the Diaspora. The ingathering of world Jewry was another central principle of Zionism, the final objective after a Jewish majority had been established in the land. It came to be believed by many Zionists that those who failed to make the *aliyah*—literally meaning 'ascent'—remained unfulfilled as Jews. Even Dr Nahum Goldmann, who disagreed with the widely held Zionist view that the Diaspora would cease to exist by dint of the immigration of all Jews to Palestine, clearly stated: 'Palestine and the Diaspora are two forms of Jewish existence, Palestine the higher, the purer, the more harmonious; the Diaspora the more difficult, the more problematic and specific; but the Jewish people form a unity existing in two spheres.'[15]

Immigration depended upon two factors, the driving force of Jewish refugee crises and the attraction Israel offered of a new future. In 1949 immigration almost overwhelmed Israel, but it was not destined to last. From 1948 until 1960 870,000 Jews came to live in Israel. During the next decade, 1961–71, 338,000 arrived, and in the period 1972–82 the number halved again to 178,000.

Since the 1970s Israel has needed a net yearly immigration of 60,000 Jews to maintain the ratio between Jews and Arabs in Palestine. Yet in the 1980s it experienced its worst immigration levels ever. In the United States, where almost six million Jews – two-thirds of Diaspora Jewry or just under half the total world Jewry—reside, a 1982 survey revealed that 80 per cent of Jewish Americans denied ever giving any serious consideration to settling in Israel.[16] In 1984 there were 19,000 Jewish immigrants to Israel, but this was exceptional. Even so, 10,000 also emigrated.[17] The next year was the worst on record, with only 12,000 immigrants and almost 17,000 emigrants, a net loss of 4,700.[18] In 1987 there was another net loss of 4,500 emigrants.[19] Much emigration has represented the loss of substantial investment in the young: 25,000 children left Israel with their parents in the years 1981–85;[20] out of 110,000 Israelis who had obtained United States citizenship up to 1986, 78 per cent matriculated from Israeli high schools.[21]

Emigration is a sensitive issue.[22] It was at its highest in the early 1950s during the period of highest immigration, and took place almost entirely among the recently arrived in Israel who did not like what they found. The level stabilized but began to increase again after 1973. Emigration today, however, occurs mainly among *sabras*, native Jewish Israelis, suggesting that the Zionist solidarity of the state is weakening, perhaps under the cumulative economic and military burden of the Arab–Israeli conflict.[23] Between 1967 and 1988 546,000 Jews migrated to Israel, but during the same period about 350,000, or 10 per cent of Jewish Israelis, left permanently, a figure predicted to double by the end of the century.[24] One survey in the mid-1980s indicated that of the 18–29 age group, the group most likely to emigrate, 20 per cent were considering doing so. Among high school pupils the figure was even higher, 27 per cent. While the vast majority of Jewish Israelis consider emigration as harmful to the country, the danger is that a growing number of Jews 'will prefer to live with Christian European neighbours to living in this unstable state with Muslim neighbours'.[25] For a hardened warrior like Yitzhak Rabin such emigration may be 'the fallout of weaklings',[26] but his cabinet colleagues did not view emigration with the same equanimity. In 1986 the government offered 17,500 Israelis who had left in 1985 financial inducements to return.[27]

Between 1967 and 1990 there was a significant change in the kind of Jew choosing to migrate to Israel. Before 1967, whatever their motives, most immigrants did not make the *aliyah* for religious or messianic reasons. During the 1980s, however, 80 per cent of immigrants were practising Orthodox Jews, and a high proportion were from the United States.[28] It was symptomatic of their outlook that half the recent immigrants from the United States chose to live in settlements in the occupied territories. New immigrants make up 20 per cent of the settler population.

An Israeli withdrawal from the territories would be a strong discouragement to *aliyah*, a fact recognized since the early 1970s.[29] It would send a message to Diaspora Jewry contradicting two principal Zionist credos, that the Jewish State had retreated from redemption of the whole Land of Israel, and that the ingathering of the Jewish people had ceased to be a prime Israeli objective.

On the other hand, it is likely that the continued failure to resolve the fate of the occupied territories, and the issue of demographic and political rights between Jews and Arabs, would also discourage further immigration. As Ben Gurion remarked sixty years ago, 'the feeling that Jews are sitting on a volcano could undermine the whole Zionist movement. Jews will see the country not as a haven but as a battlefield.[30] Even discounting the Uprising, the lack of a solution to the occupied territories will encourage an increasing number of Israeli Jews to emigrate. It is a double bind. The problem was summed up succinctly in an article entitled 'Israel's national schizophrenia' which argued that 'Israel, which presents itself as the defender of world Jewry, is a complete anomaly in the international community, and its protracted conflict—which it makes almost no effort to end—menaces Jewish communities throughout the world. They are threatened not by any hostility from the people among whom they themselves live, but rather by the protracted conflict between Israel and its neighbours.'[31]

At the end of 1989, Soviet Jews began to migrate in large numbers. At first it was thought that the demographic problem with the Palestinians might be solved. By the end of 1991, almost exactly 400,000 had arrived, and this figure was expected to exceed one million by the end of the century.[32] But even with such a massive influx, the proportion of Jews in Eretz Israel would be barely 59.5 per cent. Moreover, within the State of Israel itself the Jewish proportion of 81.5 per cent (in 1989) would still decrease by 0.5 per cent. Even the immigration of two million Jews would increase the Jewish proportion in Eretz Israel only to 62 per cent, and in the State of Israel to 84 per cent.[33] However, at the beginning of 1992 the immigration rate dropped by 50 per cent, to a rate of about 5,000 per month.[34]

Israel faces a set of fundamental demographic problems to which there are no obvious solutions. The approximately one million Jews left in the CIS reportedly have an average age of over fifty.[35] Jewish migrants still prefer to find alternative havens to Israel, for example the United States, certain Latin American countries and even Germany.[36] Israel itself has reached the limit of its present economic absorptive capacity, with approximately 40 per cent of recent immigrants unemployed. Consequently an estimated 90,000 CIS Jews with exit visas are reluctant to migrate.[37] Economic stress and increased competition for jobs are likely to accelerate emigration, mainly among recent immigrants but also possibly among *sabras*.[38] Unless Israel can attract a significantly higher proportion of young Jews, the recent immigration is bound to be eroded by the higher Arab birth rate. By 1992 Palestinians outnumbered Jews under the age of eleven in all Eretz Israel.[39] Within the State of Israel itself, Palestinians are a rapidly increasing proportion of those aged under twenty, currently 25 per cent of this age group, and they may reach 30 per cent by 2010.[40]

The failure to secure an assured majority in Israel is accompanied by a greater problem: the overall decline of world Jewry. As a result of the loss of an estimated 6 million Jews in the Nazi Holocaust, the world Jewish population stood at 11 million in 1945. It grew to a peak of 13 million in 1970 but by 1987 had declined to 12.8 million as a result of a Diaspora birth rate of 1.2 per cent, well below the replenishment level (2.1 per cent).[41] Diaspora Jewry currently numbering 9.3 million will decline to an estimated 8 million or below by the end of the century, and more rapidly thereafter.[42] The natural increase in Israel, although higher than that of most industrialized countries, will be insufficient to offset this decline.[43] Not surprisingly, in view of such dismal prognostications, a World Foundation to Promote Jewish Population Policies was established in Jerusalem in October 1987 to raise money for programmes to convince Jews to have more children.[44]

Just under half of world Jewry lives in the United States, characterized by a low birth rate and a high assimilation rate, of about 4 per 1,000 per annum.[45] As a result, the present American Jewish community of 6 million is expected to fall to about 4.6 million by the end of the century.[46]

Partly as a result of numerical decline and also as a result of unease concerning the occupied territories, Israel also faces the prospect of a political and financial decline in support from American Jewry. In the words of the public relations director of the Jewish National Fund, 'the constituency of Zionism is shrinking.'[47] American Jewish support seems to have been weakening slowly since the early 1970s and more rapidly in the 1980s.[48] There is increasing ambivalence on the part of American Jewry towards Israel.[49] Probably about two-thirds of American Jews favour a homeland for the Palestinian people in the occupied territories, an increase of about 30 per cent since 1983.[50] For Israel the loss of American Jewish financial support would not be as serious as a loss of political support, for 'the most effective sanction that the American Jewish community can employ is to refrain from lobbying for continued US economic aid.'[51]

One important factor in American Jewish attitudes is the growth in Orthodox support of Israel and the decline in that of Reform and Conservative Jews. A far higher proportion of American Orthodox Jews visit Israel than Reform or Conservative Jews.[52] There is an increasing awareness of the conflict between Orthodoxy and secularism in Israel which, in the words of the president of the United Jewish Appeal, 'has the effect of dampening enthusiasm for the Jewish State'.[53]

RELIGION AND THE NEW ZIONISM

Central to this conflict is the question of who is a Jew, one which was deliberately left unresolved in 1948 but which goes right to the heart of the identity of the Jewish State. The desire of the Orthodox camp in Israel to recast the Law of Return (automatically guaranteeing Israeli citizenship to any Jew) to deny Jewish identity to Reform and Conservative Jews, the majority in the United States, has serious implications.[54] The Labour Party resisted right-wing religious moves to make observance of the Orthodox *Halacha* (religious law) the essential definition of Jewishness lest it transform the secular basis of the state and alienate the wealthy and influential American community who would fall outside the definition. The Orthodox and the secular Right have endeavoured to amend the Law of Return in the Knesset on several occasions.[55] At the 31st Zionist Congress, in December 1987, a broad coalition of Jewish organizations, backed by the United Jewish Appeal, warned the Israeli establishment that capitulation to the Orthodox establishment on the issue would cause a severe rift with the Diaspora and would torpedo fund-raising efforts for the Jewish Agency and the World Zionist Organization.[56] It was a similar warning from American Jewry which persuaded Likud to form a new government, after the November 1988 election, with Labour rather than the religious and extreme rightist parties.

The struggle over Jewish identity draws attention to a political ideology not yet discussed. This is Messianic Zionism, which has been growing in strength over the past twenty years, and commands between 10 and 15 per cent of the Jewish vote. It claims Eretz Israel neither on the basis of the secular nationalism of Revisionist followers of Jabotinsky (who appealed to history and the use of force) nor the creed of Labour Zionism (which would possess the land by building it). Instead, it appeals purely to divine authority, tracing its inspiration back to the first Ashkenazi Chief Rabbi of the Yishuv, Abraham Yitzhak Kook.[57] Kook made the first systematic attempt to reconcile and integrate the centrality of the Land of Israel in political Zionism with religious Judaic tradition. His own dream was not one of national religious domination, though he did believe that only by the reintegration of the Torah, the People and the Land, both physically and spiritually, would 'all civilisations of the world' be 'renewed by the renaissance of our spirit.'[58] Kook attracted only a small following, viewed as somewhat eccentric by mainstream Zionists.

Kook's son, Rabbi Zvi Yehudah Kook, took this thinking concerning the land significantly further:

> We find ourselves here by virtue of the legacy of our ancestors, the basis of the Bible and history, and no one can change this fact. What does it resemble? A man left his house and others came and invaded it. This is exactly what happened to us. Some argue that there are Arab lands here. It is all a lie and a fraud! There are absolutely no Arab lands here.[59]

Shortly before the June 1967 war he delivered a sermon to *yeshiva* (religious seminary) students bewailing the partition of Eretz Israel and 'prophesying' that the Land would soon be one again.[60] For such students the June war was a fulfilment of prophecy. For secular Jews, too, who had never entered a synagogue in their lives, the capture of Jerusalem was an almost mystical experience, and they lined up in their thousands at the Wailing Wall to pray.[61] Many religious Jews throughout Israel were persuaded that the whole of Eretz Israel must now be possessed through settlement and the imposition of Israeli sovereignty. Gush Emunim is the most obvious manifestation of this outlook, but it is the tip of an iceberg.[62]

It was natural that such religious 'Whole Land of Israel' Zionists should make common cause with the more secular rightist Likud coalition. From this common cause a 'New-Zionism' has emerged, one which places far greater emphasis than previous mainstream Zionism on *acting in religious faith* to fulfil God's covenant: 'Behold, I have set the land before you: go in and possess the land which the Lord sware unto your fathers, Abraham, Isaac and Jacob, to give unto them and to their seed after them.'[63] The supposition that this view was gaining ground was confirmed in the 1988 election when the religious parties increased their Knesset representation from twelve to eighteen seats.

For Jews of the religious Right and for some of the secular Right the Palestinian Arab inhabitants are either usurpers or tolerated 'strangers' sojourning on the Land. It is a cast of mind accurately foreseen by Herzl. In 1902 he published his novel *Altneuland* (The Old New Land), which expressed his vision of utopian socialism, universal suffrage, and a welfare state in Palestine. Palestinian Arabs were to belong to and benefit from the new utopia established by Jewish settlers. Then a bigoted rabbi appears who seeks to limit membership of this utopia to Jews only. In the fiction of *Altneuland* the rabbi is worsted, rationalism and tolerance triumph.[64] In the reality of today's Land of Israel no such outcome is assured.

THE DECLINE OF LABOUR ZIONISM

By contrast with this New Zionism, the traditional vision—certainly that of the mainstream Zionist movement of the Mandate period—is now in decay. Ben Gurion's agnostic vision was of physical, rather than religious, development and redemption of the land. He saw those areas outside Israel's coastal heartland as the scene of this redemptive work, in particular in the Negev desert. His views of Jewish title to the land rested on the idea of labour 'since the only right by which a people can claim to possess a land indefinitely is the right conferred by willingness to work.'[65]

Ben Gurion hoped to settle one million Jews in the Negev, but by 1988 only 240,000, one-quarter of his target, actually lived there. Of these no fewer than 198,000 live in towns, over half of them in Beersheba, on the northern edge of the desert. Israel's first development town, Yeroham, was established in 1951, 35 kilometres south-east of Beersheba. By 1965 it had 6,500 inhabitants, the size of the average Arab village. Twenty years later it was struggling to maintain this level. As the mayor of another Negev development town observed in 1984, 'The Negev is facing disaster in terms of population growth. Many settlements will be destroyed.'[66] Apart from Beersheba itself, there are few more Jewish settlers than bedouin.

The permanency of the Jewish presence in the development areas is far from assured. Economic recession tends to hit the development towns of Galilee and the Negev harder than the richer central coastal area.[67] During 1986 many development towns in Galilee decreased in population, the result of the drying up of investment in new high-technology plants, financial difficulties of agricultural settlements, absence of jobs for young people and lack of entertainment facilities.[68]

This decline is partly a result of New Zionism's priority of redemption of the occupied territories. Between 1968 and 1985 $2 billion was invested in these settlements, at an annual rate by 1985 of $200–250 million.[69] The 1984/85 public housing budget allocation indicates the low priority of the Negev and Galilee: the West Bank 29.4 per cent; central Israel 25.6 per cent; Jerusalem 23.1 per cent; Negev 7.9 per cent; Haifa 7.2 per cent; Galilee 6.8 per cent.[70] If one looks at government per capita support for regional councils, those in the occupied territories fare far better than those within Israel's own designated development areas: West Bank settlements, Gush Etzion $230, Mateh Benyamin $245, Jordan valley $408, Samaria $357; State of Israel development areas, Sha'ar Hanegev $126, Upper Galilee $97.[71] Only 38 per cent of development towns inside the state are granted highest incentive status for industrial development, while all eighteen industrial parks in the West Bank settlements enjoy this status.[72] Redemption of the occupied territories is being achieved at the cost of eroding the Jewish economic and demographic hold on the Galilee and the Negev.

Since agriculture was the centrepiece of the young Israeli economy, it is worth noting that the passage of land into overwhelming Jewish control in 1948 led not to an expansion of agricultural lands but to a massive shrinkage. On the fertile coastal plains, large areas of hitherto Arab agricultural lands were bulldozed for urban development or allowed to fall derelict. In the Negev, Jewish settlers cultivate less than half the area cultivated by bedouin before 1948, while in the Galilee the extent of cultivation has shrunk by two-thirds since 1948. Although Jewish agriculture boasts much higher yields, this is achieved with heavy capital inputs and over-use of non-renewable water sources.[73]

Ben Gurion's maxim, that possession of the Land of Israel would come about by dint of working the land, is also now in question. During the Mandate Ben Gurion argued that the Yishuv, the Jewish community in Palestine, must not be dependent on non-Jewish labour, otherwise it would be little different from the condition of Diaspora Jewry. Unless it ceased to depend upon the labour of others and upon remittances from abroad, it would be doomed to lose its political independence as well. Today the importance of non-Jewish labour and of regular US government funding is a measure of the distance Israel has travelled away from the ideals of the Yishuv.

The labour question is particularly apparent in agriculture. The basis of Israel's agriculture is the *moshav* and *kibbutz* movements, accounting for 90 per cent of the country's agricultural production. The *moshavim* are smallholdings which benefit from co-operative membership for the purchase of necessities and the sale of produce. The better-known *kibbutzim* are socialist collectives, closely identified with Labour Zionism.[74] The state, conscious of the centrality of agriculture to its ideology, subsidizes the farming sector of the economy heavily. Nevertheless, both *moshavim* and *kibbutzim* have employed an increasing proportion of Palestinian Arab labour in order to remain economically viable. Ten years ago the secretary of the Moshav Movement saw 'the increase of hired labour in all its forms, including organized and unorganized Arab labour, as portending inestimable dangers to the state and the moshav'.[75] Insufficient Jews were willing to work for the low wages, and he considered the only solution was 'to introduce new and appropriate mechanization'.

However, increased mechanization has produced a crisis for the *moshavim*. By 1987 Israel was suffering 'a farm crisis so complicated and enormous it would make Iowans stand up and take notice'.[76] By 1987 the *moshav* debt of $1.2 billion exceeded its annual productive value of $1.1 billion. Over the next decade the number of *moshavim* is likely to reduce from 420 (providing a livelihood to 27,000 families) to only 100.[77] Even so, the survivors are likely to remain dependent on cheaper Palestinian labour.

In 1935, while trying to persuade fellow Jews of the importance of expanding the Yishuv into Galilee and the Negev, Ben Gurion warned what happened to nations without a social and economic infrastructure rooted in the countryside.

> World history recalls one frightening example which should be a lesson to us ... Hannibal ... was one of the greatest military leaders of all times ... Against him was pitted a large Roman army, larger than his own, and he defeated them time and again.
>
> Yet ultimately all his heroism and all his military and political genius did not sustain him ... For Carthage was a *city-state*, whereas Rome was a village-state, and in the desperate conflict between a city-people and a village-people, the village-people proved victorious ... Hannibal's heroism was broken by the obstinate warfare of the Roman peasants. These peasants were not taken aback by the successive defeats inflicted on them—because they were integrated into their soil and tied to their land. And they overcame Carthage and wiped it off the face of the earth without leaving a trace.[78]

Ben Gurion, of course, had in mind the creation of a Jewish village-state, but it is impossible to dismiss today's reality of the Jewish city-state and the Arab village one. Was he correct, then, in his interpretation of history and, if so, is it relevant to modern Israel? For Labour Zionists this is a painful question, for were he still alive Ben Gurion would see the decline of Jewish settlement, the spread of the Palestinian presence in Eretz Israel—by its demographic growth, its village-based society and its role in agricultural labour—as the most profound threat to the security of the Jewish State. As General Harkabi writes, 'it is precisely the backwardness of Arab societies that gives them the ability to endure, because one expression of underdevelopment is the decentralization of society—in a multiplicity of cells which are not strongly integrated.'[79]

THE FAILING VISION

Unlike the Diaspora communities, Israel is much more than an aggregate of its population. It is a symbol of collective Jewish identity. Today that identity, which possibly came closest to the Labour Zionist ideal in the Yishuv of 1948, is in crisis. The exigencies of statehood and the conflict with the indigenous people of Palestine contradict the moral values expected by world Jewry. Somehow Israel must still embody a spiritual dimension. 'If Israel becomes only a mirror image of Diaspora life,' Shlomo Avineri at the conclusion of *The Making of Modern Zionism* argues, 'if it becomes, for example, just another Western consumer society, then it will lose its unique identification for World Jewry.'[80]

The danger, as the 1988 election indicated, is that the spiritual dimension takes Israel towards theocracy. New Zionism has offered one way forward, but it is one which leaves old-fashioned Zionists deeply troubled. Whether cast in religious or secular terms, those who dissent most strongly do so largely on moral grounds. They believe New Zionism destroys democracy, equality and respect for all mankind—Jew and Gentile alike.

While New Zionism traces its lineage from Kook and Jabotinsky, the peace movement which grew in the 1970s traces its descent from spiritual leaders like Ahad Ha'am and Yitzhak Epstein at the beginning of the century and from binationalists like Judah Magnes and Martin Buber during the Mandate period. Judah Magnes, rector of the Hebrew University, defined the moral position of spiritual Zionism after the 1929 Hebron massacre:

> What is Zionism? What does Palestine mean for us? ... I can answer for myself in almost the same terms that I have been in the habit of using for many years: Immigration ... Settlement of the Land ... Hebrew Life and Culture ... If you can guarantee these for me, I should be willing to yield the Jewish State and the Jewish majority ... What I am driving at is to distinguish between two policies. The one maintains that we can establish a Jewish home here through the suppression of the political aspirations of the Arabs, and therefore a home necessarily established on bayonets over a long period ... The other policy holds that we can establish a home here only if we are true to ourselves as democrats and internationalists ... and intelligently and sincerely ... work to find a modus vivendi et operandi.[81]

For Yeshayahu Leibowitz, the present spiritual mentor of the peace movement, Israel's physical survival remains contingent on its moral survival. Thus 'the real black day was the seventh day of the Six Day War. That day we had to decide retroactively whether we had fought a defensive war or a war of conquest, and we ruled that it had been a war of conquest. Israel's decline and fall dates from that day.'[82]

THE IDEA OF DEMOCRACY

One of the essential ideas of Zionism was the revival of the Hebrew culture. In his book, *The Tragedy of Zionism*, Bernard Avishai makes an interesting argument, that 'Hebrew is so ancient that, to anyone raised in it to the exclusion of other languages, it cannot fail to convey archaic ways of thinking about politics.[83] 'Herut', he continues, the biblical word meaning freedom, implies national rather than individual freedom, and contrasts with European-derived words such as *democratia.* Avishai's thesis is that *herut* has a far stronger hold on Israeli Jews than *democratia.* The latter 'has seemed an added luxury free people enjoy, not a synonym for freedom'.[84]

As a result democracy in Israel is predicated on a Jewish (national) majority. This definition was explicitly stated in 1986 by Peres as Prime Minister, when urging increased natality: 'That which guarantees the Jewish character of the State of Israel is first and foremost its democratic character: the necessity to remain a majority.'[85] This is a long-standing feature of Labour Zionism. Half a century ago Chaim Weizmann dismissed the idea that democracy was appropriate for the Palestinian Arabs: 'They are too primitive ... and too much under the influence of Bolshevik, Catholic agitation ... to understand what we are bringing them.'[86] In 1986 Peres perceived that anti-democratic influence as terrorist, Soviet or Islamic fundamentalist.[87]

The idea of a Jewish majority is implicit even in the position of Peace Now. When it demonstrated in favour of a negotiated settlement for the occupied territories on 23 January 1988, one of its slogans was 'Yes to a democratic country with a Jewish majority and an Arab minority with equal rights.'[88] As Avishai points out, the idea of a Jewish majority is even implicit in the policies of the leftist secularist parties like Mapam and the Citizens' Rights Movement (now combined as Meretz), for otherwise it would be rational to call for a binational state—embracing both the Jewish and Palestinian Arab nations—in all Eretz Israel/Palestine (the PLO's ideal solution) or join non-Zionist parties in advocating a secular state in which neither ethnic group enjoyed special status.[89] Advocacy of Palestinian self-determination in the occupied territories implies that Meretz is anxious to preserve the Jewish character of the state, a character which would be lost if Jews ceased to be the majority.

No one has challenged the validity of this view more strongly than the late right-wing politician, Rabbi Meir Kahane: When his party, Kach, was banned from the 1988 election be observed:

> Western democracy calls for full political rights for all people, no matter who they are, Jews or Gentiles. If the Arabs were to be a majority here, then they have the right to plan the sort of state they want. Zionism states that this is nonsense. It says that this country was created as a Jewish State and a Jewish State means Jewish sovereignty, and that non-Jews can never be allowed to have sovereignty. There is a basic contradiction. That's why when we speak of giving the Arabs equal rights, that's a lie, a fraud.[90]

In view of the overwhelming appeal of a 'Jewish democracy', even to left Zionist parties, it is not surprising that only 31.5 per cent of high school pupils think that Arabs should have the right to vote in the event of annexation of the territories.[91] Up to 1984, according to Avishai, poll after poll disclosed that about 90 per cent of Israeli Jewish youth described themselves as democratic. However, polls in 1984 and 1987 indicate that 60 per cent would curtail the rights of Israeli Palestinians.[92] Furthermore, 40 per cent specifically opposed the Palestinian right to vote in Knesset elections.[93] Whether or not one subscribes to Avishai's thesis (and there must be some caution concerning how accurately youthful attitudes reflect either more general adult ones, or indeed whether youths will maintain such attitudes as they mature), there can be little doubt that the idea of democracy is under threat as Jewish opinion moves further to the right.

The threat is not solely to Arab rights. The 1982 war in Lebanon marked a substantial increase in popular disapproval of press freedom, and of criticism of government defence and foreign policy, from roughly half to two-thirds of the electorate. Furthermore, the indication was that 17 per cent explicitly preferred a non-democratic government, while another 17 per cent did not care.[94] In 1986 a survey of adults reported growing political intolerance towards those straying outside the national consensus.[95] Twenty-four per cent of Jewish Israelis wished to deny Israeli Palestinians the vote in Knesset elections. Fifty-seven per cent wished to disenfranchise Zionist Jews (i.e. Mapam and CRM) favouring a Palestinian state in the West Bank and Gaza Strip, and 70 per cent would disenfranchise all non-Zionist Jews favouring a Palestinian state (i.e. Jewish supporters of Rakah and the Progressive List for Peace (PLP). Furthermore, '68 per cent of the Jews interviewed in the survey oppose an election list running for seats in the Knesset if it "accepts the rules of democracy and recognizes Israel's right to exist but objects to the State's Jewish-Zionist character."' This would deny the two parties for which Palestinian Israelis vote, Rakah and PLP, any parliamentary legitimacy, and thereby make the vote of most Palestinians meaningless. A Tel Aviv University poll in 1988 revealed that 45 per cent of the electorate considered the country was 'too democratic'.[96]

One of the interesting findings of the poll of young Israelis in 1987 was that while journalists and Knesset members were among the least trusted elements of society, combat soldiers and army officers enjoyed the highest confidence and respect.[97] Because of its centrality in national life, the outlook of the army is an important register in the shift of attitudes nationally. For the first twenty-five years of the state, the army was fairly solidly supportive of the Labour Alignment. After the October 1973 war, presumably as a result of the Labour government's unreadiness and Sharon's inspiring generalship, most voted for Likud.[98] In the 1984 election 45 per cent of the army vote went to Likud, or to parties to the right of it, Tehiya and Kach. Another 15 per cent of the army vote went to messianic religious parties, giving the New Zionist Right 60 per cent of the army vote. In

1988 over 50 per cent of the vote went to Likud and parties of the Right, and the vote for religious parties increased also.[99]

Since the foundation of the state the military encroachment into the political domain has increased at an institutional level. This was, perhaps, inevitable for a country permanently at war, but it became more so after 1967 when the army found itself governing the occupied territories, with all the political decisions implicit in this responsibility, for it was given free rein in the least democratic domain of state activity. In 1978 for the first time an army Chief of Staff, Raphael Eitan, publicly expressed his own views on the ideological and political as well as security considerations regarding the occupied territories.[100] Previously the army had acted almost exclusively at the state level, and specific relations with individual political parties, with the exception (to some extent) of Labour, had not really existed. The period of Eitan's tenure, and his explicit encouragement of Gush Emunim settlers, brought this to an end.

Since 1978 the army's scope of activity has extended into many spheres of national life, and by the early 1980s it was 'easy to name army generals who support or identify with the Labour Movement, or with Likud or with other parties'.[101] The army's increasingly open ideological stance indicated a growing confidence that its political enterprises, particularly with regard to the territories, had assumed a legitimacy that need not remain hidden.[102]

In general, the army has remained satisfied with the way in which the civilian government has governed. One reason for this is the existence of a military-civil establishment which wields major influence not only in the political but also the economic sphere. There has been a strong military flavour to the government, with a high percentage of retired officers. Since 1967 all lieutenant-generals (Yitzhak Rabin, Haim Bar Lev, Mordechai Gur, Raphael Eitan) have achieved key political roles. So have some major-generals, for example Ezer Weizman and Ariel Sharon.[103] Many others move on retirement from the forces into the arms industry, which employs 25 per cent of the workforce, and accounts for 16 per cent of Israel's industrial exports. Even Shimon Peres, who has never served in the forces, has been closely involved in the defence establishment since the foundation of the state.

One may imagine that this military-industrial system would have a very strong point of view indeed regarding any policy evolved by a future Israeli government which cut across its own interests. For example, a peace policy which embarked upon a major run-down of arms manufacture could be faced with strong opposition not only from this military-industrial system but also from the Histadrut, anxious not to lose jobs. Military spending, it must be remembered, went up rather than down after both the 1967 and 1973 wars.

Yet the reduction of arms expenditure is an important prerequisite to any Israeli substantial economic recovery, for its economic fortunes can be directly related to the burden of war. During the years 1950–66 defence expenditure averaged 9 per cent of the annual gross national product. During this same period annual GNP growth was 10 per cent, investment accounting for 32 per cent of GNP. From 1967 to 1986 defence spending averaged 27 per cent of the GNP, and GNP growth steeply declined. Since 1980 GNP growth has been 1.5 per cent, and investment accounts now for only 22 per cent of the GNP.[104] By 1986 $500 million was being spent on military research and development compared with $100 million allocated for civil research and development.[105]

So far the army, backed by the military-industrial system, has played a major role in the running of the state, but it has not openly taken over the role of government from the elected one. However, no area of the state's activity is more liable to precipitate military intervention than the question of what to do about the occupied territories and their rebellious inhabitants. Furthermore, it is by no means certain whether, if it did intervene, it would do so on considerations purely of the strategic defence of the state or in order to take the helm in the event of a collapse of national consensus.

This raises another issue painfully well known in Israel. Since 1948 no political party has been able to form a government without taking other parties into coalition. This results from the almost absolute proportional representation system which allows any party attracting 1 per cent of the vote (increased to 1·5 per cent for the 1992 election) to be represented in the Knesset. No party has ever taken more than 38 per cent of the vote. While this may be admirable as an exercise in democracy, it has left every single administration compromised on questions of policy. Even at the height of Israel's power in 1968, the senior cabinet minister Yigal Allon concluded 'the Government contained such divergent viewpoints that every position was cancelled out from within; it was a paralysed government.'[106]

The weakness implicit in each administration reached a climax in 1984 when neither Labour nor Likud could form a government without being heavily compromised between constituent ideologies and with only the narrowest of majorities in the Knesset. In the event the rivals found it easier to form a national coalition, which brought absolute power in the Knesset but resulted in a government unable to agree on much. The 1988 election brought further polarization but no improvement in the electoral outcome. It took the largest party, Likud, seven weeks of hard negotiation before it was able to form a new coalition government.

In 1992 the Labour Party was returned to power in the most decisive election result for a decade. Yitzhak Rabin, returned to leadership of the party, offered the country firm and decisive leadership combined with the prospect of a peace settlement and the repair of Israel's damaged relations with the United States. These were the factors that accounted for the modest swing in voting. However, the electorate had voted for a peace settlement predicated on Labour's terms rather than Likud's. This implied a form of autonomy which might lead to Palestinian independence in barely 50 per cent of the West Bank and Gaza Strip. Israelis and Palestinians may take heart from this modest improvement in the prospects, but it must be remembered that such a solution is unlikely to be adequate for a substantive peace either with the Palestinian people or with Israel's neighbours. Furthermore it remains questionable how far Labour can now resolve the long-standing dilemmas of the Jewish state.

This article is reprinted from David McDowall, *Palestine and Israel: The Uprising and Beyond* (London: I.B. Tauris, 1989), pp. 163–181 and 291–296. Author has revised the original chapter for the purposes of this publication.

NOTES

1. Abba Eban, *The New Diplomacy* (London, 1983) p. 229.
2. Shlomo Avineri, *The making of Modern Zionism, the Intellectual Origins of the Jewish State* (New York, 1981) p. 13.
3. For example Peretz Smolenskin or Moshe Lilienblum who both changed their views after the 1881 pogroms. Ibid., chapters 5 and 6.
4. Ibid., chapter 13.
5. The description given of the views of Aharon Gordon. Ibid., p. 153.
6. As Ben Gurion himself said at the time of the Balfour Declaration, 'within the next twenty years, we must have a Jewish majority in Palestine'. Ben Gurion, *Mi-Ma'amad le Am* (From class to peoplehood) (Tel Aviv, 1933) p. 15, quoted by Shabtai Teveth, *Ben Gurion and the Palestinian Arabs: from Peace to War* (Oxford and New York, 1985) p. 40.
7. Sharett, *Diaries* (Tel Aviv, 1970) vol. i, p. 112, quoted by Simha Flapan, *Zionism and the Palestinians*, (London and New York, 1979) p. 154. Sharett had no doubt at all that 'our fate in Palestine will be determined not by political formulas but by the number of Jews.' Minutes of the Jewish Agency Executive, 22 November 1936, quoted by Flapan, *Zionism and the Palestinians*, p. 154.
8. Yosef Gorny, *Zionism and the Arabs 1882–1948*, (Oxford, 1987) p. 2.
9. Weizmann to Weltsch, 13 January 1924, quoted by Flapan, *Zionism and the Palestinians*, p. 72.
10. His words were addressed to a Mapai (Labour) conference. Reinhard Wiemer, 'Zionism and the Arabs after the establishment of the State of Israel' in Alexander Schölch (ed.). *Palestinians over the Green Line* (London, 1983) p. 46.
11. Ibid.
12. Ibid., p. 47; *Israel Statistical Abstract 1986* (*ISA*), p. 63. In fact, the reality is proving less adverse than Bacchi described, with a prospect now of 4.1 million Jews and 1.2 million Palestinians inside the 1949 Armistice Line.
13. *Jerusalem Post International*, 14 December 1985.
14. Israel Radio, 14 May 1986, in *News From Within*, 20 May 1986. See also *Jerusalem Post*, 5 May 1986.
15. In *Judische Rundschau*, 1919, quoted by Flapan, *Zionism and the Palestinians*, p. 127.
16. Survey by Professor Steven Cohen, cited in Bernard Avishai, *The Tragedy of Zionism* (New York, 1985) p. 354.
17. 10,000 of these immigrants were Falashas from Ethiopia, *News From Within*, 15 November 1985. On emigration, see Bank of Israel emigration figures, quoted in *Ha'aretz*, 31 May 1985, in *Israeli Mirror*, no. 734.

18. *ISA* 1986, p. 66.

19. *Middle East International*, 19 December 1987.

20. National Insurance Institute figures, *Jerusalem Post International*, 5 July 1986.

21. Ibid.

22. See for example, Haim Sadan, 'Israel's big problem', *Jerusalem Post International*, week ending 16 August 1986; Pinhas Landau, 'The issue that just won't go away', in *Jerusalem Post International*, week ending 23 May 1987; Bernard Josephs, 'Israelis seduced by the "good life" in America', in *The Jerusalem Post*, 21 September 1987.

23. *Jerusalem Post International*, 5 July 1986.

24. Avraham Schenker, *New Outlook*, March/April 1988. An expectation of 800,000 *émigrés* by the end of the century is based upon Hanoch Smith statistical estimate, based on the current *émigré* level of 12,000 per year. *Ha'aretz*, 18 May 1988, in *Israeli Mirror*, no. 779. General Matti Peled claimed in 1985 that 420,000 Jews had already left Israel. *Hadashot*, 3 December 1985, in *Israeli Mirror*, no. 745.

25. *Jerusalem Post International*, 27 December 1986. According to the Council for the Prevention of Emigration, 27 per cent of high school students thought of emigration and another 15 per cent said they would be pleased if their families left. *Ha'aretz*, 18 May 1988, in *Israeli Mirror*, no. 779.

26. Ephraim Ya'ar, 'Emigration is a normal phenomenon', *New Outlook*, January 1988.

27. *Jerusalem Post International*, 5 July 1986.

28. Ibid., 12 December 1987.

29. R. J. Isaac, *Israel Divided: Ideological Politics in the Jewish State* (Baltimore, 1976), p. 152.

30. Histadrut Executive Committee Protocols, Tel Aviv, 5 Sept 1929, quoted in Teveth, *Ben Gurion and the Palestinian Arabs*, p. 84.

31. Yael Lotan, 'Israel's national schizophrenia', in *al Hamishmar*, 10 October 1986, translated in International Centre for Peace in the Middle East, *Israeli Press Briefs*, no. 49.

32. For example see the estimate of Alfred Moses, President of the Jewish American Committee, *al Hayat*, 7 February 1992.

33. Arnon Soffer, 'Demography and the Impact of Russian Immigration by the Year 2000', in *University of Haifa News*, March 1991, and personal communication dated 17 July 1992.

34. See for example *Jerusalem Post International* 7 March and 16 May 1992.

35. *Jerusalem Post International*, 7 March 1992.

36. In the years 1989, 1990 and 1991, a total of 110,00 Soviet Jews entered the United States as legal refugees, the maximum US Government-permitted quota. The 1992 US quota is 53,000 Jews. Thus, in January 1992, while 6,200 CIS Jews entered Israel, no fewer than 4,300 went to the United States; see *Jerusalem Post International*, 18 January, 22 February and 7 March 1992.

37. *Jerusalem Post International*, 14 March and 16 May 1992; *Middle East International*, 22 August 1992.

38. A Tazpit Research Institute survey sample of 809 Soviet immigrants arriving since 1989 indicated that 29 per cent of them hoped they would be living elsewhere within five years; *Middle East International*, 21 August 1992.

39. By autumn 1988 Palestinians already outnumbered Jews under the age of eight by 630,000 to 590,000, *The Times*, 19 October 1988.

40. This assumes that the forecast in *ISA 1986*, p. 63, has not been substantially altered by recent Jewish immigration.

41. Reuven Ahlberg, 'The case against Greater Israel', *Jerusalem Post International*, 26 February-3 March 1984. Only in Israel is the birth rate higher than the replenishment rate. Ibid., week ending 14 December 1985.

42. Ibid., week ending 7 November 1987.

43. Some estimates predict an even steeper decline, of 20–25 per cent by the end of the century. Ibid., 17–24 June 1984.

44. *Guardian*, 24 October 1987.

45. G. Sheffer, 'The uncertain future of American Jewry-Israel relations', *The Jerusalem Quarterly*, no. 32, summer 1984, p. 70. Intermarriage is increasing with about 25–30 per cent of young Jews currently marrying non-Jews. *Jerusalem Post International*, 31 October 1987. Allowing for the fact that some Jews do not marry, the intermarrying proportion among those who do marry is 45 per cent. Jews 'lost' by intermarriage used to be offset by those Gentiles who

embraced Judaism on marriage, but the latter has declined from 44 per cent in the early 1970s to only 12 per cent since 1980. Ibid.

46. Report of Dr Donald Feldstein to the American Jewish Congress, reported in *Jerusalem Post International*, 8–14 April 1984.

47. David Rosenberg, 'The UJA's optimistic fundraisers', ibid., 21 February 1987.

48. Sheffer, 'The uncertain future of American Jewry-Israel relations', pp. 68, 78. See also the *Guardian*, 24 December 1987 which reported a poll in summer 1987 showing that 63 per cent of American Jews 'cared deeply' about Israel, a 15 per cent drop since 1983.

49. Even before the Uprising a substantial majority of American Jews considered public criticism of the Israeli government to be acceptable, with under-forty-year-olds feeling less attached than their elders. The decline in commitment is slight but it is real. Almost 50 per cent of American Jews, according to a poll in 1983, were 'often troubled by the policies of the Israeli government'. Sheffer, 'The uncertain future of American Jewry-Israel relations', p. 77.

50. Compare S.M. Cohen, *Attitudes of American Jews toward Israel and the Israelis*, (New York, Sept 1983) quoted in Sheffer, 'The uncertain future of American Jewry-Israel relations', p. 79, with Alex Brummer, 'The heart and mind of the Jewish voter', *Guardian*, 13 April 1988.

51. Sheffer, 'The uncertain future of American Jewry-Israel relations', p. 80.

52. For example, see the findings of Professor Steven M. Cohen in 1986, summarized in *Jerusalem Post International*, week ending 9 May 1987.

53. Rosenberg, 'The UJA's optimistic fundraisers'.

54. See on this question two contrasting books, one by an anti-Zionist Israeli, Akiva Orr, *The Unjewish State* (London, 1985) and a Zionist one, Norman Zucker, *The Coming Crisis in Israel—Private Faith and Public Policy* (Cambridge, Mass., 1973).

55. In 1986 the amendment was defeated by 61 votes to 47, in 1985 it was defeated by 62 to 51, and in the previous Knesset (1981–4) it was defeated by a far closer margin of 58 to 54. *Jerusalem Post International*, 15 February 1986 and Moshe Samet, 'Who is a Jew?' in *Jerusalem Quarterly*, no. 37, 1986, p. 134.

56. *Jerusalem Post International*, 19 December 1987.

57. For more on Rabbi Kook, see Avineri, *The Making of Modern Zionism*, chapter 16, and Ehud Sprinzak, 'The iceberg model of political extremism', in David Newman (ed.) *The impact of Gush Emunim* (Beckenham, 1985) pp. 27–8.

58. In 'The War', in Arthur Hertzberg, *The Zionist Idea* (New York, 1969), quoted by Avineri, *The Making of Modern Zionism*, p. 195.

59. Z.Y. Kook, 'Between the people and its land', *Artzi* (Jerusalem, 1983) p. 10, quoted in Yehoshafat Harkabi, *Israel's Fateful Decisions* (London, 1988) p. 150.

60. Sprinzak, 'The iceberg model of political extremism', p. 37.

61. Bernard Avishai, *The Tragedy of Zionism: Revolution and Democracy in the Land of Israel* (New York, 1985) p. 250.

62. The essential theme of Sprinzak's article.

63. *Deuteronomy*, I v 8; for a fuller discussion of God's promise, see Gwyn Rowley, 'The Land of Israel: a reconstructionist approach', in Newman (ed.) *The Impact of Gush Emunim*.

64. I have relied on Shlomo Avineri's description of *Altneuland* in *The Making of Modern Zionism*, p. 99.

65. *Igrot* (Letters) (Tel Aviv, 1971–4) vol. i, p. 71, quoted in Teveth, *Ben Gurion and the Palestinian Arabs*, p. 5.

66. The mayor of Arad, *Jerusalem Post International*, 15–21 January 1984.

67. See *News From Within*, 1 November 1985 listing the development towns most hit by high unemployment. During the 1980s there was a net loss of 15,000 from Beersheba and Dimona. All development towns in Galilee face stagnation. In 1987 the Palestinian population in Galilee grew by 19,000 while in the same year 2,500 Jews left. *Koteret Rashit*, 3 February 1988, in *Israeli Press Briefs*, no. 58.

68. *Jerusalem Post International*, week ending 29 August 1987.

69. Benvenisti, *1986 Report*, p. 51.

70. Ibid., p. 52.

71. Ibid., p. 56.

72. Benvenisti *1987 Report*, p. 61.

73. Three important articles by Moise Saltiel which show in detail the extent of dereliction and degradation of the environment are 'The sterilization of Galilee and Judaean Mountain lands', 'The desertification of the Arid Negev', and 'The concretization of the Coastal Plain', in *Israel and Palestine Political Report*, Nos. 155, 156, 161 of January, March and November 1990 respectively.

74. For descriptions, see William Frankel, *Israel Observed* (London, 1980) pp. 172–83.

75. Ibid., p. 181.

76. Thomas L. Friedman, 'Israel's tangle of farm troubles', *The New York Times*, Sunday 13 September 1987. *Kibbutzim*, since they are larger-scale ventures, have been better able to absorb spare labour by building factories.

77. Ibid.

78. David Ben Gurion, 'Our action and our direction', in Yaacov Becker (ed.), *Mishnato shel David Ben Gurion* (Tel Aviv, 1958) vol. ii, pp. 525–6, quoted by Avineri, *The Making of Modern Zionism*, p. 202.

79. Harkabi, *Israel's Fateful Decisions*, p. 63.

80. Avineri, *The Making of Modern Zionism*, p. 223.

81. Magnes, 'Like all the nations?' (pamphlet, Jerusalem, 1930) quoted in Flapan, *Zionism and the Palestinians*, p. 175.

82. Leibowitz' own verdict, *al Hamishmar*, 13 February 1983, in *Israeli Mirror*, no. 636.

83. Avishai, *The Tragedy of Zionism*, p. 303.

84. Ibid., p. 305.

85. Israel Radio, 14 May 1986, in *News From Within*, 20 May 1986.

86. Weizmann to Einstein, 30 November 1929, quoted in Flapan, *Zionism and the Palestinians*, p. 71.

87. When asked early in 1986 why there would be no elections in the occupied territories, Peres replied that elections were not possible because of the potential for terrorist subversion. Stated in response to a question following his address at Chatham House, 22 January 1986.

88. *Israel and Palestine*, no. 140, February-March 1988.

89. Avishai, *The Tragedy of Zionism*, p. 303.

90. Quoted in *Middle East International*, no. 336, 21 October 1988.

91. Avishai, *The Tragedy of Zionism*, p. 303.

92. Ibid., p. 299.

93. Dahaf poll for the Van Leer Institute, October 1987, reported in *Ha'aretz*, 26 October 1987, *Jerusalem Post International*, 7 November 1987, and *New Outlook*, February 1988.

94. In March 1982 51 per cent (already alarmingly high) disapproved of press freedom, increasing to 65 per cent by March 1983. By this date 58 per cent disapproved of criticism of government defence and foreign policy. Research by Dr Mina Tsemach, Dahaf poll, reported in *al Hamishmar*, 20 March 1983, in *Israeli Mirror*, no. 642.

95. Survey carried out by Dr Sammy Smooha, *New Outlook*, July 1986.

96. *Observer*, 12 June 1988.

97. Along with the law courts and doctors, *Jerusalem Post International*, 7 November 1987.

98. Avishai, *The Tragedy of Zionism*, p. 265.

99. Ibid., p. 340. For 1988 election results, see the *Jewish Chronicle*, 11 November 1988.

100. For a full discussion of the role of the Israeli military, see Yoram Peri, *Between Battles and Ballots, Israeli Military in Politics* (Cambridge, 1983) pp. 268ff.

101. Ibid., p. 274.

102. Ibid., p. 277.

103. Alex Mintz, 'Arms production in Israel', *Jerusalem Quarterly*, no. 42, spring 1987, p. 94.

104. Simha Bahiri, 'Guns or milk and honey', *New Outlook*, September/October 1986 and Simha Bahiri, 'Military and colonial aspects of the Israeli economy since 1967', *New Outlook*, May/June 1987.

105. Bahiri, 'Guns or milk and honey'.

106. Frankel, *Israel Observed*, p. 24.

The Strange Career of Pan-Arabism

STEPHEN HUMPHREYS

In American politics ideology is almost a synonym for political extremism. Every election campaign is filled with denunciations of left- or right-wing ideologues. Intriguingly, we hear no attacks on (or compliments for) ideologues of the center; presumably moderates are not inspired by anything as dangerous as ideas. It is not surprising, then, that we are suspicious or even fearful when politicians abroad self-consciously and proudly proclaim their adherence to this or that ideology. In their eyes, this means that their policies are not merely ad hoc solutions to separate, disconnected problems but rather flow from a comprehensive and logically integrated body of principles. In our eyes, it means that they are pursuing some mad utopian scheme, usually one hostile to vital American interests and values. Since Middle Eastern politics has been carried out in an explicitly ideological atmosphere for at least the last half century, Americans inevitably view the politicians of that region with apprehension and distrust. Europeans have tended to be more relaxed about it all, at least since they gave up their colonial empires about 1960. There are many reasons for the European frame of mind, but surely one is simply that they are accustomed to a highly ideological style of politics. Indeed, ideology is one of Europe's most enduring colonial legacies.

Guided (or misguided) by our traditional attitudes, we can make no sense of ideology in Middle Eastern politics unless we take it seriously. That in turn requires us to decide just what we are to mean by this notoriously abstract word. A full-scale analysis is out of the question, obviously, but a few comments may get us started.

To begin with, ideology arises in a context of change—in particular, the kind of massive, sudden change that threatens to overturn an existing political and social system. In the face of such disruptive forces, those who speak for the existing order must explain why it is right for things to be arranged the way they are. On the other side, dissenters will denounce what is wrong (more or less everything, as a rule) and show how they intend to set things right. It is debates of this kind that generate ideology. In formal language, we can say that ideology is a broad, systematic critique of a given sociopolitical system that both describes that system and calls on its members to defend, alter, or overthrow it. Ideology is both analysis and a call to action.

Next, ideologies are utopian. Each ideology claims that its program will establish the best possible society, a society whose rightness will be self-evident to all. This utopian goal may be portrayed as the recovery of a lost Golden Age, or it may represent the achievement of aspirations barely dreamed of in the past. Ideologies are often (almost always, in fact) connected with some metaphysical scheme, some interpretation of the ultimate nature of reality. To name only two possibilities, this metaphysics may be strictly materialist (as in Marxism-Leninism) or it may presuppose the active presence of a deity (as in the various Islamist ideologies). In any case, the claims of ideology tend to be absolute, because they are rooted in absolute truth. It is thus not surprising that ideologies readily slide toward extremism.

One final point. Ideology is conveyed to its audience in ways that are simultaneously rational and highly emotive. Ideology aims to incite people to action. To do that it must express its ideas through the use of values and symbols that inspire an intense, immediate, almost instinctive response by everyone who encounters them. A sophisticated ideology is quite able to support its program through elaborate rational arguments, but in the political arena it is more likely to resort to flag-waving and the chanting of slogans. For much the same reason, once an ideology leaves the seminar room or the salon, it prefers to keep things simple. One should never assume that a crude stump speech reflects a lack of important and complex ideas.

Of all the ideologies that have played on the Middle Eastern stage in this century—bourgeois liberalism, Marxism, Islamism—none has had a greater impact both within the region and throughout the world, none excited more hope and anxiety, than Arab Nationalism.[1] Like its cousins, the nationalisms of Turkey and Iran, Arab Nationalism aimed at the political resurrection of a people. But the nationalists of Turkey and Iran were working within the boundaries of an internationally recognized country. Arab Nationalists, in contrast, had to struggle against the artificial political divisions imposed on their homeland by a succession of foreign empires—Ottoman, French, and (most malign of all) British. In a very literal sense, Arab Nationalism sought to heal the wounds of history.

The year 1958 was the annus mirabilis of Arab Nationalism. It was a new ideology, hardly half a century old, but it already seemed the irresistible wave of the future. The energy and power of Arab Nationalism were manifested in three spectacular events: first, the February melding together of Syria and Egypt in the United Arab Republic (UAR); second, the violent overthrow of the monarchy in Iraq in July (a wonderful omen, since that was the same month that the Free Officers had seized power in Egypt six years earlier); and third, the Lebanese crisis of the autumn, which nearly led to the collapse of the strongly pro-Western regime of Camille Chamoun.

Beyond these headline-grabbing crises, 1958 marked a structural shift in Arab politics, the emergence of the progressive/reactionary split that would bedevil inter-Arab relations for the next decade and beyond. This rivalry would take many forms and pass through many phases, but initially it placed the revolutionary military regimes in the new UAR and Iraq against the conservative monarchies of Jordan and Saudi Arabia. (These alliances were marriages of convenience, to be sure; the ruling houses of Jordan and Saudi Arabia had been rivals since the end of World War I, while revolutionary zeal quickly proved unable to overcome the burgeoning rivalry—both personal and national—between Nasser of Egypt and Col. Abd al-Karim Qassem of Iraq.) The "reactionary" monarchies represented everything the new wave of Pan-Arabists despised: a commitment to traditional (supposedly despotic) forms of government, an attachment to backward social and cultural values, stagnant religiosity, alliances with reactionary social elites like big landlords, and—worst of all—subservience to foreign imperialism. The progressive states, in contrast, were led by young, future-oriented military officers. These states stood for all sorts of desirable things: cultural dynamism, rapid economic growth combined with social justice, the rise of new classes to social and political leadership (for most of the revolutionary regimes were led by men of modest rural or small-town origin), rationality and modernity, intense commitment to the Arab cause, and complete independence from foreign influence or domination. The way had already been shown by such legendary leaders as Jawaharlal Nehru of India and Sukarno of Indonesia, and the Arab generation of 1958 was determined to strike off down the same path.

By the winter of 1967, however, the glowing promise of Pan-Arabism was already a bit tarnished, and the movement had suffered some real setbacks. First of all, the UAR, the very symbol of Arab unification, had split apart (peacefully but very acrimoniously) in 1961. Nor were the wounds easily healed; increasingly radical regimes in Syria ragged Nasser for his lack of zeal for the Arab cause, and Egypt's relations with Iraq grew more and more strained. Relations among the "progressive" states quickly degenerated into what Malcolm Kerr felicitously named the Arab Cold War, an unceasing mutual barrage of vitriolic propaganda, accusations of betrayal and subversion, and stillborn reconciliations.[2] Nasser had gotten involved in a lingering civil war in the Yemen and sent the bulk of Egypt's combat-ready forces to support a beleaguered military-republican revolutionary government in that country. But in spite of all these disappointments and frustrations, Pan-Arabism was still effectively unchallenged on the ideological level, at least among the most articulate and politically mobilized groups—young professionals, university students, and army officers. Imperialism and Zionism would be harder to defeat, unity harder to achieve, than many had supposed, but victory was inevitable. If the will to struggle was there, it still waited just around the corner.

By September 1972, when I arrived in Lebanon to complete a book on the great Arab Nationalist hero Saladin (who was in fact a Kurd and grew up in the service of a Turkish-speaking dynasty), things had not improved. The Arab Nationalist program had suffered catastrophic setbacks during the previous five years, though among younger people it still remained the ideological currency of the realm. Or at least it had no viable competition, for the Islamic movement was just beginning to stir, and the old ideas of European-style liberalism were still derided as bourgeois decadence. The crushing humiliation of 1967 had left people disoriented; some were seeking to redeem the disaster through direct revolutionary action, while others had fallen into passivity. That 1967 was a terrible wound to Pan-Arabism was obvious to all; that it was in fact a death blow had yet to sink in.

But now, a quarter century later, where is Pan-Arabism, or Arab Nationalism in any form? As an effective ideology, able to mobilize and direct political action, it has failed; both Israel's unanswered invasion of Lebanon in 1982 and the Gulf War of 1990–1991 demonstrated that decisively. Arab Nationalism is of course not necessarily gone forever. As we will see, it is an ideology that embodies deepseated values and aspirations, and in a favorable milieu it may spring to life once again. But for the time being we have to ask why something once so brilliantly promising faded from the scene, and what if anything has replaced it? Arab Nationalism was not merely the victim of bad fortune and hostile circumstances, though it certainly encountered its full share of these. In its very origins and in the way it developed over half a century it had certain persistent weaknesses, and these may well have prevented it from ever achieving its full program.

First, Arab Nationalism was even in its heyday a new plant in the Arab world, with very shallow roots in the political tradition of that region. An Arab Nationalist ideology was just beginning to be articulated in the decade before World War I, chiefly in Beirut and Damascus, and it had not proceeded much beyond a few journalists, intellectuals, and army officers when war broke out. It emerged as a tangible political force only during World War I, and it did so then largely due to the failure of Ottoman policy and Ottoman arms in the Hijaz and Fertile Crescent. Even at the height of the war it was the cause of a small elite (largely in Damascus and Beirut, and to a markedly lesser extent in Baghdad) rather than of the masses. A majority of Arab military officers in the Ottoman army remained loyal to the empire down to the end of the war. The armies of the Arab Revolt, led by the Sharif Hussein of Mecca, were largely funded by British gold, and operated in close liaison with Britain's Arab Bureau in Cairo.

In the newly created Arab states of the 1920s and 1930s, however, Arab Nationalism did begin to sink deeper roots, for it provided a compelling ideology of resistance to European occupation and control under the Mandate system. By World War II it had undeniably become a broad-based popular movement in Syria, Iraq, and Palestine. At this point, however, Arab Nationalism still stirred few sympathies west of Suez. Even as late as 1940, Egypt's politicians and intellectuals chose to play only a marginal role in the movement, and the countries of North Africa (which remained under direct French rule throughout for a full decade after World War II) were fully preoccupied with their own situation.

If the concept of Arabism was a very new thing as a framework for political action, it unquestionably did have a long history as a form of ethnic identity. Down to the end of the nineteenth century, most inhabitants of North Africa, the Nile Valley, and the lands between the Mediterranean and the Tigris knew they were Arabs in the sense that they spoke the Arabic language as their native tongue. They were proud of their language and the remarkable literature it had generated over more than a millennium. Likewise, they knew that their ancestors had been the original and "most authentic" bearers of Islam, and of course they took pride in the noble lineage that they acquired from this fact. But none of these things implied in their minds that they should strive to form an Arab state. If asked to describe themselves, they would say that they were Muslims (or occasionally, Christians), residents of Damascus or Kairouan or wherever, members of such and such a clan, and subjects of the Ottoman sultan. Arabic speech was a crucial element in their cultural identity, but it had no political significance.

In the struggle for hearts and minds during the early twentieth century, Arab Nationalism—still raw and poorly articulated—had to compete with a deep-rooted and almost instinctive commitment to Islam. The relationship of Islam to Arab Nationalism was a tricky one for the publicists of the new ideology. If a person owed primary political allegiance to the Arab nation, what did that mean for the heretofore unquestioned loyalty to the worldwide Community of Believers? Whatever the historical role of the Arabs in Islam, most Muslims were not Arabs—and many Arabs were not Muslims. The early Arab Nationalists tried to make Islam a part of Arab identity by stressing its central role in their culture and history. But to many Muslims that was no solution at all, since it clearly made Islam less important than Arabism. In fact, early Arab Nationalists never quite resolved the conundrum, and they have not worked it out to this day.

It is undeniably true that Islam, in its origins, was deeply imbued with Arab elements. The Qur'an was revealed "in a clear Arabic tongue," the early Muslim Community was made up almost entirely of Arabic-speakers dwelling in the Arabian Peninsula and the Fertile Crescent, and the first conquests were aimed at uniting the peoples of this vast area within a single religiopolitical framework. But the "Arabism" of early Islam began to evaporate as the Muslim armies penetrated into non-Arab lands and as non-Arabs slowly began to accept Islam—initially to the consternation of their conquerors. By the mid-ninth century the Arabs were no longer the political-social elite of the Islamic world, except for the caliphs themselves—and the caliphs' claim to rule lay in their kinship with the Prophet, not in the distant Arabian origins of their family. Arabic still remained the language through which all educated Muslims (and increasing numbers of non-Muslims) communicated with one another, whatever ethnic group they belonged to, and it would retain that role for centuries to come. But in fact a mastery of Arabic was increasingly the province of non-Arabs, of those who had spoken something else in their childhood homes and perhaps continued to do so as adults. Ironically, very few of the leading writers of Arabic prose and poetry in the ninth and tenth centuries could trace their family trees back to the Arabian Peninsula. Moreover, in the tenth century Arabic began to be supplanted in Iran and Central Asia by a revival of written Persian, and eventually even by Turkish. By the year 1000, to be an Arab in any sense—descendant of the conquering tribal warriors of the seventh century, or native speaker of Arabic, or desert dweller—conferred little or no religious preeminence. On the contrary, in most places political power was firmly in the hands of other peoples, often proudly and self-consciously identifying themselves as Iranians, Turks, or Berbers. A Muslim was anyone who confessed that God was one and Muhammad was His apostle; Arab roots and Arab identity had very little to do with it.

The idea that political action should be driven by the fact that one was an Arab still seemed new and strange by the eve of World War I. And even as the emerging ideas of Arabism began to take hold among the political elites of the new states of the region (particularly in Iraq and Syria), a second element of weakness emerged. Arab Nationalist thinkers and publicists from the very beginning had looked at the crucial problem confronting them and their people as one of identity rather than as one of institutions. The question was, Who is an Arab? not How can the Arabs build a common political life and effective institutions of government? If Arabs believed they were Arabs and acted on that belief, it was argued, they would inevitably be able to create an Arab national state. Very few writers asked seriously how this state would be constituted, how the relationships among its many disparate regions were to be defined, and how different social groups would be represented within the political system. Such issues were vital, everyone admitted, but they were premature.

The United Arab Republic of 1958, a slapdash marriage of convenience, was the perfect embodiment of these unanswered (and almost unasked) questions. It was never wholly clear in Nasser's own thinking whether he should aim at an alliance of Arab states that he would dominate (presumably through the Arab League) or whether he should try for something more. The proposal for a United Arab Republic, launched by desperate Syrian politicians trapped between the machinations of the CIA and domestic Communists, had caught him entirely by surprise, and when the union failed he found himself trying to salvage his prestige rather than looking for alternative structures.

The historical experience of Great Britain, the United States, and France might have suggested to Pan-Arabist ideologues that political institutions and common citizenship could provide a framework within which a solid national identity could take shape. However, the Italian and German models, based on race, culture, will, and struggle against internal division and foreign rule, had far more appeal. Given the hostile attitudes toward Great Britain and France among Arab political activists during the mid-1930s—attitudes that should be readily intelligible—the victory of the Italo-German style of nationalism was perhaps inevitable.

To be fair, the problem of identity was not a trivial one for the Arabs. The earliest Arab Nationalists (perhaps they should be called protonationalists), writing in the decade before World War I, originally focused on a Greater Syria comprised of the modern countries of Syria, Lebanon, Jordan, and Palestine. During the war, they broadened their focus to include the Arabian Peninsula and Iraq. It took Arab Nationalist writers a long time to come around to the argument that all the lands between the Nile and the Tigris should be included in the Arab nation. Indeed, the first to present this argument systematically was Sati' al-Husri in the mid-1930s.[3] He is in fact an oddly paradigmatic figure for interwar Arab Nationalism. Born in Aleppo to a Turkish-speaking family of Ottoman officials, Sati' al-Husri was educated in Istanbul and spent the war years there. After World War I he took up residence in the new state of Iraq and ultimately became minister of education in that country. He emerged in the 1930s as the most sophisticated and effective spokesman for Pan-Arabism. Ironically, Turkish was his mother tongue, and though he was devoted to the Arabic language he never was fully at home in it.

Apart from uncertainties about what lands and peoples belonged to the Arab Nation, there were important and deep-rooted counter-identities at play—Egyptian, Syrian, Lebanese, Muslim, and so on. These identities had to be dealt with; except for Islam they were dismissed as "regionalism." Moreover, several Arab countries contained large non-Arab minorities, especially the Kurds in Iraq and the Berbers in Algeria—some 20 and 15 percent of the population, respectively. Morocco had an even larger Berber population than Algeria, but most Pan-Arabists were willing to recognize that it possessed a distinctive character of its own within the larger Arab world.

It followed from the fundamental propositions of Pan-Arabism that the creation of the Arab state would come about by a supreme act of will, by a revolt that would shatter the rigid but brittle cage of historical accident and misfortune that imprisoned the Arabs. It was an article of faith among the avant-grade intelligentsia that the Arabs had been kept apart solely by the selfishness of local elites and the machinations of Franco-British imperialism. But once these artificial barriers could be smashed, the Arab nation would inevitably flow together and meld into one indissoluble union. The will demanded by history was first of all the will of the whole Arab people, but it was also the heroic will of a single actor, who would embody in himself the aspirations and ideals of the whole nation.

Not entirely by his own volition and certainly not by circumstances of his own making, Gamal Abdel Nasser found himself in this role after the Suez Crisis of 1956. The problem he faced was this: whatever his stature with the Arab masses—which had become almost overwhelming even for a man of his considerable self-esteem—he had to deal with rival political elites in other Arab states. In spite of Nasser's fiery propaganda machine, these were not the entrenched elites of the "reactionary" states, the old colonial period bureaucrats and landowners, wealthy merchants and tribal chiefs, whose wealth, privilege, and toadyism the progressives loved to assail. Especially after 1958, Nasser's chief rivals were for the most part the raw, insecure radicals of Syria and Iraq who had their own vision of the Arab future. These men had just seized power and were determined to keep it in the face of domestic enemies, the CIA, and Nasser himself. In their eyes, Nasser fell far short of the unclouded vision and the pure ruthlessness that were needed to bring about the new world they envisioned so vividly.

In a sense the Pan-Arabism of the 1950s and 1960s was a surrogate for other impulses—the struggle to end the last vestiges of colonial domination, to eradicate the constant, burning humiliation of Israel, to achieve prosperity and social justice, and to realize the glorious aspirations of so many for the cultural and intellectual renewal of the Arabs. Through Arab Nationalism, the Arabs could once again become a great people who would command the respect of the world. But when Arab Nationalism—or Arab Nationalist rhetoric—did not bring those things into being but instead dragged the Arabs into the abyss of June 1967, it was inevitable that they and their leaders would look elsewhere for hope and inspiration.

In retrospect, all these points seem a sure guarantee that Pan-Arabism would have only a brief turn upon the stage. But for a moment it did triumph, or almost so. Every expert commentator in the 1960s (not only the Pan-Arabist intelligentsia, who obviously had a vital stake in the debate, but also the best-informed Western observers) took it for granted that some form of Arab Nationalism represented the future. And this universal assumption among intelligent and well-informed contemporary observers should cause us to ask whether the "failure" (as it now seems) of Pan-Arabism was rooted, not in the movement's structural flaws, but simply in the accidents of history. Suppose the Arabs had held their own in the June War—not winning the smashing victory that their propagandists had predicted, but simply stalling the Israeli offensive for three weeks or a month, long enough to compel the United Nations (or rather the United States and the Soviet Union) to intervene and compel a stand-down. In such a case might not Nasser's dominance have been restored or even heightened, in the manner of 1956? After all, a merely creditable performance in 1973 earned a tremendous surge of prestige for Sadat, and this war too might have ended very badly for Egypt had not the Americans and Soviets, fearful of a nuclear confrontation between themselves, pressured the Israelis into a cease-fire. It is in any case a possibility that deserves more serious reflection than it usually receives.

But let us grant that events might have gone differently than they did. Even so it is hard to think that the maximum Pan-Arabist program was ever attainable, if only because the existing boundaries between the Arab states—boundaries that were pure colonial fictions created out of thin air in 1920 by Britain and France for their own convenience—had become sacred and immutable by 1950. Those boundaries provided the arenas in which the struggles for independence were fought, in which established social elites and their challengers strove to control the future. It is implausible to think that the young radicals who seized power in Iraq and Syria in the mid-1960s could have been induced to surrender their own aspirations for the greater glory of Nasser—whom they despised as a waffler in any case. And of course that is all the more true today, when those young radicals, now thoroughly middle-aged or worse, have enjoyed more than two decades of almost absolute power.

If Pan-Arabism, or Arab Nationalism in any form, can no longer inspire real hope and effective political action, has anything arisen to replace it? Is it possible that the Pan-Arabist dream has been replaced by state patriotism, a devotion to Egypt or Jordan or Iraq as they exist within their present boundaries? Can we imagine that the existing Arab states have so risen in the affection and esteem of their citizens that they are now the highest goal of political action, the focus of political loyalty? It is easy enough to be dismissive. But in fact the political experience of the Arab countries has been extremely complex, and we cannot answer the question without taking account of that complexity. A satisfactory reading of the shifting balance between Arab Nationalism and state patriotism demands that we look at the Arab states one by one. Ideally, we would survey every country from Mauritania to Oman, but that is not really necessary. The main struggle for Arab Nationalism took place in the eastern Arab world, in Egypt, Syria, Iraq, and the countries adjacent to them. By focusing on these, we will have some basis for deciding whether state patriotism can fill the void left by Arab Nationalism.

The shift from Arab Nationalism to state patriotism may in fact have taken place to some degree in the Egypt of Sadat and Mubarak, but Egypt (along with Morocco) is the odd man out in the Arab world, for Egyptian intellectuals and political activists long ago developed a strong sense of their country's historical identity and cultural personality. Modern Egyptian nationalism dates back to the 1860s and 1870s, and was forever crystallized by the trauma of the British Occupation in 1882. In this context the Nasserist era (which lasted sixteen years, from his personal seizure of power in 1954 to his death in 1970) was a striking but atypical interlude. But even if Egyptians have no desire to dissolve themselves in a vast, undifferentiated Arab nation, they do not like going it alone either. Arabism is a significant element in what it means to be an Egyptian, and at some point it may well become once again the most important element.

When we turn to the countries of the Fertile Crescent and the Arabian Peninsula, however, we find few parallels to Egypt's well-articulated sense of national identity. Syria is a particularly intriguing test case for state patriotism in the Arab world, for Syria is a country that never wanted to exist at all, at least within its present boundaries.[4] Syrians quite rightly believe that the present boundaries of their country have no natural or historic roots but are rather a wholly artificial creation devised by France and Britain for their own purposes at the end of World War I. The political leaders who emerged in Syria between 1918 and 1920 had no delusions of grandeur. They hoped only for a truly independent Syria within its traditional boundaries—a region that stretches from Sinai in the south to the Taurus Mountains in the north and from the Mediterranean on the west to the Syrian Desert in the east. This region, called bilad al-Sham in Arabic (literally, "the lands of the North"), or Greater Syria, had never existed as a separate political entity with legally defined borders, but everyone knew what it was. Syrian politicians discovered very quickly that Britain and France were going to carve their homeland into pieces rigorously separated from one another and subjected to close imperial tutelage. In the Anglo-French settlement after World War I, bilad al-Sham—Greater Syria—became the modern states of Syria, Lebanon, Palestine/Israel, and Jordan.

The new Syria created by the World War I settlement was only two-thirds as large as the traditional Greater Syria. Moreover, it was isolated by being stripped of its ancient seaports, which were now located in the new entities of Lebanon and Palestine. Palestine was to be set aside for a Jewish National Home under British protection. Finally, the lands east of the Jordan (mostly desert, admittedly) were assigned by Britain to the amir Abdallah, as compensation for a host of broken promises made by the British to his father, Hussein, who had instigated and led the Arab Revolt against the Ottomans during the war.

During the interwar years Syria's politicians were compelled to focus on ridding themselves of French domination, since nothing else could be achieved until that was done. Since the final evacuation of French forces in 1946, however, Syrian leaders, whatever their political complexion, have felt it their mission to speak for some higher cause than the truncated country they inherited from the French Mandate. Even those who forswear the vast claims of Pan-Arabism have dreamed of reuniting the "historical" Greater Syria. The Syrian governments in the twelve years between independence (1946) and formation of the United Arab Republic (1958) could make no progress on either goal. They came and went with dizzying speed, leaving hardly a trace behind. By the winter of 1958, Syria's leaders were equally fearful of a CIA plot and a communist coup—and as many have remarked, even paranoids have real enemies. In desperation they turned to the one man whom they thought could save them, Gamal Abdel Nasser, by now at the peak of his prestige in Egypt.

To Nasser they offered the crown of his career, the formation of a United Arab Republic that would join together Egypt and Syria within a single state. The UAR would be the catalyst for the emergence of a dynamic and progressive Arab state stretching from the Nile to the Tigris—in effect the realization of the Arab Nationalist vision born in World War I. Nasser had serious doubts about the feasibility of the project, but against his better judgment he allowed himself to be persuaded. And thus Syria disappeared from the map, to be replaced by the rather less resonant "United Arab Republic, Northern Region." Far more upsetting to the Syrian politicians who had engineered the union, they were edged out of power and out of sight. From the Syrian perspective, the marriage proved an unhappy one in every way.

In 1961 the UAR broke up as suddenly as it had appeared, when a carefully planned conspiracy seized power in Damascus. Nasser prudently decided not to oppose the secession, and Syria was reborn. But the effort to return to "normal" lasted only a couple of years. In 1963 a mixed military-civilian coup put a new government in power and thereby founded a political system that has endured for more than three decades. The core of the new regime was the Baath ("Resurrection") party, founded in Damascus in 1943 by a Christian schoolteacher and a Sunni pharmacist. The Baath was the most ardently Pan-Arabist movement of all; its program combined a secularist worldview, populism, a vaguely Marxist socioeconomic program, and a visionary dream of a single Arab nation stretching from Morocco to Iraq. The Baath had been a fringe element in Syrian politics until the mid-1950s, but throughout that time it was building a clandestine power base in the Syrian armed forces. That was in itself not unusual: the armed forces were often a center of political dissidence and revolutionary action throughout much of the Third World during these decades.

But Syria presented an interesting twist on this pattern, for its armed forces were dominated by a deeply despised religious minority, the Alawis (or to give them their correct name, the Nusayris), who dominated the northwest coastal region and constituted about one-eighth of the population. Under French rule and early independence, the army was in effect the only channel of upward mobility for the Alawis, and they took full advantage of it. For them, the secularism, populism, and socialism of the Baath had an obvious appeal. But all this meant that a Baathist government, especially one dominated by the military, would be by definition an Alawi government. And so it turned out. In a country where two-thirds of the people are Sunni Muslims, this fact severely alienated the regime from its subjects down through the mid-1980s.

In 1966 an even more radical Baathist faction seized power. This new regime was determined to make itself the leader of the Pan-Arabist movement. To that end it sponsored a string of guerrilla attacks against Israel and mercilessly taunted Nasser for his passivity. Its efforts to put itself in the vanguard of the Arab world made little headway, but it was all too successful in setting the stage for the June War of 1967. Unlike Nasser, the Baathist junta lacked the stature to survive such a debacle. One of its members, the air force chief of staff Hafiz al-Asad, threw out his erstwhile colleagues and took charge himself.

Since seizing full power in 1971, Hafiz al-Asad—nominally a Baathist, but in fact a pure Machiavellian—has narrowed Syria's ideological focus sharply, though for tactical reasons he still attaches himself to the Arab Nationalist cause on suitable occasions. In particular, he has made himself an advocate for the more radical, "rejectionist" elements of the Palestinian resistance to Israel. However, he has played this card with such transparent cynicism that no one any longer thinks that he really believes in the Palestinian cause. Some have argued that he dreams of creating or restoring a Greater Syria. In fact he has contrived to make Lebanon a de facto Syrian protectorate for at least the last decade, and his periodic bullying of Jordan has sometimes compelled King Hussein to toe the Syrian line in regional affairs. But we could just as well see this as old-fashioned sphere-of-interest politics, intended chiefly to secure his own position in a dangerous environment. It need not imply any grand design.

Deprived of any credible higher cause and quite devoid of personal charisma, Asad has stayed in power for more than a quarter century through extraordinary political skill and when necessary through an equally extraordinary ruthlessness. He is not called the spider of Damascus for nothing. To take only the most dramatic example, his suppression of the Islamic uprising in Hama in February 1982 drowned Syria's burgeoning Islamic movement in blood.[5] In another vein, after decades of denouncing U.S. imperialism and support for Zionism in the Middle East, he joined the U.S.-led coalition against Iraq in 1990–1991. Most recently, he has entered into direct if intermittent talks with the once-despised "Zionist entity" over the future of the Golan Heights and a possible peace treaty. These talks have gone nowhere in particular, and they may well be only a tactical diversion, but it is remarkable that they have been held at all.

Under Asad as under his predecessors, then, Syria remains a country in search of its role within the Middle East—a role that lends prestige and significance to Syria but is actually within its grasp. It no longer seems likely that this role will be defined by ideology; Baathist Pan-Arabism is exhausted, and a regime like Hafiz al-Asad's can hardly inspire a spontaneous surge of state patriotism. Apart from any long-term role within the Arab world, Syrians must worry about their immediate political future, for the Asad regime is entirely a personal enterprise. Even the Baath party, with its complex apparatus reaching into every village, is simply an extension of the president. What hope does such a system have of outliving its creator? After all, even the most solidly constructed and impersonal party machinery can vanish into smoke with astonishing rapidity, as we saw in Eastern Europe between 1989 and 1991. It is hard to think that the Syrian Baath can expect a better fate. Of all the mysteries of the Asad regime, the darkest and most opaque is surely what will happen at the hour of his death.

Whatever quandaries Syria has faced in finding its place in the Arab Nationalist and post-Nationalist eras, they fade into nothingness in comparison with Lebanon's travails.[6] From World War I until 1975, Lebanon was like nothing else in the Middle East. The country was created in its modern form by the French after World War I as part of the same package deal that produced Syria, Jordan, and Palestine. Though the new Lebanon was a very small place (some 1.2 million people in 1936, and 4,000 square miles), it encompassed almost every religious sect in the Middle East, with a slight overall Christian majority. Constitutionally, Lebanon was a parliamentary democracy with a strong president. In fact it was a system of shared power, in which the bosses of the various religious sects divided up government offices (as well as the other rewards of power) among themselves and their followers. Lebanon was in a sense the elder Mayor Richard Daley's Chicago transplanted into the Middle East, though its leaders did not get the garbage collected as efficiently as he did.

No one was entirely happy with this arrangement. As Muslims gained a larger share of the population, they felt increasingly short-changed by it. Moreover, many of them wanted to align Lebanon closely with the rising forces of Arab Nationalism. On the other side, the Christians were uneasy at best about the implications of Arab Nationalism. On balance they felt a much stronger cultural affinity for the West than for the turbulent and "backward" Arab milieu in which they were imbedded. Moreover, they had no desire to abandon the only political system in the Middle East where they had the upper hand, however tenuously. In spite of such tensions, the Lebanese system worked fairly well as long as there was a modicum of prosperity and security; it even ensured a high degree of tolerance, though not mutual esteem, among the multitude of religious groups who lived there. And by 1970 there clearly seemed to be an emerging sense of a real Lebanese patriotism that could bridge the old confessional lines.

Under the stress of the decade after 1967, however—and the stress was undeniably enormous—Lebanon turned out to be less an integrated nation-state than a coalition of jealous interest groups. A hideous civil war broke out in 1975 and took at least 150,000 lives over more than a decade of intermittent fighting.

Having no ambitions of its own, Lebanon became the target of everyone else's—Syria's drive for regional paramountcy, Iran's vision of a Shiʿite revolution, Libya's hopes of revitalizing the Pan-Arabist dream, and most of all the savage struggle between the PLO and Israel. The civil war finally sputtered out in 1989, as the country's internal and external rivals fought to utter exhaustion. In a way, things have gone back to the way they used to be. The state of Lebanon still exists within its old French-drawn borders. The Lebanese have gone back to wheeling and dealing, and there is a vast program of rebuilding amid the ruins. But Lebanon is hardly an independent country any longer; it is a quasi-protectorate of Syria. In such a climate, state patriotism can be only a frail plant. Lebanon's relationship to Arab Nationalism is full of irony. It was never really a part of that movement even at its peak, but it was dragged into the struggle over Arab Nationalism's collapse and was almost destroyed by it. In the disarray of the contemporary Arab world, it is hard to know what role the Lebanese imagine for themselves.

Jordan's place in the Arab world is also uncertain though infinitely less tragic.[7] Since World War II at least, Jordan's role has been, first, to survive and, second, to serve as a broker between conflicting agendas and ideologies within the Arab world, or between the Arab countries and the West. In a very real sense, that remains its role today. The reasons for this are grounded in the country's history, size, and demography. Jordan began its career in the early 1920s as part of the British zone of control in the partition of Greater Syria. The arid regions east of the Jordan had previously been a thinly populated frontier zone (300,000 people in 1930), attached variously to Damascus or to Palestine. The first ruler of the newly created entity, the amir Abdallah, had been a significant figure in the Arab Revolt during World War I, and he should have had solid credentials within the emerging Arab Nationalist movement. But these prospects were wrecked by the chaos in Arabia and Syria after 1918. Abdallah could only restart his career when the British created a new country for him—the Amirate of Transjordan—east of the Jordan River. He was a highly ambitious and very astute politician, but he could never escape British tutelage or the taint of being regarded as a British puppet. When he was assassinated in Jerusalem in 1951, no one thought that his little state (by then called the Hashimite Kingdom of Jordan) had any future.

The Middle East produces prophets beyond number, but they seldom hit the mark. As things have turned out, Abdallah's grandson King Hussein, who took the throne in 1953, has endured and at moments even prospered against a fantastic array of crises and enemies. In the teeth of every prediction, he has built a viable state and a considerable sense of loyalty among his people, but that is very much a personal achievement. King Hussein's achievement reflects uncommon, indeed uncanny, political skill. Even when he has committed the mortal sin of backing a loser (e.g., Nasser in 1967, Saddam Hussein in 1990–1991), he has done so with an astute calculation of the gains and losses involved in his choices. He has variously played the ardent Arab Nationalist, the staunch ally of the West, the thoughtful moderate—whatever the situation at any given moment seemed to demand. Hussein's impressive acumen is not the whole story, of course; the kingdom's survival also reflects the realities of international politics—in this case, a widely perceived need both within the Middle East and among outside powers, especially the United States, to have a stable buffer state placed between Israel, Syria, Iraq, and Saudi Arabia. As to Jordan after King Hussein, it is perhaps best not to speculate about the commitment of its people to the idea of the Hashimite Kingdom.

Ideology in Jordan tends to follow the fault line of the country's sharply divided population. This fact illustrates very neatly the limits both of Pan-Arabism and state patriotism in the modern Arab world. Even after the loss of the West Bank in 1967, a majority (some 60 percent) of Jordan's citizens are Palestinian in origin, not natives of the lands east of the Jordan River. For the most part, the Palestinians of Jordan are refugees from the wars with Israel in 1948 and 1967, and in Jordan they have regarded themselves as strangers in a strange land. They have on the whole been deeply committed to the struggle to restore their Palestinian homeland. Since this struggle could only be won with the united support of all Arabs, Arab Nationalism obviously had great appeal for them. The continuing force of these feelings exploded into full view in the fall of 1990, when the Palestinians enthusiastically backed Saddam Hussein in the hope that he would at last be the longed-for champion who could face down Israel and the United States. King Hussein had no choice but to swim with this powerful current; in effect, it was Palestinian sentiment that dictated the policy he would follow. In a very vivid way, the Gulf War demonstrated state patriotism's limited role in Jordan's political life.

Iraq, like Egypt, possesses an unmistakable geographic and historical identity of its own.[8] With the fading of the Pan-Arabist dream, it should be fertile ground for a vigorous state patriotism. Saddam Hussein's appeals to the glory of ancient Assyria and Babylon undeniably have a comic aspect, but Iraqis are well aware of the great civilizations that arose in their land and take a deep pride in them. Throughout Islamic times, moreover, Iraq was always seen as a region with a character all its own; from 762 to 1258, its metropolis of Baghdad was at least the nominal capital of a vast empire stretching from the Nile deep into Central Asia. Nor is there anything vague about Iraq's "natural frontiers"; these are quite clearly marked by the Zagros Mountains on the east, the Syrian Desert on the west, and—most important—the vast alluvial plain created by the Tigris and Euphrates rivers as they exit the mountains of southeastern Turkey.

But in spite of its geographic cohesion and ancient history, Iraq is ridden with profound and apparently unassuageable tensions; these have obviously been sharply aggravated by the Gulf War and the subsequent sanctions, but they were hardly caused by these very recent events. Iraq is split by social, ethnic, religious, and socioeconomic fault lines: Sunni versus Shiʿite, Arab versus Kurd, tribal chief versus urban merchant, nomad versus peasant. Nor did Iraq have a real history of its own during the four centuries of Ottoman rule (1534–1918), when it was divided into three major provinces, centered on Mosul, Baghdad, and Basra, respectively. In the face of these challenges, it has proved almost impossible for the governments of independent Iraq since 1921 to build a stable political order founded on the consent of the governed. Stability has indeed been achieved from time to time, not least under the Baathist regime in power since 1968, but it is a stability purchased at the cost of massive repression. This repression has been directed not only against the Kurds or (especially since 1991) the Shiʿites of the deep south but against every possible dissident as well.

Iraq's ethnic and religious divisions, together with the brutal political repression it has suffered, have done much to subvert any foundations for state patriotism there. Perhaps even more important, Iraq has tried to play the leading role in defining Arab Nationalism and has pursued the constantly changing agendas of this ideology almost since the country was established in 1920. In such a milieu, a solidly grounded state patriotism has had little chance to take root. Iraq's role within the Arab world during the two decades between the world wars was mostly one of trying to assert ideological leadership, and this effort had few practical consequences. With the bloody coup d'état of 1958, however, Iraq entered the struggle for leadership alongside, then against, Gamal Abdel Nasser—a hopeless contest. The rise of the radical nationalist Baath party in the late 1960s might have given Iraq an edge during an era (the 1970s) when radicalism seemed a rising tide in the Third World. But Iraq's opportunity to reinvigorate and lead the Pan-Arabist cause was squandered by the brutal Stalinism of Saddam Hussein and a squalid quarrel with a sister-Baathist regime in Syria. In the end, Iraqi patriotism is potentially a significant force in the country. But to become genuinely effective this patriotism will have to be ethnically and religiously far more inclusive than the doctrinaire forms of Arab Nationalism that have blighted so much of Iraq's twentieth-century history.

Saudi Arabia might seem a good candidate for an effective state nationalism or local patriotism.[9] To begin with, the kingdom was never an enthusiastic participant in the Pan-Arabist dance, although it is the oldest fully independent Arab state. Its roots lie in the late eighteenth century, and it was established in its present form by the relentless campaigns and astute diplomacy of the amir (later king) Abd al-Aziz Al Saud between 1905 and 1926. As the largest state within the ancient homeland of the Arabs, it is one of the few Arab countries whose ethnic identity is not subject to debate or self-questioning. But the official ideology of Saudi Arabia has been from the beginning, and remains today, religious rather than nationalist; the mission of the kingdom and its ruling family is to promote not Arabism but an intensely traditionalist version of Islam. Thus while Saudi

Arabia was a charter member of the Arab League and has supported many of the usual Arab causes (especially the Palestinian resistance to Israel), it has vigorously and effectively resisted schemes for a union of Arab states, especially the kind of unity proclaimed by secularist-progressive leaders. The Saudis have, however, consistently supported Islamic causes of all kinds, whether missionary activity in the Philippines, funding Islamic political and social movements in Egypt and the Sudan, or providing arms to the Afghan resistance during the 1980s. King Fahd's principal title is Khadim al-Haramayn, Servitor of the Two Holy Sanctuaries (i.e., Mecca and Medina), and that fact says all we need to know about the ideological foundations of his regime.

Saudi Arabia does not face the long-term economic crisis of Egypt or the bitter sectarian and ethnic cleavages of Iraq, but it has very distinctive and quite intractable political problems of its own. In particular, the government and indeed the whole country are in a real sense synonymous with the ruling house. From the moment of its birth, Saudi Arabia has been very much a family affair; not only the throne, but every critical ministry (e.g., Defense, Interior), every provincial governorship, and a host of other government offices, is held by a senior prince of the House of Saud. Many of the kingdom's largest economic ventures belong to one or another of the princes. The Saudi regime has made considerable, indeed remarkable, efforts to "spread the wealth," and it has created a social welfare network that compares favorably to those in the European social democracies, along with a system of subsidies to politically sensitive centers. Even so, the House of Saud's strict monopoly of political power and its refusal to permit serious public debate on major issues have created serious tensions within an increasingly educated and politically aware public. Anything that goes wrong in the country can be blamed on the House of Saud—who else is there, after all? The liberal technocrats chafe, since they are denied any independent voice in policy making and face severe restrictions on their personal freedom. On the other side of the ledger, there is now a growing body of Islamic activists (many of them professional men with advanced modern educations) who denounce the regime as not Islamic enough. In their eyes the House of Saud is ridden with corruption and is all too ready to bend Islamic precepts to fit the demands of Western governments or corporations.

In the end, it is hard to think that state patriotism is the wave of the future in the Arab world; only a few of the existing Arab countries seem the right and natural focus of ultimate political loyalty. But in spite of all the weaknesses of the existing states—and many others could be cited—they have been the sole arena of political action in the Arab world for the last two decades. Pan-Arabism has fleeting moments of life—for example, the sporadic efforts by Muammar Qaddafi of Libya to construct two- or three-state federations, presumably as a step toward the ultimate goal of a unified Arab nation-state. But these federations have proved far more ephemeral than the United Arab Republic; only a few super-experts can recall that they ever existed even on paper. The only two exceptions—and in different ways each of them proves the rule—have been the wealthy but tiny United Arab Emirates in the Persian Gulf (dating back to 1969) and the more recent union of North and South Yemen (1990), which remains a tension-filled though apparently functional marriage.[10]

The most likely successor to Pan-Arabism may be the Islamic movement, which has managed to combine a universalist program with local tactics in a very effective way. The burgeoning Islamic groups espouse political and social values that are universal in principle. They have grown up within particular countries, however, and for the most part they aim only to establish an Islamic order within those countries. Very few look toward a dissolution and transformation of the present state system in the Arab world. Even the Ayatollah Khomeini envisioned a vast Islamic alliance, not a unified Islamic state. And in fact, as several commentators have shown, his own version of revolutionary Islam was so marked by Shiʿite symbols and Iranian culture that it was almost unexportable to Sunni countries.[11]

It is certainly true that in an era when Islam seems to possess enormous power to move and inspire, we could envision a situation in which Islamic movements seize power in two or three major countries—for example, Egypt and Algeria—and consequently become highly influential in the policy making of several others. This fact would certainly transform the international environment of the region, but there is no reason to think that it would reshape the existing state system in any significant way. Such an event might even harden the existing borders, for each of the various Islamist movements seems to be strongly rooted in its own local soil, to whatever degree it may be in contact with other movements or be (as with Hizbollah in Lebanon) a recipient of external financial and political support.

But all this is mere speculation, and perhaps we should close by recognizing that in some very important ways Pan-Arabism is not dead. On the contrary, it is a living and vital force. Educated Arabs (along with many from the lower strata of society) travel, work, and study widely throughout the Arab world. In so doing they have developed a spoken *koiné* that effectively bridges dialect differences, they watch Egyptian situation comedies on television, and they are aware of events everywhere among the Arabs. They retain and relish their regional differences—much like Southerners and New Yorkers—but in many ways they have indeed become one people with an acute sense of their peculiar identity. This shows up in many forms, but perhaps most characteristically in the way Arabs refer to one another as members of a family: the various Arab states are "sisters," the Arab people(s) are "brothers" to one another. Like many families, they quarrel incessantly and even violently, but against the outside world they tend to band together. When the chips are down, they believe deeply that they should support and defend one another. Such kinship language sounds odd in American and European politics, but it is an everyday part of Arab political speech. Moreover, this political kinship is taken seriously: Arabs agonized over Iraq's rape of its sister Kuwait and over the betrayal of the "family" involved in siding with outsiders (namely, the United States, Britain, and France) against one of their own, however brutal and egregious his behavior, however much he had violated the honor and integrity of the family. This deep-seated sense of Arab identity is almost certain to have political consequences. We cannot yet discern what form these will take, or what circumstances will call them forth. It is hard to imagine that the visionary Pan-Arabism of Nasser or the early Baath will ever reemerge as a serious political option, but that is not the only form in which nationalism may manifest itself or become a real force in Middle Eastern affairs.

Still, a cultural Pan-Arabism of the sort that now exists (and even flourishes) does not provide a framework for political action that goes beyond the narrow confines of state nationalism and presents a vision of a "greater destiny" or "higher good." The search among Arab politicians and intellectuals for such a framework has so far drawn a blank. If this is so, the crazy quilt of states that came into being as part of the process of colonization and decolonization must continue to provide not only the framework but also the sustenance for political life in the Arab world. To discover meaning and purpose and intellectual energy in that framework is the challenge confronting those who hope to lead the Arab world.

This article is reprinted from R. Stephen Humphreys, *Between Memory and Desire. The Middle East in a Troubled Age* (Berkeley and Los Angeles: 1999), 60–82.

NOTES

1. Arab Nationalism has many synonyms in both Arabic and English; the most common are "Arabism" (Ar., *'uruba*) and "Pan-Arabism," and I will use both terms in this chapter. There have been many varieties of Arab Nationalism over the century of its existence; they differ both as to the region that they include within the Arab homeland and as to the characteristics (language, history, race, etc.) by which they define membership in the Arab nation. Pan-Arabism is that form of Arab Nationalism which seeks to unite all the Arabic-speaking peoples from Morocco to Iraq and Oman within a single country; in the Pan-Arabist perspective, all these peoples are fundamentally and eternally one in language, race, culture, and history, in spite of regional differences between them. The best presentation of the intellectual and political milieu in which Arab Nationalism developed remains Albert Hourani's classic *Arabic Thought in the Liberal Age, 1798–1939* (London: Oxford University Press, 1962), esp. chap. 11.

2. Malcolm Kerr, *The Arab Cold War: Gamal 'Abd al-Nasir and His Rivals, 1958–1970* (orig. pub. 1965; rev. ed., New York: Oxford University Press, 1971).

3. Sati' al-Husri has been studied by William Cleveland, *The Making of an Arab Nationalist: Ottomanism and Arabism in the Life and Thought of Sati' al-Husri* (Princeton: Princeton University Press, 1971).

4. The literature on Syria is not large, but there are a few items of high quality. The French Mandate (1920–1946) is exhaustively treated in Philip Khoury, *Syria and the French Mandate: The Politics of Arab Nationalism, 1928–1945* (Princeton: Princeton University Press, 1987). Shorter, more readable, and still valuable in spite of its age is A. H. Hourani, *Syria and Lebanon: A Political Essay* (London: Oxford University Press, 1946). The period between World War II and the formation of the United Arab Republic has been brilliantly recorded by Patrick Seale, *The Struggle for Syria: A Study of Post-War Arab Politics, 1945–1958* (London: Oxford University Press, 1965). The Baathist era (since 1961) is discussed in a concise but penetrating study by Nikolaos Van Dam, *The Struggle for Power in Syria: Politics and Society under Asad and the Ba'th Party* (London: I. B. Tauris, 1996). Patrick Seale, *Asad of Syria: The Struggle for the Middle East* (Berkeley and Los Angeles: University of California Press, 1988), is important because of the author's unrivaled access to Asad while writing it but is otherwise not on the same level as his earlier book.

5. See the vivid account in Friedman, *From Beirut to Jerusalem*, chap. 4, "Hama Rules," 76–105.

6. Among many general works on Lebanon, see Kamal Salibi, *A House of Many Mansions: The History of Lebanon Reconsidered* (Berkeley and Los Angeles: University of California Press, 1988), a series of essays on crucial problems in Lebanese history. A rather jaundiced but perceptive construction of the old order in its last years is Michael Gilsenan, *Lords of the Lebanese Marches: Violence and Narrative in an Arab Society* (Berkeley and Los Angeles: University of California Press, 1996). A well-balanced but passionless survey of the civil war is Itamar Rabinovich, *The War for Lebanon, 1970–1985*, rev. ed. (Ithaca, N.Y.: Cornell University Press, 1985). A substantial journalistic account of the early 1980s is given in Friedman, *From Beirut to Jerusalem* (1989).

7. The origins of Jordan are traced in Mary C. Wilson, *King Abdullah, Britain, and the Making of Jordan* (Cambridge: Cambridge University Press, 1987). For Jordan since independence, see Kamal Salibi, *The Modern History of Jordan* (London: I.B. Tauris, 1993).

8. Phebe Marr, *The Modern History of Iraq* (Boulder, Colo.: Westview Press, 1985), is a detailed and reliable survey of the country's twentieth-century history. Saddam Hussein's Iraq is not an easy place to study. The silence was broken by an Iraqi expatriate intellectual, Kanan Makiya (writing under the pseudonym Samir al-Khalil), *Republic of Fear: The Politics of Modern Iraq* (Berkeley and Los Angeles: University of California Press, 1989). His second book, *Cruelty and Silence* (New York: W. W. Norton, 1993), has a broader agenda than Iraq but is full of valuable information about the brutal anti-Kurdish campaigns in 1988 and the Shiʿite uprisings after the Gulf War.

9. It is not easy to carry out research in Saudi Arabia, and so serious books on the country are few. On its origins, see Joseph Kostiner, *The Making of Saudi Arabia, 1916–1936* (1993). The enormous changes undergone by the country since King Faysal took the throne in 1964 must be pieced together from a variety of sources; most recently, see the useful survey of David E. Long, *The Kingdom of Saudi Arabia* (Gainesville: University Press of Florida, 1997). Issued under official auspices, William Facey, gen. ed., *The Kingdom of Saudi Arabia* (London: Stacey International; many editions since 1977), has valuable information and contributions from a number of excellent scholars, though of course it must be used critically.

10. There is now a considerable body of good work on modern Yemen, though most of it is formidably academic. In any case, the old slur about "rushing headlong into the fourteenth century" is certainly no longer applicable, if it ever was. On the 1977 elections in unified Yemen, see William A. Rugh, "A (Successful) Test of Democracy in Yemen," *Christian Science Monitor*, May 28, 1997, 19.

11. Marvin Zonis and Daniel Brumberg, *Khomeini: the Islamic Republic of Iran, and the Arab World*, Middle East Papers, no. 5 (Cambridge: Center for Middle Eastern Studies, Harvard University, 1987).

Nasser 56/Cairo 96

Reimaging Egypt's Lost Community

JOEL GORDON

In fall 1996 Egyptians lined up in record numbers—at seventeen theaters in Cairo alone—to see not the latest 'Adil Imam comedy, Nadia al-Guindi potboiler, or foreign thriller but a meticulously researched and restaged treatment of the 1956 Suez crisis, the nationalization of the Suez Canal Company by the relatively young Nasser regime and the subsequent Tripartite Aggression that did so much to put Gamal Abdel Nasser and his comrades on the world map. *Nasser 56* has already earned a place in Egyptian cinema history; it has also rallied, unnerved, and astonished people on all sides of an ongoing debate over the legacy of Nasser's eighteen-year rule. Ultimately, it will play a major role in the shaping of public memory of the man who dominates contemporary Egyptian history, of a social revolution that is recalled with increasing fondness, and of an era of cultural production that even cynics concede was golden.

Public memory, as the American historian John Bodnar suggests, "is a body of beliefs and ideas about the past that help a public or society understand both its past and present, and by implication its future." "The major focus of this communicative and cognitive process," he continues, "is not the past, however, but serious matters in the present such as the nature of power and the question of loyalty to both official and vernacular cultures" (1992, 15). Memory, the oral historian Alessandro Portelli reminds us, "is not a passive depository of facts, but an active process of creation of meanings" (1991, 52). Similarly, Robert McGlone, writing about memories of John Brown's raid on Harper's Ferry, describes the process of recall as "rescripting... not a deliberate rewriting of the past, but a transformation in the controlling expectations and logic of life situations [that] refocuses an individual's self-schema.... Rescripting adds or takes away information to make a life story coherent and believable at a particular time" (1989, 1182–83). How might this apply to the scripting of a new text about Nasser and its imaging on celluloid? Historical films raise questions about "history as a mode of knowledge, of historical accuracy, of memory and desire. . . . More than other genres, the historical film evokes a sense of the 'grand,' the visually enthralling, the huge canvass to portray the sweep of events that the past as completed action allows" (Chakravarty 1993, 183). No less for the viewers than for the filmmakers, we might add. So why Nasser? Why this particular story? How have the filmmakers, in this case scenarist, star, and director, chosen to bring the script to life? And why has the enthusiastic popular response both pleased and caused disquiet in official circles, including those that backed and promoted the project?

"ONE HUNDRED DAYS THAT CHANGED THE WORLD"

Nasser 56 is the brainchild of the veteran scenarist Mahfuz 'Abd al-Rahman in collaboration with Egypt's leading dramatic film star, Ahmad Zaki, who plays Nasser, and the veteran television director Muhammad Fadil. Originally intended as one of a series of hour-long dramatic biographies of Egyptian luminaries for television, each figure to be played by Zaki, the project blossomed into a full-length feature film on a grand scale.[1] Produced by the state-owned Egyptian Radio and Television Union (ERTU), the film was three years in the making, from initial conception to preview release in July 1995. Key portions were shot on brand-new outdoor sets at the 6 October Media Production City, the $300 million project designed to reinvigorate the flagging Egyptian film industry and maintain Cairo's virtual monopoly on Arab television production (Khalil 1996a; Saad 1996). The film then sat another full year, "frozen" is the word used by its creators, before its release in early August 1996.

Nasser 56, trumpets its ad, covers "one hundred days that changed the world." The actual span is 106 days, from June 18, 1956, Evacuation Day, until November 2, several days after the outbreak of war. The film opens with Nasser taking down the Union Jack; it closes with a famous speech from the minbar of al-Azhar Mosque. As bombs fall around Cairo, Nasser proclaims that Egypt will fight on and never surrender. Much of the action focuses on political deliberation among Egypt's leadership, formulation and implementation of the secret plan to secure the canal as Nasser addressed the nation from Alexandria on the night of July 26, and the subsequent political maneuvering of Nasser and his colleagues to defuse a crisis they cannot believe is escalating. Other well-known historical faces appear in subsidiary roles, among them military comrades Anwar Sadat, 'Abd al-Hakim 'Amr, Salah Salim, Zakariya Muhyi al-Din, 'Abd al-Latif al-Baghdadi, and Sami Sharaf and civilian associates Fathi Radwan and Mahmud Fawzi. More prominent supporting figures, such as the chief canal engineer, Mahmud Yunis, and his colleagues, are less familiar to many Egyptian viewers. There are no Egyptian villains in the piece, save for a small, rather pathetic group of old-regimistes who petition Nasser to resign in the wake of the tripartite attack.

The film was shot in black and white to effect a newsreel feel. In the opening scene the camera shoots Ahmad Zaki from a distance, a deliberate strategy to draw the audience, especially elders, into accepting an actor—and such a well-known face—as Nasser. Other characters are played by less familiar, younger actors, closer in age to their characters, also a deliberate move to keep the film from becoming a parade of stars.[2] Documentary footage of world leaders and combat punctuate this and provide broader context for the story line. The only world leaders to appear in the scenario are Nehru and Australian Prime Minister Menzies, played by opera star and character actor Hassan Kami, Egypt's master of foreign accents.[3] The black-and-white film also touches directly on a national bias for the classics, a nostalgia for black and white, from the era before color became the norm in the early seventies.[4]

Historical accuracy aside—and the debate was quickly engaged on levels great and small—the film's success rests ultimately on popular reaction to the characterization of Nasser. Ahmad Zaki has by all accounts, and with only a minimum of makeup to fill out his jaws and recede his hairline, turned in a bravura performance that captures Nasser's personality, demeanor, speech patterns, and, ultimately, charisma. This is important, because for the generations born after Nasser's death in September 1970, Zaki will, for better or worse, come to personify his subject. The filmmakers, well aware of the burden on their shoulders, paid meticulous attention to detail, shooting on location whenever possible, attempting to re-create sets based on photographic evidence, and endeavoring to balance conflicting memories about the most prosaic specifics: the physical layout of the Nasser household or the brand of cigarettes Nasser chain-smoked.

The casting of Ahmad Zaki was both a foregone conclusion, because of his personal role in promoting the project, and a natural selection. Zaki has been Egypt's premier dramatic actor since the late 1980s. Perhaps too often typecast in recent years as the poor boy trying to infiltrate the upper strata or as the social rebel, and recently reduced to plot-weak action films, he remains a powerful screen presence, a major box office draw, and occasionally a trendsetter.[5] He is also dark, rare for an Egyptian leading man (or woman), probably the darkest ever. He can, and easily does, approximate Nasser's *sa'idi* (Upper Egyptian) features. The rest is pure acting, and Zaki reportedly threw himself into the project and character, taking on Nasser's persona on and off camera.

Regardless of critical or popular reaction, the film will remain a milestone in Egyptian and Arab cinema history. It is the first film to dramatize the role of any contemporary Arab leader—with apologies to Youssef Chahine's 1963 rewriting of the Crusades, *al-Nasir Salah al-Din* (Saladin the Victorious), which portrayed the Kurdish Saladin as a pan-Arab champion, clearly alluding to Nasser—and the first Egyptian film to treat such a significant historical period in anything but caricature. A handful of Egyptian feature films in the mid- to late 1950s dramatized the Suez conflict, some as backdrop, several directly. War stories, focused on steadfast soldiers and civilians, they depicted the struggle against traitors at home—a frequent invective in early Nasserist rhetoric—as well as imperialism (Ramzi 1984).[6] *Nasser 56* decidedly has a point of view. It is a nationalist film—one Egyptian writer has called it a "quiet nationalism" (Ken Cuno, pers. com. April 1997)—but not a propaganda film in the classic sense. The target is no longer imperialism and Egyptian traitors but rather a present that has become detached from the moving spirit of a bygone era. If not a clarion call to restore that spirit, *Nasser 56* is certainly a lens through which to reimage and reassess that which has been lost.

"A MAN OF SIMPLE DREAMS"

The most critically acclaimed scenes are those that depict Nasser interacting with common Egyptians, praying in public, or at home with his family, an overworked father trying to balance politics with his children's desire for a beach vacation. In an early scene Nasser converses with a canal worker who has been sacked by European overseers, and is moved by the injustice of his plight. Up late in his study, he answers the telephone three times after midnight, only to find on the other end a peasant woman newly arrived from the village, looking for her son. The third time, flustered by her unwillingness to accept that she has not reached Hagg Madbuli, Nasser identifies himself: "I am Gamal Abdel Nasser."[7] Silence, then: "God save you, my son. [*Rabbina yansarak, ya ibni*]" ('Abd al-Rahman 1996, 32). Almost everyone's favorite scene is stolen by the veteran actress Amina Rizq, who has been playing tradition-bound matriarchs for the past forty years.[8] Here she plays a persistent peasant woman who demands and is allowed to meet the president. Once inside she relates the story of her grandfather, a peasant killed digging the canal, and presents Nasser with the man's robe, a family heirloom. "When I heard you on the radio," she asserts, "I said, by God, Umm Mustafa, this Gamal has avenged you and eased our hearts; so I am giving you this robe because you are most deserving of it" (1996, 119–20).

These scenes, products of the screenwriter's creative imagination, encapsulate persistent popular memories of Nasser as populist hero, the man of the people. Allen Douglas and Fadwa Malti-Douglas, analyzing a comic-strip biography of Nasser that appeared several years after his death, note:

> Nasser's communion with his people is so close that he shares their tragedies as well as their triumphs. He does not stand above them as all-knowing or all wise. The Egyptian leader's closeness to the people is further reflected in the frequent use of his first name without titles or appellatives, both by the narrator and by the people. (1994, 41)

They could easily be writing a contemporary script for formal and informal discussions of Nasser's personality and legacy with Egyptians from all walks of life.

Egyptians who lived the Nasser years, including many who spent time out of favor and in prison (although less so those who suffered economic dislocation), still speak with exceptional warmth about Nasser. Grand politics, successes and terrible failures aside, they recount seeing him walking the streets or driving unguarded in his car. They rarely, if ever, stopped to greet him, but, more important to their personal rescripting, feel they could have. In much the same fashion, Mahfuz ʻAbd al-Rahman has described Nasser as "a man of the utmost simplicity and modesty, . . . a man of simple dreams," for whom "the pleasures of life consisted of olives and cheese, going to the cinema, listening to Umm Kulthum" (1996, 6–7), a man who "could not comprehend a home with two bathrooms," let alone a private pool (pers. com.). In interviews Ahmad Zaki, whose career blossomed at the tail end of the 1960s, has spoken of Nasser as a father figure (Ramadan 1995).

The very depiction of Nasser, albeit imaged as Ahmad Zaki, startles. For nearly two decades his likeness was everywhere, and he remains the symbol of the iconized Arab ruler (Ossman 1994, 3). But those images came down in rapid succession following Sadat's ascension to power. Where they could not come down, as at the rarely visited monument to Soviet-Egyptian friendship at the Aswan High Dam, Nasser's profile was all but hidden by a superimposed image of the inheritor. Private establishments still display personal icons, and one bust remains in an arcade in downtown Cairo. Once the heart of the cosmopolitan city, the area is now primarily shopping turf for the lower middle class, and the arcade is particularly rich in its selection of conservative headwear for women. There is no designated monument to Egypt's most significant ruler of this century, no stadium, airport, public building, or major thoroughfare that bears his name (a Nile-side boulevard running through Imbaba officially does, but it is universally referred to as Nile Street). Nasser's tomb, unlike Sadat's, is not visited in any official commemorative capacity. There is a Nasser subway stop, but it is adjacent to a fading city center, one that is not heavily used.[9]

Nasser's name still evokes great passion, and approbation is by no means universal or unequivocal. Like any regime seeking to foment and sustain a revolution, the Nasserist state razed before building, disrupted lives and careers of opponents, and devoured some of its own. The legacies of Nasserism remain multiple and will be weighed differently by different generations, proponents of different political and social trends, sons and daughters of different social classes. Nasserism is held accountable by some for virtually every social ill facing the nation, from traffic snarls and pedestrian anarchy to the fall of social graces. Nasser has been accounted a traitor by Islamists, a prisoner of his class by leftists, a tinhorn tyrant by scions of the old parties and aristocracy.

The Nasserist political experiment is widely accepted to have failed in its stated goal of restoring a "sound" democracy. Arab Socialism, the economic strategy that produced nationalization and the creation of a vast public sector, will continue to polarize Egyptians, although the debate may increasingly turn on intentions versus consequences.[10] Nasserist foreign policy, Arabism and non-alignment, the conflict with royalist neighbors and Israel, also polarizes, and the generation that lived the period will always live in the shadows of Yemen and June 1967.

As the era grows more distant, historical perspective may help to contextualize the logic of certain directions and policies. Greater historical focus has already produced notable changes in the ways in which Nasserism has been envisioned—and debated—in the quarter century since Nasser's death. Yet, contrary to Bodnar's (1992, 13–19) thesis—which may well hold for his American context—in which vernacular traditions gradually become subsumed into an official text, in Egypt, and presumably in other countries where an official discourse quickly and effectively silenced all others, the process seems to be going in the opposite direction. Vernacular discourses, allowed a voice after two decades, quickly drowned out the official text, leaving public memory of Nasserism very much up for grabs.

Nostalgia in Egypt today is a complex phenomenon. The majority of the population was born after 1967, and many after Sadat's assassination in 1981. Less than Nasser's shadow, they have grown up in a society in which popular memory is dizzyingly multivocal. In the past two decades, during which Egyptians have been free to openly debate their history, vernacular antihistories related by representatives (some self-styled) of old-regime parties, royalists, leftist movements, and the Muslim Brothers have emerged from the underground to become standard counterorthodoxies to the official Nasserist account of the revolution. Those affiliated with the Sadat regime comprise another orthodoxy caught between competing prior legacies. The Nasserist response, official and not, has become just another vernacular tradition competing for public memory.

Ten-year anniversaries, by their very nature as discrete constructs to mark and evaluate the passage of time, provide a convenient referent. In July 1972 the country still grieved Nasser's passing yet applauded Sadat's dismantling of the state security apparatus, the release and welcome home of political prisoners and exiles, and the purging and incarceration of those who had dominated the "centers of power" (*marakiz al-quwwa*). Ten years later, when the revolution turned thirty, Egypt again faced a change in leadership, power having been transferred suddenly in a moment of national crisis. A new regime now curried favor by opening political prison doors, by prosecuting a new cohort of power abusers, and by lending freer rein to opposition voices to speak, write, and ultimately participate in government. One consequence was a frank and multi-voiced discussion of the political origins of the Nasser revolution, before and particularly after the July coup. The focus remained political, the general assessment of Nasserism critical, intensified by recollections of a period, 1952–55, when the officers squandered much of the goodwill that greeted their takeover and imposed their revolution by coercion more than charisma (Gordon 1992).

As the revolution turned forty, a pronounced shift in emphasis was under way. The exploration ten years earlier into political failure had been fueled by hopes of a truly broadened liberalism. By the early 1990s much of that hope had turned cynical. To a society riven by malaise, and at times and in certain places by interconfessional strife, Nasserism has increasingly come to represent an era of hope, unity, national purpose, social stability, and achievement. This was reflected in sentiments voiced on the street as well as in the press, official and opposition, where a growing number of Egyptians recalled a society in which there was a shared sense of community in which common, enlightened aims predominated and in which religion did not create barriers (Gordon 1997b).

Underscoring this nostalgia, and recalled increasingly by Egyptians, are recollections of a golden age of popular culture. The Nasserist state promoted and subsidized cultural production on many levels: classical Western dance and music, folklore, history, cinema, theater, radio and television drama, fiction, poetry, comedy, the fine arts. In retrospect much of it may have been hackneyed, too ideologically grounded, too often in the hands of bureaucrats rather than creative artists, some of whom left the country. Yet such assessments beg the issue of nostalgia. The faces and voices of popular movie stars and singers from the 1950s and 1960s—Fatin Hamama, ʿAbd al-Halim Hafiz, Rushdi Abaza, Shadiya—have become deified. Film classics by Salah Abu Sayf, Kamal al-Shaykh, or Barakat—before and after nationalization—and even the B-films of Niyazi Mustafa and Hilmi Rafla will never be equaled.[11] Nor will the lyrics of Salah Jahin, Ahmad Shafiq Kamil, and ʿAbd al-Rahman al-ʿAbnudi, paired with tunes by Kamal al-Tawil, Muhammad al-Muji, and Baligh Hamdi. These sentiments are echoed even by many who are otherwise highly critical of Nasserism and work to undo its economic and political legacies.[12]

The author of *Nasser 56* is quick to assert that he never has been a Nasserist. A secondary-school student with leftist links in 1952, he mistrusted the officers' motives and demonstrated against the regime. He never joined the party in any of its guises, even though he worked for the state media, and remains critical of the political order Nasserism fostered. Yet, like most of his generation, ʿAbd al-Rahman was consumed with a desire for social justice and a dream of Arab unity—and was captivated by Nasser's charisma. He admits to being dazzled by his subject in ways unfamiliar to him:

> I have written about dozens of historical figures from ʿAmru al-Qays to Baybars, from Qutuz to al-Mutanabbi and Sulayman al-Halabi. In drawing close to each of these characters I have always entered into a dispute with

> them, primarily because we are bound by our own era and circumstances . . . What is strange is that when I wrote about Gamal Abdel Nasser the opposite occurred. . . . [I]t was when I tried to come to know Gamal Abdel Nasser as a person that I became so moved. It was not the oft-told stories that affected me so much as the little tangibles. (1996, 6–7)

Implicit in the family scenes, the images of simplicity, Nasser's meals of cheese and olives or Mahmud Yunis sleeping on his office floor, the scenarist seeks to recapture and reimpart a sense of what Egypt was and has lost.

Mahfuz ʿAbd al-Rahman, like others of his generation, those who came of age under Nasserism, is rescripting the period with a focus on an enlightened community rooted in twin notions of progress and independence. His other great project in recent years has been a major revision of Khedive Ismail (1865–79), through the vehicle of a television serial that has aired over three Ramadan seasons, the prime month of television viewing (Abu-Lughod 1993b; Gordon 1997a). *Bawwabat al-Halawani* (Halawani's Gate) spins a tale of court intrigue that revolves around the romance between the musician ʿAbduh al-Hamuli and his protégée Almaz, a poor girl taken from her parents and brought up in royal circles. But the backdrop is Ismail's desire to modernize his country, the financial and political costs incurred, and, ultimately, the Suez Canal. Dismissed by much of Western scholarship and Nasser-era history as a foolish spendthrift who, entranced by Westernization, broke the state, Ismail emerges under ʿAbd al-Rahman's pen as a Renaissance man, a prisoner not of false illusions but of an international power structure that will ultimately not permit an independent Egypt.[13] In many ways the two projects, Nasser and Ismail, go hand in hand. Whatever their failings and failures, both leaders promoted cultural enrichment as a means toward liberation, and both ultimately confronted forces larger than they or Egypt.

Both projects also promote a paradigm that the state, for slightly different reasons—and obviously with less comfort in the case of Nasser—finds acceptable and beneficial in its confrontation with its most powerful vernacular challenge, Islamism. Egyptian television has always served to "produce a national community" (Abu-Lughod 1993b, 494). Yet, as Lila Abulughod and others have noted, in recent years television serials (and the cinema) have become rostrums in "the most pressing political contest in Egypt . . . the contest over the place of Islam in social and political life" (1993b, 494). Long ignored, strikingly absent from drama that purportedly depicted contemporary society, Islamist characters have become almost stock figures in television serials and the subject of one major motion picture, *Al-Irhabi* (The Terrorist; Jalal 1994; see Armbrust 1995). Always militant—and misguided—they generally meet unhappy ends at the hands of their "brothers" after recognizing the error of their ways.[14]

ʿAbd al-Rahman's reexamination of the past has always been a personal search for the drama inherent in the historical moment (ʿAbd al-Rahman (1991).

His work has spanned time and place, from early Islamic Iraq to modern Egypt. For him the dramatist has freedom to explore questions the historian cannot, but the dramatist must be bound by the historian's reliance on evidence. He is an indefatigable researcher who has battled both stolid academics, wary of the writer's craft, and, at times, popular historical and literary wisdom, against which his scripts have rubbed. ʿAbd al-Rahman's favorite anecdote involves a particularly obdurate actor who, protective of his good-guy popular image, refused to play a brother of the legendary Arab hero ʿAntar ibn Shadad, even though the script, which he had not read, revised the role, portraying the brother in a much more sympathetic light.

At the same time, like others who maintain intellectual independence yet work in or for the state-run media, ʿAbd al-Rahman participates in "a shared discourse about nationhood and citizenship" (Abu-Lughod 1993b, 494) and thus represents at once a personal and quasi-official voice. To champion Ismail is, in today's discourse, to counter the Islamist claim to authenticity, one that would view Ismail's Westernization as anathema. Likewise, to script Nasser at Suez, to depict such a powerful moment of national unity, serves, among other things, to counter social trends that are nationally divisive, even "un-Egyptian." It is notable that the original cast of characters out of which the Nasser film emerged included products and leading champions of Westernization: Rifaʿ al-Tahtawi, ʿAli Mubarak, and Taha Husayn.

This is not to suggest that state production officials who backed the project, or the creators, envisioned it consciously as a weapon in the battle against Islamism. At the same time, the green light to make a film about Nasser, and one of such scale, could not have been given without serious consideration. Support for the film clearly represented a gamble—that viewers would rally around the moment, rather than the figure, and that the moment, one of national unity in the face of specific historical foreign aggression, would not transcend historical time/place to mirror more recent national struggles with foreign creditors (World Bank, International Monetary Fund), struggles in which the government in its drive to privatize the economy is often portrayed as serving personal and foreign interests. What government officials obviously did not bank on was the degree to which the film, by so powerfully imaging the crisis, the personalities, the national moment, would underscore present-day malaise and popular perceptions of their own inadequacies—and, ultimately, the degree to which the film would resurrect the image of its hero.

"NASSER! NASSER!"

The spirit of the film, a labor of love for its creators, proved infectious to those who encountered its images, even in production. The author has recounted with impish delight how a staged workers' rally on a studio set turned real. A crowd of extras, all workers hired for the occasion—cynics will note the irony—caught sight of Ahmad Zaki and, unrehearsed, began chanting "Nasser! Nasser!" Zaki, who immersed himself in Nasser's character while on the set, spontaneously began orating in character, and the workers responded with greater vigor. Their ardor fueled Zaki's performance, and performance quickly melded into reality. The assistant director, unprepared for a sound take, shouted for a cut, but the director, Muhammad Fadil, intervened and ordered the cameras to keep rolling.

The response to the film's preview, before an invitation-only audience at the opening of the Cairo Television Festival in July 1995, provided another occasion for a spontaneous rally.[15] According to observers, people in the audience applauded, shouted encouragement, and wept openly. The inclusion of several anthems from the Suez crisis, some not heard in nearly a quarter century, punctuated the response. "The day before yesterday I saw *Nasser 56*, and my eyes filled with tears to see Ahmad Zaki embody the character of the late leader who made such great sacrifices for the sake of our national honor," wrote one attendee (Mustafa Bakri 1995).[16] Mahfuz ʿAbd al-Rahman recalls how a young man embraced him and Zaki a day after the preview and announced that he had now fulfilled his dream of meeting Nasser.

Such demonstrations before and after the preview may have given the government cause to rethink its promotion of the film. Critics lavished praise on Information Minister Safwat al-Sharif and ERTU Production Sector chief Mamduh al-Laythi and encouraged them "to undertake similar nationalist projects that reflect shining moments in Egypt's history" (Mahmud Bakri 1995). Then, suddenly, the film was put on ice, its scheduled theater release delayed indefinitely. No one offered a definitive reason. Official circles noted that final sound and print work was under way abroad. Skeptics suggested the film had been received too well, that the outpouring of emotion was not appreciated in the state's upper echelons, especially with parliamentary elections upcoming. Questions of video recording (and pirating), foreign rights, and television and satellite access complicated the matter. The Arab world was abuzz with anticipation. Syria and Libya supposedly offered to buy rights to air the film; so, according to the rumor mill, had the Saudis, but with ulterior motives.

A stalling game ensued that effectively delayed release for a full year. Cynics offered the following scenario: the fall 1995 election season was deemed inappropriate, then came Ramadan, when theaters traditionally do poorest, then the postholiday season of popular comedy-adventure blockbusters. The film did not seem to fit the calendar. In seeming incongruity with official desires to deflate, if not suppress, the film, teasers remained. A marquee arch on Gezira Island constructed before the 1995 Television Festival and left in place until the following summer featured a prominent photograph of Zaki/Nasser among other favorite productions. So did a display outside the Radio and Television Building. If those displays reached a limited audience, discerning eyes could not help but notice a final dramatic image of Zaki/Nasser on the promotional leader that identified 1995 ERTU television productions.

Ironically, the film's opening, days after the fortieth anniversary of the Suez Canal nationalization, proved far more potent than an earlier release might have been. For the great majority of adult Egyptians who lived it or were raised in its wake, the Suez crisis represents the ultimate moment of national pride, purpose, and unity. Two other historical moments in this century, pinnacles of contested political legacies, rank closely: the 1919 Revolution and the 1973 October War. Neither is as central to the historical experience or is embedded in the consciousness of Egyptians in quite the same way, in large part because the canal had been for nearly a century the key symbol of national humiliation at foreign hands. "To my generation the Suez Canal was the core of Egyptian politics," explains Mahfuz 'Abd al-Rahman.[17] When he set out to dramatize the Nasser years, 'Abd al-Rahman deliberately chose the Suez crisis because it was the one period about which there is little, if any, dispute and because it was with Suez that Nasser's star rose. Suez occurred after the disappointments of the liberal era, amid the confused early years of military rule. Nationalization and the subsequent Tripartite Aggression lodged Nasser in people's hearts and ushered in an era of regional dominance that, however flawed in retrospect, has never been recaptured. In unguarded moments even the sons and daughters of discarded pashas—no doubt Muslim Brothers as well—will admit that they stood in the streets weeping, cheering, and shouting acclaim for nationalization.

The Suez anniversary prompted a far broader retrospective for Nasser and Nasserism than any other anniversary in recent years, and certainly more than the fortieth anniversary of the revolution in 1992. Revolution Day has lost most of its meaning to the average Egyptian. It is a day off for government workers. The president addresses the nation with a text that changes little from year to year. One of the national television channels traditionally airs an afternoon matinee, one of several classic stories of evil pashas produced in the years after the revolution (*Rudd qalbi* [Return My Heart], Dhulfiqar 1957b, based on Yusufal-Siba'i's epic novel, has been the favorite). Sadat, once he felt secure in power, attempted to camouflage the revolution's anniversary behind that of Egyptian television, aired first on Revolution Day in 1960. Under Hosni Mubarak the state still acknowledges its kinship to the broad goals of the July revolution (even as it continues to dismantle fundamental pillars of its social-reform legacy in a drive to privatize the economy). But forty years later the progenitor remained largely ignored.

In 1996, however, the combined July anniversaries of revolution and nationalization inspired far greater coverage. Opposition papers sympathetic to Nasser's memory, even the Liberal party's *al-Ahrar* (July 22), published larger-than-usual special editions. The July 22 issue of *al-Hilal*, the venerable journal of popular literature and philosophy, posed the question, "What has happened to Egyptians, 1956–1996?" *Ruz al-Yusuf*, the widely read weekly of politics and the arts, abandoned its traditional "Where Are They Now?" July 23 format and asked three leading scenarists, including ʿAbd al-Rahman, to script "What If [the Free Officers coup had failed]?" Reflecting Egypt's current passion for historicals, the editors noted wryly that "writers' imaginings are worth far more than historians' truths."[18] Sawt al-ʿArab (Voice of the Arabs), the radio station most associated with Nasserism, broadcast a two-hour special on the Suez Canal, "Hadduta Misriyya" (An Egyptian Tale), that included interviews and nationalist songs. Television hired old documentary footage with nationalist songs in the background.

In addition to the celebratory atmosphere surrounding the Suez anniversary, the state has also recently decided that the time has come to participate in the shaping of public memory of Nasserism. In 1992 the government sanctioned formation of the Nasserist Arab Democratic party. By its very presence, the party has restored quasi-official legitimacy to the use of Nasser's image as political icon.[19] But the state no longer seems to be willing to consign Nasser to the Nasserists. Long-range plans are under way for a museum to be housed in the offices of the Revolutionary Command Council, a former royal rest house on the southern tip of Gezira Island Khalil 1996b; Abu al-Fath 1996). Music, too, has been appropriated: when Arab leaders gathered in Cairo in June 1996 to consider implications of a newly elected Israeli government, the theme song chosen by state-run media was "al-Watan al-Akbar" (The Greater Nation), a stirring anthem to Egyptian-Syrian unity composed by Muhammad ʿAbd al-Wahhab and Ahmad Shafiq Kamil in 1958. For Revolution Day 1996, television stations hired five movies over two days, four during prime time. The proliferation of regional broadcast in recent years—households with a reasonably good antenna now receive nine terrestrially beamed channels—added to the scope of what was unprecedented coverage of this holiday.[20] The change of heart is rather sudden and seems to be prompted both by a desire to keep in step with and to play a hand in shaping the wave of resurgent nostalgia for the Nasser era (Sipress 1995).

CONCLUSION: "WHAT HAPPENED NEXT?"

Modern history has been in vogue in Egypt for the past few years, fueled in large part by Mahfuz ʿAbd al-Rahman, Usama Anwar ʿUkasha, and other prominent scriptwriters who have penned historical dramas for television that attract wide audiences and have been extended over several seasons. The nineteenth century and prerevolutionary era of pashas and nationalist struggle are particular favorites.[21] Their influence has recently rolled over from the little to the big screen, although with much less panache or success.[22] Consequently, the tarboosh, Farouk and Queen Farida, and Ismail, have become popular images on T-shirts, in window displays of upscale shops, in television commercials geared toward young professionals, even in traditional "fast-food" eateries. The popularity of such items and images reinforces notions of creative rather than passive consumption, and should give those of us who read these melodramas as text cause to reconsider how their audiences in fact imagine them (Ang 1985; Armbrust 1996). Still, *Nasser 56*, because its subject is so recent, in the living or at least public memory of so many Egyptians, and because of its immediate political subject, is more serious business.

Demographics, the passing of the old-regime generation, the rise to prominence of the generations that lived and were shaped by Nasserism, and "serious matters in the present" point Egyptians ever more in the direction of Nasser and his era. The foundations of a resurgent nostalgia are a complex construct of political cynicism, uneven development, glaring social inequities, unfulfilled material expectations, and the vise of radical Islamist and state violence. Amid all this Egyptians are confronted daily with an alternative vision. Radio and television remain dominated by the cultural production of what was by all accounts a golden age of artistry. The songs, concert and comedy stage clips, and movies that captivated a generation still work their charms amid all that is new. Young boys in the street still croon ʿAbd al-Halim Hafiz songs (Gordon 1997a), and teenage girls still fall for Rushdi Abaza's Egyptian-Italian eyes. If their loyalties are divided and distracted by younger—and foreign—stars, they still recognize the genuine national-cultural articles for what they are.

Historical memory among Egyptian youths is short. When *Port Said* (Dhulfiqar 1957a), a propaganda film about the Suez War, aired in June 1996—on the anniversary of Evacuation Day—the newspaper movie listing explained the historical context as if describing an event much longer past. That was several months before *Nasser 56* hit the theaters. Now the Nasser generation is reliving the period, rediscovering nationalist anthems that stirred their youth. "We have waited forty years for this film," wrote one reviewer. "And because we waited so long, I found myself sitting in anticipation, my eyes, ears, and heart tuned in anticipation" (al-Ghayti 1995a). And a younger generation is asking their parents about the period. The filmmaker Yusuf Francis (who has recently directed a historical film about Howard Carter) sat near an eight-year-old boy at an evening screening who pressed his father for details, then turned to him after the film ended to ask, "What happened next?"[23] Egyptians in their twenties and early thirties are no less curious.[24]

The popular response to *Nasser 56* has taken all involved by surprise. State officials have been quick to reassert their positive role in its production, notwithstanding the obvious irony of a state-funded film glorifying nationalization in the age of privatization and championing a charismatic, idolized ruler in an era of political malaise.[25] The most cynical observers still fear the film may never make it to television, that "like many political films that the film industry has produced, it will be locked away in a can after ending its run in Egyptian theaters" (Khalil 1996). For the true believers, the Nasserist faithful, Ahmad Zaki has thrown a little water on the fire, reasserting his desire to now play his other hero, Anwar Sadat.[26] And Mahfuz ʿAbd al-Rahman has provoked unease in various circles by evincing a willingness to accept the challenge, put forth by critics who accuse him of taking the easy road via Suez, to pen *Nasser 67* as a sequel (al-Hakim 1995).[27]

Other contemporary history projects are in the works. ʿAbd al-Rahman has been scripting a serial about Umm Kulthum, and Zaki says he intends to film the life of ʿAbd al-Halim Hafiz. With the silver anniversary of the October 1973 war approaching, the Egyptian defense ministry announced its willingness to support—with guns, manpower, technical expertise, and financial aid—a silver screening of "the crossing" (*al-ʿubur*). However, a controversy over who should script the film has held up preproduction. In the Manichaean intellectual world of Nasserists and Sadatists, the leading candidate, Usama Anwar ʿUkasha, is considered to be the former, and this is deemed unacceptable by the latter. ʿUkasha retorts that his script will feature not the commander but the common soldier. This fails to appease his critics, who well sense the implicit barb. The Defense Ministry has announced its unhappiness with several draft scripts, implying a threat to withdraw support.[28]

For the time being Nasser and Suez serve as springboards for the rediscovery and rescripting of an era that so far defies official ossification. On the heels of its Egyptian success *Nasser 56* has played to audiences outside Egypt. The first screening scheduled was a single screening in Paris in June 1996 before the Egyptian opening. Shortly after its Egyptian premiere the film played to great acclaim in Gaza and the West Bank.[29] The film has since shown in several cities in the United States—"The Arab film event of the year"—and is currently available on video with English subtitles.[30] To non-Egyptian Arabs and to Arab diaspora communities the film undoubtedly conveys other particular meanings, addressing Nasser's legacy in a broader Arab context.[31] *Nasser 56* may be a flash in the pan; some certainly hope this will be the case. Conversely, it may become the Revolution Day television matinee, which, if it displaced the classics, would be a shame. Within Egypt the film clearly does speak to "serious matters of the present," and it may well inspire, or perhaps become—if it is allowed to be—the monument to Nasser that never was.

NOTES

Earlier drafts of this chapter were presented to the Colloquium on the Politics of Culture in Arab Societies in an Era of Globalization, held at Princeton University in May 1997, and to the culture studies group at the University of Illinois–Urbana. Participants' feedback was greatly appreciated. Special thanks to Walter Armbrust, Marilyn Booth, Ken Cuno, JoAnn D'Alisera, Sonallah Ibrahim, and Robert Vitalis. Funding for a broader project on Nasserist civic culture was provided by the J. William Fulbright Foreign Scholarship Board, the Joint Committee on the Near and Middle East of the Social Science Research Council, and the American Council of Learned Societies. I am, above all, deeply indebted to Mahfuz 'Abd al-Rahman and Samira 'Abd al-'Aziz for their hospitality, insight, and candor.

1. Mahfuz 'Abd al-Rahman pers. com.; all other references to 'Abd al-Rahman or *Nasser 56*, unless otherwise indicated, are from personal conversations that took place in Cairo between November 1995 and August 1996.

2. The filmmakers reportedly approached Su'ad Husni to play Nasser's wife, Tahiya, but she was unable to take part. Ahmad Zaki then suggested Firdaws 'Abd al-Hamid (al-Ghayti 1995a).

3. Kami has also played Suez Canal builder Ferdinand de Lesseps in 'Abd al-Rahman's other mammoth hit, the television series *Bawwabat al-Halawani* (Halawani's Gate), which ran three successive Ramadan seasons through 1996.

4. In a variant of this common wisdom, Mahfuz 'Abd al-Rahman told me that Egyptians will always favor an Egyptian over a foreign black-and-white film and a foreign over an Egyptian color film.

5. Zaki's filmography is long and distinguished. The great exception to the poor-boy roles is *Zawjat rajul muhimm* (Wife of an Important Man; Khan 1988), in which he plays an officer in the security police. A classic example of the poor-boy role, and a film that established a hairstyle fad for young men, is *Kaburya* (Crabs; Bishara 1990; see Armbrust 1996, 138–46). For a critique of recent disappointments, see el-Assiouty 1996.

6. Ramzi (1984) counts eight films made since that deal with the Tripartite Aggression in any way. Of these, he states, only three treated the war directly. The most noteworthy are *Bur Sa'id* (Port Said; Dhulfiqar 1957a), noted below, and *Sijin Abu Za'bal* (The Prisoner of Abu Za'bal; Mustafa 1957).

7. The simple statement may recall for some Egyptians Nasser's impromptu oration on October 26, 1954, when an assailant shot at him. Nasser repeated the phrase "I am Gamal Abdel Nasser" numerous times, invoking a willingness to die for Egypt. It was his first great public oration.

8. These characterizations have not always been positive. However, she has most often portrayed pious, doting mothers, and she is much loved. Her casting here is a master stroke, although a few people I have spoken to find the scene somewhat contrived.

9. It sits between the two main termini, at Tahrir (Liberation) and Ramsis squares, both major works projects undertaken by the Nasser regime. These subway stops are named for Presidents Sadat and Mubarak respectively.

10. The Nasserist project is increasingly recalled as noble, despite its obvious fallings; see, for example, Sid-Ahmed 1995. Alan Sipress (1995) quotes Sid-Ahmed urging Egyptians to keep Nasser's "most important legacy alive; namely his indomitable will to overcome any challenge," and notes, "Ironically, it was Nasser's will that sent Sid-Ahmed to jail for more than five years as a political prisoner."

11. As Armbrust notes in this volume, when film students and critics refer to "serious" cinema they often restrict their gaze to the 1960s when the state, through partial nationalization of the industry, sought to promote a national cinema guided by artistic rather than commercial concerns. Armbrust (and I agree) does not dispute claims that under the lead of influential public-sector artists Egyptian cinema embarked in new directions that persisted well into the 1970s. Yet he challenges the elevation of public-sector cinema by positing a "golden age before the golden age," which encompasses all commercial films made before the 1960s. My own research into Nasser-era nostalgia leads me to conclude that when people who lived the era think in terms of cinema, they recognize, consciously or intuitively, that a new generation of directors and film stars came into their own and put a distinctive stamp on Egyptian cinema in the 1950s that carried over into the following decade. Their work undoubtedly was shaped by the onset and course of the Nasser revolution and

constitutes, I would argue, a new, revolutionary cinema well before the "serious" cinema of the 1960s.

12. Key pillars of the Nasserist state—agrarian reform, subsidization, and the public sector—have undergone sustained attack in the past decade. See Hinnebusch 1993; Abdel-Moteleb 1993.

13. Prior to the serial the most common popular image of Ismail would have been in the film *Almaz wa-'Abduh al-Hamuli* (Almaz and 'Abduh al-Hamuli; Rafla 1962), in which the Khedive is a surrogate for Farouk, with all the familiar imagery of the debauched and deposed king.

14. The caricatures have become even bolder in the past few years. Two recent examples are *al-'A'ila* (The Family), written by Wahid Hamid, and *Lan a'ish fi galabib abi* (I Won't Live My Father's Way), based on a story by Ihsan 'Abd al-Quddus. In the former the mistrusted Islamist is gunned down; in the latter Islamists try to run down a failed recruit. In *al-Irhabi* the title character is also killed after rejecting his calling. The film has become an official text and was shown on the primary television channel on the last night of Ramadan in 1997.

15. The following year the festival was expanded to become the Radio and Television Festival.

16. Also see Salih 1995.

17. Comments made on *Sawt al-'Arab*, July 26, 1996.

18. The other two scriptwriters were Usama Anwar 'Ukasha, who is discussed below, and Sa'd al-Din Wahba, late president of the Cairo International Film Festival, who scripted a series of important—and popular—films in the 1960s.

19. For the past four years the Nasserist weekly, *al-'Arabi*, has featured Nasser on its masthead. During the fall 1995 election campaign, Nasser's image appeared on banners and posters, trumpeting the party—and the memories—more than the slated candidates.

20. The films were *Rudd qalbi, Allah ma'na* (God Is with Us; Badr Khan 1955), *Fi baytina rajul* (There Is a Man in Our House; Barakat 1961), *Ghurub wa-shuruq* (Sunset, Sunrise; al-Shaykh 1970), and *Shay' min al-khawf* (A Bit of Fear; Kamal 1969).

21. The most successful, in addition to *Halwani's Gate* has undoubtedly been *Layali al-Hilmiyya* (Hilmiyya Nights), written by 'Ukasha (for more on 'Ukasha, see Armbrust 1996, 16–17). But there are now scores, many rerun on regional stations.

22. The undisputed queen of historical kitsch is Nadia al-Guindi. See Hani 1995.

23. Francis was quoted in *al-Ahram*, August 12, 1996; a cartoon in this issue shows a man watching a television commercial for seventeen consecutive showings and wondering how he can divide himself to attend them all.

24. Salah Muntasir (1996) tried to play down the significance of audience turnout as curiosity. More telling, I think, is the reaction of a friend: "I was born after 1967 so I do not have any memories of the period. I was really impressed by what he did. They made him look like a savior; I do not know if that was true or not. Because my parents and husband are totally against him.... My mother told me that they had so much confidence in him and he was so impulsive and disappointed them.... I encouraged my parents to go.... I think it is more impressive to the younger generations."

25. See comments by Mamduh al-Laythi, chief of the ERTU production sector, in *al-Ahram*, August 10, 1996.

26. See *al-Ahram*, August 3, 1996; *Ruz al-Yusuf*, May 15, 1995; Adwy 1999. 'Ala' al-Sa'dani (1996) urged Zaki to reconsider, arguing that one actor should not play two such leaders.

27. Relatives of 'Abd al-Hakim 'Amr, Egypt's chief of staff, who engaged in a power struggle with Nasser in the aftermath of the defeat, was placed under house arrest, and, depending on one's take, was murdered or committed suicide, contacted 'Abd al-Rahman to express their concern over how the relationship would be treated ('Abd al-Rahman, pers. com.).

28. The war over scripting this war may well prove to be far more interesting than the final product. See Essam El-Din 1997.

29. The Gaza opening was reportedly held up when local promoters could not find proper 35 mm screening equipment. A projector had to be brought in from Egypt.

30. In the United States the film and video are available from Arab Film Distributors, based in Seattle. In addition to Seattle, the film has shown commercially in Portland, Los Angeles, Minneapolis, Cleveland, Boston, New York, and Washington, D.C., and was screened at the 1997 annual meeting of the Middle East Studies Association in San Francisco. For advertisements herald-

ing the film's importance, see *Anba' al-ʿArab* (Glendale, Calif.), May 1, 1997, and *Arab Panorama* (La Verne, Calif.), May 10, 1997. I would like to thank Yasin al-Khalesi for these ads.

31. An Arab-American community weekly published in southern California, *Beirut Times*, May 8–15, 1997, headlined "a film all Arab-American youth should see." Thanks to Yasin al-Khalesi for this information.

Iranian Revolutions in Comparative Perspective

NIKKI R. KEDDIE

The Iranian revolution of 1978–79 shocked the world and set in motion a search for causes. Most of the resulting analyses tend to locate the origins of the revolution in the errors of the shah and of various Americans, although some scholarly works assay socioeconomic explanations for the upheaval. Enough time has now passed to permit a greater range of investigations, and one written from the comparative perspective ought to be revealing. This essay will venture two types of comparison: (1) internal—comparison, on a few significant points, with other Iranian rebellions and revolutionary movements since 1890; and (2) external—comparison, more briefly, with other great world revolutions, employing theories of revolution that seem to fit the Iranian case. Both are difficult and tentative exercises, because Iran's 'Islamic revolution' appears to bear little ideological resemblance to revolutions in the West or to Iran's 'constitutional revolution' of 1905–11.

Western revolutions have tended, especially in their radical phase, to shift to the left and move toward secularism; even if religious ideology was dominant, as in the English Civil War of the 1640s, it was not fundamentalist, nor was it proclaimed by the leaders of the existing religious structure. In the Islamic revolution, however, much of the leadership came from the orthodox clergy, who propounded a return to Islamic fundamentalism. Even recent

Earlier versions of this paper were delivered in 1981 at the University of California, Irvine, Seminar on Social History and Theory and at the Conference on Islam and Social Movements, University of California, Berkeley. Thanks are due to Ira Lapidus, Edmund Burke, and Gene R. Garthwaite for suggesting revisions to the manuscript and to Eric Hooglund, Andrew Newman, and the editors and staff of the *American Historical Review* for their help in preparing it for publication.

socioeconomic theories of revolution, which tend to stress the role of the peasantry (probably because of the partial example of Russia and the clearer ones of China and other Third World countries), do not apply to either Iranian revolution; a peasantry living mainly on arid or semiarid land, dependent on landlords or others for irrigation, and unprotected by forest or mountain shelter for guerrilla warfare seems to produce neither the middle peasantry nor the close associations needed to organize politically. By contrast, the supposed impermeability of modern cities to successful mass revolution, especially in the absence of peasant support, was disproved in both Iranian revolutions; the cities were vulnerable in 1905–11 largely because the shah had no significant military force and in 1978–79 owing not only to the shah's miscalculations but also to the amazing unanimity and organization of the urban population against him.

Iranians, who in peaceable periods seem eager to please and loath to disagree openly with the powerful, whether in the home or with political superiors, have in the last 90 years engaged in an unusual number of large-scale popular revolts and revolutions. With the exception of several northern provincial revolts after World War I and the large demonstrations against the shah in the early 1960s, all of these rebellions spread to Iran's major cities, and some encompassed tribal areas as well. Indeed, Iran stands in the forefront of rebellious and revolutionary countries in the twentieth century—unmatched, to my knowledge, in the Muslim, Hindu, or Western world for the number and depth of its movements; only China, Vietnam, and possibly Russia provide competition.

This claim may be unexpected to some, not only because modern Iranian history is not generally known but also because Iran's two major twentieth-century revolutions, and especially the second, appear so aberrant. They do not fit very closely widespread ideas of what modern revolutions should be like. Yet there is no doubt that the Islamic revolution in 1978–79 provided a thoroughgoing overthrow of the old political, social, and ideological order, although what will replace it is not yet clear. And the constitutional upheaval of 1905–11 was massive enough in participation and important enough in altering the political system to deserve the name 'revolution.' Several movements that were not revolutions contained revolutionary elements. The mass rebellion against a British tobacco concession in 1890–92, the reformist-autonomist revolts in the provinces of Gilan, Azerbaijan, and Khorasan after World War I, the rebellions in Azerbaijan and Kurdistan after World War II, the mass-supported oil nationalization movement under Mosaddeq that ruled the country from 1951 to 1953, and the popular antigovernment demonstrations of the early 1960s all involved, to a greater or lesser extent, efforts to throw off foreign control over the Iranian economy and to build an independent society and state.

To attempt anything more than superficial comparisons among Iran's rebellions, not to mention comparisons between some of these upheavals and revolts in other Muslim and non-Muslim countries, requires locating the various Iranian movements of the last century within the framework of modern Iranian history. Under the Qajar dynasty (1796–1925), Iran was increasingly subject to Western economic penetration and domination, particularly by Great Britain and Russia. As in many Third World countries, Western powers exacted from Iran treaties that limited customs duties to 5 per cent, thus virtually creating a free trade area for Western imports, which often undersold Iranian handicrafts. Although Oriental carpets began to be a significant export around 1875, it is unlikely that the rise in carpet exports compensated for the fall in production of other crafts and the consequent discontent and displacement of their artisans.

In the same period the decrease in Iran's handicraft exports was partially offset by rising raw material and agricultural exports, particularly opium, cotton, and fruits and nuts. The commercialization of agriculture and carpets, which continued in the Pahlavi period (1925–79), increased economic stratification between the owners of land, water, or workshops and those who worked for them. Whether there was general immiseration or an increase in prosperity is a question on which scholars of the Qajar period have disagreed.[2] But the increase in stratification and the peasants' increased vulnerability to famine, owing to their dependence on land planted in cash crops like opium that were subject to bad market years, brought new sources of discontent to the peasantry, just as the displacement of craftsmen contributed to the grievances of middle-level urban residents. Iran did, however, have an advantage over countries like Egypt and Turkey, which had a much larger trade with Europe and far more European residents, in that the native Iranian bazaar structure remained largely intact. And wealthy import-export and local merchants and moneylenders proved important in every Iranian revolution.

The Qajars did much less than the Middle Eastern rulers of, for example, Turkey, Egypt, and Tunisia in trying to strengthen the central government and the army in order to resist further encroachments either by Western powers or by their own neighbors. Turkey saw a long series of efforts, beginning in the eighteenth century, to strengthen both its military and its technical and educational support structure; the first stage of those efforts culminated in the reforms of Sultan Mahmud in the 1820s and 1830s. And Egypt under Muhammad Ali saw even more significant transformations until Western powers limited both the economic independence and military strength of the Egyptian government in the 1840s. Iran had no parallel developments. Largely abortive reforms under Crown Prince Abbas Mirza (d. 1833) and chief ministers Amir Kabir (d. 1851) and Mirza Hosain Khan (d. 1881) left Iran without a modernized army, bureaucracy, and educational system. The small Russian-officered Cossack Brigade, founded in 1879, remained the Qajars' only modern military force.

This lack of change is not altogether surprising. Iran had much less contact with the West than did Middle Eastern countries bordering on the Mediterranean and had a very arid terrain with a scattered population. As a result, the country was very difficult to subject to centralized control. Other countries in similar circumstances—Afghanistan and Morocco, for example—also saw relatively little centralization or modernization in the nineteenth century. The shahs had to permit considerable devolution of power to groups not totally tied to the center. Among these were nomadic tribes (often organized into confederations for the main purpose of dealing with the authorities), whose mobility, mastery of gunfighting on horseback, separate languages and cultures, and geographical location (frequently near the borders) made them semi-autonomous units. Their ties to the government were frequently limited to annual payments or to cavalry duties in case of war. Even some local governors or mayors had considerable authority, although the central government exercised increasing control over them, especially under Naser ed-Din Shah (1848–96).[3]

The lack of centralization in Iran was also dependent on the increasing power and pretensions of the Shiʿi ulama. By the early nineteenth century, after a long prior evolution, the *usuli* or *mujtahidi* school of ulama won out over the rival *akhbari* school. The latter claimed that individual believers could themselves understand the Quran and the Traditions (*akhbar*) of the Prophet and the Imams and did not need to follow the guidance of mujtahids, who claimed the right of *ijtihad* ('effort to ascertain correct doctrine'). The usulis, in contrast, claimed that, although the bases of belief were laid down in the Quran and the Traditions, learned mujtahids were still needed to interpret doctrine for the faithful. As usuli doctrine developed, particularly under Mortaza Ansari, the chief *marjaʾ-e taqlid* ('source of imitation') of the mid-nineteenth century, every believer was required to follow the rulings of a living mujtahid, and, whenever there was a single chief mujtahid, his rulings took precedence over all others.[4] The usuli ulama have a stronger doctrinal position than do the Sunni ulama. While not infallible, mujtahids are qualified to interpret the will of the infallible twelfth, Hidden Imam.

In addition to doctrinal power, which extended to politics as well as religion and law, the Iranian Shiʿi ulama had economic and social power that similarly exceeded that of the ulama in most Sunni countries. Shiʿi ulama, unlike most Sunni ulama, directly collected and dispersed the *zakat* and *khums* taxes, and they also had huge *vaqf* mortmains as well as personal properties, controlled most of the dispensing of justice, were the primary educators, oversaw social welfare, and were frequently courted and even paid by rulers. Although most of the ulama were often on good terms with the crown, they resisted Qajar encroachments on their power, whereas in most Sunni states the ulama became more and more subordinate to the government. Some of the Iranian ulama worked for the state, but as the nineteenth century progressed conflicts between important ulama and the secular authorities increased.

The relative independence of the ulama facilitated their alliance with the bazaar—a term used to designate those engaged in largely traditional, urban, small-scale production, banking, and trade—and its artisans, merchants, and moneylenders. The bazaar has long been the economic, social, and religious center of towns and cities, and even in recent times has encompassed a large population and share of the economy. As early as the 1830s bazaaris complained to the government about the large-scale importation of foreign manufactures, which undermined their own production and trade. Given the long-term trade treaties limiting Iranian tariffs, there was little the government could do, short of risking war with the Western powers, even if Iranian rulers had been more energetic.

Regardless, then, of whether certain individuals or groups were better or worse off as the result of the Western impact on Iran, including British and Russian protection of Qajar rule, various groups in society had reason to be actively discontented with the Qajars and with Western incursions. Those craftsmen who were displaced had clear grievances, and many of them petitioned the government for redress. Even those merchants who prospered, however, saw that Western merchants received favored treatment—Westerners were exempt, for example, from road and municipal taxes that Iranian merchants had to pay. And the ulama were opposed to the limited steps the Qajars took toward Western education—missionaries were allowed, for instance, to teach Christians in Iran. The ulama also objected to steps toward reform and to concessions granted to Westerners. Except in the densely populated areas of heavy rainfall, like Gilan and Mazenderan on the Caspian, however, peasants were generally too scattered and too subject to landlord control of land and water to organize or coordinate movements of discontent, although those who migrated and became urban subproletarians were willing participants in urban-based rebellions, not only in the Qajar period but also, and to a greater extent, in the revolution of 1978–79.[5]

Among the discontented in the nineteenth century was also a small but growing group of intellectuals, many of whom had mercantile or government positions, who learned of Western ways. Frequently their knowledge of the West was obtained second hand, by travel to India, Istanbul, or Egypt or by temporary migration to Russian Transcaucasia. Hundreds of thousands of Iranians, mostly workers, settled semi-permanently in the Transcaucasus, which also supported a few Iranian intellectuals. Several educated Iranians, most notably Mirza Malkum Khan and Sayyed Jamal ed-Din 'al-Afghani,' also traveled as far as France and England. Those who went abroad were generally struck by Western economic development, comparative justice, and lack of arbitrary rule; their manuscript writings contain praise of Western ways and criticism of Iran's autocratic rulers, petty officials, venal clerics, and arbitrary courts, and of the low status of women.[6]

To a large degree, the recurring alliance between the bazaaris and many of the ulama on the one hand and secularized liberals and radicals on the other has been based on the existence of common enemies—the dynasty and its foreign supporters—rather than on any real agreement about goals. The ulama wanted to extend their own power and to have Shi'i Islam more strictly enforced; the liberals and radicals looked for greater political and social democracy and economic development; and the bazaaris wanted to restrict favored foreign economic status and competition. The alliance formed by many of the ulama, the bazaaris, and a few secular intellectuals first showed its power following the issuance of a tobacco concession in 1890; Iran granted to a British subject a full monopoly on the purchase, sale, and export of all tobacco grown in Iran. Not only did this follow a whole series of concessions to Europeans, but it also covered a widely grown, exported, and profitable crop rather than previously unexploited products, like most minerals. Thus, growers and merchants became aroused by the threat to their livelihood as well as by nationalistic fervor. Active and often massive protests in most of Iran's cities in 1891, largely led by ulama in partnership with bazaaris (and with some Russian behind-the-scenes encouragement), culminated in a successful boycott of tobacco dealing and smoking (as against the will of the Hidden Imam). The shah was forced to cancel the tobacco monopoly in early 1892.[7]

The tobacco rebellion of 1890–92 shared with later revolutionary and rebellious movements a substantial anti-imperialist and antiforeign component. Although this component is also found in most of the world's colonies and dependencies, anti-imperialism seems to have been stronger and to have resulted in more mass rebellions and revolutions in Iran than in other Middle Eastern countries, with the possible exception of Afghanistan. Despite the lesser degree of direct control that foreigners in Iran have had in comparison with those in many other countries of the Middle East and North Africa, Iranians, along with Afghans and a few others, have been more resistant to foreign domination than have most other peoples. Resistance has often been less obvious or militant in Iran than it has in Afghanistan, since in Iran periods of external accommodation to foreigners have alternated with periods of active rebellion. But Iranian antiforeign feeling has always been strong.

Among the territories subjugated in the original wave of Muslim conquest, Iran was the only large area that retained its own language and a great deal of its old culture, albeit considerably modified by Islam. Iran's state since 1501, Shi'i Islam appears to have been even more resistant to foreign influences than Sunni Islam. (If the comparison is extended further, both main branches of Islam seem to have been more resistant to Westernization than have the dominant religions and traditions of non-Muslim Asia and Africa; thus Iranian Shi'i Islam may be the most resistant of all non-European religions to European culture.) Part of Shi'i Islam's strength in this regard lies in its insistence on ritual purity—including prohibiting physical contact with nonbelievers, preventing nonbelievers from entering mosques and shrines, and the like. Throughout the nineteenth century certainly, and for many Iranians much longer than that, the growing economic, political, and ideological influence of Westerners was perceived largely as the usurpation of the rights of believers. Economic, political, and religious resentments were thus intertwined, although different groups tended to stress different types of grievances. Governments seen as complaisant to foreign unbelievers were considered almost as culpable as the foreigners themselves. Not just in 1891 but in the constitutional revolution of 1905–11, the oil nationalization of 1951–53 under Mosaddeq, the demonstrations of 1963 around Khomeini, and the revolution of 1978–79 Iranians held their government responsible for Western depredations.[8] A similar theme has certainly been sounded elsewhere, most notably among the Muslim Brethren and other Muslim militant groups in Egypt, Pakistan, and the Arab East, but in Iran the question of government accountability has attracted a wider and more revolutionary following. Attacks on any regime that permitted Western involvement in Iran have been strongly voiced by respected representatives of the orthodox ulama and the bazaar, which partly accounts for Iranian fervor. The strength of Iranian revulsion to foreign influence also arose from the long-held belief that Western nonbelievers were out to undermine Iran and Islam, and Shi'i Islam's encouragement of self-sacrifice to combat enemies has certainly added to resistance to foreigners based on exploitation and domination. For many, Shi'ism and nationalism were part of a single blend.

The two twentieth-century Iranian movements that clearly merit the title 'revolution'—the 'constitutional' revolution of 1905–11 and the 'Islamic' revolution of 1978–79—demonstrate the importance of this Iranian outlook. In part, the events preceding the first Iranian revolution in this century were merely a continuation and intensification of the tobacco rebellion of the 1890s. The economic and political power of Britain and Russia grew rapidly after 1892. The tobacco 'victory' saddled Iran with a £500,000 payment to the British tobacco company in compensation for its lost monopoly. On May 1, 1896, Mirza Reza Kermani, instigated by the antishah, pan-Islamic activities of Sayyed Jamal ed-Din 'al-Afghani' and his Iranian and

Shi'i circle in Istanbul, assassinated Naser ed-Din Shah. The shah's weak successor squandered far more money on courtiers and extravagant trips abroad than had his father. The son obtained the necessary monies from two Russian loans, granted on the basis of further Russian economic concessions. The British, not to be outdistanced by Russia in the race for profit in the Middle East, retaliated by requiring further concessions, chiefly the D'Arcy oil concession, which resulted in the first significant exploitation of Middle Eastern oil (following its discovery in 1908).

The Russo-Japanese War of 1904–05 and the Russian revolution of 1905 gave impetus to an Iranian opposition movement that had been growing since 1901. After a century of successive defeats, an Asian power had defeated a European power, an event that bolstered pride throughout Asia. This feeling was particularly strong in those countries, like Iran, that had experienced Russian penetration and oppression. Many considered it significant that the only Asian power with a constitution had defeated the only Western power without one, and constitutions came to be looked upon as the 'secret of strength' of Western governments. In Iran, as in a number of Asian countries, treatises explaining constitutions and their virtues began to circulate, and news of Japanese victories was happily and rapidly spread. The Russian revolution demonstrated the possibility, at least in its first stage, of a mass revolt weakening a despotic monarchy and forcing it to adopt a constitution. Both the Russo-Japanese War and the Russian revolution also effectively, if temporarily, took Russia out of Iranian internal politics, an important consideration to those who expected Russia to intervene if the power of the Qajars was threatened or weakened.[9]

The constitutional revolution began late in 1905, when respected sugar merchants raised the price of the commodity in the face of rising international prices. The merchants were bastinadoed, and a rebellion broke out in the streets. When some of the ulama took sanctuary (*bast*), the shah promised a 'house of justice' and other concessions. But the promise was not fulfilled, and a new rebellion broke out in 1906, highlighted by a new ulama *bast* in Qom and a *bast* by roughly 12,000 bazaaris at the British legation. The crown then promised to accept a constitution, and a parliament was soon elected. The constitution of 1906–07 was modeled on the Belgian constitution, with one major exception. The Iranian constitution provided for a committee of five or more mujtahids to pass on the compatibility of all laws with the Islamic *sharia*, although this provision was never enforced. The framers intended real power to reside in the parliament and its ministers, rather than in the crown, but parliament was rarely able to wrest power from the shah.

The revolution became stormy and violent when a new shah, Mohammad Ali, closed parliament by a coup in 1908. Revolutionary guerrillas (*fedayin* and *mojahedin*) held out against the crown, first in Tabriz and later in Gilan, and then marched south to take Tehran along with Bakhtiari tribesmen moving up from the south. The second constitutional period saw a split between the moderate party, led by clerics, and the democrats, who had a program of agrarian and social reform. But the British and the Russians provided the revolution's *coup de grâce* in late 1911. The Russians presented an ultimatum demanding, among other things, that the Iranians get rid of their pronationalist American adviser, Morgan Shuster. The British, who had signed an entente with Russia in 1907, went along with the Russian demands, Russian and British troops moved in during 1911–12, and parliament was closed.[10]

Although parliament passed some social, judicial, and educational reform measures, the revolution was chiefly political, aimed at reducing monarchical and foreign power through the introduction of a Western-style constitution and parliament. This instrument and this body were seen as the best means to limit Iranian autocracy. Some of the revolution's participants expected Iran and its people to be able to return to more Islamic ways (like the barber who said he would shave no more beards, now that Iran had a constitution, since shaving was non-Islamic), while a smaller number hoped to become more Western, if only to be strong enough to escape Western control. In this revolution, unlike that of 1978–79, ulama leaders did not adopt a new political ideology. Those who supported the revolution were content to occupy a high proportion of the positions in parliament and to have a veto over legislation. One of the ulama wrote a treatise defending constitutionalism as the best government possible in the absence of the Hidden Imam, but there is no evidence that it was widely read.[11] Many of the ulama accepted the constitution as a means both to limit the shah's power and to increase their own; some became disillusioned by secularist laws and trends and quit oppositional politics.

Just as the revolution of 1905–11 followed smaller 'rehearsals'—the movement against the all-encompassing concession to Baron Julius de Reuter in 1872 and the tobacco protest of 1891—so the revolution of 1978–79 built on resentments and organizations that surfaced in earlier protests and movements. The immediate post-World War II period was marked by the rise of leftist organizations, especially the Tudeh party, whose many strikes included a general strike in the oil fields, and of autonomist movements in Azerbaijan and Kurdistan, which expressed in considerable part genuine local sentiment. Then came the oil nationalization movement, which demonstrated deep anti-imperialist feeling and culminated in the nationalization of oil in 1951 and the two-year prime ministership of Mosaddeq. He was overthrown with the aid of the United States and Great Britain. Last in the series was the economic and political crisis of 1960–64, highlighted by demonstrations in 1963 that resulted in many deaths and brought about the exile of the religious leader of the movement, Ayatollah Khomeini, in 1964.

Pahlavi rule reversed the Qajars' policies on modernization and the development of the military, and after 1925 Iran was subjected to accelerated modernization, secularization, and centralization. Especially after 1961, the crown encouraged the rapid growth of consumer-goods industries, pushed the acquisition of armaments even beyond what Iran's growing oil-rich budgets could stand, and instituted agrarian reforms that emphasized government control and investment in large, mechanized farms. Displaced peasants and tribespeople fled to the cities, where they formed a discontented subproletariat. People were torn from ancestral ways, the gap between the rich and the poor grew, corruption was rampant and well known, and the secret police, with its arbitrary arrests and use of torture, turned Iranians of all levels against the regime. And the presence and heavy influence of foreigners provided major, further aggravation.

Ironically, the OPEC oil price rise of 1973 that the shah helped engineer was one cause of his undoing. He insisted on using the oil money for radical increases in investment and armaments that the economy could not bear: Iran faced galloping inflation, shortages of housing and consumer goods, and an increase of rural to urban migration that compounded the other problems. In addition, Iran became economically overcommitted as oil income fell after 1975. To cool the economy, the shah appointed Jamshid Amuzegar prime minister in 1977, but steps Amuzegar took to bring down inflation brought more hardship and discontent. A major cutback in construction, already in decline since early 1976, brought massive unemployment, which especially affected recent urban migrants, and a reduction in payments to the ulama increased the discontent of this influential class. In late 1977, partly emboldened by statements by Amnesty International, the International Confederation of Jurists, and President Jimmy Carter, Iranian intellectuals and professionals began to circulate petitions and letters calling for an extension of democratic rights.[12] A large educated and student class and a newly politicized class of urban poor, aided and influenced by the mosque network, provided the backbone for a new mass politics.

Early in 1978, the semi-official paper *Ettela'at* published an inspired and scurrilous assault on Khomeini, who was then attacking the regime from Iraq. Demonstrations with casualties ensued. Thereafter, on the traditional forty-day mourning intervals, demonstrations recurred, and religious, liberal, and leftist forces gradually coalesced against the regime. Khomeini went to France, where he could easily communicate with revolutionary leaders in Iran; the liberal National Front leadership reached an accord with him; and the shah's concessions were too few and came too late. The shah's gesture of appointing Shahpour Bakhtiar as prime minister led to Bakhtiar's expulsion from the National Front. Bakhtiar was unable to prevent Khomeini's return to Iran. And the ayatollah had become, even for many secularists, the symbolic revolutionary leader. In February 1979, air force technicians, supported especially by the Marxist guerrilla Fedayan-e Khalq and Muslim leftist guerrilla Mojahedin-e Khalq, took power for the revolutionaries in Tehran, and Khomeini's appointed prime minister, Mehdi Bazargan, took office.

Thenceforth, at least until 1983, the revolution moved ever more toward Khomeini's brand of absolutist religious radicalism. First, the National Front ministers resigned. Then, when US embassy personnel were taken hostage by young 'followers of Khomeini's line' on November 4, 1979, Bazargan and his foreign minister, Ibrahim Yazdi, were forced to resign in the face of their inability to obtain the hostages' release. Khomeini's choice for president, Abolhasan Bani Sadr, kept his post longer, but with decreasing power, and he was ousted in June 1981. Khomeini's Islamic Republican party came overwhelmingly into control of the cabinet and parliament. Once the party achieved a virtual monopoly on government, however, it lost cohesion, and increasing rumblings [were] heard of internal disagreements—dissension within the ruling groups—on such issues as further land reform, personal power, foreign policy, and succession to Khomeini's position as the holder of *velayat-e faqih* ('guardianship of the jurisprudent'). While Khomeini-type religious radicals were first in the ascendant, in early 1983 conservatives became more powerful and blocked measures for land reform and a monopoly on foreign trade. Bazaar and other middle-class influences appeared to be growing, and there were moves toward political normalization and central control over religious radicals.

Among the theories of revolution that shed light on Iran's two major upheavals in this century are James C. Davies's J-curve theory of revolution and Crane Brinton's *Anatomy of Revolution.* Davies suggests that revolutions emerge after a considerable period of economic growth followed by a shorter, sharp period of economic contraction and decline. C.-E. Labrousse had already described the economic improvements followed by a sharp downswing that preceded the French Revolution.[13] Davies's J-curve matches the prerevolutionary experience of Iran in the 1970s. To a lesser degree, the revolution of 1905–11 may also fit the model, since some scholars have a period of growth in the late nineteenth century followed by economic difficulties that stemmed from the shah's extravagance and Russia's economic and political troubles after 1904.

Apart from Davies's model, the comparative pattern that best fits the revolution of 1978–79 is Brinton's more descriptive than explanatory typology.[14] The political, economic, and financial troubles of an *ancien régime* that made rule in the old way impossible and forced accommodation with new groups were clearly seen both in the lesser crises that preceded the revolution and in the revolution of 1978–79. Such crises, in somewhat different form, were especially characteristic of the financial situation before the English (seventeenth century) and French (eighteenth century) revolutions discussed by Brinton. And political alienation of the intellectuals and the elite, including government figures, from the court was as characteristic of Iran in the 1970s as it was of Russia in the early twentieth century. The gradual and somewhat unexpected movement from demonstration to revolution, characteristic of Brinton's revolutions, has also characterized both Iranian revolutions. As late as the summer of 1978, after many major demonstrations and riots, most Iranian intellectuals voiced the view that the movement was over, having achieved its goal of liberalization with the shah's promises, especially of free elections, and many persons close to the Khomeini wing of the movement have insisted that he and his followers did not expect the shah to be ousted anytime soon.

The Iranian revolution of 1978–79 does not conform exactly to the pattern of growing radicalization fundamental to all four of Brinton's revolutions. To locate Khomeini on a right–left scale is not as easy as it may seem. On the one hand, he [was] a fundamentalist, a believer in a literalist application of scripture (except when it [did] not suit him); on the other, he [was] not only a fierce anti-imperialist, with particular dislike for encroachments by the United States and Israel, but also a man with concern for the poverty-striken, a concern that [was] manifested in such programs as free urban housing, state-supplied utilities, and further land reform, despite their scant success. Perhaps 'populist' is the closest political adjective—with the simultaneous leftist and rightist characteristics and xenophobic and sometimes fundamentalist components that that word connotes in American history. Populist rebellions that have appealed to the subproletariat in the West have sometimes turned into autocratic and even fascist movements, and some Iranians and Americans would say that this change has occurred, or is occurring, in Iran.

Brinton, in his typology of revolution, posited the fall of the radical element during a Thermidor, in which most people, overtaxed by the rule of virtue and justice, long for more accustomed, laxer ways. This deradicalization is in turn often followed by autocratic, usually military, rule; in France Napoleon succeeded the Directory, and in Russia Stalin replaced the NEP. Neither of these stages has occurred in Iran as of early 1983, but both are possibilities. Indeed, the early phases of Thermidor may be discernible; Iran has taken major steps toward normalizing its economic and political relations with ideologically divergent regimes—notably Turkey, Pakistan, and some Western and Eastern European countries. And, although much of Iran's internal and external policy has not softened as of March 1983, the growth in strength of the conservative faction in government and Khomeini's December 1982 decrees providing some protection for legal rights may be early signs of a Thermidor.

With the rise of social history, socioeconomic explanations of revolutions have become more general than Brinton's phenomenological comparisons. Although its revolution of 1978–79 can be explained in terms of socioeconomic causation (as I have attempted to do above and elsewhere), Iran fits less neatly into most existing socioeconomic comparative schemes than it does into the basic J-curve or more varied Brinton typology. The closest socioeconomic revolutionary model for Iran's experience appears to be the Marxist formula, without any of the elaborations or modifications added recently.[15] This formula, in essence, postulates that revolution occurs whenever the relations of production—particularly the control and ownership of the society's basic means of production—have changed beyond the ability of the old forms of political power and state organization to subsume the new economic order. This situation essentially obtained prior to both Iranian revolutions.

During the revolution of 1905–11 the majority of economically dominant groups and classes—the growing and often thriving class of big and medium merchants, the landlords, particularly those engaged in growing cash crops, and the tribal khans—were decreasingly represented by the Qajars. The crown made few attempts to make laws and create conditions under which trade could flourish or to build up the state so as to be able to limit foreign control. At the same time the Qajars, unlike some other Middle Eastern rulers, had no strategy for increasing the loyalty of the ulama; instead, the crown added to the causes of ulama disaffection while allowing their independent power to grow. Although Iran did not yet have a strong bourgeoisie in the modern sense, groups whose interests lay in rationalizing the economy, encouraging trade and manufacture, and decreasing foreign control, were growing in size and influence. But the last Qajar shahs tended to squander the state's funds on luxurious living and foreign travel for court favorites and members of the royal family without foreseeing the disastrous financial consequences.

In the revolution of 1978–79 the conflict between major classes and the autocracy is even clearer. The reversal of Qajar policy toward modernization helped create a sizable, well-educated stratum of society, most of the members of which became bureaucrats and technocrats; others from this stratum entered the professions and arts or private industry. Many industrialists also sprang from humble origins in the bazaar. In addition to the workers' and subproletariat's grievances over the growing privileges not only of foreigners but of the rich as well, Iran's *nouveau riche*—that is, the relatively privileged new middle and upper classes and rich bazaaris—were discontented. Their economic futures were often determined arbitrarily and irrationally by fiat from the top, while they were denied all real participation in self-government and the political process. Both the successes and the failures of modernization put different classes, from the urban poor to the new middle classes, at odds with the autocratic government. And such contradictions were also felt by national minorities, which were economically oppressed and denied their own languages and cultures.

These various disaffections coalesced in two main ideological strains that already existed in embryo in the revolution of 1905–11: the liberal or leftist desire for Westernization, and the fundamentalist wish to return to a 'pure' Islam, particularly as interpreted by Ayatollah Khomeini and those around him. The latter won out—hence the appellation 'Islamic revolution'—but the grievances behind the revolution were at least as much socio-economic as cultural.[16]

To compare the revolutions of 1905–11 and 1978–79 to each other can contribute as much to our understanding of Iran in the twentieth century as to compare them jointly to theories and paradigms developed by Western scholars. Although many points of similarity and difference can be noted, the most striking point of comparison may be stated as an apparent paradox: the constitutional revolution, despite the leading role played by many of the ulama, resulted in an almost wholly Western-style constitution and form of government, while the revolution of 1978–79, in which secular leftists and liberals—in addition to religious forces—played a major role, resulted in a self-styled Islamic republic and a constitution stressing Islam. This is not, moreover, simply a matter of constitutions. The revolution of 1905–11 was clearly secularizing in a number of spheres of life and law, while that of 1978–79 was just as clearly Islamicizing, despite the far greater Westernization of education, law, government, culture, and the economy that had taken place by then. It is true that the revolutionaries in both the first and eighth decades of this century were fighting against autocracy, for greater democracy, and for constitutionalism, so that there was much ideological continuity. Nonetheless, the ideology of the revolutionary leaders was quite different in the two revolutions. Why?

The answer to this question lies largely in the nature of the enemy perceived by each group of revolutionaries. In 1905–11 the revolutionaries were fighting against a traditionalist regime and a shah whose dynasty had made very few efforts at Westernization, including reforms of potential benefit to Iran. At the beginning of the century, therefore, non-ulama reformers in particular—but also some liberal members of the ulama—found it easy to believe that the politically and economically encroaching West, which was obviously more powerful than Iran, could be combated only if some Western ways were imitated. Nineteenth-century reformers called for Western-style armies, legal reforms, a clearly organized cabinet system, and modern economic development. For Muslims, many such ideas were justified by appropriate interpretations of the Quran and Muslim Traditions favoring change, acquiring knowledge from outside Islam, and taking the steps necessary to oppose unbelievers. When constitutions became a matter of interest after the Russo-Japanese war, the idea of adopting a Western-style constitution in order to limit autocracy and achieve the secret of Western strength gained greatly. Nor was this a ridiculous notion. Most Iranians were not yet ready to overthrow the Qajars, but many wanted to curb their arbitrary power; a constitution seemed—and under better circumstances might have been—a good way to accomplish their relatively limited objectives.

Both parts of the Iranian constitution (which lasted until 1979), the Fundamental Law of 1906 and the Supplementary Fundamental Law of 1907, were largely derived from the Belgian constitution. The clear intent was to have a constitutional monarchy of very limited power, a prime minister and his cabinet (appointments to which required the approval of parliament), and guarantees of freedom of speech, the press, and other civil rights. The provision for an appointed senate, half of whose members were to be designated by the crown as a conservative counterweight to the *majlis* ('lower house'), was not put into effect until 1950, and a key provision insisted upon by ulama leaders—for a committee of at least five leading members of the ulama to pass on the compatibility of majlis legislation with Islam—was never enforced, for reasons that have never been adequately explained. Perhaps the ulama under the leadership of Sayyed Abdollah Behbehani already so dominated the first majlis that the ulama no longer feared the passage of secular laws contrary to religious doctrine, or perhaps Behbehani secretly opposed enforcing the provision because it might have reduced his own power. In any event, revolutionary leaders in 1905–11 found their model in Western-style liberalism and constitutionalism, and many of the ulama at least permitted the adoption of the constitution. Others broke away as the implications of secularization became clearer, and many tried to block certain aspects of Westernization.[7] The growth of new bourgeois forces and of secularist ideas continued for many decades after 1911.

In 1978–79, however, the perceived enemy had changed, and the Iranian response was correspondingly different. For fifty years the Pahlavi dynasty had forced the Westernization of Iran. In the course of that Westernization the customs and beliefs as well as the prerogatives not only of the ulama but of many bazaaris and ordinary peasants, nomads, and the urban poor were attacked. Far more than the Qajars, the Pahlavis were perceived as tools of Western or Westernized powers, chiefly the United States and Israel. No longer could Iranians accept strong armies, Western-style industries, and modern legal codes and educational systems as solutions, in themselves, to Iran's problems. Even the liberal constitution had been subject to autocratic manipulation. The regime came to be seen as, among other things, too Western, and there developed among the alienated a search for roots and for a return to 'authentic' Iranian or Islamic values. The nationalism that had read modern, liberal virtues into pre-Islamic Iran—expounded by intellectuals like the nineteenth-century Mirza Aqa Khan Kermani and the twentieth-century Ahmad Kasravi—had been largely co-opted by the Pahlavi shahs. The shahs promoted pre-Islamic motifs in their speeches and in their architectural styles, and Mohammad Reza even sponsored a wasteful mythomaniacal celebration of a fictitious twenty-five-hundredth anniversary of the Iranian monarchy and abortively changed the starting date of Iran's calendar from Mohammad's *hijra* to the foundation of the pre-Islamic monarchy.

Although many educated Iranians clung to their own liberal or leftist versions of this pre-Islamic and Western form of nationalism, some important intellectuals by the early 1960s began to turn to new ideas. In a famous essay, Jalal Al-e Ahmad attacked such 'Westoxication,' suggesting that Iranians look rather to their own and Oriental ways. Later he tried to rediscover Islam for himself, although his critical account of his pilgrimage makes it doubtful that he succeeded. Clerical and lay religious opposition grew at the same time, and some intellectuals published new essays and republished with new introductions works by religious reformers like Jamal ed-Din 'al-Afghani' and the early twentieth-century Ayatollah Na'ini, who had in 1909 written the first reasoned clerical defense of a Western-style constitution as the best protection against autocracy. The important guerrilla group, the Mojahedin-e Khalq, combined new interpretations of Islam with socialist ideas that were often close to those of the great orator and hero of progressivist Islamic revolutionaries, Ali Shariati (d. 1977).[18] Significantly, none of these groups or individuals should properly be termed 'fundamentalist' or even fully 'traditionalist.' Most merely wished to escape the related evils of internal despotism and of 'Westoxication'—socioeconomic and cultural dependence on the West.

Increasing numbers of Iranians shifted to progressive versions of an indigenous Islamic ideology perceived as likely to restore Iranian self-esteem and combat Westernization. Such versions were possible because so many liberal and even leftist ideals were contained in different strands of the Islamic revival. Liberal ideals were perhaps best represented by Mehdi Bazargan and, in a more traditionalist way, by Ayatollah Shariatmadari, both of whom were important in the revolution. The more progressive interpretations of Islam came from the very popular Ayatollah Taleqani and from Shariati, and leftist ones chiefly from the Mojahedin. Many continued as late as 1978–79 to advocate enforcement of the constitution of 1906–07, although they stressed the necessity of implementing its provision for a committee comprised of five or more of the ulama to ensure the compatibility of laws with the *sharia*.

Even the interpretations of the Ayatollah Khomeini, which in the end largely won out, were not, despite their partially 'fundamentalist' emphasis on scriptural morality and punishments, really traditional. They contained new ideological elements appropriate to an Islamic revolution and to direct rule by the ulama. Khomeini's notion of direct ulama rule is new to Shiʿism, as not only Western scholars like myself but also a Muslim supporter of Khomeini has noted:

> [T]he *mujtahids* were to some extent inhibited by the doctrine of the inherent illegitimacy of political authority in the absence of the Imam. The *usuli* position did not consider the possibility of the emergence of one of the *mujtahids* as the *mujtahid* of the *mujtahids*, as the Imam himself. And this confusion was there when Imam Khomeini returned to Tehran from Paris during the Revolution. For a time he was called 'Naib-i-Imam.' It was only gradually that the word 'naib' was dropped and he became Imam Khomeini. Of course, the title of Imam does not mean that he is the twelfth Imam. It simply means that he is the leader of the *Ummah* at this moment. In other words, this is a new doctrine something akin to 'first among equals.' . . . [W]hile [people] can follow other *mujtahids* in religious matters, they can also follow Imam Khomeini as the political leader of the Islamic State, of the Revolution, indeed of the *Ummah* today. So, the Revolution has in a sense taken the Shi'ia political thought further. An actual practical difficulty has created a situation where it is possible for one of the *mujtahids* to become Imam of the *Ummah*. And this, of course, is a great advance on the earlier position of the Shi'ia political thought.[19]

The victory of Khomeini's more absolutist version of Islam, with the addition to existing doctrines of ulama power and the notion of direct rule, did not come because most people really preferred this to the more latitudinarian or progressive version of other clerical and lay Islamic thinkers but because, as a corollary to his doctrinal absolutism (as well as his charisma and leadership qualities), Khomeini was the most uncompromising opponent of the Pahlavis, of the monarchy itself, and of foreign control and cultural domination.

There is some convergence, not wholly accidental, between the 'Manichean' world outlook of Khomeini and other Muslim thinkers and the more widespread phenomenon of 'Third Worldism.' The Manichean trend sees the world as largely divided into the just Muslim oppressed and the Western or Western-tied oppressors, and the more general ideology of the Third World similarly sees itself as economically drained and culturally colonized by an imperialist West. Such perceptions of 'we' and 'they,' the Third World and the West, evince little appreciation of internal problems and class and other contradictions within either culture. Shariati, Bani Sadr, Ghotbzadeh, and others were directly influenced by varieties of Third Worldism, including the sophisticated version of Marxist dependency theory espoused by Paul Vieille, long Bani Sadr's friend and mentor, and the ideas of Frantz Fanon, whom Shariati admired. Khomeini himself [was] probably not immune to such currents. At least one student of Khomeini's thought has noted the ayatollah's brand of Third Worldism and tentatively attributed it to contacts with Palestinians in Iraq, since such arguments entered his talks and writings during his exile there.[20] The fusion of 'modern,' secular Manicheanism, 'traditional' Islam, and uncompromising hostility to monarchy, dependence, and imperialism created a revolutionary ideology that distinguished the revolutionaries from the Western and Westernized oppressors as much as the constitutionalist ideology of 1906 distinguished revolutionaries from traditional, nonmodernizing autocrats.

The blend of Islam and Third Worldism fits an anti-Western, anti-imperialist mood, particularly among students and those sections of the urban population who—in contrast to the minority of Westernized Iranians with Western-style, usually well-paying jobs in the government or private sector—were either poor or in the traditional economy. The revolutionaries in 1905–11 disliked Russian and British encroachments, but their main wrath was directed against the Qajar dynasty and its inability to organize a strong and functioning state and nation. Even though the main wrath of the revolutionaries in 1978–79 was apparently also directed against a dynasty and a shah, the cases are not really parallel. The late shah, with whatever degree of accuracy, was seen as a willing tool of the West, whose culture and economic control had pervaded Iran in a way far more offensive to most than was the case in 1905. Iranians associated things Western with their plight, and they thought their cultural and economic problems could only be solved by a return to what they saw as purely Islamic ways. Hence, the paradox of a more 'traditionalist' Islamic, more 'antimodern' reaction in the revolution of 1978–79 than in that of 1905–11 can be explained primarily as a reaction to the rapid, exploitative growth of Western influence, of Westernizing rulers, and of new forms of imperialism in the intervening period.

The disillusionment with the West and the desire to return to Islam is not unique to Iran; it is found in different forms throughout much, if not most, of the Muslim world, sometimes in revolutionary ideologies and movements. These movements do not reject modern technology but call for a return to Islamic traditions, which are interpreted differently by reformists and fundamentalists. Often, as in Iran, enthusiasm for ideas like constitutionalism and republicanism continues, but in an Islamic context. The independent power, wealth, and ideological claims of the Shi'i ulama probably allowed its members to become the first leaders of a twentieth-century Islamic revolution. The unique strength of the Shi'i ulama and their consequent revolutionary leadership does not, however, negate the possibility of related revolts and revolutions in non-Shi'i lands. Similar conditions could provide the foundation and the desire for revolt, possibly intensified by the Iranian example and military success much as the Russo-Japanese War and Russian revolution in 1905 contributed to the Iranian constitutional revolution of 1905–11. The importance of the organized network of socio-ideological ties between the Iranian ulama and Iran's urban residents bears some resemblance to the urban organization of new Muslim groups in Egypt and elsewhere, despite lesser participation by the ulama in non-Iranian movements.[21] And the widespread feeling that Western liberalism and socialism have been tried and found wanting is also important.

The changes wrought by the Iranian revolution have not run their course. Most Iranians who fought for an Islamic republic (and many were fighting rather for secular versions of justice, democracy, or even socialism) wanted a well-functioning, egalitarian state—the kind of government suggested by Shariati and by Khomeini in 1978. The growth of open discontent and its suppression in a series of small civil wars and rampant executions since the revolutionary victory is evidence that many, and probably most, were not fighting for what they got. What they did in fact get includes economic decline and upheaval, strict laws and rules (often 'Islamic' at most in the sense that literalist Quranic and other legal punishments have sometimes been enforced in Muslim countries), arbitrary trials and summary punishments (not Islamic in any sense), a scramble for wealth and power among some of the ulama, new restrictions on women, and the like. Granted, the revolution had its more positive aspects: some concern for the poor and for equalization of incomes as well as limited kinds of local self-government and self management. Some Iranians also point to the decline in US influence as a benefit of revolution, but how much this decline is a real advance in the absence of a well functioning economy and a united country is questionable. The current balance has not proved satisfactory to most Iranians, although the mullas have shown themselves far more politically organized and capable of holding onto power than many, both within and outside Iran, would have expected.

This article is reprinted from *American Historical Review*, 88 (1983), pp. 579–598. Reprinted by permission of the *American Historical Review* and the author.

NOTES

1. Fundamentalism is here used for movements calling for a return to scriptural religion. Fundamentalist movements are mostly nineteenth- and twentieth-century phenomena, and none of them aims at or achieves a true re-creation of the religious past.

2. Gad G. Gilbar has noted that in the late nineteenth and early twentieth centuries grain production fell greatly, so that wheat and barley changed from export to import commodities. The consequent rise in the price of foodstuffs resulted in bread riots, often led by clerics, and

demands that grain exports be discontinued. Large-scale merchants encouraged transferring production from grain and cotton to opium, which according to Gilbar improved the welfare of almost all groups engaged in opium production and marketing. Gilbar, 'Persian Agriculture in the Late Qajar Period, 1860–1906: Some Economic and Social Aspects,' *Asian and African Studies*, 12 (1978): 321–65. Roger T. Olson's more detailed study of opium growing and sale indicates that opium production aided the better-off but subjected poorer peasants and townspeople to large price fluctuations in agricultural staples and, occasionally, to famine. Emphasis on opium clearly increased social and economic stratification. Olson, 'Persian Gulf Trade and the Agricultural Economy of Southern Iran in the Nineteenth Century,' in Michael E. Bonine and Nikki R. Keddie, eds, *Modern Iran: The Dialectics of Continuity and Change* (Albany, N.Y., 1981), 173–89. Claiming 'a certain improvement in the standard of living of the peasants,' Gilbar stated, 'First, there are various pieces of evidence to show that peasants in many areas had a more diversified daily diet, consuming commodities which they could hardly have afforded before. Sugar, tea, tobacco, and opium are perhaps the best examples of articles which peasants consumed in large quantities in the late 19th century.' There are problems with Gilbar's analysis. Not only has he presented evidence for four commodities that are unhealthful and should not be cited as proof of a 'more diversified daily diet,' but he has also failed to note that these four items quite likely replaced nutritious ones that, by his own evidence, were becoming expensive. The experience of most modern countries suggests that a kind of dietary Gresham's Law works to supplant fruits, vegetables, and meat when less nutritious and less costly products become available, and British documents as well as travel literature support the contention that the experience of modern Iran proves no exception. Some of Gilbar's other points are more convincing, but the argument is far from settled, and Willem M. Floor, in a paper at a 1981 conference at Harvard on the Iranian revolution of 1905–11, argued for the general immiseration of Iranians in the pre-revolutionary period. For my arguments and conclusions, see Nikki R. Keddie, *Roots of Revolution: An Interpretive History of Modern Iran* (New Haven, 1981), esp. 54–57.

3. See Gene R. Garthwaite, *Khans and Shahs: The Bakhtiari in Iran* (Cambridge, 1983), and 'Khans and Kings: The Dialectics of Power in Bakhtiari History,' in Bonine and Keddie, *Modern Iran*, 159–72; Willem M. Floor, 'The Political Role of the Lutis in Iran,' *ibid.*, 83–95; Ervand Abrahamian, *Iran between Two Revolutions* (Princeton, 1982); John Malcolm *The History of Persia*, 2 (London, 1815); and Keddie, *Roots of Revolution*, chaps. 2–3. For additional information, see the numerous anthropological articles on Iranian nomads.

4. Especially see Juan R. Cole, 'Imami Jurisprudence and the Role of the Ulama: Mortaza Ansari on Emulating the Supreme Exemplar,' in Nikki R. Keddie, ed., *Religion and Politics in Iran* (New Haven, 1983), 33–46; and Mortaza Ansari, *Sirat an-Najat* (n.p. [Iran], A.H. 1300 [1883]).

5. Especially see Eric Hooglund, 'Rural Participation in the Revolution,' *Middle East Research and Information Project Reports*, 87 (1980): 3–6; and Mary Hooglund, 'One Village in the Revolution,' *ibid.*, 7–12. Ervand Abrahamian and Farhad Kazemi in a seminal article have stressed what I see as partly derivative features of the Iranian peasantry in explaining its generally nonrevolutionary character—namely, the absence of significant outside market ties and of a substantial middle peasantry, which has elsewhere been found crucial in leading peasant revolts; Abrahamian and Kazemi, 'The Non-Revolutionary Peasantry in Modern Iran,' *Iranian Studies*, 11 (1978): 259–304. The authors have understated, though less than many social and comparative historians, the roles of geography, technology, and ecology. The arid climate of most of Iran has meant that its peasants have always been less densely settled and, hence, more difficult to organize; they have been, as the authors have noted, more than usually dependent on relatively expensive underground irrigation systems that easily came under landlord control. Tribal khans' dominance over peasants may also have decreased peasant revolutionary potential. Local peasant rebellions have been frequent but could not spread, given scattered villages and strong local power. The densely populated, productive, and organized lands of China, for example, were conducive to a far more organized and organizable, and frequently rebellious, peasantry. A strong middle peasantry has largely been due to such an environment. This argument based on environment is supported by Iran's own experience; Iran's most revolutionary peasants are found in the high-rainfall, densely settled, rice-growing province of Gilan, as the authors discussed, though with less stress on ecology. Abrahamian and Kazemi have covered all of the important questions, but I would emphasize more the ecological base of the issue.

6. Especially see Hamid Algar, *Mirza Malkum Khan* (Berkeley and Los Angeles, 1973); Nikki R. Keddie, *Sayyid Jamal ad-Din 'al-Afghani'* (Berkeley and Los Angeles, 1972); and Mangol Bayat, *Mysticism and Dissent: Socioreligious Thought in Qajar Iran* (Syracuse, N.Y., 1982). Among the important primary works and analyses of Qajar reformers in Persian are Fereidun Adamiyyat, *Fekr-e Azadi* (Tehran, A.H. 1340 [1961]; Mirza Agha Khan Kermani *et al.*, *Hasht Behesht* (n.p., n.d.); Nazem al-Islam Kermani, *Tarikh-e bidari-ye Iranian* (Tehran, A.H. 1332 [1953]); Ibrahim Safa'i, *Rahbaran-e Mashruteh* (Tehran, A.H. 1344 [1965–66]; Sefatallah Jamali Asadabadi, ed., *Maqalat-e Jamaliyeh* (Tehran, A.H. 1312 [1933–34]); Iraj Afshar and Asghar Mahdavi, *Majmu'eh-ye asnad va madarek-e chap nashodeh dar bareh-ye Sayyed Jamal ad-Din mashhur be Afghani* (Tehran, 1963); and Mohammad Mohit Tabataba'i, *Majmu'eh-ye asar-a Mirza Malkum Khan* (Tehran, A.H. 1327 [1948–49]).

7. Nikki R. Keddie, *Religion and Rebellion in Iran: The Tobacco Protest of 1891–1892* (London, 1966), and the Persian, French, Russian, and English sources cited therein.

8. Richard W. Cottam, *Nationalism in Iran* (2nd edn, Pittsburgh, 1979); and Keddie, *Roots of Revolution.*

9. The change in Iranian attitudes at this time is clear in documents pertaining to Iran in the British Foreign Office. Also see Nikki R. Keddie, Religion and Irreligion in Early Iranian Nationalism, in Keddie, ed., *Iran: Religion, Politics, and Society* (London, 1980), 13–52.

10. The Persian literature on this revolution is enormous. It includes invaluable classics by Nazem al-Islam Kermani, Ahmad Kasravi, Mehdi Malekzadeh, and Sayyed Hasan Taqizadeh as well as major background works by Fereidun Adamiyyat and Homa Nateq. For the main books in English, see Edward G. Browne, *The Persian Revolution of 1905–1909* (Cambridge, 1910); and Robert A. McDaniel, *The Shuster Mission and the Persian Constitutional Revolution* (Minneapolis, 1974). Other Persian works I have found useful in studying the constitutional revolution include Amin ad-Dauleh, *Khaterat-e siyasi*, ed. Hafez Farman-Farmaiyan (Tehran, 1952); Abolhasan Bozorgomid, *Az mast ke bar mast* (n.p., n.d.); 'Haidar Khan Amu Oghli,' *Yadgar 3* (*A.H. 1325* [1946–47]): 61–80; and Mehdi Qoli Hedayat Mokhber as-Saltaneh, *Khaterat va khaterat* (Tehran, A.H. 1329 [1950–51]).

11. The defense of constitutionalism was written in 1909 by Ayatollah Na'ini. Although it is discussed by H. Algar, among others, I have seen no Persian or Western books that refer to it before its republication with an introduction by Ayatollah Taleqani in 1955; see Algar, 'The Oppositional Role of the Ulama in Twentieth-Century Iran,' in Nikki R. Keddie, ed., *Scholars, Saints, and Sufis* (Berkeley and Los Angeles, 1972). Na'ini apparently withdrew the book from circulation shortly after its publication; see Abdul Hadi Hairi, *Shi'ism and Constitutionalism in Iran* (Leiden, 1977), 124, 158.

12. The economic and political events of the 1970s are well covered in F. Halliday, *Iran: Dictatorship and Development* (Harmondsworth, Middlesex, 1979); R. Graham, *Iran: The Illusion of Power* (rev. edn, London, 1979); and Keddie, *Roots of Revolution*, chap 7.

13. See Davies, 'Toward a Theory of Revolution,' in Davies, ed., *When Men Revolt and Why* (New York, 1971), 137–47; and Labrousse, *La Crise de l'économie française à la fin de l'ancien régime et au début de la revolution* (Paris, 1944), introduction.

14. James A. Bill has noted the correspondence between Brinton's views and the events of 1978–79; see Bill, 'Power and Religion in Revolutionary Iran,' *Middle East Journal*, 36 (1982): 22–47, esp. 30. The closeness of this fit is apparent in Brinton's own summary of the patterns apparent in the four great revolutions he discussed: 'First, these were all societies on the whole on the upgrade economically before the revolution came, and the revolutionary movements seem to originate in the discontents of not unprosperous people who feel restraint, cramp, annoyance, rather than downright crushing oppression ... Second, we find in our prerevolutionary society definite and indeed very bitter class antagonisms.... Fourth, the governmental machinery is clearly inefficient, ... partly because new conditions ...—specifically conditions attendant on economic expansion and the growth of new monied classes, new ways of transportation, new business methods —... laid an intolerable strain on governmental machinery adapted to simpler, more primitive conditions. Fifth, ... many individuals of the old ruling class ... come to distrust themselves, or lose faith in the traditions and habits of their class, grow intellectual, humanitarian or go over to the attacking groups ... [T]he ruling class becomes politically inept.... [I]t is almost safe to say that no government is likely to be overthrown from within its territory until it

loses the ability to make adequate use of its military and police powers. That loss of ability may show itself in the actual desertion of soldiers and police to the revolutionists, or in the stupidity with which the government manages its soldiers and police, or in both ways.... [W]ith the attainment of power it is clear that [the revolutionists] are not united. The group which dominates these first stages we call the moderates, though to emotional supporters of the old regime they look most immoderate.... [A]t the crisis period the extreme radicals, the complete revolutionists, are in power.... This pervasiveness of the Reign of Terror in the crisis period is partly explicable in terms of the pressure of war necessities and of economic struggles as well as of other variables: but it must probably also be explained as in part the manifestation of an effort to achieve intensely moral and religious ends here on earth.... A striking uniformity ... is their asceticism or ... condemnation of what we may call the minor as well as the major vices.' Brinton, *The Anatomy of Revolution* (Vintage Books, rev. edn, London, 1965), 250–51, 550.

15. Marx and Engels' basic view is stated, with some variations, in several works from the *Communist Manifesto* onward. Recent theoretical works touching on comparative revolution and influenced to some degree by Marx include those by Theda Skocpol, Charles Tilly, Eric Hobsbawm, George Rudé, and Barrington Moore. Although these shed much light on such topics as 'primitive rebels' (Hobsbawm), the autonomy of the state (Skocpol), the nature of urban and rural rebellious crowds (Rudé), and the reasons why some societies have had major revolutions and others not (Moore), they have less to say than has Marx on the kind of forces that led to revolution in Iran. Naturally, examining the Iranian revolution is not their aim, but certainly more work now needs to be done by social historians and sociologists to produce general hypotheses or theories that will encompass the Iranian phenomenon, especially since it may not be the last of its type. Skocpol has modified some of her views in the aftermath of the Iranian revolution; see Scopkol, 'Rentier State and Shi'a Islam in the Iranian Revolution,' *Theory and Society*, 11 (1982); 265–83, with comments by Eqbal Ahmad, Nikki R. Keddie, and Walter L. Goldfrank, *ibid.*, 285–304.

16. For an important comparative discussion of the revolution of 1978–79, see Gary Sick, *All Fall Down: America's Tragic Encounter with Iran* (New York, 1985). He has covered some of the same points in preliminary fashion in a recent article; see Sick, 'Washington's Encounter with the Iranian Revolution,' in Nikki R. Keddie and Eric Hooglund, eds, *The Iranian Revolution and the Islamic Republic* (Washington, 1982), 127–31, and his transcribed remarks in the ensuing 'General Discussion,' *ibid.*, 155–68.

17. The role of the ulama in the revolution of 1905–11 has become a point of controversy, in part because scholars have let their interpretation of history reflect their view of ulama action since the early 1960s. In 1969 Hamid Algar stated even more strongly than previous authors the general view of the ulama's importance and progressivism then, but Said Amir Arjomand in various articles and Willem M. Floor in a recent re-evaluation have played down the progressive role of the ulama in 1905–11 as in other periods. See Algar, *Religion and State in Iran*, 1785–1906 (Berkeley and Los Angeles, 1969), esp. chap. 14; Arjomand, 'The Ulama's Traditionalist Opposition to Parliamentarianism, 1907–1909,' *Middle East Studies*, 17 (1981): 174–90, and 'The State and Khomeini's Islamic Order,' *Iranian Studies*, 13 (1980): 147–64; Floor, 'The Revolutionary Character of the Iranian Ulama: Wishful Thinking or Reality?' *International Journal of Middle East Studies*, 12 (1980): 501–24; and Keddie, *Religion and Politics*, 73–98.

18. On these intellectuals, see Yann Richard, 'Contemporary Shi'i Thought,' chapter 8 part 2 of Keddie, *Roots of Revolution*; and Keddie, *Roots of Revolution*, chapter 8 part 1: 'Intellectual and Literary Trends to 1960.' Among the most important works of these intellectuals, which give an idea of their criticism of the 'Westoxication' of many Iranians and suggest the alternative Islamic reforms that some of them put forth, are Jalal Al-e Ahmad, *Gharbzadegi* (Tehran, A.H. 1341 [1961–62]), and *Dar khedmat va khianat-e raushanfekran* (Tehran, n.d.); Abolhassan Bani Sadr, *Eqtesad-e tauhidi* (n.p., n.d.); Ali Shariati, *Tashayyo'-e 'Alavi va Tashayyo'-e Safavi* (n.p., A.H. 1352 [1973?]), and *Islamshenasi* (n.p., n.d.); and Ayatollah Mahmud Taleqani, *Islam va Malekiyyat dar moqayeseh be nezamha-ye eqtesadi-ye gharb* (n.p., n.d.).

19. Kalim Siddiqui [*sic*, Siddiqi] *et al.*, *The Islamic Revolution: Achievements, Obstacles, and Goals* (London, 1980). 16–17.

20. Gregory Rose, '*Velayat-e Faqih* and the Recovery of Islamic Identity in the Thought of Ayatollah Khomeini,' Nikki R. Keddie, ed., *Religion and Politics in Iran* (New Haven, 1973), 166–

88. Also see Nikki R. Keddie, 'Islamic Revival as Third Worldism,' in J.-P. Digard, ed., *Le Cuisinier et le philosophe: Hommage à Maxime Rodinson* (Paris, 1982), 275–81. Many of Khomeini's speeches are available in rough translations from the Foreign Broadcast Information Service, and some of his works are translated in Hamid Algar, ed., *Islam and Revolution: Writings and Declarations of Imam Khomeini* (Berkeley, 1981). Not yet translated is the very important early book by Khomeini, *Kashf-e Asrar* (n.p., n.d. [ca. 1944]), in which he attacked both the Pahlavi monarchy and secularist intellectuals but did not yet completely reject monarchy or call for total rule by clerics.

21. On the importance of Shi'i urban networks to the organization and fulfillment of the Iranian revolution, especially see Skocpol, 'Rentier State and Shi'a Islam.' On the economic and intellectual forces in contemporary Egypt, especially see Malcolm H. Kerr and El Sayed Yassin, eds, *Rich and Poor States in the Middle East: Egypt and the New Arab Order* (Boulder, Colo., 1982); and Fouad Ajami, *The Arab Predicament* (New York, 1981).

The Crisis of Religious Legitimacy in Iran

OLIVIER ROY

The Iranian Revolution was founded on a dual legitimacy, religious and political, which was embodied by Imam Ruhollah Khomeini. But the Constitution, the rulings of Khomeini, and the political process since his demise show that the political aspect has come to dominate and define the role of religion. This politicization, accompanied by an Iranization of supranational Shi'ism, leads to a de facto secularization, and actually undermines the traditional basis of the strength and independence of the Shi'i clergy.

The election of Iranian President Muhammad Khatami in May 1997 was an expression not only of a popular call for a more open and democratic society, but also of the increasing crisis of religious legitimacy in Iran. The Iranian Islamic Revolution was, from its inception, explicitly based on the conjunction of two legitimacies, religious and political, through the concept of *Velayat-e Faqih*, "the Mandate of the Jurist," meaning that the highest authority of the Islamic Revolution, the Guide or Leader (*Rahbar*), should be both one of the highest religious authorities (*marja'* or "source of imitation," plural *maraji'*) and *the* political leader, who "understands his time" ("*agah be zaman*") and therefore could lead a mass movement. But this congruence was realized only in the late Imam Ruhollah Khomeini's person. The Constitution stressed that Khomeini was both the highest ranking cleric and the political leader *par excellence*: thus, the ideal type of the Guide is a *faqih* (jurist) who embodies both legitimacies, before his appointment. And, in any case, after his appointment, he should be considered as both a "learned cleric" and a political leader.

But Khomeini's death in 1989 meant the end of this double legitimacy. His successor as Guide, Ayatollah 'Ali Khamene'i, was not a leading religious authority. This led to two questions: should the Guide be primarily a leading religious authority, or a political one? Second, how could an Islamic revolution bypass, through a political appointment, the highest religious authorities of the time, and even turn its back on some *shari'a* (Islamic law) requirements? Nevertheless, this conceptual crisis did not turn into a political one as long as all elections (presidential and parliamentary) selected candidates from a relatively homogeneous ruling elite from the time of Khomeini's death in 1989 until 1997. But, in May 1997, President Khatami was elected against the avowed wishes of the Guide, Khamene'i, bringing the two legitimacies into contradiction, even though, of course, the new president officially recognized the supremacy of the Guide. If the Guide, who already lacked some religious credentials, is now losing his political support, on which legitimacy is his leadership still based?

What we are witnessing since Khatami's election is the unfolding of a contradiction which already existed in the text of the Constitution: in a religious revolution, such as the Iranian Islamic Revolution, the status and role of religion is nevertheless defined by political institutions, not religious ones. Politics rule over religion. The crisis of the religious legitimacy is leading to the supremacy of politics, and subsequently to a *de facto* secularization. There is a growing tendency, not only among democrats and liberals, but also traditional clerics, to separate religion and politics, this time in order to save Islam from politics, and not, as was the case in most of the processes of secularization in Western Europe, to save politics from religion.

We can distinguish four levels of crisis: conceptual, clerical, political, and religious, leading to a complex array of positions from the different actors. As we shall see, it is a bit difficult in Iran to oppose "radicals" and "moderates," "conservatives" and "liberals," "traditionalists" and "modernists," not to speak of "leftists" and "rightists." If Khatami might qualify as a liberal, a moderate and a modernist, many of his supporters came from the radical side (and specifically from the American Embassy hostage-takers, such as Muhammad Musavi Kho'einiha and 'Ali Akbar Mohtashemi), or from the "statist-leftist" side, like Mir-Hosein Musavi or Ayatollah Hassan Sana'i, whose foundation is promoting the *fatwa* calling for the death of British writer Salman Rushdie. On the other hand, the present "radicals," who oppose the rapprochement with the United States and advocate the supremacy of the Velayat-e Faqih over democracy, may now be branded as "conservatives," because they are simply trying to "conserve" the Revolution's establishment and prevent any social and political change. To make things even more complex, many "traditionalist" clerics support Khatami out of mistrust for the concept of Velayat-e Faqih, which they see as a modern innovation that undermines the traditional pillars of the clerical order.

The cornerstone for a classification of political factions inside the Islamic regime is in fact the attitude towards Velayat-e Faqih (hereafter, for convenience, VF). It is not just a question of "opposing" or "favoring" the concept; another issue is the definition of the VF: is it primarily a religious, or primarily a political, function? Hence there are four positions, if we combine both criteria:

1) Those who favor the VF and consider that Ayatollah Khamene'i is the best qualified person for the function. Here we find all the "conservatives" who backed the candidacy of Parliament Speaker 'Ali Akbar Nateq-Nuri in the presidential elections of May 1997. These are the hardliners of the regime.

2) Those who favor the VF but do not consider Khamene'i as the right man for the job. This position is expressed in a very vocal way by Ayatollah Hosain 'Ali Montazeri, who had been designated as the successor to Imam Khomeini before March 1989 when Khomeini stripped him of the title. For them, the VF derives first from religious knowledge, and only secondarily from political ability. The faqih should be a leading *mujtahid* (a religious scholar capable of independent interpretation), and a marja', but in any case his powers are not absolute.[1]

3) Those who never accepted the VF, because it contradicts the principle of the *marja'iyya*. These represent the traditional religious leadership, the "grand ayatollahs" (*ayatollah 'ozma*), even if they did not oppose the Revolution. The main figure is the Grand Ayatollah Abu al-Qasim Musavi Khu'i, who died in 1992 in Najaf, Iraq. Many of the grand ayatollahs shared this view, including Kazem Shari'at-Madari (who died in 1983 after being stripped of his religious status by Khomeini), even if they kept silent (such as Grand Ayatollah Muhammad Reza Golpayegani). In this category were found the majority of the grand ayatollahs of the 1980s. It is ironic, then, when the Iranian system is called the "regime of the Ayatollahs," since most of the grand ayatollahs did not support it.

4) Those who never accepted the VF as a theological concept but acknowledge the need for a political leadership and accept Khamene'i as the political leader of the Revolution. In this category is Shaykh Muhammad Fadlallah of Lebanon, who, as a disciple of Ayatollah Khu'i, could not endorse the VF, but, as a radical political leader, backed the Iranian Revolution and its leadership. This view comes close to recognizing the position of Leader as actually embodied by Khamene'i today.

THE CONCEPTUAL CRISIS

The Basic Tenets of the Revolution and its Contradictions

The Iranian Revolution always claimed to have two sources: God's sovereignty and the people's will.[2] If God's sovereignty is intrinsic to the very idea of a "religious revolution," one should never forget the populist and revolutionary, arxist, origin of the Revolution. As Professor Ervand Abrahamian noted, volution is the last of the leftist, "third-worldist" and anti-imperialist revs, although it has been carried out under an Islamic cloak.[3] One of the reasons for its success was the combination of this leftist and populist trend with a recurrent traditional search for an Islamic (Shi'i) order, which attracted a large part of the clergy and traditional circles (such as the Bazaar). In the process of politicization, this traditional Shi'i Islam has been recast into a modern revolutionary millenarist terminology ("revolution" or "*enqelab*," "ideology" or "*ideolozhi*," "classless society" or "*jame'e-ye towhidi*," the "party line" transformed into "the Imam's line" or "*khatt-e Imam*," etc.).

When the Revolution succeeded, however, it had to establish a new Islamic political order, not on a *tabula rasa*, but on a clerical Islamic institution which had already existed and developed in Iran since roughly the end of the eighteenth century, and which had found a new popularity during the last decade of opposition to the Shah.[4] This clerical order was based on a collective and informal spiritual leadership of some Great Ayatollahs, each considered a person able to interpret the Divine Law (mujtahid) and thus a source of imitation (*marja'-e taqlid*) for their followers. Each mujtahid was autonomous in a certain field: he delivered "diplomas," appointed representatives, opened teaching centers, had financial autonomy through the direct collection of religious taxes, and enjoyed a large degree of autonomy from the Iranian government (mainly because most of them lived in Najaf, Iraq). Imam Khomeini became, after 1963, one of the leading figures of this clergy, and succeeded in making of it an instrument for implementing the Revolution, even if most of Khomeini's peers were a bit reluctant about his ideological conceptions, and specifically the Velayat-e Faqih.

Interestingly enough, the Iranian Islamic Revolution did not bring this existing clerical structure into power, but instead built a specific institutional framework, staffing it either with laymen (Muhammad 'Ali Raja'e, Hassan Habibi, Mir-Hosein Musavi) or middle ranking clerics, the hojatolislams (as were 'Ali Akbar Hashemi-Rafsanjani, 'Ali Khamene'i, Muhammad Musavi Kho'einiha), plus some middle ranking ayatollahs, who were not considered as maraji' (Muhammad Beheshti, Muhammad Reza Mahdavi-Kani, Ahmad Jannati). The grand ayatollahs were kept aside (Khu'i, Golpayegani, Muhammad 'Ali Araki, Muhammad Tabataba'i-Qomi) or even repressed (like Kazem Shari'at-Madari).

Article 5 of the Constitution stipulates that, in the absence of the Hidden Imam, the leadership of the Shi'i community should be entrusted in a "just and pious jurist (faqih) aware of the circumstances of his time (*agah be zaman*)," who should assume the responsibility of his office in accordance with Article 107 of the Constitution. The original 1979 Constitution stated that the faqih should be chosen from among the maraji' in one of two ways: 1) an immediate and direct recognition by the people, both as a "source of imitation" (marja') and a Guide (rahbar), or 2) a selection of one outstanding figure or of a collective leadership (three or five faqihs) through an Assembly of Experts (*Majles-e Khobregan*), made up of clerics elected by the Iranian people. Most of the provisions of the 1979 Constitution and all the amendments brought into effect in 1989 show how the requirements for the faqih shifted from religious to political qualifications, even if the Guide always has to be a cleric. Article 107 was amended in 1989: it no longer stipulates that the faqih should be among the highest ranking clerics, although it states that this was the case for Khomeini. The amended Constitution of 1989 also dropped the possibility of a direct election of the Guide by the people, as if only Imam Khomeini could have been directly recognized by the people as marjaʿ and rahbar. The disappearance of any mention of the marjaʿ in the 1989 Constitution shows clearly that the Guide, who is the supreme authority in the Islamic Republic, need not necessarily be the leading authority in religion. These dispositions underline the discrepancy between the traditional clerical establishment and the new revolutionary order. According to the Shiʿi tradition, a marjaʿ, or grand ayatollah, is usually selected by his clerical peers through a long process with little role for the *vox populi*, except that it is understood that there should be a broad consensus.[5] There is no precise and institutionalized process of appointing a grand ayatollah, and there is rarely just one at a time. That is the traditional structure. But on the contrary, according to the Iranian Constitution, there should preferably be only one Guide, and he is not appointed by his peers, because he has no peer, but by an elected body. Of course, the Assembly of Experts which elects him is made up of clerics, but they are themselves elected by ordinary Iranian citizens. Candidacies to the Assembly are screened by the Council of Guardians, itself appointed (in part) by the Guide. Thus the Council also is not an expression of the leading traditional clerical elite. In particular, they are all Iranians, excluding the Arab Shiʿis from the process of appointing the leader of the Shiʿis of the world. It is a political appointment, not a religious one. It is interesting to note that all the modalities for choosing a Guide from among the faqihs are through political means (elections) and that only the personality of Khomeini embodied ideally both legitimacies, religious and political. In the contradiction between the two legitimacies, politics explicitly prevail over religion.

In fact, after Khomeini's demise and the appointment of Khameneʾi as the new Guide, some clerical circles tried to promote either Grand Ayatollah Golpayegani or Grand Ayatollah Araki as the new marjaʿ. That would have reinstated a double order and separated the religious from the political legitimacy. But nothing was set up in official terms, even though Araki had supported the appointment of Khameneʾi as Guide and had issued some fatwas in support of the regime (including the one banning TV satellite dishes). The reason is obvious: an official endorsement of a new marjaʿ would have acknowledged the dissociation between religious authority and political function, which would be the negation of Khomeini's concept of an Islamic Revolution. But the consequence is to put the political order above the religious one.

The Prevalence of the Political State over Religion

Why, according to the Constitution as amended in 1989, need the Guide not necessarily be a marjaʿ? It might be just in case there is no marjaʿ, but why should there be no marjaʿ at a given time? The probable answer is that the distinction between marjaʿ and Guide has been established precisely because there were other marajiʿ in 1989 who were not recognized as political leaders by the revolutionary Islamist circles. Of the two conditions required to become the Guide, the real one is not having specific religious qualifications, but being "aware of the times" ("agah be zaman"): that is, to be politically minded and to promote the ideological tenets of the Revolution. It is true that during the last century, many marajiʿ took a rather quietist approach towards State power, even if they were adamant about the Islamization of law and the protection of the clergy's interests (such as Ayatollahs Abu'l-Qasim Kashani and Hosein Borujerdi). This is why, for the Constitution, a marjaʿ could be a Guide only if he is first a "political man," as Khomeini explicitly stated in a speech in March 1989.[6] During the discussions on the 1979 Constitution, Khomeini was not in favor of making the marjaʿiyya a prerequisite for being chosen as a Guide, although the opposing view prevailed.[7] It is obvious that from the beginning the prevalence of politics over religion was in Khomeini's mind. He knew all the marajiʿ of his time, of course, and was very aware that they were not prone to follow a revolutionary line.

Khomeini was able to combine the two, by stressing always the political aspect of the Revolution, even against the shariʿa. Every time Khomeini had to clarify the complex relations between religious law and revolutionary legitimacy, he opted to emphasize the latter. This prevalence of politics over religion concerns more than the issue of choosing the Leader or Guide. It touches also the realm of the religious law or shariʿa, the cornerstone of any Islamic state. Here also, the logic of the prevalence of the State is written into the Constitution, even if lip service is paid to the shariʿa (as to the Sovereignty of God): Article 36, Chapter 3 states that "the passing of a sentence must be only by a competent court and in accordance with law," meaning that a *qadi* or judge cannot simply refer to the shariʿa, but also must refer to the law of the State. No one can take the law in his own hands in the name of the shariʿa (except for a clerical court set up to deal with religious matters). Many provisions of the Constitution are not in accordance with the shariʿa (the definition of citizenship, the equality of men and women, the presence of attorneys in court proceedings, etc.).[8]

Khomeini was very keen to clarify the question of the relationship between shariʿa and Iranian law explicitly. In his famous letter to then-President Khameneʾi (6 January 1988), he stated that "the government can unilaterally abrogate legal (*shar'i*) agreements ..."[9] "Legal" here means conforming to the shari'a. It does not simply mean that the government might decide on things which are not in the shari'a (such as customs duties), which has always been the case even for very fundamentalist regimes. Khomeini explicitly states that the government might ignore or alter some shari'a requirements. Khomeini explains, for example, that the government might cancel pilgrimage, if it is in the interest of the Islamic State. The official reason for subordinating shari'a to the State law is to achieve the higher interest of the Islamic State and hence of Islam. But here again it is the political instance which decides what is essentially Islamic, in opposition to the prescribed rules of the shari'a. This assertive policy of binding shari'a to the State law explains the manner in which Imam Khomeini solved the conflict between the Parliament and Council of Guardians, whose duty is, according to the Constitution, to check the conformity with the shari'a of the laws passed by the Parliament. The Council was so adamant about its prerogatives that the issue became deadlocked: many laws were suspended in the absence of arbitration, which could come only from the Guide himself. So in 1987, Khomeini created the Expediency Council (*Majma'-e Tashkhis-e Maslahat*) as a way to deprive the Council of Guardians, in which religious lawyers had the upper hand, of the last word about the conformity with Islam of laws passed by the Parliament. Appointments to the Expediency Council were political and, as indicated by the term "*maslahat*" (the common interest) in the Council's very title, the goal of the Council was a political one.

The Accession of Khamene'i as the Rahbar

The growing discrepancy between religious legitimacy and political logic was further advanced by the appointment of Khamene'i as Guide in 1989, for not only did he not qualify as a marja' but he was even not an ayatollah, but just a hojatolislam. Soon after his appointment as Guide, he became known as ayatollah. The choice was then either to acknowledge the gap between the two legitimacies or to try to reunite them. The occasion came after the deaths of Ayatollahs Golpayegani and Araki (in 1993 and 1994, respectively), the two last maraji' living in Iran to be universally recognized. Government circles launched an offensive to have Khamene'i recognized as a marja'. This would have restored the conjunction between the two legitimacies, in favor of the State and at the expense of the clergy. But the idea was dropped in the face of a passive opposition from the clerical circles of Qom (among others, Ayatollahs Taki Bahjat, Ahmad Azari-Qomi, and Fazel Lankarani). This opposition was unspoken, but the reluctance of the high ranking clerics was so obvious that the marja'iyya could not be bestowed on Khamene'i without enlarging an already existing gap between traditionalist clerics and the ruling elites. The Association of Qom's Religious Teachers (*Jama'e-ye Modaressin-e Hawze-ye Qom*), which is comprised of some 30 leading clerics of the holy city, began to distance itself from Tehran's politics. It would be a mistake to interpret their reluctance in terms of political opposition; they support the Islamic Republic. Many clerics from Qom are simply eager to restore the credibility and the autonomy of the clergy, even if they approve of the present form of government. Few attacked directly Khamene'i's credentials for being the Guide, as Ayatollah Montazeri was to do in December 1997. But about half of the members of the Association did not openly endorse the candidacy of Nateq-Nuri for the presidency in May 1997, although he was seen as the "official" candidate endorsed by the Guide himself.

The discrepancy between the political and the clerical order has logically been coupled with a slow *de facto* de-clericalization of the political institutions. For instance, after the reform of the Expediency Council in March 1997, the six religious lawyers appointed from the Council of Guardians lost their right to vote on matters not related to constitutional issues: the majority of the members are now laymen, appointed by the Guide[10]; even those who are clerics are appointed because they are members of the ruling circles and not because of their religious qualifications.[11] In fact, the Expediency Council has become a mini-Central Committee including most of the "big shots" of the regime. At the same time, the number of clerics elected to the Parliament dropped from 125 in the first Assembly to 50 in that of 1996.[12]

The Clerical Crisis

The Islamic Revolution destroyed the pillars of the autonomy of the international Shi'i clergy, which reached its culmination precisely on the eve of the Revolution. According to the Constitution, Shi'ism is Islam *par excellence* in Iran.[13] But this promotion of Shi'ism appears to have been a mixed blessing, because it led both to the "statization" and the "Iranization" of Shi'ism.

As we saw, the Revolution has weakened the traditional Shi'i clerical structure in favor of a political organization. All the "traditional" Shi'i clerical logic (established since the eighteenth century) has been ignored or bypassed by the institutions created by the Islamic Revolution, in order to ensure Islamization. The Guide is not necessarily a marja'. The interpretation of the shari'a is no longer a clerical prerogative. The Council of Guardians is not an emanation of the higher clergy but is appointed by the Guide. The Expediency Council is a secular and purely political body. The economic and territorial autonomy of the clergy has disappeared in favor of the State's structures.

On the other hand, the traditional clerical structures are experiencing a deep crisis after the Revolution. The marja'iyya is in crisis, because the procedures for the renewing of clerical elites are no longer working. The maraji' do not play a key role in actual politics. Grand Ayatollahs Khu'i, Golpayegani, and Araki are dead. The remaining grand ayatollahs are either very old (Muhammad Qomi), or stay aloof from the Revolution (Ahmad Azari-Qomi) when they are not under house arrest (Muhammad Rouhani, Montazeri, Muhammad Shirazi in Qom, ʿAli Muhammad Sistani in Najaf). There is an obvious suspicion on the part of the State towards grand ayatollahs whose constituency is independent of the revolutionary movement. For instance, Shirazi is the spiritual leader of the Bahraini Shiʿis (among others); he never supported the VF, and two of his sons are also under house arrest.

Moreover the aging marajiʿ have been unwilling or unable to designate successors. But even if they had wanted to do so, there is a generation gap. The youngest religious scholars joined the revolutionary movement and distanced themselves from the religious establishment, except for Khomeini. Most of the clerics born in the 1930s, who could have provided the next generation of marajiʿ have devoted a large part of their time to politics (and sometimes spent time in jail under the Shah), which prevented them from pursuing their studies at the highest level; the ones who kept studying are discredited precisely because they were not involved in politics, lacking the political legitimacy that could qualify them in the eyes of the ruling political elites. That would not have been a drawback, had the clergy been able to retain its autonomy. But that autonomy is no longer the case. The religious taxes (*khoms* and *zakat*) are now distributed through the Assembly of Experts, headed by Ayatollah ʿAli Meshkini. Traditionally the *mujtahids* used to offer a stipend to their students; nowadays it comes from the State. It seems that only Montazeri has been able to keep some financial autonomy.[14] The course of studies is more and more regulated by the State, although the Association of Religious Teachers in Qom still supervises the right to teach in the holy city. The territorial immunity that the clergy enjoyed has also disappeared: Najaf and Karbala', the Shiʿite holy cities in Iraq, had been taken under Iraqi government control in 1979, and the Shiʿi rebellion in southern Iraq was crushed in February and March 1991, without any strong reaction from Tehran. In Qom, the Hizbullah groups do not hesitate to interrupt Montazeri's teaching when he is too vocal against the Guide: the "*bast*," or traditional sanctuary for religious buildings from the State's encroachment, has almost disappeared, on the grounds that in the name of the Islamic State, everything that is Islamic should be under State supervision.

But this statization has met some resistance, based more on corporatist feeling and not on a political opposition. Qom retains a certain distance from political circles, as illustrated by the role of the Association of Qom Religious Teachers. Among its 30-odd members, only 14 publicly endorsed Nateq-Nuri's candidacy for the presidency in May 1997. Some of its members also publicized their non-endorsement of the official candidate. The attacks against Montazeri have upset many clerics, even those who do not support his ideas; they defend the immunity of the clerical establishment against State encroachment. Ayatollah Taki

Behjat closed his seminary in December 1997 to protest the attacks against Montazeri.

Why has the clerical establishment been unable to resist statization? First, the clerics had to endorse the Revolution, because its avowed aim was to impose Islam and it was led by Imam Khomeini, who was seen as a grand ayatollah. Secondly, the clerical structures were not embodied in a bureaucracy. The process of building a strong hierarchy among clerics was rather recent (the nineteenth century) and never really fully achieved.[15] The system was in fact rather flexible and based on consensus. Such a consensus worked in favor of the radicals during the revolutionary period, the moderates keeping a low profile, and avoiding vocal critics of the Islamic regime. When the Revolution created a bureaucracy and imposed formal rules for choosing the leadership, it had no parallel or rival system among the clergy. And finally, many hojatolislams and middle level ayatollahs found in the new State's bureaucracy social promotion, new jobs and perquisites, and a means to provide clients or family members with such advantages.

But the "statization" of the Shi'i clergy led also to its "Iranization." As we saw, the body which elects the Guide is made up of Iranian nationals elected by Iranian citizens (even if, according to the Constitution, the Guide is not necessarily an Iranian). The obsolescence of the marja'iyya deprived Arab Shi'i clerics of any possibility to be recognized as leading religious authorities by the Iranian authorities, and even to establish direct relations with Iranian clerics not linked with the State apparatus. There is no longer a neutral place to meet, as was the case with Najaf prior to 1979. Qom is under Iranian government supervision, even indirectly. Najaf and Karbala' are under strict police control by Saddam Husayn's Iraqi government. In fact, the nationalization of the Shi'i clergy is not limited to Iran. Every state with a strong Shi'i population tries to nationalize it: Saddam Husayn can obviously not accept that an Iranian cleric could be appointed as marja' in Najaf and enjoy some of the autonomy his predecessors had. Even if Saddam is more eager to weaken or even destroy the Shi'i clergy based in Iraq than to favor it, he nevertheless tries to promote an "Arab" marja' for Iraq, most recently Muhammad Sadiq al-Sadr,[16] and maintains Ayatollah Sayyid 'Ali Sistani under house arrest. But, even when they are repressed, most Shi'i groups outside Iran shape their policy within a national framework, allying themselves with other local opposition groups; as in Iran, they choose as political leaders mid-level clerics ('Ali Mazari, Karim Khalili and Muhammad Mohaqqeq for the Afghan Hizb-e Wahdat), who usually did not have Khomeini as their marja' prior to the Revolution, but more quietist grand ayatollahs, such as Khu'i. The process of nationalization of the Shi'i clergy, and the weakening of the marja'iyya is thus not limited to Iran, but is a general phenomenon in the Shi'i areas of the Middle East.

A clear example are the Iraqi Shi'is, who endeavored as early as February

1991 to promote an *Iraqi* answer to Saddam, trying to establish a common national Iraqi front. It is symptomatic that such eminent personalities as Muhammad Bahr ol Ulum or the sons of Ayatollah Khu'i are pursuing their efforts inside a national, and even patriotic framework. What we see is the transformation of Shiʿi Islamism into "Islamo-nationalism" at the expense of the supra-national clergy; in addition, the Iranian government has more and more difficulties in imposing its views on non-Iranian Shiʿis. The paradox of the Iranian Islamic Revolution is that it has contributed to giving roots to the nation-state, by giving it a religious legitimacy at the expense of the translational solidarities.[17]

We saw that the State's logic is now prevailing, but this State is not abstract: it is the Iranian State, with its Iranian geostrategic interests. This explains why the Iranian strategic alignments have less and less to do with Islam, and even (which is relatively new) with Shiʿism. The rapprochement with Saudi Arabia and the Gulf monarchies, not to speak of the United States, the close links with Armenia and Russia against Azerbaijan (where the bulk of the population is Shiʿi), the lack of support for the Iraqi Shiʿis during the 1991 Gulf War crisis and for the Bahraini Shiʿis in 1997, all show that the clerical links which were instrumental in mobilizing the Shiʿi communities in favor of the Islamic Revolution, have either been destroyed or have become alienated from the Iranian government.

The international structures of the Shiʿi clergy are slowly unraveling. Many Arab clerics, like the Lebanese Shaykh Muhammad Husayn Fadlallah, dissociate their political support for Tehran from their choices about who should be the marjaʿ. Fadlallah has supported Sistani's candidacy for marjaʿiyya in Najaf and is not opposed to seeing his friends promoting his own candidacy. Shaykh Muhammad Mahdi Shams al-Din in Lebanon, who never supported the Islamic Revolution, is acting as if there will be no other marjaʿ: he is promoting his own teaching institutions in Khalde, with no reference to Qom. Shiʿi solidarity is expressed more and more through political channels. Iran's main leverage in Lebanon is the Hizbullah, which has its own networks of religious training, totally independent from Shaykh Shams al-Din's training centers. It is a clear case of the growing divisions brought about by the prevalence of politics inside a clerical structure which was rather homogeneous 20 years earlier (or more exactly, successfully tried to appear homogeneous).

The crisis of the marjaʿiyya is parallel to that of the Velayat-e Faqih. There could not be two kinds of leading authority, but the weakening of the first is proceeding alongside the weakening of the second. In fact, it is the very idea of a religious leadership which is dwindling, because the politicization of the function has framed it into a national and statist structure, which is in contradiction with the idea of a transnational clergy. Paradoxically, the only way to restore religious legitimacy is to withdraw from State politics, which means a "secularization" of some sort. Of course, such a move does not prevent many traditional clerics from advocating both an Islamization of law and mores, and a withdrawal from State management. As we saw in the beginning, clerics who criticize the VF do so from different perspectives. The main stream is "traditionalist," meaning that they want to keep an Islamic hand in issues of law and the constitution, but with less direct involvement in politics. For them "secularization" has no meaning, although it is probably what is going to happen. The clergy will not recover the strength it had during the first decade of the Revolution.

In fact, the vanishing of the revolutionary dreams has left the clergy largely divided. The mainstream is certainly "neo-fundamentalist," that is, stressing the shariʿa and moral order, but deeply divided on political issues, or more precisely on the VF and clerical participation in State politics. A small fringe of liberal, and even secular-minded, clerics, seems to be emerging slowly, trying to express in a religious language the new trends that are changing Iranian society, as we shall see in the fourth part of this article.

The Political Crisis

The political legitimacy of the Guide is based on the people's support, but what if elections go contrary to the Guide's will? Such a political crisis erupted after the election of President Khatami. It is no secret that his opponent, Nateq-Nuri, had the favor of the Guide. By "losing" the elections through his proxy, the Guide lost a major part of his *political legitimacy*, at the very time the function of the VF had evolved into a mainly political one. Both legitimacies are definitively moving apart, while neither is fully enjoyed by the present Guide. Worse, Khatami undeniably won his political legitimacy through the elections. In these circumstances, what remains of the Guide's function and how might the relations between him and the president evolve?

The presidential elections showed that the consensus among the ruling elite has largely eroded and that there are political issues which should be addressed. The Rafsanjani era, which was supposed to achieve a smooth liberalization without questioning the basic tenets of the regime, ended in a deadlock. No drastic changes have been undertaken. The social and economic situation is worsening every year. Growing corruption and more conspicuous wealth among the new upper classes has antagonized not only the middle class, but also the lower classes, who provided the bulk of the regime's support. Even if the *basiji* (the "Mobilization" forces, unpaid voluntary militias from the 1980–88 Iran-Iraq War) are still devoted to the Guide, they openly criticize the weakening of the revolutionary spirit and the spread of "materialism." A more and more depoliticized population, and particularly the youth who have been brought up under the Islamic regime, is fed up with the "moral order" and would like access to the kinds of entertainments which have been banned because they express "foreign cultural aggression" and "immorality" (e.g., the mixing of men and women). Sports is a field where youth has expressed its opposition. In December 1997, a throng of thousands of young women forced open the doors of the stadium where the victorious national soccer team was parading. There is a growing pressure from below, and it is time to provide some safety valve if the regime hopes to avoid more popular demonstrations.

Three issues are at stake: the alleviation of the "moral order" strictures (issues such as the forced wearing of the *chador*, co-education, free mixing of genders, entertainment, satellite dishes, etc.), multi-partyism, and economic reforms. Khatami vowed a cultural and political liberalization during his campaign and has tried to promote some changes since he has been in office (less harassment from the police, a curb on basiji interventions, promotion of women, a passport for the "liberal" Islamic thinker ʿAbdolkarim Sorush, etc.). New newspapers are flourishing, though some have been banned, and the political debate in the press is very heated. But true multi-partyism has still not been established.

In fact, Khatami endeavored first to shake the taboos on which the Islamic Revolution is based. He did not say a word against the VF, but took public stands very different from the Guide on sensitive issues of foreign policy, the main one being, of course, relations with the United States (as in his interview with CNN in January 1998). Iranian foreign policy did not drastically change after Khatami, not only because of the resistance of the conservatives (as in the speech of the Guide at the Organization of the Islamic Conference summit in December 1997), but also because the new course of Iranian foreign policy had been largely adopted before Khatami's election (rapprochement with Saudi Arabia, a lower profile against Israel, an end to the exportation of the Revolution, cooperation with Russia on the Caucasus and Central Asia, settlement of the crisis with the European Union over Iranian operations against dissidents in Europe, etc.).

In fact, Khatami is not so much charting a new course as openly questioning the taboos of the Revolution, that is, the heritage of Khomeini, which is the main critique that his opponents have brought against him, referring to the "will" of Imam Khomeini. Questioning the symbols is not merely symbolic in Iran, it has an impact in politics.

As far as the economy is concerned, Khatami is in an uneasy situation. His followers belong to different schools of thought, and the liberals in politics are not necessarily liberals in economics. To open and liberalize the economy would mean both attacking the "perks" of the *nouveaux riches* and cutting the subsidies for the poor, which would destroy the networks of clientism, patronage and social integration on which the regime is based. Reforming the economy thus faces both populist and conservative opposition. A major issue involves the "Foundations," financial holdings which manage enormous wealth without accountability. Another issue is foreign investment, desperately needed by the oil industry. That could be dealt with only through normalization of relations with the United States, that is, by adopting a new international posture.

The conservatives, whose spearhead is the Judiciary under Ayatollah Muhammad Yazdi, are waging a rear-guard faction to oppose this evolution, invoking Imam Khomeini's will. There has obviously been a conservative reaction to liberalization, which in fact predates Khatami's election: despite a relative political liberalization under Rafsanjani, the law has regularly been amended in a more "shari ʿatic" way since 1989 (the age of penal majority for women was put at nine in 1991, gender mixing was forbidden in hospitals in 1998, etc.). In fact, political liberalization has been counterbalanced with a "neo-fundamentalist" trend in law and everyday life. Many liberal newspapers and journals have been closed since spring 1998.

The Guide is in a delicate position. His only "inherited" legitimacy is as the embodiment of the revolutionary heritage and as the guarantor of its preservation. That revolutionary identity bypasses both the religious and political legitimacies, which he lacks in each case, for an "ideological" legitimacy. The danger is that an "ideology" cut off from both the political and religious legitimacies might isolate him from the people. The conservatives in fact are pressing him to dismiss the president, sooner or later, as Khomeini did with Abo'l Hassan Bani-Sadr. They are waging a guerrilla war against Khatami: for example, the Council of Guardians barred pro-Khatami candidates from running for the mid-term elections in March 1998 and for the Council of Experts elections in October of that year. But this could lead to popular uprisings, at a time when the attitude of the security forces (the police and the *Pasdaran*, the Revolutionary Guards Corps) is not certain. The other alternative would be for the Guide to act as a referee and to bring the conservatives onto the bandwagon of liberalization, ensuring a longer, but smooth transition. But for this prospect to be realized, the Guide's function has to be redefined. A solution could be to acknowledge the purely political nature of the function of the Guide, as Ayatollah ʿAli Meshkini, the head of the Council of Experts, sometimes hints. The Guide, in this sense, could become a "constitutional faqih," as there are "constitutional monarchs" in other countries, and Iran would openly become what it is already, according to its own constitution: a constitutional theocracy.

In any case, evolution has to take place from inside the system: there is no effective and credible opposition; people do not want civil war or revolution; there is room for political and ideological debate. Clerics now align themselves along a much wider spectrum of political positions, ensuring that any change would easily find a religious blessing.

The Religious Crisis

It is obvious that such heated debates on the role of Islam and politics must affect the way people relate to Islam. Is the growing weariness of the population towards the Islamic system affecting popular religiosity? The head of the movement for literacy, Hojatolislam Mohsen Qara'ati, once complained that people were neglecting their prayers.[18] Such major events as the Friday prayer at Tehran University attract fewer and fewer people. Tehran's streets do not empty at Iftar during Ramadan, as is usual in Peshawar, Cairo, or even Erzurum in "secular" Turkey. Although there is no scientific way to measure religious practices and belief, we can make some tentative remarks. The nationalization of Shi'ism is working. One of the legacies of the Revolution is surely to have linked Iranianness with Shi'ism more than ever, in place of the "Persianization," promoted by the late Shah, with its ethno-nationalist ideology. The integrative force of Shi'ism has been particularly visible since the independence of the Muslim former Soviet republics and particularly Azerbaijan: there is no yearning for a "Greater Azerbaijan" among the Iranian Azeris, just sometimes a feeling that Baku should come back into the motherland. Conversely, active solidarity towards foreign Shi'is is very limited: the plights of the Iraqi Shi'is in 1991 and of the Afghan Shi'is in August 1998 did not arouse popular concern, while an Afghan Shi'i is first of all an Afghan in the eyes of Iranian public opinion.

But the "statization" of Shi'ism is also encountering some popular resistance. We might speak of "social Shi'ism" versus "State Shi'ism." Shi'i traditional customs have been revived for socialization purposes, due to the dearth of other, more secular entertainments. "*Sofre*," or traditional receptions given on religious occasions (such as mourning), are mushrooming, and spread beyond the traditional devout middle class families. Celebrations of *'ashura* now revolve more around the neighborhood (*mahalla*), and the professional Guild or corporation (*hayat*), under the auspices of lay notables, instead of being given a political meaning, as was the case at the beginning of the Revolution.

The popularity of the concept of "civil society" (*jame'e-ye madani*) is striking. Interestingly enough, this same concept is popular in Turkey among the Islamists, and in Iran among those who would like to differentiate religion from politics. In both cases, it means a defiance towards an ideological State which has almost succeeded in its process of social integration, that is, the weakening of traditional ties of solidarity. The crisis of political Islam does not lead to a weakening of faith, but to its privatization.

This evolution is mirrored in an intellectual debate which has focused on 'Abdolkarim Sorush's works.[19] In fact, Sorush is closer to the basic tenets of the Revolution than the attacks of the Hizballah against him might suggest. He endeavors to elaborate a religious justification of the double legitimacy which is expressed in the Constitution. He contrasts "*din*" (religion), which is the direct relation between God and the faithful, and "*dark-e dini*" (the apprehension of religion), which is the way this relation is embodied at a given time in a certain system (cultural, legal and political). He stresses also the classical distinction between shari'a and *'urf* (custom), defining politics as the realm of 'urf, and giving legitimacy to a "secularization" of political action, in a society which remains for him "religious," that is, aimed at allowing a human being to experience his transcendental relation to God (which, by the way, is a very Aristotelian conception of relations between society and the "final ends"). Although Sorush does not go so far as to reformulate the main concepts of the Constitution according to his views, it is clear that he provides the "political philosophy" of the Khatamists: how to secularize politics in a society which cannot afford to reject its heritage and origin: an Islamic Revolution. To what extent this philosophy is just an intellectual tool for a political transition or a landmark in the long path to reconcile Islam with political philosophy, reopening a debate that was closed around the thirteenth century, is another question. But more than ever, what is at stake in contemporary Iran is of prime importance for the relations between Islam and politics in general.

This article is reprinted from *Middle East Journal* 53/2 (Spring 1999), 201–216. Reprinted by permission of *Middle East Journal* and the author.

NOTES

1. Montazeri has distanced himself from the concept of the VF, which he defended in the 1980s; he now favors a "*nezarat-e faqih*," that is, a supervisory power limited to the protection of the Islamic validity of the laws. Hosein 'Ali Montazeri, "Nezarat-e faqih," *Rahe Now*, no. 18, 31.5.1377 (1997–98).

2. Chapter 1, Article 1 of the Constitution states that the form of the government, an Islamic Republic, has been endorsed by "the people of Iran," "through the affirmative vote of a majority of 98.27 percent of eligible voters," implicitly making the people's will one the sources of legitimacy. Then the absolute sovereignty of God is expressed (Article 2/1), while Article 5 states that "the just and pious faqih" should exercise the "velayat" during the occultation of the Hidden Imam, and Article 6 says that "the affairs of the country should be administered on the basis of public opinion expressed by the means of elections." Text of the Constitution provided in Persian and French by the Iranian embassy in Paris. For an English translation, see (http://eurasianews.com/iran/const.htm). Analyzing the conceptual origin of the Iranian Constitution, Chibli Mallat speaks of a "dual emanation of sovereignty." See Chibli Mallat, *The Renewal of Islamic Law* (Cambridge: Cambridge University Press, 1993), p. 72.

3. Ervand Abrahamian, *Khomeynism* (London: Tauris, 1993).

4. For a history of the formation of the modern Shi'i clergy, see Said Amir Arjomand, *The Turban for the Crown* (Oxford: Oxford University press, 1988), chapter 1.

5. See Mallat, *The Renewal of Islamic Law*, p. 44.

6. Abrahamian, *Khomeynism*, p. 35.

7. Letter to the President of the Assembly of Experts in March 1989, in Mohammed Yazdi, *Qanun-e Assasi Baraye Hame* (The Constitution for Everyone) (Tehran: Amir Kabir Publishing House, 1375/1996) (text provided to the author by Nushin Yavari d'Hellencourt).

8. For a study on the discrepancies between the avowed goal of "shariatization" and the real practices of the government, see Ziba Mir Hosseyn, *Marriage on Trial, a Study of Islamic Family Law* (London: Tauris, 1993).

9. For quotations and discussions of this letter and of other declarations of Khomeini, see Mallat, *The Renewal of Islamic Law*, p. 90; and Shahrough Akhavi, "Contending Discourses on Shi'i Law on the Doctrine of Wilâyat al Faqih," *Iranian Studies* 29, nos. 3–4 (Summer-Fall 1996), pp. 262–65.

10. These include Mir-Hosein Musavi, Mohsen Nurbakhsh, Hasan Habibi, 'Ali Velayati,

Mostafa Mirsalim, 'Ali Larijani, Muhammad Hashemi, Hassan Firuzabadi, Gholamreza Aghazade, and others.

11. These include Ahmad Jannati, Muhammad Reza Mahdavi-Kani, Muhammad Kho'einiha, and others.

12. Jean Pierre Digard, Bernard Hourcade, Yann Richard, *l'Iran au XXième siècle* (Paris: Fayard, 1996), p. 208.

13. Chapter 1, Article 2–5 stresses the role of "*imama*," while Article 2–6 explicitly refers to "the *Sunna* of the Ma'sum," that is, the Shi'i Imams; and Article 12 states that "the official religion is Islam and the school is the twelve Imam Ja'fari."

14. Some clerical institutions have financial autonomy, like the religious holding Astan-e Qods in Mashhad, which manages the immense *waqf* (religious endowment) linked to the Shrine of Imam Reza. But, even if Astan-e Quds subsidizes many educational institutions, it is not in the classical framework of the *howze* (religious teaching center) under a marja''s supervision. Its manager, Ayatollah Vaez Tabassi, is one of the more influential notables behind the scenes, but he is not considered as a grand ayatollah and marja'.

15. Hosein Borujerdi, who died in 1961, was probably the first of the maraji' to be recognized as *the* only leading religious authority of his time.

16. Grand Ayatollah Muhammad Sadiq al-Sadr and two of his sons were killed in Najaf on 19 February 1999.

17. See Olivier Roy, *The Failure of Political Islam* (Cambridge: Harvard University Press, 1995).

18. Iranian Television, 26 July 1996, quoted by BBC on 30 July 1996.

19. 'Abdolkarim Sorush is the pen name of Farajollah Dabbagh, a scientist who studied epistemology and wrote extensively about philosophy and religion. He played a leading role in the "Islamization" of the university from 1981 to 1983; but he became increasingly concerned by the politicization of Islam. He has written many articles in the journal *Kyan*, advocating a separation between Islam and politics, urging a "religious civil society." He is now considered the leading figure among the liberal thinkers in Iran.

Religion, Social Structure and Political Dissent in Saudi Arabia[1]

MAMOUN FANDY

To understand the complex dynamics of Saudi dissent, we must understand the context in which this oppositional politics takes place. Explaining some central concepts such as Islam or islams, *qabila* (tribe), *'a'iliyya* and *qaraba* (tentatively translated as familialism and closeness in both spatial and social relations, respectively) is an essential first step of mapping the socio-cultural terrain. I also link this cultural sphere to both the economics and the politics of dissent by focusing on "the political economy of signs," an approach that can give us new insights into the politics of dissent.

'A'iliyya (familialism) and *qaraba* (social nearness/distance) are at the heart of the Saudi polity and make understanding the political economy of the Saudi system more than a matter of classes and economic indicators. *Qaraba* relations transform an ordinary political economy in the classical sense to a political economy of signs. This approach takes us away from the notion of the economy of state and traditional measures such as GDP to a notion of an economy that includes household and family. In what follows I explain basic concepts and describe the structure of authority and governance in the Saudi system. Next I consider religious dissent and the origin of the current opposition movements in terms of their immediate history, namely the rise of a new political language of Islamic resistance during the 1990-91 Gulf War. This includes the cultural debate that preoccupied Saudi society during 1988-89 and the intensification of this debate during the war and thereafter. Incidents that occurred during the Gulf War period are also relevant, such as the women's drive-in protest in Riyadh. Finally I explain and summarize the Letter of Demands and the Memorandum of Advice, two political initiatives that forced the government to respond. Derived from the teachings of various Islamic

shaykhs, these two documents are at the heart of opposition politics of Saudi Arabia.

RETHINKING BASIC CONCEPTS: ISLAM, FAMILY, AND THE RENTIER STATE

Islam is at the heart of both Saudi political culture and social science discourse on Saudi Arabia and Islamic societies. Given the problems associated with Islam as a term in the dominant Western discourse and in the discourse of the Islamic activists, I have opted to use islam and islams. The reason that I do not capitalize the word islam is that islam as a social text is drastically different from islam as a religion, as a written text, and as an imagined and assumed essence; I use the plural because of the many different interpretations of islam even as a social text. Not all Muslims are knowledgeable about all aspects of islam. To assume that ordinary Muslims possess full knowledge of the holy text is to essentialize and reify both social relations and the text. Muslims follow certain islamic ideas that guide their lives and provide them with a stable world outlook. Interpretations of islam vary from one person to another, from one *'alim* (religious scholar) to another, and from one culture to another.

Islam as a social text is a language with its own system of symbols that contributes to the multiplicity of interpretations. Thus islam is not a static text; it is interactive and both in-here and out-there simultaneously. Society is the ideological arena where these multiple interpretations compete using various strategies to legitimate themselves. Each and every interpretation evokes a different era of islamic history and a different school of jurisprudence to anchor its discourse and confer legitimacy on the practices of the group. Thus the islam of Saudi Arabia and how it is integrated with the larger social system and customs is different from the islams of Malaysia, Indonesia, Egypt, or the Sudan. The most stable interpretation is the one that can reproduce itself through various agents and institutions in society.

From the beginning the *'ulama* devised the system of *qiyas* (analogy) and *ijma'* (consensus) to lend the *shari'a* flexibility. In both *qiyas* and *ijma'* the *'ulama*'s personal or class interest may dictate the new laws adopted. Here the *'ulama* correspond to the intellectual strata in the Gramscian scheme where the relationship between them and the world of production is mediated by the whole fabric of society and by the complex of superstructures, of which the intellectuals are the functionaries. The intellectuals are the dominant group's deputies exercising the function of social hegemony. Thus the intellectual functions as an instrument to prepare the masses for consent. Of course, in the Muslim world intellectuals of the state have interpreted islam differently within the frame of reference of various schools of islamic jurisprudence (*madhhabs*). The four *madhhabs*, the various cultures where islam took root, and various styles of governance led to the emergence of varieties of islams at the sociopolitical level that are significantly different from an ideal, static, and literal "Islam". This is why for the purpose of social analysis I find it more analytically useful to speak of islams rather than Islam.

In Saudi Arabia, the dominant interpretation of islamic belief and practice is based on the teachings and ideas of *Shaykh* Muhammad ibn Abdul Wahhab, an eighteenth-century religious reformer who allied himself with the Saud family during the formation of the first Saudi state (1744-1811). Here the dominant interpretation is linked to the larger hegemony of the dominant group and the state. The islam of the Sunni opposition to the Saudi state is also based on the teachings of Muhammad ibn Abdul Wahhab, minus the elements that legitimize the current political order. The hegemony of the royal family and its world outlook in Saudi society is not made of islam alone, but islam mixed with *'asabiyya* (solidarity or group feeling) and the dominant ethos of *'a'iliyya* (familialism) and lies within the larger context of *qaraba* (closeness/distance both in space and social relations).

Familialism, not family, is central to this analysis. Various studies of Saudi society have focused on tribe. I try to avoid using the term tribe or use it with extreme caution, due to the pejorative connotations the term has acquired and to problems associated with its analytical utility. For the purposes of this discussion, I prefer to use the term *'a'ila* (tentatively translated as extended family) instead of tribe. One reason for this is that contemporary Saudis see themselves as part of *'a'ilas* rather than as part of tribes. For example, although the Al-Saud family is part of the 'Aniza tribe, no member of the royal family or any Saudi citizen uses this tribal name to refer to the Al-Saud or to any member of the family.

The Arabic connotation of *'a'iliyya* encompasses far more than genealogical bonds. Derived from the verb *ya'ul*, which means to protect and support, it connotes relations based on protection, interdependence, and accountability.[2] It also implies pride in household in connection with both people and animals. The reputation of the family is something beyond monetary value; it is something that cannot be lost without losing oneself. Whereas tribe connotes a clearly defined unit with lineage as the ultimate determinant of membership, *'a'iliyya* relations are more inclusive both in terms of membership and organizational cohesion. This familialism, in the sense of sponsorship, accountability, and interdependence, runs through the whole political system. A foreign worker cannot work in Saudi Arabia without a *kafil* or *'a'il* (sponsor). Small families who enter the world of business usually have a sponsor from the royal family. The king is referred to as *wali al-amr*, which translates literally as "the one who is responsible," suggesting a continuity in the patriarchal, familial organization of society. Islamic teachings also center on the family more than the tribe.[3] Women cannot leave the country without an *'a'il*, a companion or guarantor of safety. From top to bottom, familialism saturates the whole political system; the discourse of *'a'iliyya* permeates Saudi public discourse. When the king appointed his new cabinet, the main Saudi daily *al-Riyadh*, focused both the editorial and the lead articles on "the renewal of the concept of Saudi Arabia as one family." The writers conclude that "the concept of family is what governs Saudi Arabia."[4]

Ambiguity is central to Saudi politics, and conflation of concepts is dominant. Familialism and islamism converge in the common Saudi saying "*al-shuyukh abakhas*," meaning "the *shaykhs* know best." The word *shaykh* is used here to refer to multiple identities: the *shaykh* of the *qabila*, or head of the tribe; the *shaykh* of the family, or the family elder; the *shaykh* in the religious sense, or the *'alim* or man of religion; and the political rulers. Only in a specific context can we recognize whether the title refers to worldly or religious leadership. Given the ambiguity and multiple connotations of the word, the royal family can use it to establish its authority on multiple levels. By intentionally blurring or hiding the contextual referent, the state thus can exploit the word's association with various sources of power and authority.

Saudi religious opposition must be contextualized in the history of the relationship between islam and the various *'a'ilas* (families) that dominated Muslim history. With the exception of the *da'wa* (missionary) state in Medina under the leadership of the Prophet, islam historically has been secondary to the *'a'ila*; its main function has been to support the cultural hegemony of the ruling tribe/dynasty. This interaction between state and religion brought about certain adjustments to islamic practice rather than the other way around. The state was not adjusted to become islamic; rather, islamic practice was adjusted to support the state. In this arrangement, the state has used the *'ulama* to justify the policy choices of the ruling elite. The function of the *'ulama* is thus to establish the hegemony of the ruling *amir* and his family. The *'ulama* solidify the hegemony of the *amir* and his family because the interpretation of *shari'a* principles has traditionally been their exclusive domain. The *'ulama* perform this function with the assumption that the *shari'a* regulates all human activities.

In addition to problematizing dominant concepts such as Islam and tribe, a dominant approach to the study of oil states, namely the rentier model,[5] requires examination before we look at political opposition and resistance in Saudi Arabia. Currently this model dominates the discussion of the possibilities for democracy and political change in the Gulf. The central concept of rentier state theory is that assets accrued by the state from oil rent free the state from being accountable to its citizens. The model assumes that the state is autonomous, although some Saudi scholars have shown that this is not the case in Saudi Arabia.[6] Indeed, had the state been free to do what it wanted with total disregard for the power of society, we would have witnessed large-scale human rights abuses or the state would have ignored opposition demands instead of responding to them by forming the *Shura* Council in 1992 (see below). In spite of its economic determinism, the rentier model dominates the literature on the Gulf. The model links the authoritarianism of these regimes to state autonomy at the economic level. According to this model, "state-society relations seem predicated on the principle of 'no taxation, no representation.'"[7] Because citizens do not pay taxes and yet receive generous social welfare benefits from the state, they have no right to participate in government decision making. This model focuses heavily on oil and ignores indigenous social structures.

According to the rentier model, protest is positively correlated with the decline of oil prices. Citizens grow restive when their economic interests are affected, that is, when their social benefits are cut. Indeed, according to this theory, opposition to the state can be predicted according to oil booms and busts. The more oil prices increase, the more money the state has to distribute to citizens in social welfare benefits and the lesser the resistance. When prices fall so do benefits, and resistance to the state increases.

This expected pattern has not held true in Saudi Arabia. Oil prices were rising in 1979, when the Shi'a of the Eastern Province rioted and Juhaiman al-'Utaibi and his Sunni followers took over the Grand Mosque at Mecca.[8] By the mid-1980s according to the rentier model we would expect falling prices and the severe contraction in public revenues and outlays to signal a shift in the political equilibrium of Saudi Arabia. However, there was no significant protest when in 1986 the price of a barrel of oil declined sharply from $26.50 to $13.70, and the government deficit in the two years that followed increased from 52.3 to 60.9 billion Saudi riyals. Were we to deflate the price of oil by that of imported manufactured goods to get a sense of the purchasing power of oil exports, the story would be even more pronounced given the upward trend in manufactured goods' prices during this period. Had the assumption of the rentier model been sound, this period should have witnessed political turmoil. Because of the relative stability of the Saudi polity during the second half of the 1980s and the rise of opposition at times of increasing oil prices, we must look beyond the rentier model when analyzing Saudi opposition.

Oil and the purchasing power of oil have been on a downward trend since 1980, when oil prices reached their historical peak. Saudi Arabia, among other oil exporters, has seen gradual erosion in the price and purchasing power of its chief export commodity, the biggest contributor to its budget and foreign exchange earnings. Did this downward trend in prices, revenues, and expenditures by the Saudi government after 1980 coincide with increased political resistance to the state or a systematic weakening of its structures and perceived legitimacy? No. Did the boom of the 1970s lead to concentration of state power and the marginalization of the political opposition? Clearly not.

While oil has been a very important factor in solidifying the rule of the Al-Saud, it has not been the only factor. The Al-Sauds ruled central Arabia for sixty-six years (1745-1811) in the first Saudi state and for7 twenty-two years (1843-1902) in the second without oil. The third Saudi realm started in 1902, became a consolidated state by 1932, and has continued since. Similarly, oil is a reason for great power interest in the region, but it is not the source of these powers' hegemony. Given that the state existed before oil and that many describe the state as distributive, the money coming from oil rent is distributed to enforce the earlier *qaraba* hierarchy. In this argument oil becomes a downstream variable while social relations and structures are upstream variables. The rent coming from oil is distributed to consolidate an already existing hierarchy of *qaraba* relations.

A more general look at other oil-producing states serves to further discredit the assumptions of the rentier model. Although the decrease in oil prices coincided with protest in Algeria, different patterns surfaced in Venezuela, the Republic of Gabon,[9] Nigeria (trends there are much more complex), and Iran. The model has little utility in explaining the strength of the Kuwaiti parliament, where the Islamist parliamentarians have been challenging the government on various issues since 1996 and forced the resignation of one cabinet and the formation of another in 1998.[10] All these examples suggest that it is not enough to cleverly invert common American slogans into "no taxation, no representation" and "ask not what you can do for your country, ask what your country can do for you," and use them as substitutes for theory or analytical frameworks. Furthermore, rentier literature provides very little explanation in terms of either resistance or governmental human rights abuses. Although the Saudi government did not respond to Shi'a demands during the 1970s and 1980s, it has responded in the 1990s. It responded with grand steps to the demands of supposedly marginal figures (junior members of the *'ulama*), yet it ignored the demands of elite women. The question is where we locate our explanation of resistance.

THE STATE, ITS PEOPLE, AND THEIR RELIGION

Saudi Arabia is a vast country (2,240,000 square kilometers) with a population of 16.9 million people. Not all of these are Saudis; some 4.9 million are foreign nationals working in the kingdom. Saudi Arabia is a very rich country by regional standards. In addition to controlling 25 percent of the world's proven oil reserves, the country's gross domestic product (GDP) exceeds $100 billion. Administratively, it.is divided into thirteen provinces. According to the Statute of the Provinces, each province has a governor and vice governor who are appointed and dismissed by the king at the recommendation of the minister of interior.[11] Each province is ruled by a council composed of the governor, the vice governor, the managers of regional government agencies, and at least ten prominent members of the region nominated by the governor and approved by the minister of interior. They serve for a term of four years, which can be renewed.[12] Each region has a governor or *amir* (prince) and deputy *amir*, and each *imara* (region) has a council of local notables that helps the governors in running the affairs of the state. The laws for these governorates were codified in 1992 as part of a government response to the Letter of Demands and the Memorandum of Advice submitted to the king (see below). Before that time, there was no written law.[13]

According to the Basic Statute of Governance, Saudi Arabia is an Arab Islamic state and Islam is the religion of the state. At the top of the government is the king; he appoints the crown prince and can dismiss him. Abdullah, the current crown prince, is exempt from this by a royal decree since these laws were established after he was already a crown prince. The laws of succession link the royal inheritance to the sons and grandsons of the late King Abdul Aziz.[14] Beyond this the statute does not specify any mechanism for the transfer of power. Although it has been traditionally accepted that the second deputy, currently Prince Sultan, be appointed crown prince as soon as the crown prince becomes king, some members of the royal family state clearly that this is not automatic. The family must meet to decide the future crown prince.[15] A mechanism for succession satisfactory to all branches of the family has yet to be devised. Thus far the system is not one of seniority, all sons or grandsons of Abdul Aziz can be considered. Age may be a factor, but certainly it is not the only one. Given this ambiguity about the rules of succession, the Saudis may face a greater problem in the coming twenty years from within the family than from external social forces.

To analyze the legal-formal structure of the Saudi state and society is to miss the essence of how politics actually function. Formally, the government consists of the royal family, the bureaucracy, and the *'ulama*. The important question, however, is where the state ends and society begins. The royal family is the largest and most cohesive group in the kingdom with 5,000 members who are related to almost all the important tribes of Saudi Arabia through marriage. The marriage connection is central to rule, since familialism as an ideology is an important part of governance in most Arab states. Like other Saudis, members of the royal family work primarily to maximize the gain of their own family first and their other relatives second. The relatives of the Sauds inside Saudi Arabia are part of a web of social relations that could include most of the tribes. In this domain of civil society, the royal family is important at the domestic level. The formal structure, it could be argued, works well only in terms of the Saudi state's dealing with the outside world; the formal legal structure exists so that Saudi Arabia can conduct its international affairs.

Domestically, however, the royal family exists within both civil society and the state simultaneously. The Sauds may be hated as bureaucrats, regional governors, or heads of particular government agencies, yet they are loved as a magnanimous family at the level of civil society. It is that liminal nature of the royal family that makes it inside government and civil society at the same time. This is the secret of the Saud's survival and their stability in dealing with crises.

If we consider the house of Prince Salman, the governor of Riyadh, these issues become obvious. Prince Salman has five sons. One is Prince Abdul Aziz, the deputy minister of energy and oil. Another is Prince Ahmed, the owner of the Saudi publishing group called *al-Saudia li'l-Nashr wa al-Tawzi'*. Prince Ahmed is both a businessman and, as the son of Prince Salman, part of the Saudi government. What is important is that each of these princes has his own small bureaucracy that mediates his relations with both the state and society. At the level of society each *amir* has his own "mini-*majlis*," as one young prince called it. Though not as grand as the *majlis* of the governor, it is a meeting place where he brings his friends, usually young technocrats, businessmen, and colleagues from his university days. A patronage system is established in the form of a *shilla* (a group of friends/peers) as well as a following. Each *amir* also takes care of the ten to twenty families that work for his office. Thus at least 200 people are associated with each young prince. The prince's office is there to help them whenever they are in trouble with the formal structure, and in turn they are dependent on him. This circle around each *amir* shields him from other would-be beneficiaries of his largess. The role of the so-called middle class is not to compete with the royal princes but to limit others' access to them. This is why Prince Salman has an open *majlis*. There, those who are prevented from seeing him are given a chance to meet with him and be heard. Usually people leave the *majlis* praising the royal prince and cursing the non-royal gatekeepers who prevented the *amir* from hearing their cases earlier. Of course, some dissidents are outside this system and have rebelled against it.

The liminality of the royal family makes its job easier and complicates the life of the opposition. The government could respond to all the demands of any members of the opposition without doing anything to change the system. The question remains whether it is important to have formal legal rights if the system rarely works according to these rules.

The Saudi state started with an islamic mission. However, the state is not an alliance between a secular tribal leadership and a religious family, as it is conventionally perceived, with the Al-Saud family representing secular power and the Al-Shaykh family representing religion. Rather, both families are religious, although the religious credentials of the Al-Shaykh family are stronger, and both of them are prominent tribal families, although the Al-Sauds have long been more powerful. The Al-Shaykh family owes its prominence in part to being the descendants of Muhammad ibn Abdul Wahhab. However, there is nothing in Sunni islam to suggest that piety is inherited. Those members of the family known for their piety and religious learning have been appointed to religious positions, but others occupy secular positions that they owe to their family's tribal prestige. Some members of the Al-Saud family have been known for their piety, such as King Faisal, whose mother was from the Al-Shaykh family,[16] Prince Ahmed ibn Abdul Aziz, and the current crown prince, Abdullah.

Thus the relationship between the Al-Sauds and the Al-Shaykhs is not a tribal-religious alliance between one tribal and one religious family; both families are a part of the tribal and religious *'asabiyya* of Saudi Arabia.

Wahhabism, or Saudi islam, serves to separate "real" Saudis from the non-Wahhabi foreigners and from the Shi'a of the Eastern Province. These cultural signs are central to inclusion and exclusion from power, and in many cases are the main criteria. Thus what can be conceived of as corruption and nepotism in a discourse where meritocracy and legalism are the dominant criteria can be construed as another form of wealth distribution in a *qaraba*-centered discourse. Marriage lends to *qaraba* relations a degree of flexibility. Ending this system of allocating values on the basis of *qaraba* would mean ending political and economic participation as most Saudis know it. This is not to condone corruption; rather, I merely seek to explain how money and power are divvied up by the Saudi system.

Unlike many Arab countries, Saudi Arabia was spared the experience of direct colonialism. This affected the process of state building and made the political structure indigenous. Certainly, the Hashimites ruled on behalf of the Ottoman sultan in the Western Region (Hijaz), where the holy sites of Islam are located. People in the Eastern Province (Hasa) also were nominally under Ottoman control at various times. Arrangements in the northern part of Ha'il and Jabal Shammar were under the control of a local *amir*, Ibn Rashid, who was loyal to the Ottomans. Yet these Ottoman influences had very little effect. The Najd region, where the drive for state building started, was not of interest to the Ottomans. Later on Ibn Saud, the founder of the kingdom, allied himself with British, but he was never an agent of Britain in the Gulf. The British signed treaties with him to keep him away from Iraq, Kuwait, and many of the Trucial states.

Saudi Arabia was also spared the process of decolonization. The departure of colonial powers from other Arab countries left a legacy of laws and institutions that had distorted Arab societies. In Arabia by contrast the ethos of familialism, tribal customs, and religion were the law, and the informal institutions were the functioning ones. State building in the Saudi case was an indigenous process. King Abdul Aziz was a *beduin amir* who ruled according to laws that were a mix of religion and tribal customs. He also had the advantage of having learned from his predecessors. This indigenous process led to the emergence of forms of participation and structures of authority and power that are different from those in Arab countries further north.

THE 'ULAMA AND THE HEGEMONY OF ISLAMIC DISCOURSE

Saudi politics cannot be understood without understanding the role of islam at the level of formal and informal structures. The people of Saudi Arabia are known for their conservatism. About 20 percent of the Saudi public is *mutawa* (very conservative religious people) who take it upon themselves to persuade others to be strictly observant. These *mutawa* are different from what Americans refer to as *mutaween*, or morality police. *Mutaween* are known to Saudis as *al-Hayi'ah* (the Committee), after the Committee for Promoting Virtue and Preventing Vice, a formal organization associated with the state. The *mutawa* are ordinary people with no official capacity. Another 20 percent of the Saudi public is liberal. According to Saudis themselves, the remaining 60 percent of society are in between; they are conservative when they are around conservatives and liberal around liberals. These are the pragmatic Saudis. The royal family can be counted among this 60 percent. Nonetheless, the conservatives have the upper hand, since the basic conceptualization of the state and its political formula is based on the centrality of religion.

The institutionalization of specific islamic ideas, coercion, and other means of social control have maintained the hegemony of islamic discourse in the Saudi state and in Saudi society. One of the institutions that represents and reproduces this hegemony is the Council of Higher *'Ulama*. This council produces *fatwas*, books, and sermons designed to legitimate the political order. It was established in 1971 by a royal decree. The king appoints its members. The function of the Council, as the decree specifies, is "to express opinions on the *shari'a* regarding matters submitted to them by *wali al-amr* [the king]." It is also entrusted with advising the king on policy matters and with issuing *fatwas* to guide Muslims in areas of belief, prayers, and worldly affairs. The *'ulama* themselves assert that they are an independent body accountable only to the teachings of the *shari'a*; however, their *fatwas* very rarely contradict the views of the royal family. For example, the *fatwas* issued to execute those responsible for the take-over the Grand Mosque in 1979 came at the request of the royal family. During the Gulf crisis in 1990, the *'ulama* issued a *fatwa* permitting foreign troops to defend Saudi territory. In its statement, the Council asserted that "It is necessary in a situation like this that *'ulama* clarify the Islamic ruling on the matter so that the people of this country and elsewhere may be aware of the correct standpoint on it. The Council of the Senior *'Ulama* approves, therefore, of the steps taken by the ruler, may Allah lead him to success, in inviting some forces equipped with arms that frighten away anyone who thinks of invading this land."[17]

Other official religious agencies include the Committee for the Promotion of Virtue and the Suppression of Vice; the religious supervision of the Holy Mosque; the Ministry of Pilgrimage; the Directorate of Religious Research, Religious Decrees, and Promotion of Islam; and the General Department of Women's Education. Through, among others, the Committee for the Promotion of Virtue and the Suppression of Vice, hereafter referred to as the Committee, and the Directorate of Religious Research, which includes the Council of Higher *'Ulama*, the regime makes use of religion to control society;

through them also society makes use of religion to limit the power of the state.

Little has been written about the Committee, primarily because its finances are secret and its members tend to respond to questions about their exact function by merely elaborating on their full name. In essence, its members are a group of public employees and volunteers whose task is to chastise or arrest those who violate these members' perception of what is islamically appropriate—men who are not in the mosque during prayers, women who are inadequately veiled, people hosting parties at which men and women guests mix or at which alcohol is being served, and so on. In a rare interview in *al-Yamamah* magazine, the head of the agency, Dr. Abdul Aziz al-Said, stated, "We only arrest those who do wrong. After finishing the preliminary procedures, we hand them to the special branch of government that deals with their case."[18] He also said, "Our men raid the homes of evil and corruption, but of course we do it in coordination with other agencies." Two interesting facts emerge from these statements, first that arrest carries the assumption of proven guilt, and second, that while the committee arrests, the civil police have the ultimate authority. This creates an atmosphere of fear and intimidation that is a very effective means of social control, particularly of foreign workers, who are unlikely to have a network of friends and relatives in official positions to intercede for them. Although this organization seems indigenous and exotic, it functions like earlier American models such as the Charleston (Virginia) Association for the Reformation of Morals and the Alabama Society of the Suppression of Vice and Immorality. The main function of these organizations was to promote adherence to their own version of religious morality-that is, observation of the Christian sabbath and prohibition of the sale of alcoholic beverages, blasphemy, and gambling. In the future, some students may be interested in comparing these societies in the early American period and modern Saudi Arabia.

Although the alliance between the royal family and religious forces in Arabia has been central to the maintenance of the political order, this alliance has never been free from tension. Religious forces have questioned the hegemony of the ruling elite, but with very few consequences to the power of the royal family. In 1929 the *Ikhwan*, who had been instrumental in establishing Ibn Saud's power, wanted to invade other countries, such as Iraq, to form a greater Islamist state. Ibn Saud's vision of state building focused only on Arabia. Moreover, the *Ikhwan* considered Ibn Saud to be their *imam* (leader) only as long as he followed the teachings of Ibn Abdul Wahhab. In their eyes, Ibn Saud clearly had violated the Islamic codes on two counts: he declared himself King of Arabia and he signed an agreement with the British, Islam's enemy in the eyes of the *Ikhwan*. These violations provoked the *Ikhwan* to rebel. After establishing his territory, Abdul Aziz had to choose between the expansionist impulse of the *Ikhwan* and the political constraints imposed on him by major powers with interests in the surrounding area, namely Britain.[19] Realizing that the *Ikhwan* may provoke a confrontation with the British, he decided to rein them in. In 1929 he fought the *Ikhwan* at Sibla. The battle lasted only a few hours and ended in total defeat of the *Ikhwan* army. Thereafter Ibn Saud destroyed the *Ikhwan* camps, declared that religious issues would be decided only by the *'ulama*, and banned all meetings for any purpose without his prior approval.[20]

The destruction of the *Ikhwan* forces liberated Abdul Aziz from the bargains he had made with particular members of that group and consequently made religion again subordinate to secular power, although it cannot be claimed that Ibn Saud was secular himself. Like his followers, he was a religious man, or at least a mixture of religious and secular. Later the position of the *'ulama* was institutionalized; they lost autonomy and were subordinated to the state. In this the Al-Sauds are not unusual in the larger pattern of islamic history. Islam has been subordinated to the tribe or the ruling dynasty since the Umayyads (661-750) and the Abbasids (750-1258).

The second religious challenge to the Al-Saud's authority came in 1979, when two major events took place in Saudi Arabia: the takeover of the Grand Mosque and the riots in the Eastern Province. The first occurred on November 20, 1979, when Juhaiman al-'Utaibi and a few hundred of his followers took over the Grand Mosque in Mecca. The three-week fighting that followed caused heavy casualties among rebels and government forces alike. That year another incident took place in the Eastern Province, a region dominated by Saudi Arabia's Shi'a minority. The Shi'a, perhaps inspired by the success of the islamic revolution in Iran, rioted but were quelled by National Guard forces. In both cases the challenge did not come from the mainstream religious *'ulama* of Saudi Arabia or even from the dominant tribes, but from the margins of Saudi society. Generally speaking, the traditional *'ulama* support state policy, both internal and external. Even their views on dealing with Western powers usually provide legitimacy to the state's foreign policy. Using various media, such as publications, radio, and television, they propagate this hegemonic discourse legitimizing the state. This is in sharp contrast to the junior or younger or otherwise marginalized *'ulama*. Although in general all *'ulama*, senior/establishment and junior/outside the establishment, may be said to be "islamist" in that they all promote islamic values in society and islamic institutions in government, the term islamist refers specifically to the younger/outside the establishment *'ulama* who are politically active outside of the officially created and sanctioned offices, committees, and councils.

Since 1987 a debate between islamists and liberals in Saudi society has been fermenting around the issue of modernity. Central to this debate was Sheikh Awad al-Qarni's book, *Al-Hadatha fi Mizan al-Islam* (Modernity in the scale of Islam) and two taped lectures by the conservative Dr. Sa'eed al-Ghamidi entitled "al-Hadatha" (Modernity). These works accuse liberals of undermining the islamic foundations of Saudi society and the government of allowing "secular" forces to control all the major publications and the media outlets in the country. By controlling the media, the liberals were able to shape the minds of the new generation and spread Western ideas, which are, in the eyes of these islamist authors, inherently anti-islamic. The islamists also feel that the Marxist ideas that dominated socialist circles in Egypt, Syria, and Lebanon have found their way to Saudi society through these secular writers. According to the islamists, by replacing religious discourse with Western or Marxist narratives, secular writers are trying to undermine the language of the Quran. Moreover, the liberals are portrayed as agents of modernity, which itself is considered tantamount to the destruction of traditional and religious values. The Syrian poet Ali Ahmad Sa'id (Adonis) has been accused of contributing to this anti-islamic trend and consequently has been called an infidel. Indeed, Adonis is suspect because of his Shi'a background and his daring ideas.

In the late 1980s the literary pages of Saudi newspapers were among the best literary publications in the Arab world and were open to a range of ideas. Some female poets openly criticized the way women were treated within their society. Khadija al-ʿAmri rejected the notion of veiling. The islamists accused her and others of attending conferences outside Saudi Arabia unveiled. They view the increase in female columnists in the Saudi press as part of a secular conspiracy to undermine islamic values. To islamists, while media was open to liberals, authorities interfered with the distribution of al-Ghamidi's tapes.

ISLAMIC DISSENT DURING AND AFTER THE GULF WAR OF 1990-91

The Gulf War and its aftermath is a watershed in Saudi politics, or at least in the changing political language that enveloped that polity. Islamist voices became louder, and more daring demands were put to the king and the royal family. Events indicative of the changing political landscape and language include the women's drive-in in the Saudi capital, the Letter of Demands, and the Memorandum of Advice.

The confrontation between islamists and liberals crystallized when forty-five women drove their cars in a demonstration in Riyadh asking for the right to drive. Some of the women reportedly took off their veils and stepped on them. To the islamists, these acts epitomized the secular conspiracy. According to the islamists, the women, almost all of them American-educated Saudis, were emboldened by the presence of the U.S. troops to further their own interests and undermine the foundation of the society. In the eyes of islamists the women wanted to turn Saudi Arabia into America; they wanted to have complete freedom in defiance of islamic custom and law. To the islamists, therefore, these women were infidels who deserved to be killed. Islamist leaflets attacking the female drivers, accused them of being "communist whores." The leaflets listed the women's names, their husbands' names and professions, and urged the Saudi public to take action against them. The islamists also wrote to the king, Crown Prince Abdullah, and Prince Salman, the powerful governor of Riyadh, asking that the women, and those behind them, be punished.

Although nothing in islamic scriptures would prevent women from driving cars, both the regime and the islamists were disturbed by the women's protest because of the centrality of women in the kinship system of *qaraba*. Women are symbols of the presumed purity of tribal configuration and keep a specific hierarchy of relations in place; but women who are free to drive might select their own mates. Perhaps one reason why the islamists insist on the control of women is that they fear that if this stable system of social relations symbolized by who marries whom is undermined, the very bases of familialism could collapse. Women define tribal honor and the ideology of familialism; Wahhabi teachings define women. This may in part explain why so many Saudi men want to keep women out of politics. The women's drive-in sharpened splits in the royal family between liberals and conservatives and, though women are still not allowed to drive, it is an issue that is now definitely on the liberal agenda.

The perception that these women were emboldened by the presence of American troops in Saudi Arabia further intensified the attack on the alliance between the United States and Saudi Arabia. The *fatwas* of the young *'ulama* against seeking the help of non-Muslims in a war against Muslims were a part of this debate. Saudi Islamists felt that if the Americans stayed longer, they would further erode the authority of islam in the kingdom. Thus a worst-case scenario about how the Americans would eliminate islam in Saudi Arabia gained momentum. The taped sermons of 'Awad al-Qarni, Safar al-Hawali, Salman al-Auda, and Nasser al-Omar circulated in the kingdom, criticizing the presence of the foreign troops and advocating greater roles for the *'ulama* in public life. They also urged the government and the public to weed out the secularists from the Saudi media because of their danger to society.

In 1991 leading islamists presented a Letter of Demands to the king asking him to reform the Saudi system of governance by convening a *shura* (consultative) council and reforming the economic, political, and defense systems. The government asked the Council of Higher *'Ulama* to respond to the letter. This gave the government two advantages: it managed to put the demands in the hands of the *'ulama* and thus make them, at that moment, the guardians of the state, and it took the royal family out of the confrontation, making it seem a dispute between young islamists and establishment *'ulama*. The Council and the Grand Mufti of Saudi Arabia criticized the letter on the basis that advice should be private were it meant for the sake of God. If advice became a popular issue, then the aim behind it would be politicized and used to bolster the group's stature. Thus the senior *'ulama* objected to both the style and the substance of the group's advice.[21] To counter this criticism the group worked on another document, which became known as the Memorandum of Advice.

The 1992 Memorandum of Advice represents the core document of the islamist consensus (*ijma'*) concerning the kinds of reforms they expect of the Saudi government. It presents a critique of the Saudi system and its specific sectors, including: (1) the role of the *'ulama* and preachers; (2) laws and regulations; (3) the judicial system and the courts; (4) the rights of those who submit to God (*huquq al-'ibad*, not necessarily human rights); (5) public administration; (6) the economy and finance; (7) social institutions; (8) the army; (9) the information system; and (10) foreign policy. These issues are included in the Memorandum's introduction under the heading "Big Issues."[22]

This introduction reveals a great deal about the orientation and basic assumptions of the islamist groups. It starts with *Surat al-Nas*, which states that with the exception of those who do good in this world, believe in justice, and are patient, humans are likely to be a confused mass of impulses. The second verse states that what distinguishes the Muslim nation from others is that it enjoins good works toward eliminating evil, and that its members are true believers in God. Then the memorandum uses one of the Prophet's sayings, "Advice is the core of religion." This advice should be for all Muslims and their leaders.

After the memorandum provides an islamic rationale to justify its purpose, it outlines the current state of affairs in the world, which is characterized by confusion and change. It also states "the citizens of this country are given the honor of having the holy places in their land and thus they are responsible for this trust in the eyes of God." Because of these religious responsibilities and teachings, the writers wanted to present the leaders of Saudi Arabia with a list of problems that could be corrected in light of islamic teachings. Thus this memorandum fulfills its authors' islamic duty. They say: "We pray to God that this reformist advice will fall on receptive ears and that it will be accepted by the rulers of the Muslims."

The Memorandum of Advice was first sent to *Shaykh* Abdul Aziz bin Baz, Grand Mufti of Saudi Arabia, for endorsement before being sent to the king. In the letter to the *shaykh*, the authors write:

> This advice is the result of the tireless efforts of your sons, students of Islam, preachers, and university professors. More than a hundred individuals signed this. Many 'ulama have read it and corrected it. It was also endorsed by many trusted 'ulama such as Shaykh Abdullah bin Jibreen, Shaykh Safar, al-Hawali, Shaykh Salman al-Auda, and Shaykh Abdullah al-Jilali. ... Our purpose is to follow the teachings of Islam that requests advice and consultation. We would like you to read it and add what is missing and improve on it. This advice is of course an effort that is likely to have mistakes and we would want you to correct these mistakes. Whatever is good in this advice is a gift from God and whatever is wrong is our responsibility and we stand corrected. Finally we would like you to endorse it and submit it to the Custodian of the Two Holy Mosques.[23]

It is obvious that the authors have tremendous respect for the *shaykh* and are deferential toward him as well as toward the king. The letter from *Shaykh* Salman al-Audah that endorses the memorandum states that he has read the document: "I found it to be a very serious effort offering a realistic treatment for many of the social ills of this society."[24] Hawali's letter states that he has read the memorandum and finds it worthy of the attention of all officials and every responsible individual.[25]

In regard to the position of the *'ulama* in Saudi society, the memorandum identifies six areas for criticism and suggests seven ways for reform. The activists claim that the role of the *'ulama* and the religious institutions in public life is minimal and marginal: "The fact that the various ministries do not consult the *'ulama* in conducting their policy could eventually lead to separation between politics and religion, which defeats the very purpose of the establishment of the Islamic State." Moreover, the bureaucratization of the *'ulama* limits their independence. The sensitivity of state institutions toward the involvement of religious people limits their role in society. The islamists are also distressed by what they feel is the lack of exposure of the *'ulama* to the state media and the absence of any kind of media censorship to control the dissemination of material contradicting the teachings of islam. They say that the government limits the role of the mosque and imposes restrictions on preachers who dare discuss salient issues[26] and that the role of religious preachers in state institutions, such as the Ministry of Information, educational institutions, and embassies, is limited.

How do these activists want to rectify this situation? Their answer is divided into two main themes: by solidifying the position of the *'ulama* in society and by making sure that the state follows the teachings of islam. The memorandum suggests lifting all restrictions on the activities of religious activists and preachers. The state should allow greater freedom in forming civil society associations, and the religious establishment should be able to regulate these associations. The selection of the Council of Higher *'Ulama* should be based on merit, and members should be nominated based on their knowledge, piety, and sincerity; their membership in this council should not be subject to dismissal, unless there is an islamic reason for it. To ensure the islamic nature of the state, all treaties and arrangements should be subject to the Council of Higher *'Ulama* for approval. The activities of religious associations and their finances should be run by an independent group of *'ulama* and should be separated from the state budget. The government should issue a policy statement to all agencies to allow the religious people the right to promote islamic teachings. Finally, the government should allow *'ulama* from outside the kingdom to come in and conduct seminars, thus making it easier for them to exchange ideas with Saudi *'ulama*. It is also the duty of the state to have religious people in all of its embassies to make sure that all activities conform to islamic teachings. There should also be radio and television stations for the preaching of islam. This point is the core of many of Hawali's taped sermons, because the main threats to islam, according to him, are the television channels of the American Christian fundamentalists. The memorandum also requires the state to strengthen the Committee for the Promotion of Virtue and the Suppression of Vice. In essence, the writers want the equivalent of a religious supervisor in all state agencies and the *'ulama* to have an equal, if not a greater, share of power with the monarchy.

GOVERNMENT RESPONSES AND NEW SITES OF RESISTANCE

The Saudi government has used various strategies to cope with its critics and opponents since the Gulf War. These include exclusive and coercive measures as well as inclusive reform. There is no denying that the kingdom has reformed since the Gulf War. On March 1, 1992, it inaugurated the *Shura* Council (*majlis al-shura*),[27] a sixty-member consultative group appointed by the king, and for the first time the king decided to codify the *shari'a* laws and release them in a form known as the Basic Laws of Governance. The appointees of the *Shura* Council are a veritable who's who list of prominent Saudi tribes, taking into account both tribal and regional representations. Almost 70% of the members of this council had received Western educations; most of them hold doctoral degrees.[28] In 1997 the government expanded the *Shura* Council to ninety members. The government also uses financial and diplomatic power to limit the impact of opposition both inside and outside the national boundaries, and has the support of *fatwas* and publications of the official religious institutions to delegitimize the discourse of islamist groups. The mixture of coercion and cooptation is evident in the government's treatment of the Shi'a Reform Movement: members of the movement were imprisoned, but the king agreed to release them and offered them jobs in Saudi Arabia.

To compete with opposition in new global spaces and to fend off media wars by opposition groups outside the kingdom, the Saudi government has directly or indirectly purchased major media outlets in various world capitals. Saudi Arabia now dominates the Arabic visual and print media. Arab media conglomerates such as the Middle East Broadcasting Corporation (MBC), the satellite company Orbit Communications, and Arab Radio and Television (ART) are not run or controlled directly by the government but are owned either by Saudi princes or by Saudi businessmen who have close relationships with the royal family. As owners of major media outlets, Saudis control content by punishing those who are critical of Saudi Arabia or who broadcast programs offensive to Saudi social mores. For example, Orbit canceled a $150 million contract with the Arabic BBC television network because it aired a Panorama program, which, according to the Saudi government, disparaged islam. Such actions also win points with the islamists.

A new arena for criticism and defense of the Saudi system is the internet. Virtual opposition can be untouchable in that virtual critics are not restricted to "real" citizens and include Saudis outside the kingdom as well as non-Saudis. Yet, even with the opening of new arenas of opposition and despite the reforms that have been carried out since 1992, political participation in Saudi Arabia remains managed by the state. The very structure of the political system presents a formidable barrier to wider political opening.

At the center of Saudi society are the royal family and its allies, especially the Al-Shaykh family, the descendants of Muhammad ibn Abd al-Wahhab. A second, wider circle includes the aristocratic families with tribal bases. The third circle adds commercial families with limited tribal bases. Families loyal and close to the Al-Saud were given a bigger share than those whose loyalties were suspect. The families that dominate the commercial scene in Saudi Arabia—the Jufali, the Aliriza, al-Rajahi, al-Khashoqji, al-Uliyan, and bin Laden—have all benefited from the largess of the royal family. A final circle and the most remote from governance are ordinary Saudi families who are not wealthy and who lack tribal standing and thus cannot intermarry with tribal families as a way of gaining political power. Outside these concentric circles of power are some 4.9 million foreign workers, Muslims and non-Muslims alike. This "proletariat class" is both functional and disposable. It serves as an element of identity consolidation by differentiating Saudis from non-Saudis.

While the discourse of absolute authority suggests that the king's authority extends outward across these circles unimpeded, it in fact meets with resistance at each level. Any efforts by the king to allocate political power beyond a particular circle of society will encounter resistance from within all of the more exclusive circles. Thus members of the royal family will resist any extension of power to the tribal aristocracy, just as the royal family and tribal aristocracy will resist any extension of power to the wealthy merchants. Those within the more exclusive circles strive to preserve their own privileged positions in the social and political hierarchy and thus erect obstacles to political inclusion.

The lineage and the kin-ordered mode of production (*qaraba*) and the relations of production contribute to the making of a superstructure of islamic familialism in the Saudi state. Contrary to the underlying implications of the rentier model, oil wealth does not allow the royal family simply to detach itself from the other circles of power in Saudi society. Rather, wealth is filtered through and reinforces a preexisting system. Without paying special attention to the political economy of signs underlying this system and its *qaraba* context, the substance of Saudi politics could be easily missed. To see this value system at work, the political economy of signs must be uncovered. When a senior member of the royal family asks the Saudi elite, "Do you want to be governed by a Ghamidi (i.e., the islamist Safar al-Hawali)?" this says something about the currency and value of the Ghamid tribe and its exchange value in this context of social relations.[29] In an interview, some Saudis referred to a rule by the Ghamidis as "the equivalent of devaluating the Saudi riyal."[30] Regions and tribal values are reflected in Saudi slang, which categorizes citizens according to their telephone area code and electrical voltage. In area code slang, a lower number indicates the most prestigious region; in voltage slang, the highest voltage indicates the most powerful. The Ghamidis are 07 in the area code slang and 110 on the voltage scale, whereas the Sauds and other Najdi families are 01 and 220 respectively.

The Gulf War shook the signs system and symbols of the "oasis of peace" revealed the vulnerability of the *watan* (homeland), and introduced new signs of "the land of Islam" under attack both regionally and globally. Fluctuations in the cosmology of the community of believers are more threatening than fluctuations in the world of production in Saudi Arabia. This cosmology is, in part, built on notions of honor, lineage, and authority, all of which are expressed in the Saudi version of the language of islam. For this reason islamist voices have gained importance in Saudi Arabia since the Gulf War, and the government has paid heed.

NOTES

1 Adapted by Mary C. Wilson from *Saudi Arabia and the Politics of Dissent* by Mamoun Fandy, Chapter One, "Context: Concepts, Parameters, and History" pp. 21-60 (New York: St. Martin's Press, 1999).

2 Ibn Manzur, *Lisan al-Arab*, vol. 9 (Beirut: 1956), pp. 481-490.

3 See Nazih Ayyubi, *Political Islam: Religion and Politics in the Arab World* (New York: Routledge, 1991), especially the chapter entitled "The Politics of Sex and the Family," pp. 35-47.

4 *Al-Riyadh*, August 7, 1995, p. 1.

5 Rentier analysis dominates Gulf studies. Some examples of these studies include the work of Giacomo Luciani (ed.), *The Rentier State* (London: Croom Helm, 1987); Hazem Beblawi's "The Rentier State in the Arab World," in Giacomo Lucani (ed.), *The Arab State* (Berkeley:University of California Press, 1990); Jill Crystal, *Oil and Politics in the Gulf* (New York: Cambridge University Press, 1990); F. Gregory Gause, *Oil Monarchies* (New York: Council on Foreign Relations, 1994); Kiren Aziz Chaudhry, *The Price of Wealth* (Ithaca: Cornell University Press, 1997); and many more. The point is that this discourse has now become a hegemonic discourse that is no longer deterred by alternative hypotheses or alternative data; it is a self-contained discourse that reaffirms its validity and reliability via a detour of narrative.

6 Rayed Krimly, *The Political Economy of Rentier States: A Case Study of Saudi Arabia*, Ph.D. dissertation, George Washington University, 1993. Mishary al-Nuaim, *State Building in a Non-Capitalist Social Formation: The Dialectics of Two Modes of Production and the Role of the Merchant Class, Saudi Arabia, 1902-1932*, Ph.D. dissertation, University of California Los Angeles, 1986.

7 Rex Brynen, Bahgat Korany, and Paul Noble (eds.), *Political Liberalization and Democratization in the Arab World* (Boulder, Colorado: Lynne Reiner, 1995), vol. I, p. 15.

8 In 1978 the state oil revenues were $32,234 million and the price of a barrel of oil was $12.90. In 1979 the price of the barrel of oil increased to $18.60.

9 See Douglas A. Yates, *The Rentier State in Africa: Oil Rent Dependency and Neocolonialism in the Republic of Gabon* (Trenton, New Jersey: Africa World Press, 1996). Those interested in a brief summary of rentier state literature should read his first chapter.

10 On the resignation of the government as a result of pressure from the parliament, see *al-Mujtama'a*, a Kuwaiti weekly, April 2, 1998, p. 10. The Islamists have also been challenging the government since 1986 on social issues, namely the coeducational character of Kuwait University. *al-Mujtama'a*, July 8, 1996.

11 The Statute of the Provinces, Article 4.

12 *Ibid.*, Article 16.

13 For a good description of Saudi Arabia and its people, see Helen Chapin Metz (ed.), *Saudi Arabia: A Country Study* (Washington, DC: U.S. Government Printing Office,, 1993.)

14 See the Basic Statue of Governance, chapter 2.

15 For more, see interview with Prince Talal bin Abdul Aziz, *al-Quds al-Arabi*, 17 April 1998.

16 Author interview, Riyadh, 17 July 1997.

17 For the full text of the 'ulama's statement, see *Saudi Arabia* (Washington, D.C.: Official Publication of the Royal Embassy of Saudi Arabia, Fall, 1990), p. 3.

18 See *Alyamamah*, no. 1181, 20 November 1991, pp. 42-45.

19 For an excellent account of the Ikhwan movement see Muhammad Jalal Kishk, *al-sa'udiyun wal-hall al-islami* (The Saudis and the Islamic solution) (Cairo: al-al-matba'a al-faniyya, 1981), especially part 6, pp. 549-707.

20 For more on the Ikhwan see Christine Moss Helms, *The Cohesion of Saudi Arabia* (Baltimore: Johns Hopkins Press, 1981), especially chapter 8, pp. 250-272.

21 This is based on two interviews I conducted with Shaykh Saleh al-Luhaidan and Shaykh Salih al-Fawaz. Both are members of the Council of Higher 'Ulama.

22 Mudhakarat al-nasiha (The Memorandum of Advice), p. 2. It is well worth noting that whenever I talked to Mas'ari, al-Faqih, or bin Laden's representatives, each referred me to the Memorandum of Advice as the frame of reference. In fact, I received three copies of the memorandum from the three of them as part of their packages to introduce me to their organizations. Unless otherwise stated, the following information and quotations are from the memorandum.

23 From the letter to Shaykh bin Baz that accompanies the Memorandum of Advice.

24 See Salman al-Auda's letter of endorsement attached to the Memorandum of Advice.

25 Safar al-Hawali's letter of endorsement of the Memorandum of Advice.

26 This criticism of the state information system and the restrictions the state imposes on the 'ulama are central to Shaykh Salman al-Auda's message.

27 This council was organized to institutionalize an Islamic injunction that says, "and their affairs are based on consultation amongst them."

28 See my book, *Saudi Arabia and the Politics of Dissent* (New York: Palgrave, 2000) p. 40.

29 Safar al-Hawali is the most mainstream of all the Islamist critics of the Saudi regime. He was born in the al-Baha region, which lies south of al-Taif and comes from the minor but reputable Ghamid tribe. He received his doctorate from Um al-Qura University in Mecca in 1986. He is the only Saudi Islamist dissident who did not receive his doctorate from a foreign university.

30 Author interview, Jiddah, 15 July 1997.

List of Contributors

Ervand Abrahamian is Professor of History at Baruch College and the author of *Iran Between Two Revolutions* (1982), *The Iranian Mojahedin* (1989), and *Tortured Confessions: Prisons And Public Recantations In Modern Iran* (1999).

Feroz Ahmad is Professor Emeritus of History at the University of Massachusetts at Boston and the author of *The Young Turks: the Committee of Union and Progress in Turkish Politics, 1908-1914* (1969), *The Turkish Experiment in Democracy, 1950-1975* (1977), and *The Making of Modern Turkey* (1993).

Hanna Batatu (1926-2000) was Professor Emeritus of Arab Studies at the Center for Contemporary Arab Studies of Georgetown University. His publications include *The Old Social Classes and the Revolutionary Movements of Iraq* (1978) and *Syria's Peasantry, the Descendants of its Lesser Rural Notables, and their Politics* (1999).

Joel Beinin is Professor of History at Stanford University. He is the co-author (with Zachary Lockman) of *Workers on the Nile* (1988) and the author of *Was the Red Flag Flying There? Marxist Politics and the Arab-Israeli Conflict in Egypt and Israel, 1948-1965* (1990), and *The Dispersion Of Egyptian Jewry: Culture, Politics, And the Formation Of A Modern Diaspora* (1998).

Kenneth M. Cuno is Associate Professor of History at the University of Illinois, Urbana, and the author of *The Pashas Peasants: Land Tenure, Society, and Economy in Lower Egypt, 1740-1858* (1992).

Roderic H. Davison (1916-1996) was Professor Emeritus of History at George Washington University and author of *Reform in the Ottoman Empire. 1856-1876* (1963), *Turkey: A Short History* (1988), and *Essays in Ottoman and Turkish History. 1774-1923: The Impact of the West* (1990).

C. ERNEST DAWN is Professor Emeritus of History at the University of Illinois, Urbana. His publications include *From Ottomanism to Arabism: Essays on the Origins of Arab Nationalism* (1973).

PAUL DUMONT is at the Institut d'Etudes Turques, Université des Sciences Humaines de Strasbourg. He is the author of *Mustafa Kemal invente la Turquie moderne: 1919-1924* (1983) and *Du socialisme ottoman à l'internationalisme anatolien* (1997), and co-editor of *La Turquie au seuil d'europe* (1991) and *Villes ottomanes à la fin de l'empire* (1992).

MAMOUN FANDY is an independent scholar and the author of *Saudi Arabia and the Politics of Dissent* (1999).

JOEL GORDON is Associate Professor of History at the University of Arkansas and author of *Nasser's Blessed Movement: Egypt's Free Officers and the July Revolution* (1992).

URIEL HEYD (1913-1968) taught at the Hebrew University. Among his publications are *Foundations of Turkish Nationalism: the Life and Teachings of Ziya Gökalp* (1950) and *Studies in Islamic History and Civilization* (1961).

ALBERT HOURANI (1915-1993) was Reader in the Modern History of the Middle East in the University of Oxford and Emeritus Fellow of St Antony's College. His books include *Arabic Thought in the Liberal Age, 1798-1939* (1962), *The Emergence of the Modern Middle East* (1981), *A History of the Arab Peoples* (1991), and *Islam in European Thought* (1991).

STEPHEN HUMPHREYS is Professor of History and Islamic Studies at the University of California, Santa Barbara, and author of *Islamic History: A Framework for Inquiry* (1988) and *Between Memory and Desire: The Middle East in a Troubled Age* (1999), among other works.

CHARLES ISSAWI (1916-2000) was Bayard Dodge Professor Emeritus of Near Eastern Studies at Princeton University. Among his publications are *An Economic History of the Middle East and North Africa* (1982) and *Growing Up Different: Memoirs of a Middle East Scholar* (1999), and many edited volumes.

NIKKI R. KEDDIE is Professor Emerita of History at the University of California, Los Angeles. Her publications include *Sayyid Jamal al-Din al-Afghani: A Political Biography* (1974), *Iran: Religion, Politics, and Society* (1980), and *Roots of Revolution: an Interpretive History of Modern Iran* (1981), and many edited volumes.

PHILIP S. KHOURY is Professor of History and Kenan Sahin Dean of the School of the Humanities, Arts, and Social Sciences at the Massachusetts Institute of Technology. He is the author of *Urban Notables and Arab Nationalism* (1983) and *Syria and the French Mandate* (1987), and co-editor of *Tribes and State Formation in the Middle East* (1990).

ANN K. S. LAMBTON is Professor Emerita of Persian in the University of London. Her publications include *Landlord and Peasant in Persia* (1953), *State and Government in Medieval Islam* (1981), and *Continuity and Change in Medieval Persia* (1988).

ZACHARY LOCKMAN, Professor of Middle East Studies at New York University, is the co-author (with Joel Beinin) of *Workers on the Nile: Nationalism, Communism, Islam, and the Egyptian Working Class, 1882-1954* (1988) and author of *Comrades and Enemies: Arab and Jewish Workers in Palestine, 1906-1948* (1996).

ŞERIF MARDIN is Dean of the Social and Human Sciences Faculty of Sabançi University in Istanbul and author of *The Genesis of Young Ottoman Thought* (1962), *Religion and Social Change in Modern Turkey* (1989), and. *Religion, Society, and Modernity in Turkey* (1999).

DAVID MCDOWALL is a freelance writer and the author of *Palestine and Israel: The Uprising and Beyond* (1989) and *A Modern History of the Kurds* (1996).

ROGER OWEN is the A.J. Meyer Professor of History at Harvard University. His publications include *Cotton and the Egyptian Economy. 1820-1914* (1969), *The Middle East in the World Economy, 1820-1914* (1981), and *State, Power and Politics in the Making of the Modern Middle East* (1992) and several edited volumes.

DONALD QUATAERT is Professor of History and Director of the Southwest Asian and North African Program at the State University of New York at Binghamton. He is the author of *Social Disintegration and Popular Resistance in the Ottoman Empire, 1881-1908* (1983), *Ottoman Manufacturing in the Age of the Industrial Revolution* (1993), and *The Ottoman Empire, 1700-1922* (2000).

ANDRÉ RAYMOND is Professor Emeritus at the Université de Provence in Aix-en-Provence. His publications include *Artisans et Commerçants au Caire au XVIIIème siècle*, 2 vols (1973-1974), *Grandes villes arabes à l'époque ottomane* (1985), *Égyptiens et français au Caire, 1798-1801* (1998), and *Cairo* (2000).

OLIVIER ROY is Research Director in the Humanities & Social Sciences sector of the Centre National de la Recherche Scientifique in Paris. His books include *Islam and Resistance in Afghanistan* (2nd ed. 1990), *The Failure of Political Islam* (1994), and *The New Central Asia: The Creation of Nations* (2000).

AVI SHLAIM is Professor of International Relations and a Fellow of St. Antony's College in the University of Oxford. His publications include *Collusion Across the Jordan: King Abdullah, The Zionist Movement, and The Partition Of Palestine* (1988) and *The Iron Wall: Israel and the Arab World* (2000).

TED SWEDENBERG is Associate Professor of Anthropology at the University of Arkansas. He is the author of *Memories of Revolt: the 1936-1939 Rebellion and the*

Palestinian National Past (1995) and co-editor of *Displacement, Diaspora, and Geographies of Identity* (1996).

JUDITH E. TUCKER is Professor of History at Georgetown University. She is the author of *Women in Nineteenth-Century Egypt* (1985) and *In the House of the Law: Gender and Islamic Law in Ottoman Syria and Palestine* (1998).

MARY C. WILSON is Professor of History at the University of Massachusetts at Amherst. She is the author of *King Abdullah, Britain and the Making of Jordan* (1987).